Evolving Application Domains of Data Warehousing and Mining:
Trends and Solutions

Pedro Nuno San-Bento Furtado
University of Coimbra, Portugal

INFORMATION SCIENCE REFERENCE

Hershey · New York

Director of Editorial Content:	Kristin Klinger
Senior Managing Editor:	Jamie Snavely
Assistant Managing Editor:	Michael Brehm
Publishing Assistant:	Sean Woznicki
Typesetter:	Michael Brehm, Michael Killian
Cover Design:	Lisa Tosheff
Printed at:	Yurchak Printing Inc.

Published in the United States of America by
Information Science Reference (an imprint of IGI Global)
701 E. Chocolate Avenue
Hershey PA 17033
Tel: 717-533-8845
Fax: 717-533-8661
E-mail: cust@igi-global.com
Web site: http://www.igi-global.com/reference

Library of Congress Cataloging-in-Publication Data

Evolving application domains of data warehousing and mining : trends and
solutions / Pedro Nuno San-Banto Furtado, editor.
      p. cm.
  Includes bibliographical references and index.
  Summary: "This book provides insight into the latest findings concerning
data warehousing, data mining, and their applications in everyday human
activities"--Provided by publisher.
  ISBN 978-1-60566-816-1 (hardcover) -- ISBN 978-1-60566-817-8 (ebook) 1.
Data warehousing. 2. Data mining. I. Furtado, Pedro Nuno San-Banto, 1968-
  QA76.9.D37E96 2010
  006.3'12--dc22
                                    2009023836
British Cataloguing in Publication Data
A Cataloguing in Publication record for this book is available from the British Library.

All work contributed to this book is new, previously-unpublished material. The views expressed in this book are those of the
authors, but not necessarily of the publisher.

List of Reviewers

Jorge Bernardino, *ISEC, Portugal*
Ricardo Ciferri, *USP, Brasil*
Cristina Cifferi, *USP, Brasil*
Joao Pedro Costa, *ISEC, Portugal*
Rogério Costa, *PUC, Brasil*
Karen Davis, *University of Cincinnati, USA*
Christie I. Ezeife, *University of Windsor, Canada*
Helena Galhardas, *IST, Portugal*
Carson Leung, *University of Manitoba, Canada*
Patrick Martin, *Queen's University, Canada*
Rosa Meo, *Università degli Studi di Torino, Italy*
Catarina Pereira, *ISL, Portugal*
Bernardete Ribeiro, *University of Coimbra, Portugal*
David Taniar, *Monash University, Australia*
Panos Vassiliadis, *University of Ioannina, Greece*
Robert Wrembel, *Poznan University of Technology, Poland*

Table of Contents

Section 3
Foundations and Applications of Data Mining and Data Analysis

Detailed Table of Contents

Section 1
Foundation Issues in Data Warehousing and OLAP

The wide adoption of business intelligence applications has let more and more organizations to build and maintain data warehouse systems. Concepts like "unified view of data" and "one version of the truth" have been the main drive of creating data warehouses. The dynamics of the business world poses the challenges of managing large volume, complex data in data warehouses while the real-time integration and master data needs are presented. This chapter summarizes the past and present patterns of typical data warehouse architectures and describes how the concept of service-oriented architecture influences the future evolvement of data warehouse architecture. The discussion takes many real world requirements in data warehouse solutions and lists considerations on how architecture patterns can solve these requirements.

Chapter 2

Data warehouse and OLAP systems are widely required during the decision-support process, since they provide integrated data in a form that facilitates the expression of complex queries. In order to exploit both systems to their full capabilities, dimensions with hierarchies must be clearly defined. Dimensions can be of different types and they allow users to see quantified data from different perspectives. Hierarchies are important in analytical applications, since they give users the possibility of representing data at different abstraction levels. However, even though there are different kinds of hierarchies in real-world applications and some of them are already implemented in commercial tools, there is still a lack of a well-accepted conceptual model that allows decision-making users to express their analysis needs. In this chapter, we show how the conceptual multidimensional model can be used to facilitate the representation of complex hierarchies and different kinds of dimensions in comparison to their representation in the relational model and commercial OLAP tools, using as an example Microsoft Analysis Services.

Chapter 3

The Data warehouse is not an autonomous data store, because it depends upon its operational source(s) for data population. Due to changes in real-world scenarios, operational sources may evolve, but the conventional data warehouse is not developed to handle the modifications in evolved operational sources. Therefore, instance and schema changes in operational sources cannot be adapted in the conventional data warehouse without loss of information. Multiversion data warehouses are proposed as an alternative to handle these problems of evolution. In this chapter we discuss and illustrate how versioning is implemented and how it can be used in practical data warehouse lifecycle. It is designed as a tutorial for users to collect and understand the concepts behind a versioning solution. Therefore, the purpose of this chapter is to collect and integrate the concepts, issues and solutions of multiversion data warehouses in a tutorial-like approach, to provide a unified source for users that need to understand version functionality and mechanisms.

Chapter 4

The exploration of the possibility of compressing data warehouses is inevitable because of their non-trivial storage and access costs. A typical large data warehouse needs hundreds of gigabytes to a terabyte of storage. Performance of computing aggregate queries is a bottleneck for many Online Analytical Processing (OLAP) applications. Hence, data warehousing implementations strongly depend on data compression techniques to make possible the management and storage of such large databases. The efficiency of data compression methods has a significant impact on the overall performance of these implementations. The purpose of this chapter is to discuss the importance of data compression to Multidimensional Online Analytical Processing (MOLAP), to survey data compression techniques relevant to MOLAP, and to discuss important quality issues of MOLAP compression and of existing techniques. Finally, we also discuss future research trends on this subject.

Section 2
Application Issues and Trends in Data Warehousing and OLAP

Chapter 5

Christoph Quix, RWTH Aachen University, Germany
Xiang Li, RWTH Aachen University, Germany
David Kensche, RWTH Aachen University, Germany
Sandra Geisler, RWTH Aachen University, Germany

Data streams are continuous, rapid, time-varying, and transient streams of data and provide new opportunities for analysis of timely information. Data processing in data streams faces similar challenges as view management in data warehousing: continuous query processing is related to view maintenance in data warehousing, multi-query optimization for continuous queries is highly related to view selection in conventional relational DBMS and data warehouses. In this chapter, the authors give an overview of view maintenance and view selection methods, explain the fundamental issues of data stream management, and discuss how view management techniques from data warehousing are related to data stream management. They also give directions for future research in view management, data streams, and data warehousing.

Chapter 6

Nan Jiang, Cedarville University, USA

The recent advances in sensor technologies have made these small, tiny devices much cheaper and convenient to use in many different applications, for example, the weather and environmental monitoring applications, the hospital and factory operation sites, sensor devices on the traffic road and moving vehicles and so on. The data collected from sensors forms a sensor stream and is transferred to the server to perform data warehousing and mining tasks for the end user to perform data analysis. Several data preprocessing steps are necessary to enrich the data with domain information for the data warehousing and mining tasks in the sensor stream applications. In this chapter, the author presents a general framework for domain-driven mining of sensor stream applications. In this framework he is able to enrich sensor streams with additional domain information that meets the application requirements. He evaluates the proposed framework with experiments on real data for two applications: a traffic management and an environmental monitoring site.

Chapter 7

Martine Collard, INRIA Sophia Antipolis, France and University of Nice-Sophia Antipolis,
*   France*
Leila Kefi-Khelif, INRIA Sophia Antipolis, France
Van Trang Tran, I3S laboratory, University of Nice-Sophia Antipolis, France
Olivier Corby, INRIA Sophia Antipolis, France

DNA micro-array is a fastest-growing technology in molecular biology and bioinformatics. Based on series of microscopic spots of DNA sequences, they allow the measurement of gene expression in specific conditions at a whole genome scale. Micro-array experiments result in wide sets of expression data that are useful to the biologist to investigate various biological questions. Experimental micro-arrays data and sources of biological knowledge are now available on public repositories. As a consequence, comparative analyses involving several experiments become conceivable and hold potentially relevant knowledge. Nevertheless, the task of manually navigating and searching for similar tendencies in such huge spaces is mainly impracticable for the investigator and leads to limited results. In this context, the authors propose a semantic data warehousing solution based on semantic web technologies that allows to monitoring both the diversity and the volume of all related data.

Sandro Bimonte, Cemagref, UR TSCF, Clermont Ferrand, France
Marlène Villanova-Oliver, Laboratoire d'Informatique de Grenoble, France
Jerome Gensel, Laboratoire d'Informatique de Grenoble, France

Spatial OLAP refers to the integration of spatial data in multidimensional applications at physical, logical and conceptual levels. The multidimensional aggregation of geographic objects (geographic measures) exhibits theoretical and implementation problems. In this chapter, the authors present a panorama of aggregation issues in multidimensional, geostatistic, GIS and Spatial OLAP models. Then, they illustrate how overlapping geometries and dependency of spatial and alphanumeric aggregation are necessary for correctly aggregating geographic measures. Consequently, they present an extension of the logical multidimensional model GeoCube (Bimonte et al., 2006) to deal with these issues.

Section 3
Foundations and Applications of Data Mining and Data Analysis

Claudia Plant, Technische Universität München, Munich Germany, Ludwig Maximilians
Universität München, Munich, Germany
Christian Böhm, Technische Universität München, Munich Germany, Ludwig Maximilians
Universität München, Munich, Germany

Clustering or finding a natural grouping of a data set is essential for knowledge discovery in many applications. This chapter provides an overview on emerging trends within the vital research area of clustering including subspace and projected clustering, correlation clustering, semi-supervised clustering, spectral clustering and parameter-free clustering. To raise the awareness of the reader for the challenges associated with clustering, the chapter first provides a general problem specification and introduces basic clustering paradigms. The requirements from concrete example applications in life sciences and the web provide the motivation for the discussion of novel approaches to clustering. Thus, this chapter is intended to appeal to all those interested in the state-of-the art in clustering including basic researchers as well as practitioners.

Chapter 10

Chao Luo, University of Technology, Sydney, Australia
Yanchang Zhao, University of Technology, Sydney, Australia
Dan Luo, University of Technology, Sydney, Australia
Yuming Ou, University of Technology, Sydney, Australia
Li Liu, University of Technology, Sydney, Australia

This chapter aims to provide a comprehensive survey of the current advanced technologies of exception mining in stock market. The stock market surveillance is to identify market anomalies so as to provide a fair and efficient trading platform. The technologies of market surveillance developed from simple statistical rules to more advanced technologies, such as data mining and artificial intelligent. This chapter provides the basic concepts of exception mining in stock market. Then the recent advances of exception mining in this domain are presented and the key issues are discussed. The advantages and disadvantages of the advanced technologies are analyzed. Furthermore, the authors' model of OMM (Outlier Mining on Multiple time series) is introduced. Finally, this chapter points out the future research directions and related issues in reality.

Chapter 11

Symeon Papadopoulos, Aristotle University of Thessaloniki, Greece Informatics & Telematics
    Institute, Thermi, Thessaloniki, Greece
Fotis Menemenis, Informatics & Telematics Institute, Thermi, Thessaloniki, Greece
Athena Vakali, Aristotle University of Thessaloniki, Greece
Ioannis Kompatsiaris, Informatics & Telematics Institute, Thermi, Thessaloniki, Greece

The recent advent and wide adoption of Social Bookmarking Systems (SBS) has disrupted the traditional model of online content publishing and consumption. Until recently, the majority of content consumed by people was published as a result of a centralized selection process. Nowadays, the large-scale adoption of the Web 2.0 paradigm has diffused the content selection process to the masses. Modern SBS-based applications permit their users to submit their preferred content, comment on and rate the content of other users and establish social relations with each other. As a result, the evolution of popularity of socially bookmarked content constitutes nowadays an overly complex phenomenon calling for a multi-aspect analysis approach. This chapter attempts to provide a unified treatment of the phenomenon by studying four aspects of popularity of socially bookmarked content: (a) the distributional properties of content consumption, (b) its evolution in time, (c) the correlation between the semantics of online content and its popularity, and (d) the impact of online social networks on the content consumption behavior of individuals. To this end, a case study is presented where the proposed analysis framework is applied to a large dataset collected from digg, a popular social bookmarking and rating application.

Chapter 12

Cândida G. Silva, FCT, University of Coimbra, Portugal
Pedro Gabriel Ferreira, Center for Genomic Regulation, Barcelona, Spain
Paulo J. Azevedo, University of Minho, Portugal
Rui M. M. Brito, University of Coimbra, Portugal

The protein folding problem, i.e. the identification of the rules that determine the acquisition of the native, functional, three-dimensional structure of a protein from its linear sequence of amino-acids, still is a major challenge in structural molecular biology. Moreover, the identification of a series of neurodegenerative diseases as protein unfolding/misfolding disorders highlights the importance of a detailed characterisation of the molecular events driving the unfolding and misfolding processes in proteins. One way of exploring these processes is through the use of molecular dynamics simulations. The analysis and comparison of the enormous amount of data generated by multiple protein folding or unfolding simulations is not a trivial task, presenting many interesting challenges to the data mining community. Considering the central role of the hydrophobic effect in protein folding, we show here the application of two data mining methods – hierarchical clustering and association rules – for the analysis and comparison of the solvent accessible surface area (SASA) variation profiles of each one of the 127 amino-acid residues in the amyloidogenic protein Transthyretin, across multiple molecular dynamics protein unfolding simulations.

Chapter 13

Claudia Cherubini, Politecnico di Bari, Italy

Most data required for cleanup risk assessment are intrinsically characterized by a high degree of variability and uncertainty. Moreover, typical features of environmental datasets are the occurrence of extreme values like a few random 'hot spots' of large concentrations within a background of data below the detection limit. In the field of environmental pollution risk assessment constitutes a support method for decisions inherent the necessity to carry out a procedure of remediation of an area. Therefore it would be adequate to provide the analysis with elements that allow to take into account the nature of the data themselves, particularly their uncertainty. In this context, this chapter focuses on the application of an uncertainty modeling approach based on geostatistics for the parameters which enter as input in the probabilistic procedure of risk assessment. Compared with a traditional approach, the applied method provides the possibility to quantify and integrate the uncertainty and variability of input parameters in the determination of risk. Moreover, it has proved to be successful in catching and describing in a synthetic way the relations and tendencies that are intrinsic in the data set, characteristics that are neglected by a traditional classical approach.

Preface

Data warehousing and data mining are related technologies which have seen a significant boost in the last decades, in a way that many of their concepts and techniques have reached a significant level of maturity. They are applied today in most fields of human activity, from commercial to scientific or industrial areas. Today, decision support, data mining, trend analysis and pattern discovery have a large impact on businesses and science alike. This has led to the development of new solutions and approaches, some of them being incorporated into commercial tools and systems, others producing new advancement opportunities in many fields of human knowledge.

Given this evolution, it is important to understand advances that happened in those technologies concerning solutions and applications, how data warehousing and data mining technologies operate and their positive effects on many areas of human activity and knowledge. Moreover, it is very interesting to look at current developments in the underlying technologies and what research opportunities lay ahead.

The two concepts of data warehousing and data mining are in fact very much related to each other, and both research and commercial application areas need to deal with both. Warehousing refers to a multidimensional data organization, its loading, storage and analysis using typical operations that are frequently denoted as "Online Analytical Processing (OLAP)". Data mining, on the other hand, applies certain classes of algorithms to search and discover new knowledge automatically from multidimensional data sets. This means that not only data mining and data warehousing assume a similar base model, as they are related to each other in another way: data warehousing approaches are useful for basic data organization and analysis, while data mining approaches extend this to include further analysis capabilities, by applying certain objective-directed algorithms for finding new knowledge from the data sets.

This book brings together a set of papers discussing current issues in evolving application domains of data warehousing and mining, showing the trends and solutions that are currently being researched and applied concerning foundations and applications of those technologies. One important objective is to look at research results concerning actual application of the technologies, besides their foundations.

The subjects discussed along the book are relevant for both practitioners and scholars. On the practical application side, the reader will find answers to practical issues regarding how these technologies work and are to be applied, as well as cases of applications of the technologies in different fields of knowledge. The researcher and scholar, on the other hand, will have the opportunity to understand the current state-of-the-art and research-related developments and hot topics. The book also serves as a reference for advanced courses on data warehousing and mining, since it discusses state-of-the-art and advances in various relevant issues of the technologies and of their application to real-world problems.

We have been careful in the choice of chapters, by taking into consideration not only the precious input received by the team of reviewers and the quality of the chapters, but also by evaluating the importance of the subject and by structuring a book that reviews and provides new insight into some of the most interesting aspects of these technologies. One particularly important aspect of the process was to provide adequate feedback and help to the authors, and to eliminate many chapters that were not sound enough in some respect.

In the rest of the Preface we introduce the structure and contents of the book, in order to give the reader a roadmap into what is the content of sections and chapters in the book. This book is structured in such a way that readers with different objectives can all find their way directly to the parts that are most interesting to them. For instance, while a student may wish to read the book sequentially from the start to the end of it, readers specially interested in data mining may jump straight ahead into the section on data mining, and then to the section on applications of data warehousing, since those applications also include interesting parts on mining from data warehousing contexts.

STRUCTURE OF THE BOOK

The book addresses both foundational and application issues in data warehousing and mining. It presents both current state-of-the-art and research in infrastructural aspects and application areas. Trends and solutions in different domains are identified and discussed in the chapters. In the following we provide first a list of the sections and an overview of the contents of those sections. Then we provide a summary of each chapter within each section. This section is therefore a precious roadmap into the contents of the book.

The book is divided into three sections, addressing the following concerns:

*   Foundation Issues in Data Warehousing and OLAP
*   Application Issues and Trends in Data Warehousing and OLAP
*   Foundations and Applications of Data Mining and Data Analysis

Section 1 addresses foundations of data warehouses and OLAP. This section features four chapters covering current topics that include data warehouse architectures, modeling of warehouse and OLAP applications and, from a data warehouse organization perspective, management of multiple versions and compression schemes.

After addressing an important set of foundational issues in data warehousing and OLAP in the first section, section 2 proceeds with both application issues and current research trends. It covers very different application domains, including data streams, sensor data, genomics and geographical data warehouses. These are useful both for they insight into state-of-the-art in their respective domains and as research trends. Reflecting the complementarities between warehousing and mining, data mining is also present in most of the papers from this section, although in the context of warehousing and mining.

Section 3 discusses both foundations and applications of data mining technologies. The section starts with an excellent survey on data clustering, and also includes state-of-the-art information on exception mining, social network mining and risk assessment, a data analysis task. In what concerns applications, the section discusses and presents results in areas such as current applications of clustering, stock market surveillance, protein folding, social networks and risk assessment in geostatistics.

Section 1. Foundation Issues in Data Warehousing and OLAP

Chapter 1, *Data Warehouse Architectures: Practices and Trends*, by Xuegang Huang, is a high-level introductory chapter, discussing the concepts behind data warehouse architectures and past and present trends in data warehouse architectures. It considers real-world requirements for data warehouse solutions, and discusses which architectural patterns should be used to solve those requirements. It further describes how the concept of service-orientation may influence future data warehouse architectures and solutions as well.

Chapter 2, *Improving Expressive Power in Modeling Data Warehouse and OLAP Applications*, by Elzbieta Malinowski, discusses how the conceptual multidimensional model can be used to facilitate the representation of complex hierarchies and different kinds of dimensions in comparison to their representation in a relational model and commercial OLAP tools. This chapter is in itself an excellent reference on multidimensional modeling, representation and implementation issues.

Chapter 3, *From Conventional to Multiversion Data Warehouse: Practical Issues*, by Khurram Shahzad, concerns data warehouse versioning. Versioning is quite important in real-world projects, since operational sources or the data warehouse structure itself may evolve. Conventional data warehouses are not prepared to handle these modifications. The chapter, while not a comprehensive survey on the subject, takes a very practical perspective, collecting and integrating concepts, issues and solutions of multiversion data warehouses in a tutorial-like approach, to provide a unified source for users that need to understand version functionality and mechanisms.

Chapter 4, *Compression Schemes of High Dimensional Data for MOLAP*, by K. M. Azharul Hasan, surveys data compression techniques relevant to multidimensional OLAP and discusses important quality issues of MOLAP compression and of existing techniques. Compression is indeed an important issue faced in implementations of data warehouses and in particular for multidimensional OLAP, due to possibly huge size and sparsity of MOLAP representations.

Section 2. Application Issues and Trends in Data Warehousing and OLAP

Chapter 5, *View Management Techniques and Their Application to Data Stream Management*, by Christoph Quix et al., is a very interesting and insightful chapter on the subjects of view management and data stream management, starting with a suggestion that data stream processing shares many similarities with view management in data warehousing. The chapter provides an overview of view maintenance and view selection methods, explains the fundamental issues of data stream management, and discusses how view management techniques from data warehousing are related to data stream management. Finally, it provides directions for future research in view management, data streams, and data warehousing.

Chapter 6, *A Framework for Data Warehousing and Mining in Sensor Stream Application Domains*, by Nan Jiang provides insight into how data collected from sensor devices can be fed into data warehouses and mined. This is a relevant subject, since sensors are increasingly used in many different applications, from weather and environmental monitoring to hospital and factory operation sites, traffic monitoring and so on. The chapter presents a general framework for domain-driven mining of sensor stream applications, and evaluates the proposed framework with experiments on traffic management and environmental monitoring.

Chapter 7, *A Data Warehousing Approach for Genomics Data Meta-Analysis*, by Martine Collard et al., takes a very different application domain, genomics, and shows how data warehousing and mining are relevant in that context. Since experimental micro-array data and sources of biological knowledge are now available on public repositories, comparative analyses involving several experiments become conceivable and hold potentially relevant knowledge. However, manually navigating and searching for similar tendencies in such huge spaces is impracticable. In this context, the authors propose a semantic data warehousing solution based on semantic web technologies that allows to monitoring both the diversity and the volume of all related data.

Chapter 8, *A Multidimensional Model for Correct Aggregation of Geographic Measures*, by Sandro Bimonte et al., discusses aggregation issues in multidimensional, geostatistic, GIS and Spatial OLAP models. The chapter provides a good review of those models and discusses why the multidimensional aggregation of geographic objects (geographic measures) exhibits theoretical and implementation problems. The authors then proceed to propose a solution to that problem within a GeoCube multidimensional model.

Section 3. Foundations and Applications of Data Mining and Data Analysis

Chapter 9, *Novel Trends in Clustering*, by Claudia Plant and Christian Böhm, is a very interesting work featuring state-of-the-art and current trends analysis on data clustering. It is useful for both researchers and practitioners, providing an overview on emerging trends in clustering, including subspace and projected clustering, correlation clustering, semi-supervised clustering, spectral clustering and parameter-free clustering. Requirements from concrete example applications in life sciences and the web provide motivation for the discussion of novel approaches to clustering in this chapter.

Chapter 10, *Recent Advances of Exception Mining in Stock Market*, by Chao Luo et al., offers a survey of current advanced technologies for exception mining in stock markets. Additionally, it proposes and analyses improved approaches for exception mining and discusses future research directions and related issues.

Chapter 11, *Analysis of Content Popularity in Social Bookmarking Systems*, by Symeon Papadopoulos et al., embraces a very current issue of social networks and social bookmarking systems. Modern SBS-based applications permit their users to submit their preferred content, comment on and rate the content of other users and establish social relations with each other. The chapter provides a unified treatment of the phenomenon by studying four aspects of popularity of socially bookmarked content: (a) the distributional properties of content consumption, (b) its evolution in time, (c) the correlation between the semantics of online content and its popularity, and (d) the impact of online social networks on the content consumption behavior of individuals.

Chapter 12, *Using Data Mining Techniques to Probe the Role of Hydrophobic Residues in Protein Folding and Unfolding Simulations*, by Catarina Silva et. al. shows how data mining approaches, in this case hierarchical clustering and association rules mining, is useful in molecular dynamics simulation experiments related to the study of protein folding problem. The protein folding problem is the identification of rules that determine the acquisition of the native, functional, three-dimensional structure of a protein from its linear sequence of amino-acids. Its importance stems from the fact that functional properties of proteins can frequently be related to protein conformation issues, and data mining methods – hierarchical clustering and association rules – are applied on the simulation results to characterize important aspects for analysis.

Chapter 13, *A Geostatistically Based Probabilistic Risk Assessment Approach*, by Claudia Cherubini, poses the question of how to determine the levels of risk of contamination in environmental pollution risk assessment of zones, taking into consideration a high degree of variability and uncertainty that is inherent to the problem. The author uses an uncertainty modeling approach based on geostatistics for determining the parameters which enter as input to the probabilistic procedure of risk assessment. Although the focus of this work does not classify strictly as classical data mining but rather as statistical analysis, the discussion and approaches used provide insight and are relevant in any kind of analysis of spatial data.

Acknowledgment

The editor would like to acknowledge the help of all involved in the review process of the book. The reviewers provided comprehensive, critical and constructive comments, which guided both the authors and the editor in the choice and improvement of chapters.

Special thanks also goes to IGI Global, who gave me the opportunity to publish this book, and to the people from the Development Division who helped and guided me throughput the process. In particular, I would like to thank Kristin Roth, managing development editor, Rebecca Beistline and Joel Gamon, assistant book development editors who guided me through the process.

Pedro Nuno San-Bento Furtado
University of Coimbra, Portugal

Section 1
Foundation Issues in Data Warehousing and OLAP

Chapter 1
Data Warehouse Architecture:
Practices and Trends

Xuegang Huang
Danske Bank Group, Denmark

ABSTRACT

The wide adoption of business intelligence applications has let more and more organizations to build and maintain data warehouse systems. Concepts like "unified view of data" and "one version of the truth" have been the main drive of creating data warehouses. The dynamics of the business world poses the challenges of managing large volume, complex data in data warehouses while the real-time integration and master data needs are presented. This chapter summarizes the past and present patterns of typical data warehouse architectures and describes how the concept of service-oriented architecture influences the future evolvement of data warehouse architecture. The discussion takes many real world requirements in data warehouse solutions and lists considerations on how architecture patterns can solve these requirements.

INTRODUCTION

Over the past decades, the concept of data warehousing has been spread out to everywhere in the business world. Organizations have been practicing hard on achieving successful data warehouse architectures. Lessons have been learnt from those who have succeeded, as well as those who have not. Several key developments in the data warehousing industry denote the past and present of this discipline.

DOI: 10.4018/978-1-60566-816-1.ch001

Specifically, starting with very few industry vendors in the 80s such as Teradata, many IT companies like Microsoft, IBM and Oracles are extending their database management systems (DBMSs) to have sufficient support on data warehouses. The early years' data warehousing theory and engineering practices have been well recorded in the publications of Inmon (Inmon, 2005) and Kimball (Kimball & Ross, 2002).

Academic research of data warehousing technologies started in the early 90s. The database research community began with a focus on incorporating data from heterogeneous sources into a single database in order to provide a consistent and unified view of data. These early discussions, such as database snapshots (Adiba & Lindsay, 1980) and materialized views (Gupta & Mumick, 1995), motivated a big variety of subsequent research tracks such as OLAP (online analytical processing) databases (Chaudhuri & Dayal, 1997), data cube (Gray, Bosworth, Layman, & Pirahesh, 1996), multidimensional modeling (Agrawal, Gupta, & Sarawagi, 1997), multidimensional indexing and query optimization (Böhm, Berchtold, Kriegel, & Michel, 2000), and data warehousing for complex data types (Pedersen & Jensen, 1999). The research world has been putting recent attentions on improving the scalability of data warehouses on complex data types (Darmont, Boussaid, Ralaivao, & Aouiche, 2005) and how data warehouse can be seamlessly and efficiently integrated into the business intelligence process and applications (Furtado, 2006; Theodoratos, Ligoudistianos & Sellis, 2001).

Data warehouse architecture is a portfolio of perspectives on how different architecture pieces of a data warehouse system are connected and interacting with each other. It reflects how the academic research and industry development influence the data warehousing practices of different enterprises. For example, from a computing infrastructure perspective, data warehouse architecture has gone from past mainframe analytics to client/middleware/server environment, and now to service-oriented computing as well as the cloud computing concepts. With the rapid growth of information volume and more requirements arriving from the business side, many IT organizations of large business enterprises are facing the challenge of building an enterprise-wide data warehouse that integrates and manages various types of information that comes from different corners of the enterprises and provides the solid information for business analysis in a timely manner. Successful data warehouse architecture must be able to ensure the processing efficiency,

the information correctness, and propagation of metadata while managing over terabytes of data with a daily growth of over gigabytes.

As in the past decade, practices of data warehouse architecture have been focused on addressing classical issues such as the data integration needs, the data quality and metadata control, the data modeling requirements and the performance acceptance from both the data management and the analytical sides. Specifically, the data extraction, transformation, and loading (ETL) process has to manage large volumes of data in an efficient manner by allowing easy and fast scaling up/out hardware configurations. Extraction of metadata and reconciliation of data quality requirements must also be fulfilled through the data integration process in order to enable the data lineage across the whole data lifecycle in the warehouse. An enterprise-wide data model provides unified, consolidated view of the data which enables a consistent, logical representation of business data across different functional areas of a whole enterprise. As the data management side of data warehouse is focused on loading the data in an efficient manner while the analytical users are more interested in retrieving data in a fast and agile way, data warehouse architecture has to enable an easy way of finding the balance of both sides.

Built upon the past decade's research explorations, data warehouse software vendors are instantiating tools and engineering practices on these classical architecture topics. While vendors are rolling out more and more parallel-processing database and ETL engines, enterprise-wide metadata and data quality tools, and eagerly extending their center of excellence with vast amount of data warehousing practices, both the data warehouse industry and academic worlds are facing new challenges when novel concepts such as SOA, web 2.0, and cloud computing are spreading over the whole IT community. This chapter is devoted to addressing what challenges these new trends bring to the data warehouse architecture and how the different academic research can be used to contribute to the future data warehouse architecture practices to solve the new challenges. The chapter also addresses challenges and research directions on several emerging data warehousing topics, such as real time data warehousing, data privacy, and warehousing semi-structured and unstructured data.

The rest of the chapter is organized as follows. Section 2 describes data warehouse architecture practices and related research works. Section 3 explores the emerging architecture trends and describes the challenges that these trends bring to different research explorations. Section 4 summarizes the chapter and points our future directions of data warehouse architecture.

DATA WAREHOUSE ARCHITECTURE PRACTICES

IT system architecture is the conceptual design that describes the structure and behavior of the system. Likely, data warehouse architecture presents a formal description of the system, which is organized in a way that supports reasoning about its structural properties. Normally, data warehouse architecture includes definitions of basic building blocks of and describes how these building blocks are constructed, connected and interrelated to implement the overall data warehouse.

Similar to the different types of blueprints that are made in building architecture, data warehouse architecture is normally organized into different perspectives (or, views) to describe the architecture from the perspective of specific set of stakeholders and their concerns. For instance, a component-perspective describes the basic components and layers of the architecture and how they form the data warehouse system.

There are quite a few frameworks (Zachman, 1987; Kruchten, 1995) to define IT system architecture. However, we proceed to describe the data warehouse architecture in an easy-understanding way rather than following any of the existing

frameworks. We proceed to define the basic building blocks of data warehouse architecture and describe an example architecture prototype. We will then introduce a few industry practices based on the prototype architecture.

Building Blocks of Data Warehouse Architecture

There are quite a few different definitions of what is a data warehouse, such as in Inmon and Kimball's books (Inmon, 2005; Kimball & Ross, 2002). In a broad sense, the data warehouse can be seen as an organization's electronically stored data and is designed to facilitate business intelligence processes such as reporting and data analysis. To discover the basic elements in data warehouse architectures, we begin with a brief introduction of three major data warehouse architecture patterns that have been used in different industry in the past decades.

Figure 1 depicts the component-perspective of a typical type of data warehouse architecture. The figure describes a pattern where different operational systems are connected to different data marts which are then used by ad hoc queries or reporting applications. These operational systems are normally understood as systems that capture the transactions of a line of business and they should be thought of as outside the data warehouse. A data mart is a relatively small repository that contains a subset of the organization data. Data marts are normally created to serve requirements from specific business areas.

In this "point-to-point integration" architecture, end users normally access data in the data marts for certain analytical or reporting purposes. This architecture pattern allows different data marts to be directly connected to required source of data and thus enable the "fast time-to-market" requirements from the business side. However, the amount of connections between operational systems and data marts are becoming overwhelming over time. It is impossible to achieve a unified

Figure 1. Point-to-point integration architecture

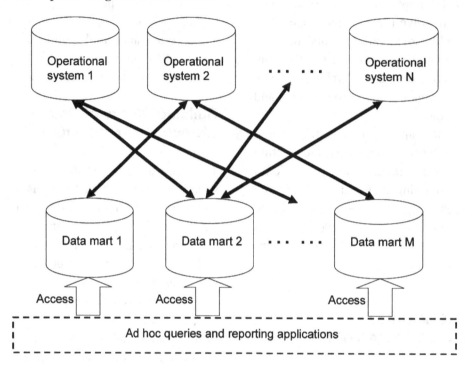

view of data in the whole organization.

Figure 2 depicts an architecture where all the operational systems deliver their production data into a single repository and data marts and different applications and users can use these production data for purposes like analysis and reporting. Here the "production data warehouse" contains production data from different operational systems. There is normally no transformation to the production data after it is loaded into the production data warehouse.

In this "production data warehouse" architecture, the management of data at different operational systems is eased by putting the data into a single repository. It becomes easier to get an overview of all kinds of data at an organization. Since the data delivery from operational system to the production data warehouse can be ensured through "service level agreement (SLA)" and there are no further operations over the data after they are loaded into the data warehouse, the efficiency for loading the data at data marts, business intel-

ligence (BI) applications or for different users to directly query the data is quite optimal. On the other hand, since there is no data transformation in the data warehouse, there can be quite a big amount of data redundancy and inconsistency within the warehouse. Specifically, when two or more operational systems contain the same area of data, such as customer information, these data will all be loaded into different tables in the production data warehouse without any further conformations and standardizations.

Figure 3 shows the typical data warehouse bus architecture defined in Kimball & Ross, 2002. This architecture is generally divided into 4 layers. The first layer contains all the operational systems. These systems deliver production data to the next layer according to the SLAs. The second layer, called "data staging area," contains data deliveries from different source systems that are temporally kept in its original format or in database, such as flat files or relational tables. The data staging area involves data extraction, transformation, and

Figure 2. Production data warehouse architecture

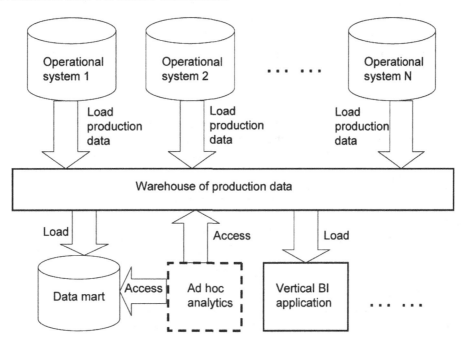

loading (ETL) operations to conform data from different sources into the target format in the next layers. This layer also contains data cleansing and standardization processes to ensure the quality of data. As in the practices recommended in Inmon, 2005, the data staging area often contains a so-called "operational data store (ODS)" where the recent operational data is kept and accessed by special applications or users for fast reporting and analytics. The third layer in this architecture is called "data presentation area" where data is organized, stored and made available for different usage purposes. As the data staging area is not open to any users, the data presentation layer is typically accessed by users. This layer is often made by a series of integrated data marts. The concept of "star-schema" and dimensional modeling provides the soil of building integrated data marts by conformed dimensions and facts. As recommend in Inmon, 2005, it may be necessary to consider building an integrated "Enterprise data warehouse (EDW)" before the layer of dimensional models to hold all the different enterprise data in a single

model and serve other data marts with data from this EDW. Having an EDW can be seen as a deviation to the enterprise bus architecture. In many real world cases of the bus architecture, one of these data marts can contain most areas of data and serve the role of primary data warehouse (similar to the purpose of the EDW). Other data marts are still connected to the data staging area in this case but are more focused on specific business areas. The "data access tools" is the fourth layer of this architecture. All the different BI tools are contained in this layer and these tools access the data in the data presentation layer for certain purpose of usage.

In this architecture, the conformed dimensions and facts provide a ground of understanding all the enterprise data in a general sense. The data staging area ensures that the quality is controlled and redundancy of data is minimized. However, since the architecture involves 4 layers, the time from when the data is loaded from operational systems to when the end-user is able to generate report based on the latest data is much longer

Figure 3. Data warehouse bus architecture

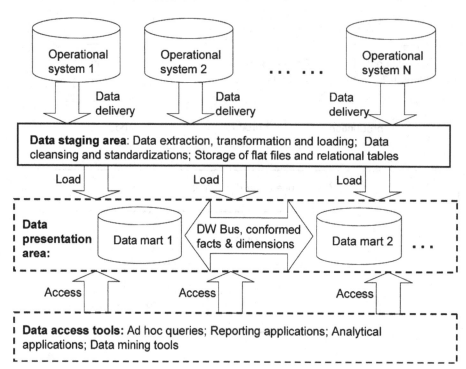

than the architectural patterns depicted in Figures 1 and 2. In addition, as being practiced by many different industries, to use a star-schema (or, a "snow-flake" schema) to model and keep a large organization data in a single, multidimensional model has not been very successful. In fact, many organizations are struggling between the loading time of the batch jobs and the query performance and the end-user side.

Although the different architectural patterns described in Figures 1, 2 and 3 have both advantages and disadvantages, all these patterns are still being practiced in different enterprises. Table 1 lists the important building blocks of data warehouse architecture.

An Architecture Prototype

To provide a background of the prototype data warehouse architecture, we present the five requirements that are most commonly used in building data warehouses.

- The data warehouse must integrate data from different business areas of the enterprise in order to ensure the "one version of truth" of data.
- The data warehouse must provide users a clear and complete catalogue of metadata.
- The data warehouse must ensure the quality of data.
- The data warehouse must have efficient performance in order to minimize the time period between the data is delivered from operational system and the data is harvested by the data access tools.
- The data warehouse must ensure usability of data when it provides data to any data access tools, methods and BI applications.

These requirements can be implemented by different data warehouse architectures with different practices. Figure 4 depicts one architecture pattern that can be shaped towards fulfilling the listed requirements. In this prototype architec-

Table 1. Building blocks of data warehouse architecture

Basic architecture element	Description
Operational system	A system that captures the transactions of a line of business
Data staging area	A storage area and a set of ETL and data quality processes
ETL operation	An operation that does data extraction, transformation, or loading
Data mart	A data silo with a subset of the whole enterprise data
Enterprise data warehouse	A data warehouse with an integrated data model that keeps the whole enterprise data
Data access tools	Tools, applications and user usage that create different BI output by accessing data in the data marts
Operational data store	A repository of most recent operational data and accessed by special applications or users for fast reporting and analytics

ture, the data staging area transforms the data and applies data quality processes before the data from operational systems is changed into an integrated data model in the enterprise data warehouse. The enterprise data warehouse normally utilizes a relational data model to keep the different business data in the whole enterprise in an integrated manner. The enterprise data warehouse either feeds data to data marts which are built upon star-schema models or directly provide data to data access tools. The metadata repository is a special tool that integrates metadata from different layers, components of the architecture in a single place in order to provide a single, unified view of all the metadata in the whole architecture.

The prototype architecture can fulfill the 5 requirements by the following practices. First, to

Figure 4. Prototype data warehouse architecture

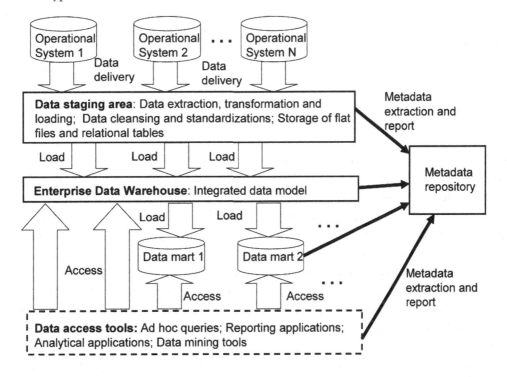

ensure one version of the truth of data, the integrated data model at the enterprise data warehouse must hold the most detailed enterprise data in a generic and versatile way so that correction and re-calculation of data will use this layer as the ground. Second, the metadata repository must include a clear metadata catalogue and the metadata can be extracted from different sources in time. Third, in the data staging area, the ETL process and data cleansing as well as standardization operations must be pre-defined according to data quality requirements so that these operations can be applied to the data from operational systems and only qualified data can be loaded into the enterprise data warehouse. Fourth, the database platform as well as the ETL tool must be tuned in order to meet the performance requirement. The direct link from the enterprise data warehouse to data access tools also provides a "short-cut" when data marts are unavailable or unnecessary to be placed between these two layers. Fifth, the data marts must be designed in an "easy to understand" format in order for users to access and use. The star-schema design is a good practice of "easy to understand" format.

Architecture Practices and Related Work

Based on the prototype architecture depicted in Figure 4, we proceed to introduce different industry practices in data warehouse architecture and describe academic research works that are related to these practices.

The data model is an essential part of data warehouses. The concept of dimensional modeling has been spread to almost every data warehouse system. However, many industry practices have proved that the dimensional modeling techniques are not able to hold different data of a whole enterprise. Instead, a few data warehouse model vendors, such as IBM and Teradata, provide industry standard models based on relational modeling and normal form theory. Historical data is a compulsory

part of any data warehouses. Although temporal database theory has been well investigated in the research community (Jensen & Snodgrass, 1999), most industry practices are focused on separating history data from the current status of entities, identifying entities that are only linked to either a time period or a time point, and finding out how the changes to each record should be applied. In the dimensional modeling theory and the discussion of slowly changing dimensions, the type 1 and type 2 updates are mostly used in the industry.

Metadata is often defined as "data about data." Data warehouses in enterprises are often in an environment where different tools are involved in the architecture. Management of these different metadata is often split into different tools due to the cost of integration. The problem of metadata integration and interpretability has recently been attracting attentions at the research community (Bernstein, 2005; Hauch, Miller, & Cardwell, 2005; Friedrich, 2005). Data lineage is a practice that quite a few metadata and ETL tools are establishing at different data warehouses (Cui & Widom, 2000). Data lineage records where data is and how it flows to, so that it is easy to securely manage the lifecycle of data when it moves across the whole data warehouse architecture. As indicated in Marco (2004), the implementation of a metadata repository is in fact very similar to building data warehouses.

Most early adaptors of data warehouses have the experience of suffering from bad quality of data. Normally, data is considered of high quality if they correctly represent the real world construct to which they refer to. The dominant industry practice of data quality is to apply quality-checking and controlling operations in the ETL processes, such as data cleansing and data standardization. These operations are normally based on data integrity rules and business logics discovered in the data modeling process. Data quality has already been a focus in the research community (Ballou & Tayi, 1999). Data quality at data warehouses often depends on the quality of delivered data from operational systems. Many industry practices indicate that data quality should in fact be controlled on the whole enterprise lifecycle rather than only at the data warehouse.

Performance management is normally a compulsory practice of any data warehouses. The study of database theories and ETL efficiency (Thomsen, Pedersen, & Lehner, 2008; Luo, Naughton, Ellmann, & Waltzk, 2006) provides the foundation of many performance tuning functionalities and practices in different vendors of database systems and ETL tools. Many database vendors are currently experiencing challenges of managing over hundreds of terabytes of data. The research work on parallel processing and data warehouse management (Datta, VanderMeer, & Ramamritham, 2002; Furtado, 2004) paves the directions that industry is heading for. The study of data federation (Haas, Lin, & Roth, 2002) is also a practice of managing large volume data warehouses.

OLAP cube is one of the most widely used data access tools in data warehouses. The research community has a quite broad study of data cube since the paper by Gray et al., 1996. Many research results in the area of data mining, such as clustering, nearest neighbor search, neutral network have been putting into practices by different BI vendors. In addition, the study of in-memory database and OLAP technologies (Lehman & Carey, 1986; Ross, 2004) has been implemented into different desktop-based analytical tools.

To summarize, different practices of data warehouse architecture come from both the engineering experiences and the results and contributions of the research community. These practices can change over the time when different trends and challenges occur to the data warehouse architecture. We proceed to describe several emerging trends in the data warehousing and software architecture world and discuss how these trends influence the practices of data warehouse architecture.

TRENDS AND CHALLENGES TO DATA WAREHOUSE ARCHITECTURE

The past decade of data warehousing practices have let different enterprises into the era of integrating and consolidating different source of information into centralized data warehouses. However, the rapidly-changing business requirements pose further challenges to the effectiveness and efficiency of having a "hub-and-spoke" data warehouse architecture. In parallel to this, the IT technology trend has entered the web 2.0 era and concepts such as service-oriented-architecture, real-time data warehousing, and master data management are widely spread. We proceed to elaborate on the major trends that are influencing the data warehouse architecture.

Service Oriented Data Warehouse Architecture

Service-oriented architecture (SOA) is a collection of services which communicate with each other. Such communications, varying from simple data delivery to coordination of multiple services, form the ground of orchestration of encapsulated enterprise services. As the basic element of SOA, a service can be understood as a well-defined, loosely coupled, interoperable, and composable software component or software agent. A service must have well-defined interfaces based on standard protocols as well as quality-of-service attributes or policies on how the interfaces can be used.

Many existing data warehouses were designed with assumptions that the workflows around them are simple and pre-defined. For example, ETL programs are often executed as one big batch window and all the transformation, conformation and data cleansing functionalities are tightly bound with each other in the program. In the SOA concept, traditional data warehouse architecture needs to be broken down into different services on the enterprise service bus. The management of data warehouse performance and data security and privacy should be laid behind these data warehouse services.

Figure 5 depicts example services based on the prototype architecture in Figure 4. Here we group the operations and components based on the major layers of the prototype architecture and form these different groups into service contracts. These data-warehouse-oriented service contracts are listed in the "enterprise service bus" which contains a complete category of all available services of an enterprise.

Compared to the prototype architecture depicted in Figure 4, SOA-enabled data warehouse architecture provides benefits such as reusability, integration, and fast "time-to-market." Specifically, a developed data standardization program, once provided as a service, can be re-used as a part of the solution to the implementation of other data quality requirements. The same service can also be called on by an operational system as part of its own data validation steps. Integration of data between the data warehouse and other enterprise

systems becomes easier because different systems can interact via the same service-oriented platform. The data warehouse architecture is able to produce data-as-a-service to end-users and other enterprise systems. When a business requirement comes, it is very easy to pick up related data or operations in the data warehouse services and form them into the solution. This "mesh-up" concept makes the implementation of business requirement fast and agile.

To guarantee these benefits, a service-oriented data warehouse architecture must contain a unified meta model and an integrated enterprise data model. The meta model ensures the smooth integration of metadata between the data warehouse and the rest of the enterprise IT systems. An integrated enterprise data model helps the whole end-user community of the data warehouse to have a unified and agreed view of data. Interoperability of the data warehouse metadata and data guarantees the orchestration of different pieces in the data warehouse architecture.

A few issues have to be addressed when SOA

Figure 5. Example data warehouse services

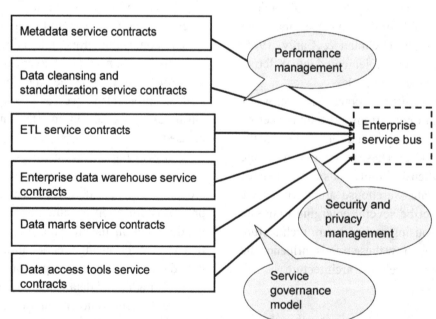

is integrated into a whole enterprise data lifecycle. In an organization which follows strict rules and regulations on data protection, the security and privacy requirements on data or services have to be implemented into both the metadata repository and the data or service model. Whether to hold the "one-version of truth" of data by physically integrating different areas of data into the enterprise data warehouse or to stay on more federated data warehouse architecture when data are logically integrated through a data federation layer poses a question to the efficiency and robustness of SOA design. Since the "master truth" of different areas of data is located at different stages of the whole data lifecycle, the SOA design has to include a logical layer which provides a centralized view of the distributed master data.

One advantage of implementing a service-oriented data warehouse architecture is the natural integration of ETL, database and BI tools on the service level. Whether ETL process is within or outside the database systems is only a matter of performance. SOA enables the easy integration of data warehouse into enterprise usage of Web 2.0 technology, and enriches the capabilities for real time data warehousing and agile master data management. These will be discussed in the rest.

How Web 2.0 Influences Data Warehouse Architecture

The concept of Web 2.0 has been spread by different tags such as "Wiki," "blog," "folksonomy," etc. One basic feature of Web 2.0 is to enable the separation of web scheme and web content so that the re-usage and re-creation of web information can be liberally maximized. As Web 2.0 has certain overlap with SOA, the rest of our discussion is focused on the specific features in Web 2.0 that are related to data warehouse architectures.

Based on the prototype architecture in Figure 5, all the relevant semantics of the data warehouse data and operations are contained in a centralized

metadata repository. When the metadata repository contains a clear, layered view of the ontology behind the metadata, the centralized repository actually enables the migration or integration of data warehouse easy and secure. Specifically, when a data warehouse has to be merged with another data warehouse based on a different data model, the integration process is mainly on the ontology of both data warehouses. In fact, the integration process can start by quietly interpreting the ontology published on the metadata site of both data warehouses and finish with a new ontology which represents data from both data warehouses in a unified meta model.

When the data access tools in the prototype architecture, such as BI dash-boards, present reports or analytical results to end-users, it is quite often that the presented results need to be re-structured or re-organized to allow different observations. Here, it becomes critical to separate the ontology and semantics of the BI reports from the data so that the re-organization becomes direct and fast.

A unified meta model that represents all parts of the data warehouse architecture is an essential part to bring Web 2.0 technologies into data warehouses. In fact, many industry vendors have been paving the way for the establishment of the Common Warehouse Model (CWM) (Medina, & Trujillo, 2002). As pointed by Friedrich, 2005, the versioning and configuration management of metadata is also quickly becoming a focus of both industry development and academic research.

Real Time Data Warehousing Architecture

The concept of real time data warehousing comes from the requirement that an organization needs to be more responsive to changing business circumstances. Ideally, an organization needs to react instantly to business needs. However, from the data warehousing technology perspective, real time requirement has to be broken down to different interpretations as it always takes time to collect and process data before it is delivered to business users.

Take the prototype architecture in Figure 5 as an example, a practice of implementing near-real-time requirements is to add an operational data store (ODS) at the data staging area such that analysis and reporting applications can access the data once they are delivered from operational systems and generate report in short time. To shorten the time of committing a record change in an operational system into the ODS or the data warehouse, the ETL processes in the data staging area can be directly linked to the databases of the operation systems. Techniques such as change data capture (CDC) and message queues can be applied in the ETL processes in order to provide a fast reflection of record change in the operational system.

Although different technologies can be applied to enable the near-real-time loading of changed data into the data warehouses and ODSs, the whole data warehouse architecture has to face the following challenges:

- Compared to the typical ways of loading large volumes of data in a bigger time period (say, per 12 hours), the near real time loading of data normally brings a good amount of execution of loading jobs with very small amount of changes to the data warehouse at each job. Such change of job execution profiles requires a sufficient configuration and scalability planning of the data warehouse platform.
- In an integrated data warehouse where the integrity of the data model is essential, the more frequent data loading brings more challenges to the modeling practices. In a case when an entity in the data model is updated based on data from records of multiple operational systems, a record change from one of the operational systems may require the other operational systems to

deliver data before the change is added to the corresponding entity in the data warehouse model.

- The more frequent loading of data with smaller amount of changes also requires that related metadata information needs to be updated at the same frequency. As the data warehouse is a multi-layered structure, a record change at an operational system naturally causes a ripple effect on all the related metadata at different layers of the data warehouse architecture. The quality of the metadata has to be maintained.

Master Data Management with Data Warehouse Architecture

Master data management (MDM) is an enterprise data management practice to actively manage and control enterprise-wide master data. Compared to data warehouses, MDM covers a broader scope by unifying critical datasets across multiple IT systems. There are very well-understood and easily identified master-data items, such as "customer" and "product" information. Data warehouses are not directly linked to an MDM solution if the solution is only focused on the real-time integration of certain master data among several operational systems. In the cases where an MDM solution is put at the downstream of an enterprise's data flow, data warehouses play a key role as the trusted source of master data.

MDM brings various benefits such as enhancement of data quality, preservation of data integrity and consistency, and reduced time-to-market on implementing business requirements. We list the following trends when MDM is applied over data warehouse architectures.

First, according to the prototype architecture in Figure 5, data quality processes are applied only at the data staging area. As a data warehousing practices, data cleansing and standardization operations must be applied to the data warehouse data flow only once. In the context of MDM, data quality must be considered multiple times during the whole enterprise data lifecycle. In the data warehouse architecture, quality of data after each "loading data" process should also be checked. The definition of data quality rules must be consistent with the enterprise's data quality discipline. If a SOA method is applied to the data staging area, the data cleansing and standardization operations in the data staging area are either services provided by other parties through the enterprise service bus or providing services to other parties through the enterprise service bus.

Second, the integrated data model at the enterprise data warehouse must be reconciled with the model of master data. One challenge of managing the consistency between the two models lies in that the data model in MDM is normally concerned with the current data while the data model in the enterprise data warehouse covers a longer history of data. Connected to the data models, there should be a single and consistent data governance model over both the master data and data in the data warehouse.

Third, the typical workflows around data warehouse architecture are normally started from an activity triggered from operational system, such as a data delivery or change of metadata. And these workflows normally finish by an activity at the data access tools side, such as a report that is generated or an analytical result is produced. When MDM is considered, the workflows have to be integrated with activities at the operational systems. Extending data warehouse architecture into SOA architecture is capable of facilitating this integration process. In service-oriented data warehouse architecture, different data warehouse services can be easily assembled into workflows.

CONCLUSION

The research and development of data warehousing technologies have evolved into the era that complex, high volume, and various types of data have to be processed and managed in a timely manner to fulfill vast amount of business requirements. The rapid-growing hardware improvement, new internet infrastructures and emerging computing frameworks are facilitating the future development of data warehouses while posing fresh challenges to the architecture design of data warehouses. This chapter is dedicated to review existing industry practices on data warehouse architectures and introduce new challenges and trends to the future of architecture design patterns for data warehouses. Compared to the classical theory of software and information system architecture, data warehouse architecture is more dependent on the different properties and aspects of its key asset, the data. Different architectural patterns in normal software system design have to be tailored to meet the demands of efficient management of data. As a conclusion of the chapter, it becomes an urgent need to both the information system architecture and database communities that a data-centric architecture discipline has to be settled for further development of data warehouse and database architectures.

REFERENCES

Adiba, M. E., & Lindsay, B. G. (1980). Database Snapshots. In *Proc. Of VLDB* (pp. 86-91).

Agrawal, R., Gupta, A., & Sarawagi, S. (1997). Modeling Multidimensional Databases. In *Proc. ICDE* (pp. 232-243).

Ballou, D. P., & Tayi, G. K. (1999). Enhancing Data Quality in Data Warehouse Environments. [CACM]. *Communications of the ACM*, *42*(1), 73–78. doi:10.1145/291469.291471

Bell, M. (2008). Introduction to Service-Oriented Modeling. In *Service-Oriented Modeling: Service Analysis, Design, and Architecture*. Hoboken, NJ: Wiley & Sons Inc.

Bernstein, P. A. (2005). The Many Roles of Meta Data in Data Integration. In *Proc. SIGMOD* (pp. 792).

Böhm, C., Berchtold, S., Kriegel, H.-P., & Michel, U. (2000). Multidimensional Index Structures in Relational Databases. *Journal of Intelligent Information Systems, 15*(1), 51–70. doi:10.1023/A:1008729828172

Chaudhuri, S., & Dayal, U. (1997). An Overview of Data Warehousing and OLAP Technology. *SIGMOD Record, 26*(1), 65–74. doi:10.1145/248603.248616

Cui, Y., & Widom, J. (2000). Lineage Tracing in a Data Warehousing System. In *Proc. ICDE* (pp. 683-684).

Darmont, J., Boussaid, O., Ralaivao, J. C., & Aouiche, K. (2005). An Architecture Framework for Complex Data Warehouses. *ICEIS,* (1), 370-373.

Datta, A., VanderMeer, D. E., & Ramamritham, K. (2002). Parallel Star Join DataIndexes: Efficient Query Processing in Data Warehouses and OLAP. *IEEE Transactions on Knowledge and Data Engineering, 14*(6), 1299–1316. doi:10.1109/TKDE.2002.1047769

Friedrich, J. R. (2005). Meta-data Version and Configuration Management In Multi-vendor Environments. In *Proc. SIGMOD* (pp. 799-804).

Furtado, P. (2004). Experimental evidence on partitioning in parallel data warehouses. In *Proc. DOLAP* (pp. 23-30).

Furtado, P. (2006). Node Partitioned Data Warehouses: Experimental Evidence and Improvements. *Journal of Database Management, 17*(2), 43–61.

Gray, J., Bosworth, A., Layman, A., & Pirahesh, H. (1996). Data Cube: A Relational Aggregation Operator Generalizing Group-By, Cross-Tab, and Sub-Total. In *Proc. ICDE* (pp. 152-159).

Gupta, A., & Mumick, I. S. (1995). Maintenance of Materialized Views: Problems, Techniques, and Applications. *IEEE Data Eng. Bull., 18*(2), 3–18.

Haas, L., Lin, E. T., & Roth, M. T. (2002). Data integration through database federation. *IBM Systems Journal, 41*(4), 578–596.

Hauch, R., Miller, A., & Cardwell, R. (2005). Information Intelligence: Metadata for Information Discovery, Access, and Integration. In *Proc. SIGMOD* (pp. 793-798).

Inmon, W. H. (2005). *Building The Data Warehouse* (4th Ed). Indianapolis, IN: Wiley Computer Publishing Inc.

Jensen, C. S., & Snodgrass, R. T. (1999). Temporal Data Management. *IEEE Transactions on Knowledge and Data Engineering, 11*(1), 36–44. doi:10.1109/69.755613

Kimball, R., & Ross, M. (2002). *The Data Warehouse Toolkit* (2nd Ed.). New York: John Wiley & Sons, Inc.

Kruchten, P. (1995). Architectural Blueprints — The "4+1" View Model of Software Architecture. *IEEE Software, 12*(6), 42–50. doi:10.1109/52.469759

Lehman, T. J., & Carey, M. J. (1986). A Study of Index Structures for Main Memory Database Management Systems. In *Proc. VLDB,* (pp. 294-303).

Luo, G., Naughton, J. F., Ellmann, C. J., & Waltzk, M. W. (2006). Transaction Reordering and Grouping for Continuous Data Loading". In *Proc. BIRTE,* (pp. 34–49).

Marco, D. (2004). *Building and Managing the Meta Data Repository: A Full Lifecycle Guide.* New York: John Wiley & Sons Inc.

Medina, E., & Trujillo, J. (2002). A Standard for Representing Multidimensional Properties: The Common Warehouse Metamodel (CWM). In *Proc. ADBIS* (pp. 232-247).

Pedersen, T. B., & Jensen, C. S. (1999). Multidimensional Data Modeling for Complex Data. In *Proc. ICDE* (pp. 336-345).

Ross, K. A. (2004). Selection conditions in main memory. *ACM Transactions on Database Systems*, *29*, 132–161. doi:10.1145/974750.974755

Theodoratos, D., Ligoudistianos, S., & Sellis, T. K. (2001). View Selection for Designing The Global Data Warehouse. [DKE]. *Data & Knowledge Engineering*, *39*(3), 219–240. doi:10.1016/S0169-023X(01)00041-6

Thomsen, C., Pedersen, T. B., & Lehner, W. (2008). RiTE: Providing On-Demand Data for Right-Time Data Warehousing. In *Proc. ICDE* (pp. 456-465).

Zachman, J. A. (1987). A Framework for Information Systems Architecture. *IBM Systems Journal*, *26*(3), G321–G5298.

KEY TERMS AND DEFINITIONS

Data Integration: Data integration is a process of transforming data at different sources into data at one or more target locations.

Data Mart: Data mart is a data silo of an organization's data. A data mart normally stores data that is oriented to a specific purpose or of a major data subject that is used for specific business needs.

Data Warehouse: Data warehouse is a repository of an organization's data. Data warehouses provide data for business intelligence applications such as reporting and analysis, dash board, balanced scorecard, etc.

ETL: Extract, transform, and load (ETL) describes a data warehouse process where data from various source locations are transformed through a data integration process into the target locations. Extract is a process of extracting data from outside sources. Transform is a process of transforming data to fit the operational requirement. Load is a process of loading the data to the end target.

Master Data Management: Master data management (MDM) is a data management discipline to actively manage master data throughout an organization. Master data represents the most correct non-transaction information of an enterprise, such as customer, product, and organization information.

System Architecture: System architecture is the design of structure and behavior of a system. Normally system architecture is represented in a conceptual diagram where different components and their connections are described.

Service-Oriented Architecture: Service-oriented architecture is a system architecture pattern that defines methods for development and integration of systems. In a service-oriented architecture, all functionalities of all the systems are designed in favor of the various business processes that these systems support. These functionalities, also termed as services, are then packaged for reuse.

Chapter 2
Improving Expressive Power in Modeling Data Warehouse and OLAP Applications

Elzbieta Malinowski
University of Costa Rica, Costa Rica

ABSTRACT

Data warehouse and OLAP systems are widely required during the decision-support process, since they provide integrated data in a form that facilitates the expression of complex queries. In order to exploit both systems to their full capabilities, dimensions with hierarchies must be clearly defined. Dimensions can be of different types and they allow users to see quantified data from different perspectives. Hierarchies are important in analytical applications, since they give users the possibility of representing data at different abstraction levels. However, even though there are different kinds of hierarchies in real-world applications and some of them are already implemented in commercial tools, there is still a lack of a well-accepted conceptual model that allows decision-making users to express their analysis needs. In this chapter, we show how the conceptual multidimensional model can be used to facilitate the representation of complex hierarchies and different kinds of dimensions in comparison to their representation in the relational model and commercial OLAP tools, using as an example Microsoft Analysis Services.

INTRODUCTION

A Data Warehouse (DW) provides users with high quality data organized in a way that facilitates expression of complex queries, ensuring at the same time efficient and accurate responses to such queries. Different systems and tools, such as **online analytical processing** (OLAP) systems, can be used

DOI: 10.4018/978-1-60566-816-1.ch002

to access and analyze the data contained in DWs. These systems allow users to interactively query and automatically aggregate data using roll-up and drill-down operations. The former operation transforms detailed data into a summarized one, e.g., daily sales into monthly sales, while the latter operation does the contrary.

The data for DW and OLAP systems is usually organized into fact tables related to several dimension tables. A **fact table** (*Sales* in Figure

Figure 1. Example of a DW for analyzing employees' sales

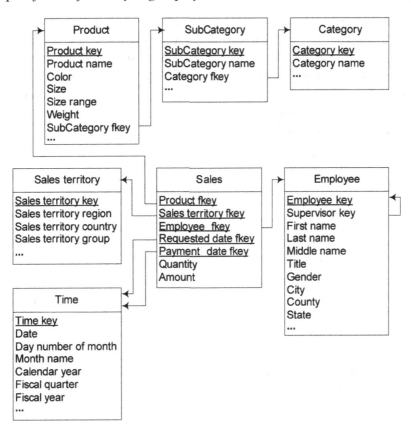

1) represents the focus of analysis (e.g., analysis of employees' sales) and typically includes attributes called **measures**. These are usually numeric values (e.g., *Quantity* and *Amount* in Figure 1) that facilitate a quantitative evaluation of various aspects of interest. **Dimensions** (e.g., *Sales territory* in Figure 1) are used to see the measures from different perspectives, e.g., according to geographic distribution of a company. Dimensions typically include attributes that form **hierarchies**. When a hierarchy is traversed from finer to coarser levels, measures are aggregated, e.g., moving in a hierarchy from a product to a subcategory will give aggregated values of sales for different products subcategories.

Hierarchies can be included in a flat table (e.g., attributes *City-County-State* in the *Employee* table in Figure 1) forming the so-called **star schema** or using a normalized structure (e.g., tables *Product*,

SubCategory, and *Category* in the figure), called the **snowflake schema**.

In order to exploit OLAP systems to their fullest capabilities hierarchies must be clearly defined. Hierarchies are important in analytical applications, since they represent data at different abstraction levels. However, in real-world situations, users must deal with different kinds of hierarchies that either cannot be represented using the current DW and OLAP systems or are represented at the logical level without the possibility of capturing the essential semantics of multidimensional applications. For example, the *Employee* table includes a hierarchy that represents the supervisor-supervisee relationship (the attributes *Employee key* and *Supervisor key*); this hierarchy is difficult to distinguish even though it may be important to consider during the analysis process. Another hierarchy in the same table can be formed by the *City*, *County*, and *State* attributes. However, the schema in Figure 1 does not reflect the real situation about the geographical division of a country where some states do not divide themselves in counties. In addition, the *Sales territory* table includes a hierarchy composed of *Sales territory region*, *Sales territory country*, and *Sales territory group*; nevertheless, the schema in Figure 1 does not represent the hierarchy clearly since some countries are not partitioned into regions, i.e., this attribute will have a null value for those countries that do not have regions. .

A similar situation has occurred with different kinds of dimensions. They have been proposed mainly by practitioners and implemented in some commercial tools due to a growing interest in having DW and OLAP systems in different application areas. Nevertheless, these different kinds of dimensions are difficult to represent using models of current DW and OLAP systems and the proposed implementation solutions are not clear for non-experienced users. An example is the so-called role-playing dimension (the *Time* table in Figure 1) which participates in the fact table several times playing different roles, i.e., in the figure indicating a date of requesting a product and paying for it.

The above-mentioned problems have brought on since the necessity of building DW systems that fulfill user expectations was ahead of formal approaches such as the ones we had for operational databases (List, Bruckner, Machaczek & Schiefer, 2002). In particular, even though DWs are databases dedicated to analytical purposes, the traditional design phases used in operational databases (i.e., requirements specification, conceptual, logical, and physical modeling) are not applied to the DW design. The latter process typically starts at a logical level skipping the conceptual level design. This situation occurs since currently there is no a well-established conceptual model for multidimensional data, even though several proposals have been emerged.

The advantage of using a conceptual model for database design has been acknowledged for several decades. Conceptual schemas are typically expressed using the ER model or the Unified Modeling Language (UML). They facilitate communication between users and designers, given that they do not require knowledge about specific features of the underlying implementation system. The conceptual schemas are also more stable due to the fact that they focus on user requirements and do not change when the target implementation platform changes.

Further, operational databases are usually developed using a relational model that has a strong formalism and many years of accumulated experience in their development. On the other hand, the multidimensional model was proposed in response to complex aggregation queries with little scientific support for establishing the correctness of such a model. Although some scientific works have formally approached the multidimensional model by proposing, among others, aggregation operators (e.g., Gray et al., 1998), summarizability conditions (Lenz & Shoshani, 1997), multidimensional normal forms (e.g., Lehner, Albrecht & Wedekind, 1998; J. Lechtenbörger & G. Vossen, 2003), and conditions for handling structural heterogeneity in hierarchies (Hurtado & Gutierrez, 2007), the usual practice in multidimensional modeling is to use "intuition" or application-ready solutions, such as proposed by Kimball and Ross (2002).

Therefore, the situation is twofold: on the one hand, there is a lack of a well-accepted conceptual multidimensional model as well as a formality and standardization of concepts related to multidimensional model; on the other hand, there is the major influence of practitioners that are proposing specific solutions for developing DWs in different application areas and of commercial tools that include solutions for managing different multidimensional elements.

In this chapter we refer to different kinds of hierarchies and dimensions already classified in

Malinowski and Zimányi (2008); these elements exist in real-world applications and are required during the decision-making process. Many of these hierarchies and dimensions can already be implemented in commercial tools, e.g., in Microsoft SQL Server Analysis Services (SSAS). However, these hierarchies and dimensions cannot be distinguished either at the logical level (i.e., star or snowflake schemas) or in the OLAP cube designer. We will demonstrate the importance of using a conceptual model, such as the MultiDim model (Malinowski & Zimányi, 2008) to facilitate the process of understanding user requirements by characterizing different kinds of hierarchies and dimensions. By using the MultiDim model as an example of a conceptual model we do not intent to suggest that this is the only model that responds to analytical needs. On the contrary, we leave to the designers the decision of using a conceptual multidimensional model among several other already existing models (e.g., A. Abelló, Samos & Saltor, 2006; Luján-Mora, Trujillo & Song, 2006; Rizzi, 2007) that may better fit their needs.

We have chosen SSAS as an example of a commercial OLAP tool, because to our knowledge, it provides different kinds of hierarchies and dimensions that can be included in the cube without incurring into any programming effort, i.e., using a wizard or the click-and-drag mechanism. We will compare the representation of different kinds of hierarchies and dimensions in the MultiDim model, in the relational logical model (star or snowflake schema), and in the SSAS OLAP cube designer.

This chapter does not focus on details as described in Malinowski and Zimányi (2008) for representing different kinds of hierarchies and dimensions. The main objective is to show how many concepts already implemented in commercial tools and accepted by the practitioners may be better understood and correctly specified if the practice for the DW design changes and includes a representation at the conceptual level.

In the next section we survey works related to conceptual modeling for DW and OLAP applications. Then, after introducing a motivating example that is used throughout this chapter, we present the main features of the MultiDim model. The following two sections refer to the conceptual representation and implementation of different kinds of hierarchies and dimensions. The last section includes conclusions.

RELATED WORK

The advantages of conceptual modeling for database design have been acknowledged for several decades and have been studied in many publications. However, the analysis presented in Rizzi (2003) shows the limited interest of the research community in conceptual multidimensional modeling. A detailed description of multidimensional models can be found in Rafanelli (2003) and Torlone (2003) and a comparison of proposals for different kinds of hierarchies in Malinowski and Zimányi (2008).

Current multidimensional models support many hierarchies (e.g., Luján-Mora et al., 2006; Rizzi, 2007; Sapia et al., 1998; Tryfona et al., 1999), in some cases, using different names for the same kind of hierarchy. Some models (e.g., Torlone, 2003) only refer to simple hierarchies. This situation is considered as a shortcoming of existing models for DWs (Hümmer, Lehner, Bauer, & Schlesinger, 2002).

Some proposals provide graphical representations based on the ER model (e.g., Sapia, Blaschka, Höfling & Dinter, 1998; Tryfona, Buisborg & Borch, 1999), on UML (e.g., Abelló, Samos & Saltor, 2006; Luján-Mora et al., 2006), or on specific new notations (e.g., Rizzi, 2007; Hüsemman, Lechtenbörger & Vossen, 2000; Tsois, Karayannidis & Sellis, 2001). Other models give only a description and/or a definition of some of these hierarchies without a graphical representation (e.g.,

Hurtado & Gutierrez, 2007; Jagadish, Lakshmanan, & Srivastava, 1999; Pedersen, Jensen & Dyrsen, 2001; Niemi, Nummenmaa, & Thanisch, 2001; Pourabbas & Rafanelli, 2003). Although Tsois, Karayannidis, and Sellis (2001) state that, without considering graphical representation, many models have the same core expressivity, we believe that a graphical support is an important feature of a conceptual model that allows both designers and users to better understand modeled concepts.

A limited number of papers refers to the representation of different kinds of hierarchies and dimensions at the logical level. Some authors (e.g., Pedersen et al., 2001) transform complex hierarchies into simple ones and implement those using star or snowflake schemas. Another approach is to include an additional structure (e.g., for non-strict hierarchies) or additional members (e.g., for unbalanced or non-covering hierarchies) (Kimball & Ross, 2002), as we will see in the following sections. Other authors (e.g., Jagadish et al., 1999) provide specific mapping to the relational model that captures the semantics of the hierarchy; however, they produce a significant number of relations and require SQL extensions for their management. On the other hand, Song, Rowen, Medsker, and Ewen (2001) have proposed several logical solutions to the problem of managing many-to-many relationships between facts and dimension tables or the so-called multivalued dimensions.

Very few authors present the mappings from the conceptual multidimensional model to the OLAP implementation platform (e.g., Han, Sapia & Blaschka, 2000; Trujillo, Palomar, Gomez & Song, 2001). Even though their conceptual models allow representing some constructs as described in this chapter (i.e., they better represent multidimensional semantics), the chosen implementation tools do not support such constructs. As a consequence, some multidimensional elements presented in the conceptual schemas must be ignored or transformed to simple ones in order to be implemented.

Some commercial products, such as Microsoft Analysis Services 2005 and Oracle OLAP 10g, can cope with some of the hierarchies and dimensions described in the following sections. However, they rely mainly on the star or snowflake structure that does not allow the designer to clearly represent the different kinds of hierarchies and dimensions or they use specific representations related to the chosen OLAP tool.

MOTIVATING EXAMPLE

In this section we briefly describe an example that we use throughout this chapter in order to show the necessity of having a conceptual model for representing different kinds of hierarchies and dimensions for the DW and OLAP applications.

The schema in Figure 2 shows an extract of the AdventureWorksDW database issued by Microsoft[1] (Microsoft, 2005). This schema is used for analysis of sales by resellers (the fact table *FactResellerSales*) and represents the measures (e.g., *SalesAmount* or *OrderQuantity,* not shown in the figure), on the level of individual products. This fact table also includes an attribute *SalesOrderNumber* that allows the user to group the products that were purchased together in the same transaction.

Sales are analyzed from different perspectives, i.e., dimensions. The *Product* dimension includes a hierarchy using the snowflake structure representing products, subcategories, and categories (the *DimProduct, DimProductSubcategory,* and *DimProductCategory* tables). The *Time* dimension (the *DimTime* table) includes attributes that allow users to analyze data considering calendar and fiscal periods of time. This dimension is also used for representing different dates, e.g., order date (when the product was ordered), due date (when the product was delivered), and ship date (when the product was shipped).

Another perspective of analysis is represented

Figure 2. An extract of the AdventureWorksDW schema

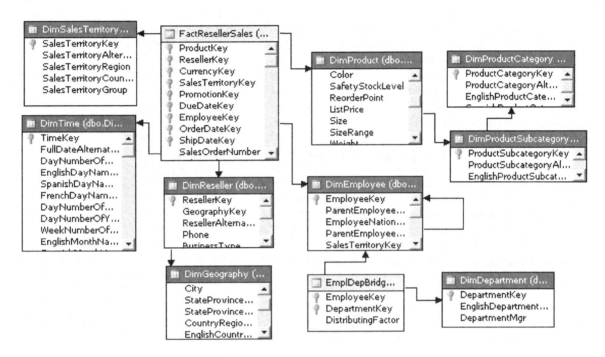

by the *DimSalesTerritory* table, which allows decision-making users to analyze measures considering the geographical distribution of a sales organization. The *DimReseller* table in Figure 2 includes stores that resell products and has attached the table *DimGeography*, which indicates geographical distribution of these stores. In addition, this schema contains an employee dimension (the *DimEmployee* table in the figure) with an organizational hierarchy of supervisors and subordinates. We slightly modified the *DimEmployee* table and deleted the attribute *DepartmentName*. Instead, we created a new table that represents different departments. Since we assigned some employees to two different departments, we had to create an additional table (the *EmplDepBridge* table in Figure 2). This table represents all assignments of employees to their corresponding departments and, in addition, includes an attribute called *DistributingFactor* that indicates how to distribute measures between different departments for employees that work in more than one department,

e.g., assign 70% of sales to the department 10 and 30% of sales to the department 14.

As can be seen in Figure 2, even though there are several hierarchies that users are interested in exploring, only the hierarchy represented as snowflake schema (e.g., *Product-Subcategory-Category*) can be distinguished. We will see in the next section how this situation can be changed using a conceptual model.

Conceptual Representation

The MultiDim model (Malinowski & Zimányi, 2008) is a multidimensional model that allows designers to represent at the conceptual level all elements required in DW and OLAP applications, i.e., dimensions, hierarchies, and facts with associated measures. In order to present a brief overview of the model[2], we use the example in Figure 3. The schema in this figure corresponds to the logical schema in Figure 2. We include in the schema only those hierarchies that are relevant

Figure 3. A conceptual representation of the logical schema from Figure 2

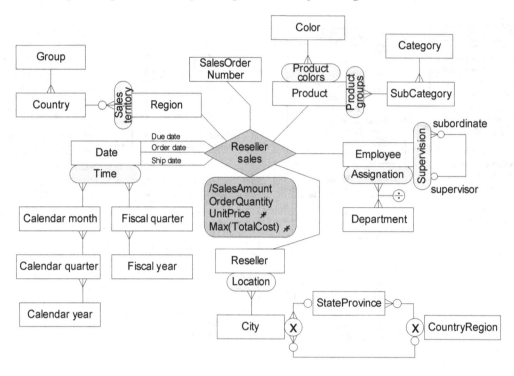

to this work and we omit all attributes since they are the same as in Figure 2.

A **schema** consists of a set of dimensions and a set of fact relationships. A **dimension** is an abstract concept that allows grouping data that share a common semantic meaning. A dimension is composed of a level or a set of hierarchies.

A **level** corresponds to an entity type in the ER model. It describes a set of real-world concepts that have similar characteristics, e.g., the *Product* level in Figure 3. Instances of a level are called **members**. A level has a set of **attributes** that describes the characteristics of their members and one or several **keys** that identify uniquely the members of a level. These attributes are not shown in Figure 1, however, they can be seen in Figure 6a, e.g., the attribute *Country name* is a key attribute for the *Country* level, while *Population* is its descriptive attribute.

A **hierarchy** comprises several related levels, which represent different data granularities, i.e., levels of detail. For example, the *Employee* level

contains specific information about employees, while the *Department* level may be used to analyze employees from the higher perspective of the department to which they are assigned. Given two related levels of a hierarchy, the lower level is called the **child** and the higher level is called the **parent**. Thus, the relationships composing hierarchies are called **parent-child relationships**. Since these relationships are used only for traversing from one level to the next, they are represented by a line to simplify the notation.

Parent-child relationships are characterized by **cardinalities**, indicating the minimum and the maximum number of members in one level that can be related to a member in another level. We use different symbols for indicating cardinalities: ━━< represents (1,n), ━O< implies (0,n), ━━━ means (1,1), and ━━O indicates (0,1). For example, in Figure 3 the child level *Product* is related to the parent level *SubCategory* with a one-to-many cardinality, which means that every product belongs to only one sub-category and that each sub-category can have many products. The cardinality between the *Employee* and *Department* levels are many-to-many, indicating that the same employee can be assigned to different departments; this hierarchy may include a symbol of ⊕ called a **distributing factor** that indicates how the measures associated with an employee are divided between departments. These and other cardinalities in the parent-child relationships lead to different kinds of hierarchies, to which we will refer in more detail in the next sections.

The hierarchies may be represented using different structures depending upon analysis purposes; to differentiate these them, we include an **analysis criterion**. For example, the *Product* dimension in Figure 3 includes two hierarchies: *Product groups* and *Product colors*. The former hierarchy comprises the levels *Product*, *SubCategory*, and *Category*, while the latter hierarchy includes the levels *Product* and *Color*.

The hierarchies include two distinguishable levels: the **leaf level** that contains the most detailed data and the **root level** representing the most general data. The leaf level must be the same for all hierarchies included in a dimension and its name is used as the dimension's name. For example, the *Product* dimension includes two hierarchies with the same leaf level *Product*, while the root levels are different for each hierarchy, i.e., the *Color* level for the *Product colors* hierarchy and the *Category* level for the *Product groups* hierarchy.

A **fact relationship** represents a focus of analysis and corresponds to an n-ary relationship between leaf levels, e.g., the *Reseller sales* fact relationship relates the *Product*, *Employee*, *Reseller*, *Date*, and *Region* levels in Figure 3. Level members may participate in a fact relationship from 0 to n times, thus defining (0,n) cardinality. To simplify the model, we omit such cardinalities. Moreover, since in some applications it may be required that the same level participates several times in a fact relationship, we define **roles**. To represent each role we use a separate link with a name between the cor-

responding level and the fact relationship, e.g., *Due date*, *Order date*, *Ship date* in Figure 3 for the *Date* dimension.

A fact relationship may contain attributes commonly called **measures**, e.g., *SalesAmount* and *OrderQuantity* in Figure 3; they are usually numeric data meaningful for the leaf members that are aggregated while traversing different hierarchy. Measures have been classified as **additive**, **semiadditive**, or **nonadditive** (Kimball & Ross, 2002; Lenz & Shoshani, 1997). We assume by default that measures are additive, i.e., they can be summarized along all dimensions. To indicate that measures are semiadditive or nonadditive, we include the symbols +! and +, respectively, next to the measure's name as shown for the nonadditive measure *UnitPrice* in Figure 3. By default, for additive measure the sum function is applied when aggregation takes place. If another function is required we include it in the schema, e.g., the maximum value for the measure *TotalCost* in Figure 3. Additionally, measures and level attributes may be calculated on the basis of other measures or attributes. We call them **derived** and use the symbol / as can be seen for the *SalesAmount* measure in Figure 3.

The conceptual schema in Figure 3 contains different kinds of hierarchies and dimensions that cannot be distinguished in the logical schema in Figure 2. We will refer to different elements of the schema in Figure 3 explaining their meaning in more detail and showing the added expressiveness of conceptual representation compared to logical and implementation ones.

Mapping to Relational Model

The usefulness of a conceptual model consists in providing different elements for representing adequately the semantic of an application. However, the conceptual schemas must be transformed into implementation schemas that are currently available for developing the DW and OLAP systems. Malinowski and Zimányi (2008) proposed the mappings of different constructs of the MultiDim model to the relational and object-relational databases. In this chapter, we will summarize the rules used for mapping to the relational model since they are required to have an in-depth understanding of implementation details, as described in the next sections.

The MultiDim model is based on the ER model, thus its mapping to the relational model is based on well-known rules, such as those described in Elmasri and Navathe (2006):

- A level corresponds to an entity type in the ER model; it maps to a relation containing all attributes of the level and includes an additional attribute for a surrogate key.
- A parent-child relationship corresponds to a binary relationship type in the ER model. Two different mappings exist, depending on the cardinality of the child role given that in order to have meaningful hierarchies we assume the maximum cardinality of the parent role equal to n:
  - If the cardinality of the child role is (0,1) or (1,1), i.e., the parent-child relationship is one-to-many, the table corresponding to the child level is extended with the surrogate key of the corresponding parent level, i.e., there is a foreign key in the child relation pointing to its parent relation.
  - If the cardinality of the child role is (0,n) or (1,n), i.e., the parent-child relationship is many-to-many, a new relation is created that contains as attributes the surrogate keys of the parent and child levels. If the parent-child relationship has a distributing factor, an additional attribute is added to the relation.
- A fact relationship corresponds to an n-ary relationship type in the ER model; it requires a new relation that includes as attributes the surrogate keys of the participating levels. Furthermore, if a level plays different roles, each role is represented by an additional surrogate key. Since measures are handled as attributes of the relationship

Figure 4. Hierarchy classification

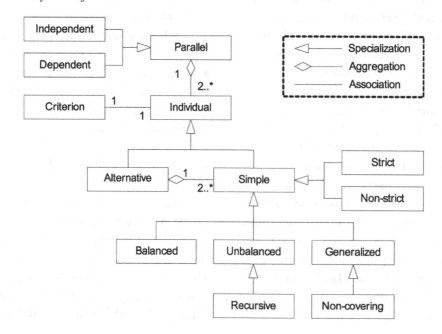

type in the ER model, for every measure an attribute is included in a relation.

In Malinowski and Zimányi (2008) some modifications were proposed to this mapping that are irrelevant for the content of this chapter.

DIFFERENT KINDS OF HIERARCHIES: THEIR REPRESENTATION AND IMPLEMENTATION

Hierarchies are very important elements in analytical processing, since they allow decision-making users to see quantified data, i.e., measures, at different levels of detail. However, even though in real-world applications users need to manage different kinds of hierarchies, the current situation is that either significant programming effort is required in order to manage these hierarchies or logical models are used that make difficult the distinction of these hierarchies.

In Malinowski and Zimányi (2008) we proposed a classification of different kinds of hierarchies as is shown in Figure 4, where we distinguish simple and alternative hierarchies. The latter hierarchies are composed of two or more simple hierarchies. Simple hierarchies include additional types: balanced, unbalanced, and gen-

eralized hierarchies. Also, unbalanced hierarchies are further specialized in recursive hierarchies, while generalized hierarchies include the special case of non-covering hierarchies. For each of these simple hierarchies, another specialization can be applied, making them strict or non-strict. Non-strict hierarchies relax the usual one-to-many cardinality between parent and child levels and allow the inclusion of child members belonging to several parent members, i.e., the many-to-many cardinalities. All these hierarchies are handled as individual hierarchies with only one analysis criterion. Finally, several individual hierarchies may be attached to the same dimension. Depending on whether they share common levels or not, they are called parallel dependent and parallel independent, respectively.

However, even though many of these hierarchies are already implemented in commercial tools, such as in SSAS, they are difficult to distinguish and the proposed implementation solutions are hard to understand. In this section, we will discuss different kinds of hierarchies and dimensions at the conceptual level using the MultiDim model as described above and the conceptual schema in Figure 3. We also include logical representation using relational tables, and cube representation using SSAS. We will show the expressiveness of the conceptual multidimensional model over other types of representations.

Figure 5. A balanced hierarchy: a) schema and b) examples of instances as included in Adventure-WorksDW

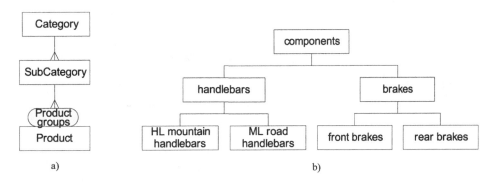

Simple Hierarchies

Simple hierarchies represent hierarchies where the relationship between their members can be represented as a tree, if all its parent-child relationships are one-to-many (Malinowski & Zimányi, 2008). These hierarchies include only one criterion for analysis. Moreover, simple hierarchies are divided into balanced, unbalanced, and generalized hierarchies.

Balanced Hierarchies

A **balanced hierarchy** is a simple hierarchy that has only one path at the schema level, e.g., the *Product groups* hierarchy in Figure 5a (also seen in Figure 3) composed by the *Product*, *SubCategory*, and *Category* levels. Since the parent-child cardinality is many-to-one, at the instance level, the members form a tree where all the branches have the same length, i.e., all parent members have at least one child member and a child member belongs to only one parent member as can be seen in Figure 5b.

Balanced hierarchies are the most common kind of hierarchies. Their mapping to the relational model gives a snowflake schema that can be later denormalized into a star schema.

For example, the *Product groups* hierarchy is represented as snowflake schema in Figure 2 composed of the tables *DimProduct*, *DimProductSubcategory*, and *DimProductCategory*. Note that there are more attributes in the *DimProduct* table that can be used for forming hierarchies, e.g., *Color*, *Size*, *SizeRange*. In the MultiDim level if the attribute is used for aggregation purposes, it should be represented as a separate level, as shown for the *Product colors* hierarchy in Figure 3. If the attribute is not represented as a hierarchy level, this indicates that the user is not interested in using it for aggregation purposes.

SSAS uses the same representation for all kinds of hierarchies (except recursive as we will see later) as shown for the *Sales Territory* hierarchy in Figure 7a.

From the above mentioned example, we see that the balanced hierarchies are distinguishable at the conceptual as well as at the logical and implementation levels. The logical level requires the snowflake representation since otherwise users would need to deduce the structure of a hierarchy considering the names of attributes found in a dimension.

Figure 6. An unbalanced hierarchy: a) schema and b) examples of instances

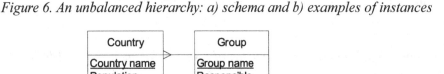
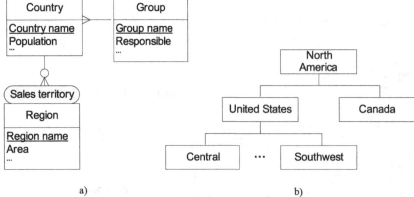

a)   b)

Figure 7. An unbalanced hierarchy in SSAS: a) schema and b), c) instances

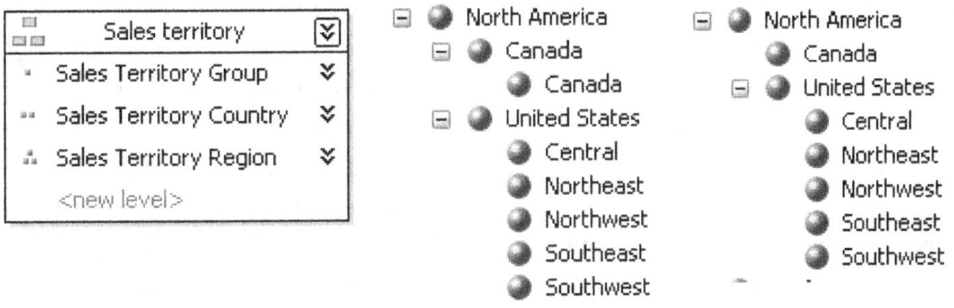

a)   b)   c)

Unbalanced Hierarchies

An **unbalanced hierarchy**[3] is a simple hierarchy that has only one path at the schema level. At the instance level some parent members may not have an associated child. This is implied by the cardinalities as shown in Figure 6a for the *Sales territory* hierarchy composed of *Region*, *Country*, and *Group* levels. Since the division in some countries (e.g., Canada) does not include regions (Figure 6b), the minimum cardinality of the parent role is 0.

Given that in the multidimensional model measures are included in the fact relationship that represents the relationships between leaf members, the unbalanced hierarchies may lead to the problem of excluding from the analysis the members of higher levels that do not have leaf members. For example, since in Figure 3 all measures are associated with the leaf level, i.e., the *Region* level, these measures will be aggregated into the higher levels, i.e., the *Country* level, only for those countries that have regions, excluding Canada from aggregation as can be seen in Figure 6b. To avoid this problem, a usual practice is to transform an unbalanced hierarchy into a balanced one by introducing null values or placeholders in missing levels, e.g., repeating the name of Canada for the *Region* member. Afterwards, the mapping for balanced hierarchies can be applied leading to the star or snowflake schema, e.g., the

DimSalesTerritory table in Figure 2 for the *Sales territory* hierarchy from Figure 3.

SSAS represents an unbalanced hierarchy as shown in Figure 7a. For displaying instances, the designers can choose between two options: to display the repeated member (Figure 7b) (the default option) or to exclude (i.e., hide) this member completely (Figure 7c). To hide a level member, designers should modify the HideMemberIf property by selecting one of the following alternatives: (1) OnlyChildWithParentName: when a parent member has one child member with a parent member name, (2) OnlyChildWithNoName: when a parent member has only one child with a null or an empty string, (3) ParentName: when a parent member have one or more child members with the same name as parent, or (4) NoName: when a parent member have one or more child members with null value. Note that this is an incorrect assignment, because in the case of unbalanced hierarchies only the first and second options should be applied, i.e., the parent member will have at most one child member with the same name, e.g., the name Canada in Figure 7b will be repeated in the missing levels until the tree representing the instances is balanced.

As can be seen, unbalanced hierarchies cannot be differentiated from other kinds of hierarchies using the logical or implementation model since these models only consider schema representations. In contrast, the MultiDim model classifies hierarchies not only at the schema but also at the instance level. Thus, by using corresponding cardinalities designers can represent this kind of hierarchy without ambiguity.

Recursive Hierarchies

Recursive hierarchies[4] are a special case of unbalanced hierarchies and represent the situation where the same level is linked by the two different roles of a parent-child relationship. Figure 3 includes a *Supervision* recursive hierarchy for the *Employee* dimension. This hierarchy represents the employee-supervisor relationship expressed by *subordinate* and *supervisor* roles of the parent-child relationship linked to the same *Employee* level. When recursive hierarchies are used all hierarchy levels most often express the same semantics, i.e., the characteristics of the children and parents are similar (or the same), e.g., where an employee has a supervisor who is also an employee.

The usual way to represent this kind of hierarchy at the logical level is by including a foreign key in the same table that contains a primary key, as can be seen in Figure 2 for the *DimEmployee* table, which includes a *ParentEmployeeKey* representing a supervisor. This implementation is called a parent-child table.

A recursive hierarchy is not represented as a hierarchy in SSAS; instead, a hierarchy symbol ![symbol] is attached to the attribute that represents a parent key. Notice that even though the conceptual (Figure 3) and logical (Figure 2) representations of these kinds of hierarchies are similar, this is not the case for the implementation model of SSAS.

Generalized Hierarchies

A generalized hierarchy occurs when a dimension includes subtypes that can be modeled as a generalization/specialization relationship (Abelló et al, 2006; Akoka, Comyn-Wattiau &Prat, 2001, Luján-Mora et al., 2006) as can be seen in Figure

8a. However, when using ER notation it is not clearly indicated whether levels may form a hierarchy since higher hierarchy levels (e.g., *Category*) may be included in supertype (e.g., *Customer*) and are not related to the other hierarchy levels in its subtypes. Therefore, in Malinowski and Zimányi (2008) we proposed a new notation as shown in Figure 8b to represent a hierarchy that clearly distinguishes different paths according to existing subtypes, e.g., a path formed by the levels *Customer-Occupation type-Category* is used for an individual customer, while a path with the levels *Customer-Business type-Category* may be traversed for a customer that is a reseller.

A **generalized hierarchy** is characterized by having at the schema level multiple exclusive paths sharing at least the leaf level; these paths may also share some other levels, as shown in Figure 8b for the *Category* level. All these paths form one hierarchy that uses the same analysis criterion. Since each member of the hierarchy belongs to only one path, as can be seen in Figure 8c[5], we use the symbol ⊗ to indicate that paths are exclusive for every member at the instance level.

Unfortunately, this kind of hierarchy is not represented as such in the AdventureWorksDW and cannot be implemented in SSAS. In general, the proposed solution is, first, to create two separate dimensions (i.e., for *Individual* and *Reseller* that, in the AdventureWorksDW, correspond to *DimCustomer* and *DimReseller*, respectively) and, second, to use separate fact tables for each of these dimensions. Another commonly-applied solution is to create one flat table with all types of customers and to include null values for the attributes not applicable for the specific type of customer. One disadvantage of these approaches is that the common levels of the hierarchy cannot be easily distinguished and managed, such as the *Customer* and *Category* levels in Figure 8b. Furthermore, the inclusion of null values requires specifying additional constraints that ensure correct queries (e.g., to avoid grouping *Business type*

Figure 8. An example of a) ISA representation and b) schema with c) instances of a generalized hierarchy

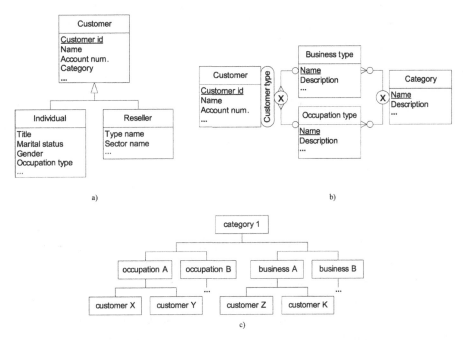

with *Occupation type* in Figure 8b). Therefore, the implementation of this kind of hierarchy currently requires a significant programming effort.

Non-Covering or Ragged Hierarchies

A **non-covering** or **ragged** hierarchy is a special case of a generalized hierarchy. It contains multiple exclusive paths sharing at least the leaf level; however, alternative paths are obtained by skipping one or several intermediate levels of other paths.

The schema in Figure 3 includes a *Location* non-covering hierarchy that is also shown in Figure 9a; this hierarchy is composed of the *Reseller*, *City*, *StateProvince*, and *CountryRegion* levels. However, as can be seen by the straight right-hand line and the cardinalities, some countries do not have division into states. Figure 9b shows some hypothetical instances that we use for this hierarchy[6]. Notice that the cities of Berlin and

Eilenburg do not have members assigned for the StateProvince level.

In order to represent non-covering hierarchy at the logical level, a solution similar to the one used for unbalanced hierarchies is applied, i.e., null values or placeholders are included in the missing members. Then, applying the mapping rules leads to a snowflake or star schema, e.g., a flat *DimGeography* table in Figure 2, with corresponding attributes in addition to the *DimReseller* table, i.e., mixing snowflake and star structures.

SSAS represents a non-covering hierarchy as shown in Figure 10a. When displaying the instances, MS provides the same four options as described for unbalanced hierarchies. However, for non-covering hierarchies, the third and fourth options should be applied, since, for our example in Figure 9b, the parent member with null value has two children. Unfortunately, SSAS does not handle this hierarchy well, since the missing level is always shown as can be seen in Figure 10b.

Figure 9. A non-covering hierarchy: a) schema and b) example of instances

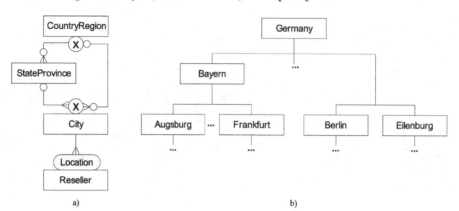

The unbalanced and non-covering hierarchies represent different situations and can be clearly distinguished using a conceptual model (respectively, the *Sales territory* and *Location* hierarchies in Figure 3). However, SSAS considers implementation details that are very similar for both hierarchies, i.e., both include placeholders or null values in missing levels and states that "it may be impossible for end users to distinguish between unbalanced and ragged hierarchies"; they even consider excluding this kind of hierarchy from the future editions of Analysis Services (Microsoft, 2005).

Unbalanced and non-covering hierarchies also differ in the process of measure aggregation. For an unbalanced hierarchy, the measure values are repeated from the parent member to the missing child members and cannot be aggregated during the roll-up operations. For the non-covering hierarchies, the measures should be aggregated for every parent member represented as placeholder or null value in order to propagate aggregation correctly to other higher levels.

Non-Strict Hierarchies

The above-mentioned simple hierarchies only include a parent-child relationship with many-to-one cardinalities, i.e., a child member is related to at most one parent member and a parent member may be related to several child members. However, in real-world applications different situations may occur, e.g., an employee can work in several departments or a mobile phone can be classified

Figure 10. A non-covering hierarchy in SSAS: a) schema and b) instances

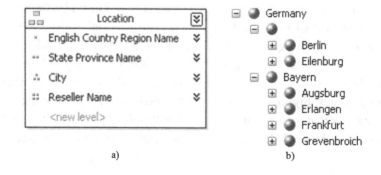

in different product categories. To represent this kind of hierarchy in the multidimensional schema, Malinowski and Zimányi (2008) define **non-strict hierarchies** as simple hierarchies that have at least one many-to-many parent-child relationships at the schema level; a hierarchy is called **strict** if all relationships have many-to-one cardinalities.

Figure 3 includes the *Assignation* hierarchy where an employee can belong to several departments. Since, at the instance level, a child member may have more than one parent member, the members form an acyclic graph (Malinowski & Zimányi, 2008). Non-strict hierarchies induce the problem of double-counting measures when a roll-up operation reaches a many-to-many

relationship, e.g., if an employee belongs to two departments, his/her sales will be aggregated to both these departments, giving incorrect results. To avoid this problem, one of the solutions[7] is to indicate, using the distributing factor symbol, that measures should be distributed between several parent members.

The mapping to the relational model provides the same solution as presented in Figure 2: the *DimEmployee*, *DimDepartment*, and *EmplDep-Bridge* tables represent the *Employee*, *Department* levels and many-to-many cardinalities with the distributing factor attribute, respectively. However, it should be noticed that the logical-level representation with three tables does not allow

Figure 11. A non-strict hierarchy in SSAS in a) a Dimension Usage and b) defining a many-to-many relationship

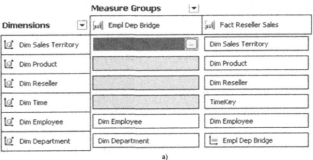

the designer to preserve the meaning of a hierarchy in order to use the roll-up and drill-down operations. This is not the case when using a conceptual model.

SSAS requires several steps in order to use this hierarchy and to obtain correct results. First, the *EmplDepBridge* table is considered as another fact table and *Employee* and *Department* dimensions are handled as separate dimensions (Figure 11a). Later on, using a cube data browser, these dimensions can be combined to form a hierarchy. In the next step, designers must define in the Dimension Usage tab that in order to aggregate a measure from the *Fact Reseller Sales* table, many-to-many cardinalities must be considered (Figure 11b) along with the intermediate measure group *Empl Dep Bridge* table. Note that the MS representation of this cardinality in Figure 11b does not clarify the possibility of performing aggregation of measures from the *Fact Reseller Sales* when rolling-up to the *Department* level. Finally, in order to use a distributing factor from the bridge table, for every measure of the fact table the Measure Expression property must be modified, e.g., for the *SalesAmount* measure we include the expression [*SalesAmount*]*[*DistributingFactor*].

Alternative Hierarchies

Alternative hierarchies, at the schema level, are composed of several non-exclusive simple hierarchies sharing at least the leaf level and accounting for the same analysis criterion (Malinowski & Zimányi, 2008). At the instance level each member participates in all composing hierarchies, thus measure aggregations can be performed as for simple hierarchies. The *Time* hierarchy in Figure 3 is an example of an alternative hierarchy, where the *Date* dimension includes two hierarchies corresponding to the usual Gregorian calendar and to the fiscal calendar of an organization.

Alternative hierarchies are used when the user requires analyzing measures from a unique

perspective (e.g., time) using alternative aggregation paths. For these kinds of hierarchies it is not semantically correct to simultaneously combine the different component hierarchies to avoid meaningless intersections, such as Fiscal 2003 and Calendar 2001. The user must choose only one of the alternative aggregation paths for his/her analysis and switch to the other one if required.

The logical-level representation provides a table for each level leading to a snowflake schema. When the denormalization process is applied, all levels are represented in the same table as it is done for the schema in Figure 2. It should be clear that while this kind of hierarchy is easily differentiated at the conceptual level, it is not possible to characterize it in the logical schema as all attributes forming both paths of alternative hierarchies are included in the flat *DimTime* table in Figure 2.

This kind of hierarchy was implemented in the MS Analysis Services issued with SQL Server 2000 with the goal of improving system performance and storage requirements. This was achieved by including a single key in a fact table and sharing aggregate values of common levels (if they exist). A name included two parts separated by a dot: the first part was common for all composing hierarchies and the second part was a unique hierarchy name, e.g., *Time.Calendar* and *Time.Fiscal* for our example.

The current version of the Analysis Services does not include this kind of hierarchy and the designers should define two different hierarchies that we call parallel: one hierarchy corresponding to calendar and another one to fiscal time periods, allowing combinations between the alternative paths (see Figure 12). This induces the existence of meaningless intersections with null values for measures and does not reuse aggregated values. The better option would be to automatically switch between composing hierarchies. However, if the users are interested in combining hierarchies representing the Gregorian and fiscal calendars and analyze only the intersections with meaningful

Figure 12. Alternative hierarchies implemented as parallel hierarchies.

| | FiscalYear ▾ | | | |
CalendarYear ▾	⊞ 2002 Sales Amount	⊞ 2003 Sales Amount	⊞ 2004 Sales Amount	Total general Sales Amount
⊞ 2001	8065435.3053			8065435.3053
⊞ 2002	8223006.4622	15921423.1918		24144429.654
⊞ 2003		12000247.3264	20202422.0988	32202669.4252
⊞ 2004			16038062.5978	16038062.5978
Total general	16288441.7675	27921670.5182	36240484.6965998	80450596.9822998

values, they should define these hierarchies as parallel instead of alternative.

Notice the difference between generalized and alternative hierarchies. Even though both kinds of hierarchies include several paths and one analysis criterion, the members use exclusive paths in generalized hierarchies and participate in all paths in alternative hierarchies. This distinction is clear in conceptual schemas and cannot be expressed in logical schemas.

Parallel Hierarchies

Parallel hierarchies represent the situation where a dimension has associated several hierarchies accounting for different analysis criteria, e.g., the *Product* dimension in Figure 3 with *Product colors* and *Product groups* hierarchies as well as the *Employee* dimension with the *Assignation* and *Supervision* hierarchies. Such hierarchies can be independent where composed hierarchies do not share levels or dependent, otherwise. The composing hierarchies may be of different kinds. For example, in Figure 3 both hierarchies of the *Product* dimension are balanced, while the *Employee* dimension includes non-strict and recursive hierarchies.

Parallel hierarchies are widely used. They are represented in the logical model either as separate tables for each level (the tables *DimProduct*, *DimProductSubcategory*, and *DimProductCategory* in Figure 2 for the *Product groups* hierarchy in Figure 3,) or as attributes of the table corresponding to the leaf level (the *Color* attribute in the *DimProduct* table in Figure 2 for the *Product colors* hierarchy in Figure 3).

SSAS allows the designer to define this kind of hierarchy as shown in Figure 13a. The composed hierarchies can be combined during the analysis process and answer the queries that refer to both hierarchies, e.g., "what are the sales figures for products that belong to the bike category and are black" as can be seen in Figure 13b.

Notice that alternative and parallel hierarchies are not differentiated at the logical level even though conceptually they are different: the composing paths in multiple hierarchies should not be combined, while this combination can be performed for parallel hierarchies.

DIFFERENT KINDS OF DIMENSIONS: THEIR REPRESENTATION AND IMPLEMENTATION

The design of DWs mainly focuses on discovering and implementing different kinds of hierarchies since they are important in analytical processing. However, as development of DWs increases and expands to different areas of human activities, the scientific community as well as practitioners face new challenges related to representation and implementation of different kinds of dimensions.

Role-Playing Dimensions

In some situations the same dimension must be used to represent its members playing different roles (Lachev, 2005; Luján-Mora et al., 2006; Malinowski & Zimányi, 2008). For example, a product can be sent to some clients, while other

Figure 13. A parallel hierarchy with two composed hierarchies in SSAS a) schema and b) instances during combination of hierarchies

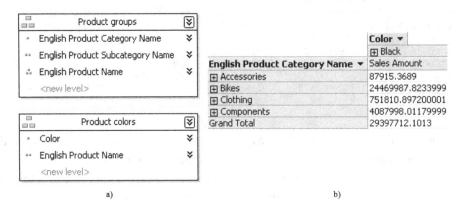

a)   b)

clients will pay for them; therefore, a client dimension is playing two different roles in participation in a fact relationship.

In Figure 3 the *Date* dimension is represented as a role-playing dimension using its members to represent order date (when the product was ordered), due date (when the product was delivered), and ship date (when the product was shipped). When this dimension is mapped to the relational model, the key attribute for the *Date* level will be included as a foreign key in the fact table as many times as different roles this level is playing. As a consequence, the relational representation will be the same as in Figure 2 for the *FactResellerSales* table, i.e., including the foreign key *DueDateKey*, *OrderDateKey*, and *ShipDateKey*.

However, as can be seen in Figure 2 and 3, the conceptual schema is much more expressive in indicating different roles than its corresponding relational mapping. The latter requires some technical knowledge and adequate naming in order to distinguish role-playing dimensions.

SSAS uses a wizard that is able to discover role-playing dimensions if several foreign keys referring to the same dimension are included in the fact table (as shown in Figure 2). Then, the role-playing dimensions (handled as virtual objects) are represented in the dimension panel (Figure 14a) and they correspond to a one time dimension included in the solution explorer panel (Figure 14b) (handled as a physical object related to the *DimTime* table).

Degenerate or Fact Dimensions

In several applications a user may require to analyze data at the lowest granularity level, e.g., an order line representing a product; however, he/she may require grouping different products according to the order to which they belong. That could be useful for applications related to, e.g., market-basket analysis. The usual practice promoted by Kimball and Ross (2002) is not to represent this order as a separate dimension in the multidimensional schema, since all data, except order number, already form part of the schema, e.g., products, date, employee who sells, reseller who buys, etc. Instead, an attribute is included in the fact table, e.g., the *SalesOrderNumber* attribute in the *FactResellerSales* table in Figure 2. This attribute is called in two different ways: (1) **fact dimensions** since it is included in the fact table playing the dimension role or (2) **degenerate dimensions** since it has only one attribute.

We consider that even though in the logical or implementation level this attribute can form part of a fact table, the conceptual schema should keep it as a dimension to indicate that users may require

Figure 14. Role-playing dimensions in SSAS a) dimension panel and b) solution explorer panel

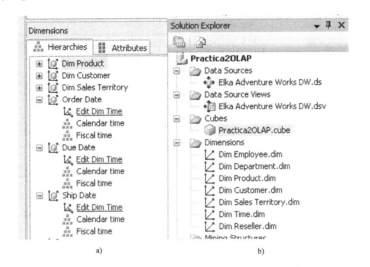

a)   b)

grouping according to dimension members, i.e., according to the order number shown in Figure 3 for the level called *SalesOrderNumber*.

SSAS allows the designer to add a new dimension using a fact table as a source table. After choosing the attribute of interest (in our example, *SalesOrderNumber*), the Dimension Usage (see Figure 15a) automatically defines a relationship between the newly-created dimension and fact table as Fact type (Figure 15 b).

Multi-Valued or Many-to-Many Dimensions

Some practitioners (e.g., Kimball & Ross, 2002) and scientists (Luján-Mora et al., 2006; Pedersen et al., 2001; Song et al., 2001) refer to the so-called "multivalued dimensions" or "many-to-many relationships between facts and dimensions" in order to represent the situation where several members of a dimension participate in the same instance of a fact relationship. An example is shown in Figure 16; it is used for the analysis of a transaction performed over clients' accounts. Since an account can be shared among different clients, aggregation of the measures *Amount* and *Cashback points* will count them as many times

as the number of account holders. This induces the so-called double-counting problem.

The double-counting problem arises since the schema does not respect multidimensional normal forms[8] (MNFs) (Lehner et al., 1998; Lechtenböger and Vossen, 2003). These forms determine conditions that ensure correct measure aggregation in the presence of generalized hierarchies. In particular, one of the conditions of the first multidimensional normal form (1MNF) requires that each measure be uniquely identified by the set of leaf levels providing the basis for correct schema design; 1MNF is then used to define the remaining MNFs.

As can be seen in our example in Figure 16, only the time and account determine the amount and cashback points of a transaction. Therefore, the schema in Figure 16 is not in the 1MNF and this schema should be transformed. Two different options exist as shown in Figure 17. The first option (Figure 17a) includes an additional fact relationship, while the second option (Figure 17b) creates a non-strict hierarchy (Malinowski & Zimányi, 2008).

Mapping both conceptual schemas from Figure 17 to the relational model will give the following tables: three tables for representing each dimension (*Time*, *Account*, and *Customer*), one *Transaction*

Figure 15. Defining fact dimension in SSAS

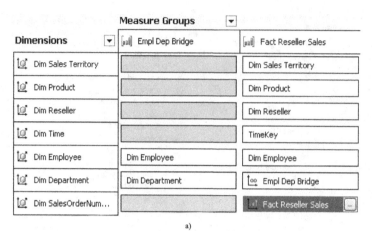

a)

b)

Figure 16. Simplified multidimensional schema for analysis of transactions

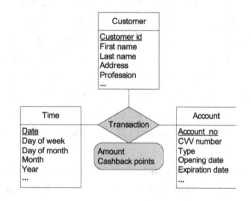

fact table containing foreign keys from the *Time* and *Account* tables and in addition, a table for representing either the *CustomerAccount* fact relationship (Figure 17a) or the *CustomerAccount* non-strict hierarchy (Figure 17b). The *Customer-Account* table will contain foreign keys from the *Customer* and *Account* tables.

In order to define multivalued dimensions in SSAS the same solution given for non-strict hierarchies should be applied, i.e., defining many-to-many relationships between the *Transaction* fact table and the *Customer* dimension table using as an intermediate table, the *CustomerAccount* table as shown in Figure 18.

Figure 17. Different options for transformation of the fact relationship from Figure 16

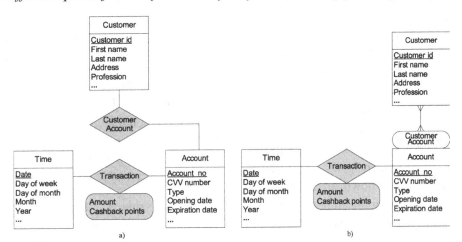

Notice that at the logical relational or OLAP implementation level there is no difference between non-strict hierarchies and multivalued dimensions. Therefore, in our opinion, it is not necessary to introduce these kinds of dimensions, since they can be transformed and implemented as non-strict hierarchies. The better choice would be to propose and explain the required transformation in order to avoid the existence of multivalued dimensions.

CONCLUSION

Data Warehouses (DWs) are defined using a multidimensional view of data, which is based on the concepts of facts, measures, dimensions, and hierarchies. On-line Analytical Processing (OLAP) systems allow users to interactively query DW data using dimensions for expanding the perspectives of analysis and hierarchies for aggregating measures through the drill-down and roll-up operations.

The ongoing practice in modeling data for DW and OLAP applications is to use a relational model and develop star or snowflake schemas. In addition, many OLAP systems also include an interface that allows the designer to represent different elements of the multidimensional schema in a more abstract way. However, neither relational tables nor OLAP interfaces are able to clearly represent different kinds of hierarchies, e.g., unbalanced or non-covering, and different kinds of dimensions, e.g., role-playing or degenerate, that exist in real-world applications. Therefore, users cannot express clearly their analysis needs and developers cannot implement them.

In this chapter we have chosen a simple analysis

Figure 18. Many-to-many relationship for representing multivalued dimensions

scenario for the analysis of sales and represented different kinds of hierarchies and dimensions at the conceptual, logical and implementation levels, for which we use the MultiDim model, relational tables, and Microsoft Analysis Services, respectively. By means of examples, we have demonstrated how the use of the conceptual model can allow a better understanding of the different elements that are required by users for analysis purposes. Then, even though mapping into the logical schema leads to well-known structures, e.g., to snowflake schema, the application semantic is better understood by using the conceptual model. Consequently, this conceptual representation may help designers choose adequate options available for implementing OLAP cubes, such as the ones included in Microsoft Analysis Services for unbalanced or non-covering hierarchies, and for role-playing or degenerate dimensions.

REFERENCES

Abelló, A., Samos, J., & Saltor, F. (2006). YAM²: a multidimensional conceptual model extending UML. *Information Systems, 32*(6), 541–567. doi:10.1016/j.is.2004.12.002

Akoka, J., Comyn-Wattiau, I., & Prat, N. (2001). Dimension hierarchies design from UML generalizations and aggregations. *Proceedings of the 20th International Conference on Conceptual Modeling*, (pp. 442-445).

Bauer, A., Hümmer, W., & Lehner, W. (2000). An alternative relational OLAP modeling approach. *Proceedings of the 2nd International Conference on Data Warehousing and Knowledge Discovery*, (pp. 189-198).

Elmasri, R., & Navathe, S. (2006). *Fundaments of database systems* (5th Ed.). Reading, MA: Addison Wesley.

Golfarelli, M., & Rizzi, S. (1998). A methodological framework for data warehouse design. *Proceedings of the 1st ACM International Workshop on Data Warehousing and OLAP*, (pp. 3-9).

Gray, J., Chaudhuri, S., Basworth, A., Layman, A., Reichart, D., & Venkatrao, M. (1997). Data cube: a relational aggregation operator generalizing group-by, cross-tab, and sub-totals. *Data Mining and Knowledge Discovery, 1*(1), 29–53. doi:10.1023/A:1009726021843

Hahn, K., Sapia, C., & Blaschka, M. (2001). Automatically generating OLAP schemata from conceptual graphical models. *Proceedings of the 4th ACM International Workshop on Data Warehousing and OLAP*, (pp. 9-16).

Hümmer, W., Lehner, W., Bauer, A., & Schlesinger, L. (2002). A decathlon in multidimensional modeling: open issues and some solutions. *Proceedings of the 4th International Conference on Data Warehousing and Knowledge Discovery*, (pp. 275-285).

Hurtado, C., & Gutierrez, C. (2007). Handling structural heterogeneity in OLAP In R. Wrembel & Ch. Koncilia (Eds.). *Data warehouses and OLAP: concepts, architectures and solutions*, (pp. 27-57). Hershey, PA: Idea Group Publishing.

Hüsemann, B., Lechtenbörger, J., & Vossen, G. (2000). Conceptual data warehouse design. *Proceedings of the 2nd International Workshop on Design and Management of Data Warehouses*, (p. 6).

Jagadish, H., Lakshmanan, L., & Srivastava, D. (1999). What can hierarchies do for data warehouses. *Proceedings of the 25th International Conference on Very Large Data Bases*, (pp. 530-541).

Kimball, R., & Ross, M. (2002). *The data warehouse toolkit: the complete guide to dimensional modeling.* Hoboken, NJ: Wiley.

Lachev, T. (2005). *Applied Microsoft Analysis Services 2005*. Prologica Press.

Lechtenbörger, J., & Vossen, G. (2003). Multidimensional normal forms for data warehouse design. *Information Systems, 28*(5), 415–434. doi:10.1016/S0306-4379(02)00024-8

Lehner, W., Albrecht, J., & Wedekind, H. (1998). Normal forms for multidimensional databases. *Proceedings of the 10ᵗʰ International Conference on Scientific and Statistical Database Management*, (pp. 63-72).

Lenz, H., & Shoshani, A. (1997). Summarizability in OLAP and statistical databases. *Proceedings of the 9ᵗʰ International Conference on Scientific and Statistical Database Management*, (pp.132-143).

List, B., Bruckner, R., Machaczek, K., & Schiefer, J. (2002). Comparison of data warehouse development methodologies: case study of the process warehouse. *Proceedings of the 13ᵗʰ International Conference on Database and Expert Systems Applications*, (pp. 203-215).

Luján-Mora, S., Trujillo, J., & Song, I. (2006). A UML profile for multidimensional modeling in data warehouses. *Data & Knowledge Engineering, 59*(3), 725–769. doi:10.1016/j.datak.2005.11.004

Malinowski, E., & Zimányi, E. (2008). *Advanced data warehouse design: from conventional to spatial and temporal applications*. Berlin: Springer.

Microsoft Corporation. (2005). *SQL Server 2005: books online*. http://technet.microsoft.com/en-us/sqlserver/bb895969.aspx.

Niemi, T., Nummenmaa, J., & Thanisch, P. (2001). Logical multidimensional database design for ragged and unbalanced aggregation hierarchies. *Proceedings of the 3ʳᵈ International Workshop on Design and Management of Data Warehouses*, (pp. 7).

Pedersen, T., Jensen, C. S., & Dyreson, C. (2001). A foundation for capturing and querying complex multidimensional data. *Information Systems, 26*(5), 383–423. doi:10.1016/S0306-4379(01)00023-0

Pourabbas, E., & Rafanelli, M. (2003). Hierarchies. In M. Rafanelli. (Ed.) *Multidimensional databases: problems and solutions*, (pp. 91-115). Hershey, PA: Idea Group Publishing.

Rafanelli, M. (2003). Basic notions. In M. Rafanelli. (Ed.) *Multidimensional databases: problems and solutions*, (pp. 1-45). Hershey, PA: Idea Group Publishing.

Rizzi, S. (2003). Open problems in data warehousing: 8 years later. *Proceedings of the 5ᵗʰ International Workshop on Design and Management of Data Warehouses*.

Rizzi, S. (2007). Conceptual modeling solutions for the data warehouse. In R. Wrembel & Ch. Koncilia (Eds.). *Data warehouses and OLAP: concepts, architectures and solutions*, (pp. 1-26.) Hershey, PA: Idea Group Publishing.

Sapia, C., Blaschka, M., Höfling, G., & Dinter, B. (1998). Extending the E/R model for multidimensional paradigms. *Proceedings of the 17ᵗʰ International Conference on Conceptual Modeling*, (pp. 105-116).

Song, I., Rowen, W., Medsker, C., & Ewen, E. (2001). An analysis of many-to-many relationships between facts and dimension tables in dimensional modeling. *Proceedings of the 3ʳᵈ International Workshop on Design and Management of Data Warehouses*, (pp. 6).

Torlone, R. (2003). Conceptual multidimensional models. In M. Rafanelli, (Ed.) *Multidimensional databases: problems and solutions*, (pp. 91-115). Hershey, PA: Idea Group Publishing.

Trujillo, J., Palomar, M., Gomez, J., & Song, I. (2001). Designing data warehouses with OO conceptual models. *IEEE Computer, 34*(12), 66–75.

Tryfona, N., Busborg, F., & Borch, J. (1999). StarER: a conceptual model for data warehouse design. *Proceedings of the 2nd ACM International Workshop on Data Warehousing and OLAP,* (pp. 3-8).

Tsois, A., Karayannidis, N., & Sellis, T. (2001) MAC: conceptual data modeling for OLAP. *Proceedings of the 3rd International Workshop on Design and Management of Data Warehouses,* (p. 5).

ENDNOTES

[1]   We do not refer to the correctness of the AdventureWorksDW schema.

[2]   The detailed model description and formalization can be found in Malinowski and Zimányi (2008).

[3]   These hierarchies are also called heterogeneous (Hurtado & Gutierrez, 2007) and non-onto (Pedersen et al., 2001).

[4]   These are also called parent-child hierarchies (Lachev, 2005; Niemi, Nummenmaa, and Thanisch, 2001).

[5]   The ellipses in the figure represent members that are not shown.

[6]   We modify the instance of the AdventureWorksDW to represent this kind of hierarchy.

[7]   Several solutions can be used as explained in Malinowski and Zimányi (2008).

[8]   We omit their descriptions; interested readers may refer to Lechtenbörger and Vossen (2003).

Chapter 3
From Conventional to Multiversion Data Warehouse:
Practical Issues

Khurram Shahzad
Royal Institute of Technology (KTH)/Stockholm University (SU), Sweden

ABSTRACT

The Data warehouse is not an autonomous data store, because it depends upon its operational source(s) for data population. Due to changes in real-world scenarios, operational sources may evolve, but the conventional data warehouse is not developed to handle the modifications in evolved operational sources. Therefore, instance and schema changes in operational sources cannot be adapted in the conventional data warehouse without loss of information. Multiversion data warehouses are proposed as an alternative to handle these problems of evolution. In this chapter we discuss and illustrate how versioning is implemented and how it can be used in practical data warehouse lifecycle. It is designed as a tutorial for users to collect and understand the concepts behind a versioning solution. Therefore, the purpose of this chapter is to collect and integrate the concepts, issues and solutions of multiversion data warehouses in a tutorial-like approach, to provide a unified source for users that need to understand version functionality and mechanisms.

INTRODUCTION

Online transaction process systems (OLTP) are used to meet day-to-day requirements of an enterprise. But OLTPs' are unable to meet decision support requirements of an enterprise, because a) their schemas are not optimized to support decision-support queries and b) they are not made to support decision making (Paulraj, 2001; Kimball, 2002).

Data is extracted from OLTP(s), transformed and loaded in data warehouse after removing inconsistencies. Therefore, the data warehouse is an integrated and materialized view of data, which is optimized to support decision making (Chaudhuri, 1997). The data warehouse works as a data source for various types of applications e.g. analytical processing, decision making OLAP, data mining tools, dashboards etc.

DOI: 10.4018/978-1-60566-816-1.ch003

Multidimensional models with central fact and surrounding dimension relations are typically used for designing a data warehouse, with two-fold benefits: on one hand they are close to the way of thinking of decision makers analyzing the data, therefore helping those users in understanding the underlying data; on the other hand, they allow designers to predict users' intentions (Rizzi, 2007).

For data population the data warehouse depends upon its operational sources (also called OLTPs). Therefore, changes in operational sources may lead to derivation of inconsistent outputs from data warehouse (Bebel, 2004). These can be divided into two types: 'i) schema changes, i.e. insert/update/delete records, ii) content changes, i.e. add/modify/ drop an attribute or a table' (Wrembel, 2004; Rundensteiner, 2000).

Inconsistent outputs, generated due to changes in operational sources, can be handled in two ways (Wrembel, 2005): 'i) evolution approach, ii) versioning approach'. According to the evolution approach, changes are made to the data warehouse and data is transformed to the changed data warehouse, after which the previous one is removed (Blaschka, 1999). But, shortcomings of the approach are identified by a number of authors [see (Bebel, 2004; Golfarelli, 2004; Golfarelli, 2006, Wrembel, 2005) for details]. Whereas, according to the versioning approach, a new version of the data warehouse is created, changes are made to the new version, data is populated in the new version and both versions are maintained (Ravat, 2006).

Most information on concepts, issues and solutions of multiversion data warehouses are spread across a number of sources in the form of white papers, conference papers, workshop papers and journal papers, and the concepts and solutions underlying versioning cannot be easily understood by a naive user from most current sources. Therefore, the purpose of this chapter is to collect and integrate concepts and solution approaches of multiversion data warehouse, in order to provide a unified source for that target audience.

The rest of the chapter is organized as follows: motivations for creating multiple versions of data warehouse are discussed in section 2; principles of versioning the data warehouse and levels of abstraction in multiversion data warehouse (MVDW) are described in section 3; a framework for version creation is presented in section 4, and a method for modeling multiversion data warehouses is presented in section 5; metadata to be stored for multiversion data warehouses is described in section 6, a method of retrieval from multiversion data warehouses is given in section 7 and in section 8 a case study is presented to discuss practical issues of implementing multiversion data warehouses. Section 9 concludes the chapter.

MOTIVATION AND REQUIREMENTS FOR DATA WAREHOUSE VERSIONS

Operational sources are structured or unstructured data stores that keep record of real-world activities by dynamically storing data about those activities (Chaudhuri, 1997; Gardner, 1998). For example, an operational store can keep record of a 'product purchase process' by storing data about: the person who purchased a product, the product that was purchased, the employee who sold the product and the order placed for purchasing the product. The data warehouse, on the other hand, is not an autonomous data store, because its information is extracted from operational sources, cleaned, transformed and loaded into it. Therefore, for population of the dimensional schema, data warehouses depend upon operational sources, and changes in operational sources may either trigger changes in the data warehouse or derivation of inconsistent results in those data warehouses (Bebel, 2004; Marian, 2001).

It is an established fact that data warehouses have four major properties: subject-oriented, time-variant, non-volatile and integrated (Paulraj, 2001; Kimball, 2002). Real-world events may bring changes to operational sources (Mitrpanont,

2006), but due to the static nature of dimensional schemas, conventional data warehouses may not be able to store some of the real-world data after the changes. Consequently, up-to-date data cannot be provided for decision-support and so decision-quality suffers. For this reason, the data warehouse should be developed in such a way that the data produced before the change and after the change could be simultaneously stored in it.

(Wrembel, 2005) has identified real-world events which may lead to changes in the data warehouse. These are: changes in borders, changes in administrative structure of an organization, new user requirements, new business markets, establishing new departments, merging the existing departments and business reengineering. In order to motivate the need for creating and maintaining multiple versions of a data warehouse, description of problems that cannot be treated in conventional data warehouse is given next. Conventional data warehouses do not adapt to some types of changes in the operational sources, which motivates the need for creating versions of the data warehouse. Here we describe the shortcomings of conventional data warehouses that were pointed-out in a number of conference, journal and workshop papers, as well as technical reports. These are:

1. *Adaptation of instances:* The data warehouse, due to its content, depends upon operational sources. Therefore, as soon as operational sources are changed, the data warehouse should also accommodate those changes. For population of the data warehouse, "extraction, transformation and loading" (ETL) components transfer data from operational sources to that data warehouse. Due to the inability of ETL to sense structure changes in operational sources, data warehouses cannot adapt to those changes. This is due to the fact that ETL is not dynamic enough to support changes in sources. This problem is also called the *incremental view maintenance* problem (Bebel, 2004; Morzy, 2003).

2. *Information loss:* Conventional data warehouses cannot keep track of changes in the structure of the data warehouse itself without loss of any information. As soon as a change comes to a data warehouse, according to the evolution approach, its schema is upgraded and data is transferred to the newly born schema (Golfarelli, 2006; Wrembel, 2005a) i.e. data is populated in the newly born schema. This way data is transferred, but old information is lost at the same time. Therefore, old information is not available for access and use by inquirers. This is called the *information loss problem*. This is due to the reason that old information is overwritten by new information. Overwriting of old information takes place because data warehouse schemas have a static structure and it is not flexible enough to store two instances of information.

3. *Schema changes in the data warehouse:* Schema changes in operational sources may lead to changes in the data warehouse schema (Golfarelli, 2006). There are several real-world changes, such as changes in borders, new user requirements and new business markets etc., which may lead to changes in the schema of the data warehouse. However, conventional data warehouses cannot handle these changes without modifications in the structure of the data warehouse existing before the schema changes. This is due to the reason that traditional data warehouses have a static structure concerning their schemas and relationships between data, therefore they may not be able to support any dynamics in their structure and contents (Wrembel, 2005 a).

4. *Tracking of evolution operations in metadata:* the operations that result in evolution of versions cannot be tracked in conventional data warehouses. As indicated above (in 3rd point), conventional data warehouses are static in nature, therefore they cannot

maintain meta-information related to evolution. Due to a limited metadata structure, it is not possible to store information about all those evolution operations that result in data warehouse evolution.

Conventionally, data warehouses rarely have the ability to handle source schema changes (Nasir, 2007; Samos, 1998), because they are not designed for that purpose. It is possible that changes in sources result in specific changes in contents of the data warehouse that cannot be handled (Golfarelli, 2004). Changes in the data warehouses include insertion/deletion/updating of fact, dimension or dimension-level (Balaschka, 1999). To be version-compatible, the metadata structure change operations need to be recorded and different versions need to be accessible in change-prepared data warehouses. Therefore, metadata structure should be extended to store a set of operations that could produce changes in the data warehouse without loss of any information. Additionally, the new solution should be easily acceptable, adoptable and usable for existing data warehouse users. For this last reason, it should be possible to interact with versions of the data warehouse using conventional SQL-like query languages with few or no extensions.

VERSIONING A DATA WAREHOUSE

In the remaining part of this chapter, the multiversion data warehouse is described as a solution to the problems discussed above. The principles of creation and management of versions in data warehouse and framework for version creation are presented in this section.

A data warehouse that is composed of multiple schema and instance versions is called multiversion data warehouse (MVDW). In MVDW, a schema version is the structure of a data warehouse, and an instance version is the dataset described by a schema version (Wrembel, 2005). It is important

to note that the concepts of simulating business scenarios and classification of versions (Bebel, 2004) (to real and alternative versions of the data warehouse), are ignored to: a) keep our focus on versioning of data warehouse and b) propagate the concept of multiversion data warehouse clearly and unambiguously.

Before describing multiversion data warehouse as a solution to the problems discussed in the previous section, basic concepts related to dimensional modeling are discussed briefly next.

Basic Concepts: Star Schema

The logical structure of a data warehouse is called a dimensional schema, which is used to store subject-oriented and time-variant data for decision support. The dimensional schema has four types: star, snowflake, constellation and star flake schema (Kimball, 2002). Out of these types, star schema is the central concept and the most often used element (Ponniah, 2001). The star schema is labeled so due to its star-like structure, as shown in Figure 1.

A dimensional model (DM) is composed of fact table(s) and a set of dimension tables (Kimball, 2002). *a) Fact table* consists of two types of attributes, called measures and key attributes. *Facts or measures* are numeric measurements to represent a critical value for an enterprise (Paulraj, 2001).

Figure 1. Example star schema

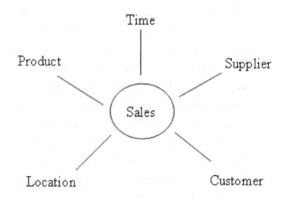

Conventionally, it is an aggregate attribute also know as calculated attribute, metrics or measure. Examples of facts are the total amount of funds allocated, funds consumed and funds in hand etc. *Key attributes* are relationship attributes, as they represent a relationship between fact and dimension tables. b) *Dimension tables* are different perspectives, which can be used for analysis of measures that are critical for the business (Paulraj, 2001). A dimension table consists of hierarchies which can be used during analysis for drilling-up, drilling down, slicing and dicing operations. Examples of dimension are, Time (Day, Month, Quarter, Year) and Product (ID, Name, Type, Category) etc.

Principles of MVDW

In order to solve the problems and to meet the requirements elicited in section 2, the multiversion data warehouse has been proposed (Rundensteiner, 2000). In multiversion data warehouses a new version of the data warehouse is created as soon as operational sources evolve, in such a way that they cannot be handled by the conventional data warehouse alone. The data produced after the change is populated in the new version of the data warehouse. Following are the main principles of multiversion data warehouse:

- *Principle 1:Ensure that real-world events do not lead data warehouse to inconsistent state.* A real-world event causes changes in OLTP and it has been established that changes in OLTP may yield inconsistencies in data warehouses. Examples of such events are: changes in administrative structure, new business markets and business reengineering (Wrembel, 2005). Therefore, DW administrator must ensure that real-world events do not yield inconsistencies in the data warehouse. Following are the high-level guidelines by which inconsistencies can be avoided.

  - *Practical guideline 1:Label the root node of DW as V0.0;*
  - *Practical guideline 2:For each change in OLTP (that can not be handled by the current data warehouse), a new version of the data warehouse should be created in such a way that each version represents a consistent state of the data warehouse;*
  - *Practical guideline 3:Once a new version is created, further data population should take place in the new version of the data warehouse.*

- *Principle 2:With an exception of the root version, each DW version is derived from a version of the data warehouse.* The initial version of the data warehouse is called root version or 0th version, and it is not derived from any previous version. As soon as the operational sources of the DW change and require a DW change, a new version is derived from the 0th version. In this case, the derived version is called the child version and the version from which it is derived is called the parent version. For accommodating a change, a new version can either be derived from the 0th version or from a current child version. This parent to child relationship is useful for understanding overtime changes in the data warehouse and for identifying dependencies between versions.

  - *Practical guideline 1:The label of version should consistently identify the version and its parent version.*
  - *Practical guideline 2:Multiple versioning graphs can be developed over a set of versions of MVDW, in order to restrict user access (see section 4.2 for details about versioning graph).*

- *Principle 3:Validity time of a version depends upon the time for which the real world change is valid for business.* Each version of the data warehouse is valid for a certain period of time. The status of version depends upon validity time of the change that brought the version. Therefore, the validity time of a version depends upon the period for which the change is valid for the business. If status of a version is 'not valid', it can not be used for analysis and decision support purposes, whereas if the status of a version is 'valid', it can be used for analysis and decision support purposes.

  ○ ***Practical guideline:****The label of a version should also include status of the version. This can be done by adding a bit to version-label. Value 1 of the status bit shows that the version is valid and value 0 shows that the version is not valid.*

- ***Principle 4:****Versions of a data warehouse share their data and schema with other versions.* Each version of the data warehouse consists of a schema version and an instance version (Bebel, 2004). The schema version is the description of the structure of the version, in the form of dimensions and facts, whereas an instance version contains information about events (see section 5.1 and 5.2 for details about data sharing and schema sharing respectively). The purpose of dividing a version into schema version and instance version is to keep the size of the data warehouse conveniently small.

  ○ ***Practical guideline:****The size of a data warehouse can be reduced by binding instance versions with several schema versions and vice versa.*

- ***Principle 5:****The process of versioning is continued as long as changes in a business are originated i.e. operational sources are evolved.* The purpose of versioning is to keep the data warehouse in consistent states along with keeping track of historical records. Therefore, for each business change that evolves the operational source,

a new version of the data warehouse is also created.

- ***Principle 6:****A version of the data warehouse represents decision-support data between two real-world events.* A data warehouse stores decision support data (Chaudhuri, 1997), whereas in the MVDW each version of the data warehouse represents a state of business at a certain time period. The state of business is valid for a certain period and, with the creation of another version, the validity of the previous version expires. So, each version of the MVDW represents decision-support data between two real-world events.

Levels of Abstraction in the MVDW

Each version of the multiversion data warehouse consists of a schema version and an instance version (Wrembel, 2005a). For each schema version, if every instance-version is stored separately, the size of the data warehouse may increase immensely. Therefore, in order to reduce the size of the data warehouse, versions are urged to share data-instance by using a data sharing scheme (Morzy, 2004). Data sharing schemes reduce the size of the data warehouse by binding data-instances with multiple versions, in this way the common data is shared between versions.

Figure 2 shows different levels of abstraction in the MVDW. The levels are: abstract level, concrete level and physical level. These levels are defined according to the information details which each level provides: a) the abstract-level contains information about high-level relationships (parent-child relationships) between versions; b) the concrete-level contains information about versioning and data sharing between versions; c) the physical level contains information about physical storage of data.

Figure 2. Different levels of abstraction in multiversion data warehouse

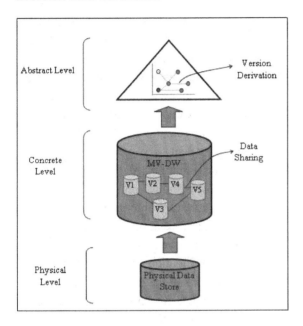

Figure 3. Version creation framework

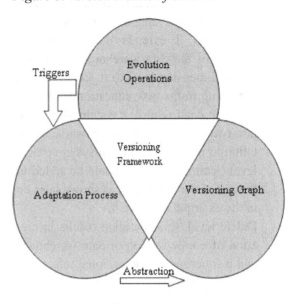

FRAMEWORK OF VERSION CREATION

As soon as a business change occurs, change in operational sources is triggered and, as a result, operational sources evolve. However, the data warehouse is not designed to handle operational source changes. Therefore, a framework is needed that facilitates adjustment of the data warehouse in order to adapt to changes in the operational source.

The framework takes the dimensional schema and evolution operations as input and produces a new version of the data warehouse, while extending the versioning relation. The framework called 'Versioning framework', is composed of evolution operations, versioning graph and adaptation process, as shown in Figure 3: *a) Evolution operations* are responsible for triggering changes in the data warehouse; *b) Versioning derivation graph* shows high-level relationship between versions and *c) Adaptation process* is a phenomena that can be used for adaptation of change in the data warehouse.

Evolution Operations

It is not possible to clearly anticipate market and business trends before the development of a data warehouse (Golfarelli, 2004; Mitrpanont, 2006). Therefore, it is difficult to capture all the evolving requirements on data warehouses in advance. In reality, changes in business strategies, changes in business markets, establishing new departments, independence of countries and redevelopment of boundaries or other events may trigger evolution operations. These are the operations which often lead to development of new versions of the data warehouse. These operations are (Morzy, 2004; Balaschka, 1999): insert level, delete level, insert attribute, delete attribute, connect attribute to dimension level, disconnect attribute from dimension level, connect attribute to fact, disconnect attribute from fact, insert classification relationship, delete classification relationship, insert fact, delete fact and insert dimension into fact. The following brief introduction to these operations is adapted from Blaschka's work (Balaschka, 1999):

- Insert level, this operation results in creation of a new version of the data warehouse and it extends the dimensional schema of the data warehouse by adding a new dimension level to it. For example, according to the new education system of Sweden, each semester system is divided into two learning periods. To handle adaptation to this new education system a new level (learning period) should be added to the dimensional schema, as shown later on in the example of figure 8;
- Delete level, this operation results in creation of a new version of data warehouse and it squeezes the dimensional schema of the data warehouse by deleting a dimension level from it. For example, departments may be dissolved and programs directly offered by schools. To handle this change, the level (department) should be deleted from dimensional schema, as shown later in the example of figure 8.
- Insert attribute, this operation results in creation of a new version of the data warehouse and it extends the dimensional schema of the data warehouse by inserting an attribute to it. An example is the addition of complexity level to the course dimension in Figure 8;
- Delete attribute, this operation results in the creation of a new version of the data warehouse and it squeezes the dimensional schema of the data warehouse by deleting an attribute. For example, removal of course description attribute from course dimension in Figure 8;
- Connect attribute to dimension level, this operation results in the creation of a new version of the data warehouse by connecting attribute to dimension level;
- Disconnect attribute from dimension level, this operation results in the creation of a new version of the data warehouse by removing an attribute from a dimension level;

- Connect attribute to fact, this operation results in the creation of a new version of the data warehouse and it modifies the dimensional schema of the data warehouse by connecting attribute to fact;
- Disconnect attribute from fact, this operation results in creation of a new version of the data warehouse and it modifies the dimensional schema by disconnecting attribute from fact.
- Insert classification relationship, this operation results in the creation of a new version of the data warehouse and it inserts a classification relation to the dimensional schema of the data warehouse.
- Delete classification relationship, this operation results in the creation of a new version of the data warehouse and it deletes a classification relation from the dimensional schema of the data warehouse.
- Insert fact, this operation results in creation of a new version of the data warehouse and it extends the fact table of the dimensional schema by inserting a new fact.
- Delete fact, this operation results in the creation of a new version of the data warehouse and it squeezes the fact table of the dimensional schema by deleting a fact from it.

Versioning Graph

A graphical representation is based on a set of graphical notations that facilitates using, understanding and management of systems (Kitano, 2003). Therefore, GUI-based systems are widely demanded worldwide. So, in order to, a) know about the number of versions of data to get a high-level view of versions; b) identify relationships between versions of the data warehouse to identify dependencies; c) track versioning history and to easily navigate between versions; and d) to identify the active version of the data warehouse, a versioning graph is proposed to be used (Wrembel, 2005a).

A version derivation graph, as shown in Figure 4, can be integrated with a graphical interface tool to provide visualization of versions and their relationships. In the interface, each version is represented by a labeled node. The label of a node is a name and a number that indicates a relationship between versions e.g. in $V_{1,0,1}$, V is the name of version, first 1 is the identification number of the version, 0 is identification of its parent version and last 1 shows the status of the version which could be 0 or 1. Dotted lines indicate parent-child relationships between versions i.e. tail of dotted line is toward parent version and head is towards child version. The version from which a version is derived is called parent version and the derived version is called child version.

In order to meet the initial decision support requirements of an enterprise, a zero[th] version of the data warehouse is developed. It is called the root version and represented by root node in versioning graph, with label $V_{0,0,1}$. First 0 means that it is the root version, and the second 0 means it has no parent version and 1 represents active status of version. Every version is valid for a certain period of time and it is represented by 1 if the version is valid or active, otherwise by 0 i.e. inactive status or not available for use.

The versioning graph is embedded in a graphical interface, and it is available for administrators to modify. Using this interface an administrator can manage operations such as: delete a version completely, insert a new version, change relationship between versions and edit identification of a version.

Change Adaptation Process

Creation of a new data warehouse version depends upon the change brought about by the evolution operations. Here, we present a process called change adaptation process, which can be used to adapt changes in operational source of data warehouses. The sequence of steps is shown in Figure 5 and their brief explanation is as follows:

- **Source change identification:** the purpose of this step is to identify changes in operational sources of the data warehouse. This is done by comparing the schema before change with the newly developed schema or schema developed after the change. By doing the comparison, changes in sources can be identified.
- **Version creation:** in this step the administrator has to create a new version of the data warehouse explicitly, in order to adapt

Figure 4. Version derivation graph (adapted from Bebel, 2004)

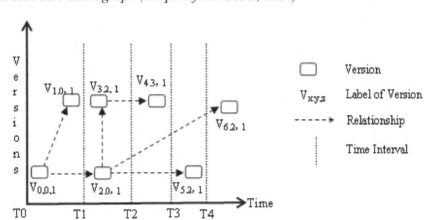

changes into the data warehouse. The earlier version is called parent version and the derived version is called child version. As soon as a new version is created, a label is assigned to it and relationship is created between them [parent and child version].

- **Schema adaptation:** in this step the dimensional schema is upgraded in such a way that it can handle changes in schema. This can be done by adding or removing dimension tables, fact tables, attributes, levels or relationship etc. Contents before changes in source are reflected from parent version whereas the contents after the change are reflected in the new version.

- **Schema sharing:** data warehouse versions can partially share their schemas e.g. dimensions tables or fact tables can be shared between versions. In this step shared tables are identified by the administrator. If a table T is evolved as a result of change, the table T cannot be shared by parent and child version. Whereas, if table X doesn't change, the table x can be shared by parent and child version. For example, if a course offering is changed it will not affect the relationship of department and school. Therefore, the tables [schools,

department, program, time, employees and university_fact] can be shared with parent version.

- **Data Sharing:** in order to reduce data redundancy in the presence of versions of the data warehouse, data is shared amongst tables from different versions. According to this approach, single instance of data is stored at physical level and shared by different tables at logical level. This is done by attaching a bitmap to each record of table for each data warehouse version (Bebel, 2004). The value of bitmap could be 1 or 0.

- **Reconfigure ETL:** due to changes in dimension and fact tables, often the ETL component may not be able of extracting, transforming and loading the data into the data warehouse. Therefore, it is required to reconfigure ETL to fulfill demands of new versions of the data warehouse. For example, if "comprehensive exam" is added in the requirements of each degree, it is required to add a new version of the data warehouse by extending the dimensional schema in a way that is capable of accommodating change in academics. Also, ETL cannot populate the extended schema (new

Figure 5. Change adaptation process

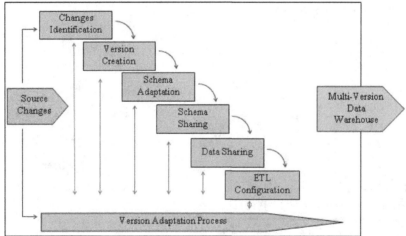

version of data warehouse), therefore, it should be reconfigured to populate the new version of the data warehouse.

MODELING THE MULTIVERSION DATA WAREHOUSE

The versioning graph presented in the section 4.2 gives a high-level view of versions of data warehouse and identifies relationships between versions. However, the versioning graph doesn't give detailed information about sharing dimensions and facts between versions. In addition to that, changes in dimensional schemas cannot be represented by the versioning graph.

Modeling dimensional schemas of a multiversion data warehouse addresses the problem of specifying overtime changes in the data warehouse due to evolution operations. It is also important to note that modeling dimensional schemas of a conventional data warehouse is neglected here to keep the focus on modeling structural changes and schema sharing between versions. Interested readers may read (Tryfona, 1999) for more insight into modeling of a dimensional schema.

Modeling Schema Sharing

Various approaches for modeling of a single dimensional schema have been presented in the literature (Tryfona, 1999. Feyer, 2002). However, those approaches are not appropriate for modeling multiple versions of a data warehouse, because schema sharing and changes in dimensional schemas are not included. In this section, we discuss the way in which schema sharing and changes in dimension schema can be represented, while modeling MVDW.

The size of the data warehouse can be reduced by sharing schema between different versions. Before describing a way of modeling versions, a set of constructs that are used for modeling are presented in Figure 6. Solid nodes (filled node or colored node) are used to represent a fact table with a label F_{vi}, where F is the name of the fact and vi is the identification number of the version to which the Fact table belongs. In contrast, an empty node (hollow node) is used to represent a dimension table with label $D_yL_{z\cdot p}$, where D_y is the name of the dimension and in L_z, z is the level to which the dimension table belongs. To represent two tables at the same dimension level, p is an integer value added to make each label unique.

Within a version, a straight line is used to represent a relationship between dimension and fact tables, whereas dotted lines (with arrows) are used for relationships between tables across the version. Furthermore, to clearly identify schema-sharing tables, those are encircled by a dotted rectangle.

For modeling MVDW, consider a root version V0 of the DW at time T0 having fact table F_{v1} and dimensions {D1, D2... D5}. The details of dimensions are as follows:

$D1 = \{ D_1L_{1.0}\}$, $D2 = \{ D_2L_{1.1}, D_2L_{2.0}, D_2L_{2.1}\}$,

$D3 = \{ D_3L_1, D_3L_2\}$, $D4 = \{ D_4L_1\}$,

$D5 = \{ D_5L_1, D_5L_2\}$ $D6 = \{ D_6L_1, D_6L_2\}$

Assume that a business change occurs that ultimately triggers creation of a new version (V1.0)

Figure 6. Modeling constructs

of the data warehouse after time T1. Similarly, after time T2, another version (V2.1) is created from version V1.0. Also assume that after time T3 a third version (V3.2) is created from V2.1.

Figure 7 shows the way in which changes in structure of dimensional schema can be modeled, in the presence of overtime changes and evolving requirements of users. The X-axis represents status of data warehouse version with the passage of time and Y-axis represents various dimension and fact tables. Figure 7 also shows presence of version V0 at time interval T_0. At time T_1 version V1.0 is generated, at T_2 version V2.1 is generated and at T_3 version V3.2 is generated.

As described in the principles of creation of versions in data warehouses in section 3.2, different versions of the data warehouse can share dimension and fact tables. Shared dimension and fact tables are surrounded by square boxes, as shown above in Figure 7 by dotted lines. Also, the label of shared boxes is extended by adding identification of versions in curly brackets e.g. {V0, V1.0}.

For relationship between tables, a dotted line starts from child version headed towards parent version. For example, the dimension table D_3L_1 and D_3L_2 is part of version V1.0. If shared dimension table D_3L_1 is related with dimension $D_9L_{2.0}$, the relationship is represented by dotted line (called relationship line) starting from version V1.0 to V0. Otherwise, if fact table F_{v2} is related with dimension $D_{14}L_1$ and $D_{13}L_{1.0}$, the relationship is represented by a dotted line (called relationship line) starting from version V3.2 to V2.1.

Instance Sharing

Conventionally, the size of a data warehouse varies from gigabytes to terabytes (Chaudhury, 1997). Therefore, physically storing multiple copies of each record is not practical because, it will immensely increase the size of the data warehouse. A solution to this problem is found by avoiding physical storage of redundant data by implementing data sharing techniques between versions.

Figure 7. Modeling schema sharing

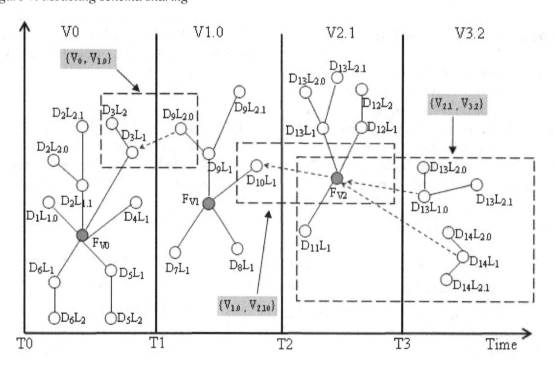

Instance sharing approaches are also known as data sharing approaches. According to this approach (Wrembel, 2005a), a record is physically stored in a data warehouse only once and shared by one or more versions. The data common between versions is stored in parent version and shared by child versions. In case of changes, a new record of only the changed data is stored physically in the new version. Relationship between schema and instance version is given in Figure 8.

Sharing of a record stored by the parent version is done by attaching a bitmap with each record and for each version. So, one bitmap gives the information whether a particular record is attached with the version or not. If the value of the bit is 0 the record is not shared with the version, whereas if the value of the bit is 1 it is shared with the version. Let A1, A2 ....An be the attributes of the table in parent version (V0.0) with data values Di1,Di2, ... where I is the row id. Let V1.0 ... Vw.x, Vq.r, Vy.z be the child versions of the data warehouse. The parent version shares data with all versions with an exception of Vq.r. Generally, the bitmap will look like shown in Table 1.

In case versions of the data warehouse are maintained in such a way that each version has its own data physically stored, the size of the data warehouse will become much larger. By using the data sharing approach, the size of the data warehouse will be greatly reduced. However, at the same time query performance will be impacted as well. Therefore a balance between query performance and size of the data warehouse should be maintained.

METADATA IN MULTIVERSION DW

In order to support the data warehouse lifecycle managing relationships between versions for data sharing and for retrieval from multiversion data warehouse, multifaceted data is required to be

Table 1. Data sharing scheme between versions of data warehouse

A1	A2	...	An	V1.0	...	Vw.x	Vy.z
D11	D12		D1n	1		1	1
D21	D22	...	D2n	1		1	1
...	...	...	...				
Dp1	Dp2	...	Dpn	1		1	1

Figure 8. Relationship among schema and instance versions (adopted from Bebel, 2006)

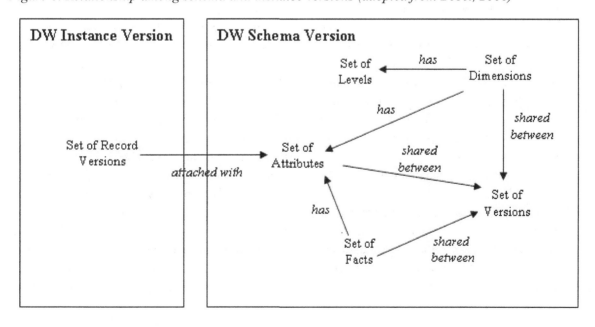

53

maintained. In this section we discuss, motivation of maintaining metadata, identify metadata to be stored and a meta-model for storage of metadata.

The data dictionaries available with database management systems cannot store metadata about multiversion data warehouse due to its complex nature. Metadata is complex because it includes metadata about dimensional schemas, data instances, evolution operations, data sharing scheme as well as metadata about versioning relationships. The reasons to that are as follows:

- Basic versioning metadata includes version identification, version validity time and version creation time etc. In the absence of versioning metadata, versions cannot be identified and no operation on versions is possible;

- Versioning relationship metadata includes label of parent version, child version, shared dimensions and facts etc. In the absence of version relationship metadata, shared dimensions cannot be identified and history of versions cannot be used.

- Metadata about data sharing includes the information about binding of dimensional schemas and data instances. In the absence of data sharing metadata, separate instances are required for each version of the data warehouse, which increases redundancy.

- Metadata about evolution operations is the information about operations that results in creation of new versions of the data warehouse. In the absence of evolution operations metadata, history of changes in business cannot be tracked and evolution operations cannot be maintained.

We have classified data into three groups. a) Static metadata, the metadata that remains static throughout the life cycle of the data warehouse. It is the basic information about data warehouse, e.g. the information about root version is fixed i.e. dimension tables, fact tables, relationship between them, possible operations on the data warehouse and so on; b) Versioning metadata, the metadata about data warehouse versions e.g. evolution operations applied on data warehouse schema, new fact tables produced, new dimension tables produced; c) Dynamic metadata, the data that could change all the time and is not related to versioning (e.g. information about integrated schema). Details about integrated schema are given in section 6.2.

Before presenting the metaschema for storing data multiversion data warehouse, let us enlist the metadata produced in multiversion data warehouse lifecycle (Wrembel, 2005): i) Schema description includes metadata about fact tables, dimensions, dimension levels, attributes and relationships; ii) Integrity constraints include information about the constraints applied on the data warehouse for maintaining data consistency; iii) Basic versioning metadata includes information about version identifier, version status, version label; iv) Schema and data sharing metadata includes information about tables that are shared between schemas and contents that are shared between versions; v) Versioning relationship; vi) Schema integration information; vii) Content of every DW instance version; viii) Sharing fact and dimension data between DW versions.

Figure 9 shows a simplified metaschema for storing metadata given above. In the metaschema, information about version at the basic level is stored. Operations that are possible on a data warehouse schema are stored in a separate table. Metadata about the operations applied on data warehouse versions is maintained separately in a metaschema table. The dimension and fact tables that are attached with versions are maintained separately. The tables in version can be dimension or fact tables, therefore we have created separate tables for both types of tables. Fact_table has all metadata about fact tables and BasicFAttribute has metadata about its attributes, whereas versions are maintained separately. Similarly, information about dimensions and their attributes and versions of attributes and dimension tables are maintained in separate tables. Finally, for information about retrieval from data warehouse through integrated schema and mapping of attributes of integrated schema to versions of data warehouse are stored in other tables.

RETRIEVAL FROM THE MULTIVERSION DW

Retrieval and use of complete and consistent information for decision-support is the original objective of versions. Information required for user is spread across versions and users may not be able to retrieve this information (Golfarelli, 2006). This is due to the inability of conventional SQL to be used for retrieval of data from multiple versions simultaneously.

Two types of approach are used depending on the type of users and required functionality: 1) for expert users (skilled and capable of writing complex queries), the "SQL extensions" approach is used, based on SQL with versioning-related extensions; 2) for basic users, who which to use basic SQL syntax only, the "transparent querying" approach is available.

SQL Extensions Approach

According to this approach, extensions to the query language are proposed by adding clauses to conventional SQL. Users can query the current version of the data warehouse or a set of data warehouse versions. A query that deals with a single version of the data warehouse is called mono-version query. In contrast, a query written to retrieve data from multiple versions is called multiversion query.

Figure 9. Generic metamodel for metadata about MVDW

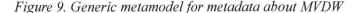
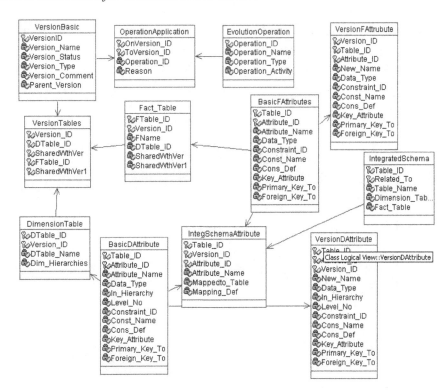

According to (Morzy, 2004), the user has the possibility to retrieve data from the following:

1) Querying current DW version: this can be done by using conventional SQL i.e. without extension from query language. By default each query is executed on the current version of DW;

2) For querying multiple versions, the user has to specify the versions involved for retrieval. This demands extensions to clauses of the query, from date 'begin date' to 'end date'. This will specify valid time of the involved versions. This way, data from all the versions which are valid in the time period will be retrieved. Generally, the query can be written as,

Select $A_1, A_2 \ldots A_n$
From $T_1, T_2 \ldots T_m$
Where $Join_1$ and $Join_2 \ldots Join_x$
Group by A_t
Version begin date 'YYYY-MM-DD'
End date 'YYYY-MM-DD';

As an output to this query, a number of partial results are produced. Each result represents output of each version of the data warehouse. So, if 'B'

is the total number of versions that are valid between 'begin date' and 'end date', then B number of partial results will be produced.

3) Querying a single version: data will be retrieved from the specific version, mentioned in the query.

Select $A_1, A_2 \ldots A_n$
From $T_1, T_2 \ldots T_m$
Where $Join_1$ and $Join_2 \ldots Join_x$
Group by A_t
Version = 'Vy.z'
Where Vy.z is the identifier of the version.

4) merging results of partial queries: in this case the user can access data from more than one version and the result will not appear in the form of partial results as stated in case 2. Instead as a result of execution of the query, a single output will be produced.

Select $A_1, A_2 \ldots A_n$
From $T_1, T_2 \ldots T_m$
Where $Join_1$ and $Join_2 \ldots Join_x$
Group by A_t
Version begin date 'YYYY-MM-DD'

Figure 10. Multiversion data warehouse explorer (adopted from Morzy, 2004)

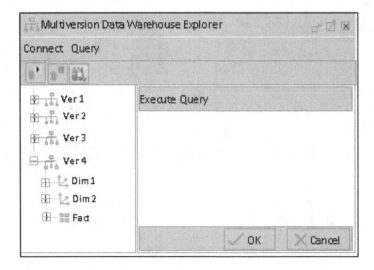

Merge into 'Vy.z';

Conventional database management systems cannot process clauses like version and merge. Therefore Morzy *et. al.* have implemented a prototype tool to support this kind of extended features, as shown in Figure 10.

Transparent Querying Approach

According to this approach, extensions to query language are not required for retrieval from multiple versions of the data warehouse, and the whole approach revolves around the concept of transparency. 'Transparency refers to separation of high-level semantics of a system from lower-level implementation issues' (Ozsu, 1991). By using this approach, a user can query MVDW without paying any attention to versions and data associated with each version.

In a query, transparency is provided at three levels i) source transparency, by this transparency a user can retrieve data from multiple versions without specifying any information about versions in from clause of the query. ii) analysis transparency, by this transparency a user can retrieve data from multiple versions without specifying any information about versions in where clause of the query. iii) projection transparency, by this transparency a user can retrieve data from multiple versions without specifying any information about versions in select clause of the query.

Conventional database management systems cannot provide transparency, therefore a prototype is implemented by Nasir, *et. al.* 2006, as shown below in Figure 11.

Comparison of Approaches

Both SQL extension and transparent querying approaches have advantages and disadvantages of their own. Brief descriptions of these are as follows:

Figure 11. Synthetic warehouse builder (adapted from Nasir, 2006)

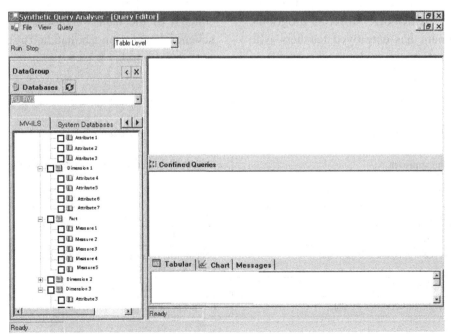

UNIVERSITY DATA WAREHOUSE: A CASE STUDY

In this section we present a versioning case study for illustration purposes. The Royal Institute of Technology (known as KTH) is a leading technology institute in Stockholm, Sweden. It has a number of Schools and each School consists of departments. Undergraduate, graduate and post graduate programs are offered by each department. School of Information and Communication Technology (SICT) is situated in Kista Science City and it has two major departments, Microelectronics and Information Technology (IMIT) and Computer and Systems Science (DSV). A program, Masters in Nanoelectronics is offered by IMIT, whereas Masters in Information Systems Engineering (EMIS) is one of the 60 credits degrees offered by DSV.

Figure 12 shows a dimensional schema of the university data warehouse. The schema has five dimensions, {Program, Student, Courses, Time and Employee} and a fact table {UniversityFact}. The dimension named 'Program' has three hierarchal levels, at highest level the university has 'Schools'. A school consists of 'Departments', which offer different programs. Each department has employed teachers who teach different courses, which are offered in different semesters.

Over time changes & problems: As a part of making a common education standard in EU, KTH has raised its Master's degree requirement from 60 European credits (ECTS) to 90 ECTS. At the same time, credits of each course are changed from 5 to 7,5 ECTS. After a while, a semester was divided into two learning periods.

The multidimensional schema of the university data warehouse shown in figure 10 cannot *adapt new instances* i.e. changes in degree requirements from 60 to 90 ECTS cannot be stored in the data warehouse. Also, degree requirement was raised from 60 to 90 credits in 2007, a change valid for all the students admitted from 2007 onwards. However, if the degree requirement is raised in the data warehouse, this will wrongly apply to students from prior years. This is due to the reason that old information is overwritten by new information (*information loss problem*). Overwriting of old information takes place because the data warehouse schema has a static structure in what concerns the schema, and it is not flexible enough to store two instances of data. Similarly, in the case of redesign of the university's semester plan, when semester is divided into two learning period (LP's), it requires changes in the dimensional schema of the data warehouse. However, this schema change cannot be handled by conventional data warehouses.

Table 2. Comparison of SQL extension and transparent querying approaches

Query extension approach	Transparent querying approach
Query writing becomes very complex when versions are increased.	Query writing is simplified even in the presence of large number of versions.
By default partial results are produced.	Partial results cannot be produced.
Results can be merged by using a clause 'merge'.	By default, results are merged.
A set of versions can be included in the result.	Data from all the active versions is produced and it is not possible to limit the result to certain versions.
Can be used by expert users only.	Can also be used by non-expert users.
Querying single/current version is possible.	It is not possible to query single/current version.

Figure 12. Multidimensional schema for the university data warehouse

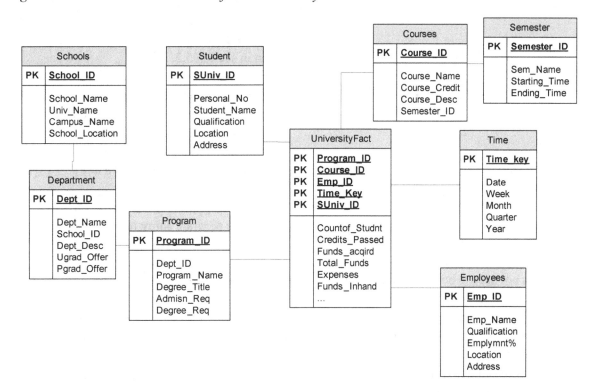

Evolution operations: There are two types of changes in the example. a) Data changes, the change which results in change in the data of the DW; b) Schema changes, in which the schema of the data warehouse is changed. In case of change in degree requirements and increase in credits of each course, data changes come into play, whereas for the change in which a semester is divided into two learning periods, this modification can be handled by adding another level to in the dimension of programs (i.e. a level above course and below semester). This type of change is called schema change.

MVDW for the University case: The problems mentioned above motivate the need for using a multiversion data warehouse for storing complete and consistent information including overtime changes in data.

According to the practical guidelines of principle 1 (given in section 3.2), we label the root version with V0.0. Due to changes in degree re-quirements and changes in credits of courses the DW will be inconsistent. Therefore, a new version of the DW is derived from the root version after time T1 and labeled as V1.0. Once a new version is created, next data must be transferred to the new version, labeled as V1.0. It is important to note that a version V1.0 is created, but there is no change in the schema of the data warehouse.

In order to handle the division of a semester into two learning periods, after interval T2, it is required to create a new version of the data warehouse as well. The new version is labeled as V2.1 and is derived from V1.0. The versioning graph for the University DW is shown in Figure 13.

As shown in Figure 13, the root version of university data warehouse is V0.0 and after time T1 a new version (V1.0) is derived. Another version (V2.1) is derived after time T2. In Figure 14, we show the way in which schema sharing can be modeled in accordance with the description given in section 5.1.

Figure 13. Schema versioning graph for the university case

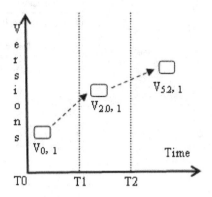

There is no schema change in V1.0, therefore schema does not need to be shared between V1.0 and V0.0. In contrast, in V2.1 schema change takes place by adding a level 'LP' to one of the dimensions. Therefore, schema sharing takes place between V1.0 and V2.1.

In order to keep the size of the data warehouse small, data stored by the version V0.0 is shared by

V1.0 and V2.1. Table 3 shows the way in which data can be shared between versions of the data warehouse. This is in accordance with the method given in section 5.2.

For retrieval from the MVDW, let us consider a query that retrieves the number of students per year and program. By using the query extension approach (given in section 7.1), the SQL becomes:

Select ProgramName, year, sum(passedstudents)

    From Program, Universtyfact, Time

    Where program **joinwith** university fact

    And universityfact **joinwith** time

    Group by programname, year

    Version begin date 'T1'

    Merge into 'V0.0';

In contrast, the same query using the transparent querying method (given in section 7.2) can be written as:

Select ProgramName, year, sum(passedstudents)

Figure 14. Modeling schema sharing for the university case

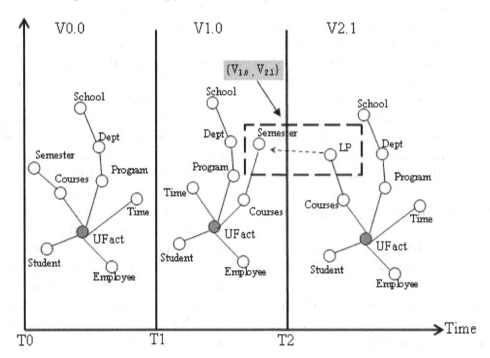

Table 3. Data sharing scheme between versions of the data warehouse

School_ID	School_Name	Univ_Name	Campus_Name	S_location	V1.0	V2.1
1	SICT	KTH	Kista	1	1	1
...	...	...	...	...	...	...

From Program, Universtyfact, Time
Where program **joinwith** university fact
And universityfact **joinwith** time
Group by programname, year;

CONCLUSION

This chapter has focused on describing multi-version data warehousing concepts as a solution for handling shortcomings of conventional data warehouses. Real-world changes in business scenarios may subject to changes in operational sources of the data warehouse. These changes in operational sources may result in production of inconsistent results from the data warehouse (DW) due to the inability of the DW to adapt to the new instances. Also, transformation of data from changed operational sources to data warehouse may result in information loss problems. Similarly, conventional data warehouses don't have the ability to handle schema changes.

The versioning data warehouse is an approach to overcome deficiencies of conventional data warehouses in handling change. According to this approach, twelve possible operations are possible which can result in changes to the data warehouse. For each change which can result in deficiencies, a new version of the data warehouse (called child version) is created from the previous version (called parent version) by a change adaptation process. The relationship between parent and child versions can be represented by a versioning graph and the versions can share schemas as well as instances.

We have also discussed the necessary metadata. The metadata for the data warehouse lifecycle is complex in nature, and it includes metadata about operations, versions, schema sharing and instance sharing. We also discussed querying the multiversion DW. Conventional SQL cannot be used to retrieve data from multiple data warehouse versions, therefore extensions to SQL were also described in this chapter.

Finally, we have presented a practical illustrative example of application of the multiversion data warehouse approach. The discussion and illustration of the approaches that we provided in this chapter are a useful aid to anyone dealing with the versioning issues in practical data warehouse lifecycle.

REFERENCES

Bebel, B., Eder, J., Koncilia, C., Morzy, T., & Wrembel, R. (2004). Creation and Management of Versions in Multiversion Data Warehouse. In *Proceedings of ACM Symposium on Applied Computing,* (pp. 717-723), Cyprus.

Bebel, B., Krolinkowski, Z., & Wrembel, R. (2006). Formal approach to modelling a multi-version data warehouse. *Bulletin of the Polish Academy of Sciences, 54*(1), 51–62.

Blaschka, M., Sapia, C., & Höfling, G. (1999) On Schema Evolution in Multidimensional Databases, In *Proceedings of the International Workshop on Data Warehouse and Knowledge Discovery,* (LNCS 1676, pp. 153-164). Berlin: Springer.

Chaudhuri, S., & Dayal, U. (1997). An overview of data warehousing and OLAP technology. *ACM SIGMOD, 26*(1), 65–74. doi:10.1145/248603.248616

Feyer, T., & Thalheim, B. (2002). Many-Dimensional Schema Modeling. In *Proceedings of the 6th East European Conference on Advances in Databases and Information Systems,* (LNCS 2435, pp. 305 – 318). Berlin: Springer

Gardner, S. R. (1998). Building the Data Warehouse. *Communications of the ACM, 41*(9), 52–60. doi:10.1145/285070.285080

Golfarelli, M., Lechtenborger, J., Rizzi, S., & Vossen, G. (2004). Schema Versioning in Data Warehouses, In Proceedings of *ER Workshops*, (LNCS 3289, pp. 415 – 428). Berlin: Springer.

Golfarelli, M., Lechtenborger, J., Rizzi, S., & Vossen, G. (2006). Schema Versioning in Data Warehouses: Enabling Cross Version Querying via Schema Augmentation. *Data & Knowledge Engineering, 59*(2), 435–459. doi:10.1016/j.datak.2005.09.004

Golfarelli, M., & Rizzi, S. (1998). A Methodological Framework for Data Warehouse Design, In *Proceedings of ACM international Workshop on Data Warehouse and OLAP,* (pp. 3-9).

Kimball, R. (2002). *The Data Warehouse Toolkit: The Complete Guide to Dimensional Modeling,* (2nd Ed.). New York: John & Wiley & Sons.

Kitano, H. (2003). A Graphical Notation for Biochemical Networks. *BIOSILICO, 1*(5), 169–176. doi:10.1016/S1478-5382(03)02380-1

Marian, A., Abiteboul, S., Cobena, G., & Mignet, L. (2001). Change-Centric Management of Versions in an XML Warehouse. In *Proceedings of the 27th International Conference on Very Large Databases,* (pp. 581-590).

Mitrpanont, J. L., & Fugkeaw, S. (2006). Design and Development of a Multiversion OLAP Application. In *Proceedings of ACM Symposium on Applied Computing,* (pp. 493-497), France.

Morzy, T., & Wrembel, R. (2003). Modeling a Multiversion Data Warehouse: A Formal Approach. In *Proceedings of the International Conference on Enterprise Information Systems,* France.

Morzy, T., & Wrembel, R. (2004). On querying versions of multiversion data warehouse. In *Proceedings of 7th ACM international Workshop on Data Warehouse and OLAP*, (pp. 92 - 101), USA.

Nasir, J.A., & Shahzad, M. K. (2007). Architecture for Virtualization in Data Warehouse. In Sobh. T (Ed.) *Innovations and Advanced Techniques in Computer and Information Sciences and Engineering* (pp. 243-248). Berlin: Springer.

Nasir, J. A., Shahzad, M. K., & Pasha, M. A. (2006). Transparent querying multiple version of data warehouse. *Information Technology Journal, 5*(2), 250–259. doi:10.3923/itj.2006.250.259

Ozsu, T., & Valduriez, P. (1991). *Principles of Distributed Database Systems,* (2nd Ed.). Upper Saddle River, NJ: Prentice-Hall Publishers.

Paulraj, P. (2001). *Data Warehousing Fundamentals: A Comprehensive Guide for IT Professionals.* New York: John and Wiley Sons.

Ravat, F., Teste, O., & Zurfluh, G. (2006). A Multiversion based Multi-dimensional Model. In *Proceedings of Data Warehousing and Knowledge Discovery,* (LNCS 4081, pp. 65-74). Berlin: Springer.

Rizzi, S. (2007). Conceptual Modeling Solutions for the Data Warehouse. In J. Wang, (Ed.), *Data Warehousing and Mining: Concepts, Methodologies, Tools, and Applications* (pp. 1-26). Hershey, PA: IGI Global Publishers.

Rundensteiner, E. A., Koeller, A., & Zhang, X. (2000). Maintaining Data Warehouses over Changing Information Sources. *Communications of the ACM, 43*(6), 57–62. doi:10.1145/336460.336475

Samos, J., Saltor, F., Sistac, J., & Bardes, A. (1998). Database Architecture for Data Warehousing: An Evolutionary Approach, In *Proceedings of 9th International Conference on Database and Expert Systems Applications,* (LNCS 1460, pp. 746-75612). Berlin: Springer.

Tryfona, N., Busborg, F., & Christiansen, J. G. B. (1999). StarER: A Conceptual Model for Data Warehouse Design, In *Proceedings of the 2nd ACM International Workshop on Data Warehousing and OLAP,* (pp. 3-8).

Wrembel, R., & Bebel, B. (2005). Metadata Management in a Multiversion Data Warehouse, In Proceedings of *International Conference on Ontologies, Databases and Applications of Semantics,* (LNCS 3761, pp. 1347- 1364). Berlin: Springer.

Wrembel, R., & Morzy, T. (2005a). Multiversion Data Warehouses: Challenges and Solutions. In *Proceedings of the 3rd International Conference on Computational Cybernetics,* (pp. 139-144).

Yin, R. K. (2003). *Case Study Research: Design and Methods,* (3rd Ed.). San Francisco, CA: SAGE Publications.

Chapter 4
Compression Schemes of High Dimensional Data for MOLAP

K. M. Azharul Hasan
Khulna University of Engineering and Technology (KUET), Bangladesh

ABSTRACT

The exploration of the possibility of compressing data warehouses is inevitable because of their non-trivial storage and access costs. A typical large data warehouse needs hundreds of gigabytes to a terabyte of storage. Performance of computing aggregate queries is a bottleneck for many Online Analytical Processing (OLAP) applications. Hence, data warehousing implementations strongly depend on data compression techniques to make possible the management and storage of such large databases. The efficiency of data compression methods has a significant impact on the overall performance of these implementations. The purpose of this chapter is to discuss the importance of data compression to Multidimensional Online Analytical Processing (MOLAP), to survey data compression techniques relevant to MOLAP, and to discuss important quality issues of MOLAP compression and of existing techniques. Finally, we also discuss future research trends on this subject.

INTRODUCTION

Data compression is widely used in data management to save storage space and network bandwidth. The main benefits that are achieved in data compression are well described by Bassiouni 1985 for different contexts and applications. The most obvious advantage of data compression is that of reducing the storage requirement for the database.

Reducing the storage requirement of databases is equivalent to increasing the capacity of the storage medium. Since compressed data are encoded using a smaller number of bytes, transfer of compressed information from one place to another requires less time and hence results in a higher effective transfer rate. Since data compression reduces the loading of I/O channels, it becomes feasible to process more I/O requests per second and hence achieve higher effective channel utilization. Most importantly, however, is the application of data compression

DOI: 10.4018/978-1-60566-816-1.ch004

in reducing the cost of data communication in distributed networks. In order to use or interpret compressed data, it is necessary to restore the information to its uncompressed format. To do this, a decoding algorithm must be available, and performance concerns are relevant for that operation. In some applications, data compression can also lead to other types of improvement in system performance. For example, in some index structures it is possible through compression to pack more keys into each index block. When the database is searched for a given key value, the key is first compressed and the search is performed against the compressed keys in the index blocks. The net effect is that fewer blocks have to be retrieved and thus the average search cost is reduced.

On-line Analytical Processing (OLAP) is a database acceleration technique used for deductive analysis. The main objective of OLAP is to have constant-time or near constant-time answers for many typical queries. There are two types of OLAP, namely ROLAP (Relational OLAP) and Multidimensional Online Analytical Processing (MOLAP). In ROLAP, the data is usually stored in the form of "summary tables". ROLAPs are built on top of standard relational database systems, whereas MOLAPs are based on multidimensional database systems. The data structures in which ROLAPs and MOLAPs store datasets are fundamentally different. ROLAPs use relational tables as their basic data structure and MOLAPs store their datasets as multidimensional arrays. Those large multi-dimensional arrays are used as basic data structures for scientific computations, business analysis, and visualization, where huge amounts of data manipulation are necessary. The multi-dimensional rectangular arrays, both dense and sparse depending on the context, form the fundamental abstract data structure used in different computation schemes. One area where multidimensional arrays are commonly used is data warehousing and Online Analytical Process-

ing (OLAP), which often requires extraction of statistical information for decision support.

In MOLAP applications, data compression is important because database performance strongly depends on the amount of available memory. A MOLAP is a set of *multidimensional datasets* and is designed to allow for the efficient and convenient storage and retrieval of large volumes of data that is closely related, viewed and analyzed from different perspectives. The multidimensional arrays that are linearized to store multidimensional datasets normally have high degree of sparsity and need to be compressed. It is therefore desirable to develop techniques that can access the data in their compressed form and can perform logical operations directly on the compressed data. Multidimensional arrays are good to store dense data, but most datasets are sparse, which wastes huge memory, since a large number of array cells are empty and thus are very hard to use in actual implementations. In particular, the sparsity problem increases when the number of dimensions increases. This is because the number of all possible combinations of dimension values increases exponentially, whereas the number of actual data values would not increase at such a rate. Efficient storage schemes are required to store such sparse data for multidimensional arrays for MOLAP implementations. In this chapter, a survey of the compression schemes for multidimensional data is presented. The data compression techniques are not only important for data warehousing implementation but also for any kind of large database implementation such as Scientific and Statistical Databases (SSDB).

Some of the most relevant issues concerning data compression are: the ability to perform efficient and random searching in compressed databases for a given logical position in the original database; and then the ability to provide an efficient mapping from arbitrary positions in the compressed data back to the corresponding logical position in the original database.

There are two types of compression, namely lossless and lossy compression. In lossless data compression, the decompressed data is an exact replica of the original data. On the other hand, in lossy data compression, the decompressed data may be different from the original data. Typically, there is some distortion between the original and reproduced data. Data compression must be lossless for typical MOLAP applications.

In this chapter we review MOLAP compression schemes, discuss important issues related to compression of MOLAP and existing techniques and also discuss future trends. The chapter is structured as follows: section 2 describes compression mechanisms of many existing MOLAP compression schemes. Section 3 reviews other related work in MOLAP compression. Section 4 discusses some relevant quality issues in MOLAP compression and existing compression schemes and section 5 discusses future trends. Section 6 discusses some limitations of compression schemes and section 7 concludes the chapter.

COMPRESSION SCHEMES FOR MULTIDIMENSIONAL ARRAYS

Efficiently computing aggregations on compressed data warehouses is crucial once the large multidimensional databases are to be compressed for storage and efficiency reasons. This compression must be lossless for data warehousing applications, in order to allow the original data to be fully recovered from its compressed form. In this section we discuss several compression schemes that are applied to MOLAP. We start by discussing multidimensional array linearization, which may be used as part of many compression schemes. After that we review a set of compression techniques that includes chunk-offset compression, compressed row or column storage, extended Karnaugh map representation, header compression, BAP compression, run-length en-

coding, bitmap compression and finally history offset compression.

The compression techniques usually provide two mappings. One is *forward mapping,* computing the location in the compressed dataset given a position in the original dataset. The other one is *backward mapping,* computing the position in the original dataset given a location in the compressed dataset. A compression method is called *mapping-complete* if it provides forward mapping and backward mapping. The term logical database and physical database is used to refer to the uncompressed and compressed database respectively.

Some mapping complete compression schemes such as header compression, BAP compression, run length encoding, and bit map compression first transform the multidimensional data into a linearized array using the array linearized function. Then the linearized data are compressed by a mapping complete compression method. Li and Srivastava (2002) applied this idea for implementing compressed MOLAP using header compression method. Hence those mapping complete compression schemes are used for compressing higher dimensional data sets after linearizing the data using the array linearization function.

Multidimensional Array Linearization

Figure 1 is an example of mapping a relational table to multidimensional array. In Traditional Multidimensional Array (TMA) based implementation of a MOLAP scheme, each of the kth column of an n column relational table is mapped to the kth dimension of the multidimensional array. Each column value is mapped to a unique subscript and the measure value (i.e. sales value) of the relational table is inserted into the corresponding cell in the multidimensional array. Therefore, each record of the relation can be expressed as one cell in the multidimensional array, if each column of the relation is assigned to each dimension of the

Figure 1. Representation of relational table using multidimensional array

Product	Store	Time	Sales
P1	S1	T1	100
P2	S2	T2	200
P3	S3	T2	300
P4	S4	T3	400

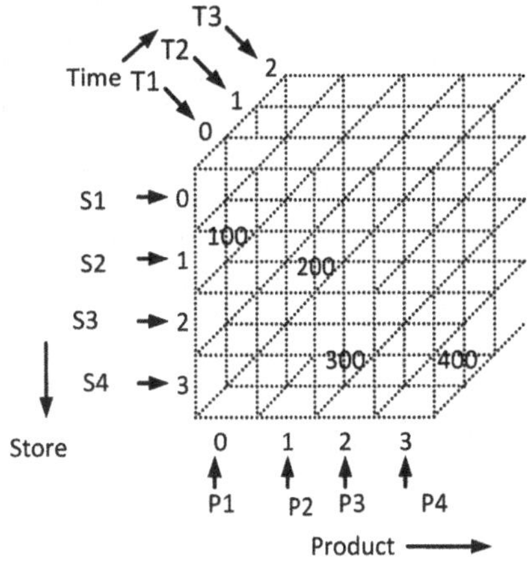

multidimensional array and the column value of each column of the relation is positioned on the axis of coordinates of each dimension of the multidimensional array.

As can be seen in the example of Figure 1, since the fact data is stored as contents of each cell, the multidimensional array becomes n-1 dimensional for an n-column relational table. Using multidimensional array methods, the linearization is done as described below. After the linearization of the array, the offset values of the array cells that correspond to actual records in the relation are stored (Hasan et. al; 2007).

Let $A(d_1, d_2, ..., d_n)$ be an n dimensional array with length of each dimension $d_1, d_2, ..., d_n$. The n-dimensional array can be mapped into a single *linearized array* by an array linearization function. Assume that the value of the ith dimension of A is encoded into $(0, 1, ..., d_i - 1)$ for $A(d_1, d_2, ..., d_n)$ $d_1, d_2, ..., d_n$ $(0, 1, ..., d_i - 1)$ $1 \le i \le n$ be an n dimensional array with length of each dimension $d_1, d_2, ..., d_n$. The n-dimensional array can be mapped into a single *linearized array* by an array linearization function. Assume that the value of the ith dimension of A is encoded into $(0, 1, ..., d_i - 1)$ for $1 \le i \le n$. The *array linearization function* for the multidimensional arrays (Li & Srivastava, 2002) of A is

$$F(x_1, x_2, ..., x_n) = d_1 d_2 ... d_{n-1} x_n$$
$$+ d_1 d_2 d_3 ... d_{n-2} x_{n-1} + ... + d_1 x_2 + x_1$$

If the subscript of dimension k is a_k and the length of dimension d_i are known then

$$f(x_n, x_{n-1}, ..., a_k, ..., x_1) = d_1 d_2 d_3 ... d_{n-1} x_n$$
$$+ d_1 d_2 ... d_{n-2} x_{n-1} + d_1 d_2 ... d_{k-1} a_k + ... + x_1$$

$x_j = 0, 1, 2, ..., d_j - 1$ where $1 \le j \le n$, $x_j = 0, 1, 2, ..., d_j - 1$ $1 \le j \le n$ $j \ne k$ where $1 \le j \le n$ $j \ne k$,

The logical position of the array indices $(x_1, x_2, ..., x_n)$ is determined by the above function for forward mapping and is denoted by $(x_1, x_2, ..., x_n)$ $F(x_1, x_2, ..., x_n)$ is determined by the above function for forward mapping and is denoted by $F(x_1, x_2, ..., x_n)$. The *reverse array linearization function* of the multidimensional array of A for backward mapping is defined as follows:

$$R - F(Y) = (y_1, y_2, ..., y_n)$$
where
$$y_n = Y \bmod d_n$$
$$y_i = [...[Y / d_n]...] / d_{i+1}] \bmod d_i \quad for\ 2 \le i \le n - 1$$
$$y_1 = [[...[[Y / d_n] / d_{n-1}]...] / d_3] / d_2]$$

Figure 2. Multidimensional array chunking

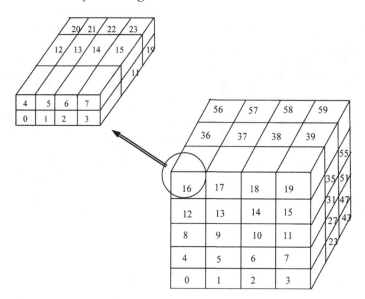

The logical position (i.e. offset value) is calculated for the records using the forward mapping function F and stored on a data structure (Hasan et, al; 2007) along with the measure value. The backward mapping algorithm R-F is used to determine the coordinates of the corresponding multidimensional array.

Chunk-Offset Compression

One common MOLAP approach stores data in chunked multidimensional arrays. Indices into an array are obtained by a normalization process that maps attribute values to integers.

In this scheme the large multidimensional arrays are broken into chunks for storage and processing (Sarawagi & Stonebraker 1994). Consider some normalized n-dimensional array A, whose dimensionality is $|d_1| \times |d_2| \times ... \times |d_n|$. The chunks can be formed by breaking each d_i into several ranges. Within A, two positions are in the same chunk iff, in every dimension, they fall within the same range. In memory or disk, values within a chunk are stored consecutively. Figure 2 shows a 3 dimensional array divided into sixty chunks (4×5×3) that are numbered in row-major fashion.

Chunk 16 is itself 4×2×3 array whose 24 cells are numbered in row-major order and are stored contiguously (Owen, 2002).

In chunk-offset compression, for each valid array entry, a pair (OffsetInChunk, data) is stored.

The offset inside the chunk (OffsetInChunk) can be computed using the multidimensional array linearization function described before. The reverse array linearization function is used for backward mapping to get the original coordinates of the array.

Compressed Row/ Column Storage for Multidimensional Arrays

Compressed Row Storage (CRS) and Compressed Column Storage (CCS) (Barret et, al; 1994 and White & Sadayappan, 1997) are commonly used due to their simplicity and purity with a weak dependence relationship between array elements in a sparse array.

The CRS scheme uses one one-dimensional floating point array VL and two one-dimensional integer arrays RO and CO to compress all the nonzero elements along the rows (columns for CCS) of the multidimensional sparse array. The

Figure 3. The CRS compressing scheme for sparse multidimensional array

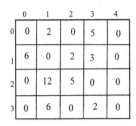 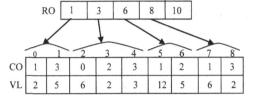

The original array   The compressed array

base of these arrays is 0. Array VL stores the values of nonzero array elements. Array RO stores information of nonzero array elements of each row (columns for CCS). If the number of rows is k for the array then RO contains k+1 elements. RO[0] contains 1, RO[1] contains the summation of the number non zero elements in row 0 of the array and R[0]. In general, RO[i] contains the number of nonzero elements in (i-1)th row of the array plus the contents of RO[i-1]. The number of non zero array elements in the ith row can be obtained by subtracting the value of RO[i] from RO[i+1]. Array CO stores the column (rows for CCS) indices of nonzero array elements of each row (columns for CCS). Figure 3 shows an example of CRS scheme for a two dimensional array.

In Figure 3, the number of nonzero element of row 1 can be found by RO[2]-RO[1] = 3. The column indices of the nonzero array elements of row 1 are stored in CO[RO[1]-1], CO[RO[1]], and CO[RO[1]+1] i.e CO[2], CO[3], and CO[4], since there are 3 nonzero array elements exist in row 1. Finally the values of the nonzero array

elements of row 1 can be found in VL[2], VL[3], and VL[4]. Based on this scheme, a sparse array of dimension 3 can be compressed adding one more one dimensional integer array JO which stores the third dimension indices of the nonzero array elements of each row. For higher dimensional sparse arrays more one dimensional integer arrays are needed.

EKMR Based Compression

A basic array representation scheme named Extended Karnaugh Map Representation (EKMR) is proposed by Chun et al; 2002, 2003. In this scheme, an n-dimensional array is represented by a set of 2 dimensional arrays.

A more concrete example based on the row-major data layout is given in Figure 5. In Figure 5(a), a three dimensional array based on the TMA(3) with a size of 3×4×5 is shown in a 2D view as three 4×5 two-dimensional arrays. Its corresponding EKMR(3) with a size of 4×15 is given in Figure 5(b).

Figure 4. 3-input K-map and its corresponding EKMR(3)

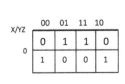 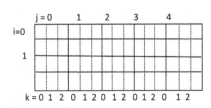

(a) K-map for 3 input function   (b) EKMR(3) scheme unction

The idea of the EKMR scheme is based on the Karnaugh map (K-map). Consider a 3 input K-map and its corresponding EKMR(3) in Figure 4. Let A[k][i][j] denote a three-dimensional array based on Traditional Multidimensional Array TMA(3) with a size of 3×4×5. The corresponding EKMR(3) of array A[3][4][5] is shown in Figure 4(b). The analogy between the EKMR(3) and the 3-input Karnaugh map is that the index variables i, j, and k correspond to the variables X, Y, and Z, respectively. According to the 3-input Karnaugh map, a three dimensional array based on the TMA(3) can be presented by a two-dimensional array based on the EKMR(3). The EKMR(3) is represented by a two-dimensional array with the size of 4×(3 × 5). Here, index variable i is used to indicate the row direction and the index variable j is used to indicate the column direction. The index variable i is the same for both EKMR and TMA representations and the index variable j of EKMR is a combination of the index variables j and k of TMA (See Figure 5). The basic difference between TMA(3) and the EKMR(3) is the placement of elements along the direction indexed by k. The relative position makes the fundamental difference when using EKMR as array representations. The EKMR(4) can be obtained in the similar way. The EKMR(4) is also represented in by two dimensional array. The EKMR(n) for n dimensional array is represented by $d_n \times d_{n-1} \times ... \times d_{n-5}$ EKMR(4) and a one dimensional array that links all the EKMR(4) where d_i ($5 \leq i \leq n$) is the length of the corresponding dimension. For example a 2×3×4×2×3×5 six dimensional array can be represented by six EKMR(4) each of size 12×10.

Compressing the Sparse Array

The EKMR array can then be compressed using the CRS or CCS schemes described before in this chapter. The scheme uses one one-dimensional floating point array V and two one-dimensional integer arrays R and CK to compress a multi-

Figure 5. (a) A three dimensional TMA (b) The corresponding EKMR

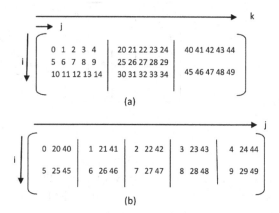

dimensional sparse array based on the EKMR scheme. It can be implemented in two ways: EKMR Compressed Row Storage (ECRS) and EKMR Compressed Column Storage (ECCS). [REMOVED SHAPE FIELD]

The ECRS (or ECCS) scheme compresses all the nonzero array elements along rows (columns for ECCS). Array V stores the values of non zero array elements. Array R stores information of nonzero array elements of each row. R[i] contains the number of nonzero elements in (i-1)th row of the array plus the contents of RO[i-1] and the contents of R[0] is 1. The number of non zero array elements in the ith row can be obtained by subtracting the value of R[i] from R[i+1]. Array CK stores the column (rows for ECCS) indices of nonzero array elements of each row (columns for ECCS). Figure 6 shows an example of ECRS scheme for a 4×8 sparse array based on EKMR(3). The compressed elements of the array can be accessed as described in CRS scheme in this chapter.

The EKMR(4) can also be compressed using the one dimensional arrays R, CK, and V as discussed above. Since EKMR(n) can be represented by $d_n \times d_{n-1} \times ... \times d_{n-5}$ EKMR(4) (d_i ($5 \leq i \leq n$) is the length of the corresponding dimension), the higher dimensional (more than 4) data sets can be generalized as follows: Using the arrays R, CK and V each EKMR(4) is compressed then a pointer array with size $d_n \times d_{n-1} \times \ldots \times d_{n-5}$ is used to link the arrays R, CK, and V in each EKMR(4).

Header Compression

The header compression method (Eggers & Shohani, 1980) is used to suppress sequences of missing data codes, called *constants*, in linearized arrays by counts. This method makes use of a *header* that is a vector of counts. The odd-positioned counts are for the unsuppressed sequences, and the even positioned counts are for suppressed sequences. Each count contains the cumulative number of values of one type at the point at which a series of that type switches to a series of the other. The counts reflect accumulation from the beginning of the linearized array to the switch points. In addition to the header file, the output of the compression method consists of a file of compressed data items, called the *physical file*. The original linearized array, which is not stored, is called the *logical file*.

In the following example, L represents the uncompressed form of a database, where 0's are the constant to be suppressed and the V's are the unsuppressed values. H represents the header database/file which contains the number of data or constants where odd position represents the data and even position represents constants. The physical, compressed form of the data is represented by P.

L: V_1 V2 0 0 0 0 0 0 0 0 V_3 V_4 V_5 V_6 V_7 0 0 V_8 V_9 V_{10} 0 0 0

H: 2, 9, 7, 11, 10, 14

P: V_1 V_2 V_3 V_4 V_5 V_6 V_7 V_8 V_9 V_{10}

BAP Compression

The BAP compression method (Li et al; 1987) consists of three parts: Bit Vector (BV), Address Vector (AV), Physical Vector (PV) and therefore called BAP compression method.

Let DB=$\{x_1, x_2, \ldots, x_n\}$ be a logical database and c be the constants. The physical vector PV is the vector of non-constants in DB, that is,

Figure 6. The ECRS compressing scheme for a three dimensional sparse array based on EKMR(3)

$$\begin{bmatrix} 0 & 5 & 1 & 0 & 0 & 0 & 3 & 0 \\ 2 & 0 & 0 & 9 & 0 & 5 & 0 & 6 \\ 4 & 0 & 3 & 0 & 0 & 7 & 0 & 2 \\ 3 & 0 & 0 & 2 & 0 & 0 & 0 & 1 \end{bmatrix}$$

(a) The original EKMR

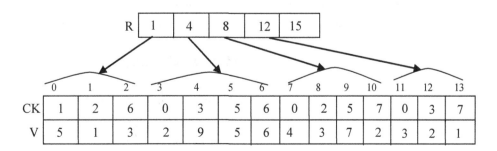

(b) The compressed EKMR

$PV=(y_1,y_2,...,y_n)$ where y_i are in DB and $y_i \neq c$.

The y_i are arranged according to their logical order in DB. No compression algorithm is applied on PV because it stores only non-constants values. The Bit Vector BV indicates the locations of constants and non-constants in the database. The bit vector is

$BV=(b_1,b_2,...,bn)$ where $b_i=1$ if $x_i \neq c$ and $b_i=0$ if $x_i=c$ for $1 \leq i \leq N$.

where BV consists of N bits.

The Address Vector AV is typically small and is used as an index for searching the database. It is stored in main memory rather than secondary storage. In addition to efficient compression fast forward and backward mapping between logical and physical databases is also important. To do this, BV is divided into subvectors of D bits each. The subvectors are compressed independently. This division of BV into subvectors makes the Address Vector AV sufficiently small to store it in main memory.

BV can be compressed by run-length encoding method (also discussed in this chapter). The division of BV into subvectors imposes a division of the database DB into $d=\lceil N/D \rceil$ sections, each consisting of D elements. The address vector is defined as:

$AV=(a_1,a_2,a_3,...a_d)$

Where $a_1=0$ and for $i \geq 2$, a_i is the relative position in PV of the last non-constant element in the $(i-1)^{th}$ section of DB if such a non-constant exists, otherwise we set $a_i=a_{i-1}$.

Consider an example where DB=(1, 0, 0, 7, 0, 0, 0, 0, 0, 0, 0, 18, 0, 0, 0, 13, 0, 0, 0, 0, 9, 0, 0, 37) and constants are 0 and D=5, Then

BV=(1, 0, 0, 1, 0, 0, 0, 0, 0, 0, 0, 0, 1, 0, 0, 0, 1, 0, 0, 0, 0, 1, 0, 0, 1)

PV=(1, 7, 18, 13, 9, 37)

AV=(0, 2, 2, 3, 4)

Run Length Encoding

Run Length Encoding (RLE) is based on the idea to replace a long sequence of the same symbol by a shorter sequence in a linearized array. RLE is a very simple form of data compression in which *runs* of data (that is, sequences in which the same data value occurs in many consecutive data elements) are stored as a single data value and count, rather than as the original run. This is most useful on data that contains many such runs. The sequence of length *l* of a repeated symbol '*s*' is replaced by a shorter sequence, usually containing one or more symbols of '*s*', a length information and sometimes an escape symbol. RLE replaces a string of repeated symbols with a single symbol and a count (*run length*) indicating the number of times the symbol is repeated. For example the string "aaaabbcdeeeeef-ghhhij" is replaced with "a4b2c1d1e5f1g1h3i1j1". The numbers indicate that they are values, not symbols. One of the major disadvantages of the classical run-length encoding is that they cannot support updates to the database without completely readjusting the runs. The method assumes that the data is primarily static.

The RLE scheme is modified by Stabno & Wrembel (2007) using the well known Huffman coding (Dipperstein, 2008). They developed a compression technique called Run-length Huffman (RLH) based on RLE. In RLH, the encoded symbols and their corresponding bit strings are represented as the Huffman tree. The Huffman tree is used for both compressing and decompressing. The distances between bits of value"1" are encoded in this scheme. This modified run length encoding is next compressed using Huffman encoding.

Bitmap Compression

A bitmap compression scheme consists of a bitmap and a physical database which stores the non-constant values of a linearzed array. The bitmap is employed to indicate the presence or absence of non-constant data.

Original data: a_1, c, c, a_2, c, c, c, a_3.
Compressed data
Bit map: 10010001.
Physical database: a_1, a_2, a_3.

The access time for both forward and backward mapping for the bitmap scheme is O(N), where N is the number of bits in the bitmap, or equivalently the number of elements in the database.

History Offset Compression

The history offset compression scheme (Hasan et al; 2005, 2006) is based on extendible array proposed by Rosenberg, 1974 and Otoo & Merrett, 1983. Conventional schemes for storing arrays do not support easy dynamic extension of an array. An extendible array, however, does not store an individual array; rather, it stores an array and all its potential extensions. The scheme is an *n*-dimensional rectangular array that grows by adjoining blocks, which are subarrays of dimension *n-1*, within which each subarray storage allocation is in row-major or lexicographic order.

The Notion of Extendible Array

An *n* dimensional extendible array *A* has a history counter *h* and three kinds of auxiliary tables for each extendible dimension $i(i = 1, ..., n)$. See Figure 7. These tables are history table H_i, address table L_i, and coefficient table C_i. The history tables memorize extension history *h*. If the size of *A* is $[d_n, d_{n-1}, ..., d_1]$ and the extended dimension is *i*, for an extension of *A* along dimension *i*, contiguous memory area that forms an $n - 1$ dimensional subarray *S* of size $[d_n, d_{n-1}, ..., d_{i+1}, d_{i-1}, ..., d_2, d_1]$ is dynamically allocated. Then the current history counter value is incremented by one, and it is memorized on the history table H_i, also the first address of *S* is held on the address table L_i. Since *h* increases monotonously, H_i is an ordered set of history values. As the subarrays are n-1 dimen-

sional for an n dimensional extendible array the linearization function F becomes

$$F(x_1, x_2, ..., x_{n-1}) = d_1 d_2 ... d_{n-2} x_{n-1}$$
$$+ d_1 d_2 d_3 ... d_{n-3} x_{n-2} + ... + d_1 x_2 + x_1$$

The coefficients of above function F is n-2 dimensional. As the extendible array is two dimensional in Figure 7 the coefficient table is void is there. When the number of dimension is more than two in an extendible array then the coefficients are computed and stored in the coefficient table. The actual data is stored in the subarrays that construct the extendible array. The three kinds of tables are auxiliary tables only. With the cost of the small auxiliary tables the multidimensional array can be extended dynamically in any direction without reallocation of the data already stored. Such advantages make it possible to apply the extendible array in a wide area of application where dynamic treatment of the array is necessary (Hasan et, al; 2007).

Using these three kinds of auxiliary table, the address of an array element can be computed as follows. Consider the element <4,3> of the extendible array in Figure 7. Compare $H_1[4] = 7$ and $H_2[3] = 6$. Since $H_1[4] > H_2[3]$, it can be proved that the element <4,3> is involved in the extended subarray *S* occupying the address from 60 to 63. The first address of *S* is known to be 60, which is stored in $L_1[4]$. Since the offset of <4, 3> from the first address of S is 3, the address of the element is determined as 63. Note that such a simple computational scheme can be used to access an extendible array element only by preparing small auxiliary tables. The superiority of this scheme in element accessing speed and memory utilization is shown by Otoo & Merrett 1983 comparing with other schemes such as hashing (Rosenberg & Stockmeyer, 1977).

Figure 7. Realization of 2 dimensional extendible array

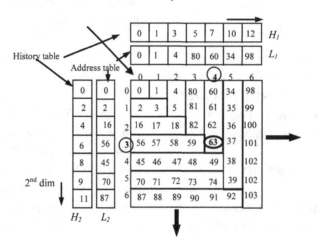

Compressing by History Offset Compression

Using coordinate method, Each element of an *n* dimensional extendible array can be specified by its *n* dimensional coordinate like $<x_1, x_2, ..., x_n>$. In this technique, an element is specified using the pair of *history value* and *offset value* of the extendible array. Since a history value is unique and has one to one correspondence with the corresponding subarray, the subarray including the specified element of an extendible array can be referred to uniquely by its corresponding history value *h*. Moreover, the *offset value* (i.e., logical location) of the element in the subarray can be computed by using the addressing function and this is also unique in the subarray. Therefore, each element of an *n*-dimensional extendible array can be referenced by specifying the pair *(history value, offset value)*.

In the coordinate method, if the dimension of the extendible array becomes higher, the length of the coordinate becomes longer proportionally. Since an *n*-column record can be referenced by its *n* dimensional coordinate $<x_1, x_2..., x_n>$ in the corresponding multidimensional array, the storage requirement for referencing records become large if the dimension is high. On the contrary, in the

history offset compression, even if the dimension is high, the size of the reference is fixed in short.

As the data incrementally grows over time, the extension of the array should be a characteristic of MOLAP systems. (Rotem & Zhao, 1996) pointed out some reasons for extension, such as to add new values to a dimension, a new level of aggregation or a completely new dimension. History offset compression (Hasan et, al; 2006, and 2007) allows easy extension, since it is based on extendible arrays. This allows the array to be extended dynamically without reallocating the existing data that is already stored. The degree of compression of the history offset compression approach is heavily dependent on the number of dimensions and the length of each dimension, because the size of each subarray is determined by $\prod_{i=1}^{n-1} d_i$, where n is the number of dimensions. If n and d_i are large, then the size of the subarray overflows the address space even for 64 bit machines. Moreover, for a k-bit processor, if b bits are used for storing history values and rest of the k-b bits are used to store offset values in history offset compression, then the maximum history value is 2^b and the maximum offset value that can be stored is 2^{k-b}. But these are small numbers with respect to large data warehouses. Unless some special treatment is done, the array size will overflow soon, even if the k bits are used both for history and offset values. For a query of the form *"column name<value or column name>value or column name between value1 and value2"*, it is necessary to visit different subarrays in the extendible array, whereas in traditional multidimensional arrays the records are organized linearly in only one stream, hence the query time of traditional arrays outperforms that of the extendible array. But when the compression scheme is applied, then the retrieval time is very similar for both the cases (Hasan et, al; 2007), while there is a gain concerning extension capability when history offset compression is used.

ADDITIONAL RELATED WORK AND PERFORMANCE ISSUES

In this section we review briefly other related work on the issue of MOLAP compression and performance.

The performance of accessing elements of large multidimensional arrays is strongly affected by the order of the dimensions, since the array is stored by a predetermined order of dimensions or axes. The multidimensional array having a number of dimensions n can be accessed or linearized in n! ways (Rotem & Zhao, 1996). Hence, the performance of aggregation computation for a slice of an array might greatly differ depending on which slice operation is done (Shimada et, al; 2006 and Seamons & Marianne, 1994).

To cope with the dimension dependency, array chunking can be employed (Zhao et, al; 1997) to get uniform treatment of all the dimensions. An n-dimensional array is divided into small sized n-dimensional chunks and each chunk is stored as a contiguous page on the secondary storage. The dimension dependency becomes moderate by chunking, but chunk size and shape have great effects on array chunking: large chunk sizes may cause unnecessary data to be read for queries with small result sets; On the other hand, small chunk sizes may require more disk accesses to retrieve all chunks required to answer a query. Moreover, the chunk shape influences the number of chunks retrieved in answering a query. It is shown by Zhao et, al; 1997 that the optimal dimension order for chunking multidimensional arrays is $|d_1| \leq |d_2| \leq |d_3| \leq \ldots |d_n|$ here d_i denotes the size of the dimension.

In order to have a good compression rate for data cubes, image compression approaches can also be applied, where simple blocks are compressed using many image compression formats including JPEG in David et, al; (1998). The images are divided into arbitrarily shaped regions through adaptive (Pennec & Mallat, 2000) or non-adaptive algorithms (Emmanuel & David, 1999). It is not clear *a priori* that more complex shapes or algorithms lead to more efficient storage. Another argument for block-coded data cubes is that many efficient buffering schemes for OLAP range queries rely themselves on block coding (Geffner, et, al; 1999 and Lemire, 2002).

Bitmap indices can be used for two important purposes-, namely basic bitmap index and bitmap compression or bitmap index compression (Stabno & Wrembel, 2007). Beside the basic bit map compression, there are also ideas of bitmap compression like Byte-aligned Bitmap Compression (Antoshenkov & Ziauddin 1996), Word-Aligned Hybrid (Wu et. al; 2004) (Stockinger & Wu 2007), and Approximate Encoding (Apaydin et, al; 2006). The first two techniques use the basic RLE compression (discussed in this chapter) algorithm where continuous vectors of bits with the same bit value (either "0" or "1") are represented as one occurrence of the value and the number of the values. Byte-aligned Bitmap Compression divides a bitmap into 8-bit words, whereas Word-Aligned Hybrid divides a bitmap into 31-bit words. Both techniques offer the best compression ratio for bitmaps describing rows ordered by the value of an indexed attribute. The set of bitmaps is treated as a Boolean matrix in Approximate Encoding technique. The matrix is constructed in a compressed form called Approximate Bitmap where multiple hash functions are used to encode into Approximate Bitmap to compress the Boolean matrix. For each vector of bits in the matrix, hashing string *hs* is constructed as the function of a row number and a column number in the matrix. The positions pointed by the hash values are set to "1" in Approximate Bitmap. The efficiency of bitmap compression ratio can be improved by reordering columns in bitmap matrices which is an NP-complete problem and only ordering heuristics can be applied.

The authors of (Stabno and Wrembel, 2007) show that the performance of Run Length Huffman(RLH) is better than *Word-Aligned Hybrid* or Byte-aligned Bitmap Compression because the Huffman tree is stored in main memory. Although decompressing bitmaps compressed by RLH requires a larger number of operations than in the case of *Word-Aligned Hybrid* and Byte-aligned Bitmap Compression, the fact that the tree is stored in-memory compensates. One major drawback of bitmap compression schemes is the need to update the bitmap. To modify a bitmap compressed by RLH, it is necessary to decompress the whole bitmap, then to modify the frequencies, and finally compress the bitmap again. All these operations are necessary because when updates occur the frequencies of distances change and hence the run-length encoding also changes. In order to improve the efficiency concerning bitmap updating, a new approach of modified RLH called RLH-1024 is also proposed by (Stabno and Wrembel, 2007).

Kaser & Daniel (2003) employs block coded data cubes for Hybrid OLAP (HOLAP) compression for two important operations of OLAP, namely slice and normalization. The slice fixes one of the attributes and the normalization can be viewed as a tuple of permutations. They also showed that depending on whether there is a very dense or a very sparse block, MOLAP and ROLAP are more efficient respectively. There is also work on compression of ROLAP datasets (Dehne et, al; 2001, Ng & Chinya 1997, and Sismanis et, al; 2002).

TRENDS IN MOLAP COMPRESSION

The state of the art of the trends in MOLAP compression and implementation can be summarized as follows:

- Implementing the dense part of the array as MOLAP and sparse part as ROLAP. This approach is termed as Hybrid OLAP (HOLAP). The dense chunks are compressed for MOLAP implementation and sparse chunks are compressed for ROLAP compression. The array is also considered at multiple levels for higher dimensions. Vendors such as Speedware and Microsoft are applying this approach. P. Kaser & Daniel (2003) show that for large multidimensional arrays, proper normalization can lead to more efficient storage in HOLAP contexts that store dense and sparse chunks differently. The uncompressed multidimensional array may be sparse in some areas and have some dense clusters of data in others(Owen, 2002). If certain chunks of the array are sufficiently dense then those chunks are more efficient than the sparse representation. The formation of dense chunks is important and it allows better array compression. If the normalization and selection of chunk boundaries are done carefully, then the data can be clustered. But this is an NP-problem even for a simple two-dimensional case. This problem is of the Maximum-Edge-Biclique form (Owen, 2002). Rotem et, al; (2007) treat each chunk as dense array. The block addressing is done in two levels: the first level concerns locating the block that an element falls into, and the second level concerns the location of the element within the block. The chunking process is equivalent to the block partitioning method used for matrices. For extremely large multidimensional arrays, a B+ tree storage scheme can be used for the first level chunk organization. The accessing of array elements in multi levels is also used in EKMR (Chun et, al;, 2003) scheme when the number of dimension is more than four. Kaser & Daniel, (2003) and Owen (2002) determine some ways to store data cubes using different coding for dense regions than for sparse ones. A single dense sub-cube is found and the remainder is considered sparse.

- Compressed implementation of flexible and extendible MOLAP, so that the dynamic treatment of the array becomes feasible. In both scientific and MOLAP data storage, the data grows incrementally over time and as such the array storage mapping must be extendible (Rotem & Zhao, 1996 and Tsuji et, al; 2008). Hence, incremental maintenance of the data cube is an important future MOLAP implementation and research issue (Kim & Lee, 2006 and Jin et, al; 2008). The incremental maintenance of the data cube means the propagation of its changes. Generally the amount of changes during the specified time is much smaller than the size of the source relation. Therefore, it is necessary to compute only the changes of the source relation and reflect this into the original data cube. Kim & Lee (2006) introduces incremental data cube maintenance for ROLAP and Jin et, al; 2008 employed the same approach for MOLAP data cube computation. A MOLAP array is extendible if the array bounds are allowed to grow by admitting new array elements that are appended to the storage space but without reorganizing previously allocated elements.

- Applying indexing techniques on compressed data warehouses. The storage requirement for the indices will also be reduced because the size of the database has been reduced by compression. Bitmap indices are designed for different query types including range, aggregation and join queries. The basic idea is to indicate whether an attribute in a tuple is equal to a specific value or not (O'Neil & Quass, 1997) and Chan & Ioannidis (1998). Queries whose predicates involve attributes indexed by bitmap indexes can be answered fast by performing bitwise AND, or OR, or NOT operations on bitmaps, which is a big advantage of bitmap indexes. The size of a bitmap index strongly depends on the cardinality of an indexed attribute. For attributes of high cardinality, indexes would be very large and hence the performance of data access with the support of such indexes might deteriorate (Wu & Buchmann, 1998). The dynamic bitmap index is constructed dynamically (Sarawagi, 1997) using vertical partition of the table, where each column stores a compressed representation of the values in the corresponding indexed column. In bitmap join index (Vanichayobon & Gruenwald, 1999) an index is created for a join attribute of two tables so that the actual join needs not be performed. This is effective for low cardinality data. Considering different criteria, a data cube is partitioned and compressed by Buccafurri, et, al; 2003 by substituting each block with a few summary information. Three 64-bits indexing techniques for compressed data warehouses are presented, namely 2/3LT, 2/4LT and 2/pLT indexes (LT stands for Level Tree). The 2/3LT index is balanced and suitable for distributions with no strong asymmetry, the 2/4LT is for biased for a distribution, and 2/pLT (p for peak) captures distribution having few high-density peaks. All the three types of indices use 32 bits of storage.

SOME LIMITATIONS OF MOLAP COMPRESSION

The main limitations of compression include address space limitations for multidimensional array (Hasan et, al; 2005), excess overhead, disruption of data properties, limited portability, and reduced reliability (Bassiouni 1985).

The address space for a linearized array is one of the main disadvantages of multidimensional array linearization and MOLAP implementations. If the number of dimensions and length of a dimension increase, then the address space overflows soon, even for 64 bit machine. Hence in most cases the MOLAP implementation using traditional multidimensional arrays is efficient if the number of dimensions is limited and it does not overflow the address space.

The overhead incurred by the compression process to encode data and the expansion process to recover original data is one of the most serious disadvantages of data compression. For some applications, this overhead could be considerable enough to discourage any consideration for employing data compression. In stable databases like scientific/statistical databases (where changes in the database are not frequent) the expansion process has greater impact on the performance of the system than the compression process.

Many data compression schemes disrupt data properties that may be important for some applications. For example, by not preserving the lexical order of compressed data, efficient sorting and searching schemes can become inapplicable.

The size of a compressed database is usually unknown in advance, and depends on the compression method and the contents of the database. Different records having the same length may produce compressed records with different sizes. This uncertainty of the output length creates dif-

ficulties in space allocation and in updating records within compressed files.

CONCLUSION

In this chapter we have motivated the importance of MOLAP compression and provided a survey of common compression mechanisms. We also reviewed additional related work, described trends and limitations of compression schemes. The multidimensional array based MOLAP implementation is widely used, but this scheme suffers from inadequate address space, dimension dependency and dynamic extension issues during runtime. We have argued that chunking of arrays overcomes the dimension dependency and multidimensional extendible arrays overcome the dynamic extension problem. Within future trends, we identified the use of indexes and especially bitmap indexing in compressed data warehouses. We also discussed the use of HOLAP, where MOLAP compression techniques can be applied concerning dense regions and the rest are implemented as ROLAP.

REFERENCES

Antoshenkov, G., & Ziauddin, M. (1996). Query processing and optimization in oracle rdb. *The VLDB Journal*, 5(4), 229–237. doi:10.1007/s007780050026

Apaydin, T., Canahuate, G., Ferhatosmanoglu, H., & Tosun, A. S. (2006). Approximate encoding for direct access and query processing over compressed bitmaps. In *Proceedings of Conference on Very Large DataBases (VLDB)*, (pp. 846–857).

Barret, R., Berry, M., Chan, T. F., Dongara, J., Eljkhhout, V., Pozo, R., et al. (1994). *Templates for the solution of linear systems: Building blocks for the iterative methods*, (2nd ed.). Philadelphia: SIAM.

Bassiouni, M. A. (1985). Data Compression in Scientific and Statistical Databases. *IEEE Transactions on Software Engineering*, *11*(10), 1047–1057. doi:10.1109/TSE.1985.231852

Buccafurri, F., Furfaro, F., Sacca, D., & Sirangelo, C. (2003). A quad tree based multiresolution approach for compressing datacube. *SSDBM, 2003*, 127–140.

Chan, C., & Ioannidis, Y. (1998) Bitmap index design and evaluation. *ACM SIGMOID* (pp. 355-366).

Chun, Y. L., Yeh, C. C., & Jen, S. L. (2002). Efficient Representation Scheme for Multidimensional Array Operations. *IEEE Transactions on Computers*, *51*(3), 327–345. doi:10.1109/12.990130

Chun, Y. L., Yeh, C. C., & Jen, S. L. (2003). Efficient Data Parallel Algorithms for Multidimensional Array Operations Based on the EKMR Scheme for Distributed Memory Multicomputers. *IEEE Transactions on Parallel and Distributed Systems*, *14*(7), 625–639. doi:10.1109/TPDS.2003.1214316

Chun, Y. L., Yeh, C. C., & Jen, S. L. (2003). Efficient Data Compression Method for Multidimensional Sparse Array Operations Based on EKMR Scheme. *IEEE Transactions on Computers*, *52*(12), 1640–1648. doi:10.1109/TC.2003.1252859

Datta, A., & Thomas, H. (2002). Querying Compressed Data in Data Warehouses. [Dordrecht, The Netherlands: Springer Netherlands.]. *Journal of Information Technology Management*, *3*(4), 353–386. doi:10.1023/A:1019772807859

David, L., Vetterli, M., Daubechies, I., & Ron, A. (1998). Data compression and harmonic analysis. *IEEE Transactions on Information Theory*, 44.

Dehne, F., Eavis, T., & Andrew, R. (2001). Coarse grained parallel on-line analytical processing (OLAP) for data mining. In *Proceedings of ICCS 2001*.

Dipperstein, M. (2008). *Huffman Code Discussion and Implementation*. Received March 4, 2009 http://michael.dipperstein.com/huffman/index.html.

Eggers, S., & Shohani, A. (1980). Efficient Access of Compressed Data. In *Proceedings of sixth int'l conference on Very large Databases*, 205-211.

Emmanuel, J. C., & David, L. D. (1999) Curvelets - a surprisingly effective nonadaptive representation for objects with edges. In *Curves and Surfaces*.

Geffner, S., Agrawal, D., Abbadi, A. E., & Smith, T. R. (1999) Relative prefix sums: An efficient approach for querying dynamic OLAP data cubes. In *Proceedings of International Conference of Data Engineering (ICDE)*, (pp. 328–335). Washington, DC: IEEE CS.

Hasan, K. M. A., Kuroda, M., Azuma, N., Tsuji, T., & Higuchi, K. (2005). An extendible array based implementation of relational tables for multidimensional databases. In *Proceedings of 7th International Conference on Data Warehousing and Knowledge Discovery (DaWaK'05)* (pp. 233-242). Heidelberg: Springer-Verlag.

Hasan, K. M. A., Tsuji, T., & Higuchi, K. (2006). A Parallel Implementation Scheme of Relational Tables Based on Multidimensional Extendible Array. *International Journal of Data Warehousing and Mining*, *2*(4), 66–85.

Hasan, K. M. A., Tsuji, T., & Higuchi, K. (2007). An Efficient Implementation for MOLAP Basic Data Structure and Its Evaluation, In *Proceedings of DASFAA 2007*, (LNCS 4443, pp. 288 – 299). Heidelberg: Springer-Verlag.

Hierachical Data Format (HDF) group. (2004). *HDF5 User's Guide*. National Center for Supercomputing Applications (NCSA), University of Illinois, Urbana-Champaign, Illinois, UrbanaChampaign, release 1.6.3. edition.

Jin, D., Tsuji, T., Tsuchida, T., & Higuchi, K. (2008). An Incremental Maintenance Scheme of Data Cubes.In *Proceedings of* DASFAA 2008: (pp. 172-187). Heidelberg: Springer-Verlag.

Karen, C., & Gupta, A. (2006). Indexing in Datewarehouses: Bitmaps and Beyond. In Wrembel & Koncilia (Eds.) *Data Warehouses and OLAP*. Hershey, PA: IGI Global.

Kaser, O., & Daniel, L. (2003). Attribute value reordering for efficient hybrid OLAP. In *Proceedings of DOLAP'03*, New Orleans, Louisiana, November 7, 2003 (NRC 46510).

Kim, M. H., & Lee, K. Y. (2006) Efficient incremental maintenance of data cubes. In *Proceedings of the 32nd international conference on Very large data bases*, (pp. 823 – 833). San Francisco: Morgan Kaufman.

Lemire, D. (2002). Wavelet-based relative prefix sum methods for range sum queries in data cubes. In *Proceedings of CASCON*.

Li, J., Rotem, D., & Wong, H. K. (1987). A New Compression Method with Fast Searching on Large Databases. In *Proceedings of* 13th *international conference on Very large data bases*, (pp. 311-318). San Francisco: Morgan Kaufman.

Li, J., & Srivastava, J. (2002). Efficient Aggregation Algorithms for Compressed Data warehouses. *IEEE Transactions on Knowledge and Data Engineering, 14*(3), 515–529. doi:10.1109/TKDE.2002.1000340

Maintenance, D. A. S. F. A. A. *2008,* (LNCS 4947, pp. 682-685). Heidelberg: Springer-Verlag.

Ng, W., & Chinya, V. R. (1997). Block-oriented compression techniques for large statistical databases. *IEEE Transactions on Knowledge and Data Engineering, 9*(2), 314–328. doi:10.1109/69.591455

O'Neil, P. & Quass, (1997). Improved query performance with variant indexes. In *SIGMOID*, (pp. 38-49).

Otoo, E. J., & Merrett, T. H. (1983). A storage scheme for extendible arrays. *Computing, 31*, 1–9. doi:10.1007/BF02247933

Owen, K. (2002). *Compressing MOLAP arrays by attribute-value reordering: An experimental analysis*. UNBSJ ASCS Technical Report TR-02-001.

Pennec, E. L., & Mallat, S. (2000). *Image representation and compression with bandelets*. Technical report, École Polytechnique.

Rosenberg, A. L. (1974). Allocating storage for extendible arrays. *Journal of the ACM, 21*, 652–670. doi:10.1145/321850.321861

Rosenberg, A. L., & Stockmeyer, L. J. (1977). Hashing schemes for extendible arrays. *Journal of the ACM, 24*, 199–221. doi:10.1145/322003.322006

Rotem, D., Otoo, E. J., & Seshadri, S. (2007). *Chunking of Large Multidimensional Arrays*. Lawrence Berkeley National Laboratory, University of California, University of California, 2007, LBNL-63230.

Rotem, D., & Zhao, J. L. (1996) Extendible arrays for statistical databases and OLAP applications. In *Proceedings of Scientific and Statistical Database Management*, (pp. 108-117). Washington, DC: IEEE Computer Society.

Sarawagi, S. (1997). Indexing OLAP Data. *IEEE Data Eng. Bull., 20*(1), 36–43.

Sarawagi, S., & Stonebraker, M. (1994). Efficient organization of large multidimensional arrays. In *Proceedings of International Conference on Data Engineering (ICDE)*, (pp. 328-336). Washington, DC: IEEE CS.

Seamons, K. E., & Marianne, W. (1994) Physical schemas for large multidimensional arrays in scientific computing applications. In *Proceedings of Scientific and Statistical Database Management*, (pp. 218–227). Washington, DC: IEEE Computer Society.

Shimada, T., Fang, T., Tsuji, T., & Higuchi, K. (2006). Containerization Algorithms for Multidimensional Arrays. *Asia Simulation conference*, (pp. 228-232). Heidelberg: Springer-Verlag.

Shoshani, A. (1997). OLAP and statistical databases: Similarities and differences. In *Proceedings of ACM-PODS Conference*, (pp. 185–196).

Shoshani, A. (1997). Olap and Statistical database: Similarities and differences. *Proceedings of the sixteenth ACM SIGACT-SIGMOD-SIGART*, (pp. 185 – 196).

Sismanis, Y., & Deligiannakis, A. Roussopoulus, & Kotidis, Y. (2002). Dwarf: Shrinking the peta-cube. In *ACM SIGMOD 2002*, (pp. 464–475).

Stabno, M. Wrembel R. (2007). RLH: bitmap compression technique based on run-length and huffman encoding. In *DOLAP 2007*, (pp. 41-48). New York: ACM.

Stockinger, K., & Wu, K. (2007). Bitmap indices for data warehouses. In R. Wrembel & C. Koncilia, (Ed.), *DataWarehouses and OLAP: Concepts, Architectures and Solutions*. Hershey, PA: Idea Group Inc.

Tsuji, T., Jin, D., & Higuchi, K. (2008). Data Compression for Incremental Data Cube

Vanichayobon, S., & Gruenwald, L. (1999). *Indexing techniques for data warehouses' queries*. Technical report, University of Oklahoma, School of Computer Science.

White, J. B., & Sadayappan, P. (1997). On improving the performance of sparse matrix-vector multiplication. *Proc. Int'l Conf. High Performance Computing*, (pp. 711-725).

Wu, K., Otoo, E. J., & Shoshani, A. (2004). On the performance of bitmap indices for high cardinality attributes. In *Proc. of Int. Conference on Very Large Data Bases (VLDB)*, (pp. 24–35). San Francisco: Morgan Kaufman.

Wu, M. C., & Buchmann, A. (1998). Encoded bitmap indexing for data warehouses. In *Proc. of Int. Conference on Data Engineering* (ICDE), (pp. 220–230). Washington, DC: IEEE CS.

Zhao, Y., Deshpande, P. M., & Naughton, J. F. (1997). An array based algorithm for simultaneous multidimensional aggregates. *ACM SIGMOD*, (pp. 159–170).

Section 2
Application Issues and Trends in Data Warehousing and OLAP

Chapter 5
View Management Techniques and Their Application to Data Stream Management

Christoph Quix
RWTH Aachen University, Germany

Xiang Li
RWTH Aachen University, Germany

David Kensche
RWTH Aachen University, Germany

Sandra Geisler
RWTH Aachen University, Germany

ABSTRACT

Data streams are continuous, rapid, time-varying, and transient streams of data and provide new opportunities for analysis of timely information. Data processing in data streams faces similar challenges as view management in data warehousing: continuous query processing is related to view maintenance in data warehousing, multi-query optimization for continuous queries is highly related to view selection in conventional relational DBMS and data warehouses. In this chapter, we give an overview of view maintenance and view selection methods, explain the fundamental issues of data stream management, and discuss how view management techniques from data warehousing are related to data stream management. We also give directions for future research in view management, data streams, and data warehousing.

INTRODUCTION

The management of views is a fundamental problem in the design and maintenance of data warehouse systems. Materialized views speed up query process-

DOI: 10.4018/978-1-60566-816-1.ch005

ing, but require additional storage and need to be maintained in case of updates of the base data. In order to balance the efficiency of query processing and view maintenance, *view selection* techniques have been proposed which select a set of views that approximates optimal costs for query processing and view maintenance.

Data warehouses rely heavily on analysis of up-to-date information to support decision makers. The advent of a new class of data management applications, namely data stream management systems (DSMS), provides new opportunities for analysis of timely information. A data stream is a continuous, rapid, time-varying, and transient stream of data. There are connections between DSMS and view management. Whereas continuous query processing is related to view maintenance in data warehousing, multi-query optimization for continuous queries is highly related to view selection in conventional relational DBMS and data warehouses. In this chapter, we give an overview of view maintenance and view selection methods, explain the fundamental issues of data stream management, and discuss how view management techniques from data warehousing are related to data stream management.

The chapter is structured as follows: section 2 briefly explains the roles of views in data warehouses. Section 3 gives an overview of view maintenance methods and classifies them according to various criteria. Then, section 4 explains the view selection problem and presents a taxonomy of existing view selection techniques. Section 5 discusses issues and challenges in data stream management and summarizes recent results in research on data streams. Section 6 discusses the relationship of view management techniques to data stream management. Similarities, differences and possible connections between data stream management and view management are discussed. Finally, section 7 summarizes the chapter and points out directions for future research in view management, data streams, and data warehousing.

Views in Data Warehousing

A view can select or restructure data in such a way that an application can use the data more efficiently. Different from On-Line Transaction Processing (OLTP) systems, which focus at managing the common data operations, data warehouses aim at supporting data analysis (i.e., On-Line Analytical Processing, OLAP) and are known for their vast volume of data and complexity of queries. The response time of queries, if evaluated from base tables, is usually too long for users to tolerate as a huge amount of data has to be processed. Therefore, it is a common practice to pre-compute summaries of base tables in order to reduce the query response time. The following example illustrates the benefit of materializing views:

Example 1 Consider the TPC-D benchmark (Serlin, 1993), modeling a data cube of sales with three dimensions: part, supplier, and customer. We denote the base table as *R(part; supp; cust; sales)*. The following query is posed by users:

Q: SELECT part, SUM(sales) AS total
FROM R
GROUP BY part;

The following two materialized views can both benefit Q:

V_1: SELECT part, cust, SUM(sales) AS total
FROM R
GROUP BY part, cust;

V_2: SELECT part, supp, SUM(sales) AS total
FROM R
GROUP BY part, supp;

It depends on the statistics of the data to decide which view is better in terms of query response or storage cost. For instance, the statistics of the TPC-D database are as follows:

- R: 6M rows
- V_1: 6M rows
- V_2: 0.8M rows

It is easy to see that materializing V_2 will benefit answering Q, because V_2 is much smaller to scan than the base table. Meanwhile, V_1 is not quite useful since it has a comparable size to the base table.

Nonetheless, materialization of views comes at some price. On the one hand, materializing views takes up storage. On the other hand, once a view is materialized, we have to take care of the maintenance problem (cf. Section 3). Materializing views can benefit query response time at a cost of increasing storage and maintenance overhead. It is interesting to note that query response time degrades with too much extra view materialization. Kotidis (2002) attributes the phenomenon to the competition of memory buffers among materialized views.

VIEW MAINTENANCE

View maintenance is the process of updating a materialized view after the base tables, from which the view has been derived, have been updated (Gupta and Mumick, 1995). As the recomputation of the views from scratch is usually too expensive, incremental methods are used to compute the changes to the view which result from changes of the base data. However, in some special cases (e.g., update or deletion of a complete relation) it might be more efficient to recompute the view from scratch instead of using an incremental view maintenance method. In the following, we will refer to incremental view maintenance methods when speaking about view maintenance.

We first introduce the problem in Section 3.1, before we discuss several view maintenance methods in more detail according to a classification in Section 3.2.

Description of the View Maintenance Problem

Consider Example 1 from Section 2. Suppose we want to group customers in view V_1 by nation for which we have to join the table R with the customers table:

SELECT R.part, R.cust, C.nationkey, SUM(sales) AS total

FROM R, Customer as C

WHERE R.cust=C.custkey

GROUP BY part, R.cust, C.nationkey;

In order to maintain the view after an update to the base relations R or *Customer*, we can distinguish the following cases:

- A tuple is inserted, deleted or modified in R.
- A tuple is inserted, deleted or modified in *Customer*.

The effect of the updates to base relations of the materialized view can be computed by rewriting the definition of view V_1 using relations representing only the inserted and deleted tuples from the base relations. For simplicity, we represent a modification of a tuple as deletion followed by an insertion, knowing that this representation is inaccurate and might be inefficient. There are maintenance methods which consider modifications separately (Urpí and Olivé, 1992). To keep the example simple, we just focus on the join between R and C in the view V_1:

The insertions to V_1 can then be computed by the expression:

$$V_{1,ins} = R_{ins} \bowtie C \cup R' \bowtie C_{ins}$$

where R_{ins} and C_{ins} represent the tuples inserted into R and C, respectively, and R' denotes the relation R after the update (e.g., including newly inserted tuples and old tuples) (Hanson, 1987; Ceri and Widom, 1991; Gupta et al., 1993).

In a similar way, the deleted tuples from V_1 can be computed as:

$$V_{1,del} = R_{del} \bowtie C \cup R \bowtie C_{del}$$

Please note that the set of deleted tuples of a relation is only joined with the former state of the other relation in order to get the deleted tuples of the join relation.

Then the new state of the view V_1 can be computed as:

$$V'_1 = V_1 - V_{1,del} \cup V_{1,ins}$$

This principle of using the delta relations in a semi-naive method (Ullman, 1989) to compute the resulting changes in the view is the basis for most view maintenance methods which we will discuss in more detail in the following.

Classification of View Maintenance Techniques

View maintenance techniques can be distinguished according to several criteria. So far, we have considered only the relational model with expressions in relational algebra. There are approaches which consider other *query languages* and *data models* for view maintenance. Furthermore, even in the relational case, we can consider more complex operators in the query language such as aggregation. These issues will be discussed in Section 3.2.1.

View maintenance approaches can be also distinguished by the type of *information* they require to maintain a view. A classical example are *self-maintainable views* which can be maintained using only the update information (i.e., without accessing the original base relations). In the example above, we could maintain the view only using the modified tuples and the materialized view if there is a foreign key constraint between *R.cust* and *C.custkey*. Self-maintainable views and similar methods will be discussed in Section 3.2.2.

Finally, the desired quality of the materialized view is also an important issue. Some view maintenance approaches relax certain *quality constraints* (such as the timeliness of the view or the accuracy of the result) in order to optimize the view maintenance process. We discuss these methods in Section 3.2.3.

Query Language and Data Model

Algorithms related to view maintenance have been first studied in the context of integrity constraint checking for relational databases (e.g., (Buneman and Clemons, 1979; Bernstein et al., 1980; Nicolas, 1982)). Early works on view maintenance were based on Select-Project-Join (SPJ) queries expressed in relational algebra (Blakeley et al., 1986; Hanson, 1987) or even only project queries (Shmueli and Itai, 1984).

In the context of deductive databases, Datalog and its variants have been used to study incremental view maintenance (Gupta et al., 1992; Harrison and Dietrich, 1992; Urpí and Olivé, 1992). The counting solution presented by Gupta et al. (1992) counts the number of alternative derivations for a tuple in a view. The view is maintained by updating the counts incrementally using rewritten rules of the original Datalog program. However, this method does not work for recursive Datalog programs, as a tuple might have infinitely many derivations in this case. The DRed algorithm (Gupta et al., 1993; Toroslu and Kocabas, 1997) can be used also for the maintenance of recursive views. It first computes all the tuples which are potentially deleted by an update of the base relations and then tries to rederive these tuples using the new state of the database. Finally, all inserted tuples are computed using a method similar to the method sketched above.

The maintenance of views including aggregation has been studied especially in the field of data warehouses. Gray et al. (1997) introduced the cube operator and also distinguished between types of aggregation functions: distributive, algebraic, and holistic. Distributive aggregate functions can be also computed by combining results from disjoint sets. For example, MIN, MAX and SUM are distributive functions. COUNT is distributive unless DISTINCT is used. Algebraic functions can be computed by some combination of distributive aggregate functions, e.g., AVG can be expressed as SUM/COUNT. The remaining aggregate functions are called holistic functions, as their value can only be computed taking the whole relation into account (e.g., median) (Mumick et al., 1997). Therefore, most view maintenance methods just consider distributive and algebraic functions, as only those can be maintained efficiently.

The approach by Mumick et al. (1997) uses summary delta tables which compute the aggregate functions for those tuples which have been inserted or deleted in a view. The results of the summary delta tables are then combined with the previous values in the view. Thus, it can be applied only to algebraic and distributive aggregate functions.

Methods for maintaining views using non-distributive aggregate functions have been proposed (Li and Wang, 2006; Palpanas et al., 2002). The approach by Li and Wang (2006) can be applied to the median function and is based on the quotient cube (Lakshmanan et al., 2002) which partitions a cube into several cells with similar behavior. The aggregate values need then to be maintained only if a cell is affected by an update and not for all tuples of the base relation. A similar idea is used by Palpanas et al. (2002) which recomputes the values only for affected groups.

Views using outer joins are common in data integration and data warehousing, but they cannot easily be maintained using the scheme described above. Suppose we want to maintain a view with an outer join between R and S, then if a tuple is inserted into R, it might be necessary to remove a tuple from S for which previously there was no matching tuple in R. These special characteristics of outer joins have to be taken into account in view maintenance. Larson and Zhou (2007) present a method which can efficiently maintain outer join views. It also exploits foreign key constraints: in the example above, if the join is between a foreign key in R and a key in S, then if a tuple is inserted into S, we can directly insert the tuple extended with null values into the view, as there can be no matching tuple in R because of the foreign key constraint. In other cases, the maintenance of the view is done in two phases: a primary delta table represents all tuples which need to be inserted into the view; the secondary delta removes those tuples with extended null values from the view which now have a joining tuple in the other relation.

The secondary delta can be computed using the primary delta and either the base tables or the view. Other approaches for the maintenance of outer join views (Griffin and Kumar, 1998; Gupta and Mumick, 2006) are either less efficient, incorrect, or incomplete (Larson and Zhou, 2007).

Maintenance of views over XML data has also been considered. Early approaches studied maintenance of views over the semistructured data model (Abiteboul et al., 1998; Zhuge and Garcia-Molina, 1998) which provides only a rough, graph-based abstraction of XML data (e.g., the order of XML elements is not represented in the semistructured data model). Liefke and Davidson (2000) use a subset of the XML-QL query language (which can be seen as a predecessor of XQuery), supporting also restructuring operations such as regrouping, flattening and aggregations. However, ordered data structures are not supported. In an order-sensitive approach (Dimitrova et al., 2003) queries are expressed in an XML algebra in which corresponding update propagation operations can be defined for each operation. However, these update propagation operations need to be processed by a special query engine and require the materialization of intermediate results.

These weaknesses have been identified by El-Sayed et al. (2006) who also present a framework for maintenance of views defined in XQuery. The framework works in three phases: validate, propagate and apply. In the validate phase, update trees are generated from the source updates, and it is verified whether these update trees are relevant for a view. Multiple update trees can be combined to a batch update tree if they are semantically related. In the propagate phase, the update trees are used to derive incremental maintenance plans (IMPs) from the XQuery views. The IMPs generate delta update trees which represent the updates to be performed on the view extents. These delta update trees are then applied in the last phase, in which the necessary modifications to the materialized views are done.

Information

With respect to the information which is used to maintain a view, the class of *self-maintainable views* is most important. A view is self-maintainable if it can be maintained using only the view and the modifications. Whether a view is self-maintainable depends also on the type of modification which has to be considered, e.g., it has been stated that in general views with a join of two or more relations are not self-maintainable with respect to insertions (Gupta et al., 1996).

However, as sketched by the example above, if key and foreign key constraints are considered, many views including joins are self-maintainable in practicable applications (Quass et al., 1996). Many views can be easily made self-maintainable by either including certain columns of the base relations in the view, or by creating auxiliary views which contain additional data to enable self-maintenance of views (Quass et al., 1996).

The opposite problem to self-maintainable views is the following (Staudt and Jarke, 1996): views should be maintained as efficient as possible without taking into account the materialized views. This is the case, for example, for applications which extract the data of the view from a database and store it in some application specific cache on the client side; maintenance of the view has still to be done in the database on the server side where the base relations are stored. The approach recomputes the views and intermediate results only as much as necessary. The results can then be sent as update messages to the client application. This method is also useful if views are defined by a hierarchy of views (i.e., a view is defined by other views instead of base relations), as the intermediate views are not recomputed completely for view maintenance.

Similar ideas are used by Sawires et al. (2006) which consider the maintenance of XPath views in *loosely coupled systems*, i.e., the system managing the base data and the system holding the materialized views are only loosely coupled and cannot query each other. The method tries to identify irrelevant updates for a view, such that further computations can be avoided. Furthermore, it checks whether a view is self-maintainable with respect to a certain update.

Quality Constraints

Normally, the view maintenance method should deliver a complete, correct and accurate result, i.e., we do not tolerate any kind of incorrectness. However, many applications, especially in web-based systems, can accept a certain degree of incorrectness or inaccuracy as long as the efficiency of the system is guaranteed.

Top-k views are an example where a certain inaccuracy can usually be tolerated (e.g., in a search engine delivering the k best results). A method for maintaining a top-k view more efficiently by making it more self-maintainable is presented by Yi et al. (2003). By allowing the actual value of k to vary between k and a k_{max}, the view can usually be maintained without doing an expensive scan over the base relation.

Another important quality factor to be considered is the timeliness of the data in the materialized view. In the context of data warehouse systems, often a daily maintenance of the views is sufficient. This means, that the update propagation is usually done during a period of the day at which OLAP users do not lock the data warehouse with long running queries (e.g., at night time). However, the definition of 'night time' in a global organization might be not possible. On the other hand, the requirement to access the most recent data is becoming more and more important in many data warehouse applications.

Therefore, some approaches have considered *online view maintenance*, i.e., maintaining a view while the data warehouse is being used for queries. Quass and Widom (1997) presented a first approach in this area. They developed an algorithm that allows view maintenance transactions to run concurrently with query transactions by using two versions of the database and avoiding locking.

A different paradigm has been proposed by Zhou et al. (2007). Whereas most approaches trigger the view maintenance process when an update occurs, in this approach the maintenance can be deferred until the system has resources available to process the view maintenance task, or a user accesses a view which is affected by the update. By doing so, the burden of view maintenance is removed from the update transactions.

VIEW SELECTION

View selection addresses the problem of choosing materialized views in the design process of data warehouses. Informally, it can be stated as, given an estimated query workload and possibly also sets of candidate views, to select a set of views, such that some operation goals (e.g., average query response time, maintenance costs, or both) are optimized and meanwhile some resource constraints are satisfied. View selection, view maintenance, and answering queries using views (Halevy, 2001) comprise a relatively complete framework for query processing in data warehousing.

In this section, we discuss the challenges of and solutions to the view selection problem. We first state the formal framework of the view selection problem and some theoretical aspects based on the framework (Section 4.1). We then describe a taxonomy that we use to classify view selection techniques (Section 4.2). The main body of view selection approaches in the static setting is then discussed (Section 4.3), where the query workload is assumed to be known in advance. Finally, dynamic view selection approaches are introduced (Section 4.4).

Theoretical Perspectives

We focus on static view selection in this section and start by introducing a model treating the view selection problem as an optimization problem.

View selection is handled as an optimization problem, which can be described as a tuple *(S;V;M;Q)*, where S is the schema together with some size estimation model, *V* is the set of all the possible views to choose from, *M* is a quantity denoting the space available for materializing views, and *Q* is a set of queries. The problem is to find a subset of *V* that optimizes the queries against *Q* while the storage requirement is no larger than *M*. The overall evaluation cost is formulated as a weighted sum over *Q*:

$$E(V) = \Sigma_{q \in Q} E(q, V) \times f_q$$

where f_q denotes the frequency of query q, and $E(q, V)$ is the minimal possible evaluation cost of q using the selected views V. Besides the cost of queries, view maintenance can be considered in a similar way:

$$U(V) = \Sigma_{v \in V} U(v) \times f_v$$

where f_v denotes the frequency of updating view v, and $U(v)$ is the cost of updating the view. Thus, the task is a multi-goal optimization problem:

$$C(V) = E(V) + \alpha U(V)$$

where α is a positive weight parameter adjusting these two goals. Normally, these two goals lead to different solutions if considered separately. For example, given a large enough storage, minimizing query evaluation requires all queries in the workload to be materialized as views, while update cost is minimized when only base relations are stored.

The view selection problem is known to be *NP-hard*, since even the simplest form in a hypercube has a reduction from the set cover problem (Harinarayan et al., 1996).

Figure 1. Classification of view selection techniques

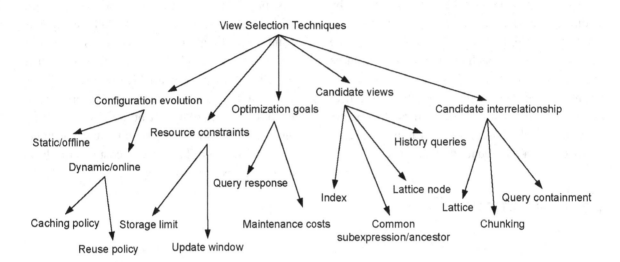

A Taxonomy of View Selection Approaches

The taxonomy which we used for classifying view selection techniques is illustrated in Figure 1.

Configuration Evolution

One most characteristic dimension of view selection techniques is whether the selected views evolve over time. Most of the techniques are offline/static and will not change once the selection is done. In contrast, online/dynamic approaches, such as WATCHMAN (Scheuermann et al., 1996) and DynaMat (Kotidis and Roussopoulos, 1999), adjust the view selection following similar ideas as semantic caching (cf. Section 4.4). Inside the scope of dynamic view selection, there are two significant issues: namely the caching policy and the reuse policy. The caching policy is the way how the view cache admits/evicts views, while the reuse policy describes how the cached views are used to speed up later queries.

Resource Constraints

Due to the vast volume of data in OLAP systems, storage space is usually the first issue to be considered. However, regarding materialized views, the limit on maintenance time also becomes vital. Too much materialization can make the maintenance time prohibitively long and hence decrease the availability of the OLAP systems.

Optimization Goals

Ideally, view selection techniques are aimed at query response time. However, this goal is usually too expensive to achieve. Many existing approaches opt for some other relevant measures such as the benefit of a unit storage space. It has been shown that materializing additional views may reduce the overall maintenance costs in presence of a set of pre-determined materialized views (Ross et al., 1996; Labio et al., 1997). With the costs of extra storage decreasing dramatically, the update window, however, keeps shrinking.

Therefore, many approaches (e.g., (Gupta and Mumick, 2005; Theodoratos and Sellis, 1997; Mistry et al., 2001)) aim at optimizing maintenance costs instead of query response. It is also easy to incorporate both query evaluation costs and materialized view maintenance costs in the goal function (cf. Section 4.1).

Candidate Views

In general, there are prohibitively many views that can be materialized. Even restricted to possible combinations of selections and group-bys, the number of candidate views is already exponential in terms of the size of the queries. Therefore, the scope of candidate views has to be confined to allow feasible tools. Most of the static view selection techniques (cf. 4.3) restrict themselves to a given set of candidate views. For example, a natural scope is defined by all the aggregation possibilities in the data cube (Gray et al., 1997), which can be modeled as nodes in a lattice. Dynamic view selection approaches (cf. section 4.4) make use of a windowed query history of users as a candidate domain. Another type of candidates are the views that are common subexpressions or ancestors of queries. They are not optimal for a single query, but they can benefit more than one query and hence be a globally optimal choice. Moreover, indexes can be also deemed as a special type of views.

Interrelationship Modeling

Candidate views have interactions. Selection of one view may render materialization of another view useless, while several views may have overlapping information and therefore duplications. Dependencies between aggregations in a data cube are modeled using a lattice. Analytic queries involving selection and aggregation can be modeled using hyperplanes covering. Chunks in view selection approaches for MOLAP (Zhao et al., 1997) usually have more intricate relationships

such as part-of. Modern tuning tools shipped with commercial database management systems rely on query optimizers to explore implicit interrelationships between candidate views (Zilio et al., 2004; Dageville et al., 2004; Agrawal et al., 2004).

Static View Selection

Most of the view selection techniques follow the paradigm of *static view selection* (or *data warehouse configuration*) (Theodoratos and Sellis, 1997), which selects views from a given input candidate view set under storage and/or maintenance constraints. The materialized views, once determined offline, will not change over time. Therefore, this line of work is good for cases where the queries are relatively fixed or similar. When the query patterns of the users change dramatically, view selection has to be redone.

In the seminal work of Harinarayan et al. (1996), both the query workload and the candidate views are taken from the nodes in the data cube, which are various group-bys for aggregation. The interrelationship between candidates is then represented by a lattice. For example, the database in Example 1 gives rise to the lattice depicted in Figure 2.

The edges in the lattice depict dependency relationships. One view is dependent on another,

Figure 2. The lattice for the TPC-D database

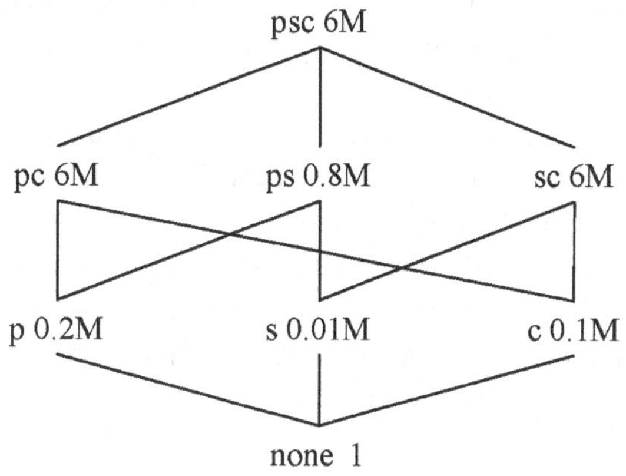

if it can be computed using solely data in the latter view. An aggregation query can be answered using any of its ancestors, i.e., the views it transitively depends on. With the lattice model at hand, the benefit of materializing a view *v* wrt. *S*, the set of views already selected, is defined as the gain in terms of costs:

$$B(v, S) = \sum_{w \preceq v} \max(0, E(w, S) - E(w, v))$$

where ≼ is the partial order represented in the lattice, *E(w;v)* is the evaluation cost of query *w* using view *v*, and *E(w;S)* is the minimal evaluation cost of *w* using *S*, i.e., $E(w; S) = min_{u \in S}\{E(w; u)\}$. A greedy algorithm is then adopted to select the most beneficial view per storage space (Benefit-Per-Unit-Space) up to the storage limit.

Gupta et al. (1997) extend the framework to accommodate index selection while the query workload is extended to allow both aggregation and selection (also called *slice* (Gray et al., 1997)). An index, regarded as a special view, is selected only after the view it is defined over is selected. A greedy algorithm is employed to choose at each step a physical structure, either a view or an index, to maximize the benefit per unit space.

In the above case when slice queries are considered, the lattice is no longer sufficient to express the interrelationship of candidate views. A bipartite query-view graph is used in (Gupta et al., 1997), in which there are a set of edges between a query and a view, each labeled with the evaluation of the query against the view using a different index.

There is a trade-off between distribution of storage space between views and indices if there are global space constraints. Bellatreche et al. (2000) introduce a procedure that iteratively approximates a solution and in the dynamic case maintains it as query workloads change and data is added or removed.

The interrelationship modeling is further extended to so-called AND-OR view graphs in (Gupta, 1997). A lattice is then a special case called OR view graph, in which each AND-arc consists of only one edge. Maintenance costs can be incorporated into the framework either as constraints (Gupta and Mumick, 2005), or in the optimization goal (Gupta, 1997). Gupta and Mumick (2005) present a relatively complete summary of various aspects of the general framework.

It is shown that the benefit measure of the result of the greedy algorithm is at least 63% of the benefit of the optimal solution without index selection (Harinarayan et al., 1996), and 46% with index selection (Gupta et al., 1997). Interestingly, Shukla et al. (1998) show that the Benefit-Per-Unit-Space (BPUS) greedy strategy is equivalent to a simpler heuristic algorithm which picks the view with the smallest size at each iteration step.

Another line of work (Theodoratos and Sellis, 1997, 1999; Theodoratos et al., 2001; Yang et al., 1997; Baralis et al., 1997) is influenced by multiple query optimization techniques (Sellis, 1988; Roy et al., 2000), with the aim of finding reusable common sub-expressions of queries. Theodoratos and Sellis (1997) model the problem as a state space search problem, where each state is a multi-query graph specifying Select-Join queries. State transitions achieved by cutting edges or merging nodes represent local modifications of the candidate views selected. Though the exhaustive search gives the optimal view set regarding both query evaluation and maintenance costs, it is exponential and a storage limit is not taken into account. The work is extended in (Theodoratos and Sellis, 1999) to incorporate storage limit, and in (Theodoratos et al., 2001) to allow for projection in queries.

Yang et al. (1997) consider a slightly broader range of queries including aggregation. Their approach proceeds in two steps. The first step is to generate multiple view processing plans (MVPPs), which are query processing plans for multiple queries using intermediate views. With an emphasis on shared join computation, they map the MVPP generation problem into a 0-1 integer programming problem. In the second step, given an optimal MVPP, cost driven optimization with heuristics is performed to select views under storage constraints.

Because of the high complexity in the techniques above, heuristics pruning the search space are necessary. Baralis et al. (1997) explore some heuristics to reduce the search space and promote reuse of views. A view is worth considering if it corresponds to a user query or it is the least common ancestor (in the lattice) of two worthy views. They also observe that it is often advantageous to group by key attributes instead of non-key attributes in terms of reuse.

Mistry et al. (2001) propose a framework tightly integrated with a query optimizer to select materialized views with the goal of reducing overall maintenance costs. The query optimizer is used to select an optimal maintenance plan out of a search space consisting of recomputation plans and incremental plans for materialized views. Given an optimal maintenance plan, a cost driven greedy algorithm is employed to select appropriate additional views.

The lattice based techniques assume that the candidate views are given as input, i.e., nodes in the lattice. Approaches based on multiple query optimization explore a broader scope, including the original queries in the workload and their common subexpressions. Therefore, sub-optimality may result from their restricts over the candidate views.

AutoAdmin ((Chaudhuri and Narasayya, 2007), http://research.microsoft.com/DMX/ autoadmin/) is an industrial strength view selection tool emphasizing practical SQL queries and scalability for commercial settings. The project started dealing with automatic index selection (Chaudhuri and Narasayya, 1997), and

was extended (Agrawal et al., 2000) to allow for selection of materialized views.

The approach has several advantages. First, it is tightly integrated with the query optimizer, and hence the selected structures are surely to be made use of during query evaluation. Second, neither a restricted set of candidate views has to be provided in advance nor the interrelationships between candidate views have to be modeled explicitly. Third, a query language as rich as SQL is considered with effective heuristics to ensure (near-)optimality.

Dynamic View Selection

Static view selection techniques, though very effective, still suffer from a variety of problems. First, they rely on a pre-compiled query workload, and may not perform well for ad hoc queries. Second, the resource constraints such as space and maintenance time may change over time, while the materialized views are fixed once selected. Third, static view selection is usually unable to meet both the space bound and the maintenance bound at the same time. For example, if space is sufficiently large, we can materialize transient views, which can be dropped before the update window. Finally, in order to adapt to the evolution in reality, administrating efforts such as monitoring and reconfiguration cannot be avoided. Based on the above observations, another paradigm of view selection techniques, called *dynamic view selection* or *view caching*, is proposed to remedy such problems.

Caching can be roughly divided into two categories: *physical caching* and *semantic caching*. *Physical caching* refers to the mechanism employed in operating systems and traditional relational databases, where some physical storage unit such as a page or a tuple is kept in cache. *Semantic caching* takes advantage of high level knowledge about the data being cached, and keeps track of the semantic description of the cached data (Dar et al., 1996). In particular, caching of views or queries is semantic caching, since the cache manager knows both the data and their query expressions. Dar et al. (1996) focus on selection queries and the cache space is divided into disjoint semantic regions bounded by boolean constraints. Thus, a query q with selection Q can be decomposed into two parts: $Q \wedge C$ and $Q \wedge \neg C$, where C is a boolean expression for the cache. The missing part is then computed from the base relations, while the in-cache part can be directly fetched. *Chunk caching* is a kind of semantic caching specific to chunk based organization (Zhao et al., 1997). Chunks have finer granularity than views or tables and are thus more flexible and may be more efficient in answering overlapping queries mainly involving aggregations (Deshpande and Naughton, 2000; Deshpande et al., 1998).

WATCHMAN (Scheuermann et al., 1996) is a cache manager targeted at OLAP. It employs a simple hit-or-miss strategy and relies on temporal locality of queries to gain benefits. That is, each query is taken as a unit for admission and replacement. No explicit modeling of interrelationship between queries and views are needed.

DynaMat is a more advanced system introduced in (Kotidis and Roussopoulos, 1999, 2001), which considers queries using group-bys and equality based selections. Each query is represented by a hyperplane in the hypercube of multidimensional data. A cover-or-miss strategy is employed, that is, a cached view can benefit any query computable from it, which is reduced to coverage of hyperplanes. Due to the restricted query type, an R-tree like view index can be built over the cached views to search in the cache to answer queries. Though DynaMat is more flexible than WATCHMAN, it does not allow combinations of cached views to answer queries. For instance, one query may be covered by the union of two cached views. Deshpande et al. (1998) propose using fine granularity of cache units, namely chunks, which are organized in a hierarchy of aggregation levels. A multidimensional query is then decomposed to chunks at the same aggregation

level, with missing chunks computed from raw data. The work is further extended by Deshpande and Naughton (2000) to allow aggregation from lower level cached chunks. Due to decomposability, chunk caching is proved to be useful in distributed caching (Kalnis et al., 2002). In contrast to DynaMat, chunk caching searches for chunks covered by the query instead of making use of a materialized view covering the query.

Dynamic view selection techniques enjoy the benefit that no candidate views need to be specified in advance because the candidates are just history queries or their fragments. All the techniques restrict the query language to a relatively simple class so that the interrelationship modeling between candidate views or between views and queries is usually analogous to some geometric relationship that is efficient to reason about. In principle, the relationship between views and queries can be handled using the techniques of answering queries using views (Srivastava et al., 1996; Halevy, 2001).

Another most significant issue in view caching is the admission and replacement control, i.e., how to decide which view is admitted and which view is replaced. If space allows, caching data is in general beneficial. Hence, when a new view is considered for admission and there is enough free space for the view, it is always admitted. The situation is more complicated, if the free space is not sufficient for the new view. The caching policy is usually determined by two factors: a benefit metric and a recency metric. The benefit metric represents an estimation of the benefits of caching a query. Recency of the queries is also important because of the temporal locality.

Whenever there is not enough free space for caching a new query, a candidate replacement subset of cached queries is chosen and the benefit of the candidate subset is compared to the benefit of the new query. If the new query is more beneficial then the candidate subset is replaced by the new query, otherwise admission is refused. Scheuermann et al. (1996) adopt the *cost save ratio* (CSR), which measures the percentage of total query costs saved due to hits in the cache. Because of the chunking organization in (Deshpande et al., 1998), a simple metric of coverage of base tables is adopted for measuring benefits of cached chunks.

Recency metrics of caching are well studied in the literature. One well known strategy is *Least Recently Used* (LRU), which discards the oldest data cached. The strategy is extended to *LRU-K* by O'Neil et al. (1993) to take advantage of recent access patterns. Deshpande et al. (1998) utilize the *CLOCK* algorithm (Silberschatz et al., 2002), an efficient approximation of LRU.

There are two ways to use the benefit metric and the recency metric simultaneously. One way is to consider the recency and benefit in parallel: first use LRU to select a candidate set and then use benefit to decide on replacement (Scheuermann et al., 1996). The other way is to use an aging strategy to obtain benefit in the recent time window and then use the windowed benefit for both candidate set selection and replacement decision (Deshpande et al., 1998).

DATA STREAM MANAGEMENT

Whereas in traditional database management systems different queries are posed against static data, in many applications a relatively fixed set of processing tasks must be evaluated against an ever changing sequence of data tuples. Such monitoring applications (Abadi et al., 2003) evaluate their queries against streams of data. In contrast to a database that entirely resides in a set of (virtual) files, a *data stream* is a rapidly flowing stream of structured data that is so vast in its amount that it is usually impossible to store the complete data on persistent memory.

Common examples of monitoring applications are analysis of financial tickers, web click stream analysis, traffic monitoring, or network traffic analysis. The characteristics of this family of applications have quite some implications on storage and query processing that make it impossible to use conventional DBMSs for such tasks.

These new requirements gave rise to a new class of data management systems, so called *data stream management systems* (DSMS) (Babcock et al., 2002). Although there are similarities between data stream management systems and conventional database management systems, the requirements of data stream analysis necessitate new types of queries and new query evaluation techniques.

Issues in DSMS include that special care has to be taken in incremental computation of stateful operators like joins and aggregations, because they could block a query. Queries are usually only evaluated over a window of most recent data, since otherwise the amount of data would grow unbounded. All operators must process incoming tuples incrementally. Furthermore, continuous query evaluation must take into account common subexpressions of queries registered with the streams to execute the same operators only once and stream the results to subsequent operators of concurrent queries.

This section surveys different aspects of DSMSs and queries against data streams. After giving a formal definition of the notion of a data stream, we describe different possibilities to define the portions of streams to be used for query answering. These methods, called window models, are a particularly characteristic feature of DSMSs and a means for computing approximate query answers. Due to the amount of incoming data, storage of streaming data is often only possible in an aggregated form. Therefore, we conclude the discussion with a survey on different techniques to produce such synopses or digests of streaming data.

For the remainder of this section we adopt some definitions by Arasu et al. (2006) since most other models can be reduced to their model. We restrict the discussion to relational data streams. A stream is defined as a tuple consisting of a relational tuple and a timestamp.

Definition 1*(Data Stream)* A *stream S* is a (possibly infinite) bag (multiset) of elements <s; τ>, where *s* is a tuple belonging to the schema of *S* and τ ∈ *T* is the *timestamp* of the element.

There is no bound for the number of tuples with the same timestamp, except that this number must be finite. It must not be allowed for queries to perform transformations on timestamps. Therefore, Arasu et al. (2006) chose to not include the timestamp into the schema since the abstract semantics′of their query language relies heavily on timestamps. However, often it is necessary to include the timestamp into query predicates. This can be achieved by mirroring the timestamp in the schema.

Please note that assignment of timestamps to data stream tuples is a quite nontrivial problem. We abstain from dwelling on this topic and just assume that appropriate timestamps are provided. Please refer, for instance, to Srivastava and Widom (2004) for a detailed discussion on time management in data streams.

To illustrate the notion of data streams, we will give examples from the field of road traffic. For traffic applications, such as traffic state estimation and forecasting, data describing the flowing traffic has to be gathered, also called traffic monitoring. In Germany this is predominantly done by inductive loops, which are embedded into the road surface and connected with processing units at the road side. Other data sources are weather stations or data from vehicles themselves (also called Floating Car Data, FCD). The acquired data, for example the mean speed or traffic volume, can be represented as data streams flowing from the detectors to a central control unit. Two data stream schemas for traffic management could be for example: *MeasurementStation(SectionID; Speed; Volume; Temperature;Humidity)* and *FCD(VehicleID; PosLatitude; PosLongitude; Speed)*

Stream Query Languages

A variety of data stream query languages have been proposed. In the *Aurora* system (Abadi et al., 2003) a graphical notation allows the user to explicitly provide query plans. Query operators (called *boxes* in Aurora) are composed to a lattice. This realization has been chosen since the authors deem the optimization of the joint query plan for multiple declarative continuous queries as too difficult. However, still some optimizations are performed by Aurora based on runtime statistics gathered during query execution. The successor of Aurora, *Borealis* (Abadi et al., 2005), extends these concepts to distributed stream processing.

However, most continuous query languages lend their concepts from relational query languages and algebra and extend this by new constructs for handling streaming data. In fact, besides SQL being known to most developers (Stonebraker et al., 2005), this approach is advantageous because it allows to build on the large body of knowledge acquired about relational databases. Obviously, it is still necessary to adapt relational operators to the new requirements for handling data streams.

The problem of streams of data that are too large for persistent storage and require incremental evaluation of *continuous queries*, was first realized in the context of the *Tapestry* system (Terry et al., 1992). In the Tapestry system, the user specifies a query in a relational query language (TQL) which is transformed by some normalization steps into an *incremental query*. This incremental query is installed as a stored procedure in a relational DBMS and periodically executed to compute (almost) only the new results for the original query. However, this model blinded out some of the fundamental problems that are researched in current DSMS since the query was not really continuous.

Jagadish et al. (1995) introduced the *chronicle* data model to maintain views with aggregation operators. The chronicle data model is also based on a subset of relational algebra shown to have tractable complexity of maintaining views. Although the authors do not mention the term data stream, the requirements that have motivated the development of the chronicle data model are the same as for DSMSs. Their system is used for maintenance of materialized views. Its query language is basically a´restriction of SQL with some special extensions. It allows for queries including relations, views, and chronicles. In this scenario, a chronicle is a sequence of tuple insertions. It is modeled as a relation with an extra sequencing attribute, which can be regarded as a timestamp. Based on the chronicle materialized views are maintained. Thus, like a data stream query, a materialized view is a result set being continually updated.

Arasu et al. (2006) developed the *continuous query language* CQL. A formal abstract semantics for CQL as well as some details about its query plans are given. The language has been (almost completely) implemented in the DSMS prototype system STREAM.

The central idea of CQL is to reuse the large body of research that has been conducted in the area or relational databases. CQL therefore is comprised of a set of *stream-to-relation* operators that are essentially window definition operators (cf. section 5.2), the *relation-to-relation* operators well known from the relational algebra and three *relation-to-stream* operators that produce streams from relations.

The approach requires the definition of a relation $R(\tau)$ corresponding to a stream at a certain point in time (the instantaneous relation).

Definition 2 *(Relation)* A relation R is a mapping from each time instant in T to a finite but unbounded bag of tuples belonging to the schema of R.

Furthermore, CQL allows operations integrating static data with streaming data.

Window Models

A database models the state of the domain of discourse at the current time. Queries are evaluated once on the complete database and in return produce an iterator over the result set. On the other hand, queries in a DSMS are registered once with the incoming data streams and are continuously being evaluated. Thus, the query must produce records incrementally as it is evaluated against new incoming tuples.

Whereas some query operators like projection and selection can be evaluated without state on a per-tuple basis, other operators, such as join, aggregation, or sorting, need to consider every available tuple before producing a result. A requirement that cannot be fulfilled due to the potentially infinite size of data streams. In such cases only an approximate result can be produced. A natural way of approximating continuous query results is to define a window over which the query is evaluated. This is actually often the desired semantics of queries. For instance, if continuous queries are used for decision support based on financial tickers, the user is likely more interested in recent information than in historic data.

One way to categorize window models is the way to determine which elements are currently in the window and which are not, i.e., which records fulfill the validity criterion of the window definition. The most important decision criterion in data stream applications is time. To be usable for window models the records in a data stream have to be comparable, i.e., they must be monotonously sortable according to some ordering. One method is to use time stamps, where *implicit timestamps* (created when the tuple streams in) and *explicit timestamps* (an existing attribute of the tuple) can be distinguished (Babcock et al., 2002). Another possibility to make records sortable are unique sequence numbers.

In our traffic state estimation example, we are mostly interested in monitoring recent data streaming in from the stationary and mobile detectors.

Box 1. A time-based window

```
SELECT SectionID, AVG(Speed)
FROM MeasurementStation (Range 60 seconds] AS m
GROUP BY SectionID
```

Box 2. A window using partitioning

```
SELECT SectionID, LaneNo, AVG(Speed)
FROM
MeasurementStation (PARTITION BY LaneNo RANGE 2
minutes]
GROUP BY SectionID
```

Therefore, a time-based window can be defined which only selects measured data from the last 60 seconds. A CQL query with a time-based window is shown in Box 1.

To always gather the most recent results, the window "moves" along the stream. This idea is also called sliding window, because the window is sliding with the data stream flow. If we are interested in the stream records of the last five minutes every minute, the single windows overlap. This idea of defining the granularity of sliding is defined in CQL using a slide parameter. If we are interested in a window representing records from the last five minutes every five minutes the windows are disjoint. This is also called tumbling windows and has been used for instance in the Aurora system (Carney et al., 2002). Carney et al. (2002) extend the idea of tumbling windows by a latch window operator, which is also capable of storing intermediate results between two successive windows. Defining a coarse granularity for window sliding may improve overall performance of the DSMS running the query. However, the granularity heavily depends on the application's requirements.

Another technique to define a validity criterion for data stream elements are tuple-based windows (Arasu et al., 2003b, 2006). In tuple-based window models the number of the last N tuples which are valid for the current window is defined. This idea is further specialized by defining partitioned windows (Arasu et al., 2003b, 2006). A partitioned window definition takes a set of attributes from the stream's schema and a window size N as input. The stream is, similar to a grouping operation, partitioned into substreams

by the attribute values. The window contains the last N records of each group.

For our traffic application we now assume, that for each lane of the highway the traffic is monitored separately. Hence, we introduce a new attribute LaneNo in the MeasurementStation data stream schema. The query in Box 2 analyzes speed and traffic volume for each lane separately and creates a substream for each by using the PARTITION BY operator from CQL.

Li et al. (2005) define a sliding window by using parameters for the size of the window (RANGE), the sliding step (SLIDE) and the attribute over which range and size are defined (WATTR).

Furthermore, windowing techniques can be distinguished according to the definition of their bounds (also called edges (Patroumpas and Sellis, 2006)). Suppose we want to track velocities on a freeway section after a specific event happened, for example, an accident. We want to analyze the change in average velocity since the moment that the accident happened, and want to monitor it until the situation has been solved. In this case we would fix the lower bound of the window, such that it marks the time of the accident in the stream. The upper bound of the window is progressing with new data records streaming in. These kinds of windows are called *landmark windows*. Specifically, landmark windows are categorized in upper-bound and lower-bound windows, depending on the edge which is fixed (Patroumpas and Sellis, 2006). Of course, a landmark window with a lower bound suffers from the same problems like any data stream. Due to the ever-growing size of the window, the amount of resources required for query evaluation also grows. Hence, such a query usually must be deregistered after some time. Finally, both bounds can be fixed, yielding so called fixed-bound windows, which enable selection of records in a certain interval of time in the stream (if available).

Especially in data warehousing it may be interesting to aggregate values for different granularities of time. At each aggregation level along the time dimension a value has to be calculated based on the records seen so far. Therefore, a landmark window can be used, which aggregates the data streaming in to an aggregation level, such as one hour. This approach guarantees that there always exists a preliminary value for the current hour. After one hour, the lower bound of the window may be shifted. This idea is called *tilted time frame* (Han et al., 2007). Three different scaling options are described. In the natural tilted time frame model, the time scale is natural, which means that time portions are mapped as they occur (15 minutes represented by 15 slots, 4 quarters by 4 slots and so on). Other models are the logarithmic tilted time frame model using a logarithmic time scale and progressive logarithmic tilted time frame model which stores snapshots of the data in logarithmic scale according to their actuality.

Synopsis Construction

As we have seen in the previous sections, a data stream is an unbounded sequence of tuples, which is not feasible or desirable to be stored and queried in its entirety. Especially, space complexity is an important issue in data stream processing. Hence, DSMS aim at processing each tuple in a one-pass manner.

Besides window models, another option for approximating data streams for queries are synopses. *Synopses* provide a summarization of the data stream using specific algorithms and can be stored using the available resources. The stored summary can then be used to answer user queries with a satisfactory accuracy. Other application fields of synopses are query optimization (using approximate join estimation), computation of aggregate statistics and data mining (Aggarwal and Yu, 2007). This section will give a brief overview of synopses. A detailed discussion is beyond the scope of this chapter and the interested reader is referred to more detailed literature (Babcock et al., 2002; Aggarwal and Yu, 2007).

There exist different synopsis techniques introduced for traditional databases and time series analysis. An easy approach to build a synopsis of a stream is sampling. For example, random sampling selects randomly tuples from the data stream and stores them as a summary. However, it depends on the variety of the stream data if the selected samples constitute an adequate representation. Sampling poses the advantage that the multi-dimensional data representation of the data stream is kept and is therefore well suited for data mining applications (Aggarwal, 2006). *Reservoir sampling techniques* are a probabilistic method which collects tuples in a *reservoir* either without restriction (unbiased) or the size of the reservoir is restricted by an unbiased or biased function, which determines, if a tuple is added to the reservoir or not (Aggarwal, 2006).

Sliding windows as already introduced in Section 5.2 can be seen as a special case of reservoir sampling, which are temporally biased as they only take into account recent tuples. *Concise sampling* improves reservoir sampling by summarizing the distinct values of a stream which are assumed to fit into memory (Aggarwal and Yu, 2007).

Histograms have already successfully been applied for approximate query answering in traditional database systems (Poosola et al., 1999). Histograms partition data into buckets according to a partitioning rule, where each bucket represents a set of attribute values. The attribute values are represented on the x-axis of the histogram and their quantity or frequency on the y-axis. If a user query, such as a range query is issued, it can be easily answered approximately using histograms. There are different types of histograms, such as equi-width, equi-depth, or v-optimal histograms

(Poosola et al., 1999; Babcock et al., 2002). Each type has a different approach to construct the buckets which influences obviously the accuracy of the histogram.

Further techniques building synopses for data streams are based on wavelets. Wavelets have been used in a variety of fields, especially in signal processing and data and image compression. In the database area they have been used for selectivity estimation (with wavelet-based histograms), query approximation (e.g., data cube approximation) and clustering (Keim and Heczko, 2001). The general process of using wavelets for these applications is the decomposition of the input data by means of the wavelet transformation, processing the approximated data in wavelet space, i.e., in its decomposed representation, and finally retransforming the results by wavelet synthesis. The decomposition is done in several levels, where on each level the data is more and more summarized. In the wavelet space the coefficients of the higher levels can give information about trends in the overall data while coefficients of the lower level represent local trends (Aggarwal and Yu, 2007). Applied to data streams, the wavelet-based approaches have also to obey space and memory limitations and have to cope with the one-pass characteristics and continuous updates of data streams. Gilbert et al. (2003) present an approach to create wavelet-based synopses for data streams, where the data stream represents the input signal for the wavelet transformation. As data streams, they update the synopsis of the data read so far striving at the calculation of the highest B-term approximation. For this approximation only a small set of wavelet base coefficients, the B- term coefficients, is used which provide the highest 'energy', i.e., which best describe the stream data. The reconstructed stream based on the B-coefficients is then called the best B-term approximation, which poses a minimal sum squared error compared to the original data.

Sketches are also a common synopsis technique in data streams. Essentially, these methods have

been borrowed from time series analysis and are based on the principles of random projection. Random projection is used to map vectors (data points) from a high-dimensional space to a lower dimension. A well known sketching technique in data streams are Alon-Matias-Szegedy (AMS) sketches introduced by Alon et al. (1999). AMS sketches are based on the notion of so called frequency moments. For example let $A = (a_1; a_2; ...; a_m)$ be a sequence of elements and $N = \{1; 2; ...; n\}$ be the domain of the a_i. Then the frequency moments are defined by

$$F_k = \sum_{i=1} nm_i^k$$

where m_i is the number of occurrences of an element in a data stream and n the dimension of the value domain. F_0 is then the number of distinct elements in the data stream, F_1 the entire number of elements and F_2 the repeat rate (or Gini's index of homogeneity) and F_∞ the most frequent item's multiplicity. The frequency moments measure has been used by Alon et al. (1999) to create a randomized join-size estimator for data streams, where the values of the data streams are projected on a family of random variables to estimate the join size following the idea of random linear projection.

The AMS sketches technique has been used for data streams in several approaches. For example, Cormode and Garofalakis (2007) enhance the AMS sketches technique to approximate complex aggregate queries on probabilistic data streams (so called probabilistic AMS sketches), i.e., to each tuple an independent existence probability is assigned according to a certain probability distribution. Rao and Moon (2006) extend the idea of AMS sketches to build one-pass sketches for streams of labeled trees (e.g., XML documents). A very efficient sketch technique addressing the counting problem (i.e., counting the distinct values in a data set) are Flajolet-Martin (FM) sketches (Flajolet and Martin, 1985). The authors propose a one-pass counting approach for the distinct values in a database by using a family of hash functions and least significant bits to create a sketch.

Ganguly et al. (2003) adopt the idea of FM sketches by introducing a data structure called 2-level hash sketch and proposing algorithms implementing union, difference and intersection over the 2-level hash sketches. The 2-level hash sketch uses two independent families (levels) of hash functions to determine the bit vector, where the first family are randomizing hash functions projecting values uniformly over a range while the second family distributes the values uniformly over the binary domain.

Towards Automatic Synopsis Selection

Zhang et al. (2005) adopt similar ideas to view selection to achieve shared computation for multiple aggregations over data streams. They opt for per unit time processing costs utilizing shared synopses called phantoms. Phantoms are hash tables for aggregations of finer granularity than the original queries, of which the interrelationship is modeled in a similar way as a lattice. Under an assumption of a fixed total memory, maintaining more phantoms may increase the collision rates, which in turn increases the costs. They start with the set of original queries, and select at each step greedily a most beneficial phantom until the benefit becomes negative. Based on their collision rate based cost model, the benefit of incorporating an additional phantom is derived from a sub-optimization procedure, which selects the optimal space allocation to minimize the overall costs for a given set of phantoms.

Up to now, state-of-the-art data stream systems are still limited to special cases of computation/ synopsis sharing. In the STREAM prototype ((Arasu et al., 2003a), http://infolab.stanford. edu/stream/), subplan sharing is limited to exact subexpression matching, while synopsis sharing remains largely unexplored (Motwani et al., 2003). Babu et al. (2005) discuss sharing a join

index for multiway joins. In the Telegraph project ((Chandrasekaran et al., 2003), http://telegraph. cs.berkeley.edu/) data/computation sharing is confined to avoidance of copying base tuples and maintaining independent indexes, called state modules, for each base table (Raman et al., 2003; Madden et al., 2002).

Although view selection techniques are highly interesting for automatic synopsis selection in stream processing, there are a few challenges to be resolved first:

- Modeling the interrelationships between synopses, such as subsumption.
- Selection of a cost model for cost estimation in stream processing.
- Choice of the optimization target: throughput, per-unit-time-cost, or quality-of-service.
- Integration of synopsis sharing with operator scheduling.
- Adaptability of these methods for continuous data streams.

VIEW MANAGEMENT TECHNIQUES AND DATA STREAM MANAGEMENT

In this section we explore the relationship of view maintenance and view selection techniques to data stream management systems. In particular continuous query processing is related to view maintenance whereas view selection techniques can be applied to continuous query planning.

Continuous Queries and View Maintenance

According to (Arasu et al., 2006) materialized views are a form of continuous queries. Views are continually updated when the underlying base relations are updated. Incremental view maintenance techniques are applied to avoid re-evaluation of the view definition on complete base relations. Early implementations of continuous query semantics (Jagadish et al., 1995; Liu et al., 1999) were basically systems that defined a continuous query as a view and periodically re-evaluated the query by updating the view.

However, there are also fundamental differences between incremental view maintenance and continuous query evaluation. In contrast to view maintenance, periodical updates processed in a batch-like mode are not an option in stream data management. Instead, DSMSs adopt a pipelined approach to query evaluation. Insertions to and deletions from the instantaneous relations are handled by the query operators as soon as they occur (albeit operators are scheduled following some policy). Thus, it is not necessary to poll the base relations for changes.

As discussed in Section 3.2 view maintenance techniques have been implemented for different data models and with different query languages. Predominantly, data streams are based on the relational model and can be continuously queried with extensions of SQL. There exist also systems which offer continuous queries for XML data, such as the NiagaraCQ system using XML-QL (Chen et al., 2000).

In view maintenance, self-maintainability is desired, i.e., maintenance of the view without access to the base relations. These base relations correspond to the instantaneous relations specified by the streams and their window definitions in a continuous query. Although, it is of course desirable to evaluate continuous operators incrementally without accessing the underlying instantaneous relation, it is often (as in the case of holistic aggregation operators) inevitable to scan the whole window to evaluate an operator.

Also, in view maintenance any tuple can be deleted from the underlying base relations. In DSMS, instantaneous (base) relations are append-only. Though, if a window is defined, tuples are removed from the instantaneous relation either time-based or order-based. They are only removed in the same order in which they were inserted. It

is not possible to remove a tuple from the stream. Eventually, any tuple will flow out of a bounded window and hence be not further considered for evaluation.

Thus, with respect to the information dimension in the classification of view maintenance approaches, answering continuous queries cannot be restricted to self-maintainability. On the other hand, the strict order of tuple removal from the instantaneous relation may offer some advantages.

Data streams produce a vast amount of data which sets new challenges for the (real-time) processing of data. Efficient techniques for rapid processing of incoming tuples are required. The rate of changes to the instantaneous relations is usually considerably higher than in view maintenance. This causes new challenges for efficient evaluation of operators. Highly optimized operators such as the state-slice join described in section 6.3 allow fast, and truly continuous query evaluation.

However, in general the high data arrival rates in DSMS require query answers to be approximated. Thus, as opposed to view maintenance which usually requires exact answers, results to continuous queries are usually only approximated. This approximation is implemented by window models as described in Section 5.2 and synopsis depicted in Section 5.3. The timeliness is an inherent property of data streams. As streams are continuously flowing in the instantaneous relations are updated as window operators slide on and therefore guarantee an immediate incorporation of changes.

Instead of considering stream data management as a special case of view maintenance, it may be beneficial to swap sides and regard view maintenance as a special case of stream data management. This could allow to leverage the efficient data stream query operators for fast incremental view maintenance. Such an approach would be very similar to real-time data warehousing or online view maintenance (Quass and Widom,

1997; Luo and Yu, 2008) where updates should be propagated immediately (or only with a short delay) to the materialized views.

Continuous Query Evaluation and View Selection

Due to the high arrival rates of data in a DSMS, it aims at processing queries in-memory only. Multiple queries are evaluated against the same set of data streams simultaneously. Therefore, it is vital that queries are not processed in an isolated fashion with an individual plan for each query. Instead, joint query plans should be used which facilitate sharing of resources such as memory and CPU time. A shared operator in a joint query plan can be regarded as a materialized view that is used for answering the queries represented by its parent operators.

Continuous query optimization therefore concentrates on finding efficient query plans for executing multiple queries in parallel. This is similar to batch processing of simple relational queries where identification of common subexpressions is utilized for optimization of execution plans. Thus, instead of creating an individual execution plan for each query, a DSMS must create a single execution plan for a workload of registered queries and must adapt it to changing circumstances, such as varying data arrival rates. This problem is very similar to the view selection problem. In particular, speaking in terms of our view selection classification hierarchy, continuous query planning can be seen as a case of dynamic view selection whereas no reuse policy is required in this case. Candidate views are common subexpressions of continuous queries.

Furthermore, regarding the resource constraints, a DSMS has to cope at the same time with limited storage due to the aim of in-memory query processing and time constraints, because queries must be evaluated in real-time. However, the optimization goals of query response time and maintenance costs are identical in this case.

DSMS usually make use of such joint query plans. In Aurora, (Carney et al., 2002) the user explicitly defines the joint query plan manually using a graphical language, in which each operator is represented as a box. The user adds so-called *connection points* to a query plan. Aurora collects runtime statistics and loops through the subnetworks between connection points and then locally optimizes each such subnetwork if necessary by applying a set of heuristics.

The *STREAM* system creates joint query plans from declaratively defined queries. However, it merges only exactly matching subexpressions (Motwani et al., 2003). Thus, if a new query is added, an individual query plan is produced for that new query. If possible, operators from the new query plan are merged with matching operators from the existing joint query plan. Although this approach produces some resource sharing, it suffers from eventual deterioration of the joint query plan while queries are registered and deregistered.

Although some systems address the issue of creating joint query plans, there is still much opportunity for research on joint query planning. In particular, the area of continuous query plan adaptation is yet not comprehensively explored. Query optimization for continuous queries must consider statistics about relations, streams and subqueries such as selectivity and arrival rates. However, in the case of DSMS these estimators may fluctuate. Therefore, joint query plans must be adapted to these changing parameters. Algorithms are required that are able to efficiently update joint query plans such that optimal plans (for different quality requirements, e.g., memory or CPU time) can be approximated.

Optimization of Stream Joins

The particular characteristics of window operators cause new problems for stateful operators in a DSMS which must be considered for resource sharing and query plan optimization as well. One family of stateful operators are aggregation functions. Arasu and Widom (2004) present techniques for efficient resource sharing in computation of aggregation functions. However, here we concentrate on sharing of join processing.

Usually in query planning, selections are pushed down under joins so as to reduce the amount of tuples that must be processed by the join operator. In multi-query processing, it may instead be useful to do the opposite, that is, to pull up selection predicates over joins so as to reuse join results for multiple queries with different selection predicates. Obviously, it is best to pull down as many selection predicates as possible. In a DSMS, however, due to windowing it is not uncommon that simply pulling up the other predicates produces highly memory- and CPU-inefficient query plans. Reusing without adaptation view selection or multi-query optimization algorithms means to assume all window definitions are identical. However, window definition may only intersect or even be disjoint. In that case the supposedly common subexpressions may not be common at all.

To overcome this problem, Wang et al. (2006) present a way to push down every selection predicate as far down as possible by cutting the windows into pieces and placing selection operators in between. The windows of a join operator's input streams are cut into slices. The slices are handled by distinct join operators that are pipelined such that each operator contributes join results to the queries whose windows end with the corresponding slice. Tuples that do not match the window slice are pipelined to the subsequent join operator. Two algorithms are presented, one to produce a memory-optimal and one to produce a CPU-optimal query plan for the join.

In fact, both, multi-query optimization or view selection as well as efficient handling of window definitions are required to produce efficient joint query plans for a workload of continuous queries.

CONCLUSION AND OUTLOOK

In this chapter we presented a comprehensive survey on view management and data stream management systems. View maintenance and view selection are of particular importance in data warehouse systems, since decision support requires complex analytical queries. Whereas view maintenance addresses efficient methods for updating views if their base relations are changed, view selection is the problem of choosing a set of views to be materialized in order to minimize a cost function. View selection must carefully trade off query response time, storage space, and view maintenance costs.

Data stream management systems deal with new query planning and processing requirements in systems generating tremendous amounts of data that can only be processed once due to high arrival rates of tuples. Typical applications again need to pose analytical queries over these streams. There are special challenges to be solved, such as dealing with the new data models containing sliding windows or efficiently creating synopses of data. Other issues are related to existing problems. Continuous query planning is highly related to multi-query optimization and view selection as the high performance requirements suggest to share computation and resources in query processing. On the other hand, continuous query processing is related to view maintenance.

The relatively new field of stream data management offers many opportunities for research. Resource sharing through joint query planning needs further work. In particular adaptive query planning for continuous queries is a requirement since the statistics underlying query plans may change during execution. As we have seen in the context of the state-slice operator, query plans must also deal with the new issues arising from window models.

View maintenance and processing of continuous queries in data streams can both benefit from new methods using only limited information to compute the effects of base data updates. Methods, which take into account that the system managing the base data and the system processing the view data are only loosely coupled (such as (Sawires et al., 2006)) can be useful also for the processing of updates in DSMSs.

Although theoretical results show that, even for quite simple situations (e.g., conjunctive queries (Afrati et al., 2007) and data cubes (Harinarayan et al., 1996)), the view selection problem remains intractable, the field of static view selection is relatively mature (cf. Section 4.3). Dynamic view selection techniques, although quite effective, are limited in aspects such as candidate enumeration, interrelationship modeling, etc. Therefore, we deem it quite an interesting direction to migrate the results achieved in the static setting to the dynamic setting. Besides the direction of developing a principled framework for dynamic view selection, query processing in DSMSs also poses new challenges to view selection techniques, which we described already in Section 5.4.

ACKNOWLEDGMENT

This work is supported by the DFG Research Cluster on Ultra High-Speed Mobile Information and Communication UMIC at RWTH Aachen University, Germany (http://www.umic.rwth-aachen.de).

REFERENCES

Abadi, D. J., Ahmad, Y., Balazinska, M., Çetintemel, U., Cherniack, M., Hwang, J.-H., et al. (2005). The design of the borealis stream processing engine. In *Proc. 2nd Biennal Conference on Innovative Data Systems Research (CIDR)*, (pp. 277–289), Asilomar, CA.

Abadi, D. J., Carney, D., Çetintemel, U., Cherniack, M., Convey, C., & Lee, S. (2003). Aurora: a new model and architecture for data stream management. *The VLDB Journal, 12*(2), 120–139. doi:10.1007/s00778-003-0095-z

Abiteboul, S., McHugh, J., Rys, M., Vassalos, V., & Wiener, J. L. (1998). Incremental maintenance for materialized views over semistructured data. In A., Gupta, O., Shmueli, & J., Widom, (Eds.), *Proceedings 24th International Conference on Very Large Data Bases (VLDB)*, (pp. 38–49). New York: Morgan Kaufmann.

Afrati, F. N., Chirkova, R., Gergatsoulis, M., & Pavlaki, V. (2007). View selection for eal conjunctive queries. *Acta Informatica, 44*(5), 289–321. doi:10.1007/s00236-007-0046-z

Aggarwal, C. (2006). On biased reservoir sampling in the presence of stream evolution. In Dayal et al.

Aggarwal, C., & Yu, P. S. (2007). A survey of synopsis construction in data streams. In C. Aggarwal, (Ed.), *Data Streams: Models and Algorithms*, (pp. 169–207). Berlin: Springer.

Agrawal, S., Chaudhuri, S., Kollár, L., Marathe, A. P., Narasayya, V. R., & Syamala, M. (2004). Database tuning advisor for Microsoft SQL Server 2005. In Nascimento et al., (pp. 1110–1121).

Agrawal, S., Chaudhuri, S., & Narasayya, V. R. (2000). Automated selection of materialized views and indexes in SQL databases. In A. E. Abbadi, M. L. Brodie, S. Chakravarthy, U. Dayal, N. Kamel, G. Schlageter, & K.-Y. Whang, (Eds.), *Proc. 26th Intl. Conference on Very Large Data Bases (VLDB)*, (pp. 496–505), Cairo, Egypt. San Francisco: Morgan Kaufmann.

Alon, N., Matias, Y., & Szegedy, M. (1999). The space complexity of approximating the frequency moments. *Journal of Computer and System Sciences, 58*, 137–147. doi:10.1006/jcss.1997.1545

Arasu, A., Babcock, B., Babu, S., Datar, M., Ito, K., Nishizawa, I., et al. (2003a). STREAM: The Stanford Stream Data Manager. In A. Y. Halevy, Z. G. Ives, & A. Doan, (Eds.), *Proc. ACM SIGMOD Intl. Conference on Management of Data*, (p. 665), San Diego, California, USA. New York: ACM.

Arasu, A., Babu, S., & Widom, J. (2003b). An abstract semantics and concrete language for continuous queries over streams and relations. In *Proc. Intl. Conf. on Data Base Programming Languages.*

Arasu, A., Babu, S., & Widom, J. (2006). The CQL continuous query language: semantic foundations and query execution. *The VLDB Journal, 15*(2), 121–142. doi:10.1007/s00778-004-0147-z

Arasu, A., & Widom, J. (2004). Resource sharing in continuous sliding-window aggregates. In Nascimento et al., (pp. 336–347).

Babcock, B., Babu, S., Datar, M., Motwani, R., & Widom, J. (2002). Models and issues in data stream systems. In L. Popa, (Ed.), *Proc. 21st ACM Symposium on Principles of Database Systems (PODS)*, (pp. 1–16), Madison, Wisconsin. New York: ACM Press.

Babu, S., Munagala, K., Widom, J., & Motwani, R. (2005). Adaptive caching for continuous queries. In *Proc. 21st Intl. Conf. on Data Engineering (ICDE)*, (pp. 118–129), Tokyo, Japan. New York: IEEE.

Baralis, E., Paraboschi, S., & Teniente, E. (1997). Materialized views selection in a multidimensional database. In Jarke et al., (pp. 156–165).

Bellatreche, L., Karlapalem, K., & Schneider, M. (2000). On efficient storage space distribution among materialized views and indices in data warehousing environments. In *Proc. 9th Intl. Conference on Information and Knowledge Management (CIKM)*, (pp. 397–404). New York: ACM.

Bernstein, P. A., Blaustein, B. T., & Clarke, E. M. (1980). Fast maintenance of semantic integrity assertions using redundant aggregate data. In *Proc. 6th Intl. Conference on Very Large Data Bases (VLDB)*, (pp. 126–136), Montreal, Canada. Washington, DC: IEEE Computer Society.

Blakeley, J. A., Larson, P.-A., & Tompa, F. W. (1986). Efficiently updating materialized views. In *Proceedings ACM SIGMOD International Conference on Management of Data*, (pp. 61–71). New York: ACM.

Buneman, O. P., & Clemons, E. K. (1979). Efficiently monitoring relational databases. *ACM Transactions on Database Systems, 4*(3), 368–382. doi:10.1145/320083.320099

Carney, D., Centintemel, U., Cherniack, M., Convey, C., Lee, S., Seidman, G., et al. (2002). Monitoring streams - a new class of data management applications. In *VLDB.*

Ceri, S., & Widom, J. (1991). Deriving production rules for incremental view maintenance. In *Proceedings of 17th International Conference on Very Large Data Bases (VLDB)*. San Francisco: Morgan Kaufmann.

Chandrasekaran, S., Cooper, O., Deshpande, A., Franklin, M. J., Hellerstein, J. M., Hong, W., et al. (2003). TelegraphCQ: continuous dataflow processing for an uncertain world. In *Proc. 1st Biennal Conference on Innovative Data Systems Research (CIDR)*, Asilomar, CA.

Chaudhuri, S., & Narasayya, V. R. (1997). An efficient cost-driven index selection tool for Microsoft SQL Server. In Jarke et al., (pp. 146–155).

Chaudhuri, S., & Narasayya, V. R. (2007). Self-tuning database systems: A decade of progress. In Koch, C., Gehrke, J., Garofalakis, M. N., Srivastava, D., Aberer, K., Deshpande, A., et al (Eds.), *Proceedings 33rd Intl. Conf. on Very Large Data Bases (VLDB)*, (pp. 3–14), Vienna, Austria.

Chen, J., DeWitt, D. J., Tian, F., & Wang, Y. (2000). NiagaraCQ: A Scalable Continuous Query System for Internet Databases. In W. Chen, J. F. Naughton, & P. A. Bernstein, (Eds.), *Proceedings of the ACM SIGMOD International Conference on Management of Data,* pages 379–390, Dallas, Texas. New York: ACM.

Cormode, G., & Garofalakis, M. (2007). Sketching probabilistic data streams. In L. Zhou, T. W. Ling, & B. C. Ooi, (Eds.), *Proc. ACM SIGMOD Intl. Conf. on Management of Data*, Beijing, China. New York: ACM Press.

Dageville, B., Das, D., Dias, K., Yagoub, K., Zaït, M., & Ziauddin, M. (2004). Automatic SQL tuning in Oracle 10g. In Nascimento et al., (pp. 1098–1109).

Dar, S., Franklin, M. J., & Jónsson, B. Thorn., Srivastava, D., & Tan, M. (1996). Semantic data caching and replacement. In Vijayaraman et al., (pp. 330–341).

Dayal, U., Whang, K.-Y., Lomet, D. B., Alonso, G., Lohman, G. M., Kersten, M. L., et al. (Eds.). (2006). *Proc. 32nd Intl. Conference on Very Large Data Bases (VLDB)*. New York: ACM Press.

Deshpande, P., & Naughton, J. F. (2000). Aggregate aware caching for multi-dimensional queries. In C. Zaniolo, P. C. Lockemann, M. H. Scholl, & T. Grust, (Eds.), *Advances in Database Technology – 7th International Conference on Extending Database Technology (EDBT)*, Konstanz (LNCS 1777, pp. 167–182). Berlin: Springer.

Deshpande, P. M., Ramasamy, K., Shukla, A., & Naughton, J. F. (1998). Caching multidimensional queries using chunks. In L. M. Haas, & A. Tiwary, (Eds.), *Proc. ACM SIGMOD Intl. Conference on Management of Data,* (pp. 259–270), Seattle, Washington, USA. New York: ACM Press.

Dimitrova, K., El-Sayed, M., & Rundensteiner, E. A. (2003). Order-sensitive view maintenance of materialized XQuery views. In I.-Y. Song, S. W. Liddle, T. W. Ling, & P. Scheuermann, (Eds.), *Proceedings 22nd International Conference on Conceptual Modeling (ER)*, (LNCS Vol. 2813, pp. 144–157), Chicago, USA. Berlin: Springer.

El-Sayed, M., Rundensteiner, E. A., & Mani, M. (2006). Incremental maintenance of materialized XQuery views. In L. Liu, A. Reuter, K.-Y. Whang, & J. Zhang, (Eds.), *Proceedings 22nd International Conference on Data Engineering (ICDE)*, Atlanta, GA. Washington, DC: IEEE Computer Society.

Flajolet, P., & Martin, G. N. (1985). Probabilistic counting techniques for data base applications. *Journal of Computer and System Sciences, 31*, 182–208. doi:10.1016/0022-0000(85)90041-8

Ganguly, S., Garofalakis, M., & Rastogi, R. (2003). Processing set expressions over continuous update streams. In *Proc. ACM SIGMOD Intl. Conference on Management of Data*, San Diego, CA. ACM.

Gilbert, A. C., Kotidis, Y., Muthukrishnan, S., & Strauss, M. J. (2003). One-pass wavelet decompositions of data streams. In *IEEE Transactions on Knowledge and Data Engineering*.

Gray, J., Chaudhuri, S., Bosworth, A., Layman, A., Reichart, D., & Venkatrao, M. (1997). Data cube: A relational aggregation operator generalizing group-by, cross-tab, and sub-totals. *Journal Data Mining and Knowledge Discovery, 1*(1), 29–53. doi:10.1023/A:1009726021843

Griffin, T., & Kumar, B. (1998). Algebraic change propagation for semijoin and outer-join queries. *SIGMOD Record, 27*(3), 22–27. doi:10.1145/290593.290597

Gupta, A., Jagadish, H. V., & Mumick, I. S. (1996). Data integration using self-maintainable views. In Apers, P. M. G., Bouzeghoub, M., and Gardarin, G., editors, *Proc. 5th International Conference on Extending Database Technology (EDBT)*, Avignon, France, (LNCS Vol. 1057 pp. 140–144). Berlin: Springer.

Gupta, A., Katiyar, D., & Mumick, I. S. (1992). Counting solutions to the view maintenance problem. In *Workshop on Deductive Databases*, (pp. 185–194).

Gupta, A., & Mumick, I. S. (1995). Maintenance of materialized views: Problems, techniques and applications. *IEEE Quarterly Bulletin on Data Engineering. Special Issue on Materialized Views and Data Warehousing, 18*(2), 3–18.

Gupta, A., Mumick, I. S., & Subrahmanian, V. S. (1993). Maintaining views incrementally. In P. Buneman, & S. Jajodia, (Eds.), *Proceedings of the ACM SIGMOD International Conference on Management of Data*, (pp. 157–166). Washington, DC: ACM Press.

Gupta, H. (1997). Selection of views to materialize in a data warehouse. In F. N. Afrati, & P. G. Kolaitis, (Eds.) *Proceedings of the 6th International Conference on Database Theory (ICDT)*, Delphi, Greece (LNCS Vol. 1186, pp. 98–112). Berlin: Springer.

Gupta, H., Harinarayan, V., Rajaraman, A., & Ullman, J. D. (1997). Index selection for OLAP. In A. Gray, & P.-Å. Larson, (Eds.), *Proceedings of the 13th International Conference on Data Engineering (ICDE)*, (pp. 208–219), Birmingham, UK. Washington, DC: IEEE Computer Society.

Gupta, H., & Mumick, I. S. (2005). Selection of views to materialize in a data warehouse. *IEEE Transactions on Knowledge and Data Engineering, 17*(1), 24–43. doi:10.1109/TKDE.2005.16

Gupta, H., & Mumick, I. S. (2006). Incremental maintenance of aggregate and outerjoin expressions. *Information Systems, 31*(6), 435–464. doi:10.1016/j.is.2004.11.011

Halevy, A. Y. (2001). Answering queries using views: A survey. *The VLDB Journal, 10*(4), 270–294. doi:10.1007/s007780100054

Han, J., Chai, Y. D., Chen, Y., & Dong, G. (2007). Multi-dimensional analysis of data streams using stream cubes. In C. Aggarwal, (Ed.), *Data Streams - Models and Algorithms*, (pp. 103–123). Berlin: Springer.

Hanson, E. N. (1987). A performance analysis of view materialization strategies. *SIGMOD Record, 16*(3), 440–453. doi:10.1145/38714.38759

Harinarayan, V., Rajaraman, A., & Ullman, J. D. (1996). Implementing data cubes efficiently. In H. V. Jagadish & I. S. Mumick, (Ed.), *Proc. ACM SIGMOD International Conference on Management of Data*, Montreal, Quebec, Canada, (pp. 205–216). New York: ACM Press.

Harrison, J. V., & Dietrich, S. W. (1992). Maintenance of materialized views in a deductive database: An update propagation approach. In *Workshop on Deductive Databases, JICSLP*, (pp. 56–65).

Jagadish, H. V., Mumick, I. S., & Silberschatz, A. (1995). View maintenance issues for the chronicle data model (extended abstract). In M. Yannakakis (Ed.), *Proc. 14th ACM Symposium on Principles of Database Systems (PODS)*, San Jose, CA, (pp. 113–124). New York: ACM Press.

Jarke, M., Carey, M. J., Dittrich, K. R., Lochovsky, F. H., Loucopoulos, P., & Jeusfeld, M. A. (Eds.). (1997). *Proc. 23rd International Conference on Very Large Data Bases (VLDB)*, Athens, Greece. San Francisco: Morgan Kaufmann.

Kalnis, P., Ng, W. S., Ooi, B. C., Papadias, D., & Tan, K.-L. (2002). An adaptive peer-to-peer network for distributed caching of OLAP results. In M. J. Franklin, B. Moon, & A. Ailamaki, (Eds.), *Proc. ACM SIGMOD International Conference on Management of Data*, Madison, Wisconsin. New York: ACM.

Keim, D., & Heczko, M. (2001). Wavelets and their applications in databases. In A. Reuter, & D. Lomet, (Eds.), *Proceedings of the 17th International Conference on Data Engineering (ICDE)*, Heidelberg. Washington, DC: IEEE Computer Society.

Kotidis, Y. (2002). Aggregate view management in data warehouses. In J. Abello, P. M. Pardalos, & M. G. C. Resende, (Eds.), *Handbook of Massive Data Sets*, (pp. 711–741). Norwell, MA: Kluwer Academic Publishers.

Kotidis, Y., & Roussopoulos, N. (1999). DynaMat: a dynamic view management system for data warehouses. In A. Delis, C. Faloutsos, & S. Ghandeharizadeh, (Eds.), *Proceedings of the ACM SIGMOD International Conference on Management of Data*, (pp. 371–382), Philadelphia. New York: ACM Press.

Kotidis, Y., & Roussopoulos, N. (2001). A case for dynamic view management. *ACM Transactions on Database Systems*, *26*(4), 388–423. doi:10.1145/503099.503100

Labio, W., Quass, D., & Adelberg, B. (1997). Physical database design for data warehouses. In A. Gray, & P.-Å. Larson, (Eds.), *Proceedings of the 13th International Conference on Data Engineering (ICDE)*, (pp. 277–288), Birmingham, UK. New York: IEEE Computer Society.

Lakshmanan, L. V. S., Pei, J., & Han, J. (2002). Quotient cube: How to summarize the semantics of a data cube. In *VLDB* (2002), (pp. 778–789).

Larson, P.-Å., & Zhou, J. (2007). Efficient maintenance of materialized outer-join views. In *Proc. 23rd Intl. Conference on Data Engineering (ICDE)*, (pp. 56–65), Istanbul, Turkey. Washington, DC: IEEE.

Li, C., & Wang, S. (2006). Efficient incremental maintenance for distributive and non-distributive aggregate functions. *Journal of Computer Science and Technology*, *21*(1), 52–65. doi:10.1007/s11390-006-0052-6

Li, J., Maier, D., Tufte, K., Papadimos, V., & Tucker, P. A. (2005). Semantics and evaluation techniques for window aggregates in data streams. In F. Özcan, (Ed.), *Proceedings of the ACM SIGMOD International Conference on Management of Data*, Baltimore, Maryland, USA. New York: ACM.

Liefke, H., & Davidson, S. B. (2000). View maintenance for hierarchical semistructured data. In Y. Kambayashi, M. K. Mohania, & A. M. Tjoa, (Eds.), *Proceedings Second International Conference on Data Warehousing and Knowledge Discovery (DaWaK)*, (LNCS Vol. 1874, pp. 114–125), London. Berlin: Springer.

Liu, L., Pu, C., & Tang, W. (1999). Continual queries for internet scale event-driven information delivery. *IEEE Transactions on Knowledge and Data Engineering*, *11*(4), 610–628. doi:10.1109/69.790816

Luo, G., & Yu, P. S. (2008). Content-based filtering for efficient online materialized view maintenance. In *Proc. 17th ACM Conference on Information and Knowledge Management (CIKM)*, (pp. 163–172), New York. New York: ACM.

Madden, S., Shah, M. A., Hellerstein, J. M., & Raman, V. (2002). Continuously adaptive continuous queries over streams. In M. J. Franklin, B. Moon, & A. Ailamaki, (Eds.), *Proc. ACM SIGMOD International Conference on Management of Data*, (pp. 49–60), Madison, Wisconsin. New York: ACM.

Mistry, H., Roy, P., Sudarshan, S., & Ramam-ritham, K. (2001). Materialized view selection and maintenance using multi-query optimization. In T. Sellis, & S. Mehrotra, (Eds.), *Proceedings of the ACM SIGMOD International Conference on Management of Data*, (pp. 307–318), Santa Barbara, CA. New York: ACM Press.

Motwani, R., Widom, J., Arasu, A., Babcock, B., Babu, S., Datar, M., et al. (2003). Query process-ing, approximation, and resource management in a data stream management system. In *Proc. 1st Biennal Conference on Innovative Data Systems Research (CIDR)*, Asilomar, CA.

Mumick, I. S., Quass, D., & Mumick, B. S. (1997). Maintenance of data cubes and summary tables in a warehouse. In *ACM SIGMOD*, (pp. 100–111).

Nascimento, M. A., Özsu, M. T., & Renée, J. Miller, D. K., Blakeley, J. A., & Schiefer, K. B., editors (2004). *Proc. 30th Intl. Conference on Very Large Data Bases (VLDB)*, Toronto, Canada. San Francisco: Morgan Kaufmann.

Nicolas, J.-M. (1982). Logic for improving integ-rity checking in relational data bases. *Acta Infor-matica, 18*, 227–253. doi:10.1007/BF00263192

O'Neil, E. J., O'Neil, P. E., & Weikum, G. (1993). The LRU-K page replacement algorithm for database disk buffering. In P. Buneman, & S. Jajodia, (Ed.), *Proceedings of the ACM SIG-MOD International Conference on Management of Data*, (pp. 297–306), Washington, DC. New York: ACM Press.

Palpanas, T., Sidle, R., Cochrane, R., & Pirahesh, H. (2002). Incremental maintenance for nondis-tributive aggregate functions. In *VLDB* (2002), (pp. 802–813).

Patroumpas, K., & Sellis, T. K. (2006). Window specification over data streams. In *Current Trends in Database Technology - EDBT 2006 Workshops*, (pp. 445–464).

Poosola, V., Ganti, V., & Ioannidis, Y. E. (1999). Approximate query answering using histograms. *Bulletin of the IEEE Computer Society Technical Committe on Data Engineering*, (pp. 1–10).

Quass, D., Gupta, A., Mumick, I. S., & Widom, J. (1996). Making views self-maintainable for data warehousing. In *Proc. 4th Intl. Conference on Parallel and Distributed Information Systems (PDIS)*, (pp. 158–169), Miami Beach, FL. Wash-ington, DC: IEEE Computer Society.

Quass, D., & Widom, J. (1997). On-line warehouse view maintenance. In J. Peckham, (Ed.), *Proceed-ings of the ACM SIGMOD International Confer-ence on Management of Data*, (pp. 393–404), Tucson, Arizona. New York: ACM Press.

Raman, V., Deshpande, A., & Hellerstein, J. M. (2003). Using state modules for adaptive query processing. In *Proceedings of the 19th Interna-tional Conference on Data Engineering (ICDE)*, pages 353–366, Bangalore, India. Washington, DC: IEEE Computer Society.

Rao, P., & Moon, B. (2006). Sketchtree: Approxi-mate tree pattern counts over streaming labeled trees. In L. Liu, A. Reuter, K.-Y. Whang, & J. Zhang, (Eds.), *Proceedings 22nd International Conference on Data Engineering (ICDE)*, Atlanta, GA. Washington, DC: IEEE Computer Society.

Ross, K. A., Srivastava, D., & Sudarshan, S. (1996). Materialized view maintenance and integrity constraint checking: Trading space for time. In H. V. Jagadish, & I. S. Mumick, (Eds.), *Proc. ACM SIGMOD Intl. Conference on Manage-ment of Data*, (pp. 447–458), Montreal, Quebec, Canada. New York: ACM Press.

Roy, P., Seshadri, S., Sudarshan, S., & Bhobe, S. (2000). Efficient and extensible algorithms for multi query optimization. In W. Chen, J. F. Naughton, & P. A. Bernstein, (Eds.), *Proceedings of the ACM SIGMOD International Conference on Management of Data*, (pp. 249–260), Dallas, Texas. New York: ACM.

Sawires, A., Tatemura, J., Po, O., Agrawal, D., Abbadi, A. E., & Candan, K. S. (2006). Maintaining XPath views in loosely coupled systems. In *Dayal* et al. (2006), (pp. 583–594).

Scheuermann, P., Shim, J., & Vingralek, R. (1996). WATCHMAN: A data warehouse intelligent cache manager. In Vijayaraman et al. (pp. 51–62).

Sellis, T. K. (1988). Multiple-query optimization. *ACM Transactions on Database Systems, 13*(1), 23–52. doi:10.1145/42201.42203

Serlin, O. (1993). The history of DebitCredit and the TPC. In J. Gray, (Ed.), *The Benchmark Handbook*. San Francisco: Morgan Kaufmann.

Shmueli, O., & Itai, A. (1984). Maintenance of views. In *Proceedings ACM SIGMOD International Conference on Management of Data*, (pp. 240–255). New York: ACM.

Shukla, A., Deshpande, P., & Naughton, J. (1998). Materialized view selection for multidimensional datasets. In A. Gupta, O. Shmueli, & J. Widom, (Eds.), *Proceedings 24th International Conference on Very Large Data Bases (VLDB)*, New York. San Francisco: Morgan Kaufmann.

Silberschatz, A., Galvin, P., & Gagne, G. (2002). *Operating System Concepts*, (6th Ed.). New York: John Wiley.

Srivastava, D., Dar, S., Jagadish, H. V., & Levy, A. Y. (1996). Answering queries with aggregation using views. In Vijayaraman et al. (pp. 318–329).

Srivastava, U., & Widom, J. (2004). Flexible time management in data stream systems. In A. Deutsch, (Ed.), *Proc. 23rd ACM Symposium on Principles of Database Systems (PODS)*, (pp. 263–274), Paris, France. New York: ACM.

Staudt, M., & Jarke, M. (1996). Incremental maintenance of externally materialized views. In Vijayaraman et al. (pp. 75–86).

Stonebraker, M., Çetintemel, U., & Zdonik, S. B. (2005). The 8 requirements of real-time stream processing. *SIGMOD Record, 34*(4), 42–47. doi:10.1145/1107499.1107504

Terry, D. B., Goldberg, D., Nichols, D. A., & Oki, B. M. (1992). Continuous queries over append-only databases. In M. Stonebraker, (Ed.), *Proc. ACM SIGMOD International Conference on Management of Data*, (pp. 321–330), San Diego, CA. New York: ACM Press.

Theodoratos, D., Ligoudistianos, S., & Sellis, T. K. (2001). View selection for designing the global data warehouse. *Data & Knowledge Engineering, 39*(3), 219–240. doi:10.1016/S0169-023X(01)00041-6

Theodoratos, D., & Sellis, T. (1997). Data warehouse configuration. In Jarke et al. (1997).

Theodoratos, D., & Sellis, T. K. (1999). Designing data warehouses. *Data & Knowledge Engineering, 31*(3), 279–301. doi:10.1016/S0169-023X(99)00029-4

Toroslu, I. H., & Kocabas, F. (1997). Effective maintenance of recursive views: Improvements to the dred algorithm. In *Proceedings International Conference on Logic Programming (ICLP)*, (pp. 213–225).

Ullman, J. D. (1989). *Principles of Database and Knowledge-Base Systems*, (Vol. 2). New York: W.H. Freeman & Company.

Urpí, T., & Olivé, A. (1992). A method for change computation in deductive databases. In L.-Y. Yuan, (Ed.), *Proceedings 18th International Conference on Very Large Data Bases (VLDB)*, (pp. 225–237). San Francisco: Morgan Kaufmann.

Vijayaraman, T. M., Buchmann, A. P., Mohan, C., & Sarda, N. L. (Eds.). (1996). *Proceedings of 22th International Conference on Very Large Data Bases (VLDB)*, Mumbai (Bombay), India. San Francisco: Morgan Kaufmann.

VLDB. (2002). *Proc. 28th Intl. Conference on Very Large Data Bases (VLDB)*, Hong Kong, China. San Francisco: Morgan Kaufmann.

Wang, S., Rundensteiner, E. A., Ganguly, S., & Bhatnagar, S. (2006). State-slice: New paradigm of multi-query optimization of window-based stream queries. In Dayal et al., (pp. 619–630).

Yang, J., Karlapalem, K., & Li, Q. (1997). Algorithms for materialized view design in data warehousing environment. In Jarke et al., (pp. 136–145).

Yi, K., Yu, H., Yang, J., Xia, G., & Chen, Y. (2003). Efficient maintenance of materialized top-k views. In *Proceedings of the 19th International Conference on Data Engineering (ICDE)*, (pp. 189–200), Bangalore, India. Washington, DC: IEEE Computer Society.

Zhang, R., Koudas, N., Ooi, B. C., & Srivastava, D. (2005). Multiple aggregations over data streams. In F. Özcan, (Ed.), *Proceedings of the ACM SIGMOD International Conference on Management of Data*, pages 299–310, Baltimore, Maryland, USA. New York: ACM.

Zhao, Y., Deshpande, P. M., & Naughton, J. F. (1997). An array-based algorithm for simultaneous multidimensional aggregates. In J. Peckham, (Ed.), *Proceedings of the ACM SIGMOD International Conference on Management of Data*, Tucson, AR (pp. 159–170). New York: ACM Press.

Zhou, J., Larson, P.-Å., & Elmongui, H. G. (2007). Lazy maintenance of materialized views. In C. Koch, J. Gehrke, M. N. Garofalakis, D. Srivastava, K. Aberer, A. Deshpande, et al (Ed.), *Proceedings 33rd Intl. Conf. on Very Large Data Bases (VLDB)*, (pp. 231–242), Vienna, Austria.

Zhuge, Y., & Garcia-Molina, H. (1998). Graph structured views and their incremental maintenance. In *Proceedings of the 14th International Conference on Data Engineering (ICDE)*, pages 116–125, Orlando, Florida. Washington, DC: IEEE Computer Society.

Zilio, D. C., Rao, J., Lightstone, S., Lohman, G. M., Storm, A. J., Garcia-Arellano, C., & Fadden, S. (2004). DB2 Design Advisor: integrated automatic physical database design. In Nascimento et al., (pp. 1087–1097).

Chapter 6

A Framework for Data Warehousing and Mining in Sensor Stream Application Domains

Nan Jiang
Cedarville University, USA

ABSTRACT

The recent advances in sensor technologies have made these small, tiny devices much cheaper and convenient to use in many different applications, for example, the weather and environmental monitoring applications, the hospital and factory operation sites, sensor devices on the traffic road and moving vehicles and so on. The data collected from sensors forms a sensor stream and is transferred to the server to perform data warehousing and mining tasks for the end user to perform data analysis. Several data preprocessing steps are necessary to enrich the data with domain information for the data warehousing and mining tasks in the sensor stream applications. This chapter presents a general framework for domain-driven mining of sensor stream applications. The proposed framework is able to enrich sensor streams with additional domain information that meets the application requirements. Experimental studies of the proposed framework are performed on real data for two applications: a traffic management and an environmental monitoring site.

INTRODUCTION

Networks of thousands of sensors present a feasible and economic solution to some of our most challenging problems, such as real-time traffic modeling, weather and environmental monitoring, and military sensing and tracking. Recent advances in sensor technology have made possible the development of relatively low cost and low-energy-consumption micro sensors, which can be integrated in a wireless sensor network. These devices - Wireless Integrated Network Sensors (WINS) - will enable fundamental changes in applications spanning the home, office, clinic, factory, vehicle, metropolitan area, and the global environment.

Concerning the needs of the user for knowledge discovery from sensor streams in these application domains, new data warehousing, data mining techniques have to be developed to extract meaningful,

DOI: 10.4018/978-1-60566-816-1.ch006

useful and understandable patterns for the end users to perform data analysis. Many research projects have been conducted by different organizations regarding wireless sensor networks; however, few of them discuss the sensor stream processing infrastructure, and the data warehousing and data mining issues need to be addressed in the sensor network application domains. There is a need for new methodologies in order to extract interesting patterns in a sensor stream application domain. Since the semantics of sensor stream data is application dependent, the extraction of interesting, novel, and useful patterns from stream data applications becomes domain dependent.

Some data warehousing and data mining methods have been recently proposed to mine stream data, for example in (Manku 2002, Chang 2003, Li 2004, Yang 2004, Yu 2004, Dang 2007), the authors proposed algorithms to find frequent patterns over the entire history of data streams. In (Giannella 2003, Chang 2004, Lin 2005, Koh 2006, Mozafari 2008), the authors use different sliding window models to find recently frequent patterns in data streams. These algorithms focus on mining frequent patterns with one scan over the entire data stream.

In (Chi, 2004), Chi et al considers the problem of mining closed frequent itemsets over a data stream sliding window in the Moment algorithm, and in (Li, 2006), the authors proposed the New-Moment algorithm which uses a bit-sequence representation of items to reduce the time and memory needed. The CFI-Stream algorithm in (Jiang, 2006) directly computes the closed itemses online and incrementally without the help of any support information. In (Li, 2008), Li et al proposed to improve the CFI-stream algorithm with bitmap coding named CLIMB (Closed Itemset Mining with Bitmap) over data stream's sliding window to reduce the memory cost.

Besides pattern mining in data stream applications, as the number of data streaming applications grows, there is also an increasing need to perform association mining in data streams. One example application is to estimate missing data in sensor networks (Halatchev, 2005). Another example application is to predict frequency of Internet packet streams (Demaine, 2002). In the MAIDS project (Cai, 2004), an association mining technique is used to find alarming incidents from data streams. Association mining can also be applied to monitor manufacturing flows (Kargupta, 2004) to predict failures or generate reports based on accumulated web log streams. In (Yang, 2004), (Halatchev, 2005), and (Shin, 2007), the authors proposed using two, three, and multiple frequent pattern based methods to perform association rule mining.

In general, these approaches have focused on mining patterns and associations in data streams, without considering an application domain. As a consequence, these methods tend to discover general patterns, which for specific applications can be useless and uninteresting. Stream patterns are usually extracted based on the concept of pattern frequency. With no semantic or domain information, the discovered patterns cannot be applied directly to a specific domain.

In this book chapter, we present a data warehousing and mining framework where the users give to the data the semantics that is relevant for the application, and therefore the discovered patterns will refer to a specific domain. We will also discuss the issues needed to be considered in the data warehousing and mining components of this framework for sensor stream applications.

The remaining of the chapter is organized as follows: in the background section, we present some basic concepts about sensor data applications and the data warehousing and mining issues needed to be considered in stream data applications. Following with the background information, we present a framework for domain-driven data warehousing and mining from sensor streams. The case study section shows the experimental results with real data in two application domains. Finally, we conclude the chapter and discuss the future trends.

BACKGROUND

In this section, the background information is reviewed and discussed for two main areas: the sensor stream application domain and the data warehousing and mining issues needed to be considered in this specific domain. These are covered in the following two subsections, respectively.

Sensor Stream Application Domain

A data stream is a sequence of items that arrive in a timely order. Different from data in traditional static databases, data streams are continuous, unbounded, usually come with high speed, and have a data value distribution that often changes with time (Guha, 2001). A data stream is represented mathematically as an ordered pair (r, Δ) where: r is a sequence of tuples, Δ is the sequence of time intervals (i.e. rational or real numbers) and each $\Delta_i > 0$.

Applications that rely on data streams can be classified into offline and online streaming. Offline streaming applications are characterized by regular bulk arrivals (Manku, 2002). Generating reports based on accumulated web log streams is an example of mining offline data streams because most of reports are made based on log data that

is collected over a relatively large period of time. Online streaming applications are characterized by real-time updated data that needs to be quickly processed as the data arrives. Predicting frequency of Internet packet streams is an application of mining online data streams because the prediction needs to be made in real time. Other potential online data streaming applications include stock tickers, network measurements, and evaluation of sensor data. In online data streaming applications, data is often discarded soon after it arrives and has been processed, because of the high update rate and huge resulting amount of data.

Figure 1 shows an example of wireless sensor stream applications. In this figure, the sensors generate a series of sensor streams with domain information, such as the sensor identifiers, sensor locations, time stamps, sensed values at a particular time, and power left for the particular sensor, etc. The information is reported to the server through single-hop or multiple-hop routings. General stream mining methodologies do not have a mechanism to connect the domain information of each application to the reported sensor values; correspondingly the discovered patterns and their relationships with each sensor could not be connected together.

Figure 1. Wireless sensor stream application

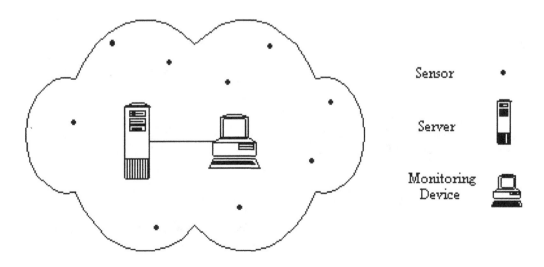

Moreover, concerning the needs of the user for queries about particular sensors, mining the whole set of information from all the sensors may not always be necessary and effective. Connecting the sensors' domain information with reported values will make it easy when the mining task only associated with part of potential sensors. It will also save computing power and memory spaces, which consequently provide higher quality of service in the wireless sensor networks. More data warehousing and mining issues in the sensor stream application domain will be discussed in the following subsection.

Data Warehousing and Mining Issues

As shown in Figure 2, there are several stages in the sensor stream processing infrastructure, namely the data collecting stage, the data preprocessing stage, the data storage and processing stage, and the data reporting and analysis stage. In this subsection, we discuss the data warehousing and mining issues needed to be considered in each of these stages, respectively.

Data Collecting Issues

In the sensor stream application domain, data is gathered through wireless sensors and is delivered

to the server or multiple servers for centralized or distributed processing and computing through single-hop or multiple-hop routing. Different data warehousing and mining techniques need to be considered regarding to the different computing models, for example, the centralized computing, distributed or parallel computing, etc. In this book chapter, we focus our discussion to the centralized computing, in which there is one server to collect and process all the delivered data from multiple sensors.

Data Preprocessing Issues

After the data is delivered to the server, before it can be processed, several data preprocess steps need to be performed to get the data ready for the processing unit and connect it with domain information. We discuss each of the steps in the following paragraphs.

Data Extraction

The first step of the data preprocessing stage is data extraction. In this step, the package sent from a particular sensor is extracted and information associated with the data warehousing and mining tasks is collected.

Figure 2. Sensor stream processing infrastructure

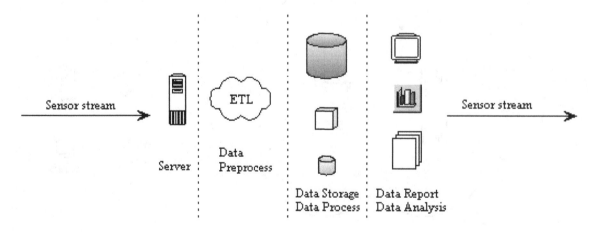

Questions need to be considered in this step include: which information we need to extract? Why we need to collect the information? How the collected data can work with the data warehousing and mining tasks and process? After the needed information is extracted and collected from the data transportation package, some Meta data information regarding the application domain can be gathered from the end user or from the collected information. For example, the data description of the application domain, the data ranges, and data type, etc. All these associated information can be loaded to the framework after being transferred to the required format.

Data Transformation

In the data transformation step, data is transformed to the formats that are able to be processed by the processing unit. The Meta data is used to generate indicator flags which reflect the data's effectiveness, i.e. missing, corrupted or not. Each set of information from a particular sensor is connected together with the sensor's identifier, so that it is easier to identify the sensor relationships and perform data analysis. More of the detail information will be discussed in the framework section.

Questions need to be considered in this step include: What are the source data formats? What are the target data formats? How to perform the data transformation? What kind of data can be regarded as corrupted? How the transformed data can work with the data warehousing and mining task and process? What is the Meta data? What are the usage and constraints of the data? After the data transformation task is complete, all the information can be loaded to the processing system and is ready to be processed.

Data Loading

Data loading is the last step of the data preprocessing stage. In this step, the extracted and transformed data is loaded into the processing system.

Things need to be considered in this step are: If the data coming rate can be kept with the data processing rate? The speed of the mining system should be faster than the data coming rate, otherwise data approximation techniques, such as sampling and load shedding, need to be applied. If so, the questions needed to be considered include: Which kind of speed adjusting techniques are suitable to use? How it will affect the accuracy of the mining result? What is the maximum allowable error rate specified by the end user? How we can apply the selected technique to the application system?

Data Storage and Processing Issues

After the data is being preprocessed, the next fundamental issue we need to consider is how to optimize the storage and process the collected information to perform the data warehousing and mining tasks. We will discuss the related issues in the following subsections.

One important thing in the data stream application domain different from the traditional application domains is that due to the continuous, unbounded, high speed characteristics of data streams, there is a huge amount of data in both offline and online data stream applications. Thus, there is not enough space to store and accumulate all the stream data and wait for bulk offline processing as in traditional database applications. One scan processing of data and compact data storage structure are preferable in this environment.

Data Storage

In this stage, data is stored in different data structures associated with the relative data warehousing and mining tasks. Efficient and compact data structure is needed to store, update and retrieve the collected information. This is done to the bounded memory size and huge amounts of data stream characteristics. Furthermore, the data structure needs to be incrementally maintained since it is not possible to rescan the entire input due to the huge amount of stream data and requirement of rapid online querying speed.

Questions need to be considered in this stage include: What information we need to store to process the data warehousing and mining tasks? What data structures we use to store the data and/or Meta data? How and when we update the stored information? Is the data structure efficient to perform the data mining and retrieving tasks? The data storage stage is directly related with the data processing stage, where the data warehousing and mining tasks are performed.

Data Processing

In the data processing stage, different data warehousing and mining tasks are performed based on the user's query. This is the main stage of the data processing system where different data warehousing and data mining methodologies are used to discovery knowledge or potential important information.

The first issue need to be addressed in this stage is the data processing model. According to (Zhu, 2002), there are three stream data processing models, Landmark, Damped and Sliding Windows. The Landmark model mines all collected information over the entire history of stream data from a specific time point called landmark to the present. The Damped model, also called the Time-Fading model mines information in stream data in which each transaction has a weight and this weight decreases with age. Older transactions contribute less weight towards the mining results. The Sliding Windows model finds and maintains most recent information in sliding windows. Only part of the data streams within the sliding window are stored and processed at the time when the stream data flows in. The size of the sliding window may be decided according to the applications and

system resources. All these three models can be converted to one another. Choosing which kind of data processing model to use largely depends on the application needs.

The next issue need to be considered in this stage is which data warehousing and data mining methods are suitable in the application environment? A number of questions need to be considered: Should we use an exact or approximate algorithm to perform the mining task? Can the error rate be guaranteed if it is an approximate algorithm? How to reduce and guarantee the error? What is the tradeoff between the accuracy and processing speed? Is the data processed within one pass? Can this method handle a large amount of data? What are the mechanism to maintain and update the data structure and mining results? Is the method resource aware? Can the processing methods handle timeline queries and/or multidimensional stream data?

Data Reporting and Analysis Issues

Data reporting and analysis is the last stage in the sensor stream processing infrastructure, where the mining results are monitored, analyzed and reported. What monitoring and visualization techniques and devices to use is largely application dependent.

Questions need to be considered in this stage include: What is the suitable layout and structure of the reporting interface? How the end users set parameters in the queries? For example, from the pick lists or drop down menus? What is the maximum query response time requested by the end users? What visualization techniques are appropriate to use in a particular application domain?

After discussing the issues needed to be considered in the data warehousing and mining in sensor stream application domain, in the next section we present a framework where the domain-driven data warehousing and mining tasks are used for knowledge discovery in sensor steam applications.

A FRAMEWORK FOR DOMAIN-DRIVEN DATA WAREHOUSING AND MINING FROM SENSOR STREAMS

As shown in Figure 3, raw data is collected from the sensor stream application, which includes the data from wireless sensor networks and data profile from a particular application domain. It is known that raw sensor stream data requires a lot of work to be transformed into data that is ready to be processed (processed data level in Figure 3). The processed data is generated for any application domain, and therefore is application independent. They can be used, for instance, to build applications of transportation management, environmental monitoring, urban planning, etc. On the other hand, the domain information is application dependent, and therefore, will contain only the entities of processed sensor stream data that are relevant to the sensor stream application, as shown in the application level in Figure 3.

Data warehousing and data mining are on the top level, and are also application dependent. In data warehousing and data mining tasks, the user is interested in patterns and/or their relationships about a specific problem or application. For instance, transportation managers are interested in patterns about traffic conditions, accidents, etc., but are not interested in, for instance, patterns of weather conditions.

In data stream mining, in general, mining has been directly performed over raw stream data or sensor databases, and the background sensor network information has not been integrated to the mining process. For data warehousing and mining in sensor stream applications, sensor streams need to be integrated with domain information, the discovered pattern information will not be meaningful to the end user or data analyst until it connects with the sensor stream domain information.

In our framework, shown in Figure 3, in the Application Domain level, we proposed to generate domain-enriched sensor data streams,

Figure 3. Proposed framework for sensor stream application domain

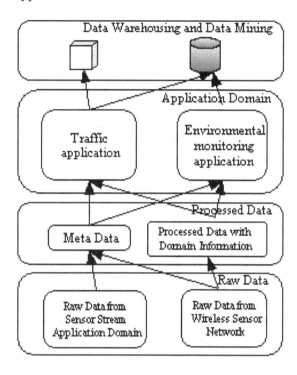

using the connected sensor identifier and sensor value information to find important patterns and relationships among sensors. Let $D = \{d_1, d_2,\ldots, d_n\}$ be a set of n sensor identifiers, and $V = \{v_1, v_2,\ldots, v_m\}$ be a set of m sensor values. A sensor value with domain information is a combination of sensor identifier D and sensor value V, denoted as $J = D.V$. For example, $d_n.v_m$ means that a sensor with identifier d_n has the value v_m.

In this framework, there are basically four abstraction levels as shown in Figure 4. On the bottom is the data: raw data from wireless sensor network and from sensor stream application domain. Raw data is obtained from the integration of sensor package information from server and sensor stream application domain. Data from the wireless sensor networks contains the information from wireless sensors, such as sensor locations, time stamps, sensor values, etc. Data from sensor stream application domain contains data descrip-

Figure 4. Architecture of a domain-driven framework for sensor stream application

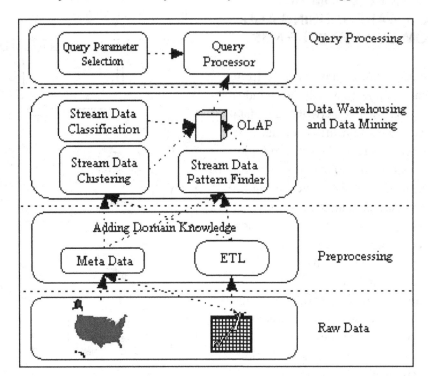

tion and constraints, such as data description, data range, data type, etc.

The second level is the preprocessing tasks, where the raw data are preprocessed and integrated with the domain information, and the sensor identifier are connected with sensor values. For data warehousing and mining, another fundamental task is the transformation of the data in different granularity levels. This is essentially important for sensor stream data, where both space and time need to be aggregated in order to allow the discovery of patterns. The user may aggregate both space and time in different granularities.

On the third level of the framework are the data warehousing and data mining tasks. Once the raw data are preprocessed and transformed, different data mining tasks can be applied. For example, data classification, data clustering, pattern and association discovering, and online data analytic processing, etc. These tasks can be combined together to get different mining results requested by the end users.

On the top of the framework is the query processing component, where the end users select query parameters and their queries can be answered based on the mining results. Different end users' requests can be answered at the same time according to their specified query parameters.

CASE STUDY

In this section we describe two different applications and present some experiments to show the usability of the framework for sensor stream application domain. Our experiments were performed with different data warehousing and data mining methods.

The Traffic Management Sensor Stream Application

The simulation data of the traffic management application was collected in year 2000 at various locations throughout the city of Austin, Texas. The data represents the current location, the time interval, and the number of vehicles detected during this interval. All sensor nodes report to a single server. The sensors are deployed on city streets, collect and store the number of the vehicles detected for a given time interval. The vehicle counts taken as sensor readings that are used as input for our simulation experiments are traffic data provided by (Austin, 2003).

Framework Setup and Implementation

As discussed in the framework for domain-driven data warehousing and mining from sensor streams, raw data was collected from the traffic sensor stream application and being transformed into data that was ready to be processed. The data was then enriched with the domain information from the traffic sensor network, and ready to be processed by different data warehousing and mining processes. The mining results were used to answer different user queries at requests. Below, we describe the process in each stage of the framework setup and implementation for the traffic management sensor stream application.

Raw Data Stage

At the raw data stage, which is on the bottom level of our proposed framework for sensor stream application domain, raw data is collected from the traffic management sensor stream application network. This information includes each sensor's current location, sensor identifier, the time interval for the reported value, and the number of vehicles detected during this time interval. The collected data was then transferred to the data preprocessor to be cleaned, integrated and added with domain information for the traffic management sensor stream application.

Data Preprocessing Stage

At the data preprocessing stage, the collected raw data was first integrated into a single sensor stream sequenced by their arrival time stamps. It was then cleaned to map the actual vehicle counts to ten different traffic states which represent the heavy or light levels of current traffic status at each sensor location during the reported time interval. The cleaned data was then enriched with the domain information; in this case, the sensor identifier was integrated with associated sensor values reported during different time intervals. The Meta data is used to generate indicator flags which reflect the data's effectiveness, i.e. missing, corrupted or not. In this case we define the data which no reporting value is missing, and the data reporting value is not within the specified vehicle count range is corrupted. After the preprocessing each sensor reading is connected by a particular sensor identifier, a sequence number represents the time interval the sensor reading was reported, and the Meta data contains the locations of each sensor represented by each sensor identifier.

Data Warehousing and Data Mining Stage

At the data warehousing and data mining stage, which is on the third level of the domain-driven framework, different data warehousing and data mining tasks can be performed on the preprocessed data enriched with domain information. In this case, we perform data clustering and classification tasks based on the sensor locations, and perform data association mining task in each sensor cluster to find out the interesting patterns and associations between the sensor readings. We then use the discovered relationships between these sensor readings to perform missing sensor data estimation based on the sensor readings related with the missing sensor reading. Please refer to (Jiang, 2007) for the detailed algorithm description of this approach.

Query Processing Stage

At the query processing stage, which is on the top level of the domain-driven framework, different users' query can be fulfilled at the users' specified query criteria at the same time. The end user will specify their query parameters on their online queries, in this case, the support, confidence threshold, and the sliding window size of their online association queries, or specify they would use the system recommend parameter values. The query processor then use these specified parameters as query criteria to pass the request to the data warehousing and mining components and retrieve the query results for different end users' requests.

Performance Study

The performance of our proposed framework is studied by means of simulation. Several different data warehousing and data mining experiments are conducted in order to evaluate the proposed framework while using the Average Window Size (AWS) approach, the linear interpolation approach, the linear trend approach, the Window based Association Rule Mining (WARM) approach (Halatchev, 2005), and the Closed itemsets based Association Rule Mining (CARM) approach (Jiang, 2007).

All these methods are applied to our proposed framework to answer the user's request for missing sensor value estimation. The AWS approach uses the average value of the missing sensor readings in the current sliding window as the estimated value. The linear interpolation approach uses the linear interpolation of the missing sensor's neighbor readings as the estimated value. The linear trend uses the linear regression trend for the missing sensor readings as the estimated value. The WARM approach (Halatchev, 2005) is a revised data warehousing technique for sensor network database based on the relationship between two sensors. And the CARM approach is a pattern and association mining approach for stream data application based on multiple sensor relationships. We compared the estimation accuracy, running time and memory space usage when applying each method to our proposed framework.

Performance Study of Estimation Accuracy

The evaluation of the estimation accuracy of the missing values is done by using the average Root Mean Square Error (RMSE):

$$RMSE = \frac{1}{numStates} \sqrt{\frac{\sum_{i=1}^{\#\,estimations} (Xa_i - Xe_i)^2}{\#\,estimations}}$$

where X_{ai} and X_{ei} are the actual value and the estimated value, respectively; #estimations is the number of estimations performed in a simulation run; and numStates is the number of states in which the actual readings are distributed.

The expression $\sqrt{\dfrac{\sum_{i=1}^{\#\,estimations} (Xa_i - Xe_i)^2}{\#\,estimations}}$ represents the standard error and is an estimate of the standard deviation under the assumption that the errors in the estimated values (i.e. X_{ai} - X_{ei}) are normally distributed. Thus, the RMSE allows the construction of confidence intervals describing the performance of different candidate missing value estimators. The smaller the RMSE (the standard deviation), the better the estimated results.

From Figure 5, we can see that CARM gives the best result of the above approaches in the proposed framework regarding the estimation accuracy, followed by the WARM approach. The linear interpolation, AWS, and linear trend approaches perform no better than WARM and CARM approaches. The main reason might be that it only considers the relationship between the neighbor nodes, while CARM and WARM find

Figure 5. Performance study of average and maximum estimation accuracy

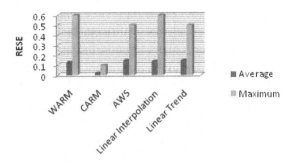

Figure 6. Performance study of running time

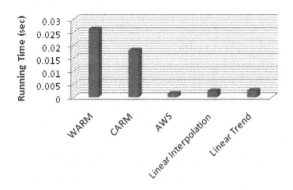

out more of the relationships between the existing sensors. Also from this figure, we can see that the CARM approach provides better estimation accuracy than the WARM approach does. This is because CARM performs the estimation based on the associations from multiple sensors derived by a compact and complete set of information, while WARM performs the estimation based on the associations derived by two sensors as frequent patterns in the data structure.

Performance Study of Running Time

Figure 6 illustrates the running time in seconds of AWS, linear interpolation, linear trend, WARM and CARM approaches in the proposed framework. The experimental results show that in terms of running time, the WARM and CARM approach are outperformed by AWS, linear interpolation and linear trend approaches. The CARM approach is faster than the WARM technique. This is because in the AWS, linear interpolation, linear trend approaches, the calculation is based on relationships in a certain sensors reading trend, while for WARM and CARM the calculation is based on relationships between not only the missing sensors previous readings but also the other sensors' readings that related with the missing sensor reading.

Performance Study of Memory Usage

Figure 7 illustrates the memory usage of AWS, linear interpolation, linear trend, WARM and CARM approaches in the proposed framework. The experimental results show that in terms of memory space, the WARM approach is outperformed by all other four approaches. The results of the simulation experiments show that for all processed sensors the needed memory space using WARM, is higher than that using CARM. This is because the lattice data structure in CARM uses less memory space than the cube data structures in WARM, and it stores only the condensed closed patterns. And for the AWS, linear interpolation, and linear trend approach, they only need to store and process information regarding the missing sensor's readings.

Figure 7. Performance study of memory usage

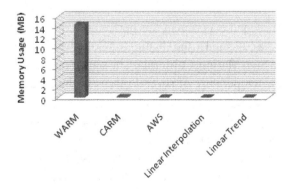

Analysis Summary

In this section, we discussed how to setup and implement a traffic management sensor stream application in the domain-driven framework for data warehousing and mining from sensor streams. We described the process of the framework setup in each implementing stage: the raw data stage, data preprocessing stage, data warehousing and data mining stage, and the query processing stage.

The performance of our proposed framework is studied by means of simulation. Several different data warehousing and data mining experiments are conducted in order to evaluate the proposed framework while using the Average Window Size (AWS) approach, the linear interpolation approach, the linear trend approach, the WARM approach (Halatchev, 2005), and the CARM approach (Jiang, 2007). All these methods are applied to our proposed framework to answer the user's request for missing sensor value estimation. We compared the estimation accuracy, running time and memory space usage when applying each method to our proposed framework.

Our performance study shows that the proposed domain-driven framework can be applied to different data warehousing and mining tasks. For the traffic management sensor stream application, the closed pattern based association mining to estimate missing sensor data online is an area worth to explore.

The Environmental Monitoring Sensor Stream Application

A second experiment was performed over sensor data collected in the Huntington Botanical Garden in Sam Marino, California. The sensor reports the air temperature of several places in the gardens for different time intervals.

The simulation data of the environmental monitoring application was collected in year 2008 at various locations throughout the sensor network in Huntington Botanical Garden. The data represents the current location, the time interval, and the air temperature of detected environment during this interval. All sensor nodes report to a single server. The sensors are deployed on different places of the botanical garden, collect and store the air temperature detected for a given time interval. The actual air temperatures are taken as sensor readings that are used as input for our simulation experiment.

Framework Setup and Implementation

As discussed in the domain-driven framework for data warehousing and mining from sensor streams, raw data was collected from the environmental monitoring sensor stream application and being transformed into data that was ready to be processed. The data was then enriched with the domain information from the environmental monitoring sensor network, and ready to be processed by different data warehousing and mining processes. The mining results were used to answer different user queries at requests. Below, we describe the process in each stage of the framework setup and implementation for the environmental monitoring sensor stream application.

Raw Data Stage

At the raw data stage, which is on the bottom level of our proposed framework for sensor stream application domain, raw data is collected from the environmental monitoring sensor stream application network. This information includes each sensor's current location, sensor identifier, the time interval for the reported value, and the air temperature detected during this time interval. The collected data was then transferred to the data preprocessor to be cleaned, integrated and added with domain information for the environmental monitoring sensor stream application.

Data Preprocessing Stage

At the data preprocessing stage, the collected raw data was first integrated into a single sensor stream sequenced by their arrival time stamps. It was then cleaned to round up the detected air temperature to its nearest integer value which represents the temperature at each sensor location during the reported time interval. The cleaned data was then enriched with the domain information; in this case, the sensor identifier was integrated with associated sensor values reported during different time intervals. The Meta data is used to generate indicator flags which reflect the data's effectiveness, i.e. missing, corrupted or not. In this case we define the data which no reporting value is missing, and the data reporting value is beyond the specified temperature range is corrupted. After the preprocessing each sensor reading is connected by a particular sensor identifier, a sequence number represents the time interval the sensor reading was reported, and the Meta data contains the locations of each sensor represented by each sensor identifier.

Data Warehousing and Data Mining Stage

At the data warehousing and data mining stage, which is on the third level of the domain-driven framework, different data warehousing and data mining tasks can be performed on the preprocessed data enriched with domain information. In this case, we perform data association mining task in each sensor cluster from the Huntington Botanical Garden sensor network application to find out the interesting patterns and associations between the sensor readings. We then use the discovered relationships between these sensor readings to perform missing sensor data estimation based on the sensor readings related with the missing sensor reading.

Query Processing Stage

At the query processing stage, which is on the top level of the domain-driven framework, different users' query can be fulfilled at the users' specified query criteria at the same time. In this case, the temperatures at different locations during the specified time interval. If the query information is not missing, it can be directly retrieved from the sensor network database. Otherwise, the request was send through the data estimation component in the data warehousing and mining level and the estimated results are retrieved for different end users' requests.

Performance Study

Several different data mining techniques are conducted in order to evaluate the proposed framework using the Average Window Size (AWS) approach, the linear interpolation approach, the linear trend approach, and the CARM approach (Jiang, 2007). All these methods are applied to our proposed framework to answer the user's request for missing sensor air temperature value. We compared the estimation accuracy, running time and memory space usage when applying each method to our proposed framework.

Performance Study of Estimation Accuracy

The evaluation of the estimation accuracy of the missing values is done by using the average Root Mean Square Error (RMSE).

From Figure 8, we can see that CARM gives the best result of the above approaches regarding the estimation accuracy. The AWS, and linear series approaches perform no better than CARM approaches. The main reason might be that it only considers the relationship between the neighbor nodes, while CARM find out all of the relationships

Figure 8. Performance study of average estimation accuracy

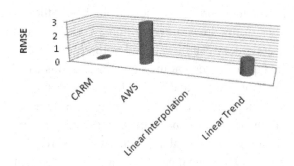

Figure 10. Performance study of memory usage

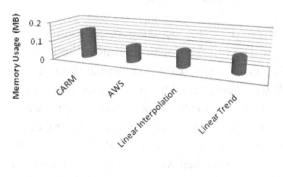

between the existing sensors. The linear interpolation method fails to report the missing temperature value, because it predicates the missing value based on the missing readings neighbor reported values. Therefore, when there are two consecutive missing values on the same sensor, this method couldn't calculate the estimated result.

Performance Study of Running Time

Figure 9 illustrates the running time in seconds of AWS, linear interpolation, linear trend, and CARM approaches. The experimental results show that in terms of running time, the CARM approach are outperformed by AWS, linear interpolation and linear trend approaches. This is because in the AWS, linear interpolation, linear trend approaches, the calculation is based on relationships in a certain sensors reading trend, while for CARM the calculation is based on relationships between

Figure 9. Performance study of running time

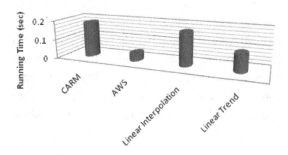

multiple sensor readings of the missing senor and the other related sensors.

Performance Study of Memory Usage

Figure 10 illustrates the memory usage of AWS, linear interpolation, linear trend, and CARM approaches in MB. The experimental results show that in terms of memory space, the CARM approach is outperformed by all other three approaches. This is because CARM stores the relationships of multiple sensor readings, and for the AWS, linear interpolation, and linear trend approach, they only need to store and process information regarding the missing sensor's readings.

Analysis Summary

In this section, we discussed how to setup and implement an environmental monitoring sensor stream application in the domain-driven framework for data warehousing and mining from sensor streams. We described the process of the framework setup in each implementing stage: the raw data stage, data preprocessing stage, data warehousing and data mining stage, and the query processing stage.

The performance of our proposed framework is studied by means of simulation. Several different data mining techniques are conducted in order to evaluate the proposed framework using the Average

Window Size (AWS) approach, the linear interpolation approach, the linear trend approach, and the CARM approach (Jiang, 2007). All these methods are applied to our proposed framework to answer the user's request for missing sensor air temperature value. We compared the estimation accuracy, running time and memory space usage when applying each method to our proposed framework.

Our performance study shows that the proposed domain-driven framework can be applied to the environmental monitoring sensor stream application for different data warehousing and mining tasks. For the missing sensor value application component in the sensor network application, the closed pattern based association mining approach is an area worth to explore.

CONCLUSION AND FUTURE TRENDS

Sensor stream applications are becoming very common with the advances in technologies for sensor devices. There data are normally available as stream data with very little or no semantics. This makes their analysis and knowledge extraction very complex from an application point of view. Most sensor stream mining works have focused on the streaming properties without considering the background of sensor domain information.

In this chapter we have addressed the problem of mining sensor stream system from an application point of view. We presented a framework to preprocess sensor streams for domain-driven data mining. The objective is to integrate domain information that is relevant for stream data warehousing and data mining.

We have evaluated the framework with real data from two different stream data application domains, which shows that the framework is general enough to be used in different application scenarios. This is possible because the user can choose the domain information that is important for data warehousing and mining tasks.

Domain-driven data mining is an open research field, especially for spatial, temporal sensor stream data. We believe that in the future new data warehousing and mining algorithms that consider data semantics and domain information have to be developed in order to extract more interesting patterns and associations in different application domains.

REFERENCES

Austin, F. I. (2000). *Austin Freeway ITS Data Archive*. Retrieved January, 2003 from http://austindata.tamu.edu/default.asp.

Cai, Y. D., Pape, G., Han, J., Welge, M., & Auvil, L. (2004). MAIDS: Mining alarming incidents from data streams. *International Conference on Management of Data*.

Chang, J. H., Lee, & W. S. (2004). A sliding window method for finding recently frequent itemsets over online data streams. *Journal of Information Science and Engineering*.

Chang, J. H., Lee, W. S., & Zhou, A. (2003). Finding recent frequent itemsets adaptively over online data streams. *ACM SIGKDD International Conference on Knowledge Discovery and Data Mining*.

Chi, Y., Wang, H. X., Yu, P. S., & Muntz, R. R. (2004). Moment: Maintaining closed frequent itemsets over a stream sliding window. *IEEE International Conference on Data Mining*.

Dang, X. H., Ng, W. K., & Ong, K. L. (2007). Online mining of frequent sets in data streams with error guarantee. *Knowledge and Information Systems*.

Demaine, E. D., Ortiz, A. L., & Munro, J. I. (2002). Frequency estimation of internet packet streams with limited space. *European Symposium on Algorithms*.

Giannella, C., Han, J. W., Pei, J., Yan, X. F., & Yu, P. S. (2003). Mining frequent patterns in data streams at multiple time granularities. *Data Mining: Next Generation Challenges and Future Directions*, AAAI/MIT.

Guha, S., & Koudas, N. (2002). Approximating a data stream for querying and estimation: Algorithms and performance evaluation. *International Conference on Data Engineering*.

Halatchev, M., & Gruenwald, L. (2005). Estimating missing values in related sensor data streams. *International Conference on Management of Data*.

Jiang, N., & Gruenwald, L. (2006). CFI-Stream: Mining Closed Frequent Itemsets in Data Streams. *ACM SIGKDD international conference on knowledge discovery and data mining*.

Jiang, N., & Gruenwald, L. (2007). Estimating missing data in data streams, *the International Conference on Database Systems for Advanced Applications*.

Kargupta, H., Bhargava, R., Liu, K., Powers, M., Blair, P., Bushra, S., et al. (2004). VEDAS: A mobile and distributed data stream mining system for real-time vehicle monitoring. *SIAM International Conference on Data Mining*.

Koh, J. L., & Shin, S. N. (2006). An approximate approach for mining recently frequent itemsets from data streams. *The 8th International Conference on Data Warehousing and Knowledge Discovery*.

Li, H. F., & Cheng, H. (2008). Improve frequent closed itemsets mining over data stream with bitmap. *Ninth ACIS International conference on software engineering, artificial intelligence, networking, and parallel/distributed computing*.

Li, H. F., Ho, C. C., Kuo, F. F., & Lee, S. Y. (2006) A new algorithm for maintaining closed frequent itemsets in data streams by incremental updates. *Six IEEE International Conference on Data Mining Workshop*.

Li, H. F., Lee, S. Y., & Shan, M. K. (2004). An efficient algorithm for mining frequent itemsets over the entire history of data streams. *The International Workshop on Knowledge Discovery in Data Streams*.

Lin, C. H., Chiu, D. Y., Wu, Y. H., & Chen, A. L. P. (2005). Mining frequent itemsets from data streams with a time-sensitive sliding window. *SIAM International Conference on Data Mining*.

Manku, G. S., & Motwani, R. (2002). Approximate frequency counts over data streams. *International Conference on Very Large Databases*.

Mozafari, B., Thakkar, H., & Zaniolo, C. (2008). Verifying and mining frequent patterns from large windows over data streams. *IEEE International Conference on Data Engineering*.

Shin, S. J., & Lee, W. S. (2007). An online interactive method for finding assoication rules data streams. *ACM 16th Conference on Information and Knowledge Management*.

Yang, L., & Sanver, M. (2004). Mining short association rules with one database scan; *International Conference on Information and Knowledge Engineering*.

Yu, J. X., Chong, Z. H., Lu, H. J., & Zhou, A. Y. (2004). False positive or false negative: Mining frequent itemsets from high speed transactional data streams. *International Conference on Very Large Databases*.

Zhu, Y. Y., & Shasha, D. (2002). StatStream: Statistical monitoring of thousands of data streams in real time. *International Conference on Very Large Databases*.

Chapter 7
A Data Warehousing Approach for Genomics Data Meta–Analysis

Martine Collard
INRIA Sophia Antipolis, France and University of Nice-Sophia Antipolis, France

Leila Kefi-Khelif
INRIA Sophia Antipolis, France

Van Trang Tran
I3S laboratory, University of Nice-Sophia Antipolis, France

Olivier Corby
INRIA Sophia Antipolis, France

ABSTRACT

DNA micro-array is a fastest-growing technology in molecular biology and bioinformatics. Based on series of microscopic spots of DNA sequences, they allow the measurement of gene expression in specific conditions at a whole genome scale. Micro-array experiments result in wide sets of expression data that are useful to the biologist to investigate various biological questions. Experimental micro-arrays data and sources of biological knowledge are now available on public repositories. As a consequence, comparative analyses involving several experiments become conceivable and hold potentially relevant knowledge. Nevertheless, the task of manually navigating and searching for similar tendencies in such huge spaces is mainly impracticable for the investigator and leads to limited results. In this context, the authors propose a semantic data warehousing solution based on semantic web technologies that allows to monitoring both the diversity and the volume of all related data.

INTRODUCTION

DNA micro-arrays are now widely used for mRNA expression profiling and have applications in a variety of biological issues. Numerous laboratories have collected micro-array data that are available on public databases and web sites. For instance, the Gene Express Omnibus[1] (GEO) or the ArrayExpress[2] repositories provide public availability of data on

DOI: 10.4018/978-1-60566-816-1.ch007

gene profiles for the entire scientific community. Thus, it has recently appeared useful for biologists to take advantage of these archives of responses for different purposes.

Despite the genome wide dimension of micro-arrays and their expression data, results published in scientific media generally focus on the hundred first differentially expressed genes among thousands of a whole genome, and real discussions are on ten of them only. So novel statistical analyses may be led on archived data in order to explore them more deeply, and confirm original results or discover new knowledge.

Another use of these public archives is for comparative analyses. New micro-array experimental data may be compared to previous ones in order to highlight similar and specific responses to a particular biological test.

A third use of these expression datasets is to involve multiple data sets in a new meta-analysis. In order to highlight similar and specific biological responses to a particular biological test, it seems promising to transversally analyze the largest set of related data. Combined analyses of multiple data sets and their issues have focused either on differential expressions (Rhodes et al., 2002, Choi et al., 2003) or on co-expressed genes (Eisen et al., 1998, Lee et al., 2004). (Hong and Breitling, 2008) evaluated three statistical methods for integrating different micro-array data sets and concluded that meta-analyses may be powerful but have to be led carefully.

Nevertheless, biologists that are interested in studying micro-array data and finding novel knowledge face a very complex task. Navigating manually into huge amounts of diverse data stored in these public repositories is such a tedious task that they finally lead restricted studies and make limited conclusions. Systems like GEO for the NCBI[3], ArrayExpress[4] for the EBI[5], Gemma[6] or Genepattern[7] allow investigators to share data and analyses results, they provide user-friendly tools allowing the analysis of global expression data, as collected by DNA micro-array experiments.

There are still critical points, on one hand to combine directly data sets derived from different experimental processes and micro-arrays, and on another hand, to take benefit from the whole set of related information.

In this context, our approach is to enable meta-analyses involving multiple types of source data including aggregated or synthetic data and semantic aspects.

This chapter presents the semantic data warehousing approach AMI (*Analysis Memory for Immunosearch*) that we designed in order to facilitate storage and intelligent querying of:

- gene expression data from multiple experiments,
- refined data (aggregate or synthetic) resulting from statistical analyses and data mining methods,
- data and metadata representing all related information from the biological domain.

All these different kinds of information may be considered as dimensions of the semantic data warehouse. Refined data may be considered as facts in a standard data warehouse. One idea is to take advantage of semantic relationships among metadata for querying this data warehouse and provide relevant comparative analyses. Technical solutions in AMI knowledge base and search engine are based on semantic web techniques such as semantic annotation languages and underlying ontologies.

The work realized within the AMI project aims in a final stage at providing the scientist user with semi-automatic tools facilitating navigation and comparative analyses into a whole set of comparable experiments and multiple sources of information related to a particular bi- 3 Data warehousing approach for Genomics Data Analysis biological process. This work was done in collaboration with the Immunosearch company[8] whose projects focus on human biological responses to chemicals. In a first step, AMI is devoted to human skin biological reactions only.

Table 1. Gene expression data from a micro-array

Probe	Symbol	c_1	c_2	...	...	c_j	...	...	...	c_n
$probe_1$	$gene_1$	exp_{11}	exp_{12}	...	...	exp_{1j}	...	...	...	exp_{1n}
$probe_2$	$gene_2$	exp_{21}	exp_{22}	...	...	exp_{2j}	...	...	...	exp_{2n}
...	...	...	...	...	...	...	...	...	...	...
$probe_i$	...	...	exp_{i2}	...	...	exp_{ij}	...	...	...	exp_{in}
...	...	...	...	...	...	...	...	...	...	...
$probe_p$	...	...	exp_{p2}	...	...	exp_{pj}	...	...	...	exp_{pn}

The chapter is organized in seven sections: the second section "MICRO-ARRAYS EXPERIMENTS" presents micro-array experiment basic principles and guidelines of micro-array data processing and analysis. The third section "AMI OVERVIEW" details our motivations in designing the AMI approach and the framework of this semantic data warehouse. In the fourth section "STANDARD META-ANALYSES OF DNA MICRO-ARRAYS", we discuss standard meta-analyses approaches and we provide some experimental results that justify the AMI data warehouse oriented approach. The fifth section "EXPRESSION DATA, SYNTHETIC DATA AND METADATA" details data storage and representation in AMI; it presents XML-based representations of statistical results on micro-array gene expression data and metadata describing them. In the sixth section "SEMANTIC WEB TECHNOLOGIES FOR META-ANALYSES", we show how semantic web technologies provide a useful insight into the wide diversity of the data warehouse. We conclude in the seventh section.

MICRO-ARRAYS EXPERIMENTS

In this section, we introduce main concepts and standards of micro-array domain and we give some insights in most frequent methods applied to analyze their data.

Gene Expression Data

Micro-arrays are arrays of genetic material. This technology consists on printing DNA brands (DNA sequences) on a chip of plastic or glass and making them hybridize with similar radioactively labeled DNA sequences (*probes*) extracted from a tissue of interest. The number of hybridizations gives an estimation of the gene expression for the gene matching the probe hybridized Affymetrix[9] micro-arrays that become a standard, use a technique that synthesizes probes *in situ* while in two channels micro-arrays technology, DNA sequences are directly deposed on the chip. Whatever the kind of chip, three steps are followed: labeling with fluorescent dyes, hybridization and image scanning. After probes are hybridized, the light emitted is captured by a scanner and the chip produces an image that produces a result in its turn since the image is processed to extract numeric data.

Gene expression data may be seen as the Table 1 where each column c_j represents a particular condition or sample (tissue, kinetic...). Generally one column at least represents a control condition. Each item exp_{ij} represents the expression of a probe $probe_i$ with its matching $gene_i$ under the condition c_j. Some columns may refer to so called *replicates* that measure gene expression in similar conditions to ensure more robustness. Raw gene expression data need to be pre-processed before statistical and data mining analyses.

In the two next sections, we give some details on pre-processing methods and then we discuss main analysis methods.

Micro-Array Data Pre-Processing

Raw intensities (that are stored in so called *CEL* files in the case of Affymetrix micro-arrays) need to be pre-processed in order to smooth errors and variability. Then the normalization step is mandatory since the experimental process often introduces much noise into data. Normalization methods are generally fitted to a kind of micro-array.

The *LOWESS* (Locally Weighted Linear Regression) method (Cleveland and Devlin, 1979) was designed for two channels micro-arrays. The *RMA* (Robust Multiarray Analysis) method (Irizarry, 2003) is fitted to arrays with replicates (or multi-arrays); it operates a quantile transformation in order to obtain the same quantiles over all arrays.

Micro-Array Data Analysis

Differentially Expressed Genes

One standard analysis on gene expression data consists on searching for genes that behave differently under two given conditions (control/treatment, time1/time2...). Statistical hypothesis tests are mostly used.

The *fold-change* calculated for each gene as the ratio of the average expression under a condition and the average expression under another condition may be used to determine which genes are differentially expressed but depends on an arbitrary threshold. Standard t-tests are performed as an hypothesis test. A very frequent approach is to perform an Analysis of Variance (ANOVA), either a one way or a two way ANOVA, that are fitted to data sets with multiple samples. An ANOVA returns a *p-value* as a level of significance that a gene or a group of genes are differentially expressed. One way ANOVA are applied when one

criterion only has an influence on data variance.

Co-Expressed Genes

Another frequent analysis on micro-arrays data is intended to search for genes that have similar behaviour over conditions. They are called *co-expressed genes*. Numerous attempts have been done to design clustering methods for the identification of groups of co-expressed genes. Hierarchical methods have been particularly developed to address the specific issues of these data.

Standards and Ontologies for Micro-Arrays Experiments

The scale and complexity of micro-array experiments require the adoption of standards and *ontologies* so that data from micro-array experiments can be exploited in full. Here is a list of some used standards (see also (Stoeckert et al., 2002)):

- Gene Ontology (Ashburner et al., 2000) is a controlled vocabulary widely used to describe genes and gene products (their function and location),
- MIAME (Brazma et al., 2001) is a standard that defines the minimal information that is required to understand the experiment and the data,
- MINiML10 (MIAME Notation in Markup Language) is a data exchange format optimized for micro-array gene expression data. It is defined in XML and allows the capture of every MIAME information,
- MAGE11 is a standard for the representation of micro-array expression data that would facilitate the exchange of micro-array information between different data systems: For example, MAGE-OM is a stable specification for the standard representation of data in a database and MAGE-ML defines a common format for data transfer from one database to another,

- MGED Ontology (Whetzel et al., 2006) is a framework of micro-array concepts that reflects the MIAME guidelines and MAGE structure. It provides controlled terms to describe a micro-array analysis,
- OBI (Ontology for biomedical investigations) (Smith et al., 2007) models the design of an investigation, protocols, instrumentation and material used and data generated. The adoption of such standards for the management and sharing of micro-array data is essential and provides benefit to the research community.

AMI OVERVIEW

Analyzing a unique experiment dataset like presented in the previous section is a first mandatory step for evaluating a micro-array experiment. But results are obviously more valuable when compared to other experiments. This section is organized in two subsections. In the first subsection, we first present some practical scenarios that motivated the design of AMI. Then in the second one, we describe our approach to provide a semantic solution to comparative analyses.

Motivations

Statistical analyses on gene expression data are mainly conducted in order to identify differentially expressed gene between two conditions. Let us consider the two following experiments:

1. the gene expression analysis on Nickel allergy as described in (Pedersen et al., 2007) and its datasets with kinetic gene expression of Nickel exposure at 0h,7h, 48h and 96h after exposure,
2. the gene expression analysis on psoriasis as described in (Sa et al., 2007)and its datasets with gene expression for exposure to 8 cytokines such as IL20 or IL1b.

Series GSE6281 and 7216 are described in section "STANDARD META-ANALYSES OF DNA MICRO-ARRAYS" below.

In this kind of data, it is quite typical to search for up-regulated genes at 48h compared to 7h for instance or up-regulated genes in *IL20* exposure compared to control on the basis of statistical techniques. Such statistical results lead then the scientist to numerous comparative investigations not only on the same dataset but on similar gene expression datasets produced by human skin biological reaction experiments.

For instance, investigators in such a situation would obviously try to ask questions like these ones: ''*Which are the genes that are differentially expressed in Nickel allergy and are not expressed in cytokine exposure?*'' or ''*If gene CCL19 is over-expressed in Nickel exposure at 48h, is it expressed in other Nickel allergy experiments too?*''. Multiple information sources may be useful for answering: datasets from the same laboratory, public datasets as described above, scientific publications on the same issues, etc.

After studying differential gene expressions, clustering methods are frequently applied for identifying similarities among genes or samples. Gene clustering results still raise new questions on cluster meaning. Semantic data like concepts defined in domain ontologies like the Gene Ontology (GO) are useful for annotating a cluster with its most descriptive properties related to biological processes or molecular functions. For instance, a biologist may probably wonder for instance "*Which biological processes can be most likely associated with clusters including genes CCL19 and IL2RA?*", or more widely "*What are the other analyses in which genes CCL19 and IL27RA were clustered together and what are the semantic annotations of the clusters?*".

Answers to comparative questions as shown above should be obviously more relevant if queries took into account a wider catalogue of experiments and connected sources of information. While so-called *meta-analyses* techniques (see the next section) are able to involve multiple datasets, they are essentially adapted to similar micro-arrays datasets and do not provide semantic enhancements.

The main goal in our approach is to provide the investigator (most frequently biologist) with enhanced semantic access capabilities to multiple and huge sources of various data in order to lead robust comparative analyses on gene expression data. We have thus designed a semantic data warehouse which central component is a knowledge base built on semantic annotations and ontologies.

More precisely, we aim at providing functionalities for multiple scenarios that may access a variety of relevant sources of information. For instance an AMI user should be able to:

- select interesting publications, annotate them and store such annotations,
- store explicit background knowledge and annotate it as facts and rules,
- enhance previous statistical and data mining analyses on downloaded public raw expression datasets and store results as annotations,
- store all expression datasets on a new local experiment, lead statistical and data mining analyses on them and store results as annotations,
- lead meta-analyses on comparable selected datasets and store results as annotations,
- query the AMI data warehouse for comparative analysis by confrontation of knowledge from all related sources.
  - *AMI Analysis Tools* allow the users to process data transformations for further combined meta-analysis and to run statistical and data mining tasks such as differentially expressed gene analysis or co-expressed genes clustering on relevant subspaces of the data set. Such results on absolute gene expression and differential gene

expression are stored in a relational database and clustering models are described in XML files according the PMML[12] formalism defined by the Data Mining Group[13] (DMG).

- *Annotation Storing Tools* generate for each relevant source of information, specific semantic annotations based on the domain ontologies. As illustrated in Figure 1 semantic annotations are generated by different tools: *GEAnnot* annotates experiments and their experimental conditions (3), *GMineAnnot* annotates synthetic statistical data (5), *MeatAnnot* annotates scientific publications (2) and *KnowAnnot* annotates background knowledge (1).
- *AMI Querying Tools* allow to navigating into the knowledge base and retrieve experiments, conditions or genes according to more or less complex criteria. This tool generates exact answers and approximate answers extracted according similarity links in ontologies or deduced answers obtained by logic inference rules.

Framework

In AMI, thanks to underlying ontologies, each available source of relevant information on a genomic experiment is represented as a set of semantic annotations. A search engine relying on semantic ontological links ensures powerful and intelligent querying functions which may retrieve interesting and approximate answers to a query as well as inferred knowledge deduced from logical rule annotations.

Ontologies are formal representations of a set of concepts within a given domain and relationships between those concepts. They allow to reason and to draw inferences about the properties of that domain. In AMI, we re-used some existing

Figure 1. Global overview of flow processing in AMI

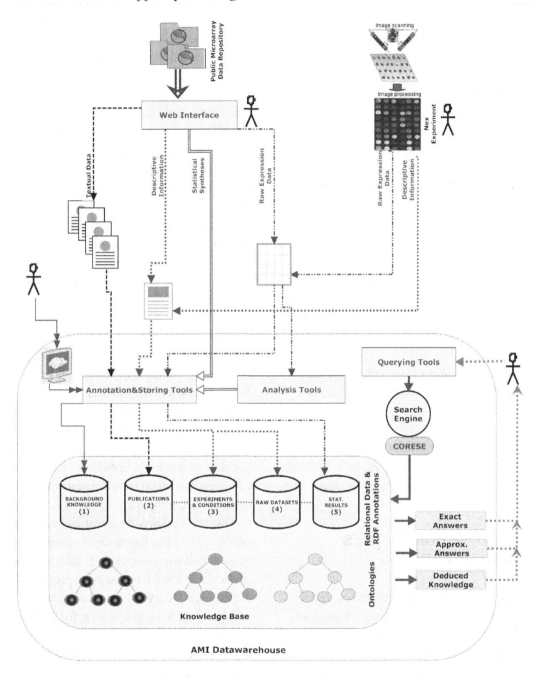

ontologies (such as UMLS[14] (Unified Medical Language System) semantic network, OntoDerm (Eapen, 2008) and GO) and we designed new specific ones.

Figure 1 gives an overview of data flow processing that is detailed below.

In AMI, we consider a whole set of information that may be useful for the investigator:

- Description of experiments (laboratory, micro-array, contributors...) and their conditions (tissue, treatment, subject, culture...),

- Raw expression data that either are downloaded from public repositories (like CEL files from GEO database) or produced by local micro-array experiments,
- Synthetic data obtained from numeric raw expression data by processing transformation, statistical and data mining tools, and also related statistical results downloaded from public sites,
- Related scientific publications selected by investigators from public repositories like PUBMED[15]
- Implicit background knowledge of the investigators.

All these data are processed by *AMI Analysis Tools* and/or *Annotation Storing Tools*. These modules produce semantic annotations and relational data that may be then queried by *AMI Querying Tools*.

In summary, in this section, we have presented examples of data analysis scenarios that demonstrate the need of a powerful semantic querying system. Then we have detailed the AMI framework that provides capabilities to process either semantic enhanced meta-analyses on synthetic data or standard meta-analyses on raw data.

STANDARD META-ANALYSES OF DNA MICRO-ARRAYS

Meta-analyses on multiple independent expression data sets are one option to provide more comprehensive view for cross-validation of previous results and comparison with novel analyses than individual ones. For instance, for the particular issue of human skin biomarkers identification, it should be valuable to group together expression data like GSE6281, GSE7216, GSE6475 and GSE9120 series (see subsection "Description of data sets") respectively on Nickel allergy on skin biopsies, reactions of human keratinocytes to cytokines IL-19, IL-20..., inflammatory acne on

skin biopsies, reactions of human keratinocytes to IL-1 and to search for differentially expressed genes or gene clusters.

A so-called standard meta-analysis consists of applying a set of statistical techniques to combine and analyze results from multiple independent datasets. Indeed while DNA micro-array technology allows measuring simultaneously the expression levels of thousands genes under various conditions and provide genome-wide insight, the weak number of samples (conditions) in each study is a limit to the power of the statistical inferences. Therefore with the increasing amount of public expression data, a new interest appeared in combining independent datasets from multiple studies in order to increase the sample size and elicit more genetic markers (Moreau et al., 2003). Growing volumes of experiments offer new opportunities but amplify the challenging statistical and computational complexity too. In fact, when combining different data sets, one has to consider at least data scales, distributions, and sample similarity. Specific mathematical methods to pre-process and transform data sets are necessary to obtain a valid integrated data set. Some recent attempts have been done to address and solve new statistical issues raised when different datasets are combined.

This section aims at presenting main proposed solutions of standard meta-analyses on expression datasets and their limits. It is structured in two subsections. The first subsection presents diverse recent meta-analyses methods and discusses mainly integration and search for differentially expressed genes issues. In the second subsection we present conclusive tests that demonstrate how carefully meta-analyses have to be driven.

Overview of Methods

For the purpose of demonstration, we first give some examples of datasets that could be typically involved in a meta-analysis. Then we present solutions for addressing data integration issues, and techniques for eliciting differentially expressed genes. We conclude with classification techniques that were employed on combined datasets.

Description of Data Sets

We consider four experiments series (GSE6281, GSE7216, GSE6475 and GSE9120) available on the GEO website. These data are related to skin reactions; they come from 85 Affymetrix micro-arrays (either HG-U133 Plus 2.0 array or HG-U133A 2.0 array) experiments on human skin allergic contact dermatitis. In both series GSE6281 and GSE7216, cRNAs were extracted from skin biopsies and a genome wide expression analysis was carried out on the same HG-U133 Plus 2.0 array (platform GPL570) gene chip containing 54675 probe sets, while the hybridized cRNA of series GSE6475 and GSE9120 were prepared using the gene chip HG-U133A 2.0 Array containing 22277 probe sets. Table 2 provides some details on these datasets.

The GSE6281 serie introduced in (Pedersen et al., 2007) used a high density oligonucleotide array for gene expression profiling in human skin during the elicitation of allergic contact dermatitis. Samples are part of an analysis of gene expression time-course. Skin biopsies from normal and nickel-exposed skin were obtained from 7 nickel-allergic patients and 5 non-allergic controls at four different time points 0h, 7h, 48h and 96h during elicitation of eczema. In addition, one nickel-allergic patient and one healthy control were recruited for immunocytochemistry study.

The GSE7216 serie contains gene expression data on primary human keratinocytes receptors for the cytokines IL-19, IL-20, IL-22, and IL-24 (Sa et al., 2007). The effects of all cytokines on cultured human keratinocytes and in a reconstituted human epidermal culture system were evaluated by comparison with controls.

In the GSE6475 serie, the gene expression profiles in acne patients were studied in order to identify the specific genes involved in inflammatory acne (Trivedi et al., 2006). Skin biopsies were obtained from an inflammatory papule and from normal skin in six patients with acne. Biopsies were also taken from normal skin of six subjects without acne. Gene array expression profiling was led to compare lesional with nonlesional skin in acne patients, and nonlesional skin from acne patients with skin from normal subjects. This experiment studied gene expression changes in inflammatory acne lesions and potential therapeutic targets in inflammatory acne.

To characterize the molecular effects of IL-1 in epidermis, the GSE9120 serie studied the human epidermal keratinocytes treated with IL-1a compared to control cells at 1h, 4h, 24h, and 48h time points (Yano et al., 2008). This comparative analysis was led for comprehensive investigations defining the targets of IL-1 in epidermal keratinocytes and understanding the nature of the inflammatory response and the gene products that mediate the effects of IL-1 in these cells.

Procedure of Integration

The variability in experimental environments such as RNA sources, micro-array production, or the

Table 2. Characteristics of example datasets

Series	Affymetrix	Data Type	Nb of probesets	Description	Size
GSE6281	U133 Plus 2.0	Raw Data	54675	Contact Allergy	34
GSE7216	U133 Plus 2.0	Raw Data	54675	IL-10 Cytokine Family	25
GSE6475	U133A 2.0	Raw Data	22277	ACNE	18
GSE9120	U133A 2.0	Raw Data	22277	Keratinocytes+I1b	8

use of different platforms, can cause bias because of distortion among distribution, scale of intensity expression, etc. Such systematic differences present a substantial obstacle to the analysis of micro-array data, which may result in inconsistent and unreliable information. Therefore, one of the most pressing challenges in meta-analyses is how to integrate results from different micro-array experiments or combine data sets prior to the specific analysis. In general, in order to perform efficiently the meta-analysis, the procedure of combining independent datasets falls into three steps detailed below: identification of common probesets, normalization and transformation of distribution.

Identifying a List of Common Probesets

Since data sets come from different chips or different platforms, it is essential to guarantee that same probesets (homonyms) in combined data match identical (or approximately identical) oligo sequences. To obtain a more stringent subset of matched probesets/sequences, mapping common genes on the basis of probeset sequences comparison is more reliable and conservative. Only common probesets that share the same target sequences are selected in datasets (Jiang et al., 2004).

Per Data Normalization

Differences in treatment of two samples, especially in labelling and in hybridization, bias the relative measures on any two arrays. Individual normalization of data sets is done to compensate for systematic technical differences between data samples within a same data set, to see more clearly the systematic biological differences between samples. (Jiang et al., 2004) proposed the simplest method for per chip normalization in which the expression of each probe set in each array was divided by the median of the data. But normalization of individual data sets is generally

performed via known existing methods. Standard procedures as RMA (Robust Multiarray Analysis) or LOWESS (Cleveland and Devlin, 1979) are frequently used and provide more robust normalizations (see section "MICRO-ARRAYS EXPERIMENTS").

Distribution Transformation

After per chip normalization, scales and distributions of two data sets may still be different. Data distributions vary greatly between two raw and even normalized data sets. Therefore, a distribution transformation method is needed to ensure data sets similar distribution before combining them (Jiang et al., 2004, Kim et al., 2007).

A simple transformation method is to transform the gene expression ratios of each data set on the basis of a *reference data* by the pooled standard deviation and mean expression values to have similar expression patterns in corresponding experimental group (Kim et al., 2007). For instance, one of data sets is selected to be the reference. Then each other data is transformed on the basis of this reference. (Jiang et al., 2004) proposed a distribution transformation based on a Cumulative *Distribution Function* (CDF) that transforms each data set Y according to the following equation:

$$z = F_X^{-1}(F_Y(x)),$$

where X is the reference and $F_X(x)$ and $F_Y(x)$ are respective distribution functions.

Consequently Z and X have the same distribution.

Once integration and transformation is processed, statistical analyses may be driven on these new data. The two following subsections are devoted to this subject.

Identifying Differentially Expressed Genes

Recently, several propositions (Hong and Breitling, 2008, Hu et al., 2006, Rhodes et al., 2002, Kim et al., 2007) have shown potential solutions to overcome the challenges in computational meta-analysis. Rhodes et *al.* (Rhodes et al., 2002) applied a meta-analysis via Fisher's inverse χ^2 test by combining *p-values* results associated with four datasets on prostate cancer. They tried to determine genes that are differentially expressed between clinically localized prostate and benign tissue. The method validated and confirmed sets of significantly similar genes across studies. (Choi and Kim, 2003) used a standard *t*-test statistic, defined as *effect size* to identify differentially expressed genes, as the summary statistic for each gene from each individual dataset. They then proposed a hierarchical modelling approach to assess both intra- and inter-study variation in the summary statistic across multiple datasets. This model-based method estimated an overall effect size as the measurement of the magnitude of differential expression for each gene through parameter estimation and model fitting.

Besides these two approaches on p-values and effect size, (Hu et al., 2006) compared a quality-weighted strategy with the traditional quality-unweighted strategy, and examined how the quality weights influence two commonly used meta-analysis methods: combining p-values and combining effect size estimates. This study demonstrated that the quality-weighted strategy can lead to larger statistical power for identifying differentially expressed genes than the quality-unweighted strategy and that the combination of multiple datasets identifies many more differentially expressed genes than individual analysis of either of the datasets.

In summary, p-values and effect size approaches that have been employed in meta-analyses for differential gene expression analysis are fitted to very similar studies where differential expression refer to similar pairs of conditions over studies. This is an important limitation.

Approaches in Classification

Data mining and machine learning methods including classification methods and clustering techniques have been proposed to analyse multiple expression datasets (Jiang et al., 2004, Lee et al., 2004). (Jiang et al., 2004) used a Random Forest method and Fisher's Linear Discrimination (FLD) to select lung adenocarcinoma marker genes from two different gene expression data sets in order to predict normal and patient samples. Fisher's Linear Discrimination is a traditional classification method that has computational efficiency, while Random Forest is based on growing a set of decision trees on bootstrapped samples. (Lee et al., 2004) presented a co-expression link method for studying the functional relevance and reproducibility of the co-expression patterns from an analysis of gene co-expression in the large-scale analysis of mRNA co-expression of 60 large human data sets (3924 micro-arrays) from the Stanford micro-array Database[16] (SMD) and the Gene Expression Omnibus. The principle of co-expression link method is that a gene has a co-expression link if it has same profile across at least two data sets. After filtering, each gene expression profile was compared to all others using the standard Pearson correlation coefficient. A co-expression link between two genes was confirmed if the link was observed in more than one data set. The authors found that a substantial number of correlated expression patterns occur in multiple independent data sets. This confirmation of correlated expression provides a useful way to improve the confidence in any particular correlated expression pattern. This study showed that co-expression patterns that are confirmed are more likely to be functionally relevant.

Table 3 summaries all these existing methods for meta-analyses.

Table 3. Summary of the methods of meta-analysis

Paper	Chip	Statistical Method	Data Mining
(Hong and Breitling, 2008)	Simulated data	Fischer's χ^2, Effect size, Rank Product	
(Hu et al., 2006)	Affymetrix	Fischer's χ^2, Effect size,	
(Jiang et al., 2004)	Affymetrix	FLD	Hierarch. Clust., Rand. Forest
(Kim et al., 2007)		ANOVA	Hierarch. Clust.
(Lee et al., 2004)	Affymetrix		Coexpression, GO
(Rhodes et al., 2002)	Affymetrix	Fischer's χ^2,	
(Moreau et al., 2003)	Review	P_{min}, Fischer's χ^2,	

In summary, in this subsection, we have discussed different approaches for analyzing combined gene expression data. We can observe that the experiments that are mentioned involve very identical studies and micro-arrays technologies. In the next section, we present experimental tests that confirm these limits.

Experimental Tests

As seen above, the variability in experimental environments such as RNA sources, micro-array production, or the use of different platforms, can cause biases because of variations among distributions, scale of intensity expression, etc. Such systematic differences present a substantial obstacle to the co-analysis of multiple micro-array data, resulting in inconsistent and unreliable information.

In this section we present experimental tests that combine data from identical Affymetrix chips. It is organized in three subsections. In the first and the second subsections we show that in this special condition, we may apply a quite simple technique to combine data. Then in the third subsection, we describe interesting tests on combined Affymetrix data sets; we present comparative tests between individual analyses and meta-analyses combining different expression datasets that demonstrate how carefully the last ones have to be considered.

RMA-Based Transformation and Integration

With Affymetrix micro-arrays, various methods have been proposed for transforming and normalizing gene expression arrays. Here we use the RMA method (described previously) that is based on quantile transformation for the transformation of distribution. This transformation gives the same distribution to each array by taking the mean quantile and substituting it as the value of the data item in the original arrays. We applied it for transforming combined Affymetrix datasets in order to obtain the same distribution. Let us assume that we have J datasets from identical Affymetrix chips, then the algorithm for data integration and transformation is described by the following steps:

1. build the X array of dimension $N \times J$ where each array is a column,
2. sort each column of X to give X_{sort}
3. compute each row mean in X_{sort} and assign this mean to each element in the row to get X'_{sort}
4. compute $X_{normalized}$ by rearranging each column of X'_{sort} to have the same ordering as original X

The example below illustrates the method.

Example 1

1. Sort columns of original matrix:

$$x = \begin{bmatrix} 4 & 7 & 2 & 9 \\ 5 & 2 & 8 & 5 \\ 1 & 3 & 5 & 8 \\ 8 & 2 & 3 & 4 \end{bmatrix} \Rightarrow x_{sort} = \begin{bmatrix} 1 & 2 & 2 & 4 \\ 4 & 2 & 3 & 5 \\ 5 & 3 & 5 & 8 \\ 8 & 7 & 8 & 9 \end{bmatrix}$$

2. Compute row means:

$$x_{sort} = \begin{bmatrix} 1 & 2 & 2 & 4 \\ 4 & 2 & 3 & 5 \\ 5 & 3 & 5 & 8 \\ 8 & 7 & 8 & 9 \end{bmatrix} \Rightarrow \begin{bmatrix} 2.25 \\ 3.50 \\ 5.25 \\ 8.00 \end{bmatrix}$$

3. Set mean for all columns:

$$\begin{bmatrix} 2.25 \\ 3.50 \\ 5.25 \\ 8.00 \end{bmatrix} \Rightarrow x'_{sort} = \begin{bmatrix} 2.25 & 2.25 & 2.25 & 2.25 \\ 3.50 & 3.50 & 3.50 & 3.50 \\ 5.25 & 5.25 & 5.25 & 5.25 \\ 8.00 & 8.00 & 8.00 & 8.00 \end{bmatrix}$$

4. Unsort columns to original order:

$$x'_{sort} = \begin{bmatrix} 2.25 & 2.25 & 2.25 & 2.25 \\ 3.50 & 3.50 & 3.50 & 3.50 \\ 5.25 & 5.25 & 5.25 & 5.25 \\ 8.00 & 8.00 & 8.00 & 8.00 \end{bmatrix} \Rightarrow x_{normalized} = \begin{bmatrix} 3.50 & 8.00 & 2.25 & 8.00 \\ 5.25 & 2.25 & 8.00 & 3.50 \\ 2.25 & 5.25 & 5.25 & 5.25 \\ 8.00 & 3.50 & 3.50 & 2.25 \end{bmatrix}$$

This method of distribution transformation is robust, simple and easy for application. While other methods only perform the distribution transformation for two datasets, the advantage of RMA is that it allows combining multiple individual datasets and normalizing them globally. The following section presents a comparative study that gives a proof of its efficiency.

Comparative Study

Here, we compare the RMA-based integration method proposed above with the CDF reported in (Jiang et al., 2004). A two-sample Kolmogorov-Smirnov test is used to compare the distribution (repartition) of the data combined by CDF and the data combined by RMA-based procedure described in the previous subsection. The test provides the maximal distance between two samples. In this test, we obtained a distance before and after combining the data that was around $D = 0.07$ with p-value$<2.2e^{-16}$. This result demonstrates similar results between CDF and our RMA-based procedure on these data. We combined data of the Affymetrix GSE6475 and GSE9120 series (described previously in this chapter). Figure 2 that plots intensity densities on two different data samples, shows three curves for each sample:

1. the "*single data via RMA*" curve represents GSE6475 data transformed via standard RMA normalization,
2. the "*meta data via RMA*" curve represents GSE6475 data combined and transformed in a meta-analysis way with GSE9120 data via a RMA-based transformation as described in the previous subsection,
3. the "*meta data via CFD*" curve represents GSE6475 data combined and transformed in a meta-analysis way with GSE9120 data via a CFD transformation as described in the previous subsection on "Procedure of integration".

We can observe that RMA and CFD transformations give results very close one to the other.

In fact, the quantile normalization method used in RMA is a specific case of the CDF transformation $z = F_X^{-1}(F_Y(x))$, where we estimate F_Y by empirical distribution of each array and F_X using the empirical distribution of averaged sample quantiles. However, our procedure does

Figure 2. Transformed distribution comparison between data density in single GSE6475 data (1) and combined GSE6475-GSE9120 transformed via RMA (2) and CDF (3) on two samples

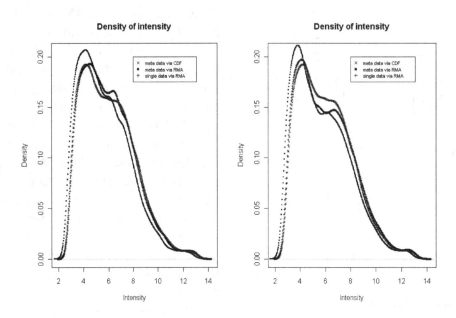

not need the individual normalization (per chip normalization) and per gene normalization. It directly takes the raw data CEL files of the raw data set and uses only one time the RMA procedure. That is the simplest procedure and reduces the complexity time of computation while returning similar results.

Furthermore we have led another test: from the combined GSE6475-GSE9120 data transformed via RMA and CDF, we have looked for differential expressed genes between ACNE and Normal Skin within GSE6475 data. Table 4 provides results on differential expressed genes found in these data. The third and fourth columns give the number of differential expressed genes found when using CDF and RMA. The fifth column indicates the number of differentially expressed genes found in both cases. We can observe that differentially expressed genes given by both methods are identical in a great majority.

In the following section, we present results of meta-analyses combining Affymetrix data that are transformed with the RMA-based method described above.

Tests on Human Skin Allergic Data

In this section, we show experimental results obtained when comparing individual analyses with meta-analyses on gene expression. Our goal is to observe if individual analysis results are retrieved when data are combined into a meta-analysis. We show that the statistical relevance of meta-analyses is only significant when raw expression data are combined and then normalized.

We have conducted several tests on meta-analyses combining the series GSE6281 and GSE7216 as an example to ensure more reliability in identification of human skin reaction biomarkers. We detail below results obtained with a meta-analysis on GSE6281 and GSE7216 series for differential expression search. GSE6281 datasets provide gene expression between time points (0h, 7h, 48h, 96h) over *control* subject and *patient* subject and GSE7216 datasets provide gene expression between *IL-10* family of cytokines in reconstituted human epidermis and control subject. Both are resulting from experiments on the same Affymetrix chip HG-U133 Plus 2.0 Array. Such

Table 4. Comparison CDF versus RMA via elicitation of differentially expressed genes

Data	Comparison	CDF	RMA	Gene in common
GSE6475 with RMA normalization	ACNE-NormalSkin	223	239	216
GSE6475 with Median normalization	ACNE-NormalSkin	214	239	213

an integration of datasets in a meta-analysis would be useful to confirm the relevance of individual analyses on specific Nickel-allergy biomarkers or on reconstituted skin reactions for instance. We present a first test on pre-normalized expression data and a second one on raw data as CEL files that are normalized after combination. For differential expression analysis, we used a one-way ANOVA (Analysis Of VAriance) via linear regression model, defined as in section "MICRO-ARRAYS EXPERIMENTS", to identify a set of differentially expressed genes between two different groups of samples, the treatment group (Test) and untreated control (Control) group.

These tests show that combining data may introduce much noise since in these meta-analyses, we do not retrieve afterwards previous results of individual analyses obtained from each dataset separately. Furthermore results presented below show that it is very important to combine raw CEL data rather than pre-normalized data sets.

Integration of Normalized Datasets

We had previously conducted individual analyses on GSE6281 datasets in order to extract differentially expressed genes on:

- *control* subject at 7h compared to 0h
- *control* subject at 48h compared to 7h
- *patient* subject at 7h compared to 0h
- *patient* subject at 48h compared to 7h

Here we compared meta-analysis results with individual analysis by a one-way ANOVA. In Table 5 we can observe:

- in the second column, the number of differentially expressed genes elicited by individual analyses on GSE6281 data only in each of the four cases,
- in the third column, the number of differentially expressed genes elicited by a meta-analysis combining pre-normalized GSE6281 and GSE7216 data in each of the four cases (we applied the RMA-based transformation method presented previously),
- in the fourth column, the number of differentially expressed genes common in the two previous lists.

We used the same *p*-value and fold change for each of these comparisons.

We observe an important dissimilarity between individual and meta analysis: a large number of

Table 5. Comparison of differentially expressed genes elicited by an individual analysis on GSE6281 and a meta-analysis on pre-normalized data of GSE6281-GSE7216 series

Comparison	Individual analysis	Meta-analysis	Gene in common
control-7h/0h	219	353	142
control-48h/7h	15	59	7
patient-7h/0h	223	413	146
patient-48h/7h	3069	5238	2849

genes is lost, the expressed genes are not coherent. One explanation comes from the method of transformation distribution that results in two normalizations. Another reason could be on the inadequacy of data to be combined.

Table 6 gives similar results on GSE7216 data. We had previously conducted similar individual analyses on GSE7216 datasets in order to extract differentially expressed genes for the cytokines on reconstituted skin compared to control. We observe an important distortion again.

These results demonstrate that meta-analyses combining pre-normalized datasets may provide unreliable information.

Integration of Raw Data and Normalization

In this test we combined raw data from GSE6281 CEL files (34 files) and GSE7216 CEL files (25 files). We used the Bioconductor[17] package *affy* to read CEL files and to normalize them globally with RMA procedure by quantile normalization as shown previously in the subsection on "RMA-based transformation and integration".

On Table 7 and Table 8 that compare new meta-analyses and previous individual analyses with the same *p*-value and fold change, we have:

- in the second column, the number of differentially expressed genes elicited by individual analyses on GSE6281 and GSE7216 data only in each of the four cases,
- in the third column, the number of differentially expressed genes elicited by a meta-analysis combining raw CEL data of GSE6281 and GSE7216 series in each of the four cases (we applied the RMA-based transformation method),
- in the fourth column, the number of differentially expressed genes common in the two previous lists.

While meta-analysis results are closer to individual ones, we still find an important distortion in genes found in common.

This first test on the integration of only two individual data series conducted on the same gene chip shows how meta-analyses should be conducted carefully. Integrating pre-normalized data may be irrelevant. For Affymetrix series, CEL raw data are more adequate for combination. When datasets result from different gene chips, further problems occur: it becomes essential to guarantee that probe sets on different chips correspond to identical (or approximate identical) oligo sequences. In such cases, meta-analyses must pre-process data with probeset sequence

Table 6. Comparison of differentially expressed genes elicited by an individual analysis on GSE7216 and a meta-analysis on pre-normalized data of GSE6281-GSE7216 series

Comparison	Individual analysis	Meta-analysis	Gene in common
IL19-control	82	1103	70
IL20-control	207	1438	192
IL22-control	606	2608	576
IL24-control	363	2020	347
IL26d-control	0	858	0
KGF-control	224	1619	197
IFNg-control	253	1875	248
IL1b-control	214	2121	196

Table 7. Comparison of differentially expressed genes elicited by an individual analysis on GSE6281 and a meta-analysis combining raw CEL data of GSE6281-GSE7216 series

Comparison	Individual analysis	Meta-analysis	Gene in common
control-7h/0h	219	280	142
control-48h/7h	15	42	8
patient-7h/0h	223	308	164
patient-48h/7h	3069	4655	2798

Table 8. Comparison of differentially expressed genes elicited by an individual analysis on GSE7216 and a meta-analysis combining raw CEL data of GSE6281-GSE7216 series

Comparison	Individual analysis	Meta-analysis	Gene in common
IL19-control	82	90	77
IL20-control	207	247	189
IL22-control	606	701	580
IL24-control	363	429	349
IL26d-control	0	2	0
KGF-control	224	254	202
IFNg-control	253	291	242
IL1b-control	214	267	199

comparison and select common probe sets only for data integration (Jiang2004).

In summary, in this section, we have introduced issues of gene expression meta-analyses that concern mainly the integration of heterogeneous data. We have observed that their statistical relevance is only effective when data are coming from very identical studies and micro-arrays technologies, thus motivating the design of a tool like AMI that allows to leading meta-analyses at a more synthetic level. Indeed the AMI framework will allow either to drive standard meta-analyses on gene expression data (as described in this section) or to start from preliminary results (synthetic data) provided by individual statistical analyses and to mine them for extracting potentially interesting knowledge. In the next section, we give details on the representation and the storage of these various data types in AMI.

EXPRESSION DATA, SYNTHETIC DATA AND METADATA

This section is dedicated to the representation and the storage of raw data on gene expression intensity (first subsection), to synthetic or refined data that result from previous analyses on raw expression data (second subsection) and to metadata that are one important underlying support to semantic capabilities in AMI (third subsection). These data are stored in the AMI knowledge base as detailed below.

Representation of Expression Data

One goal of the AMI data warehouse is to give the capability to store raw datasets (represented by (4) in Figure 1) that contain gene expression intensities and to explore more deeply original experimental results with further so called *in silico* individual or meta analyses. These data may be downloaded from public repositories or may be the result of local experiments.

Representation of Statistical Results

As stated in the AMI overview, another main goal in designing the semantic AMI data warehouse is to provide the capability to keep in memory synthetic data that are provided by statistical analyses, and in a way that should facilitate information retrieval on fuzzy and semantic criteria. In a first stage, we plan to consider two kinds of statistical and data mining results that are differential gene expression between two given conditions and clustering models on gene expression intensities. Differential gene expression are stored into relational tables and clustering models are stored as XML representations (represented by (5) in Figure 1); each of them is discussed in following paragraphs.

Differentially Expressed Genes

While gene expression data table have much more lines (genes) than columns (conditions), for instance 50000 genes for 50 conditions, analyses of pair-wise differentially expression among conditions provide huge amount of resulting data too. Search for differentially expressed genes is frequently processed by one-way or two-ways ANOVA algorithms. As presented previously (see section "MICRO-ARRAYS EXPERIMENTS"), an ANOVA method will provide results as a list of genes with their p-values over two conditions.

For instance Table 9 gives an excerpt of ANOVA results for the search of differentially expressed genes between gene expressions at 7h and at 0h on *Control* conditions in the GSE6281 series described previously. The first three columns give information on the gene probeset, the fourth column gives the intensity ratio between conditions, the fifth column give the p-value and the last column give the differential expression level (+, - for up- or down- regulation) deduced from a threshold.

In AMI, we keep only synthetic data obtained from p-values and fold-change that indicates up- and down- regulation of genes over two conditions. These data are stored in relational tables like raw expression intensity data.

Data Mining Models of Gene Expressions

For storage and intelligent retrieval of data mining models, standard representation formats like XML and PMML and semantic annotations formats like RDF are perfectly fitted to AMI requirements. The Predictive Model Markup Language (PMML) is an XML-based language that provides a way for applications to define statistical and data mining models and to share models between PMML compliant applications. It was defined by the Data Mining Group[18]. In this section, we present PMML extensions we have defined for clustering models. RDF annotations are detailed in next sections. A PMML clustering model as illustrated by Figure

Table 9. Example of results after an ANOVA on gene expression

Probe	Symbol	Description	Fold change7h/0h	p-value7h/0h	Exp
240717_at	ABCB5	ATP-binding cassette sub-family B (MDR/TAP)	0.5235	0.01219	+
232081_at	ABCG1	ATP-binding cassette sub-family G (WHITE)	1.6253	0.00124	-
...	...	...	...	...	...

3 is defined as a quite rich sequence of elements and attributes among which we are interested with: *ComparisonMeasure* for the distance or similarity measure used for clustering, *ClusteringField* for attributes on which the clustering is based, Cluster} for describing each resulting cluster, *modelName, modelClass, algorithmName* and *numberOfClusters*. In the example shown in Figure 3, we only keep these ones.

A cluster model basically consists of a set of clusters. The standard PMML representation of clusters is rather simple but extensions may be defined thanks to the element *Extension*.

We have extended this PMML representation for hierarchical clustering. One required evaluation of clustering models on gene expression is to check the semantic meaning of clusters. Indeed, when clusters of genes are elicited, one main issue is to check their soundness and understand the common characteristics of their items (genes). One obvious way is to search for genes that were annotated by domain ontologies like GO.

Let us consider as examples, the two clusters *Cluster_GSE6281_hclust_1* and *Cluster_GSE6281_hclust_2* that were elicited from

GSE6281 data when searching for co-expressed genes. We applied a hierarchical clustering model which clusters gather genes that have similar expression profiles over the 4 time points: 0h, 7h, 48h and 96h. Figures 4 and 5 provide a description of each cluster with: in the column *Probe* the probeset name, in the column *Symbol* the gene name and in the third column the gene description for each cluster. We observe for instance that cluster *Cluster_GSE6281_hclust_1* includes genes CCL5, CCL19, CCL22 that are chemokines.

GO annotations that annotate the most part of genes in each cluster are shown partly in Figures 6 and 7. Each cluster is annotated by a list of its most descriptive GO concepts. For each GO concept, the number of genes annotated and the annotation frequency in the cluster are given. These figures illustrate cluster annotations from the *Molecular function* GO ontology only.

The PMML extension we defined provides:

- the list of gene names in the cluster,
- and the list of GO concepts that annotate its genes ; annotations are split according to the three ontologies in GO (''Molecular

Figure 3. Cluster representation in PMML

```
<xs:element name="ClusteringModel">
  <xs:complexType>
    <xs:sequence>
      ...
      <xs:element ref="ComparisonMeasure"/>
      <xs:element ref="ClusteringField" .../>
      <xs:element ref="Cluster" .../>
      ...
    </xs:sequence>
    <xs:attribute name="modelName" .../>
    <xs:attribute name="algorithmName" .../>
    <xs:attribute name="modelClass" ...>
      ...
    <xs:attribute name="numberOfClusters" type="INT-NUMBER" use="required"/>
  </xs:complexType>
</xs:element>
```

function}", "Biological process}" and "Cellular component}"). Each concept is associated to its frequency in the cluster.

In Figure 8, we can observe that cluster *Cluster_GSE6281_hclust_1* annotation contains the two concepts GO:0005198 and GO:0043531 that are the most descriptive for it ; they refer to "*cytoskeleton*" and "*nucleotide binding*". As stated above, the PMML representation keeps the information on the number of occurrences for each annotation and frequency in the cluster. For instance 10 genes among the 26 genes into the cluster are annotated by "*cytoskeleton*" and 4 only with "*nucleotide binding*". Theses annotations provide the semantic meaning of each cluster and are essential for a comprehensive of the investigator.

In this section, we have presented how XML may be used to represent synthetic results of data analyses. In the next section, we show how semantic aspects that represent the domain knowledge may be represented by metadata via ontologies.

Metadata on Differentially Expressed Genes and Genes Clusters

Ontologies provide an organizational framework of concepts and a system of hierarchical and associative relationships for a domain. They are useful for reuse and sharing and moreover the formal structure coupled with hierarchies of concepts and relations between concepts offers the opportunity to draw complex inferences and reasoning. In AMI, we reused the existing ontology MeatOnto (Khelif et al., 2007) to annotate

Figure 4. Cluster_GSE6281_hclust_1

Probe	Symbol	Description
209309_at	AZGP1	alpha-2-glycoprotein 1, zinc-binding
216935_at	C1orf46	chromosome 1 open reading frame 46
217087_at	C1orf68	chromosome 1 open reading frame 68
210072_at	CCL19	chemokine (C-C motif) ligand 19
207861_at	CCL22	chemokine (C-C motif) ligand 22
1405_i_at	CCL5	chemokine (C-C motif) ligand 5
206149_at	CHP2	calcineurin B homologous protein 2
219529_at	CLIC3	chloride intracellular channel 3
231930_at	ELMOD1	ELMO/CED-12 domain containing 1
221950_at	EMX2	empty spiracles homeobox 2
220276_at	FLJ22655	hypothetical protein FLJ22655
203697_at	FRZB	frizzled-related protein
203698_s_at	FRZB	frizzled-related protein
1568983_a_at	GABPB2	GA binding protein transcription factor, beta subunit 2
221470_s_at	IL1F7	interleukin 1 family, member 7 (zeta)
201124_at	ITGB5	integrin, beta 5
1568617_a_at	KIAA1543	KIAA1543
237120_at	KRT77	keratin 77
207710_at	LCE2B	late cornified envelope 2B
1557570_a_at	LOC285084	hypothetical protein LOC285084
207720_at	LOR	loricrin
207114_at	LY6G6C	lymphocyte antigen 6 complex, locus G6C
228885_at	MAMDC2	MAM domain containing 2
1554195_a_at	MGC23985	similar to AVLV472
213568_at	OSR2	odd-skipped related 2 (Drosophila)
226435_at	PAPLN	papilin, proteoglycan-like sulfated glycoprotein

Figure 5. Cluster_GSE6281_hclust_2 excerpt

Probe	Symbol	Description
1569410_at	RP1-14N1.3	filaggrin 2
206177_s_at	ARG1	arginase, liver
207324_s_at	DSC1	desmocollin 1
209292_at	ID4	inhibitor of DNA binding 4
210426_x_at	RORA	RAR-related orphan receptor A
210479_s_at	RORA	RAR-related orphan receptor A
213369_at	PCDH21	protocadherin 21
215704_at	FLG	filaggrin
220414_at	CALML5	calmodulin-like 5
223816_at	SLC46A2	solute carrier family 46, member 2
229254_at	MFSD4	major facilitator superfamily domain containing 4
232459_at	CYBRD1	cytochrome b reductase 1
232530_at	PLD1	phospholipase D1, phosphatidylcholine-specific

Figure 6. Most frequent GO annotations in Cluster_GSE6281_hclust_1

GO ID	Description	Occurence Number	Frequency
GO:0005198	cytoskeleton	10	0.3846
GO:0043531	nucleotide binding	4	0.1538
GO:0005515	cytoskeleton organization and biogenesis	2	0.0769
GO:0005507	protein modification process	2	0.0769

Figure 7. Most frequent GO annotations in Cluster_GSE6281_hclust_2

GO ID	Description	Occurence Number	Frequency
GO:0004190	skin development	33	0.037
GO:0005044	membrane	26	0.029
GO:0008186	ATP binding	26	0.029
GO:0051020	membrane	26	0.029
GO:0008396	cholesterol catabolic process	24	0.027
GO:0004931	apoptosis	18	0.020

biomedical publications and we developed two new ontologies: GEOnto for experiments and conditions, and GMineOnto to annotate statistical and mining results on numeric experimental data. These annotations provide descriptive metadata stored in the AMI knowledge base (represented by (3) in Figure 1).

MeatOnto

MeatOnto (Khelif et al., 2007) is devoted to concepts related to biomedical literature resources. Briefly, it is based on two sub-ontologies: UMLS semantic network that integrates the Gene Ontology enriched by more specific relations to describe the biomedical domain (biomedical concepts and their interrelations), and DocOnto that describes

Figure 8. Cluster extended PMML representation in AMI

```
<ClusteringModel modelName="Clustering_GSE6281_hclust_1"
        functionName="hierarchical_clustering" algorithmName="hclust"
        modelClass="agglomerative" numberOfClusters="5">
        <MiningSchema>
                <MiningField name="0h" usageType="active"/>
                <MiningField name="7h" usageType="active"/>
                <MiningField name="48h" usageType="active"/>
                <MiningField name="96h" usageType="active"/>
        </MiningSchema>
        <ComparisonMeasure kind="correlation"/>
        <Cluster name="Cluster_GSE6281_hclust_1" size="26">
                <Extension>
                        <X-GeneList>
                                AZGP, C1orf46, C1orf68, CCL19, CCL22, CCL5,
                                CHP2, CLIC3, ELMOD ...
                        </X-GeneList>
                        <X-AnnotationList ontology="go" type="Molecular Function" >
                                <X-Annot GO:0005198 nboccu=10 freq= 0.2333/>
                                <X-Annot GO:0043531 nboccu=4   freq=0.1/>
                                . . .           ...
                        </X-AnnotationList>
                        <X-AnnotationList ontology="go" type="Biological Process">
                        ....
                        </X-AnnotationList>
                        <X-AnnotationList ontology="go" type="Cellular Component">
                        ....
                        </X-AnnotationList>

                </Extension>
        </Cluster>

        <Cluster name="2" size="884">
        ...
        </Cluster>
</ClusteringModel>
```

metadata about scientific publications and links documents to UMLS concepts.

GEOnto

GEOnto (Gene Experiment Ontology) allows describing an overall micro-array experiments (e.g. PubmedId, keywords...) and its experimental conditions (exp. sample, treatment...). GEOnto concepts are also defined in ontologies such as MGED or OBI (mentioned in section "STANDARD META-ANALYSES OF DNA MICRO-ARRAYS"), but they are differently structured in GEOnto. Indeed,

the goal of MGED and OBI is to describe all the design of an investigation (protocols and instrumentation used, material used, data generated and kind of analysis performed), while the goal of GEOnto is to describe experimental conditions fitted for a semantic search.

GEOnto includes a set of general concepts that are applicable across various biological domains (in vivo, inductor, subject, sample, etc.) and domain-specific concepts that are relevant only to a given domain. In a first step, we limit it to dermatology (skin, eczema, contact dermatitis, etc.) but GEOnto can be extended towards other biologic fields.

To build GEOnto, we rely on:

- a corpora of experiment descriptions used to pick out candidate terms (e.g. "*bioSample*", "*treatment*", "*patch test*", etc.),
- dialogs with biologists for organizing the concepts and validate the proposed ontology (e.g. "*patch test*" is a "*topical delivery*" which is a "*delivery method*" and a "*treatment*" is "*delivered via*" a "*delivery method*"),
- existing ontologies UMLS and OntoDerm (Eapen, 2008) to extract specific concepts (e.g. UMLS was used to enrich the concept *cell of the epidermis* and OntoDerm to enrich the concept *derm disease*)

Figure 9 presents some concepts and relationships of GEOnto.

GMineOnto

GMineOnto provides concepts for the description of models that result of data mining algorithms application on gene expression data. In this first stage, we focus on clustering models. Concepts defined by GMineOnto describe the clustering method, process and tool, and the set of clusters discovered. External domain ontologies like GO are linked with GMineOnto by the relationship between a cluster and one of their most descriptive concepts. As presented previously, the PMML representation of a given cluster includes all semantic annotations and their frequency into the cluster. These annotations are thoroughly used for cluster interpretation. GMineOnto relationship between a cluster and an external concept allows annotating a cluster with its most descriptive and discriminative characteristics. Figure 10 gives a fragment of the ontology where external concepts are in grey.

Figure 9. Fragment of GEOnto

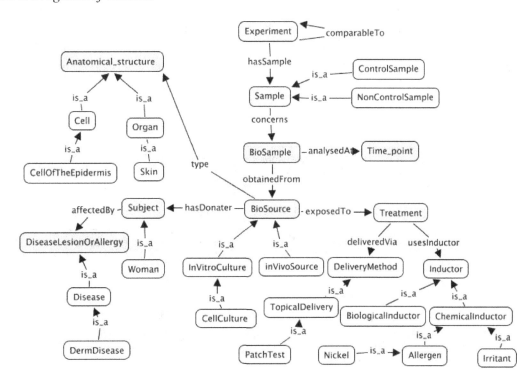

In summary, in this section, we have first described which synthetic data are stored and semantically annotated in the AMI data warehouse. We have presented the underlying ontologies that support the annotation process.

SEMANTIC WEB TECHNOLOGIES FOR META-ANALYSES

One of the originalities of the AMI approach is to take advantage of semantic annotations, about expression data and related information, for querying the AMI knowledge base. This section is organized in two subsections. The first subsection details the different kinds of annotations in AMI and the second subsection shows how they are involved in a semantic search among data.

Semantic Annotations

Annotating a resource tends to associate the most relevant descriptive information to it. Here we detail the AMI approach for annotating the different types of resources (see AMI Annotation&Storing Tools in Figure 1). This includes annotations on scientific papers, on micro-array experiments, on statistic and data mining results and on the implicit

knowledge of biologists. These annotations are detailed in the subsections below.

Annotation of Scientific Papers

Here is an example of a sentence extracted from a scientific paper:

"In vitro assays demonstrated that only p38alpha and p38beta are inhibited by csaids." Our purpose is to extract, from this sentence, relevant biomedical concepts and the relationship expressed between these concepts.

AMI reuses here an existing module called MeatAnnot (Khelif et al., 2007). Starting from a scientific paper, MeatAnnot generates a structured annotation, based on the MeatOnto ontology, which describes interactions between genes/proteins and other concepts. The annotation process consists on three steps:

(i) Instances of MeatOnto concepts and relationships are detected in the sentence: "*p38alpha*" and "*p38beta*" are detected as instances of the concept "*Gene_or_Genome*", "*csaids*" is detected as instance of the concept "*Pharmacologic_Substance*",

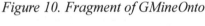

Figure 10. Fragment of GMineOnto

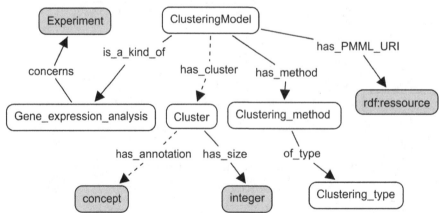

and an instance of the relation *"inhibits"* is detected in the sentence of the given example,

(ii) Concepts instances are linked by a relationship according to the ontology and grammatical structure: the instances *"p38alpha"* and *"p38beta"* (subjects of the verb to inhibit) are linked to the instance *"csaids"* (object of the verb to inhibit) by the relationship *"inhibits"*,

(iii) A structured annotation describing this interaction is generated as shown on Figure 11.

Annotation of Genomic Experiments

Here is an example of an experiment description given in natural language:

"The experiment has the accession number GSE6281 in the GEO repository. It is referred in a published article (PubmedID 17597826) describing this experiment: Gene expression time-course in the human skin during elicitation of allergic contact dermatitis. The type of study is described by the keyword allergic response, and GSM144309 and GSM144311 refer to two samples that make up this experiment. The sample GSM144435 concerns a patch test with 5% nickel sulfate taken from a nickel allergic woman (age range 33-49). The patch test was exposed for 7h immediately followed by a skin biopsy..."

Our purpose is to extract relevant information describing this type of experiment and to use this information to generate semantic annotations based on GEOnto.

We can distinguish two types of experiments: so-called *public* experiments selected by biologists from the public repositories and so-called *local* experiments led directly by the biologist. While local experiments can be easily annotated using a dedicated editor to describe them, it is more difficult to annotate public experiments that are already described in a variety of ways and not necessarily in a usable format. That's why we focused on controlled experiment descriptions: we chose to annotate experiments selected from public repositories supporting MIAME. This kind of repositories allows authors to publish their data in a usable format. For example, experiments submitted to GEO are published in MINiML files. Both MIAME and MINiML are described above in subsection "Standards and ontologies for microarrays experiments". We chose to annotate these files and thus to generate a semantic annotation of the experiment.

Biologists who submit individual MIAME-compliant records to GEO provide their data in three sections: *Platform*, *Samples*, and *Series*.

- A *platform* record describes the micro-array used in the experiment (e.g. Affymetrix GeneChips).

- A *sample* record describes the biological material under examination and the quantification measurements derived from those samples. Sample information is supplied in two sections: (i) a data table that includes normalized quantification measurements from hybridization or SAGE library and

Figure 11. Example of MeatAnnot annotation

```
<meat:Pharmacologic_Substance rdf:about='#csaids'>
    <meat:inhibits><meat:Gene_or_Genome rdf:about='#p38alpha'/></meat:inhibits>
    <meat:inhibits><meat:Gene_or_Genome rdf:about='#p38beta'/></meat:inhibits>
</meat:Pharmacologic_Substance>
```

(ii) descriptive information regarding the biological source material, and the protocols performed in the experiment (e.g. organism, age, treatments...)

- A *serie* record links together a group of related Samples and provides a focal point and description of the study as a whole.

While it is not possible to check automatically if the MINiML information is accurate, the annotation process cannot be completely automated. Indeed, information contained in the *serie* and the *platform* records can be automatically extracted to annotate the study as a whole, since these parts are usually clearly inserted by biologists, but the information contained in the descriptive part of the *sample* records is not easy to process automatically since biologists have no standard syntax to conform.

Thus GEOnto relies on two annotating subprocesses: an automatic one and a semi-automatic one. They are described below (see Figure 12):

- Automatic annotation: general information on the study as a whole is automatically extracted from the MINiML file using XPATH (XPath is a language for addressing parts of an XML document). These data such as title, contributors, PubmedID, type of array, keywords, associated samples/experimental conditions... are used to generate automatically an RDF annotation based on GEOnto.
- Semi-automatic annotation: Information describing each sample record such as subjects (type, age, disease, allergy...) and treatments (inductor, delivery method, delivery time...) is usually not well structured in the MINiML file. For example, the treatment protocol (describing treatments applied to the biological material prior to extract preparation) is most of the time a unique global description repeated for all the sample records. Therefore, it seems to

be impossible to extract automatically the terms describing each treatment protocol and assign them automatically to the corresponding sample records. The solution we chose was to design an annotation editor that:

- Proposes for each concept (e.g. inductor, disease, allergy, subject, age, cell...) all candidate-instances extracted from the MINiML file (e.g. 'nickel' for the concept 'inductor', 'contact dermatitis' for 'disease', 'nickel allergy' for 'allergy'...). The extraction is automatic. Briefly, it is based on a comparison of words in the text with concepts labels in the GEOnto ontology and instances in existing annotations.
- Allows the biologist to complete (by adding relevant terms that have not been extracted) and structure the description of each sample record (experimental condition). For example, a biologist will associate the use of the inductor 'nickel' to the sample 'GSM144435' while the sample 'GSM144362', which uses an empty patch test, will not be associated to an inductor.
- Builds automatically RDF annotations.

RDF annotations obtained from these two sub-processes give a relevant and structured description, based on GEOnto, of what is important to know about the experiment.

Annotation of Statistic Analyses and Data Mining Results

GMineAnnot takes a PMML file as input data and generates semantic annotations about statistic analysis and data mining results models based on GMineOnto. These annotations focus on the

Figure 12. Processing flows in GEAnnot

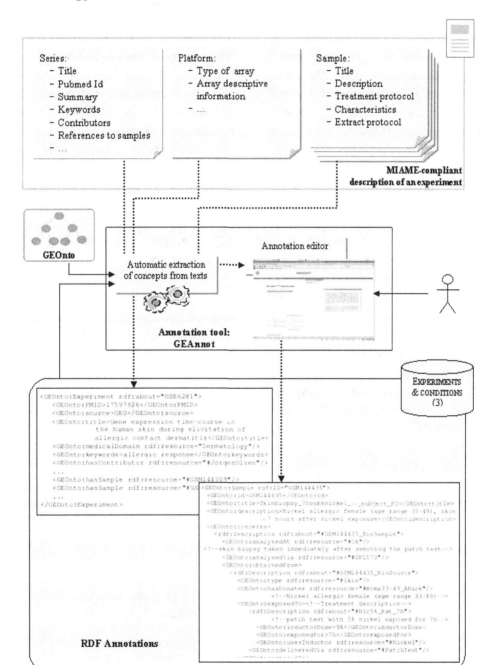

clustering method and on concepts that best describe each cluster. Figure 13 illustrates such an annotation: it concerns the PMML data (described in section "Representation of statistical results") for a gene clustering model on GSE6281 data.

Annotation of Implicit Knowledge

The module KnowAnnot produces annotations describing the implicit background knowledge of biologists. These annotations can reduce silence (non-retrieved answers) in the information retrieval phase.

As shown in Figure 1, information retrieval in the AMI data warehouse relies on the semantic search engine CORESE (Corby et al., 2006). The CORESE rule language is perfectly fitted to this kind of annotations. Indeed, CORESE provides an inference mechanism to deduce new facts from declared annotations. In AMI, rules are a good mean to reflect the implicit expert knowledge. For instance, the following information: *When the sample studied in an experimental condition is taken from a subject affected by psoriasis, then this condition is most likely using the IL22 inductor* is an example of such knowledge that is never explicitly stated while admitted by experts in skin reactions. It would be translated like shown in Figure 14.

One challenge addressed in AMI is to succeed in building a system based on this kind of knowledge rules. In a first stage, biologist background knowledge is collected and coded by an expert.

Semantic Search

The AMI querying tools propose an *intelligent* information retrieval system that retrieves data stored in different types of resources (semantic annotations, databases and XML documents). It is based on the semantic search engine CORESE (Corby et al., 2006) which allows navigating and reasoning on the whole annotation set and takes into account the ontology concept relation hierarchies. New features have been added to CORESE in order to query not only semantic annotations but also data stored in XML documents and in standard databases using XPATH and SQL embedded in SPARQL. Indeed relational and XML data provide relevant supplementary information in addition to RDF annotations.

SQL Embedded in SPARQL: An Example

In many cases, an answer to a user query should combine annotated information with relational and XML data. Let us consider the following query: *"In which others experiments using a Nickel treatment, CCL19 gene is up-regulated"*. In this example, the information about experiments using a Nickel treatment can be found into annotations on experiments, while information about gene CCL19 behaviour (up-regulated) is stored in the relational database.

The idea here is to query the database using SQL embedded in SPARQL. It was introduced

Figure 13. Example of a clustering annotation

```
<GMine:ClusteringModel rdf:about='Clustering_GSE6281_hclust_1'>
    <GMine:hasCluster rdf:resource="#ClusterGSE6281_hclust_1"/>
    <GMine:hasCluster rdf:resource="#ClusterGSE6281_hclust_2"/>
    <GMine:hasMethod rdf:resource="#Clust_Method_12"/>
    <GMine:hasPmml rdf:resource="...uri.../PmmlGSE6281.xml"/>
    <GMine:concerns rdf:resource="&GEOnto;GSE6281"/>
    ...
</GMine:ClusteringModel>
<GMine:Cluster rdf:ID="ClusterGSE6281_hclust_1">
    <GMine:relatedTo rdf:resource="&go;GO0005198 "/>
    <!--'GO:0006955' refers to ' cytoskeleton' in GO-->
    <GMine:relatedTo rdf:resource="&go;GO0043531">
    ...
</GMine:Cluster>
```

Figure 14. Example of a rule describing biologist knowledge

```
IF:      {?c        rdf:type                    GEOnto:ExperimentalCondition
          ?c        GEOnto:concerns             ?s
          ?s        GEOnto:obtainedFrom         ?subj
          ?subj     GEOnto:affectedBy           GEOnto:psoriasis}
THEN: {?s          GEOnto:exposedTo            ?t
          ?t        GEOnto:usesInductor         GEOnto:IL22}
```

in the semantic search engine CORESE, a new function *sql* with four arguments: the database URL, the username, the password and the query. The purpose of this function is to evaluate the SQL query on the given database.

Figure 15 shows the CORESE query that matches the following question: *"In which others experiments using a Nickel treatment, CCL19 gene is up-regulated"*

In this example:

- The SPARQL query retrieves all conditions (*?condition}*) using a Nickel treatment (*?treatment GEOnto:usesInductor GEOnto:Nickel*) and the URI of the database (*?dbURI*) where the information about genes behaviour is stored .
- The sql function evaluates the SQL query (*'SELECT distinct inCondition FROM...'*)

on the referred database *?dbURI* and returns the list of condition URIs where CCL19 gene is up-regulated (*gene='CCL19' and behaviour='up-regulated'*)

- The SPARQL query filters conditions contained into the previous list returned by the SQL clause (*Filter (?condID=sql(...))*.

The result is a list of triples. Each triple contains:

- the experiment URI (e.g. *GSE6281*),
- the condition identifier (e.g. *GSM144309*),
- the description of the condition (e.g. *Female (age range 33-49), skin biopsy from upper dates taken 7 hours after nickel exposure*).

Figure 15. Example of a CORESE query using SQL embedded in SPARQL

```
prefix GEOnto:<http://.../GEOnto#>
Select ?experiment ?cond_id ?desc
where {
    ?experiment      rdf:type                         GEOnto:Experiment
    ?experiment      GEOnto:DB_URI                    ?dbURI
    ?experiment      GEOnto:hasExperimentalCondition  ?condition
    ?condition       GEOnto:id                        ?condID
    ?condition       GEOnto:description               ?desc
    ?condition       GEOnto:concerns                  ?bioSample
    ?bioSample       GEOnto:exposedTo                 ?treatment
    ?treatment       GEOnto:usesInductor              GEOnto:Nickel
Filter(?condID=sql(?dbURI,"log","pwd",
                "SELECT distinct inCondition FROM GENE_BEHAVIOUR
                where gene='CCL19' and behaviour='up-regulated"))
}
```

Figure 16. Example of a CORESE query using XPATH embedded in SPARQL

```
prefix GMine:<http://.../GMine#> go:<http://.../GO#>
Select ?cluster ?expe ?molfunc
Where {
    ?clustering      GMine:hasPmmlURI      ?pmmlURI
    ?clustering      GMine:hasCluster      ?cluster
    ?clustering      GMine:concerns        ?expe
    ?cluster         GMine:relatedTo       ?molfunc
    ?molfunc         rdf:type              go:GO0003674
    Filter(xsd:string(?cluster)= xpath(?pmmlURI,"//PMML/ClusteringModel/Cluster[
        contains(Genes,'CCL19')and contains(Genes,'CCL5')]/Name/text()"))
}
    <!--'GO0003674 refers to 'molecular_function' in the Gene Ontology-->
```

XPATH Embedded in SPARQL: An Example

Descriptions of gene clusters are stored in a PMML document referred by semantic annotations. So it is easier to answer to the query *"Which molecular functions are associated to clusters containing both genes CCL19 and CCL5 "* by combining the information stored into annotations and into PMML documents. This can be done via XPATH code embedded in SPARQL through the semantic search engine CORESE.

It was introduced in the semantic search engine CORESE, a new function xpath with two arguments. The first argument is the URI of an XML document. The second argument is an XPath expression. The purpose of this function is to evaluate the XPath expression on the given XML document.

Figure 16 shows the CORESE query that matches the question: *"which molecular functions are associated to clusters containing both genes CCL19 and CCL5"*.

In this example:

- The SPARQL query retrieves all existing clusters (*?cluster*) and the molecular functions (*?biofunc*), experiment identifier (*?expe*) and PMML URI(*?pmmlURI)* associated to each retrieved cluster.

- The function *xpath* evaluates the XPATH expression *"//PMML/.../Cluster[contains(Genes,'CCL19')...]..."*: it returns the list of all clusters that contain both genes 'CCL19' and 'CCL5'. The search process is performed on the PMML documents (*?pmmlURI}*) referred in the clusters annotations.

- The SPARQL query filter on clusters (*?cluster*) contained on the list returned by the XPATH query *(Filter(xsd:string(?cluster)=xpath(...)).*

The result is a list of triples. Each triple contains:

- the cluster URI (*?cluster*) (e.g. *Cluster_GSE6281_hclust_1*),
- the experiment identifier (*?expe*) attached to the cluster (e.g. *GSE6281*),
- the biological functions (*?molfunc*) associated to the cluster (e.g. *cytoskeleton*).

In summary, in this section, after a first section that details semantic annotations, we have shown how SQL and XPATH functions associated with the CORESE search engine give to AMI the ability to provide semantic answers and inferred knowledge while incorporating all related original data.

CONCLUSION AND FURTHER WORKS

In this chapter we have presented the AMI solution that provides an intelligent tool for retrieving relevant information in comparative analyses of gene expression data with semantic aspects.

We have explained the need for biologists to access multiple sources of information to infer valuable new knowledge. And we have shown that so called meta-analyses were not fitted to encompass a wide variety of data.

The AMI framework was designed both to integrate all useful data and to retrieve them thanks to semantic tools that are able to use semantic concepts and relationships and to give approximate answers and infer new knowledge.

Major research effort presented in the chapter was first done on collecting requirements of future users (biologists) to fit their specific demand and on the way semantic web techniques would be employed. Some experiments have been conducted for testing the semantic solution feasibility.

Current works are devoted to AMI implementation and consist partly on studying solutions to collect all heterogeneous related data in order to drive real scale tests on the system.

AKNOWLEDGMENT

This work was partially supported by the Immunosearch[8] project

REFERENCES

Ashburner, M., Ball, C., Blake, J., Botstein, D., Butler, H., & Cherry, J. (2000). Gene ontology: tool for the unification of biology. the gene ontology consortium. *Nature Genetics, 25*(1).

Brazma, A., Hingamp, P., Quackenbush, J., Sherlock, G., Spellman, P., & Stoeckert, C. (2001). Minimum information about a microarray experiment (miame)- toward standards for microarray data. *Nature Genetics, 29*(4), 365–371. doi:10.1038/ng1201-365

Choi, I., & Kim, M. (2003). Topic distillation using hierarchy concept tree. In *ACM SIGIR conference*, (pp. 371–372).

Choi, J., Yu, U., Kim, S., & Yoo, O. (2003). Combining multiple microarray studies and modeling interstudy variation. *Bioinformatics (Oxford, England), 19*(1), i84–i90. doi:10.1093/bioinformatics/btg1010

Cleveland, W., & Devlin, S. (1979). Robust locally weighted regression and smoothing scatterplots. *Journal of the American Statistical Association, 74*, 829–836. doi:10.2307/2286407

Corby, O., Dieng-Kuntz, R., Faron-Zucker, C., & Gandon, F. (2006). Searching the semantic web: Approximate query processing based on ontologies. *IEEE Intelligent Systems, 21*(1), 20–27. doi:10.1109/MIS.2006.16

Eapen, B. R. (2008). Ontoderm - a domain ontology for dermatology. *Dermatology Online Journal, 14*(6), 16.

Eisen, M., Spellman, P., Brown, P. O., & Botstein, D. (1998). Cluster analysis and display of genome wide expression patterns. *Proceedings of the National Academy of Sciences of the United States of America, 95*(25), 14863–14868. doi:10.1073/pnas.95.25.14863

Hong, F., & Breitling, R. (2008). A comparison of metaanalysis methods for detecting differentially expressed genes in microarray experiments. *Bioinformatics (Oxford, England), 24*(3), 374–382. doi:10.1093/bioinformatics/btm620

Hu, P., Greenwood, C., & Beyene, J. (2006). Statistical methods for meta-analysis of microarray data: A comparative study. *Information Systems Frontiers, 8*(1), 9–20. doi:10.1007/s10796-005-6099-z

Irizarry, R. et al (2003). Summaries of affymetrix genechip probe level data. *Nucleic Acids Reseach, 31.*

Jiang, H., Deng, Y., Chen, H.-S., Tao, L., Sha, Q., & Chen, J. (2004). Joint analysis of two microarray gene-expression data sets to select lung adenocarcinoma marker genes. *BMC Bioinformatics, 5,* 81. doi:10.1186/1471-2105-5-81

Khelif, K., Dieng-Kuntz, R., & Barbry, B. (2007). An ontology based approach to support text mining and information retrieval in the biological domain. *J. UCS, 13*(12), 1881–1907.

Kim, K., Ki, D., Jeong, H., Jeung, H., Chung, H. C., & Rha, S. Y. (2007). Novel and simple transformation algorithm for combining microarray data sets. *BMC Bioinformatics,* 8. doi:10.1186/1471-2105-8-8

Lee, H., Hsu, A., Sajdak, J., Qin, J., & Pavlidis, P. (2004). Coexpression analysis of human genes across many microarray data sets. *Genome Research, 14,* 1085–1094. doi:10.1101/gr.1910904

Moreau, Y., & Aerts, S., Moor1, B., Strooper, B., & Dabrowski, M. (2003). Comparison and meta-analysis of microarray data: from the bench to the computer desk. *Trends in Genetics, 19,* 570–577. doi:10.1016/j.tig.2003.08.006

Pedersen, M. B., Skov, L., Menne, T., Johansen, J., & Olsen, J. (2007). Gene expression time course in the human skin during elicitation of allergic contact dermatitis. *The Journal of Investigative Dermatology, 127*(11), 2585–2595. doi:10.1038/sj.jid.5700902

Rhodes, D., Barrette, T., Rubin, M., Ghosh, D., & Chinnaiyan, A. (2002). Interstudy validation of gene expression profiles reveals pathway dysregulation in prostate cancer. *Cancer Research, 62,* 4427–4433.

Sa, S., Valdez, P., Wu, J., Jung, K., Zhong, F., & Hall, L. (2007). The effects of il-20 subfamily cytokines on reconstituted human epidermis suggest potential roles in cutaneous innate defense and pathogenic adaptive immunity in psoriasis. *Journal of Immunology (Baltimore, MD.: 1950), 178*(4), 2229–2240.

Smith, B., Ashburner, M., Rosse, C., Bard, J., Bug, W., & Ceusters, W. (2007). The obo foundry: Coordinated evolution of ontologies to support biomedical data integration. *Nature Biotechnology, 25*(11), 1251–1255. doi:10.1038/nbt1346

Stoeckert, C., Causton, H., & Ball, C. (2002). Microarray databases: standards and ontologies. *Nature Genetics, 32,* 469–473. doi:10.1038/ng1028

Trivedi, N., Gilliland, K. L., Zhao, W., Liu, W., & Thiboutot, D. M. (2006). Gene array expression profiling in acne lesions reveals marked upregulation of genes involved in inflammation and matrix remodeling. *The Journal of Investigative Dermatology, 126,* 1071–1079. doi:10.1038/sj.jid.5700213

Whetzel, P. L., Parkinson, H., Causton, H. C., Fan, L., Fostel, J., & Fragoso, G. (2006). The MGED Ontology: a resource for semantics-based description of microarray experiments. *Bioinformatics (Oxford, England), 22*(7), 866–873. doi:10.1093/bioinformatics/btl005

Yano, S., T., B., Walsh, R., & Blumenberg, M. (2008). Transcriptional responses of human epidermal keratinocytes to cytokine interleukin-1. *Journal of Cellular Physiology, 214*(1), 1–13. doi:10.1002/jcp.21300

ENDNOTES

1. http://www.ncbi.nlm.nih.gov/geo/
2. http://www.ebi.ac.uk/micro-array-as/aer/
3. http://www.ncbi.nlm.nih.gov/
4. http://www.ebi.ac.uk/micro-array-as/ae/
5. http://www.ebi.ac.uk/
6. http://www.bioinformatics.ubc.ca/Gemma
7. http://www.broad.mit.edu/cancer/software/genepattern/index.html
8. http://www.immunosearch.fr
9. http://www.affymetrix.com
10. http://www.ncbi.nlm.nih.gov/projects/geo/info/MINiML.html
11. http://www.mged.org/Workgroups/MAGE/mage.html
12. Predictive Model Markup Language
13. http://www.dmg.org/
14. http://www.nlm.nih.gov/research/umls/
15. http://www.ncbi.nlm.nih.gov/PubMed/
16. http://genome-www5.stanford.edu/
17. http://www.bioconductor.org/
18. http://www.dmg.org/.

Chapter 8
A Multidimensional Model for Correct Aggregation of Geographic Measures

Sandro Bimonte
Cemagref, UR TSCF, France

Marlène Villanova-Oliver
Laboratoire d'Informatique de Grenoble, France

Jerome Gensel
Laboratoire d'Informatique de Grenoble, France

ABSTRACT

Spatial OLAP refers to the integration of spatial data in multidimensional applications at physical, logical and conceptual levels. The multidimensional aggregation of geographic objects (geographic measures) exhibits theoretical and implementation problems. In this chapter, the authors present a panorama of aggregation issues in multidimensional, geostatistic, GIS and Spatial OLAP models. Then, they illustrate how overlapping geometries and dependency of spatial and alphanumeric aggregation are necessary for correctly aggregating geographic measures. Consequently, they present an extension of the logical multidimensional model GeoCube (Bimonte et al., 2006) to deal with these issues.

INTRODUCTION

A Data Warehouse (DW) is a centralized repository of data acquired from external data sources and organized following the multidimensional model (Kimball, 1996) in order to be analyzed by On-Line Analytical Processing (OLAP) systems. Multidimensional models rely on the concepts of *facts* and *dimensions*. Facts are described by values called *measures*. Dimensions, structured in *hierarchies*, permit to analyze facts according to different analysis axes and at different levels of detail. An instance of a dimension is a set of *members* organized according to the hierarchies. An instance of the conceptual model is represented by a hypercube whose axes are the dimension members at the finest levels. Each cell of a hypercube contains the value

DOI: 10.4018/978-1-60566-816-1.ch008

of the detailed measure. This basic cube (also called *facts table*) is then enhanced with cells that contain aggregated values of the measures for each combination of higher level's members. Aggregation operators applied on the measures must be specified in the conceptual model and depend on the semantics of the application. The classical functions used to aggregate numeric measures are the standard SQL operations "COUNT", "SUM", "MIN", "MAX" and "AVG". The multidimensional model allows pre-computation and fast access to summarized data in support of multidimensional analysis through OLAP operators which permit to explore the hypercube. Drill operators (Roll-Up and Drill-Down) permit to navigate in the dimensions hierarchies aggregating measures. Cutting operators (Slice and Dice) select and project a part of the hypercube. The multidimensional model and OLAP operators have been formalized in some logical models (Abello et al., 2006) as a support to correct aggregation of measures which plays a central role in multidimensional analysis (Pedersen et al., 2001). They define constraints on the aggregation functions in compliance with the semantics of the measure and explicit the dimensions that can be used in the multidimensional queries.

Most of 80% of transactional data contain spatial information, which represents the form and the location on the earth surface of real world objects (Franklin, 1992). The heterogeneity of physical spaces and the strong spatial correlation of thematic data (Anselin, 1989) are not taken into account into multidimensional models. Then, a new kind of systems have been developed, which intended to integrate the spatial component of the geographic information into multidimensional analysis: Spatial OLAP (SOLAP) (Bédard et al., 2001). Spatial OLAP allows decision-makers to explore, analyze and understand huge volume of geo-spatial datasets, in order to discover unknown and hidden knowledge, patterns and relations. This useful information can help spatial analysts and decision-makers to validate and reformulate

decisional hypothesis, and to guide their spatial decision making processes. SOLAP technologies have been usefully applied in several domains: geo-marketing, urban, health, environment, crisis management, etc. (Bédard et al., 2001) as they allow non-computer science users to exploit databases, statistical analysis and spatial analysis tools without mastering complex query languages and Geographic Information Systems functionalities, and understanding underlying complex spatial datasets. SOLAP redefines main multidimensional concepts: spatial dimensions, spatial measures and spatial aggregation functions. In this approach, spatial measures are not numerical values, but spatial objects (geometries) which are aggregated using spatial aggregation functions (union, intersection, etc.) (Shekar et al., 2001). As shown in this work, SOLAP models only partially support dependency of spatial and numerical values, which can lead to wrong aggregation of spatial and numerical measures (geographic measures).

In this paper, we identify a three-step aggregation process for the correct aggregation of geographic measures, and we formalize it by providing an extension of the logical multidimensional model, GeoCube (Bimonte et al., 2006). The model provides a set of rules to ensure the valid aggregation of geographic measures.

This paper is organized as follows. In the Section "Background", we introduce main concepts of geographic data and Spatial OLAP. Section "Related Work" discusses aggregation issues in multidimensional databases, GIS, geostatistic and Spatial OLAP domains. We investigate the problem of the correct aggregation of geographic measures in the Section "Research Motivations". The extension of the multidimensional model Geo-Cube is presented in Section "Correct Geographic Multidimensional Aggregation". Conclusions and discussions about implementation issues are given in the Section "Conclusion and Discussion".

BACKGROUND

Geographic Data

Geographic data are objects or phenomena of the real world described by both a *spatial* component and a *semantic* component (Degrene & Salgé, 1997). The spatial component gives the object's geometry and its position on the earth's surface (e.g. shape of a department). The semantic component is a set of descriptive properties (e.g. name and population of a department) and of spatial, thematic and map generalization relationships that the object shares with other (geographic) objects (e.g. a department belongs to a region). Map generalization is the process of obtaining less detailed maps at different scales (Weibel & Dutton, 2001).

Geographic Information Systems (GIS) are main tools to handle geographic information (Longley et al., 2001). GIS allow storing, visualizing and analyzing geographic data. GIS store geographic data using two different models: vector and raster models (Rigaux et al., 2002). The raster model represents the space as a single continuous space by means of a grid. Thematic data are associated with each cell of the grid. The vector model represents the space through geographic objects. A *geographic object* is a set of spatial objects composed by points. Alphanumeric attributes are associated with each spatial object. Querying and analyzing methods for geographic data extends classical ones, explicitly exploiting its spatial component (Longley et al., 2001). Some models, representing the geographic information as a set of uniform geographic objects have been proposed in literature (Erwig & Schneider, 2000; Guting, 1998; Guting & Schneider, 1995, Voisard & David, 2002). They provide classical GIS operators such as spatial selection, overlay, merge, fusion, etc (Longley et al., 2001). These operators allow selecting geographic objects using thematic and spatial predicates (i.e. "Which

cities are located at 50 Km far from Paris?") and creating new geographic objects by splitting and/ or aggregating geographic objects. Aggregation of geographic objects is performed using spatial aggregation functions (i.e. union, centroid, etc.) (Tao & Papadias, 2005) to aggregate the spatial component, and alphanumeric aggregation functions to aggregate alphanumeric attributes (SUM, AVG, etc.) (Rigaux et al., 2002). Spatial disaggregation functions are used to split geographic objects. A spatial disaggregation is a spatial function that does not preserve all the original geometries into its final result (i.e. intersection, centroid, etc.).

Spatial OLAP

Integration of spatial data in OLAP leads to the definition of Spatial OLAP (SOLAP). (Bédard et al., 2001) define SOLAP as "*a visual platform built especially to support rapid and easy spatio-temporal analysis and exploration of data following a multidimensional approach comprised of aggregation levels available in cartographic displays as well as in tabular and diagram displays*". SOLAP systems integrates OLAP and GIS functionalities into a unique framework allowing visualizing measures on maps, and triggering OLAP and spatial analysis operators by simply interacting with the cartographic interactive component of the SOLAP client (Rivest et al., 2005; Escribano et al., 2007).

In order to exploit the spatial component into OLAP systems, SOLAP re-think main OLAP concepts: dimensions and measures. SOLAP models, using the vector model, introduce geographic information as analysis axes thanks to *spatial dimensions* (Bédard et al., 2001; Fidalgo et al., 2004; Malinowski & Zimányi, 2005). A spatial dimension is described by *spatial hierarchies* that are characterized by the presence of the geometric attribute at the different levels (spatial levels). Spatial hierarchies, usually very complex, can present spatial and classical levels. Members of different

Figure 1. Multidimensional application with a geographic measure

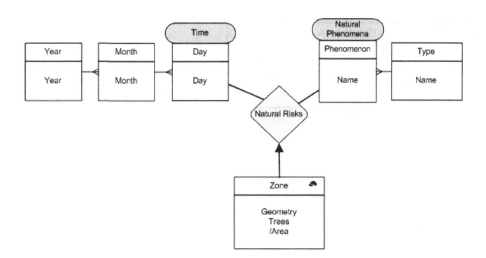

spatial levels are related by topologic inclusion or intersection relationships (Malinowski & Zimányi, 2005). An example of spatial hierarchy is French administrative organization, which groups cities into departments and departments into regions. A topological inclusion relationship exists between these geographic objects.

Spatial data can be also used as analysis subject using the concept of *spatial measure*. Different definitions of spatial measure can be found in literature: a collection of pointers to spatial objects or the result of topological or metric operators (Bédard et al., 2001; Malinowski & Zimányi, 2004; Stefanovic et al., 2000). In (Bimonte et al., 2006), the concept of *geographic measure* is introduced as a geographic object representing a real world entity and described by some alphanumerical attributes and geometry. Aggregation of geographic measures corresponds to the aggregation of their alphanumeric and spatial attributes by means of classical, spatial and user-defined aggregation functions.

An example of SOLAP application concerns the monitoring of natural phenomena in a park (Figure 1). The dimensions of that spatio-multidimensional application are time and the type of phenomenon (e.g. fire, landslide, etc.). "Time"

dimension is described by a calendar hierarchy ("Day" < "Month" < "Year"). "Natural Phenomena" dimension groups phenomena (i.e. fire, avalanche, etc.) into categories of phenomena (i.e. dangerous, etc.).

The measure is the damaged zone, which is described by a geometry, the number of damaged trees and the area. The area is a derived measure as it is calculated using other measures (Abello et al., 2006). Then, to calculate the area for the aggregated geographic object, no aggregation function is applied. It is calculated using the geometry resulting from the spatial aggregation.

Figure 2 shows an example of the facts table and the cartographic representation of two geographic measures.

The model allows users to answer queries like: *"What regions have been damaged by fires during 1978 ?"*. This query implies the aggregation of the geometry and the number of damaged trees.

Some works study the aggregation of spatial and numerical measures in spatial data warehouses. Performance is fundamental for SOLAP analysis. Then, several authors, focusing on numerical measures and spatial dimensions, integrate spatio-temporal indexes with pre-aggregation techniques

Figure 2. Facts table and cartographic representation of geographic measures

Day	Phenomenon	Zone
28-8-78	Fire	Zone A
19-8-78	Fire	Zone B
...	...	...

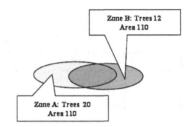

(i.e. Tao & Papadias, 2005; Rao et al., 2003Zhang & Tsotras, 2005). These methods speed-up aggregation computation on evolving user-defined spatial hierarchies. While numerical aggregation functions have been well defined (i.e. SUM, MIN, MAX, etc.), a standard set of spatial aggregation functions for spatial measures (geometries) has not been defined yet. (Shekar et al., 2001) classify spatial aggregations as distributive, algebraic, and holistic in order to grant summarazability (c.f. Sec "Multidimensional Models") in spatial data warehouse. Lopez & Snodgrass (2005), and Silva et al., (2008) formally define a set of spatial and numerical aggregation functions (i.e. AvgArea, Count_AtNorth, etc.). In addition to the conceptual aspects of spatial aggregation, some efforts have been done for improving queries computation in large spatial data warehouses. They provide indexes materialization, selection of aggregated measures and computational geometry algorithms (i.e. Stefanovic et al., 2000; Han et al., 1998).

Finally, some models have been proposed for spatial data warehouses, which formally define SOLAP main concepts: spatial dimensions, spatial measures, multidimensional operators and aggregation functions. In particular, the correct aggregation of geographic information is a quite complex task, which raises some unresolved problems as described in the next sections.

RELATED WORK

In this Section, we investigate problems and solutions related to aggregation of geographic data according to different models: logical multidimensional models, GIS models, geostatistic models and logical SOLAP models.

Multidimensional Models

The correct aggregation of measures is of crucial importance in the multidimensional analysis process. The correctness of aggregation depends on both the semantics of the measure and the multidimensional structure of the data warehouse (Horner et al., 2004; Pedersen et al., 2001). For example, the sum of pollution values has no sense, while the max or the min operators can safely be applied. Also, it is possible to sum the populations of cities of a region, but to sum these values on the time dimension is not correct (the same inhabitants would be counted several times). This problem is known in OLAP literature as *Additivity* (Kimball, 1996). A measure is: (1) *Additive* if the sum operator can be applied on all dimensions (2) *Semi-additive* if the sum can be applied on a subset of dimensions (3) *Non additive* if the sum makes no sense whatever the dimension. The correct aggregation means providing *aggregation constraints* (i.e. a control on the type of the aggregation, considering the semantics of the measure (i.e. the nature of the measure) and used dimensions). Some logical multidimensional models define explicitly the type of aggregation functions that can be applied to measures (Abello et al., 2006; Lenher, 1998; Pedersen et al., 2001; Trujillo et al., 2000). These models, based on the definitions introduced by Rafanelli & Ricci (1983), classify measures according to three different types of aggregation functions that can be applied to them: $\sum$ (data can be added together, e.g. population), ω (data can be used for average calculations, e.g. temperature) or c (constant data implying no application of aggregation operators, e.g. name). Considering only the SQL standard aggregation functions (AF) applying to each type of data (c, ω and $\sum$), an inclusion relationship exists so that $AF_c = \{COUNT\} \subset AF_\omega = \{AVG, MIN, MAX, COUNT\} \subset AF_\sum = \{SUM, AVG, MIN, MAX, COUNT\}$. This inclusion relationship allows deducing that "$\sum$ data" which can be summed can also be averaged and identified as the minimum or the maximum of a set (as "ω data") and that "ω data" can also be counted as "c data". By transitivity, "$\sum$ data" can also be counted.

Geostatistic Models

The aggregation of geographic information is crucial in spatial analysis especially in the geostatistic domain. Spatial aggregation operators (*i.e.* union, convex hull, etc.) and the management of aggregations applied to alphanumeric attributes have been widely discussed. Different frameworks, dealing with the type of alphanumeric attributes and with their aggregation functions have been proposed to address the issue of disjoint spatial units aggregation into bigger spatial units (Charre et al., 1997; Chrisman, 1974; Chrisman, 1998). Alphanumeric attributes are grouped into classes and they are associated with particular aggregation rules. For example, a rule defines that attributes representing relative values such as the temperature or the population density, can be aggregated using a weighted average. Another rule expresses that attributes used to represent raw quantitative

values, such as the number of inhabitants, can be aggregated using the SUM operator. For the *disaggregation* process (moving to smaller units), the sum is forbidden as it makes non-sense (Charre et al., 1997; Chrisman, 1974; Egenhofer & Frank, 1986). Finally, we underline that the concept of *analysis dimension* is not present. Indeed, all the aggregation rules are defined exclusively on the spatial dimension, while we claim that performing analysis on other dimensions (e.g. time dimension) can reveal itself interesting.

GIS Models

Spatial aggregation operators have been formalized and implemented in Geographic Information Systems (GIS) (Rigaux & Scholl, 1995; Voisard & David, 2002; Longley et al., 2001). In all these approaches, unlike the geostatistic solutions, the semantics of alphanumeric attributes are not taken into account. This lack is also evident from the implementation point of view. Nowadays, commercial GIS systems (*i.e.* ArcGIS, MapInfo, etc.) implement only union and splitting operators. They provide a simple control on the aggregations applied to alphanumeric attributes using only their type (*i.e.* numeric, alphanumeric, etc.) but not their semantics. These tools propose some numeric aggregation functions (*i.e.* sum and average) for the numeric attributes and some particular methods, as for example the usage of a default value or of the count operator, for textual attributes. They do not consider the semantics of the attributes. Therefore, it is possible to sum temperatures or population densities, which makes no sense. Moreover, all other spatial aggregation operators (*i.e.* the convex hull, etc.) only create new geometries without aggregating alphanumeric attributes.

Spatial OLAP Models

Some SOLAP logical models have been proposed in literature (Ahmed & Miquel, 2005; Damiani &

Spaccapietra, 2006; Jensen et al., 2004; Pourabbas, 2001; Sampaio et al, 2006, Silva et al., 2008).

Ahmed & Miquel (2005) define a spatial dimension according to the raster model as an infinite set of members. They simulate this "infinite" set using interpolation functions to calculate measures in every point of the analysis region represented by spatial dimensions. Pourrubas (2003) provides a formal framework to integrate multidimensional and geographic databases. The model handles spatial dimensions in which members of different levels are related by topological inclusion relationship. These models only handle numerical SQL aggregation functions. Sampaio et al. (2006) define a logical model for spatial data warehouse using the object-oriented approach. Spatial measures and numerical measures can be aggregated using SQL spatial and numerical aggregation functions. The model does not provide any support for correct aggregation. Damiani & Spaccapietra (2006) define a model in which all levels of a spatial dimension can be used as measures, allowing multi-granular analysis. The model aims at supporting measures as geographic objects, but it does not explicitly represent spatial and alphanumeric attributes. Then, no aggregation constraint is defined on measures (attributes of geographic objects).

Silva et al., (2008) define formally the elements of a spatial data warehouse with particular attention to aggregation functions for spatial data. They introduce a set of aggregation functions that combine numerical and spatial functions. These aggregation functions are classified according to whether numerical aggregation is scalar, distributive or holistic, and whether spatial aggregation is unary or n-ary function. However, these aggregation functions are not associated with any aggregation constraints and numerical functions are applied exclusively to metric values of spatial data (i.e. perimeter, etc.).

Only, Jensen et al., (2004) and Pedersen et al., (2001) define logical multidimensional models for spatial data warehouses taking into account aggregation constraints. In particular, Jensen et al., (2004) propose a model for location-based services. It supports partial inclusion of spatial dimension members granting imprecise measures. Measures are numerical and alphanumeric values. The model extends (Pedersen et al., 2001) and it grants correct aggregation of non-spatial measures by classifying measures according valid aggregation functions (c.f. the Section "Multidimensional Models"). Nevertheless, the model does not explicitly represent spatial measures nor associated aggregation constraints.

Pedersen & Tryfona (2001) investigate pre-aggregation in multidimensional applications with spatial measures. In particular, they study the pre-aggregation of alphanumeric attributes associated with spatial measures. In other words, they investigate the correct aggregation of alphanumeric attributes of geographic objects according to their spatial components. The model represents measures as bottom levels of dimensions. Aggregated measures are less detailed dimensions levels. Since a topological inclusion relationship always exists between spatial objects at different levels, the model does not allow applying spatial disaggregation functions. Then, only union can be used. Spatial disaggregation functions, such as intersection or centroid, can not be applied.

To conclude, few SOLAP models consider aggregation constraints on spatial and numerical measures without correctly support aggregation of geographic measures. Indeed, as shown in the next section, correct aggregation of geographic measures should take into account: semantics of measures, used dimensions, overlapping geometries and dependency between spatial and alphanumeric functions.

RESEARCH MOTIVATIONS

The aggregation of geographic measures raises several problems from both theoretical and implementation points of view. In particular,

Figure 3. Decomposition of geographic measure (Step 1)

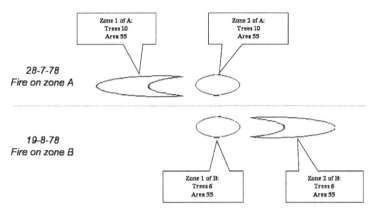

alphanumeric and spatial functions used for the aggregation are dependent: used spatial function dictates alphanumeric functions that are allowed for non-spatial attributes. This implies a redefinition of the OLAP *additivity* concept for spatio-multidimensional databases. Existing spatio-multidimensional models do not completely investigate this issue, which covers different research domains: multidimensional databases, geostatistic models and Geographic Information Systems (GIS) as discussed in the previous section. Let us consider the application of Figure 1, and let us suppose we need to get information at the year level. A Roll-Up operation on the year level aggregates the geographic measures Zone A and Zone B. In such a situation, how to aggregate these geographic objects?

Using union to aggregate the geometries, queries like: "*Where and how many trees have been damaged by some fires during 1978?*" (Query 1) can be answered.

To calculate the number of damaged trees aggregating on the time dimension, we propose to apply the average operator, as the number of trees is non-additive, and then to sum all these averages in order to have the total of trees in the merged zone. More in details, Zone A (resp. Zone B) is first splitted into two zones (Zone 1 of A and Zone 2 of A (resp. Zone 1 of B, and Zone 2 of B)), and then its alphanumeric attributes values

are recalculated (trees and area) (Figure 3). Please note that a user-defined function is used to calculate alphanumeric non-derived attributes of geographic measure. The number of trees is calculated as a weighted average on the surface. Areas of Zone 1 of A and of Zone 2 of A are the same (55), and a weighted average on the surface is used for the number of trees. Then, this latter is the same (10) for the two new zones. By the same way, spatial and alphanumeric attributes values of Zone 1 of B and Zone 2 of B are calculated.

Then, using these geographic objects, we calculate another set of geographic objects applying the average to the number of trees for the geographic objects with the same geometry and coordinates (Figure 4). We use average because the aggregation is made on the time dimension, which requires not counting several times the same tree. For instance in figure 3, Zone 2 of A and Zone 1 of B have the same geometry and coordinates, and some trees (note that the number of trees varies in time) (Figure 3). Then, from these two geographic objects, we create a new geographic object Zone V2 whose geometry is the same as the ones of Zone 2 of A and Zone 1 of B and whose number of trees is the average (8=(10+6)/2) (Figure 4).

Finally, we apply union to these zones and sum the numbers of trees (Figure 5). In particular, the geometry of Zone E is the union of the geometries

Figure 4. Vertical aggregation of trees using average

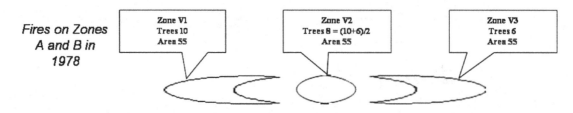

Table 1. Roll-up on the time dimension

Year	Phenomenon	Aggregated Zone
1978	Fire	Zone E
...	...	...

of Zone V1, Zone V2 and Zone V3. The number of trees is the sum of the number of trees of Zone V1, Zone V2 and Zone V3 (24= 10+8+6). Without this approach, damaged trees for the Zone E will be erroneously 32 as it is the union of Zone A and Zone B and as the associated sum operation does not consider that the damaged trees of the Zone 2 of A, Zone 1 of B are counted twice when aggregating on the time dimension. Finally, the result of the Roll-Up operator is shown in table 1.

Let us use another spatial function: *intersection*. In the OLAP context, intersection (Shekar et al., 2001) is a spatial aggregation function, but it should be better to considered it as a spatial disaggregation function following the geostatistic approach (c.f. Sec. "Geographic Data" and "Geostatistic Models").

In this case, the multidimensional query is: "*Where and how many trees have been damaged by all fires during 1978?*" (Query 2). The number of trees cannot be calculated using the sum of the averages because it is not representative of the number of trees in the intersected zone. Therefore, instead of applying sum, we apply a weighted average on the area (Figure 6). Consequently, the number of trees of Zone E is the same than the one of Zone V2 (8). Damages trees are not counted twice.

These two examples show that:

1. aggregation process has to take into account overlapping geometries and
2. alphanumeric aggregation functions applied to the descriptive attributes of geographic measures depend on their semantics ($\sum$: measures that can be summed, ω: measures that can be averaged, c: measures that can be only counted), on used dimensions (as for classical OLAP measures), and on spatial function (as in geostatistic models). In other words, additive measures cannot be added if a spatial disaggregation function is used.

Finally, the aggregation process of geographic measures can be seen as a three-step process using two alphanumeric aggregation functions (noted φ and κ) for each alphanumeric attribute and a spatial function (spatial aggregation or spatial disaggregation) for the spatial attribute.

The three steps are:

Figure 5. Aggregation of park's zones on the time dimension.

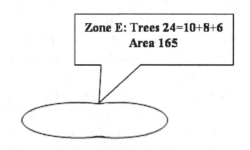

Figure 6. Aggregation of park's zones on the time dimension

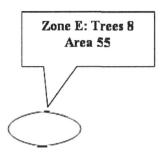

- *Step 1: Calculate disjoint geographic objects Calculate the set of geographic objects whose geometries are obtained using the intersection operator on the geographic measures (i.e.Figure 3). Alphanumeric attributes are calculated using user-defined functions. Geographic objects with the same geometry and coordinates could be created.*
- *Step 2: Vertical Aggregation Geographic objects created at step 1 with the same geometry and coordinates are unified to create one geographic object, by applying an aggregation function (κ) to the alphanumeric attributes (i.e.Figure 4). These aggregations have to be coherent with the semantics of the measures and with the dimensions used in the multidimensional query (Semantic of the measures "$\sum$, ω, c data" cf. Sec. "Multidimensional Models").*
- *Step 3: Horizontal Aggregation Aggregate the geometries of original geographic measures. Aggregate the alphanumeric attributes of the geographic objects created at step 2 (i.e.Figures 5 and 6). The alphanumeric aggregations (φ) have to be coherent with the semantics of the measure ($\sum$, ω, c) and with the used spatial function.*

It is important to underline that this process can be applied also to lines, points, etc.

To best of our knowledge, no work deals with this problem.

As discussed in Section "Related Work", existing spatio-multidimensional models (Abello et al., 2006; Damiani & Spaccapietra, 2006; Pourabbas, 2001, Sampaio et al., 2006, Silva et al., 2008) do not introduce any constraint on spatial and alphanumeric functions.

Jensen et al. (2004) do not extend aggregation constraints for spatial measures. Moreover, since the model provides a symmetrical representation of measures and dimensions and since it does not support dimensions attribute, each attribute of a geographic object has to be represented as a dimension which implies aggregating attributes separately. This means that the model cannot support the dependency of spatial and alphanumeric functions in the aggregation process.

Only Pedersen & Tryfona, (2001) model the dependency of spatial and alphanumeric functions, but as described above, they restrict spatial functions to union, discarding spatial disaggregation functions. This limits the analysis capabilities of the model because, as shown by our case study, spatial disaggregation functions could be necessary for spatial analysis.

CORRECT GEOGRAPHIC MULTIDIMENSIONAL AGGREGATION

In this section we introduce the base concepts of the logical multidimensional model GeoCube (Bimonte et al., 2006) and its extension to correctly aggregate geographic measures.

An Overview of the GeoCube Model

Bimonte et al., (2006) present a logical multidimensional model called GeoCube, which supports measures and dimension members as geographic objects. *GeoCube* allows the usage of a set of spatial and/or alphanumeric attributes as one single complex measure (*geographic measures*).

It also proposes user-defined aggregation functions for each attribute of the geographic object representing the aggregated measure. GeoCube also provides an algebra that redefines common OLAP operators.

Data Model

The main concepts of multidimensional data model are: *Entity*, *Hierarchy* and *Base Cube*. The concepts of *Entity Schema* and *Entity Instance* permit to represent indifferently the data of the analysis universe: dimension members and measures. An Entity is a set of attributes and functions used to represent derived attributes (data calculated using other data). Derived attributes are necessary to model metric attributes (i.e. area, perimeter, etc.) of geographic objects.

Entity Schemas and their instances are organized into hierarchies (*Hierarchy Schema* and *Hierarchy Instance*). The *Base Cube* represents the facts table.

In what follows, we only provide the definitions that are necessary to describe the framework we propose.

Definitions. (Entity Schema and Entity Instance).

An Entity Schema S_e is a tuple $\langle a_1, \ldots a_n, [F] \rangle$ where:

- a_i *is an attribute defined on a domain* $dom(a_i)$
- *F, if it exists, is a tuple* $\langle f_1 \ldots f_m \rangle$ *where* f_i *is a function defined on a sub-set of attributes* $a_1 \ldots a_k$.

An Instance of an Entity Schema S_e is a tuple t_i such as

- *If F exists then* $t_i = \langle val(a_1), val(a_n), val(b_1), \ldots val(b_m) \rangle$ *where* $val(a_i) \in dom(a_i)$ *and* $val(b_j) = f_j(val(a_1), \ldots val(a_k))$

- *If F does not exist,* $t_i = \langle val(a_1), \ldots val(a_n) \rangle$ *where* $val(a_i) \in dom(a_i)$

F permits to model derived measures and/or dimension attributes.

Definition. (Geographic Entity Schema).

An *Entity Schema* S_e is a *Geographic Entity Schema* if the domain of one attribute is a set of spatial objects.

Example 1. In the case study presented previously, the geographic measure representing the zones is $S_{zone} = \langle$ geometry, nbDamagedTrees, $f_{area} \rangle$ where f_{area}: dom(geometry) $\rightarrow$ N is a function to calculate the area of a zone. An instance of S_{zone} is $\langle$ pt01, 20, 110 $\rangle$ (Zone A) (Figure 2).

Entities are organized in hierarchies thanks to the concepts of *Hierarchy Schema* and *Hierarchy Instance*. A level of a hierarchy is an *Entity Schema* and a member is an *Entity Instance*. The *Hierarchy Schema* organizes levels into a lattice. Thanks to the *Hierarchy Instance*, the members' levels are organized in a tree structure. The root is an instance of the *Entity Schema* which represents the top level of the lattice represented by the *Hierarchy Schema*. Leafs are the instances of the *Entity Schema* which represents the bottom level of the lattice.

This definition allows modeling non-balanced and non-strict hierarchies, which are necessary for spatio-multidimensional applications (Malinowski & Zimányi, 2005).

Definition. (Hierarchy).

A Hierarchy Schema is a tuple $H_h = \langle L_h, \lfloor_h, \lceil_h, \ddagger_h \rangle$ where:

- L_h *is a set of Entity Schemas,*
- $\lfloor_h$ *and* $\lceil_h$ *are two Entity Schema and* $\lceil_h$ *contains one instance ('all'),*
- $\ddagger_h$ *is a partial order defined on the levels of the hierarchy* $(L_h \cup \lfloor_h \cup \lceil_h)$ *and* $\ddagger_h$ *is a lattice where* $\lfloor_h$ *and* $\lceil_h$ *are respectively the bottom and the top levels of the order.*

We call *Entity Schema levels $(L(H_h))$* the entities belonging to the set $\{L_h \cup L_h \cup \lceil_h\}$

An Instance of a Hierarchy H_h is a partial order $\uparrow_h$ defined on $L(H_h)$, such as:

- *if $t_i \uparrow_h t_j$ then $S_i \ddagger h\ S_j$, where $t_i \in I(S_i)$ and $t_j \in I(S_j)$*
- *$\forall\ t_i$ not belonging to the top level, then $\exists\ t_j$ such as $t_i \uparrow h\ t_j$*
- *$\forall\ t_i$ not belonging to the bottom level, $\exists\ t_j$ such as $t_j \uparrow h\ t_i$*

Schema and data of the spatio-multidimensional application are represented by *Base Cube*. *Base Cube Schema* defines dimensions (Hierarchies) and measures (e.g. the spatio-multidimensional application schema of Figure 1). The instance of the *Base Cube* represents facts table data (e.g. data of Figure 2). In our approach, dimensions and measures are (geographic) objects, for example phenomena and zones. Then, our model must define measures in the same way as dimensions levels. Following the approach of Vassiliadis (1998), we define a *Base Cube* as a tuple of *Hierarchies* and a boolean function which represents the tuples of the facts table. Here, the bottom levels of the hierarchies are (geographic) objects. They can be used as dimensions and measures. This definition allows defining measures as (geographic) objects, and not as numerical value.

Example 2. The multidimensional model of figure 1 is represented by the Base Cube Schema $BC_{naturalrisks} = \langle H_{natural\_phenomena}, H_{time}, H_{zone}, \delta \rangle$ where $H_{natural\_phenomena}$, H_{time} and H_{zone} are the hierarchies representing the phenomena, time and zones. δ: $I(S_{phenomen}) \times I(S_{day}) \times I(S_{zone})$ is a boolean function defined on the bottom levels of the hierarchies. The instance of $BC_{naturalrisks}$ represents the facts table (Figure 2).

In this application, each bottom level of a hierarchy (object and/or geographic object) can be used as measure.

Multidimensional Query Model

Base Cube represents the basic cuboid, which is represented by measures values associated with the most detailed levels of all hierarchies. These measures are not aggregated. Then, in order to represent a multidimensional query (i.e. cuboid), we introduce the concepts of *Aggregation Mode* and *View*. A multidimensional query defines the dimension levels used (e.g. "Type" and "Year"), the (geographic) object used as measure ("Zone") and a set of aggregation functions (*Aggregation Mode*) to aggregate its attributes (e.g. union for geometry and sum for number of trees) (Figure 7). For simplicity, we provide only the definition of the *Aggregation Mode* and we give a example of *View*.

Aggregation Mode defines a function for each non-derived attribute of the *(Geographic) Entity* representing the measure. The result of the aggregation is another *(Geographic) Entity* whose attributes values are calculated using these functions.

Definition. (Aggregation Mode).

An Aggregation Mode Θ_k is a tuple $\langle S_a, S_b, \Phi \rangle$ where:

- S_a *is an Entity Schema $\langle a_1, ... a_m, [F_a] \rangle$ (the detailed measure)*
- S_b *is an Entity Schema $\langle b_1, ... b_p, [F_b] \rangle$ (the aggregated measure)*
- *Φ a set of p ad-hoc aggregation functions ϕ_i*

An *Aggregation Mode* defined on geographic objects (geographic measures) is called *Geographic Aggregation Mode*.

Definition. (Geographic Aggregation Mode)

An Aggregation Mode $\Theta_k = \langle S_a, S_b, \Phi \rangle$ is a Geographic Aggregation Mode if S_a and S_b are Geographic Entity Schemas.

Figure 7. Geographic aggregation mode: Zones of a park

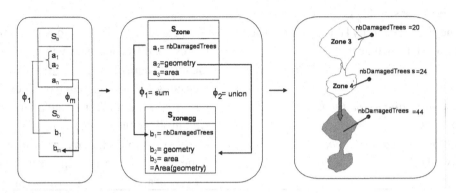

Example 3. Let the aggregation of the geographic Measures S_{zone} be represented by the *Entity Schema* $S_{zone\_agg} = \langle$ geometry, nbDamagedTrees, F$\rangle$.

The area is a metric attribute of the damaged zone and so it can be directly and univocally calculated using the geometry. For this reason, it has to be considered as a derived measure. Then, an example of *Geographic Aggregation Mode* for the zones is $\Theta_{zone} = \langle S_{zone}, S_{zone\_agg}, \Phi_{union} \rangle$ where Φ_{union} is the set of functions:

1. $\phi_{geometry}$: $dom(S_{zone}.geometry)^n \rightarrow dom(S_{zone\_agg}.geometry)$, i.e. the Geometric Union
2. $\phi_{nbtrees}$:$dom(S_{zone}.geometry, S_{zone}.nbDamagedTrees)^n \rightarrow dom(S_{zone\_agg}.nbDamagedTrees)$, i.e. the sum

An example of aggregation of two geographic measures (Zone 3 and Zone 4) using Θ_{zone} is shown in figure 7. S_{zone} is a schema entity with attributes a_1 (the number of trees damaged by fires), a_2 (the geometry of the region) and a a_3 area attribute a_3 (a_3 is derived from the geometry). Zone 3 and Zone 4 in the figure are two S_{zone} entities. $S_{zone-aggreg}$ is another schema entity, which represents the result of aggregating Zone 3 and Zone 4 (as shown in the dark grey area in the right panel of the figure). The attribute b_1 in $S_{zone-aggreg}$ is the result of applying the operator

ϕ_1 (sum) to attribute a_1, and the attribute b_2 is the result of applying the operator ϕ_2 (union) to attribute a_2.

GeoCube introduces the concept of *View* to represent the result of a multidimensional query. A *View* is a tuple of a *Base Cube* (the facts table), the set of *Entity Schema*s used for the multidimensional query, and an *Aggregation Mode* which defines the *Entity* used as measure and aggregation functions to aggregate it.

Example 4. The multidimensional query *Where and how many trees (which zones) have been damaged by some fires during 1978?"* (Query 1, *cf.* Sec. "Research Motivations") is represented by the *View* $V_{zones-year} = \langle BC_{naturalrisks}, \langle S_{phenomenon}, S_{year} \rangle, \Theta_{zone}, \gamma \rangle$. This query aggregates geographic measures along the time dimenson. We note that the *View* is composed of the *Base Cube*, the levels used in the query $S_{phenomenon}$ (phenomena) and S_{ye}(years) and the *Aggregation Mode* Θ_{zone} which defines S_{zone} as measure and establishes how to aggregate it. The instance of $V_{zones-year}$ is shown in Table 1.

Correct Geographic Aggregation

In order to formalize the constraints that ensure the correct aggregation of geographic measures according to the algorithm described in the Section "Research Motivations", we formalize the semantics of alphanumeric attributes of geographic measures and the dependency of spatial and alphanumeric functions, and then we introduce the constraints.

Semantics of Alphanumeric Attributes of Geographic Measures

Following the approach to ensure correct aggregation, described in the Section "Multidimensional Models", we introduce the functions *DimensionsMeasure* and *SemanticsMeasure*.

They classify aggregation functions of attributes of geographic objects in three different groups, called *aggregation types*: AF_Σ, AF_ω and AF_c, where $AF_\Sigma > AF_\omega > AF_c$, ">" being a total order. Functions classified as AF_Σ can be applied to measures that can be summed, AF_ω are functions that can be applied to measures that can be averaged, and AF_c are functions that can be applied to measures that can be only counted.

SemanticsMeasure takes into account the semantics of attributes. It takes as input an alphanumeric attribute and returns an aggregation type (AF_Σ, AF_ω, AF_c). For example, functions that can be applied to the number of trees are AF_Σ, as number of trees can be summed.

Definition. (SemanticsMeasure)

For each Entity Schema S_e, we assume a function SemanticsType: $A(S_e) \rightarrow \{AF_\Sigma, AF_\omega, AF_c\}$ which returns the aggregation type.

□

DimensionsMeasure takes into account the semantics of attributes, and used dimensions levels. It takes as input an alphanumeric attribute and the dimensions levels of the *View*, and it returns an aggregation type (AF_Σ, AF_ω or AF_c). For example, functions that can be applied to the number of trees aggregating on the time dimension are AF_ω, as the number of trees cannot be summed on the time dimension (some trees must not be counted twice.

Definition. (DimensionsMeasure).

For each Entity Schema S_e and set of levels of a View V_e, we assume a function DimensionsMeasure: $A(S_e) \times L(V_e) \rightarrow \{AF_\Sigma, AF_\omega, AF_c\}$ which returns the aggregation type.

Example 5. In our example, SemanticsMeasure(nbDamagedTrees) = AF_Σ, because the sum of number of trees makes sense, and DimensionsMeasure(nbDamagedTrees, S_{year}, $S_{phenomenon}$)= AF_ω, because number of trees is not additive on the time dimension (the level S_{year}, which is not the most detailed level of the "Time" dimension, is used in the multidimensional query).

Dependency of Spatial and Alphanumeric Functions

In order to model dependency of spatial and alphanumeric functions, we introduce a function *SpatialType*, which takes as inputs the type of spatial function (AF_U, AF_Ω) and the semantics of the alphanumeric attribute (*SemanticsMeasure*), and returns the *aggregation type (AF_Σ, AF_ω, or AF_c)* that can safely be applied to the alphanumeric attribute. Let us note spatial aggregation functions as AF_U, and spatial disaggregation functions as AF_Ω. Then, spatial functions classified as AF_U allows summing additive data (e.g. number of trees) because they preserve the set of input geometries in the result (i.e. union, convex hull, etc.). AF_Ω do not allow summing data as they leave out some spatial objects (i.e. centroid, intersection, etc.).

Definition. (SpatialType function).

We define a function SpatialType: $\{AF_U, AF_\Omega\} \times \{AF_\Sigma, AF_\omega, AF_c\} \rightarrow \{AF_\Sigma, AF_\omega, AF_c\}$ as defined in Table 2.

The function *SpatialType* models the dependency of spatial and alphanumeric functions as defined by the Step 3 of our algorithm. In particular, when using spatial aggregations (AF_U), it is possible to sum additive alphanumeric attributes (AF_Σ) values of geographic

Table 2. SpatialType function

SpatialType	AF_Σ	AF_ω	AF_c
AF_U	AF_Σ	AF_ω	AF_c
AF_Ω	AF_ω	AF_ω	AF_c

measure (SpatialType(AF_U, AF_Σ) = AF_Σ). For example, when using the union, it is possible to sum number of trees as it is additive (AF_Σ): *SpatialType(UNION, AF_Σ) = AF_Σ* (see Figure 5). . When using spatial disaggregations (AF_Ω), it is not possible to sum alphanumeric attributes values of geographic measures, but it should be possible to use average (AF_ω) or count (AF_c) (SpatialType(AF_Ω, AF_Σ)= AF_ω). For example, when using intersection, it is not possible to use sum, even if number of trees is additive (AF_Σ): SpatialType(INTERSECTION, AF_Σ) = AF_ω (see Figure 6). .

Finally, if the alphanumeric attribute is not additive (AF_ω or AF_c) and spatial aggregation is used, then it is not possible to add alphanumeric attribute values (SpatialType(AF_U, AF_ω) = AF_ω and SpatialType(AF_U, AF_c)= AF_c).

Correct Geographic Aggregation Mode

Before defining the Correct Geographic Aggregation Mode, we need to introduce the concept of *overlay*. The GIS operator overlay takes as inputs two maps and overlays them one on the top of the other to form a new map. The *Union Overlay* is an operator that takes as inputs 2 maps and returns a map whose geometries are the set of all disjoint geometries obtained by applying the topological

intersection among all features. Figure 8 shows an example of overlay of two maps whose geometries are polygons.

Using the definitions previously given, we formalize the three steps of our algorithm by defining two functions (*DisjGeoObjects* and *OverlayGeoObjects)* and two constraints (*Vertical Aggregation Constraint* and *Horizontal Aggregation Constraint*) for the *Geographic Aggregation Mode*.

These two constraints allow the Geographic Aggregation Mode ensuring a correct geographic aggregation of geographic measures.

In particular, each alphanumeric aggregation function ϕ of the *Geographic Aggregation Mode* is decomposed in two functions: κ and φ used to calculate attributes values of the geographic objects created at Step 2 and 3 respectively. Then, the two constraints are defined on κ and φ according to the requirements of the *Vertical* and the *Horizontal* steps respectively.

The *Vertical Aggregation Constraint* defines correct functions for κ considering disjoint geographic measures using the function *DisjGeoObjects* (see Figure 3), and taking into account semantics and used dimensions (i.e. *DimensionsMeasure*) of the alphanumeric attributes (e.g. number of trees cannot be summed on the time dimension).

For example, in order to calculate geographic objects of Figure 3 resulting from an aggregation on the time dimension, the *Vertical Aggregation Constraint* does not allow using the sum ($\kappa_{nbDamagedTrees}$ = AVG) because number of trees is not additive on the time dimension ($\kappa_{nbDamagedTrees} \in AF_\omega$ = Min(DimensionType(nbDamagedTrees, S_y

Figure 8. Union overlay

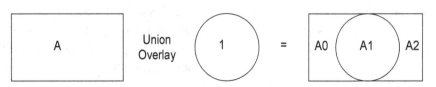

$_{ear}$,S_{type}), where DimensionType(nbDamagedTrees,S_{year},S_{type})= AF_ω).

The *Horizontal Aggregation Constraint* defines correct functions for φ taking into account the semantics of the alphanumeric attributes thanks to the function *SemanticsType* (e.g.. number of trees can be summed), and the dependency between spatial and alphanumeric functions thanks to the *SpatialType* function (when using intersection, it is not possible to sum the number of trees).

For example, in order to aggregate geographic objects resulting from Vertical Aggregation Step of figure 3, the *Horizontal Aggregation Constraint* does not allow using the sum for number of trees. Therefore, $\varphi_{nbDamagedTrees}$ = Weighted Average on surface because a spatial disaggregation (intersection) is used for geometry (Figure 6).Indeed, sum is not representative of number of trees in the intersection region ($\varphi_{nbDamagedTrees} \in AF_\omega$ = SpatialType(AF_Ω, Min(SemanticType(nbDamagedTrees)))).

By this way, user chooses the functions φ and κ, and the model avoids building any non-sense aggregated geographic measures.

In the following, we formally introduce the *Correct Geographic Aggregation Mode* and then the functions *DisjGeoObjects* and *OverlayGeoObject*.

Definition. (Correct Geographic Aggregation Mode)

Let:

- V_e *be a View* (See example 4: $V_{zones\text{-}year}$ = ⟨B-$C_{naturalrisks}$, ⟨$S_{phenomenon}$, S_{year}⟩, Θ_{zone}, γ⟩)
- t_1 ...,t_n *be instances of the Geographic Entity which must be aggregated: input instances* (See Zone A and Zone B, Figure 2)
- t_i^{D1}, ... t_i^{Dr} *be the instances calculated using DisjGeoObjects on input instances: vertical instances* (See Zone 1 of A, Zone 2 of A, Zone 1 of B and Zone 2 of B, Figure 3)

- t_1^d ...,t_m^d *be the instances calculated using OverlayGeoObjects on input instances and t_i^d have the same geometry and coordinates than t_i^{D1}, ... t_i^{Dr} of the vertical instances* (See Zone V1, Zone V2 and Zone V3, Figure 4)
- *SpatialAggregationType be the spatial function type {AF_U, AF_Ω}*
- *geomAggregate be the result of the spatial aggregation on the geometries of t_1 ...,t_n*
- *The alphanumeric aggregation function ϕ_i of Φ_e be defined by means of:*
- φ_i *(t_i^d .a_m, ... t_i^d.a_p t_i^d.geom) (Horizontal Aggregation)*
- κ_i *(t_i^{Di}.a_m,...,t_i^{Di}.a_l) (Vertical Aggregation)*

such as:

1. $\phi_i = \varphi_1$
2. $t_i^d.a_i = \kappa_1^r(t_i^{Di}.a_m,...,t_i^{Di}.a_l)$

then the Geographic Aggregation Mode Φ_e is correct if are respected the following constraints:

1. Vertical Aggregation Constraint:

   $\kappa_i \in$ Min(DimensionsMeasure(a_m, S_{11},... S_{lm}),...,DimensionsMeasure(a_l, S_{11}, ..., S_{lm}))

2. Horizontal Aggregation Constraint: $\varphi_i \in$ *SpatialType(SpatialAggregation Type, Min(SemanticsMeasure(a_m),..., SemanticsMeasure(a_l))*

Definition. (DisjGeoObjects)

DisjGeoObjects is a function which takes as inputs n Geographic Entity Instances and returns $l \geq n$ Geographic Entity Instances whose geometries are obtained using the geometric intersection operator.

Figure 3 shows the results of the *DisjGeoObjects* function on geographic objects of figure 2.

Figure 9. Correct Geographic Aggregation Mode on Time dimension and using spatial union

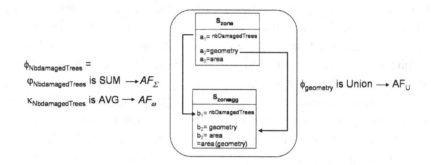

Definition. (OverlayGeoObjects)

OverlayGeoObjects is a function which takes as inputs n Geographic Entity Instances representing n maps and returns m≥ n Geographic Entity Instances whose geometries are obtained using the Union Overlay.

Figure 4 shows the results of the *Overlay-GeoObjects* function on geographic objects of figure 3.

We present now the two *Geographic Aggregation Modes* for our case study: the first uses union and the second intersection. We show how the *Geographic Aggregation Mode constraints* oblige the user to use sum only in the first case. Moreover, these examples show how the user is forced to aggregate the number of trees considering the semantics of the attributes and the used dimensions.

Example 6. Let us consider the query *"Where and how many trees have been damaged by some fires during 1978?"* (Query 1, *cf.* Sec "Research Motivations"). We define a *View* with a *Correct Geographic Aggregation Mode*, which uses average for the *Vertical Aggregation* and sum and union for the *Horizontal Aggregation* (Figure 9).

Formally, let $V_{zones\text{-}year} = \langle BC_{naturalrisks}, \langle S_{phenomenon}, S_{year} \rangle, \Theta_{zone}, \gamma \rangle$ represent the Query 1 where:

- DimensionsMeasure(nbDamagedTrees, S_{year}, S_{type}) = AF_ω
- SemanticsMeasure(nbDamagedTrees) = AF_Σ

- Geographic Aggregation Mode $\Theta_{zone} = \langle S_{zone}, S_{zone\_agg}, \Phi_{union} \rangle$ where Φ_{union} is (Figure 5)
  1. $\phi_{geometry}$: $dom(S_{zone}.geometry)^n \rightarrow dom(S_{zone\_agg}.geometry)$ is Union
- $\phi_{geometry}$ is AF_U (spatial aggregation)
  2. $\phi_{nbDamagedtrees}$: $dom(S_{zone}.geometry, S_{zone}.nbDamagedTrees)^n \rightarrow dom(S_{zone\_agg}.nbDamagedTrees) = \varphi_{nbDamagedTrees}$ where:
- $\varphi_{nbDamagedTrees}$ is SUM
- $\kappa_{nbDamagedTrees}$ = Average

The multidimensional query $V_{zones\text{-}year}$ defines a *Correct Geographic Aggregation Mode* because the *Geographic Aggregation Mode Constraints* are satisfied:

1. $\kappa_{nbDamagedTrees} \in AF_\omega$ =Min(DimensionType(nbDamagedTrees, S_{year}, S_{type})

(It is not possible to apply the sum operator to numbers of trees because this measure is not additive on time dimension)

2. $\varphi_{nbDamagedTrees} \in AF_\Sigma$ =SpatialType(AF$_U$,Min(SemanticsType(nbDamagedTrees)))

(It is possible to apply the sum to the numbers of trees for the geographic objects resulting from *VerticalAggregation* because the spatial function is union and it is a spatial aggregation)

The Geographic Aggregation Mode Θ_{zone} uses

Figure 10. Correct geographic aggregation mode on time dimension and using spatial intersection

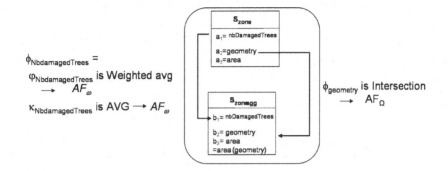

spatial Union ($\phi_{geometry}$) to aggregate geometry. The aggregation of the number of damaged trees is performed using the AVG for the vertical aggregation ($\kappa_{nbDamagedTrees}$), as the number of damaged trees is not additive on time dimension (DimensionsMeasure(nbDamagedTrees, S_{year}, S_{type}) = AF_ω), and the SUM ($\varphi_{nbDamagedTrees}$) for the horizontal aggregation, as $\phi_{geometry}$ is a spatial aggregation (AF_U).

Example 7. Let us suppose now we want to answer to the query "*Where and how many trees have been damaged by all fires during 1978?*" (Query 2, *cf.* Sec "Research Motivations"). We define a *View* with a *Correct Geographic Aggregation Mode*, which uses an interpolation function and intersection for the *Horizontal Aggregation*, and average for the *Vertical Aggregation* (Figure 10).

Let $\Theta_{zone} = \langle S_{zone}, S_{zone\_agg}, \Phi_{intersect} \rangle$ (Query 2) where $\Phi_{intersect}$ is:

1. $\phi_{geometry}$: $\mathrm{dom}(S_{zone}.\mathrm{geometry})^n \rightarrow \mathrm{dom}(S_{zone\_agg}.\mathrm{geometry})$ is Intersection
   - $\phi_{geometry}$ is AF_Ω (spatial disaggregation)
2. $\phi_{nbDamagedtrees}$: $\mathrm{dom}(S_{zone}.\mathrm{geometry}, S_{zone}.\mathrm{nbDamagedTrees})^n \rightarrow \mathrm{dom}(S_{zone\_agg}.\mathrm{nbDamagedTrees}) = \varphi_{nbTrees}$ where:
   - $\varphi_{nbDamagedTrees}$ is Weighted Average on surface
   - $\kappa_{nbDamagedTrees}$ = Average

The multidimensional query $V_{zones-year}$ uses a *Correct Geographic Aggregation Mode* because the *Geographic Aggregation Mode constraints* are satisfied:

1. $\kappa_{nbDamagedTrees} \in AF_\omega = \mathrm{Min}(\mathrm{DimensionType}(\mathrm{nbDamagedTrees}, S_{year}, S_{type}))$

(The sum cannot be applied to numbers of trees because this measure is not additive on time dimension)

2. $\varphi_{nbDamagedTrees} \in AF_\omega = \mathrm{SpatialType}(AF_\Omega, \mathrm{Min}(\mathrm{SemanticType}(\mathrm{nbDamagedTrees})))$

(The sum cannot be applied to numbers of trees of the geographic objects resulting from *VerticalAggregation* because the spatial function is intersection and it is a spatial disaggregation).

The Geographic Aggregation Mode Θ_{zone} uses spatial Intersection ($\phi_{geometry}$) to aggregate geometry. The aggregation of the number of damaged trees is performed using the AVG for the vertical aggregation ($\kappa_{nbDamagedTrees}$), as the number of damaged trees are not additive on time dimension (DimensionsMeasure(nbDamagedTrees, S_{year}, S_{type}) = AF_ω), and the Weighted Average on surface ($\varphi_{nbDamagedTrees}$) for the horizontal aggregation, as $\phi_{geometry}$ is a spatial disaggregation (AF_Ω).

We have presented and illustrated the approach we propose for Correct Geographic Aggregation

Mode. To complete our case study, we have to recall that no aggregation function is provided to get the value of the attribute representing the area of the damaged zone. Indeed, the area is a derived measure calculated using the geometry resulting from the spatial aggregation of the component geographic objects.

CONCLUSION AND DISCUSSION

Spatial OLAP refers to the integration of spatial data in OLAP. Correct aggregation is crucial in multidimensional analysis. In this paper, we provide an overview of solutions for aggregation of geographic objects in multidimensional, geostatistic, GIS and SOLAP models. By introducing a case study concerning the monitoring of natural phenomena, we define the aggregation of geographic measures as a –three-step process in which two constraints on aggregation functions are defined. They extend classical OLAP aggregation constraints with dependence between spatial and alphanumeric aggregation functions applied to the attributes of geographic measures. We present an extension of the logical multidimensional model GeoCube (Bimonte et al., 2006), which formalizes our approach. Alphanumeric aggregation functions are decomposed into two aggregation functions and two constraints are applied to them to take into account the additivity of the measures and the dependency of spatial and alphanumeric aggregation functions. By this way, GeoCube ensures the correct aggregation of geographic measures. This requirement is not supported by existing spatio-multidimensional model. Indeed, most of SOLAP models do not provide any aggregation constraint for aggregation functions. Jensen et al. (2004) define aggregation constraints, but they reduce spatial measures to classical data without taking into account the spatial component of the geographic information. Finally, only Pedersen & Tryfona (2001) provide a model that explicitly supports aggregation constraints for spatial and alphanumeric data. The model supports overlapping geometries and aggregation constraints as well as our 3-step framework. However, it supports only partially the dependency of spatial and alphanumeric functions as it does not allow disaggregation functions. We have addressed this issue in this paper

Currently, we are working on the implementation of our framework in the SOLAP system GeWOlap (Bimonte et al., 2006b). We are implementing the three steps of our framework using PL/SQL functions and user-defined aggregation functions provided by Oracle. Semantics of measures (valid aggregation functions) are defined in XML files representing the multidimensional application in the ROLAP Server Mondrian. Semantics of measures have to be parsed before any OLAP query computation in order to verify dependencies between spatial and alphanumeric functions. The main issues of this approach deal with performances in large spatial data warehouses. Developing ad-hoc pre-aggregation and indexing techniques for geographic measures are our future work.

ACKNOWLEDGMENT

Authors wish to thank Pr. Pierre Dumolard for precious discussions and material on GIS and geostatistics.

REFERENCES

Abelló, A., Samos, J., & Saltor, F. (2006). YAM2: a multidimensional conceptual model extending UML. *Information Systems, 31*(6), 541–567. doi:10.1016/j.is.2004.12.002

Ahmed, T., & Miquel, M. (2005). Multidimensional Structures Dedicated to Continuous Spatiotemporal Phenomena. In *Proceedings of the 22th BNCOD* (pp. 29-40). Berlin: Springer.

Anselin, L. (1989). *What Is Special about Spatial Data? Alternative Perspectives on Spatial Data Analysis,* (Technical Report). Santa Barbara, CA: National Center for Geographic Information and Analysis.

Bédard, Y., Merrett, T., & Han, J. (2001). Fundaments of Spatial Data Warehousing for Geographic Knowledge Discovery. In *Geographic Data Mining and Knowledge Discovery* (pp. 53-73). London: Taylor & Francis.

Bimonte, S., Tchounikine, A., & Miquel, M. (2006). GeoCube, a Multidimensional Model and Navigation Operators Handling Complex Measures: Application in Spatial OLAP. In *Proceedings of the 4th ADVIS* (pp. 100-109). Berlin: Springer-Verlag.

Bimonte, S., Wehrle, P., Tchounikine, A., & Miquel, M. (2006). GeWOlap: A Web Based Spatial OLAP Proposal. In Meersman, R., Tari, Z., & Herrero, P. (Eds.), In *Proceedings of the Workshop on Semantic-Based Geographical Information Systems* (pp. 1596-1605). Berlin: Springer.

Charre, J., Dumolard, P., & Le Berre, I. (1997). *Initiation aux pratiques statistiques en geographie.* Paris: Masson.

Chrisman, N. (1974). *Attributes of geographic entities.* Technical Report, Harvard Laboratory for Computer Graphics, Cambridge, MA.

Chrisman, N. (1998). Rethinking Levels of Measurement in Cartography. *Cartography and GIS, 25*(4), 231–242. doi:10.1559/152304098782383043

Damiani, M., & Spaccapietra, S. (2006). Spatial Data Warehouse Modeling. In *Processing and Managing Complex Data for Decision Support* (pp. 1-27). Hershey, PA: IGP.

Degrene, J., & Salge, F. (1997). *Les systèmes d'information géographique,* (2nd Ed.). Paris: Presses Universitaires de France.

Egenhofer, M., & Frank, A. U. (1986). Connection between Local and Regional: Additional Intelligence Needed. In *Proceedings of the 18th International Congress of FIGURE*

Egenhofer, M., & Frank, A. U. (1992). Object-Oriented Modeling for GIS. *URISA Journal, 4*(2), 3–19.

Erwig, M., & Schneider, M. (2000). Formalization of advanced map operations. In *Proceedings of the 9th Int. Symp. on Spatial Data Handling* (pp. 3-17).

Escribano, A., Gomez, L., Kuijpers, B., & Vaisman, A. (2007). Piet: a GIS-OLAP implementation. In *Proceedings of the ACM 10th International Workshop on Data Warehousing and OLAP* (pp. 73-80). New York: ACM Press.

Fidalgo, R., Times, V., Silva, J., & Souza, F. (2004). GeoDWFrame: A Framework for Guiding the Design of Geographical Dimensional Schemas. In *Proceedings of 6th International Conference on Data Warehousing and Knowledge Discovery* (pp. 26-37). Berlin: Springer.

Franklin, C. (1992). An Introduction to Geographic Information Systems: Linking Maps to databases. *Database, 15*(2), 13–21.

Guting, R. (1998). Geo-Relational Algebra: A model and query language for geometric database systems. In *Proceedings of the EDBT* (pp. 506-527).

Güting, R., & Schneider, M. (1995). Realm-based spatial data types: the ROSE algebra. *The VLDB Journal, 4*(2), 243–286. doi:10.1007/BF01237921

Han, J., Stefanovic, N., & Koperski, K. (1998). Selective Materialization: An Efficient Method for Spatial Data Cube Construction. In *Proceedings of 6th PAKDD Conference* (pp. 144-158). Berlin: Springer.

Horner, J., Song, I., & Chen, P. (2004). An Analysis of Additivity in OLAP Systems. In *Proceedings of the 7th DOLAP* (pp. 83-91). New York: ACM Press.

Jensen, C., Kligys, A., Pedersen, T., & Timko, I. (2004). Multidimensional data modeling for location-based services. *The VLDB Journal, 13*(1), 1–21. doi:10.1007/s00778-003-0091-3

Kimball, R. (1996). *The Data Warehouse Toolkit.* New York: John Wiley.

Lehner, W. (1998). Modeling large scale OLAP scenarios. In *Proceedings of the 6th EDBT* (pp. 153–167).

Longley, P., Goodchild, M., Maguire, D., & Rhind, D. (2001). *Geographic Information Systems and Science.* New York: John Wiley & Sons.

Lopez, I., & Snodgrass, R. (2005). Spatiotemporal aggregate computation: A survey. *IEEE Transactions on Knowledge and Data Engineering, 17*(2), 271–286. doi:10.1109/TKDE.2005.34

Malinowski, E., & Zimányi, E. (2004). Representing spatiality in a conceptual multidimensional model. In *Proceedings of the 12th ACM GIS* (pp. 12-22). New York: ACM Press.

Malinowski, E., & Zimányi, E. (2005). Spatial Hierarchies and Topological Relationships in SpatialMultiDimER model. In *Proceedings of the 22th British National Conference on Databases* (pp. 17-22). Berlin: Springer.

Pedersen, T. B., Jensen, C., & Dyreson, C. (2001). A foundation for capturing and querying complex multidimensional data. *Journal of Information Systems, 26*(5), 383–423. doi:10.1016/S0306-4379(01)00023-0

Pedersen, T. B., & Tryfona, N. (2001). Pre-aggregation in Spatial Data Warehouses. In *Proceedings of the 7th International Symposium on Spatial and Temporal Databases* (pp. 460-478).

Pourabbas, E. (2003). Cooperation with Geographic Databases. In *Multidimensional databases: problems and solutions* (pp. 393-432). Hershey, PA: IGP

Rafanelli, M., & Ricci, F. (1983). Proposal of a logical model for statistical databases. In *Proceedings of the 2nd International Workshop on Statistical and Scientific Database Management,* (pp. 264-272).

Rao, F., Zhang, L., Yu, X., & Li, Y. & Chen, Y. (2003). Spatial hierarchy and OLAP-favored search in spatial data warehouse. In *Proceedings of the 6th ACM International Workshop on Data Warehousing and OLAP* (pp. 48-55). New York: ACM Press.

Rigaux, P., & Scholl, M. (1995). Multi-Scale Partitions: Application to Spatial and Statistical Databases. In *Proceedings of the 4th International Symposium on Advances in Spatial Databases,* (pp. 170-183). Berlin: Springer-Verlag

Rigaux, P., Scholl, M., & Voisard, A. (2002). *Spatial databases with applications to Gis.* New York: Academic Press.

Rivest, S., Bédard, Y., Proulx, M., Nadeaum, M., Hubert, F., & Pastor, J. (2005). SOLAP: Merging Business Intelligence with Geospatial Technology for Interactive Spatio-Temporal Exploration and Analysis of Data. *Journal of International Society for Photogrammetry and Remote Sensing, 60*(1), 17–33. doi:10.1016/j.isprsjprs.2005.10.002

Sampaio, M. C., Sousa, A. G., & Baptista, C. (2006) Towards a logical multidimensional model for spatial data warehousing and olap. In *Proceedings of the 9th ACM international workshop on Data warehousing and OLAP* (pp. 83-90). New York: ACM Press.

Shekar, S., Lu, C., Tan, X., Chang, S., & Vatsrai, R. (2001). Map Cube: A Visualization Tool for Spatial Data Warehouses. In *Geographic Data Mining and Knowledge Discovery* (pp. 74-90). London: Taylor & Francis

Silva, J., Times, V., Salgado, A., Souza, C., Fidalgo, R., & Oliveira, A. (2008). A set of aggregation functions for spatial measures. In *Proceedings of the ACM 14th International Workshop on Data Warehousing and OLAP* (pp. 25-32). New York: ACM Press.

Stefanovic, N., Han, J., & Koperski, K. (2000). Object-Based Selective Materialization for Efficient Implementation of Spatial Data Cubes. *IEEE TKDE, 12*(6), 938–958.

Tao, Y., & Papadias, D. (2005). Historical spatio-temporal aggregation. *ACM Transactions on Information Systems, 23*(1), 61–102. doi:10.1145/1055709.1055713

Trujillo, J., Palomar, M., & Gómez, J. (2000). An Object Oriented Approach to Multidimensional Databases & OLAP Operations. *International Journal of Computer and Information Science, 2*(3), 75–85.

Vassiliadis (1998). Modeling Multidimensional Databases, Cubes and Cube Operations. In *Proceedings of 10th International Conference on Scientific and Statistical Database Management* (pp. 53-62). Alamitos, CA: IEEE Computer Society.

Voisard, A., & David, B. (2002). A Database Perspective on Geospatial Data Modeling. *IEEE TKDE, 14*(2), 226–243.

Weibel, R., & Dutton, G. (2001). Generalizing Spatial Data and Dealing with Multiple Representations. *Geographic Information Systems and Science*. New York: John Wiley & Sons (pp. 125-155)

Zhang, D., & Tsotras, V. (2005). Optimizing spatial Min/Max aggregations. *The VLDB Journal, 14*(3), 170–181. doi:10.1007/s00778-004-0142-4

KEY TERMS AND DEFINITIONS

Spatial OLAP: Visual platform built especially to support rapid and easy spatio-temporal analysis and exploration of data following a multidimensional approach comprised of aggregation levels available in cartographic displays as well as in tabular and diagram displays

Spatial Data Warehouse: Subject-oriented, non volatile, time variant and integrated repository of spatial data that is designed to facilitate reporting and spatial analysis.

Multidimensional Model: Conceptual model for the multidimensional analysis of huge datasets, based on the concepts of dimensions, facts and measures.

Geographic Information System: Information system for capturing, storing, analyzing, managing and presenting data that are spatially referenced

Spatial Decision Support System: Interactive, computer-based system designed to support a user or group of users in achieving a higher effectiveness of decision making while solving a semi-structured spatial problem

Section 3
Foundations and Applications of Data Mining and Data Analysis

Chapter 9
Novel Trends in Clustering

Claudia Plant
Technische Universität München, Munich Germany, Ludwig Maximilians Universität München, Munich, Germany

Christian Böhm
Technische Universität München, Munich Germany, Ludwig Maximilians Universität München, Munich, Germany

ABSTRACT

Clustering or finding a natural grouping of a data set is essential for knowledge discovery in many applications. This chapter provides an overview on emerging trends within the vital research area of clustering including subspace and projected clustering, correlation clustering, semi-supervised clustering, spectral clustering and parameter-free clustering. To raise the awareness of the reader for the challenges associated with clustering, the chapter first provides a general problem specification and introduces basic clustering paradigms. The requirements from concrete example applications in life sciences and the web provide the motivation for the discussion of novel approaches to clustering. Thus, this chapter is intended to appeal to all those interested in the state-of-the art in clustering including basic researchers as well as practitioners.

INTRODUCTION

In many applications, for example in medicine, life sciences, physics and market observation, terabytes of data is collected every day. Consider for example metabolite profiling (Baumgartner & Graber 2008). As an evolving branch of life sciences, Metabolomics studies the highly complex metabolism of cells, tissues, organs and organisms. One major focus of research is on identifying subtle changes related

to disease onset and progression. Small molecules involved in primary and intermediate metabolism are called metabolites. Metabolite profiling provides techniques to quantify the amount of metabolites in a sample. Due to recent advances of high-throughput technologies such as tandem mass spectrometry (MS/MS) hundreds of metabolites can be detected from a single blood sample. As a second example consider web usage. For each user accessing a page, the corresponding web server logs information including IP address, time of access, file path, browser and amount of transferred data.

DOI: 10.4018/978-1-60566-816-1.ch009

Huge volumes of web server log data is generated every day and its potential for commercial and non-commercial applications such as designing online shops or providing users with personalized content in digital libraries (Zaiane & al. 1998) is far from being fully exploited.

In both applications scenarios, extraction of information from the massive amounts of data is a non-trivial, highly challenging task. In both scenarios we want to learn unknown regularities and structure in the data with very little previous knowledge. In metabolite profiling, we want to gain novel insights how certain diseases change the pattern of metabolites. Simple statistic tests often applied in biomedicine can provide valuable information. However, only a tiny part of the information potentially available in the data can be accessed but large parts remain unexplored. There may be several sub-types of the disease each associated with a unique pattern of altered metabolism. Also in the healthy controls there may be different types of normal yet unexplored metabolic patterns. Similarly, in the second scenario we want to find groups of users with similar behavior to provide them personalized content.

As an important area within data mining, clustering aims at partitioning the data into groups such that the data objects assigned to a common group called cluster are as similar as possible and the objects assigned to different clusters differ as much as possible. With the term 'data objects'

we denote the instances subjected to a cluster analysis. Often, data objects can be represented as a feature vectors. In the scenario of metabolite profiling, the data objects are the subjects. Each subject is represented by a vector composed of the amounts of the measured metabolites. The dimensionality of the resulting feature space equals the number of metabolites. Alternatively, it could also be interesting to cluster the metabolites in the space defined by the subjects with the objective to identify groups of metabolites having similar prevalence across subjects.

Figure 1 displays examples of different types of clusters in vector data. The simplest type of a cluster is a spherical Gaussian. An example in two-dimensional space is depicted in Figure 1(a). Both coordinates follow a Gaussian distribution and are statistically independent from each other. As we will see in the next section, basic clustering algorithms can reliably detect such clusters. More complicated are correlation clusters with orthogonal major directions, as depicted in Figure 1(b). The objects of this cluster follow a line in one-dimensional space which is characterized by a strong linear dependency between the coordinates. In addition, the major directions of the cluster are orthogonal and can be detected by Principal Component Analysis. Figure 1(c) displays a non-linear correlation cluster. There exists a distinct dependency between the two coordinates but this dependency cannot be captured by a linear

Figure 1. Different types of clusters in vector data: (a) spherical Gaussian; (b) correlation cluster; (c) non-linear correlation cluster; (d) non-Gaussian cluster with non-orthogonal major directions

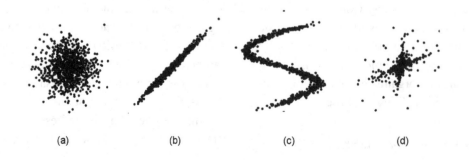

(a)   (b)   (c)   (d)

model. Linear and non-linear correlation clusters frequently occur in high dimensional vector data, such as metabolic data. Typically, such clusters exist in a subset of the dimensions only. Figure 1(d) displays a non-Gaussian correlation cluster with non-orthogonal major directions. Besides the cluster, there are some outliers. Noise points and outliers are common in real-world data.

This chapter provides a survey on novel trends in clustering. We will especially focus on highlighting the conceptual similarities and differences among approaches. In addition, a special focus will be on the applicability to real-world problems. Thus, we hope to provide conceptual survey which is valuable and maybe even inspiring for different groups of readers: scientists and students but also for practitioners looking for solutions in a concrete application. We can only provide a very incomplete snapshot focusing on some current and emerging vital trends and already apologize for all the important approaches which are missing.

We will discuss novel algorithms which are suitable to detect clusters in high dimensional feature space, including linear and non-linear correlation clusters with orthogonal and non-orthogonal major directions in noisy real-world data, as depicted in Figure 1(b)-(d). We will focus not only on vector data but also introduce solutions for clustering other types of data, for example graphs or data streams. For example in the internet scenario, it is interesting to cluster the users according to their behavior. The file path allows tracking the path of users within a website and can be represented as a graph. For online shop design, it would be interesting to cluster the users based on their file paths. The result could help to improve the structure of a website for specific groups of customers.

Most approaches to clustering require defining a suitable representation of the data objects, for example as feature vectors or graphs together with a notion of object similarity. In most applications, this is challenging and a mathematical similarity measure which fully agrees with the needs of the application may not even exist. In information retrieval, this problem is commonly referred to as the *semantic gap*. External side information which is often available in the form of expert knowledge can be very helpful to cope with this problem. For example it is known from literature that some metabolites are similar since they fulfill a common function in the organism. Semi-supervised clustering, an emerging research area which has recently attracted much attention focuses on integrating such side information into clustering. We will discuss some interesting solutions. Besides a suitable representation of the data objects and a notion of similarity, most clustering algorithms require input parameters which are often difficult to estimate, for example the number of desired clusters. We will introduce some recent approaches to parameter-free clustering which avoid crucial parameters by the application of information-theoretic concepts.

BACKGROUND

To make this chapter self-contained, and to illustrate some of the challenges associated with clustering, we will briefly discuss two fundamental clustering paradigms: iterative partitioning clustering and hierarchical density-based clustering. These two paradigms introduce two very different cluster notions which have been taken up and further elaborated by many other approaches.

For illustration and comparison, we introduce iterative partitioning clustering on the algorithm K-means (Duda & Hart 1973). K-means requires a metric distance function in vector space. In addition, the user has to specify the number of desired clusters K as an input parameter. Usually K-means starts with an arbitrary partitioning of the objects into K clusters. After this initialization, the algorithm iteratively performs the following two steps until convergence: (1) Update centers: For each cluster, compute the mean vector of its assigned objects. (2). Re-assign objects: Assign each object to its closest center. The algorithm converges as soon as no object changes its cluster assignment during two subsequent iterations. In most cases, fast convergence can be observed. The optimization function of K-means is well defined. The algorithm minimizes the sum of squared distances of the objects to their cluster centers. This optimization goal coincides well with our definition of the clustering problem provided in the beginning: Objects assigned to a common cluster should be as similar as possible. The second aspect of the definition that objects in different clusters should differ as much as possible is implicitly addressed at the same time. However, finding a global minimum of the objective function is a NP-hard problem (see for example Meila 2008). The objective function is non-linear and non-convex, which implies that no efficient algorithm can be provided to detect the global minimum exactly. K-means converges to a local minimum of the objective function in a very acceptable time frame. In many cases, the result is close to optimal and K-means is thus among the most wide-spread clustering algorithms. In practice it is useful to try different random initializations and keep the best result. There are many algorithms following the K-means paradigm, perhaps most importantly the expectation maximization (EM) algorithm (Dempster et al. 1997) to detect Gaussian mixture models with fuzzy cluster assignment. As K-means, the EM algorithm consists of two steps which are iterated until convergence: (1) Update centers to maximize the log-likelihood of the data (this step is often called M-step where M stands for maximization) and (2) assign objects proportionally to their likelihood to all centers (this step is called E-step where E stands for expectation, since the expected value of the log-likelihood is computed). Another important branch of iterative partitioning clustering consists of K-medoid methods such as PAM (Partitioning around Medoids) (Kaufmann & Rousseeuw 1990) or CLARANS (Clustering Large Applications based on Ran-

domized Search) (Ng & Han 1994). Instead of the mean, these methods select objects from the data set as cluster representatives. Therefore, also non-vector metric data can be clustered. However, selecting a suitable K is major problem with all these algorithms.

To avoid the problems with parameterization and local minima, hierarchical or density-based clustering can be an attractive alternative. Single Link (Jain & Dubes 1988) is the basic algorithm for hierarchical clustering. As result, this algorithm produces a tree-style visualization of the hierarchical cluster structure which is often called dendrogram. At the lowest level of the hierarchy all objects are represented as singleton clusters. In each step the closest pairs of objects are merged to form a cluster at the next higher level. Besides the distance function, no parameterization is required. There is no objective function to be minimized and the result is determinate. The runtime of Single Link is quadratic in the number of objects, which is acceptable in most applications. However, the result is often hard to interpret, especially for large data sets, since the visualization is the only output of the algorithm. If a partitioning into distinct clusters is desired, it is difficult to find a suitable level for horizontally cutting the hierarchy. In the presence of noise objects, the so-called Single Link effect can occur: Clusters may get connected by a chain of noise objects. Popular variants of Single Link which are somewhat less prone to the Single Link effect are Average Link and Complete Link. These algorithms introduce distance functions between sets of objects for clustering. In Average Link the average distance between two sets of objects is applied, in Complete Link the maximum distance.

Strongly related to the cluster notion of Single Link is the idea of density-based clustering. In density-based clustering, clusters are regarded areas of high object density which are separated by areas of lower object density. The algorithm DBSCAN (Density-Based Spatial Clustering of Applications with Noise) proposed in (Ester et al. 1996) formalizes this idea by two parameters: *MinPts* specifying a number of objects and ε specifying a volume. An object is called *core object* if it has at least *MinPts* objects within its ε− neighbourhood. If one object *P* is in the ε-neighbourhood of a core-object *Q*, then *P* is said to be *directly density reachable* from *Q*. The *density-connectivity* is the symmetric, transitive closure of the *direct density reachability*, and a *density-based (ε, MinPts)-cluster* is defined as a maximal set of density-connected objects. It can be proven that an *(ε, MinPts)-cluster* can be detected by collecting all density reachable objects starting from an arbitrary core object which is implemented in DBSCAN. See Figure 2 for an illustration of the definitions of DBSCAN. As K-means, DBSCAN determines a non-hierarchical, disjoint partitioning of the data set into clusters. However, the number of clusters does not need be specified in advance and the algorithm is robust against noise objects. Nevertheless, the number of clusters detected by DBSCAN depends on the choice of the parameters ε and *MinPts*. For some data sets even no suitable parameterization exists, for example in the case of various object densities in different areas of the data space or in the case of a hierarchical cluster structure. To cope with these problems, the algorithm OPTICS (Ordering Points to Identify the Clustering Structure) (Ankerst et al. 1999) has been proposed which is a hierarchical extension of DBSCAN but also related to Single Link. The main idea of OPTICS is to compute all possible clusterings for varying ε simultaneously during a single traversal of the data set. The output of OPTICS is a linear order

of the data objects according to their hierarchical cluster structure which is visualized in the so-called reachability-plot. OPTICS is equivalent to Single-Link if the *MinPts*-Parameter of OPTICS is set to one. OPTICS avoids the Single Link effect if *MinPts* is set to larger values.

We introduced K-means and Single Link as representatives of two different clustering paradigms. It is important to point out that clustering algorithms differ in their cluster notion. K-means provides a well defined objective function which intuitively coincides with our idea of clustering. But this specific objective function also narrows the type of clusters which can be detected: Only spherically shaped Gaussian clusters are captured by this definition. Single Link has a more general cluster notion: Arbitrarily shaped dense areas of the feature space are regarded as clusters. As discussed, the algorithms further differ in the need for parameter settings and the type of the result. When introducing recent clustering paradigms, we will always re-visit these points since they are essential for the choice of a suitable clustering algorithm for a certain application.

Figure 3 (a) displays a simple two-dimensional data set consisting of three Gaussian clusters. For comparison, Figure 3(b) displays the result of the iterative partitioning EM algorithm and Figure 3(c) the result of the hierarchical algorithm Single Link on this data set. Correctly parameterized with K=3 the result of EM clustering is a Gaussian mixture model with a good fit to the data. This result includes location and variance of each cluster which is often important for interpretation. The result of Single Link is a hierarchical visualization of the cluster structure. The three clusters are clearly visible in the dendrogram. However, the dendrogram always implies a hierarchical structure, even if there is no distinct cluster hierarchy in the data as in this example. In contrast to the result of EM, the dendrogram does not provide a model on the data. But note that Single Link does not require any input parameters whereas the result of EM strongly depends on a suitable parameterization.

Figure 2. Definitions of DBSCAN

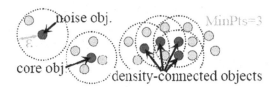

Figure 3. Clustering basics: (a) example data set with three spherical Gaussian clusters; (b) Gaussian mixture model obtained by EM clustering; (c) dendrogram obtained by Single Link

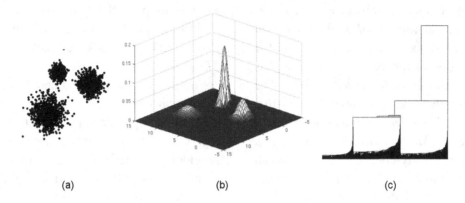

(a)   (b)   (c)

In summary, let us point out that both algorithms are suitable to detect the clusters in this simple toy example. In addition, the choice of a specific algorithm always comes along with characteristic benefits and drawbacks.

Detecting clusters in real-world data is usually much more difficult. The data are often represented in a high dimensional sparse feature space. Commonly, the data contains noise objects and features which are not relevant for clustering. Or the data has a complex non-vector structure. In the following, we will see that basic algorithms like K-means, EM, Single Link and DBSCAN are not sufficient to cope with the challenges emerging from modern applications, such as our example scenarios in life sciences and web usage. We will discuss some of the most vital research topics in clustering addressing the major challenges of clustering real-world data.

SUBSPACE CLUSTERING AND PROJECTED CLUSTERING

In metabolite profiling, hundreds of quantified metabolites can be detected from the serum samples of thousands of subjects. In this scenario, the data are represented in a very high dimensional vector space, regardless if we intend to cluster the subjects or the metabolites. When clustering such data with the basic algorithms as K-means or Single Link we face problems related to the so-called *curse of dimensionality*. The curse of dimensionality subsumes all the strange effects in high dimensional vector spaces which make clustering, indexing and classification difficult. With increasing dimensionality, more and more objects are located at the boundaries of the feature space and the distances between objects assimilate, for details see for example (Weber et al. 1998). The curse of dimensionality can already be visualized at the transition from one- to two-dimensional spaces, as Figure 4(a) demonstrates. In one dimensional space there are two distinct clusters, denoted by C1 and C2. Adding a single noise dimension significantly worsens the cluster structure. When adding more dimensions, we often see no cluster structure in the dendrogram. The result of K-means and EM is very unstable over different runs with different random initializations, since no distinct minimum of the objective function exists. The curse of dimensionality can significantly affect the result of basic clustering algorithms starting already at a moderate dimensionality of about ten. Global dimensionality reduction like Principal Component Analysis (PCA) can be applied to

Figure 4. Subspace and Projected Clustering. (a) The curse of dimensionality: In one-dimensional space there are two distinct clusters C1 and C2. In two-dimensional space the cluster structure is blurred due to one noise dimension; (b) and (c): Objects can be differently clustered in different subspaces. For example, in the subspace spanned by the features A and B, object 1 is clustered together with the objects 2, 3, and 4. In the subspace spanned by C and D, object 1 clustered together with the objects 2, 5, and 6. This information is preserved in subspace clustering but not in projected clustering

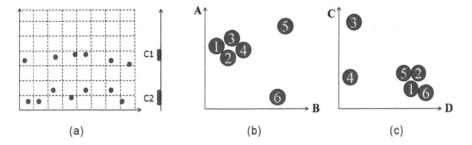

transform the data to a lower dimensional space. However, at least for clustering, PCA is not the best choice to cure the curse of dimensionality. PCA preserves the overall variance in the data. This implies, if the data has high variance without cluster structure in the full dimensional space, the clustering can not be much better in a subspace selected by PCA.

Subspace clustering is a better solution. Many high dimensional data sets exhibit rich cluster structures in axis-parallel subspaces which are spanned by subsets of the features. In our metabolite scenario, clusters of patients can only be identified in a subspace spanned by a subset of the metabolites. In addition, patients can be clustered differently in different subspaces. See Figure 3 (b) and (c) for an illustration of this effect. The subspace clustering problem is highly complex since a vector space of dimensionality d has 2^d-1 axis-parallel subspaces. Thus, an exhaustive search for the best subspaces is infeasible in higher dimensions. The algorithm CLIQUE (Clustering in Quest) (Agrawal et al. 1998), the fundamental approach to subspace clustering, introduces a monotonic criterion for object density which allows effective pruning in combination with bottom-up search. To define the density criterion, the data space is partitioned by

an axis-parallel grid into equal-sized units of width ε. Only units whose densities exceed a threshold τ are retained. A cluster is defined as a maximal set of connected dense units. This cluster notion allows effective pruning of the search space using the upwards monotonicity of the density criterion: Only subspaces containing dense units may be part of a higher dimensional subspace cluster. Successive modifications of CLIQUE with similar algorithmic paradigm include ENCLUS (Entropy-based Subspace Clustering) (Cheng et al. 1998) and MAFIA (Merging Adaptive Finite Intervals) (Nagesh et al. 2000). A drawback of these methods is the use of grids. In general, the efficiency and the accuracy of these approaches heavily depend on the positioning and resolution of the grids. Objects that naturally belong to a cluster may be missed or objects that are naturally noise may be assigned to a cluster due to an unfavorable grid position. The algorithm SUBCLU (Density-connected Subspace Clustering) (Kailing et al. 2004) avoids this problem by defining a monotonic density criterion relying on concepts of density-based clustering without grids. More precisely, the core object property of DBSCAN is applied in the definition of the density criterion. As a grid cell, the core object property is upwards monotonic.

Recently proposed algorithms like SURFING (Subspaces Relevant for Clustering) (Baumgartner et al. 2004), SCHISM (Support and Chernoff-Hoeffding Bound-based Interesting Subspace Miner) (Sequeira & Zaki 2004) and DUSK (Dimensionality-unbiased Subspace Clustering) (Assent et al. 2007) refrain from a cluster notion based on a monotonic density criterion, since this leads to major problems. With increasing dimensionality, the object density naturally decreases. Therefore, a fixed density criterion implicitly specifies the dimensionality of subspace clusters which can be detected by the algorithm. Parameterization of such algorithms is difficult. Subspace clusters of various dimensionalities cannot be detected in a single run of the algorithm. However, with the fixed density criterion, also the monotonicity property is dropped and heuristic search strategies are required. SURFING and DUSK propose criteria to rate the interestingness of subspaces for clustering based on statistics of the data distribution which allow detecting subspace clusters of various dimensionalities. SCHISM also employs a variable density criterion and heuristic search but uses a grid-based data quantization as CLIQUE. All described algorithms apply bottom-up search, which implies that at least parts of the subspace clusters must be visible in the one-dimensional subspaces.

An alternative solution to the curse of dimensionality in clustering is projected clustering. In contrast to subspace clustering, algorithms for projected clustering assign each data object to only one distinct cluster and determine the best subspace, or the best projection, for this cluster. Instead of performing a bottom-up search, most algorithms for projected clustering start in the full dimensional space and, similar to K-means, iteratively optimize some objective function. The first approach to projected clustering is the algorithm PROCLUS (Projected Clustering) (Aggarwal et al. 1999). Provided with the input parameters K and *l*, PROCLUS returns a partitioning of the data into K clusters having an average dimensionality

l. Objects not fitting well to any of the clusters are assigned to noise. To achieve comparability of distances among objects assigned to subspace clusters of different subspace dimensionality, the Manhattan distance is normalized by the subspace dimensionality. In the initialization stage, PROCLUS selects initial medoids as cluster representatives from the data objects. In the iterative phase, the set of medoids and their associated subspaces are refined using a greedy hill-climbing technique. After this iterative search, an additional pass over the data is performed for refinement of clusters, medoids and associated subspaces.

Procopiuc et al. (2002) introduce an alternative notion of projected clusters, called optimal projective clusters, together with an algorithm called DOC (Density-based Optimal Projective Clustering) to find such clusters. An optimal projective cluster is defined using two parameters: α specifying a fraction of the data objects and ω specifying the width of a hypercube. An optimal projected cluster is defined as a set of points C associated with a subspace of dimensions D such that C contains more than α% points of the objects and the projection of C onto the subspace spanned by D is contained in a hyper-cube of width ω. Based on Monte-Carlo sampling, the algorithm DOC returns approximations of the optimal projected clusters. DOC does not require the user to specify K, but the parameterization remains difficult for the same reasons as discussed for subspace clustering with a fixed density criterion. In addition, the cluster notion of DOC does not care about the data distribution inside the hypercube representing a cluster. Not always the hypercube contains exactly one cluster, it may contain several clusters, noise points and empty space as well. The algorithm PreDeCon (Subspace Preference Weighted Density- connected Clustering) (Böhm et al. 2004) partially avoids the problems of difficult parameterization and undesired behavior in the presence of noise by extending the basic concepts of density-based clustering to projected clustering. In this approach, the notion of subspace preference clusters is introduced which are defined as density-based clusters in subspaces. The dimensions of the subspace of a cluster are determined by selecting directions of low variance within the $\varepsilon-$ neighbourhood of core objects.

CORRELATION CLUSTERING

The detection of correlations between different features in a given data set is a very important data mining task. High correlation of features may result in a high degree of co-linearity or even a perfect one, corresponding to approximate linear dependencies between two or more attributes. These dependencies can be arbitrarily complex, one or more features might depend on a combination of several other features. In the data space, dependencies of features are manifested as lines, planes, or, generally speaking, hyper-planes exhibiting a relatively high density of data objects compared to the surrounding space. See Figure 1(b) for an example of a correlation cluster in two-dimensional space. Knowing of correlations is traditionally used to reduce the dimensionality of the data set by eliminating redundant features. However, detection of correlated features may also help to reveal hidden causalities which are of great interest to the domain expert. Recently, correlation clustering has been introduced as a novel concept of knowledge discovery in databases to detect dependencies among features and to cluster data objects sharing a common pattern of dependencies. It corresponds to the marriage of two widespread ideas: First, correlation analysis usually performed by Principle Component Analysis (PCA) and, second, clustering which aims at identifying local subgroups of data objects sharing high similarity. Correlation clustering groups the data set into subsets called correlation clusters such that the objects in the same correlation cluster are all associated to a common hyper-plane of arbitrary dimensionality. In addition, many algorithms for correlation cluster analysis also require the objects

of a cluster to exhibit a certain density, i.e. feature similarity. When comparing correlation clustering with subspace and projected clustering, we can observe, that in correlation clustering, the clusters exist in an arbitrarily oriented subspace rather than in an axis-parallel one. Therefore, correlation clustering is sometimes also referred to as *generalized subspace clustering*.

Correlation clustering has been successfully applied to several application domains. For example, customer recommendation systems are important tools for target marketing. For the purpose of data analysis for recommendation systems, it is important to find homogeneous groups of users with similar ratings in subsets of the attributes. In addition, it is interesting to find groups of users with correlated affinities. This knowledge can help companies to predict customer behaviour and thus develop future marketing plans. In molecular biology, correlation clustering is an important method for the analysis of several types of data. In metabolic screening, the collected data usually contain the concentrations of certain metabolites in the blood of thousands of patients. In such data sets, it is important to find homogeneous groups of patients with correlated metabolite concentrations indicating a common metabolic disease. Thus, several metabolites can be linearly dependent on several other metabolites. Uncovering these patterns and extracting the dependencies of these clusters is a key step towards understanding metabolic or genetic disorders and designing individual drugs. A second example where correlation clustering is a sound methodology for data analysis in molecular biology is DNA micro-array data analysis. Micro-array data comprise the expression levels of thousands of genes in different samples such as experimental conditions, cells or organisms. Roughly speaking, the expression level of a gene indicates how active this gene is. The recovering of dependencies among different genes in certain conditions is an important step towards a more comprehensive understanding of the functionality of organisms which is a prominent aspect of systems biology. When the samples represent some patients, it is important to detect homogeneous groups of persons exhibiting a common linear dependency among a subset of genes in order to determine potential pathological subtypes of diseases and to develop individual treatments.

One of the first approaches to correlation clustering (there called generalized projected clustering) was ORCLUS (for Oriented Clustering), proposed in (Aggarwal & Yu, 2000). As a variant of K-means, this algorithm requires the user to specify in advance the number of clusters K, as well as the subspace dimensionality of the clusters, l. Like K-means, the algorithm performs a loop until convergence, in which points are assigned to clusters and cluster representatives are re-determined. In ORCLUS, the cluster representatives correspond to the mean vectors, complemented by a linear subspace which is determined according to the Eigenvectors of the associated points. A number l_c of these Eigenvectors is selected where l_c decreases in each iteration step from full dimensionality to the user-specified final dimensionality l. In addition, the number of clusters is also decreased from step to step by a user-defined parameter α. The general idea of ORCLUS is that each cluster is associated to its own individual subspace which is arbitrarily oriented. This set of subspaces is searched by first partitioning the data set into spherical clusters (of full dimensionality) and then successively stripping off noisy dimensions. In the case of clearly separated correlation clusters this method performs well. However, when correlation clusters touch each other, the initial search in full dimensionality may be misleading, and the algorithm may easily fail to separate neighbouring clusters with different subspace orientation.

An approach particularly addressing this problem is 4C (Computing Clusters of Correlation-connected Objects), as proposed in (Böhm et al. 2004). 4C is founded on the paradigms of density-based partitioning clustering (for DBSCAN, cf.

the background section) and Principal Component Analysis (PCA). A point P is considered as a core object if its ε-neighbourhood not only contains a sufficiently high number (parameter *MinPts*) of neighbouring points but also has a dimensionality of at most l, as determined by the PCA of the neighbouring points. To allow imperfect correlations, a dimension is considered flat if the corresponding Eigenvalue is below a specified threshold d. Each core object is then associated to an ellipsoid which exactly reflects the extension of the neighbouring points: It is extended (with radius ε) in l dimensions and flat (with radius ε/κ where κ is usually set to $1/d$) in the remaining dimensions. Two objects are directly density reachable from each other if both objects are mutually located in their ε-neighbourhood with respect to their associated ellipsoids. The remaining definitions of correlation connection and correlation reachability are then defined like the density connection and density reachability, respectively in the DBSCAN algorithm (symmetric and transitive closure of the direct correlation reachability). A correlation cluster is a maximal set of correlation density connected objects. Like the DBSCAN algorithm, 4C starts by selecting an arbitrary starting object, determining whether it is a core object and if so, putting its neighbours into a queue called seed list. The cluster is extended by iteratively taking neighbours out of the seed list and performing them in the same way, until the seed list is empty. Then a new, unprocessed object is selected as the next starting object, until all objects have been considered. The algorithm is well able to handle difficult situations where points of different clusters are close together. Likely, the points located at the boundary, will not be assigned to any of the correlation clusters (because their neighbourhood is not flat in a sufficient number of dimensions) but the remaining database points are not touched by this problem. The difficulty with this method is the selection of the radius ε: If ε is chosen too large, then too many points which actually belong to different correlation clusters are located in the neighbourhood, and an incorrect subspace dimension may be determined. In contrast, if ε is chosen too small, no core objects may be found. A hierarchical extension of 4C called HiCO which is based on the hierarchical density-based clustering notion of OPTICS (cf. the background section) and PCA has also been proposed (Achtert et al. 2006). A further extension, DiSH (Achtert et al. 2007) considers more general, network-based relationships between correlation clusters.

In (Tung et al. 2006) the authors propose CURLER, a method for finding and visualizing clusters even with a nonlinear correlation. CURLER uses the concept of micro-clusters that are generated using a variant of EM clustering. The micro-clusters are merged to discover correlation clusters. The merging of micro-clusters is based on the concept of co-sharing, i.e. the co-sharing level of two micro-clusters corresponds to the total amount of points which are associated to both clusters simultaneously. From the set of all micro-clusters, an arbitrary starting object is selected, and, like in OPTICS or Single Link, in each step that cluster is selected as the next micro-cluster in the micro-cluster order which has the highest co-sharing level to the starting object or any of the previously placed micro-clusters. CURLER also defines a visualization technique similar to the reachability-plot of OPTICS. CURLER improves over ORCLUS and 4C as the correlations underlying the clusters are not necessarily linear. Thus, also clusters like the example in Figure 1(c) can be detected. Furthermore, as a fuzzy approach, CURLER assumes each data object to belong to all clusters simultaneously, but with different probabilities for each cluster assigned. By merging several clusters according to their co-sharing level, the algorithm on the one hand becomes less sensitive to the predefined number K of clusters, thus also overcoming a severe limitation of any K-means related approach. On the other hand, the user cannot directly derive a model describing the correlations, since the original K models are no longer present in the resulting clustering. Therefore, one can say that the algorithm can handle arbitrary non-linear correlations but is not able to identify the type of correlation.

The most important problem of all approaches previously presented in this section is the missing robustness with respect to noise objects and correlation clusters which are close to each other. All the applied techniques, iterative methods, density-based methods and micro-clusters are to some degree sensitive to the situation when the correlation cannot be determined by looking at the full-dimensional local neighbourhood of an object. The algorithm CASH (Clustering in Arbitrary Subspaces based on the Hough transform) presented in (Achtert et al. 2008) tackles this problem by a sophisticated parameter space transformation: Instead of clustering the points directly, the idea is first to replace each point by the (infinite) set of all possible, λ-dimensional planes in which the point is contained. For low (two or three) dimensional applications from image processing domains, this idea is already well-known, and denoted by the term Hough transform. In these low dimensional domains, the infinite set of all lines or planes can easily be discretely represented by a finite selection of some possible sample planes (for example sampled by discrete angles). Matching planes can easily be determined by counting of accumulators, where each accumulator corresponds to one possible plane. In higher dimensional spaces, a sufficient discretization of all possible planes is not possible due to the curse of dimensionality. But the set of all possible planes passing through a point can also be represented by a function. If the planes are represented by Euclidean coordinates, these functions are linear functions. If the planes are represented by spherical coordinates (which is advantageous because orthographic planes cannot be represented in Euclidean coordinates) then the functions are trigonometric (combinations of sine and cosine functions). Points sharing a common plane are determined by those trigonometric functions which have a common intersection at an

Figure 5. Transformation of the objects into parameter space for correlation clustering as performed by the algorithm CASH: (a) correlation cluster in original space; (b) representation of the objects as trigonometric functions in parameter space

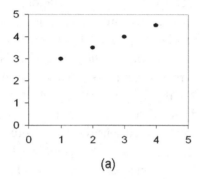
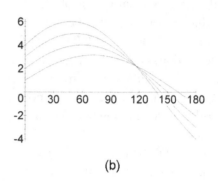

(a)   (b)

arbitrary point of the parameter space. See Figure 5 for an illustration of the transformation to parameter space. The algorithm CASH decomposes the trigonometric functions recursively until a point in the parameter space is found in which many trigonometric functions coincide. That means, even if different planes intersect each other or are hidden in a noisy environment, the points in the parameter space representing the correlation clusters exists and can be found. With increasing dimensionality the number of required decompositions of the trigonometric functions increases. Therefore, also the processing time increases, but is still of cubic order in the number of dimensions. Of all algorithms presented in this section, CASH reveals least sensitivity with respect to noise objects and intersecting clusters.

SEMI-SUPERVISED CLUSTERING

Semi-supervised clustering is an emerging area which evolved from an important need of numerous applications: integrating side-information or supervision into clustering. Semi-supervised clustering may be beneficial for bridging the so-called semantic gap in human-computer interaction. Often, purely feature-based similar-ity measures can not satisfactorily represent the complex human notion of similarity. Consider for example clustering web pages, which may contain images, text and hyperlinks. It is difficult to define an appropriate similarity measure based on the content of the web pages. As a valuable source of side information, ratings of users on the similarity of some selected pages can be integrated into clustering. As an example from biomedicine, consider clustering of gene expression data. The expression levels of thousands of genes can be measured simultaneously using the micro-array technology. Clustering is often applied to detect functionally related genes. There are two major challenges associated with clustering gene expression data: First, the curse of dimensionality, which can be addressed by subspace or projected clustering. Secondly, there exists a huge amount of side information on functionally related genes, where most of this knowledge is contained in publications available in biomedical literature databases. Similar to the webpage example, the side-information is often incomplete, i.e. there are genes for which we have expression measurements but no literature information. As demonstrated in (Zeng et al. 2007), semi-supervised clustering exploiting both sources of knowledge, the feature information of gene expression as measured in the micro-array experiment and the literature information outperforms conventional clustering.

Most algorithms for semi-supervised clustering model potentially incomplete side-information by a set of constraints. Must-link constraints are established between pairs of objects which should be clustered together, for example two genes which are known to be functionally related from literature, and cannot-link-constraints are established between objects which should be assigned to different clusters. This set of constraints is then incorporated into a modified clustering algorithm. Following the classification of clustering algorithms introduced in the background section, we can assign most algorithms for semi-supervised clustering into the classes of iterative partitioning and hierarchical density-based algorithms.

The first iterative partitioning algorithm for semi-supervised clustering is COP-K-means introduced in (Wagstaff et al 2001). COP-K-means extends K-means with must-link and cannot-link constraints formulated as described above. The cluster assignment step of the basic K-means algorithm is modified as follows: Objects with cannot-link constraints must be assigned to different clusters. If this is not possible, i.e. if no cluster exists to host an object, the algorithm aborts. Note that supervision is only used for the cluster assignment of the objects for which side information is available, also often called the *labeled* objects, and not for the other objects, called the *un-labeled* objects. Shental et al. (2003) propose a constrained version of the EM algorithm. Must-link constraints can be respected by a modification of the E- step: For two objects with a must-link constraint, only the proportion of probability respecting the constraint is considered. The incorporation of cannot-link-constraints is more complex since they are not transitive. To incorporate both types of constraints into EM, a Markov network is applied. Because of the probabilistic nature of the EM algorithm, supervision not only affects the clustering of the labeled objects, but implicitly also the clustering of the un-labeled objects.

The MPCK-means (Metric Pairwise Constraint K-means) algorithm proposed in (Bilenko et al. 2004) integrates constraints and metric learning into K-means and thereby explicitly extends the influence of supervision to the un-labeled objects. For each cluster, Euclidean distance is parameterized with a weight matrix which is updated in each iteration of the algorithm. The update rule for the weight matrix considers the constraint violations inside a cluster proportionally to their severity. If for example the cluster contains two cannot-link objects which are very close together, the metric needs to be altered more drastically as if these points are already far away from each other. In the second case it is likely that the objects are assigned to different clusters in the next iteration even without any metric change. Although each cluster has its own associated weight matrix, in the update step global metric learning is performed by the linear transformation best representing the metric changes in all clusters. In (Basu et al. 2004) this idea is theoretically liked to Hidden Markov Random Fields (HMRF) and extended to the Bregman divergences, a wide range of distance functions including cosine similarity for text data. The foundation on HMRF allows defining a kernel for semi-supervised graph clustering (Kulis et al. 2005).

Due to the different cluster notion, hierarchical and density-based algorithms to semi-supervised clustering integrate supervision information in different ways. The first algorithm in this category is the CCL (Constrained Complete Link) algorithm proposed by (Klein et al. 2002) which integrates constraints into Complete Link clustering. Before clustering, the constraints are used to modify the distance matrix between objects: the distance between must-link objects is set to zero. To preserve the metric property of the data space, distances between other objects are adjusted by a shortest-path algorithm. The distance between cannot-link objects is set to a value larger than the maximal distance occurring in the data set. Cannot-link constraints are implicitly propagated during clustering. The result of the CCL algorithm is of other type (dendrogram) but besides this very similar to the result of COP-K-means. Both algorithms perform clustering without violating any of the constraints. This rigid preservation of constraints can lead to very unnatural clustering results if the constraints do not agree well with the data distribution. Consider for example the data set displayed in Figure 6. The labeled objects are visualized by larger symbols and the clustering results are marked by different colors and are additionally annotated. The result of COP-K-means in Figure 6(a) only respects the constraints and not the data distribution. The recently proposed hierarchical density-based algorithm HISSCLU (Böhm & Plant 2008) alleviates this problem by proposing a different way of incorporating supervision into density-based clustering. Instead of for formulating pair-wise must-link and cannot-link constraints, the labeled objects are utilized as seeds for cluster expansion. Density-based clusters are expanded starting at each labeled object simultaneously. During this cluster expansion process, labels are propagated to the un-labeled objects. In areas of the feature space where conflicts caused by differently labeled objects exist, a local distance weighting is applied. Similar to MPCK-means,

HISSCLU achieves more natural results in the case of inconsistent information provided by the data and the supervision (for comparison Figure 6(b) displays the result of MPCK-means and Figure 6(c) the result of HISSCLU). Experiments demonstrate that, especially in the case of some wrongly labeled objects (for example originating from erroneous user ratings), the local metric adaptation applied in HISSCLU outperforms the global metric learning scheme of MPCK-means. In addition, HISSCLU provides a visualization of the hierarchical cluster structure which displays how consistent both sources of information actually are.

In this section, our major focus is on algorithms closely interrelating supervision and clustering. It should be mentioned that there are several recent approaches focusing on methods for global (Xing et al. 2003, Bar-Hillel et al. 2003) or local (Chang & Yeung 2004) metric learning from supervision information which can be used prior to an arbitrary clustering algorithm. Yip et al. (2005) propose a semi-supervised algorithm for projected clustering which is an interesting option to cope with the curse of dimensionality. Their algorithm SSPC (Semi-supervised Projected Clustering) considers not only supervision for objects in the form of

Figure 6. Results of semi-supervised clustering. The example consists of three clusters containing six labeled objects of two different classes. (a) COP-K-means: unnatural clustering respecting the constraints; (b) MPC-K-means: Although it contains uniformly labeled objects, the cluster on top is split into two parts (c3 and c4) due to the limitations of K-means; (c) HISSCLU: Most natural result by density-based clustering and local distance weighting (Figure from Böhm & Plant 2008)

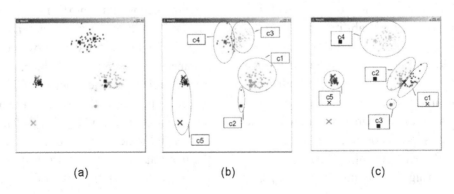

(a) (b) (c)

class labels but also supervision for dimensions. This type of supervision is modeled by specifying dimensions which are relevant for certain classes. The algorithmic paradigm of SSPC is similar to the algorithms PROCLUS and ORCLUS with some modifications. Most importantly, labeled objects and labeled dimensions are used for initialization and the parameter *l* specifying the average cluster dimensionality is replaced by a more intuitive parameter specifying the maximum variance for relevant dimensions.

SPECTRAL CLUSTERING

Spectral clustering considers the clustering problem from the perspective of graph theory. The data is provided by a similarity matrix from which a weighted graph is constructed. For many types of data the graph representation is very natural, for example for social networks where the nodes are different people and the edges represent friendship. The clustering problem is to find a partitioning of the graph such that the edges between different clusters have a very low weight. Different objective functions for a good partitioning have been proposed. If for example a partitioning into two clusters is desired, the Minimum Cut objective function (minCut) just removes the edge having the lowest weight. The minCut problem can easily be solved (Stoer & Wagner 1997) but leads to an undesired partitioning in many cases for example by simply removing a single outlying vertex from the graph. One option to circumvent this problem is to request that the clusters should be reasonably large. This is implemented in the objective function Ratio Cut (rCut) first introduced by (Hagen & Kahng 1992) which considers the ratio between the weight of the cut edges and the size of the resulting clusters. As an alternative, the objective function Normalized Cut (nCut) (Shi & Malik 2000) considers the connectivity between clusters, expressed by the weight of the cut edges as in rCut, but in relation to the within

cluster density which is expressed by the sum of weights of the edges within the clusters. Several further objective functions for balanced graph partitioning have been proposed, for example minMaxCut (Ding et al. 2001) which sums up the weights within each cluster separately and thus strikes to obtain individual clusters of high object density. Introducing balancing constraints however makes the graph partitioning problem NP-hard (Wagner & Wagner 1993).

Spectral clustering proposes algorithms to solve relaxed forms of the balanced graph partitioning problem. Most algorithms for spectral clustering such as (Shi & Malik 2000, Ng et al. 2002) follow a similar paradigm. After creating a weighted similarity graph from data, the Laplacian of this graph is constructed. The similarity graph is represented by a symmetric adjacency matrix A. The unnormalized Laplacian of a graph is obtained by subtracting the adjacency matrix from the degree matrix, i.e. $L = D-A$. The spectrum of the Laplacian obtained by Eigenvalue decomposition has interesting properties for clustering, for example the number of constant Eigenvectors coincides with the number of connected components of a graph. Usually, we have a fully connected graph in clustering. In this case, the clusters can be detected by mapping the data objects to the space spanned by the first K Eigenvectors and performing standard K-means. It can be proven that this procedure yields an approximation of balanced graph partitioning. The algorithms differ in the ways if and how the Laplacian is normalized. Thereby, different objective functions can be optimized. Recall that the objectives of clustering are two-fold: First, the objects in different clusters should be as dissimilar as possible and secondly the objects within one cluster should be as similar as possible. The simplest case of no normalization of the Laplacian addresses only the first goal. Performing K-means in the Eigenvector space approximates the rCut objective function which only considers balance in the number of objects which is achieved by K-means. To explicitly require within cluster similarity, normalization with the inverted degree matrix is required. The algorithm proposed in (Shi & Malik 2000) approximates the optimal nCut by decomposing a normalized Laplacian defined as D$^{-1/2}$ L. It can be proven that minMaxCut can be approximated by the same generalized Eigenproblem. Ng et al. (2002) propose symmetric normalization of the Laplacian, i.e. D$^{-1/2}$ L D$^{-1/2}$. This paper also provides derivations of spectral clustering from the perspectives of perturbation theory and random walks on graphs. Figure 7 provides an example of non-Gaussian vector data clustered with this algorithm. It becomes evident that the transformation of the clustering problem to the graph-cut perspective allows detecting arbitrarily shaped clusters.

Dhillon (2001) and Zha et al. (2001) propose algorithms for simultaneously clustering documents and words of a word-document co-occurrence matrix based on the spectral clustering idea. Documents and words are arranged in a bipartite graph and objective functions similar to nCut for bipartite graph partitioning are introduced. A more general framework for spectral clustering of multi-type relational data is introduced in (Long et al. 2006). This method allows simultaneously clustering objects of multiple types which are related to each other, for example web pages, queries and web users. Technically this is achieved by collective factorization of related matrices.

Unlike many algorithms for partitioning clustering, spectral clustering requires no assumptions on the data distribution and the algorithms can be easily implemented using standard linear algebra packages. However, the result strongly depends on the construction of the similarity matrix and a suitable choice of the number of clusters K. Bach and Jordan (2003) propose a technique for metric learning to construct the similarity matrix together with a novel algorithm approximating nCut by weighted K-means in Eigenvector space. Zelnik-Manor and Perona (2004) propose guidelines for parameter settings. Another limitation of spectral methods is that they require decomposing an $n \times n$ matrix for a data set of n points and are therefore not suitable for very large data sets. Fowlkes et al. (2004) propose a sampling-based method to approximate spectral clustering of large data sets. As an alternative, Dhillon et al. (2004) propose a weighted kernel-K-means algorithm to minimize Ncut without matrix decomposition.

PARAMETER-FREE CLUSTERING

Most approaches to clustering introduced so far suffer from a common problem: To obtain a good result, the user needs to select suitable values for parameters such as the number of clusters K in K-means and related approaches, density thresholds

Figure 7. Spectral Clustering following Ng et al. (2002): (a) Data set with two non-linear correlation clusters; (b) Color coded visualization of the normalized Laplacian; (c) Second largest Eigenvector provides cluster indicators which can be trivially separated by bisecting K-means

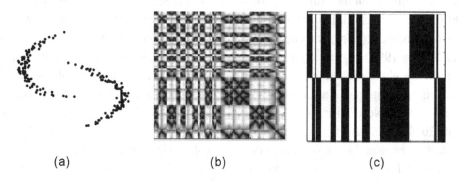

(a)   (b)   (c)

or neighbourhood sizes in density-based clustering, or the subspace dimensionality in projected clustering. In practice, the best way to cope with this problem often is to run the algorithm several times with different parameter settings. Thereby, suitable values for the parameters can be learned in a trial and error fashion. However, this process is very time consuming. Confronted with a large data set to be clustered only a few trials are feasible, or suitable parameter settings need to be estimated from a small sample. Anyhow, it cannot be guaranteed that at least useful values for the parameters are obtained by this procedure. The large number of parameters required in many algorithms even conflicts with the unsupervised nature of the clustering problem as introduced in the beginning. The goal of clustering is to find a natural grouping of the data without requiring any background knowledge. But without background knowledge, it is often very difficult to specify appropriate parameter settings.

Recently, parameter-free clustering therefore has attracted increasing attention. Most approaches, such as the algorithms X-Means (Pelleg & Moore 2001), G-Means (Hammerly & Elkan 2003) and OCI (Böhm et al. 2008) are founded on information theory and closely related concepts. The basic idea is to relate clustering to data compression. Assume that data consisting of feature vectors should be transferred via a communication channel from a sender to a receiver. Without clustering, each coordinate needs to be fully coded by transforming the numerical value into a bit string. If the data exhibits regularities, clustering can drastically reduce the communication costs. For example the EM algorithm can be applied to determine a model for the data. With this model, the data can be compressed very effectively since only the deviations from the model need to be encoded which requires much less bits than the full coordinates. In addition, the model itself needs to be encoded and transferred. The model can be regarded as a codebook which allows the receiver to de-compress the data again.

This basic idea, often referred as the Minimum Description Length Principle (MDL) (Grünwald 2005) allows comparing different clusterings: Assume we have two different clusterings A and B of the same data set. We can state that A is better than B if it allows compressing the data set more effectively than B. Note that we consider the overall communication cost comprising data and model here and not only the code length spent for the data. Thereby we achieve a natural balance between the complexity of the model and its fit to the data. Closely related ideas developed by different communities include the Bayesian Information Criterion (BIC), the Aikake Information Criterion (AIC) and the Information Bottleneck method (IB) (Tishby et al. 2000).

A first line of papers are based on the Information Bottleneck method. The fundamental idea behind IB is compressing only the relevant characteristics of the data which leads to a lossy compression. To judge relevance, besides the data a second source of information is required which is often called the *auxiliary variable*. Therefore, these approaches are also related to semi-supervised clustering but are discussed here because of their information theoretic foundation. Relevance is defined as the amount of information that the data provide about the auxiliary variable. The clustering problem is considered as finding a lossy compression of the data preserving as much information on the auxiliary variable as possible. IB is particularly useful for co-occurance data such as words and documents. In this context it is interesting to discover clusters of words which contain relevant information on the documents (Slonim & Tishby 2000, Dhillon et al. 2003). This principle has been extended by Slonim et al. (2001) to the multivariate information bottleneck technique which allows extracting different meaningful partitions of the data simultaneously. As demonstrated in (Tishby & Slonim 2000), the IB principle can also be applied for clustering general metric data. This algorithm first transforms the similarity matrix of the data into a Markov process by assigning a state of a Markov chain to each data object and the transition probability between states is defined as an exponential function of the pair-wise distances. A transition matrix is defined whose entries specify the transition probabilities between the different states. Using this transition matrix, a random walk with an infinite number of steps would provide no information on the starting point. For clustering, it is interesting to consider the information loss on the starting point for a random walk of some fixed number of steps t. The rate of information loss is slow if the random walk is stabilized by structures in the data, for example if it remains within one cluster. IB is applied to find a partitioning of the data into clusters which best predicts the information loss after t steps of random walk (which is the auxiliary variable in this case). However, this approach is not completely parameter-free since a suitable number of steps t needs to be selected.

The second category of approaches directly focus on parameter-free partitioning clustering and are based on MDL and related ideas such as BIC. For these methods, the data itself is the only source of knowledge. Information-theoretic arguments are applied for model selection during clustering and, in contrast to the approaches based on IB, these approaches involve a lossless compression of the data. The work of Still and Bialek (2004) provides important theoretical background by using information-theoretic arguments to relate the maximal number of clusters that can be detected by partitioning clustering with the size of the data set. The algorithm XMeans (Pelleg & Moore 2000) combines the K-means paradigm with the Bayesian Information Criterion for parameter-free clustering. XMeans involves an efficient top-down splitting algorithm where intermediate results are obtained by bisecting K-means and are evaluated with BIC. However, due to the properties of K-means, only spherically Gaussian clusters can be detected. The algorithm G-means (Gaussian means) introduced in (Hamerly & Elkan 2003) has been designed for parameter-free correlation

clustering. G-means follows a similar algorithmic paradigm as XMeans with top-down splitting and the application of bisecting K-means upon each split. However, the criterion to decide whether a cluster should be split up into two is based on a statistical test for Gaussianity. Splitting continues until the clusters are Gaussian, which implies of course, that non-Gaussian clusters can not be detected. The algorithm PG-means (Projected Gaussian means) (Feng & Hamerly 2006) is similar to G-means but learns models with increasing K with the EM algorithm. In each iteration, various one-dimensional projections of the data and the model are tested for Gaussianity. Experiments demonstrate that PG-means is less prone to over fitting than G-means. Figueiredo and Jain (2002) propose a parameter-free EM algorithm based on the MDL principle. In contrast to XMeans which applies BIC to evaluate intermediate results, an MDL-based model selection criterion is directly integrated into EM. Due to the properties of EM Gaussian data is assumed, but the algorithm can be supplied with a covariance matrix and thus supports the same cluster notion as G-means and PG-means.

It turns out that the underlying clustering algorithm and the choice of the similarity measure are already some kind of parameterization which implicitly comes with specific assumptions. The commonly used Euclidean distance for example assumes Gaussian data. In addition, the algorithms discussed so far are very sensitive with respect to noise objects or outliers. These problems are addressed by the recently proposed algorithm RIC (Robust Information-theoretic Clustering) (Böhm et al. 2006). This algorithm can be applied for post-processing an arbitrary imperfect initial clustering. This approach is based on MDL and introduces a coding scheme especially suitable for clustering together with algorithms for purifying the initial clusters from noise. The coding scheme for a cluster is illustrated in Figure 8. Each coordinate of each cluster is associated with a probability density function (PDF). Best

Figure 8. Parameter-free clustering. Coding scheme for cluster objects of the RIC algorithm. In addition to the data, type and parameters of the PDF need to be coded for each cluster. (Figure from Böhm et al. 2006)

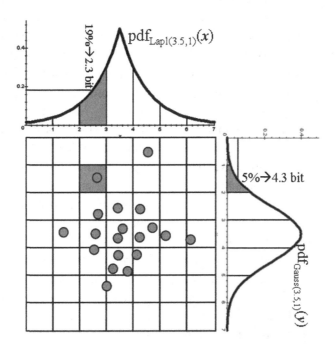

compression can be achieved if the value of a coordinate is encoded with a bit string of length anti-proportional to its likelihood. In a first step, RIC removes noise objects from the initial clusters, and then merges clusters if this allows for more effective data compression. The algorithm can operate with arbitrary data distributions which can be described by PDFs. However, a fixed set of PDFs needs to be selected in advance. The algorithm OCI (Outlier-robust Clustering using Independent Components) (Böhm et al. 2008) provides parameter-free clustering of noisy data and allows detecting non-Gaussian clusters with non-orthogonal major directions as the example in Figure 1(d). Technically this is achieved by defining a very general cluster notion based on the Exponential Power Distribution (EPD) and by integrating Independent Component Analysis (ICA) into clustering. The EPD includes a wide range of symmetric distribution functions, for example Gaussian, Laplacian and uniform distri-

butions and an infinite number of hybrid types in between. Beyond correlations detected by PCA which correspond to correlation clusters with orthogonal major directions, ICA allows to detect general statistical dependencies in data.

FUTURE TRENDS

In this section, we point out some further trends from which we believe that they will attract even more attention in the future; one is clustering of uncertain data. Uncertainty is a natural element in many applications, for example due to the limited resolution and accuracy of data acquisition techniques or due to the application of aggregated features. Sometimes uncertainty is even willingly introduced, for example by adding small perturbations to the data to mask sensitive features in privacy-preserving data mining (Aggarwal 2007). Some recent papers focus on clustering uncertain data, such as (Hamdan & Govaert 2005, Kriegel & Pfeifle 2005, Ngai et al. 2006). These approaches model uncertain objects by probability density functions and propose adapted versions of partitioning clustering such as K-means (Ngai et al. 2006), EM (Hamdan & Govert 2005) and DBSCAN (Kriegel & Pfeifle 2005). A special case of uncertainty is clustering moving objects, for example for location-based services. In this case, specialized algorithms can be applied, for example (Li et al. 2004) since the location of the data objects is usually described in two-dimensional space but with an additional temporal dimension.

The temporal dimension is even more emphasized in clustering data streams. In a streaming environment the data objects are coming into the system at a very high rate, consider for example sensor measurements or the click streams of users on a website. The goal of clustering is thus to provide at any time a good clustering of the sequence of objects seen so far. Algorithms for clustering data streams have to be very efficient to keep pace with high-throughput streams. Usually, complete re-clustering is not feasible and efficient incremental algorithms are needed. Designing algorithms with limited memory usage is an additional challenge arising of the special properties of massive streams which do not allow storing all objects. Clustering of streaming data has recently attracted much attention with a lot of research papers, for example (O'Callaghan et al. 2003, Aggarwal et. al. 2003, Nasaroi et al. 2003), to mention a few. To cope with the special requirements of data streams, for example (Aggarwal et. al. 2003) introduces CluStream, a general framework. The fundamental idea of CluStream is to divide the clustering process into two steps. The micro-clustering phase involves efficient online collecting of statistical data from the stream. Initial micro-clusters are created by applying K-means to the first objects of the stream. Whenever a new object of the stream arrives, the micro-clusters are updated by either assigning the new object to one of the micro-clusters or creating a new cluster, if the object does not fit to any of the existing clusters. Each micro-cluster is associated with statistical information, including for example its radius. In the macro-clustering phase the final clustering result is determined with a variant of K-means. As input parameters, the user needs to specify the timeframe of interest *h* and the desired number of clusters K. Multiple runs of this algorithm allow a flexible exploration of stream clusters over various time frames. A very different approach to clustering noisy multidimensional streaming data has been proposed by (Nasraoui et al. 2003). Inspired by the immune system of living organisms, this paper introduces a model for an artificial immune system suitable for clustering. Data objects of the stream are regarded as antigens which are presented to the lymphocytes. In the immune system of living organisms, antigens are roughly speaking substances which are responsible to initiate an immune response by generating antibodies. If the amount of antibodies exceeds a certain threshold, the lymphocytes become active and kill infected cells. The artificial immune system model allows for automatically detecting clusters and outliers. Two interesting recent approaches for streaming data even addressing several challenges discussed in this chapter simultaneously are the work of Aggarwal et al. (2004) for projected clustering of high-dimensional data streams and the approach of Aggarwal and Yu (2008) for clustering uncertain streaming data. We are convinced that the special requirements of the streaming environment will continue to promote creative research in clustering.

There is a huge variety of approaches for clustering other special types of data. One interesting direction which we want mention is clustering graphs. Unlike spectral clustering focusing on detecting clusters within one graph, the objective here is to find clusters in a database of graph structured objects. Especially in biology and chemistry large amounts of graph structured objects are collected, representing for example chemical compounds or molecular structures. However, only relatively few papers, such as (Tsuda & Kudo 2006) focus on clustering such type of data.

Not only the amount of data collected in modern applications is rapidly increasing but also the structure of data becomes more and more rich, diverse and complex. Therefore, integrative clustering of information from different sources will continue to attract much attention. Related to semi-supervised clustering is the task of clustering of multi-represented objects. As discussed, algorithms for semi-supervised clustering typically consider only relatively simple types of side information such as constraints or labels. The goal of multi-represented clustering is integrative clustering of several equally complex sources. First approaches have been proposed for different underlying clustering paradigms, for example spectral clustering (De Sa 2005), the EM algorithm (Bickel & Scheffer 2004) and density-based clustering (Achtert et al. 2006).

The presentation of highly specialized methods for the needs emerging from the application side may lead to the impression that the research community working on clustering (which is anyhow split up into different sub-communities originating from data mining, databases, machine learning, statistics and physics) is continuously diversifying. But there is also a lot of effort on integration. Theoretical work on similarities or even equivalence of at first glance completely different clustering paradigms not only leads to interesting insights but can also result in substantial gains in effectiveness and efficiency. As mentioned, (Dhillon et al 2004) demonstrate the equivalence of the normalized cut objective function in spectral clustering with weighted kernel K-means. This allows more efficient spectral clustering without matrix decomposition. Song et al. (2007) provide a unified view of many clustering algorithms including K-means, spectral and hierarchical clustering, regarding the clustering problem as maximization of dependence between the data objects and their cluster labels. A formulation of

this idea using the Hilbert-Schmidt Independence Criterion and kernel methods is elaborated. In addition, the authors provide guidelines for practical application. The trend towards a unified view is not restricted to clustering paradigms only, but also on integrating clustering and closely related techniques from mathematics and statistics, especially techniques for matrix factorization and dimensionality reduction. Ding and He (2004) explore the relationship between K-means clustering and Principle Component Analysis (PCA). Principle Components actually are the continuous solutions of the cluster membership indicators obtained by K-means. This result allows providing lower bounds on the optimality of K-means. In addition, K-means can significantly profit from PCA: PCA provides a good initialization for K-means, and there is a theoretical justification to apply PCA as a preprocessing for dimensionality reduction before K-means (at least for data of moderate to medium dimensionality). These examples demonstrate that the integrative view of different clustering paradigms and related techniques not only has a theoretical value but also has an impact on the application of clustering algorithms in practice. We believe that this research direction has great potential in the future.

But not only within clustering there is a trend towards unification. Clustering also fruitfully integrates into other related research areas. Within data mining and machine learning there are close relationships to the areas of classification and outlier detection. The evolving research area of semi-supervised learning is crossing the borders between traditional unsupervised clustering without external knowledge and classification, which is the classical task within supervised learning. The goal of outlier detection is to find the exceptional objects of a data set. To specify what exceptional or outstanding means in the context of the given data set, it is necessary to have an idea about what is normal or common. Therefore, outlier detection is closely related to clustering and we expect further interactions between these areas in the future. Going beyond data mining, we expect that there will be even more interaction of clustering with other research areas, for example information retrieval, indexing, parallel and distributed computing.

CONCLUSION

At first glance, the problem specification of clustering as introduced in the introduction seems to be very simple: Find a natural partitioning of the data into groups or clusters such that the objects assigned to a common cluster are as similar as possible and objects assigned to different clusters differ as much as possible. This very general problem specification is highly relevant in a large variety of applications, wherever an overview on huge amounts of data is desired. With the technological progress, larger amounts of data can be acquired and stored at decreasing costs. Thus, the practical relevance of clustering is constantly increasing. We have seen that clustering is indeed not a trivial task at all. Finding a natural grouping of a small set of objects may be easy for humans because of our advanced cognitive abilities, most importantly our ability to focus on relevant information and our ability to intuitively select a suitable level of abstraction. However, the problem size in real applications exceeds our processing capability by orders of magnitude. Thus, we need efficient and effective algorithms for automatically clustering large complex data sets. Recent developments in clustering are exactly addressing the following questions:

1. How can we automatically find out which part of the information potentially contained in the data actually is relevant for clustering?

2. How can we exploit the cognitive abilities of humans or other types of expert knowledge to improve the clustering result?

3. How can we automatically select a suitable level of abstraction in clustering?

Automatically selecting that information from data which is relevant for clustering is very challenging. If the data is represented in a high dimensional vector space, approaches to subspace and projected clustering provide solutions to this problem. Subspace clustering aims at automatically detecting interesting dimensions for clustering and preserves the information that objects can be clustered differently in different subspaces. Projected clustering detects clusters which are associated with a specific subspace where each object is exclusively assigned to one cluster. Clusters in real-world data are not restricted to axis-parallel subspaces, but can be associated with arbitrary linear or non-linear hyper-planes and subspaces. Correlation clustering focuses on detecting such clusters, which are characterized by specific patterns of linear or non-linear feature dependencies. Especially the result of subspace, projected and correlation clustering provides interesting insights on why objects are clustered together which is very important for interpretation. For example we can learn from correlation clustering of metabolic data that a specific pattern of linear dependency of metabolites is characteristic for certain disorder. For general metric data represented by a similarity matrix, spectral clustering algorithms are very suitable. Selecting relevant information for clustering in this context means learning a suitable similarity measure. Recent approaches propose techniques for automatically adjusting the similarity measure by metric learning to improve the cluster structure.

Semi-supervised approaches to clustering address the second question. These approaches demonstrate that the clustering result can be substantially improved by external side information. This side information is usually obtained by human experts or other sources of knowledge, such as literature databases. Most algorithms require side information only for very few data objects to obtain good results. Therefore, semi-supervised clustering provides the potential to combine the cognitive abilities of humans with the computing power of machines for clustering.

The third question is mainly addressed by approaches to parameter-free clustering. To be most informative to the user, the clustering result must have a suitable level of abstraction. The clustering should concisely summarize the important characteristics of the data without over fitting. For most clustering algorithms the resolution of the result depends on input parameters which are difficult to estimate. Approaches to parameter-free clustering automatically select a suitable level of abstraction by introducing ideas from information theory into clustering.

There are many challenges for clustering in the future, which cannot all be mentioned here. Definitely, there is a strong need for highly scalable techniques and for techniques which can combine data originating from different sources. The development of novel techniques will be promoted by the needs of novel applications. Clustering is an important step on the path from data to knowledge and will therefore continue attracting the attention of generations of researchers to come.

REFERENCES

Achtert, E., Böhm, C., David, J., Kröger, P., & Zimek, A. (2008). Robust Clustering in Arbitrarily Oriented Subspaces. In *Proc. of SIAM International Conference on Data Mining (SDM)* (pp. 763-774).

Achtert, E., Böhm, C., Kriegel, H.-P., Kröger, P., Müller-Gorman, I., & Zimek, A. (2006). Finding Hierarchies of Subspace Clusters. In *Proc. of European* Conference *on Principles and Practice of Knowledge Discovery (PKDD)* (pp. 446-453).

Achtert, E., Böhm, C., Kriegel, H.-P., Kröger, P., Müller-Gorman, I., & Zimek, A. (2007). Detection and Visualization of Subspace Cluster Hierarchies. In *Proc. of International* Conference *on Database Systems for Advanced Applications (DASFAA)* (pp. 152-163).

Achtert, E., Kriegel, H.-P., Pryakhin, A., & Schubert, M. (2006). Clustering Multi-represented Objects Using Combination Trees. In *Proc. of Pacific-Asia Conference on Knowledge Discovery and Data Mining (PAKDD)* (pp. 174-178).

Aggarwal, C. C. (2007). On Density Based Transforms for Uncertain Data Mining. In *Proc. of IEEE International Conference on Data Engineering (ICDE)* (pp. 866-875).

Aggarwal, C. C., Han, J., Wang, J., & Yu, P. S. (2003). A Framework for Clustering Evolving Data Streams. In *Proc. of International Conference on Very Large Data Bases (VLDB)* (pp. 81-92).

Aggarwal, C. C., Han, J., Wang, J., & Yu, P. S. (2004). A Framework for Projected Clustering of High Dimensional Data Streams. In *Proc. of International Conference on Very Large Data Bases (VLDB)* (pp. 852-863).

Aggarwal, C. C., Wolf, J. L., Yu, P. S., Procopiuc, C., & Park, J. S. (1999). Fast algorithms for projected clustering. In *Proc. of ACM SIGMOD International Conference on Management of Data (SIGMOD)* (pp. 61-72).

Aggarwal, C. C., & Yu, P. S. (2000). Finding Generalized Projected Clusters in High Dimensional Space. In *Proc. of ACM SIGMOD International Conference on Management of Data (SIGMOD)* (pp. 70-81).

Aggarwal, C. C., & Yu, P. S. (2008). A Framework for Clustering Uncertain Data Streams. In *Proc. of IEEE International Conference on Data Engineering (ICDE)* (pp. 150-159).

Agrawal, R., Gehrke, J., Gunopulos, D., & Raghavan, P. (1998). Automatic Subspace Clustering of High Dimensional Data for Data Mining Applications. In *Proc. of ACM SIGMOD International Conference on Management of Data (SIGMOD)* (pp. 94-105).

Assent, I., Krieger, R., Müller, E., & Seidl, T. (2007). DUSC: Dimensionality Unbiased Subspace Clustering. In *Proc. of IEEE International Conference on Data Mining (ICDM)* (pp. 409-414).

Bach, F., & Jordan, M. (2003). Learning Spectral Clustering. In *Proc. of 16th Annual Conference on Advances in Neural Information Processing Systems (NIPS)*.

Bar-Hillel, A., Hertz, T., Shental, N., & Weinshall, D. (2003). Learning Distance Functions using Equivalence Relations. In *Proc. of International Conference on Machine Learning (ICML)* (pp. 11-18).

Basu, S., Bilenko, M., & Mooney, R. J. (2004). A Probabilistic Framework for Semi-supervised Clustering. In *Proc. of ACM SIGKDD International* Conference *on Knowledge Discovery and Data Mining (KDD)* (pp. 59-68).

Baumgartner, C., & Graber, A. (2008). Data Mining and Knowledge Discovery in Metabolomics. In Masseglia, F., Poncelet, P. Teisseire, M. (Eds.) *Successes and New Directions in Data Mining.* (pp. 141-166). Hershey, PA: IBI Global.

Baumgartner, C., Kailing, K., Kriegel, H.-P., Kröger, P., & Plant, C. (2004). Subspace Selection for Clustering High-Dimensional Data. In *Proc. of IEEE International Conference on Data Mining (ICDM)* (pp.11-18).

Bickel, S., & Scheffer, T. (2004). Multi-View Clustering. In *Proc. of IEEE International Conference on Data Mining (ICDM)* (pp. 19-26).

Bilenko, M., Basu, S., & Mooney, R. J. (2004). Integrating Constraints and Metric Learning in Semi-supervised Clustering. In *Proc. of International Conference on Machine Learning (ICML)* (pp. 81-88).

Böhm, C., Faloutsos, C., & Plant, C. (2008). Outlier-robust Clustering using Independent Components. In *Proc. of ACM SIGMOD International Conference on Management of Data (SIGMOD)* (pp. 185-198).

Böhm, C., Kailing, K., Kröger, P., & Zimek, A. (2004). Computing Clusters of Correlation Connected Objects. In *Proc. of ACM SIGMOD International Conference on Management of Data (SIGMOD)* (pp. 455-466).

Böhm, C., & Plant, C. (2008). HISSCLU: A Hierarchical Density-based Method for Semi-supervised Clustering. In *Proc. of International Conference on Extending Database Technology (EDBT)* (pp. 440-451).

Chang, H., & Yeung, D.-Y. (2004). Locally Linear Metric Adaptation for Semi-supervised Clustering. In *Proc. of International Conference on Machine Learning (ICML)* (pp. 153-160).

Cheng, C.-H., Fu, A.-C., & Zhang, Y. (1999). Entropy-Based Subspace Clustering for Mining Numerical Data. In *Proc. of ACM SIGKDD International* Conference *on Knowledge Discovery and Data Mining (KDD)* (pp. 84-93).

De Sa, V. R. (2005). Spectral Clustering with two Views. In *Proc. of International Conference on Machine Learning (ICML). Workshop on Learning with Multiple Views.*

Dempster, A. P. Laird, N. M. & Rubin, D. B. (1977). Maximum Likelihood from Incomplete Data via the EM Algorithm. In *Journal of the Royal Statistical Society, 39,* 1-31.

Dhillon, I. S. (2001). Co-clustering Documents and Words using Bipartite Spectral Graph Partitioning. In *Proc. of ACM SIGKDD International Conference on Knowledge Discovery and Data Mining (KDD)* (pp. 269–274).

Dhillon, I. S., Guan, Y., & Kulis, B. (2004). Kernel K-means: Spectral Clustering and Normalized Cuts. In *Proc. of ACM SIGKDD International Conference on Knowledge Discovery and Data Mining (KDD)* (pp. 551-556).

Ding, C. H. Q., & He, X. (2004). K-means Clustering via Principal Component Analysis. In *Proc. of International Conference on Machine Learning (ICML)* (pp. 225-232).

Ding, C. H. Q., He, X., Zha, H., Gu, M., & Simon, H. (2001). A Min-max Cut Algorithm for Graph Partitioning and Data Clustering. In *Proc. of IEEE International Conference on Data Mining (ICDM)* (pp.107–114).

Duda, R. O., & Hart, P. E. (1973). *Pattern Classification and Scene Analysis*. Hoboken, NJ: John Wiley & Sons.

Ester, M., Kriegel, H.-P., Sander, J., & Xu, X. (1996). A Density-based Algorithm for Discovering Clusters in Large Spatial Databases with Noise. In *Proc. of ACM SIGKDD International Conference on Knowledge Discovery and Data Mining (KDD)* (pp.226–231).

Feng, Y., & Hamerly, G. (2006). PG-means: Learning the Number of Clusters in Data. In *Proc. of 19th Annual Conference on Advances in Neural Information Processing Systems (NIPS)* (pp. 393-400).

Figueiredo, M. A. T., & Jain, A. K. (2002). Unsupervised Learning of Finite Mixture Models. [PAMI]. *IEEE Transactions on Pattern Analysis and Machine Intelligence, 24*(3), 381–396. doi:10.1109/34.990138

Fowlkes, C., Belongie, S., Chung, F. R. K., & Malik, J. (2004). Spectral Grouping Using the Nyström Method. [PAMI]. *IEEE Transactions on Pattern Analysis and Machine Intelligence, 26*(2), 214–225. doi:10.1109/TPAMI.2004.1262185

Grünwald, P. (2005). A Tutorial Introduction to the Minimum Description Length Principle. In P. Grünwald, I. J. Mynung, & M. Pitt, (Eds.) *Advances in Minimum Description Length: Theory and Applications*. Cambridge, MA: MIT Press.

Hagen, L., & Kahng, A. (1992). New Spectral Methods for Ratio Cut Partitioning and Clustering. *IEEE Trans. Computer Aided Design, 11*(9), 1074–1085.

Hamdan, H., & Govaert, G. (2005). Mixture Model Clustering of Uncertain Data. In *IEEE International Conference on Fuzzy Systems* (pp. 879–884).

Hamerly, G., & Elkan, C. (2003). Learning the K in K-means. In *Proc. of 16th Annual Conference on Advances in Neural Information Processing Systems (NIPS)*.

Jain, A. K., & Dubes, R. C. (1988). *Algorithms for Clustering Data*. Upper Saddle River, NJ: Prentice-Hall.

Kailing, K., Kriegel, H.-P., & Kröger, P. (2004). Density-connected Subspace Clustering for High Dimensional Data. In *Proc. of SIAM International Conference on Data Mining (SDM)* (pp. 246-257).

Kaufman, L., & Rousseeuw, P. J. (1990). *Finding Groups in Data: An Introduction to Cluster Analysis*. Wiley series in probability and mathematical statistics. Chichester, UK: John Wiley and Sons.

Klein, D., Kamvar, D., & Manning, C. (2002). From Instance-Level Constraints to Space-Level Constraints: Making Most of Prior Knowledge in Data Clustering. In *Proc. of International Conference on Machine Learning (ICML)* (pp. 307-314).

Kriegel, H.-P., & Pfeifle, M. (2005). Density-based Clustering of Uncertain Data. In *Proc. of ACM SIGKDD International Conference on Knowledge Discovery and Data Mining (KDD)* (pp. 672–677).

Kulis, B., Basu, S., Dhillon, I. S., & Mooney, R. J. (2005). Semi-supervised Graph Clustering: a Kernel Approach. In *Proc. of International Conference on Machine Learning (ICML)* (pp. 457-464).

Li, Y., Han, J., & Yang, J. (2004). Clustering moving objects. In *Proc. of ACM SIGKDD International Conference on Knowledge Discovery and Data Mining (KDD)* (pp.617–622).

Long, B., Zhang, Z., Wu, X., & Yu, P. S. (2006). Spectral clustering for Multi-type Relational Data. In *Proc. of International Conference on Machine Learning (ICML)* (pp.585-592).

Meila, M. (2008). The Uniqueness of a Good Optimum for K-means. In *Proc. of International Conference on Machine Learning (ICML)* (pp. 625-632).

Nagesh, H., Goil, S., & Choudhary, A. (2000). A Scalable Parallel Subspace Clustering Algorithm for Massive Data Sets. In *Proc. of IEEE International Conference on Parallel Processing* (pp.477-).

Nasraoui, O., Uribe, C. C., Coronel, C. R., & Gonzales, F. (2003). TECNO-STREAMS: Tracking Evolving Clusters in Noisy Data Streams with a Scalable Immune System Learning Model. In *Proc. of IEEE International Conference on Data Mining (ICDM)* (pp. 235-242).

Ng, A., Jordan, M., & Weiss, Y. (2002). On Spectral Clustering: Analysis and an Algorithm. [Cambridge, MA: MIT Press.]. *Advances in Neural Information Processing Systems*, *14*, 849–856.

Ng, R. T., & Han, J. (1994). Efficient and Effective Clustering Methods for Spatial Data Mining. In *Proc. of International Conference on Very Large Data Bases (VLDB)* (pp. 144-155).

Ngai, W., Kao, B., Chui, C., Cheng, R., Chau, M., & Yip, K. Y. (2006). Efficient Clustering of Uncertain Data. In *Proc. of IEEE International Conference on Data Mining (ICDM)* (pp. 436-445).

O'Callaghan, L., Meyerson, A., Motwani, M., Mishra, N., & Guha, S. (2002). Streaming-Data Algorithms for High-Quality Clustering. In *IEEE International Conference on Data Engineering (ICDE)* (pp.685-).

Pelleg, D., & Moore, A. (2000) X-means: Extending K-means with Efficient Estimation of the Number of Clusters. In *Proc. of International Conference on Machine Learning (ICML)* (pp. 727–734).

Procopiuc, C. M., Jonesý, M., Pankaj, K., Agarwal, M., & Muraliý, M. (2002). A Monte Carlo Algorithm for Fast Projective Clustering. In *Proc. of ACM SIGMOD International Conference on Management of Data (SIGMOD)* (pp. 418–427).

Shi, J., & Malik, J. (2000). Normalized Cuts and Image Segmentation. *IEEE Transactions on Pattern Analysis and Machine Intelligence*, *22*(8), 888–905. doi:10.1109/34.868688

Slonim, N., & Tishby, N. (2000). Document clustering using Word Clusters via the Information Bottleneck Method. In *Proc. of International ACM/SIGIR Conference on Research and Development in Information Retrieval* (pp. 208-215).

Song, L., Smola, A. J., Gretton, A., & Borgwardt, K. M. (2007). A Dependence Maximization View of Clustering. In *Proc. of International Conference on Machine Learning (ICML)* (pp.815-822).

Stoer, M., & Wagner, F. (1997). A Simple Min-cut Algorithm. *Journal of the ACM, 44*(4), 585–591. doi:10.1145/263867.263872

Tishby, N., Pereira, F. C., & Bialek, W. (2000). The Information Bottleneck Method. In *CoRRphysics/0004057*.

Tishby, N., & Slonim, N. (2000). Data Clustering by Markovian Relaxation and the Information Bottleneck Method. *Proc. of 13th Annual Conference on Advances in Neural Information Processing Systems (NIPS)*, (pp. 640-646).

Tsuda, K., & Kudo, T. (2006). Clustering Graphs by Weighted Substructure Mining. In *Proc. of International Conference on Machine Learning (ICML)*, (pp. 953-960).

Wagner, D., & Wagner, F. (1993). Between Min-cut and Graph Bisection. In *Proc. of International Symposium on Mathematical Foundations of Computer Science (MFCS)*, (pp. 744–750).

Wagstaff, K., Cardie, C., Rogers, S., & Schroedel, S. (2001). Constrained K-means Clustering with Background Knowledge. In *Proc. of International Conference on Machine Learning (ICML)*, (pp.577-584).

Weber, R., Schek, H.-J., & Blott, S. (1998). A Quantative Analysis and Performance Study for Similarity-search Methods in High-dimensional Spaces. In *Proc. of International Conference on Very Large Data Bases (VLDB)*, (pp. 194-205).

Xing, E., Ng, A., Jordan, M., & Russell, S. (2003). Distance Metric Learning, with Application to Clustering with Side-information. In *Proc. of 15th Annual Conference on Advances in Neural Information Processing Systems (NIPS)*, (pp. 505-512).

Yip, K. Y., Cheung, D. W., & Ng, M. K. (2005). On Discovery of Extremely Low-Dimensional Clusters using Semi-Supervised Projected Clustering. In *IEEE International Conference on Data Engineering (ICDE)*, (pp. 329-340).

Zaiane, O. R., Man, X., & Han, J. (1998). Discovering Web Access Patterns and Trends by Applying OLAP and Data Mining Technology on Web Logs. In *IEEE Forum on Research and Technology Advances in Digital Libraries (ADL)*, (pp. 19-29).

Zelnik-Manor, L., & Perona, P. (2004). Self-Tuning Spectral Clustering. In *Proc. of 17th Annual Conference on Advances in Neural Information Processing Systems (NIPS)*, (pp. 1601-1608).

Zeng, E., Chengyong, Y., Tao, L., & Narasimhan, G. (2007). On the Effectiveness of Constraints Sets in Clustering Genes. In *IEEE International Conference on Bioinformatics and Bioengineering (BIBE)*, (pp. 79-86).

Chapter 10
Recent Advances of Exception Mining in Stock Market

Chao Luo
University of Technology, Sydney, Australia

Yanchang Zhao
University of Technology, Sydney, Australia

Dan Luo
University of Technology, Sydney, Australia

Yuming Ou
University of Technology, Sydney, Australia

Li Liu
University of Technology, Sydney, Australia

ABSTRACT

This chapter aims to provide a comprehensive survey of the current advanced technologies of exception mining in stock market. The stock market surveillance is to identify market anomalies so as to provide a fair and efficient trading platform. The technologies of market surveillance developed from simple statistical rules to more advanced technologies, such as data mining and artificial intelligent. This chapter provides the basic concepts of exception mining in stock market. Then the recent advances of exception mining in this domain are presented and the key issues are discussed. The advantages and disadvantages of the advanced technologies are analyzed. Furthermore, our model of OMM (Outlier Mining on Multiple time series) is introduced. Finally, this chapter points out the future research directions and related issues in reality.

INTRODUCTION

Stock market is a place where buyer and seller trade for company stock and derivatives. It has become an important part of the economic activities all over the world. The transaction volume of stocks keeps increasing significantly all the time. However, there are some illegal behaviors which impair the development of stock market, and some people try to maximize their profit by breaking the rules of stock

DOI: 10.4018/978-1-60566-816-1.ch010

markets, even breaking relevant laws. The above illegal behaviors are referred to as market abuse, anomalies or exceptions in stock markets.

Stock market surveillance is responsible for the detection of illegal behaviors in stock markets. The technologies play important roles in effective market surveillance. With the development of stock market, the technologies of market surveillance have evolved from simple rule based approaches to advanced approaches based on artificial intelligence and data mining. In particular, the researches on how to effectively utilize the advanced technologies for the task of surveillance have been developed in most stock exchanges. These researches can be summarized as exception mining in stock markets.

In this chapter, we will present a comprehensive literature review on the recent advances of exception mining in stock markets. Various approaches are currently being used for the detection of exceptions by researchers all over the world. For example, outlier mining technologies have been researched and utilized in some exchanges. Most of the publications in this area focus on the specific technologies. So it is necessary to summarize the current advances of exceptions mining in stock markets. By doing so, we expect to provide a clear picture of the technologies utilized in this area. We hope it can provide guidance to professionals and researchers in this area to find the appropriate solutions for their own purposes.

The rest of this chapter is organized as follows. Section 2 will introduce the related background of stock market and stock surveillance. Some important concepts and issues, such as the concept of insider trading and market manipulation, will be described and illustrated with real-life examples. Section 3 will discuss recent technologies for stock market surveillance, such as rule-based approaches, statistic methods, outlier detection technologies, etc. The technologies will be analyzed and compared, and their strength and weakness will be pointed out. A detailed introduction of

our current research, outlier mining on multiple time series, will be given in Section 4. Section 5 will discuss some future research directions in exception mining in stock market. The chapter will be concluded in the last section.

BACKGROUND OF STOCK MARKET AND STOCK SURVEILLANCE

Stock Market

Stock market is the platform where the buyer and seller trade for stock and its derivatives (Cheng 2006, Allen 1992, Lucas 1993). It is one of the most important sources for companies to raise money (Jain 2005). The business is able to be traded publicly in the form of stock. The accumulation of additional capital makes companies expansion by selling shares of ownership of the company in a public market. In addition, exchanges provide the liquidity which affords investors the ability to quickly and easily sell securities (Charest 1978). Stock market has become an important part of the dynamics of economic activity. Nowadays it has become an indicator of economy and can influence the social mood. For example, when the stock market is on the rise, the economy is considered to be positive; otherwise, the economy is regarded as upsetting. Therefore, the stock market is regarded as the primary indicator of a country's economic strength and development (Jain 2005).

The stocks are listed and traded on stock exchanges. Exchanges act as the clearinghouse for each transaction in stock markets (John & Narayanan 1997). They guarantee payment to the seller of a security by collecting and delivering the shares. The risks for buyers or sellers are expected to be eliminated or controlled to some extent. Exchanges also take the responsibilities of regulations of stock markets (Bettis et al. 1998). They have the duty to provide fair and transparent platform for all participants.

Stock Surveillance

Stock surveillance plays a vital role in ensuring market confidence by providing continuous, real-time monitoring of activity in the equities and derivatives markets (Schinasi et al. 1999). However, stock surveillance also faces many challenges. Surveillance needs to detect any suspicious trading from the rise and fall of prices and volumes of stocks. There are various types of illegal trades and breaking of rules and regulations in stock markets. The stock market surveillance is responsible for the detection of these behaviors. In particular, surveillance monitors for two key market abuses, insider trading (Bettis et al. 1998) and market manipulation (Aggarwal & Wu 2006).

Insider Trading

There are different definitions of insider trading in different stock exchanges. Generally speaking, insider trading is the trade based on non-public information. The insiders normally refer to managers, directors, employees or major shareholders of companies who own the undisclosed inside information. The inside information refers to the company announcements, annual reports or other news which have significant influence on the movements of stock (Minenna 2003, Szockyj & Geis 2002).

A real-life case of insider trading in Hong Kong Stock Exchange (HKEx) is as follows. Taylor Ho, the financial controller, company secretary and an executive director of Ngai Hing Hong Company Limited (NHH), bought 1 million NHH shares on 21st July 1995. He knew that the Annual Report for NHH would have positive impact and the price of NHH would rise. In fact, when the Annual Report of NHH was announced on 18th July 1995, the price increased significantly. In the following day, Taylor sold NHH shares and made much profit. As a result, the Securities and Futures Commission (SFC) investigated the case and proved that Taylor made insider trading and Taylor was fined HK$1,000,000.

The regulations of insider trading also vary from exchange to exchange all over the world. In most exchanges, insider trading is regarded as severe and illegal, and insiders are often punished with imprisonment (Fishman & Hagerty 1992, Garfinkel & Nimalendran 2003). An interesting issue is that there are always debates on whether insider trading should be prohibited. Some financial researchers argue that insider trading benefit the stock markets by providing liquidity and should not be banned. However, most of the financial research proved that insider trading impair stock markets and should be prohibited definitely (Leland 1992).

Stock Market Manipulation

Stock market manipulation is another kind of market abuse. It describes a deliberate attempt to interfere with the free and fair operation of the market and create artificial, false or misleading appearances with respect to the price of, or market for, a stock. This is typically done either by spreading false or misleading information in order to influence others to trade in a particular way, or by using buying and selling orders deliberately to affect prices or turnover, in order to create an opportunity for profit (Allen 1992, Felixson & Pelli 1999).

The following is a case of market manipulation in HKEx. Three manipulators were proved to have conducted market manipulation on the GP Nano Technology Group Limited. The SFC investigated the case and found that they bought and sold the stock of GP Nano at the same price, and sometimes they bought the same stock at a higher price and sold at a lower price from 18th January 2002 to 11th June 2002. They also made frequent intra-group trades among themselves. Their intentions were not to trade normally, but to make a false impression of active trade for GP Nano Technology stocks and attract others to invest on the stock. These market manipulation trades led to the increase of turnover of the stock. As a

Table 1. Market manipulation

Types of Manipulation	Descriptions
Corner	Buying up a substantial volume of a security in order to manipulate the price.
Matched Orders	A person buys a security and subsequently places buy and sell orders for that security at the same time.
Pools	Same as a matched orders. Involving more than two parties trading on the basis that the transaction will be reversed later.
Wash trade	Buyer is also seller or is associated with seller. There is no change in the beneficial ownership of the securities.
Marking the close	Buying or selling securities or derivatives contracts at the close of the market in an effort to alter the closing price of the security or derivatives contract.
Market Stabilisation	Trading in a security at the time of a new issue in order to prevent a decline in the price of the security.
Parking and Warehousing	Hiding the true ownership of securities
Pump & dump/Ramping	Buying at increasingly higher prices. Securities are sold in the market (often to retail customers) at the higher prices
Short Selling	A market transaction in which an investor sells stock he does not have or he has borrowed in anticipation of a price decline.

result, each of them was sentenced two months imprisonment suspended for 12 months.

In general, stock market manipulation can be classified into trade-based market manipulation and information-based market manipulation (Aggarwal & Wu 2006). The information-based manipulation is defined as disseminating false information which misleads other participants about the value or trading volume of a security. Trade-based market manipulation refers to the buying or selling of a security which aims to mislead or deceive other participants about the value or trading volume of the security. There are a variety of strategies of market manipulation, and the most important types of market manipulations are shown in Table 1 (Schinasi et al. 1999).

Market Surveillance Process

A qualified surveillance function is expected to capture all the anomalies from a large amount of complex market records, while avoiding false alerts so as to reduce the waste of time and human resources on the investigation of alerts (Buta & Barletta 1991). It consists of the following four steps.

- **Step 1. Generating Alerts:** Generating alerts is the start of a stock market surveillance process. The exchanges monitor the transaction records and generate alerts if there are suspicious trades identified. The technology of generating alerts plays an important role on the efficiency of surveillance and in the whole process of stock market surveillance (Smith 1995).

- **Step 2. Analyzing Alerts:** This step is done by regulation staff. The alerts generated are reported to regulators. The regulators analyze the alerts and replay the historical transaction records. If they think the alert are really suspicious, then a case investigation will be started. Otherwise, the alerts will be ignored (Brown & GoldSchmidt 1996).

- **Step 3. Case Investigation:** This step normally spends a long time to enquiry the persons involved. The regulators have to find adequate evidence to validate that the suspicious parties have committed illegal behavior. The persons involved need to give reasonable explanation for their trades or behaviors in stock markets.

- **Step 4. Jurisdiction:** The court makes decision and sentences based on relevant laws. Most countries have made laws for regulation in stock markets. For example, Securities Disclosure of Interests Ordinance (SDIO) is to regulate the insider trading in Hong Kong. SDIO specifies the definition of insiders and what constitutes insider trading, and outlines the notification procedure and the penalties for failing to report (Wong et al. 2000).

TECHNOLOGIES FOR EXCEPTION MINING IN STOCK MARKET

The technologies on stock market surveillance have been developed for decades from the simple rule-based technology to advanced artificial intelligent technologies. Many researchers have made contributions on stock market surveillance. The well-known technologies for market surveillance will be surveyed in this section.

Rule Approaches

The rule approaches are the initial way to monitoring stock markets. Normally a set of parameters are predefined based on experience (Smith 1995). If the real value is larger than the predefined parameter, an alert will be generated. In practice, the price and volume are used to measure the performance of stock. For example, assume that the parameter of price movement is set to $2. If the price of one stock is $8 on the first day, and rises to $11 on the next day, an alert will be generated, because the increase is $3, larger than the predefined threshold $2.

In order to improve the effectiveness of the rule approaches, the threshold is often set as a specific percentage to the prior value. For example, assume we set the movement percentage parameter as 10%. If the price on the first day is $20, and price on the next day is $21, then there is no alert generated. However, if the price yesterday is $5, and the price today is $6, then an alert will be generated because the rise percentage is 20%, larger than the predefined threshold 10%. For both of the above cases, the prices rise by the same amount, but they have different results.

The rule approaches have the advantage of simplicity, and sometimes can effectively capture some types of market abuse. However, the limitation of the rule approaches is their low accuracy. They tend to generate too many alerts and most of the alerts are not related to any market abuse or illegal behaviors.

Basic Statistic Methods

By considering the movement trend of price or volume over time, the basic statistical technique, such as the mean and standard deviation is also utilized in surveillance process (Smith 1995).

The use of the mean and standard deviation assumes that the values for each measure are normally distributed. In order to reduce the number of alerts generated, the standard deviations are tuned accordingly. The traditional approach regards the returns out of $\mu \pm 3\sigma$ as outliers, where μ and σ are respectively the mean and variance of Gaussian distribution (Smith 1981). The stock measures, however, are generally non-normal, which show themselves as excess kurtosis and skewness.

The statistical tests are used to test whether the price and volume data are normally distributed. The stability of the distributions in different time periods is also tested by statistical tests. However, in practice, the price and volume movements of most of stocks are not normally distributed. An alternative way is to identify the distribution by curve fitting technologies (Alhanaty & Bercovier 1998). In addition, the price and volume of most stocks are not stable and it is difficult to identify the underlying distribution over time. Therefore, the basic statistic methods are inappropriate to monitor stock movements.

Outlier Identification

Outliers refer to the data points which are grossly different from or inconsistent with the rest of data (Han & Kamber 2001). The usual strategy for outlier mining is to find a model that aims at maximally capturing the information of the normal data and take samples inconsistent with the model as outliers. Based on the above strategy, numerous successful outlier mining models have been proposed, which can be further categorized into four approaches: the statistical approach, the distance-based approach, the deviation-based approach, and the density-based approach.

Outlier Test

Dixon (1950) firstly introduced his ratio R to test outliers from a sample. It is proved to be robust and applicable to any distribution (Chernick 1982). In the Dixon Ratio Test, the range of the test values is calculated, and the results are utilized to measure variation of the stock markets. The Dixon Ration R is calculated by the difference between the two highest values and the range of all samples. Let H_1 be the highest value and H_2 be the second highest value. Let LV be the lowest value.

$R = (H_1 - H_2) / (H_1 - LV)$ (1)

The closer the value of R is to one, the more likely that the highest value is from another distribution and an outlier to the current set of values.

The Dixon Ration Test is used to detect the extremely deviated data set from the rest of the data. However, it fails to identify outliers where all the top k highest values are outliers. Therefore, in our research, we used the modified Dixon Ration to test outliers. We define LA be the average value of all values except the highest values by replacing the H_2 in formula 1 with LA (Luo et al. 2008). Our Test Ratio is calculated as following:

$R = (H_1 - LA) / (H_1 - LV)$ (2)

This adjustment makes the R fit to measure the multiple outliers.

Outlier Detection in GARCH Models

Generalized Autoregressive Conditional Heteroskedasticity (GARCH) model was introduced by Bollerslev (1986). It is an econometric model for modeling and forecasting time-dependent variance, and hence volatility, of stock price returns. It represents current variance in terms of past variances. The parameters in the model are usually determined by Maximum Likelihood Estimation applied to the likelihood function.

The GARCH model is typically called the GARCH (1, 1) model. The (1, 1) in parentheses is a standard notation in which the first number refers to how many autoregressive lags, or (Autoregressive Conditional Heteroscedasticity) ARCH terms (Gourieroux 1997), appear in the equation, while the second number refers to how many moving average lags are specified, which here is often called the number of GARCH terms. Sometimes models with more than one lag are needed to find good variance forecasts.

The GARCH model is a popular approach to abnormal return detection. Franses and Dijk (2000) researched on this issue and adapted the outlier detection method proposed by Chen and Liu (1993). The critical values for the relevant test statistic were generated, and their methods were evaluated in an extensive simulation study. This outlier detection and correction method was applied to 10 years of weekly return from 1986 to 1995 on the stock markets of Amsterdam, Frankfurt, Paris, Hong Kong, Singapore and New York, which amounts to approximately 500 observations. Franses and Dijk (2000) used weekly data from 1996 to 1998 to evaluate the out-of-sample forecast performance of conditional volatility with GARCH (1, 1) models estimated on the series before and after outlier correction. The result shows that correcting for a few outliers yields substantial improvements in out-of-sample forecasts.

Variance-Based Outlier Mining (VOMM)

Qi and Wang (2004) proposed a Variance-based Outlier Mining Model (VOMM), a general outlier model based on principal curve (Zhang & Wang 2003) to find outliers on daily closing price. The design of VOMM aims to solve the outlier mining problem where outliers are highly intermixed with normal data. In VOMM, the information of data is decomposed into normal and abnormal components according to their variances. With minimal loss of normal information in the VOMM, outliers are viewed as the top k samples holding maximal abnormal information in a dataset. The principal curve is a smooth nonparametric curve passing through the "middle" of the dataset and describes the normal information with a nonlinear summary of the data.

In stock market, the daily closing price is affected not only by daily random fluctuation, but also long-term trend. If we consider the long-term trend as normal information and the daily random fluctuation as abnormal information, it is difficult to separate the abnormal information from the normal information. Therefore, VOMM is an appropriate approach to handle this issue. Qi and Wang (2004) applied VOMM to analyze the daily INDEXSH (Integrate Index in Shanghai Stock Exchange of China) during the period of 1st January 1998 to 31st December 2001. To evaluate the experimental results, the stock analyst was asked to detect the outliers of INDEXSH in the same period of time. The authors also collected the significant events happened in this period of time to evaluate the results. The results showed that VOMM is feasible to identify the outliers of INDEXSH. In addition, the authors compared VOMM with the Gaussian model (Smith 1981) and GARCH model (Franses & Dijk 2000) on the same datasets, and the results indicate that VOMM perform better than Gaussian model and GARCH model.

As a general outlier mining model, VOMM is applicable in many applications. However, stock market is very complicated and the anomalies may affect and/or be reflected in many measures, including closing price, volume, price range, depth, spread, trading, etc. Therefore, it is far from enough to detect outliers from closing price only, and multiple measures in stock market need to be considered.

Case-Based Reasoning for Market Surveillance

Case-based reasoning (CBR) is the process of solving new problems based on the solutions of similar past problems (Buta & Barletta 1991). CBR builds a case database to store the past problems and their solutions. Whenever an input is coming, a case-based system will search its case database for an existing case that matches the input. If a past case is identified to exactly match the input problem, the system will immediately provide a solution for the problem. If, on the other hand, there are no past cases matching the input, system will try to retrieve a case that is similar to the input situation but not exactly appropriate to provide as a complete solution. The case-based system must then find and modify those small portions of the retrieved case that do not meet the input specifications. This will also provide a complete solution, but it generates a new case that can be automatically added to the case database. Then, the system is updated when new cases are stored in case database. Normally, to build a case database, terms and classified cases need to be defined by experts.

Buta & Barletta (1991) presents a CBR approach for market surveillance. Their approach aims to evaluate trading patterns in the context of additional company, industry, and market data, and identify possibly suspicious trades. By using CBR, the time cost of analyzing suspicious stock trade is reduced significantly. They also introduced an intelligent market monitor (IMM) for processing transactions. It is a market surveillance application at the Toronto Stock Exchange (TSE). Their system uses CBR to identify the transactions by the alert filter and process the features of current situation, such as the interest rates, company news and so on.

However, CBR is an approach that accepts anecdotal evidence as its main operating principle. There is no guarantee that the solutions for the input are correct without the statistically relevant data to test and to support it.

Expert System (ES)

An expert system (Lucas 1993) is a traditional application of artificial intelligence which aims to reproduce the performance of one or more human experts. Most expert systems are commonly used in a specific problem domain. Expert system is able to analyze information input by using a set of rules. The expert system may also provide mathematical analysis of the problems, and has the ability of reasoning to generate solutions. A simple decision tree or fuzzy logic may be utilized in an expert system. An important component of expert system is the aid of human workers or a supplement of information.

The New York Stock Exchange (NYSE) uses a series of ES called ICAS (Integrated Computer-Assisted Surveillance) (Francis 1989). The ICAS system has the abilities of identifying questionable trades and analyzing the trades with other external information. It finally specifies the most likely instances of insider trading and produces alerts for supervisors.

Lucas (1993) reports on the development of an experts system for stock market surveillance in the America Stock Exchange (AMEX). The system provides recommendations and a number of significant data for regulators. For example, it computes and displays the maximum potential gain or loss avoidance from insider trading based on the information of price, volume, etc. The expert system finally prints a report with salient data and related information for audit trail purposes.

Relational Knowledge Discovery

The National Association of Securities Dealers (NASD) (Bessembinder 1999) uses the probability relational model to identify the most dangerous brokers' trade. The NASD is a self-regulatory organization of the securities industry responsible for the operation and regulation of the Nasdaq stock market and over-the-counter markets. It watches over the Nasdaq to make sure that the market operates correctly. In 2007, the NASD merged with the New York Stock Exchange's regulation committee to form the Financial Industry Regulatory Authority, or FINRA.

Neville et al. (2005) reports the usage of relational probability trees (RPTs) for the task of surveillance. RPTs extend probability estimation trees to a relational setting. Due to their selectivity and intuitive representation of knowledge, tree models are often easily interpretable. This makes RPTs an attractive modeling approach for NASD examiners. The RPT learning algorithm adjusts for biases towards particular features due to the unique characteristics of relational data. Specifically, three characteristics, concentrated linkage, degree disparity and relational autocorrelation, can complicate the efforts to construct good statistical models, leading to feature selection bias and discovery of spurious correlations. By adjusting for these biases, the RPT algorithm is able to learn relatively compact and parsimonious tree models.

It is successful in reality, but it is difficult to run the above system for other stock exchanges in that it depends heavily on the qualified data collected by Central Registration Depository (CRD). NASD's task of ranking brokers for examination has three characteristics that are common to many knowledge discovery tasks, but that are rarely addressed in combination. Accurate ranking of brokers is inherently probabilistic, relational, and temporal.

Graph Clustering

A clustering algorithm divides records in a given database into groups or clusters such that records within a cluster are similar to each other and records from different clusters are dissimilar. In graph clustering, data sets can be represented as weighted graphs, where nodes correspond to the entities to cluster and edges correspond to a similarity measure between those entities (Kannan et al. 2000). The problem of graph clustering is well studied and the literature on the subject is very rich (Everitt 1980, Jain & Dubes 1988). The best known graph clustering algorithms attempt to optimize specific criteria such as k-median, minimum sum, minimum diameter, etc. Other algorithms are application-specific and take advantage of the underlying structure or other known characteristics of the data.

Palshikar and Apte (2008) research on collusion set detection by using graph clustering. Their research aims to assist to identify stock market manipulation. In stock market, some stock market manipulations take the form of collusion set of traders. For example, a group of traders have "heavy trading" among themselves in order to make false impression of some stocks and attract the other investors to buy. Palshikar and Apte (2008) utilize graph clustering to solve this problem. In their model, The label φ (u, v) on a directed edge (u, v) is the total quantity of shares sold by u to v. Therefore, the higher is the edge label, the closer is the vertices in terms of "heaviness" of trading. The authors test their models on synthetic trading data and real data sets. The results show that the graph clustering can effectively detect the collusion set.

One obvious limitation of the proposed approach is the failure of classifying the detected collusion set in stock markets, such as marking the end and matched orders.

Correlating Burst Events on Streaming Stock Market Data

Burst events refer to the events of importance happening within the same time frame. Identification of the burst events can significantly help monitoring or surveillance tasks. In particular, the identification of burst events is very critical to recognize anomalous activity for applications of fraud detection. For example, in stock market, some market manipulations take the form of burst events, and burst detection technologies are utilized to capture suspicious activities in large stock market volumes (Lerner & Shasha 2003).

Vlachos et al. (2008) provide a solution for monitoring and identification of correlated burst patterns in multi-stream time series database. The authors firstly identify the burst sections in datasets, and then store them for easy retrieval in an efficient in-memory index. The burst detection scheme imposes a variable threshold on the examined data and takes advantage of the skewed distribution that is typically encountered in many applications. The detected bursts are compacted into burst intervals and stored in an interval index. The index facilitates the identification of correlated bursts by performing very efficient overlap operations on the stored burst regions. Their approach was tested on financial stock data at the NYSE and the target burst patterns are the events in stock trading volumes during the days before and after the 9/11 event. The results showed that it efficiently detected the burst events from multi-stream time series datasets.

A possible extension of this research is the detection of cross-correlation between multiple data-streams based on their burst characteristics.

Artificial-Immune- Abnormal-Trading-Detection System (AIAS)

As a biologically inspired system, natural immune system (NIS) has been researched on a variety of areas, such as feature extraction, self-regulation and adaptability and so on. A NIS comprises a complex system of cells, molecules and organs that jointly represent an identification mechanism capable of perceiving and combating exogenous infectious microorganisms, which contain many antigens that are substances that can trigger immune responses, resulting in production of antibodies as part of the body's defence against infection and disease to neutralize related antigens.

Generally speaking, an artificial immune system (AIS) is a specific computational algorithm which takes its inspiration from the way how a NIS learns to respond to those exogenous invaders. It simulates the key features, such as adaptability, pattern recognition, learning, and memory acquisition of the NIS in order to deal with the problems (Dasgupta 1998) in computer security, anomaly detection, fault diagnosis, pattern recognition and a variety of other applications (Timmis et al. 2003) in science and engineering. As one of the main areas of the financial market, the stock market has an important concept –noise, which is defined as the fluctuations of price and volume that can confuse interpretation of market direction. Accordingly, those investors undertaking trades which generate such confusions are termed as noise traders. Some noise traders are described as essential players of the stock market (Black 1985) whereas some insiders illegitimately take advantage of exclusive information which is still unavailable to the public to trade securities and disclose some information through a public signal consisting of a noisy transformation of his or her own private information (Gregoire 2001). Some market manipulators try to influence the price of a security in order to create false or misleading patterns of active trading to bring in more traders. Often, the newly brought-in traders further cause significant or even disastrous deviation of security prices from the underlying values of the related assets resulting to the failure of correct interpretation of the market direction.

Lee & Yang (2005) proposed an expansile and adaptive abnormal-trading detection system

with the characteristics of good self-learning and memory capacities. Their artificial abnormal detection system has the following advantages. Firstly, its adaptivity means that the system is able to learn the trading patterns of different stocks; and also that it is able to learn the different trading patterns of the same stock according to each economic period, trading period, and the locality of financial markets. Secondly, it is anticipated that better proxies will be continuously found; the expansibility allows those newly discovered proxies be added to the system. Thirdly, the system can be used as a tool to compare proxies so as to search for a more proper proxy for a specified stock in a certain period at a certain place. Finally, those proxies used in the system will be eliminated or superseded before they are out of date. Thus with the continuous introduction of the new proxies into the system, the limited memory capacity of the system can be effectively utilized.

AIAS was tested and evaluated on high-frequent artificial and real stock market data. The test on real stock market is to see whether AIAS is able to detect one recorded insider trader case. It is recorded that insider trader trades occurred on 24 April, 2001, just before Qantas announced at the end of April 2001 that it would take over the operations of Impulse Airlines. As a result, AIAS detected three suspicious transactions on 20th and two on 24th respectively. It matches the insider trading case which happened on 24 April 2001.

AIAS needs to be researched on its time usage, and its ability of detecting anomalies needs to be improved and tested on more datasets.

Other Techniques

Some other techniques used for exception mining in stock market surveillance are decision tree, logistic regression, neural network, etc.

Decision tree is a predictive model that maps from observations about an item to conclusions about its target value (Utgoff 1989). In the tree structures, leaves represent classifications and branches represent conjunctions of features that lead to those classifications (Utgoff 2004). The machine learning technique for inducing a decision tree from data is called decision tree learning. A well-known decision tree algorithm is C4.5 (Quinlan 1993).

Logistic regression is a model used to predict the probability of occurrence of an event by fitting data to a logistic curve (Hosmer & Stanley 2000). It makes use of several predictor variables that may be either numerical or categorical. For example, the probability that a person has a heart attack within a specified time period might be predicted from knowledge of the person's age, sex and body mass index. Logistic regression is used extensively in the medical and social sciences as well as marketing applications, such as prediction of a customer's propensity to purchase a product or cease a subscription.

Neural network (NN) is a network of artificial neurons that uses a mathematical or computational model for information processing (Muller & Insua 1995). In most cases, a neural network is an adaptive system that changes its structure based on external or internal information that flows through the network.

Donoho (2003) researches on the solution of early detection of insider trading by using data mining technologies. His research was inspired by McMillian's hypothesis that people with inside information leave evidence in option trading data that might predict news. In order to automate the analysis and discover unknown relationships, he made use of different data mining technologies to replace the large amount of human intuition and manual analysis in McMillian's method. The utilized technologies include C4.5, backwards stepwise logic regression and neural networks. The experimental data in the research came from three sources: option trading, stock trading, and news. Stock and option data were available on all U.S. companies for which options are trades (about 2160 companies). News covered these

companies plus others. The date range for which all three data sources were available covered a six-month time period from March 11, 2003 to Sept 17, 2003. An expert model was used in order to evaluate the results. All three algorithms produced lift over random and over the expert model, but no algorithm clearly outperformed the others.

OUTLIER MINING ON MULTIPLE TIME SERIES IN STOCK MARKET

From the literature review, we can see that most of the exceptions detection technologies handle a single time series. It will be beneficial if we could integrate multiple time series, such as price, index, trade amount, etc. This is the motivation of our research on outlier mining on multiple time series (OMM). In this section, the design of OMM, the experiments and the evaluation of OMM are illustrated.

Outlier Mining on Multiple Time Series (OMM)

The idea of OMM is motivated to improve the accuracy of stock market surveillance. In Shannon's information theory, information is defined as that which removes or reduces uncertainty (Cover & Thomas 1991). For outlier detection task, more information means higher accuracy of an outlier detection model, since the identified outliers are more likely to be different from the remaining data. For example, it is less accurate to measure a stock and identify the outliers by using price information only. The results will be more reasonable if we add one or more measures, such as volume, volatility and liquidity.

In the design of OMM, the key issue is how to integrate multiple time series. There are two main potential approaches for this. One is to integrate the multiple time series before the outlier mining process, and the other is to run outlier mining on individual time series first and then integrate the results. In our research, we choose the latter because it keeps the original features of individual time series. This approach also facilitates utilizing the previous research outcomes.

Another issue is which measures to select as the multiple time series for exception mining. For the task of stock market surveillance, there are some valuable experiences from financial experts which can guide the choosing of measures. Price is the most important measure of stock performance. We can also use the outcomes of previous financial research to choose measures. For example, there are a great deal of financial research on the relationship between the abnormal behavior and the response of stock. Meulbroek (1992) conducted research on the relationship between insider trading, price movement and trading amounts. Their conclusion is that there is an association between these elements. Fishe & Robe (2002) also made a similar conclusion. Therefore, the price movement and trading amount are regarded as good measurements for anomalies. The price movement can be measured by price return and price fluctuation range during one day. Price fluctuation range is presented by the difference between the highest price and the lowest price in one day.

Our OMM consists of two components: generators of outliers on individual time series and integrators of multiple time series. The generators of outliers produce outliers by using existing outlier mining technologies. Currently, we use VOMM (Qi & Wang 2004) to carry out the task, because it has been proved to be an effective and efficient outlier mining technology applied in stock market surveillance. The outliers generated will be utilized by the integrators. The integrator of multiple time series is to integrate the multiple time series in order to refine the results. There are two proposed approaches in our research. One is based on major voting (V-BOMM) technology and the other is based on probabilities (P-BOMM).

Description of V-BOMM and P-BOMM

In order to illustrate our proposed OMM clearly, we provide an example and demonstrate how the V-BOMM and P-BOMM work.

Given 100 points on three time series X, Y and Z, which are described as: $[P_1(x_1, y_1, z_1), P_2(x_2, y_2, z_2),..., P_{100}(x_{100}, y_{100}, z_{100})]$, where $x_1, x_2, ..., x_{100}$ represent the values of each points on X, $y_1, y_2, ..., y_{100}$ represent the values of each points on Y, and $z_1, z_2, ..., z_{100}$ represent the values of each points on Z.

First, we generate three lists of candidate outliers on each time series by using VOMM. The number of candidate outliers is determined based on domain experience. Generally speaking, the less the candidate outliers are, the result is more accurate, but the coverage is worse. In this example, we choose 3 candidate outliers on each time series. Assume that the list of candidate outliers obtained from time series X is $[P_1, P_3, P_5]$, and the candidate outliers from Y and Z are respectively $[P_1, P_3, P_{10}]$ and $[P_1, P_5, P_2]$. After that, V-BOMM is used to refine the candidate outliers. The V-BOMM produces the final outliers with majority voting. There are 3 time series in total, so the majority should be no less than 2. That is, if a point appears in 2 or more lists of candidate outliers, it will be regarded as one of the final outliers. In the above example, P_1, P_3 and P_5 are the final outliers because they appear in 2 or 3 of the above lists. On the contrary, P_{10} and P_2 are not included as the final outliers because they only appear in one candidate list.

The P-BOMM produces the final points ranked with the probabilities of being an outlier. First, we generate three lists of candidate outliers on each time series by VOMM. At the same time, an outlier test ratio is calculated based on Formula (2). This ratio gives the probability of being an outlier for each point. For example, one list of candidate outliers could be $[\{P_1, 98\%\}, \{P_3, 92\%\}, \{P_9, 88\%\}]$ on

Table 2. Examples of original alerts

No.	Date	Time	Type	Threshold	Value
8	13/06/2005	9:30:00	Price Change Rate	0.04	0.04
18	24/05/2006	9:30:03	Turnover Rate	1000000	2167700
23	21/11/2005	9:25:00	Price Change Rate	0.04	0.05
24	27/03/2006	9:25:00	Price Change Rate	0.04	0.1
33	27/03/2006	9:25:05	Price Change Rate	0.08	0.1

time series X, and one is [{P_1, 97%}, {P_{23}, 91%}, {P_9, 96%}] on time series Y and [{P_{33}, 87%}, {P_3, 92%}, {P_9, 97%}] on time series Z. Then all the points are ranked as [{P_1, 98%}, {P_9, 97%}, {P_3, 92%}, {P_{23}, 91%}, {P_{33}, 87%}] by taking the maximum of the probability for each point. The last step is to determine the number of final outliers. We choose the top k outliers from the ranked list as the final outliers. The value of k can be set based on the specific application, If we set $k=3$, then the final outliers are P_1, P_9 and P_3.

The proposed V-BOMM and P-BOMM use the principle curve algorithm as the kernel. The principle curve is applied on the three individual time series. The computation complexity of principle curve is $O(n^2)$ (Zhang & Wang 2003). Therefore, the computation complexity of our proposed OMM is also $O(n^2)$.

Application Background and Data

The Shanghai Stock Exchange (SSE) is a Chinese stock exchange based in Shanghai, with a market capitalization of nearly US$3.02 trillion in 2007 making it the largest exchange in mainland China. It is a non-profit organization directly administered by the China Securities Regulatory Commission (CSRC). The proposed OMM was tested and evaluated with the data from SSE. The data are daily trade records in SSE from 1 June 2004 to 3 Mar 2006. It has the 425 trading days. The attributes of the data sets include the highest price, the lowest price, the closing price and trade amounts.

Based on the relevant financial knowledge, we constructed daily price return, daily price range and daily trade amount as the three time series and each of them was assigned with the same weight on experiments. The daily amount was the original attribute of raw data, but the daily price return was calculated out from the raw data:

Price Return = $(P_1 - P_2) / P_2$, (3)

where P_1 is the current closing price and P_2 is the previous closing price. The daily price range was calculated with the following equation:

Daily Price Range = $P_3 - P_4$ (4)

where P_3 is the daily highest price and P_4 is the daily lowest price.

We chose the real Alerts generated by China stock exchange during 1 June 2004 to 3 Mar 2006 as a benchmark, which is the same as that of our experimental data. Rules were set by surveillance staff to detect the abnormal movement of turnover exception and price change rate exception. Some examples of rules are shown in Table 2.

and $VOMM^k_{trade\_amounts}$.

- **Stage 2:** Run Voting-based OMM on Daily Price Return data, Daily Price Range data and Trade Amount data respectively, and choose the top k ($k=60,50,40,30,20,10$) samples as outliers on each measure. The outcomes are vectors named as $V\text{-}BOMM^k$ ($k=60,50,40,30,20,10$)

- **Stage 3:** Run the Probability-based OMM on the three data respectively, and choose the top k ($k=60,50,40,30,20,10$) samples as

Table 3. Output of experiments.

	k =60	k =50	k =40	k =30	k=20	k =10
$VOMM^k_{trade\_amounts}$	18	17	16	15	13	9
$VOMM^k_{trade\_amounts}$	17	17	16	16	15	9
$VOMM^k_{trade\_amounts}$	15	15	13	13	13	9
V-BOMM^k	20/52	20/45	17/32	17/27	16/19	9/9
P-BOMM^k	21	20	20	20	16	10

outliers. The outcomes are vectors named as *P-BOMM^k* (*k*=60,50,40,30,20,10).

The experimental results are shown in Table 3. The columns stand for the factor *k*, the expected number of outliers. For example, *k*=20 means that the top 20 samples are regarded as outliers, while the rest of the samples are regarded as normal. The observation in each row stands for the alerts which are exactly identified by corresponding methods. For example, the value 16 on row 1 and column 4 means that 16 alerts are identified by VOMM methods on price return time series. One special case is the observation of V-BOMM, where the left value stands for the number of real alerts detected, while the right value stands for the calculated number of outliers.

We evaluate the experiments results and com-

pare the performance of the five methods according to the four measures: accuracy, precision, recall and specificity. They are calculated based on the following formula:

$Accuracy = (TP+TN) / (TP+FN+FP+TN)$ (5)
$Specificity = TN / (FP+TN)$ (6)
$Precision =TP / (TP+FP)$ (7)
$Recall = TP / (TP+FN)$ (8)

The *TP* represents the number of detected outliers those are real alerts; *FP* stands for the number of detected which are not actual alerts; *FN* represents the number of the identified normal days which are real alerts and *TN* stands for the number of identified normal days which are not alerts.

The Tables 4, 5, 6, & 7 show the values of the accuracy, specificity, precision and recall for different methods. From these tables, we can

Table 4. Accuracy evaluation

	k =60	k =50	k =40	k =30	k =20	k =10
$VOMM^k_{price\_return}$	0.894	0.913	0.932	0.951	0.965	0.969
$VOMM^k_{price\_range}$	0.889	0.913	0.932	0.955	0.974	0.969
$VOMM^k_{trade\_amounts}$	0.88	0.904	0.918	0.941	0.965	0.969
V-BOMM^k	0.922	0.939	0.955	0.967	0.981	0.972
P-BOMM^k	0.908	0.927	0.951	0.974	0.979	0.974

Table 5. Specificity evaluation

	$k=60$	$k=50$	$k=40$	$k=30$	$k=20$	$k=10$
$VOMM^k_{price\_return}$	0.896	0.918	0.941	0.963	0.983	0.998
$VOMM^k_{price\_range}$	0.894	0.918	0.941	0.965	0.988	0.998
$VOMM^k_{trade\_amounts}$	0.889	0.913	0.933	0.958	0.983	0.998
$V\text{-}BOMM^k$	0.921	0.938	0.963	0.975	0.993	1.00
$P\text{-}BOMM^k$	0.903	0.926	0.950	0.975	0.990	1.00

Table 6. Precision evaluation

	$k=60$	$k=50$	$k=40$	$k=30$	$k=20$	$k=10$
$VOMM^k_{price\_return}$	0.300	0.340	0.400	0.500	0.650	0.900
$VOMM^k_{price\_range}$	0.283	0.340	0.400	0.533	0.750	0.900
$VOMM^k_{trade\_amounts}$	0.250	0.300	0.325	0.433	0.650	0.900
$V\text{-}BOMM^k$	0.385	0.444	0.531	0.630	0.842	1.000
$P\text{-}BOMM^k$	0.350	0.400	0.500	0.667	0.800	1.000

Table 7. Recall evaluation

	$k=60$	$k=50$	$k=40$	$k=30$	$k=20$	$k=10$
$VOMM^k_{price\_return}$	0.857	0.810	0.762	0.7143	0.619	0.429
$VOMM^k_{price\_range}$	0.810	0.810	0.762	0.762	0.714	0.429
$VOMM^k_{trade\_amounts}$	0.714	0.714	0.619	0.619	0.619	0.429
$V\text{-}BOMM^k$	0.952	0.952	0.810	0.810	0.762	0.429
$P\text{-}BOMM^k$	1.000	0.952	0.952	0.952	0.762	0.477

see that the accuracy, precision and specificity decrease with the increase of the k value. However, the recall increases with the increase of k. By comparing the methods, it is obvious that our proposed V-BOMM and P-BOMM perform better than the outlier mining on single outlier mining, and they have improved accuracy, precision, recall and specificity.

FUTURE RESEARCH TOPICS

Although there are a couple of existing techniques on exception mining in stock market, there are still many open issues on this research, and there are also some possible research topics which have potential to stock market surveillance. This section will present future research topics in this area.

Application of Market Microstructure Theory

Market Microstructure is a branch of finance concerned with the details of how exchange occurs in markets (Frino & Segara 2008, Harris 2003). While the theory of market microstructure applies to the exchange of real or financial assets, more evidence is available on the microstructure of financial markets due to the availability of transaction data from financial markets. The major thrust of market microstructure research examines the ways in which the working process of a market affects determinants of transaction costs, prices, quotes, volume, and trading behavior.

O'Hara (1997) defined market microstructure as "the study of the process and outcomes of exchanging assets under a specific set of rules. While much of economics abstracts from the mechanics of trading, microstructure theory focuses on how specific trading mechanisms affect the price formation process." The market microstructure theory is one of the most important theories in finance. It is a rapid growing specialization of financial economics. It can help us understand stock markets and the elements in stock markets. The key elements in stock market include the trading protocol, participants, information, regulations, technologies and instruments. Market microstructure also provides the measures of market quality and efficiency, such as the liquidity, transparency, volatility and transaction cost and risk.

In order to utilize microstructure efficiently in stock market surveillance, we need to consider all the elements and their relationships. For instance,

there are a variety of definitions of insider trading from different exchanges, and there are also different regulations for market manipulations in different exchanges. In addition, the emerging markets have different performance with the mature markets, such as NYSK. There are two kinds of markets: one is floor stock markets, like NYSK; another kind of markets is electric markets where the trades occur automatically by computers. Therefore, there are no general models which fit everywhere. The produced models should be based on specific environments.

The market microstructure theory provides some measures of stock markets including return, abnormal return, volume, volatility, spread (Gopikrishnan & Stanley 2005). These measures play important roles in stock market surveillance.

- Return refers to the gain or loss for a single security or portfolio over a specific period. It is usually quoted as a percentage. The popular equation to calculate return is $VOMM_{price\_return}^{k}$, where R_t is the return over the period from time t to time t-1, P_t is the trading price at time t, and P_{t-1} is the trading price at time t-1.

- Abnormal return is the difference between the actual return of a single security or portfolio and the expected return over a specific period. The expected return is the estimated return based on an asset pricing model, using a long run historical average or multiple valuations. Brown and Warner (1985) gave the following formula to measure the abnormal return: $AR_{jt} = R_{jt} - (\alpha_j + \beta_j R_{mt})$, where AR_{jt} is the abnormal return for the security j at time t, R_{jt} is the observed return for the security j at time t, R_{mt} is the observed return for the market index at time t, and α_j, β_j are the estimated parameters using previous return observations.

- Volatility is a statistical measure of the

dispersion of the value of a market measure for a security over a specific period. It frequently refers to return volatility which is the standard deviation of the returns over the period. A higher volatility means that the price of a security can change dramatically over a short time period in either direction. The formula of return volatility is $VOMM^k_{price\_range}$, where V is the return volatility over a time range of T and R_t is the return.

- Spread is the difference between the bid and ask price of a security. The formula to compute spread is $S = P_b - P_a$, where S is the spread, P_b is the bid price and P_a is the ask price. Spread is used to measure the market liquidity, which refers to the ability of securities to be bought or sold in the market without causing a significant movement in the price and with minimum loss of value. Commonly, the wider the spread is, the lower the liquidity is.

Application of Semi-Supervised Classification

Time series classification has attracted great interest in the last decade. However current research assumes the existence of large amounts of labeled training data. In reality, such data are often very difficult or expensive to obtain. Therefore, a semi-supervised technique for building time series classifiers is valuable in many domains (Ratsaby & Venkatesh 1995).

The idea of using unlabeled data to help classification may sound initially unintuitive. However, several studies in the literature have indicated the utility of unlabeled data for classification. Learning from both labeled and unlabeled data is called semi-supervised learning (SSL) (Chapelle et al. 2006). Because semi-supervised learning requires less human effort and generally achieves higher accuracy, it is of great interest both in theory and in practice. There are many semi-supervised learning methods proposed in the literature. Based on their underlying assumptions, they can be organized into five classes: SSL with generative models, SSL with low density separation, graph-based methods, co-training methods and self-training methods.

The task of time series classification is to map each time series to one of the predefined classes. However, the identified exceptions in stock market are few in reality. It means that the labeled examples are rare, but unlabeled data is abundant. For example, there are only about 30 insider trading cases found in Hong Kong Stock Exchange from 1997 to 2007, and it is almost impossible to train a good classifier based on these few identified cases. An alternative way is to use the semi-supervised classification technology to construct accurate classifiers with few labeled examples.

Shape-Based Analysis

The shape-based analysis is another possible way of identifying exceptional patterns (Fu et al. 2007). It is significant to define the movement pattern based on the shape of time series. For example, the time series may change in the order of increase, decrease and then increase again, which form a shape of wave. This approach is based on the assumption that there exist unique shapes of time series corresponding to some exceptions in stock market. The frequent shapes on multiple time series are identified first, and then the exceptional shapes are to be found. However, it is challenging to define the shapes of time series movement and the similarity between two time series. Another challenge is how to split the time slides to compare time series.

In the shape-based analysis, the identification of perceptually important points (PIPs) is the most important issues. By identifying the PIPs, we can measure or compare the multiple time series. In particular, it is challenging to identify the PIPs on stock market data, such as the price return, volume and volatility.

Statistical-Based Analysis

The statistical analysis is also possible to identify exception patterns on multiple time series. A combination of counts, frequency, or distribution of data may be a potential way of identifying the exceptions. It is also challenging to define the statistical measures on proper time slides. For example, marking the close is a typical manipulation in most stock exchanges. The manipulator normally places a lot of small orders just near the close of the market in order to influence the closing price change. Therefore, a possible method of identifying this type of manipulation is to analyze the combination of frequency of order, the price change and times slide by statistical methods.

There are many complex relationships between elements in stock market. It is more challenging to identify the abnormal behaviors hidden in these elements. The Bayesian Networks or Markov Chains are possible tools to discover the relationship between multiple time series data on stock markets.

Sequential Pattern Mining for Exception Detection

The traditional outliers in time series are statistically based and an outlier is a specific data point corresponding to a specific time. For example, one point is significantly different from the rest of data. However, the exceptions in stock market often spans over a period of time, and their impacts on the stock prices, volumes, indexes, etc., are also shown over a time span, instead of at a single time point. For example, when an insider trading happens, the price may change abnormally over a long period of time. Therefore, it would be more effective to detect exceptions by analyzing the changing of time series over a period of time. The idea is to convert time series

into sequences and then use sequential pattern mining techniques (Agrawal & Srikant 1995) to find normal sequential patterns and exceptional sequential patterns in stock markets. At first, every time series is discretized into a sequence of "1" and "0" or a sequence of digits or symbols (e.g., "up" and "down"). Then techniques for sequential pattern mining are used to find frequent sequential patterns P1. After that, we can use sequential patter mining to find sequential patterns (P2) highly associated with known illegal trades, such as insider trading and market manipulation. By comparing P1 and P2, we can find which sequential patterns are truly associated with exceptional trading and which are associated with them by chance. The above sequential pattern mining can be done to find the sequential patterns in a single long time series. It can also be done on multiple time series of the same measure of many stocks. Moreover, it is also interesting to mine for sequential patterns on the multiple time series of a single stock on multiple measures, such as price, volume, spread, index, etc.

CONCLUSION

Exception mining is very important for stock market surveillance. This chapter has summarized the literature of technologies which have been used or researched for stock market surveillance. These include the simplest rule-based approaches, basic statistic approaches, outlier detections, graph clustering, C4.5, logistic regression, neural networks, etc. We also have presented our OMM (Outlier Mining on Multiple time series) model, which improves the accuracy of outlier mining by integrating multiple time series. The proposed P-BOMM and V-BOMM are proved to perform better than the outlier mining on single time series.

There are still many open issues in this area. We pointed out several potential research directions in stock market surveillance. The financial knowledge, in particular, the market microstructure theory, is the valuable support to stock market surveillance. Semi-supervised classification is an appropriate tool to handle the data set with a large amount of unlabelled data, but few labeled data. Shape-based analysis, statistical analysis and sequential pattern mining also provide potential solutions of exception mining for stock market surveillance.

REFERENCES

Aggarwal, R. K., & Wu, G. J. (2006). Stock market manipulations. *The Journal of Business*, *78*(4), 1915–1953. doi:10.1086/503652

Agrawal, R., & Srikant, R. (1995). Mining sequential patterns. In *Proceedings of the Eleventh International Conference on 1995*, (pp. 3-14).

Alhanaty, M., & Bercovier, M. (1998). Curve fitting and design by optimal control methods. In *Information Visualization*, (pp. 108-113). Washington, DC: IEEE.

Allen, F., & Gorton, G. (1992). Stock price manipulation,market microstructure and asymmetric information. *European Economic Review*, *36*, 624–630. doi:10.1016/0014-2921(92)90120-L

Bessembinder, H. (1999). Trade Execution Costs on NASDAQ and the NYSE: A Post-reform comparison. *Journal of Financial and Quantitative Analysis*, *34*(3), 387–407. doi:10.2307/2676265

Bettis, J. C., Duncan, W. A., & Harmon, W. K. (1998). The effectiveness of insider trading regulations. *Journal of Applied Business Research*, *14*(4), 53–70.

Black, F. (1985). Noise. *The Journal of Finance*, *41*(3), 530–531.

Bollerslev, T. (1986). Generalized autoregressive conditional heteroscedasticity. *Journal of Econometrics*, *31*, 307–327. doi:10.1016/0304-4076(86)90063-1

Brown, P. & GoldSchmidt, P. (1996). Alcod idss: Assisting the australian stock market surveillance team's review process. *Applied Artificial Intelligence*, *10*, 625–641. doi:10.1080/088395196118452

Buta, P., & Barletta, R. (1991). Case-based reasoning for market surveillance. *Artificial Intelligence on Wall Stree.* (pp. 116-121). Washington, DC: IEEE.

Chapelle, O., Scholkopf, B., & Zien, A. (2006). *Semi-Supervised learning.* Cambridge, MA: MIT Press.

Charest, G. (1978). Dividend information, stock returns and market efficiency-II. *Journal of Financial Economics*, *6*(2/3).

Chen, C., & Liu, L. M. (1993). Joint estimation of model parameters and outlier effects in time series. *Journal of the American Statistical Association*, *88*, 284–297. doi:10.2307/2290724

Cheng, L., Firth, M., Leung, T., & Rui, O. (2006). The effects of insider trading on liquidity. *Pacific-Basin Finance Journal*, *14*, 467–483. doi:10.1016/j.pacfin.2006.01.006

Chernick, M. R. (1982). A note on the robustness of Dixon Ratio Test in small samples. *The American Statistician*, *36*, 140. doi:10.2307/2684033

Cover, T. M., & Thomas, J. A. (1991). *Elements of information theory.* Hoboken, NJ: Wiley.

Dasgupta, D. (1998). *Artificial immune systems and their applications.* Berlin: Springer.

Dixon, W. J. (1950). Analysis of extreme values. *Annals of Mathematical Statistics*, *21*, 488–506. doi:10.1214/aoms/1177729747

Donoho, S. (2004). Early detection of insider trading in option market. In *The Tenth ACM SIGKDD international conference on Knowledge discovery and data mining*, (pp. 420-429). New York: ACM Press.

Everitt, B. (1980). *Cluster analysis*. New York: Halsted Press.

Felixson, K., & Pelli, A. (1999). Day end returns: Stock price manipulation. *Journal of Multinational Financial Management, 9*(2), 95–127. doi:10.1016/S1042-444X(98)00052-8

Fishe, R. P., & Robe, M. A. (2002). *The impact of illegal insider trading in dealer and specialist markets: evidence from a natural experiment*. Technical report, Securities and Exchange Commission.

Fishman, M., & Hagerty, K. (1992). Insider trading and the efficiency of stock prices. *The Rand Journal of Economics, 23*(1), 106–122. doi:10.2307/2555435

Francis, T. (1989). Expert system tools are Wall Street's newest creation. *Wall Street Comput. Rev.,* 26-40.

Franses, P. & Dijk, D. (2000). *Outlier detection in GARCH models*. Econometric institute research report EI-9926/RV.

Frino, A., & Segara, R. (2008). *Trade execution, arbitrage and dealing in Australia*. Upper Saddle River, NJ: Pearson Education.

Fu, T., Chung, F., Luk, R., & Ng, C. (2007). Stock time series pattern matching: Template-based vs. rule-based approaches. *Engineering Applications of Artificial Intelligence, 20*, 347–364. doi:10.1016/j.engappai.2006.07.003

Garfinkel, J. A., & Nimalendran, M. (2003). Market structure and trader anonymity: An analysis of insider trading. *Journal of Financial and Quantitative Analysis, 38*(3), 591–610. doi:10.2307/4126733

Gopikrishnan, V.P.P. & Stanley, H.E. (2005). Quantifying fluctuations in market liquidity: Analysis of the bid-ask spread. *The American Physical Society*, 1–7.

Gourieroux, C. (1997). *ARCH models and financial applications*. Berlin: Springer-Verlag.

Gregoire, P., & Huangi, H. (2001). *Insider trading, noise trading and the cost of Equity*.

Han, J., & Kamber, M. (2001). *Data Mining: concepts and techniques*. San Francisco: Morgan Kaufmann Publishers.

Harris, L. (2003). *Trading and Exchanges, Market microstructure for practitioners*. New York: Oxford University Press.

Hosmer, D. W., & Stanley, L. (2000). *Applied logistic regression*. Hoboken, NJ: Wiley.

Jain, A. K., & Dubes, R. C. (1988). *Algorithms for clustering data*. Englewood Cliffs, NJ: Prentice-Hall.

Jain, P. K. (2005). Financial market design and the equity premium: Electronic versus floor trading. *The Journal of Finance, 60*(6), 2955–2985. doi:10.1111/j.1540-6261.2005.00822.x

John, K., & Narayanan, R. (1997). Market manipulation and the role of insider trading regulations. *The Journal of Business, 70*(2), 217–247. doi:10.1086/209716

Kannan, R., Vempala, S., & Vetta, A. (2000). On clusterings - good, bad and spectral. *IEEE Symposium on Foundations of Computer Science*, (pp. 367—377). Los Alamitos, CA: IEEE Computer Society.

Lee, V. C., & Yang, X. J. (2005). Development and test of an artificial-immune-abnormal trading-detection system for financial market. *Advances in Intelligent Computing*, (pp.410-419). Berlin: Springer.

Leland, H. E. (1992). Insider Trading: Should it be prohibited? *The Journal of Political Economy, 100*(4), 859–887. doi:10.1086/261843

Lerner, A., & Shasha, D. (2003). The virtues and challenges of ad hoc + streams querying in finance. *IEEE Data Eng Bull,* 49–56.

Lucas, H. (1993). Market expert surveillance systems. *Communications of the ACM, 36*, 27–34. doi:10.1145/163298.163301

Luo, C., Zhao, Y., Cao, L., Ou, Y., & Liu, L. (2008). Outlier mining on multiple time series data in stock market. In *Proc. of the Tenth Pacific Rim International Conference on Artificial Intelligence (PRICAI 08), 2008.*

Meulbroek, L. K. (1992). An emrirical analysis of illegal insider trading. *The Journal of Finance, 47*, 1661–1699. doi:10.2307/2328992

Minenna, M. (2003). Insider trading, abnormal return and preferential information: Supervising through a probabilistic model. *Journal of Banking & Finance, 27*, 59–86. doi:10.1016/S0378-4266(01)00209-6

Muller, P., & Insua, D. R. (1995). Issues in bayesian analysis of neural network models. *Neural Computation, 10*, 571–592.

Neville, J., Simsek, O., Jensen, D., Komoroske, J., Palmer, K., & Goldberg, H. (2005) Using relational knowledge discovery to prevent securities fraud. *the eleventh ACM SIGKDD international conference on Knowledge discovery in data mining*, (pp. 449-458). New York: ACM Press

O'Hara, M. (1997). *Market microstructure eheory.* London: Blackwell Publishing.

Palshikar, G. K., & Apte, M. M. (2008). Collusion set detection using graph clustering. *Data Mining and Knowledge Discovery, 16*(2), 135–164. doi:10.1007/s10618-007-0076-8

Qi, H., & Wang, J. (2004). A model for mining outliers from complex data sets. *The 2004 ACM symposium on Applied computing*, (pp. 595-599). New York: ACM Press.

Quinlan, J. R. (1993). *C4.5: Programs for machine learning.* San Francisco: Morgan Kaufmann.

Ratsaby, J., & Venkatesh, S. S. (1995). Learning from a mixture of labeled and unlabeled examples with parametric side information. In *proceedings of the Eighth Annual Conference on Computational Learning Theory*, (pp. 412-417).

Schinasi, G. K., Drees, B., & Lee, W. (1999). Managing global finance and risk. *Finance & Development, 36*(4), 38–41.

Smith, C. R. (1995). Tracking the elusive insider. *Wall Street and Technology, 12*, 48–50.

Smith, J. (1981). *The probability distribution of market returns: a logistic hypothesis.* PhD dissertation, University of Utah.

Szockyj, E., & Geis, G. (2002). Insider trading pattern and analysis. *Journal of Criminal Justice, 30*, 273–286. doi:10.1016/S0047-2352(02)00129-0

Timmis, J., Bentley, P., & Hart, E. (2003). Artificial immune systems. In *Proceedings of Second International Conference, ICARIS 2003*, Edinburgh, UK.

Utgoff, P. E. (1989). Incremental induction of decision Trees. *Machine Learning, 4*, 161–186. doi:10.1023/A:1022699900025

Utgoff, P. E. (2004). Decision tree induction based on efficient tree restructuring. *Journal of Machine Learning*, 5-44. Berlin: Springer.

Vlachos, M., Wu, K. L., Chen, S. K., & Yu, P. S. (2008). Correlating burst events on streaming stock market data. [Amsterdam: Kluwer Academic Publishers.]. *Data Mining and Knowledge Discovery, 16*(1), 109–133. doi:10.1007/s10618-007-0066-x

Wong, M. C. S., Cheung, Y. L., & Wu, L. (2000). Insider trading in the Hong Kong stock market. *Financial Engineering and the Japanese Markets, 7*(3), 275–288.

Zhang. J. & Wang, J. (2003). An overview about principal curves. *Chinese journal of computers, 2*, 129-146.

Chapter 11
Analysis of Content Popularity in Social Bookmarking Systems

Symeon Papadopoulos
Aristotle University of Thessaloniki, Greece Informatics & Telematics Institute, Thermi, Thessaloniki, Greece

Fotis Menemenis
Informatics & Telematics Institute, Thermi, Thessaloniki, Greece

Athena Vakali
Aristotle University of Thessaloniki, Greece

Ioannis Kompatsiaris
Informatics & Telematics Institute, Thermi, Thessaloniki, Greece

ABSTRACT

The recent advent and wide adoption of Social Bookmarking Systems (SBS) has disrupted the traditional model of online content publishing and consumption. Until recently, the majority of content consumed by people was published as a result of a centralized selection process. Nowadays, the large-scale adoption of the Web 2.0 paradigm has diffused the content selection process to the masses. Modern SBS-based applications permit their users to submit their preferred content, comment on and rate the content of other users and establish social relations with each other. As a result, the evolution of popularity of socially bookmarked content constitutes nowadays an overly complex phenomenon calling for a multi-aspect analysis approach. This chapter attempts to provide a unified treatment of the phenomenon by studying four aspects of popularity of socially bookmarked content: (a) the distributional properties of content consumption, (b) its evolution in time, (c) the correlation between the semantics of online content and its popularity, and (d) the impact of online social networks on the content consumption behavior of individuals. To this end, a case study is presented where the proposed analysis framework is applied to a large dataset collected from Digg, a popular social bookmarking and rating application.

DOI: 10.4018/978-1-60566-816-1.ch011

INTRODUCTION

The emergence of Web 2.0 technologies and the widespread use of applications integrating such technologies have transformed the way people experience and act in online settings. In the first days of the Web, people were excited to browse through and consume online content (mostly static web pages) that was prepared and published by website owners or administrators. Nowadays, digital content consumption – e.g. online article reading, picture viewing and video watching – still appears to be one of the main activities for most internet users[t]. However, the advent of the Web 2.0 application paradigm has transformed the established "browsing-based" online content consumption behavior of users. This change was possible by means of offering users a host of rich interactivity features, such as content sharing, rating as well as online community building. Thus, users of today's Web 2.0 applications are empowered to share, organize, rate and retrieve online content. In addition, users are exposed to the content-related activities of other users and can even form online relations to each other. Consequently, online content consumption

within a modern Web 2.0 application constitutes an overly complex phenomenon with interesting dynamics which have not been thoroughly investigated yet.

Social Bookmarking Systems (SBS) hold a prominent place among Web 2.0 applications with respect to content consumption since they provide a platform where users are provided with two significant features:

- Submitting and sharing bookmarks (links) to online resources, e.g. articles, photos or videos, which they consider interesting.
- Indicating their preference or disapproval to bookmarks submitted by other users, by voting for or against the interesting-ness/ appeal of online resources and by commenting on them.

In addition to these two features which are fundamental for an SBS, there are two other optional groups of features, namely Taxonomic and Social-Community features. Taxonomic features pertain to the possibilities offered to users for assigning bookmarks to a predefined topic-scheme or for tagging them with freely chosen keywords.

Table 1. Taxonomic and social/community features of several social bookmarking services

Application name / URL	Type of Bookmarks	Taxonomic Feats		Social/Community Feats	
		Tags	Topics	Friends	Groups
Digg.com	News		+	+	
www.**StumbleUpon**.com	General	+		+	
www.**propeller**.com	News	+	+	+	+
www.**reddit**.com	News		+	+	
www.**fark**.com	News		+		
www.**newsvine**.com	News	+	+	+	+
delicious.com	General	+		+	
www.**blinklist**.com	General	+		+	
www.**clipmarks**.com	General	+		+	
furl.nt	General	+	+		+
www.**citeulik**.org	Ciations	+			+
bibsonomy.org	Citations	+			+

Social-Community features enable the users to create "friendship" relations with each other (which can be unilateral or mutual) or to create groups of topical interests. A number of social bookmarking applications have been recently launched. Systems such as *delicious* are meant to be used as general bookmark organization and sharing applications, while there are also social bookmarking applications focused on online news such as *Digg* and *newsvine*, and even niche bookmarking services such as *CiteULike*, used only for bookmarking citations to research articles. Table 1 lists some of the most popular SBS along with their features.

There has been a recent surge in the usage of social bookmarking applications, many of which currently attract several million of unique users per month. An illustrative overview of usage statistics pertaining to the most popular SBS is provided in Table 2, where the top 10 social bookmarking applications are ranked based on the number of unique monthly visitors they attract. Several additional web popularity metrics are provided in the same table, namely the number of inbound links, the Google Page Rank and the Alexa Rank. According to the table, *Digg*, *StumbleUpon*, propeller and *reddit* are the most popular social

bookmarking applications in terms of the number of unique visitors per month. Although *delicious* is the oldest bookmarking application from this list and features the largest number of bookmarks, it appears to attract a smaller number of visitors than its main competitors.

The widespread and intense use of such applications is responsible for the ceaseless creation of massive data sets where the content consumption patterns of users are imprinted. The description and analysis of the intricate phenomena related to these patterns could provide answers to a series of interesting questions:

- What kinds of distributions emerge in the content consumption behavior of the masses?
- How does the attention attracted by a particular online resource evolve over time?
- Is there correlation between the content of a resource (semantics) and its popularity?
- What is the impact of social networking on the consumption of online content?

This chapter provides insights into such questions by investigating recent and ongoing research

Table 2. Top 10 Social Bookmarking services ranked by averaging the number of unique visitors as provided by Compete[a] and Quantcast[b]. The number of inbound links was collected from Yahoo! Site Explorer. The data were collected in June 2008.

Site	Monthly Visitors		Inbound Links	Page Rank	Alexa Rank
	Compete	Quantcast			
Digg	**23,988,437** (1)	**19,906,963** (1)	27,589,161 (6)	8	**114**
StumbleUpon	2,338,242 (3)	1,331,110 (3)	160,863,707 (2)	8	372
propeller	1,521,706 (5)	6,055,679 (2)	8,590,778 (7)	7	876
reddit	2,489,583 (2)	1,115,655 (5)	4,859,451 (8)	8	4,074
fark	368,566 (7)	1,235,481 (4)	2,915,127 (9)	5	1,938
newsvine	625,115 (6)	986,471 (6)	66,154,514 (3)	8	6,923
delicious	1,632,204 (4)	420,043 (9)	**462,168,833** (1)	**9**	1,161
blinklist	307,673 (9)	510,838 (7)	43,226,590 (5)	7	5,613
clipmarks	322,011 (8)	448,437 (8)	460,278 (10)	6	6,208
furl	153,987 (10)	79,462 (10)	60,312,568 ()	8	15,914

efforts in the area of Web 2.0 data mining as well as by carrying out an analysis of a large dataset collected from Digg. The next section provides an account of existing studies on the analysis of content consumption behavior within Web 2.0 applications, organized around four research tracks. The third section formalizes a framework for the analysis of content-related phenomena in SBS. The application of this framework is illustrated in the fourth section, with Digg used as a case study. The final two sections of the chapter present an outlook on future trends in this area and conclude the chapter respectively.

BACKGROUND

Considerable research interest has been recently developed in the analysis and modeling of the content consumption behavior of Web 2.0 application users. Much of this research is focused on the mining of web log data where the user transactions are recorded. In our study, we have identified four major research tracks addressing the study of phenomena that arise through the online content consumption by masses of users:

1. *Statistical analysis:* The monitoring of the activities of large user masses enables the application of powerful statistical analyses in order to study the distributional properties of observed variables and to make inferences about the recorded data.
2. *Temporal data mining:* The analysis of content consumption patterns over time is crucial for in-depth understanding of the dynamics emerging in the phenomena that take place within social bookmarking applications. Discovering trends and periodic patterns as well as producing summaries of multiple data streams is the focus of this perspective.
3. *Content semantics:* The lexical and semantic analysis of the content that is consumed

within SBS provides insights into the interests of the masses and has broad implications in the design of effective Information Retrieval (IR) systems.
4. *Social network effects:* The influence of the users' online social environment on their content consumption behavior is increasingly important for describing diffusion processes and viral phenomena arising in the SBS user communities.

In order to gain a high-level understanding of the phenomena emerging in complex systems such as SBS, researchers commonly employ statistical analysis techniques; more specifically, they inspect and analyze the distributional properties of the variables observed in the system under study. Previous studies of social, biological and computer systems have confirmed in a series of phenomena the emergence of highly-skewed distributions, frequently taking the form of a *power law*. Power-law distributions – commonly referred to as Zipf's laws or Pareto distributions – provide a statistical model for describing the "rich-get-richer" phenomena frequently appearing in complex systems. Two noteworthy survey studies on power laws are provided by Newman (2005) and Mitzenmacher (2004). In an attempt to explain the emergence of such distributions in complex systems, a series of generative models have been recently proposed; among those, one of the most prominent is the *preferential attachment* model by (Barabási & Albert, 1999). Later in the chapter, we will confirm that the interest attracted by online resources in Digg, as well as the voting patterns of SBS users follow highly-skewed patterns that can be often well approximated by a power law.

Furthermore, analysis of the temporal aspects of phenomena similar to the ones appearing within SBS-like environments provides further insights into the evolution of variables such as the intensity of user activity, or the number of votes that an online resource collects. For instance, the temporal analysis of the user posting and commenting activity in Slashdot, a social bookmarking and public discussion application focused on technology news, revealed that the time intervals between a post and its comments closely follow a log-normal distribution with periodic oscillatory patterns with daily and weekly periods (Kaltenbrunner et al., 2007a). Subsequently, the same authors managed to predict the future Slashdot user activity based on their past behavior by creating prototype activity profiles (Kaltenbrunner et al., 2007b). Another related study is provided by Cha et al. (2007) where the authors analyze the temporal video viewing patterns in YouTube[4] and Daum[5]. In line with these studies, we devote part of this chapter to analyzing the story popularity evolution in Digg as well as the temporal activity profiles of its users.

Another aspect of content popularity pertains to the correlation between the popularity of bookmarked online items (as quantified by number of votes or hits) and their semantics, which are conveyed by means of their textual features[6]. Considerable work has been carried out with the goal of separating between different classes of content based on machine learning methods that make use of features extracted from their text (Yang & Pedersen, 1997). For instance, automatic methods based on machine learning have been devised for differentiating between positive and negative online product reviews (Dave et al., 2003; Pang et al., 2002; Turney, 2002). Further text classification problems involve the automatic classification of textual items based on their utility (Zhang & Varadarajan, 2006) or their quality (Agichtein et al., 2008). In part of the case study presented in this chapter, we examine the potential of automatically predicting whether a given bookmarked item will become popular or not based on its textual content. Although this problem is very complex to tackle by means of the machine learning paradigm adopted in the aforementioned studies, we can establish significant correlations between the popularity of content items and their textual features.

Finally, the study of social network effects on the behavior of users constitutes another analysis perspective for content popularity in social bookmarking applications. In (Richardson & Domingos, 2002), evidence is provided supporting the significance of network effects on a customer's online purchase behavior. In an effort to exploit such effects, Song et al. (2007) propose an information flow model in order to exploit the different information diffusion rates in a network for improving on recommendation and ranking. On the other hand, an empirical study by Leskovec et al. (2007) based on an online recommendation network for online products (e.g. books, music, movies) indicated that there is only limited impact of a user's social environment on his/her purchasing behavior. Finally, the study by Lerman (2007) concludes that the users of Digg tend to prefer stories that their online friends have also found interesting. Here, we define two measures of social influence on (a) content popularity and (b) users' voting behavior, conceptually similar to the ones introduced by Anagnostopoulos et al. (2008). Then, we carry out a set of experiments to quantify the extent of the social influence effects on bookmarked content popularity and consumption in Digg.

SBS ANALYSIS FRAMEWORK

This section introduces the *Diggsonomy* framework, which aims at facilitating the study and the description of the phenomena arising in social bookmarking applications. This framework was originally presented in (Papadopoulos et al., 2008); here, we repeat the definition of the framework. The framework considers an SBS and the finite sets U, R, T, S, D, which stand for the sets of users, resources, timestamps, social relations and votes on resources respectively. Note that T is an ordered set.

Definition 1 (Diggsonomy): Given an SBS, its derived Diggsonomy B is defined as the tuple B

= (U, R, T, S, D), where $S \subseteq U \times U$ is the social network of the SBS users, and $D \subseteq U \times R \times T$ is the users' voting set, modeled as a triadic relation between U, R, and T.

Definition 2 (Personomy): The Personomy P_u of a given user $u \in U$ is the restriction of B to u, i.e. $P_u = (R_u, S_u, D_u)$ with $D_u = \{(r, t) \in R \times T \mid (u, r, t) \in D\}$, $S_u = \pi_U(S)$ and $R_u = \pi_R(D_u)$.

Definition 3 (Vote-history): The Vote-history for a particular resource (story) r, denoted as H_r is defined as the projection of the Diggsonomy D on $U \times T$ restricted on r, i.e. $H_r = \pi_{U \times T}(D \mid r) \subseteq U \times T$. The user u_0 for whom the statements $(u_0, t_0) \in H_r$ and $\forall\ t \in \pi_T(H_r)$, $t_0 < t$ hold is called the submitter of the story.

The framework is inspired by the Folksonomy definitions appearing in (Mika, 2005) and (Hotho et al., 2006a). The major difference is that the Diggsonomy formalism enables the description of the temporal aspects of content rating. The notation introduced by this framework will form the basis of the following discussion, which will be organized around the four analysis perspectives that were introduced in the background section:

- Analysis of statistical properties of variables measured in an SBS.
- Temporal analysis of content popularity and user behavior.
- Semantic aspects of popularity.
- Impact of social networks on popularity.

In the rest of this section, each of these perspectives will be discussed separately and existing analysis approaches will be reviewed.

The Heavy Tails of Social Bookmarking

A widely researched and empirically supported model for popularity (and variables generated by skewed distributions) is the power-law distribution. A comprehensive review of the properties observed in such distributions is provided in

(Newman, 2005). According to this model, the probability density function of the skewed variable should be described by the following law:

$$p(x) = Cx^{-a} \qquad (1)$$

In Equation (1), α is called the exponent or the scaling parameter of the power law (the constant C is part of the model in order to satisfy the requirement that the distribution sums to 1). A straightforward way to empirically identify a power-law is to plot its histogram. However, this might be tricky in practice since the tail of the distribution would appear very noisy (due to the regular histogram binning which is not appropriate for distributions of this nature). A potential solution to this problem would be to employ logarithmic binning; however, a more elegant way to deal with the problem is to calculate and plot the Cumulative Distribution Function (CDF), $P(x)$. Based on Equation (1), we get:

$$P(x) = \int\limits_0^\infty p(x')dx' = C\int\limits_0^\infty x'^{-a}\,dx' = \frac{C}{a-1}x^{-(a-1)}$$

$$(2)$$

It appears from Equation (2) that the cumulative distribution function $P(x)$ also follows a power law, but with a different exponent (α-1). Since $P(x)$ is derived by integrating over $p(x)$, the resulting curve has a much smoother tail (integration acts as a low-pass filter), thus rendering clear the power-law nature of the distribution. Also, an important consideration when modeling skewed distributions with power-laws (and other related models) is the range of values for which the power law approximates sufficiently well the real distribution. Typically, a value x_{min} can be identified such that Equation 1 is a reasonable approximation for the distribution only for $x \geq x_{min}$. The employed approach for estimating the parameters α and x_{min} of the power law will be described in the case study section.

A set of quantities measured within real-world complex systems have been reported to exhibit power-law behavior (Newman, 2005). Examples of such quantities are the frequency of words in the text of the *Moby Dick* novel, number of citations to scientific papers, number of calls received AT&T telephone customers and others (Newman, 2005). Recent research on social web data has confirmed the power-law nature of a series of Web 2.0 originating distributions, e.g. tag usage in delicious (Hotho et al., 2006a) and (Halpin et al., 2007), number of votes to questions/answers in the Yahoo! Answers system (Agichtein et al., 2008), video popularity in YouTube and Daum (Cha et al. 2007) and story popularity in Digg (Papadopoulos et al., 2008).

Apart from the classic power-law distribution of Equation (1) reported in the aforementioned works and used for the subsequent analysis of Digg popularity, a set of more elaborate models have recently been proposed in the literature for modeling skewed distributions. For instance, the Discrete Gaussian Exponential is proposed by Bi et al. (2001) as a generalization of the Zipf distribution (i.e. power-law) to model a variety of real-world distributions, e.g. user click-stream data. Furthermore, statistical analysis of the distribution of 29,684 Digg stories by Wu and Huberman (2007) resulted in a log-normal distribution model for the data. The truncated log-normal distribution was also found by Gómez et al. (2008) to accurately describe the in- and out-degree distributions of the Slashdot user network formed on the basis of their participation in the online discussion threads. Finally, the recently formulated Double Pareto log-normal distribution was presented by Seshadri et al. (2008) as an accurate model for a set of variables in a social network created by mobile phone calls.

There are significant benefits in recognizing and understanding the heavy-tail nature of skewed distributions. As pointed by Bi et al. (2001), typical statistical measures such as mean, median and standard deviation are not appropriate for summarizing skewed distributions. In contrast, parametric models, such as the power-law or the log-normal distribution, convey a succinct and accurate view of the observed variable. Furthermore, comparison of the observed variable with the fitted model may reveal deviant behavior (outliers). Similar benefits of employing a parsimonious model such as the power-law to summarize and mine massive data streams that depict skewed distribution were reported in (Cormode & Muthukrishnan, 2005). Finally, the work in (Cha et al., 2007) demonstrated the utility of understanding the heavy-tail content consumption patterns by demonstrating a potential for 40% improvement in video content consumption (in YouTube) by alleviating information delivery inefficiencies of the system (e.g. by recommending niche content lying in the long tail of the distribution). Later in the chapter, we will confirm the emergence of heavy-tail distributions in Digg.

Temporal Patterns of Content Consumption

The study of the temporal aspects of online content consumption and rating in the context of a Web 2.0 application has been beneficial for a series of tasks, e.g. planning an online campaign, anticipating voluminous requests for content items or detecting malicious user activities. For instance, by analyzing the temporal activity patterns of Slashdot users (i.e. posting and commenting on posts of others), the authors of (Kaltenbrunner et al., 2007b) could predict with sufficient accuracy the future comment activity attracted by a particular post. Similarly, the study by Cha et al. (2007) presents an analysis of the temporal video content popularity patterns observed in YouTube and demonstrates the potential for short-term popularity prediction. Furthermore, studies of the temporal aspects of story popularity in Digg were carried out by Lerman (2007) and Papadopoulos et al. (2008). In both studies, it was confirmed that Digg stories when moved to the front page of the site go through a staggering popularity growth phase, thus anticipating voluminous user requests for particular content items.

The temporal data appearing within a bookmarking system are usually generated by means of recording event timestamps; specifically, the set of instances when a story collects votes from users constitute the popularity timeline of the particular story (cf. $\pi_T(H_r)$ of Definition 3) and the instances when a user gives votes to stories form his/her activity timeline (cf. $\pi_T(D_u)$ of Definition 2). For convenience, we will denote the raw timestamp set comprising the event instances of object i (where i can either denote a story or a user) in an ordered fashion as $T_i = \{t_0, t_1 .... t_N\}$. The first step in analyzing such data is to select a small but sufficiently representative subset of stories or users and then to inspect their timestamp sets on an individual basis.

However, these timestamp sets are not time series in a typical sense, i.e. they are not the result of measuring the value of a variable at regular intervals. Thus, in order to visually convey the information contained in them in a meaningful way, we consider two kinds of time series based on these raw timestamp sets: (a) the time series of the aggregate count of events at time t, and (b) the time series of the count of events falling in the interval *[t-Δt, t+Δt]*. For ease of reference, we shall denote the aforementioned time series as *N(t)* and *n(t)* respectively. Figure 1 illustrates the characteristics of such time series for a small sample of Digg story popularity time series.

A complication arises when attempting to study the temporal behavior of numerous SBS entities (stories or users) in an aggregate manner: The entities of interest are active in different time intervals and have different activity rates. In order to overcome this complication, we consider the projection on T of the Vote-history set H_r, denoted by $T_r = \pi_T(H_r)$. For each story, we perform the following transformation:

$$T_r = \frac{T_r - \min(T_r)}{\max(T_r) - \min(T_r)} \qquad (3)$$

Figure 1. Two alternatives for inspecting event-based time series: (a) cumulative number of Diggs, (b) number of Diggs per hour. Here, three sample Digg story popularity curves are shown

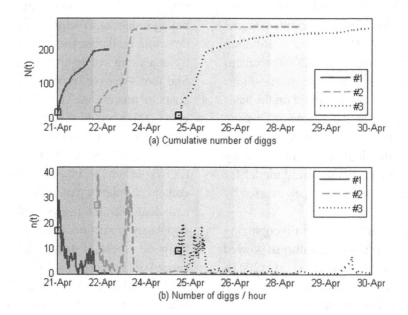

(a) Cumulative number of diggs

(b) Number of diggs / hour

where *min(T)*, *max(T)* return the minimum and maximum timestamp values of the input timestamp set. In that way, it is possible to normalize the temporal activity of an SBS entity to an artificial temporal space spanning the interval [0, 1], which makes it possible to perform a set of operations between time series, e.g. addition, subtraction, averaging and so on. This possibility is of significance since we are particularly interested in deriving an "average" time series which is representative of hundreds or even thousands of time series. Figure 2 depicts the effect of the transformation on the set of time series of Figure 1 (under the representation *n(t)*, i.e. number of events per time interval). One should note that while the transformation removes the notion of temporal scale from the individual time series, it preserves their structural characteristics.

Finally, it is possible to apply the transformation of Equation 3 to a subsequence of a given time series and in that way to map a particular "phase" of a time series to the *[0, 1]* interval with the purpose of comparing the evolution of the phenomenon within this phase to its evolution within the full lifetime of the time series. Comparison between time series phases provides additional insights to the understanding of temporal phenomena, especially in cases where there is prior knowledge that a phenomenon takes place in more than one phases.

Semantic Aspects of Content Popularity

In a social media website where a stream of online stories is continuously flowing through the site's pages, one could argue that the popularity (number of votes) of a given resource (e.g. news article) will strongly correlate with the semantic content featured by the story as well as the linguistic style of the story text. Stories usually appear in the form of a short title and description which should provide sufficient incentive to readers to read the whole story and then vote in favor of it. Therefore, one could attempt to predict which stories will draw the attention of the masses by

Figure 2. The effect of the proposed time series normalization

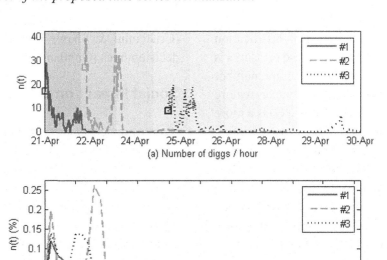

plain inspection of their textual content. In other words, one could cast the problem of popularity prediction as a text classification task, comprising a feature extraction and a training step (exploited by some machine learning algorithm).

Text classification usually takes place by processing a corpus of documents (bookmarked content items in our case), extracting all possible terms from them and considering them as the dimensions of the vector space where the classification task will be applied. This is commonly referred to as the Vector Space Model (VSM) in the Information Retrieval literature (Salton et al., 1975). However, due to the extremely large variety of vocabulary in large corpora (millions of unique terms), the dimensionality of such a vector space is frequently prohibitive for direct application of the model. The problem gets even worse when combinations of more than one term are considered as text features. For that reason, feature selection (or reduction) techniques are crucial in order to end up with a manageable set of dimensions that are sufficient for the classification task at hand.

In (Yang & Pedersen, 1997), a series of measures were evaluated regarding their effectiveness to select the "proper" features (i.e. these features that would result in higher classification performance). The simplest of these measures is the *Document Frequency* (DF), i.e. the number of content items where the particular feature (term) appears. *Information Gain* (IG) is a more sophisticated feature selection measure. It measures the number of bits of information obtained for class prediction (popular vs. non-popular) by knowing the presence or absence of a term in a document. Further, *Mutual Information* (MI) is an additional criterion for quantifying the importance of a feature in a classification problem; however, Yang & Pedersen (1997) found this measure ineffective for selection of discriminative features. In contrast, they found that the χ^2 *statistic* (CHI), which measures the lack of independence between a term and a class, was quite effective in that re-

spect. Finally, another interesting feature selection measure introduced in the aforementioned paper is the *Term Strength* (TS), which estimates the term importance based on how commonly a term is likely to appear in closely-related documents.

Assuming that a subset of terms from the corpus under study have been selected as features, each content item is processed so that a feature vector (corresponding to the selected feature space) is extracted from it. Then, it is possible to apply a variety of machine learning techniques in order to create a model that permits classification of unknown pieces of texts to one of the predefined classes. Previous efforts in the area of sentiment classification (Dave et al., 2003; Pang et al., 2002) have employed Support Vector Machines (SVM), Naïve Bayes, as well as Maximum Entropy classifiers to tackle this problem.

In our case study, we investigated the potential of popularity prediction based purely on textual features. We conducted a series of feature extraction and text classification experiments on a corpus of 50,000 bookmarked articles. The feature selection measures used to reduce the dimensionality of the feature space were DF and CHI. For the classification task, three standard methods were used: Naïve Bayes (Duda et al., 2001), SVM (Cristianini & Shawe-Taylor, 2000) and C4.5 decision trees (Quinlan, 1993).

Social Impact on SBS Usage

It was previously argued that story popularity depends on the textual content of the particular story. However, it is widely recognized that readers do not select their content in isolation. Users of social bookmarking applications form online relations and are constantly made aware of the preferences and content consumption patterns of other SBS users. Therefore, one would expect the emergence of viral phenomena in online content consumption within an SBS. The value of understanding and exploiting viral phenomena has been already acknowledged in online knowledge sharing communities, for e.g. improving online advertising campaigns (Richardson & Domingos, 2002), understanding viral marketing dynamics (Leskovec et al., 2007) and identifying experts (Zhang et al., 2007). Therefore, we introduce here two measures in order to quantify the social influence on the content rating process. We name these two measures, the u*ser Social Susceptibility* (SS) I_u, and the *story Social Influence Gain* (SIG) I_r.

Definition 4 (Social Susceptibility - SS): The social susceptibility of a given user u denoted by I_u quantifies the extent to which his/her voting behavior (as expressed by his voting set D_u) follows the behavior of his/her friends' voting behavior (denoted by D_u').

$$I_u = \frac{|D_u'|}{|D_u|}, \text{ where}$$

$$D_u' = \{(r_u, t_u) \in D_u \mid \exists f \in S_U, (r_u, t_f) \in D_f, t_f < t_u\}$$

$$(4)$$

Definition 5 (Social Influence Gain - SIG): The social influence gain for a given story r denoted by I_r is a measure of the extent to which r has benefited from the social network of the story submitter.

$$I_r = \frac{|H_r'|}{|H_r|}, \text{ where}$$

$$H_r' = \{(u, t_k) \in H_r \mid \exists (u_0, t_0) \in H_r, u_0 \in S_U, t_0 < t_k\}$$

$$(5)$$

and u_0 is the submitter of the story as defined in Definition 3.

SS and SIG are similar in nature to the concept of *Social Correlation* as discussed in (Anagnostopoulos et al., 2008). Social Correlation (SC) within an SBS can be defined either for two users, u_1, u_2 as the Jaccard coefficient of the sets R_{u1} and R_{u2} (cf. Definition 2) or for a single user u as the proportion of his/her stories that are common with the stories of the users of his/her social network.

Here, we adopt the latter definition since it is directly comparable with the SS of a user, i.e. it can be derived by removing the temporal constraint from Equation 4. Note that SC may be attributed to a combination of the following: (a) an inherent tendency of friends to have similar interests (homophily), (b) some external factor causing two users to vote in favor of the same story (confounding) and (c) the possibility for users to see through the Digg interface which stories their friends have already dugg (influence). By imposing temporal constraints in Equations 4 and 5, we attempt to isolate the effect of (a) and (b) in order to use SS and SIG as measures of social influence rather than measures of generic SC.

CASE STUDY: SOCIAL BOOKMARKING PATTERNS IN DIGG

Since the case study for the discussion of the chapter is based on data collected from Digg, a short introduction on the specifics of the application will precede the presentation of the data analysis in order to facilitate the interpretation of the derived results. The basic rationale of Digg is the discovery of interesting web resources (or *stories* as they are commonly called in Digg-speak) by means of empowering simple users to submit and then collectively decide upon the significance (or interesting-ness) of the submitted web items (mostly news items, images and videos). In other words, Digg can be considered as an example of a Social Media application. When a story is submitted, it appears in the *Upcoming* section of the site, where stories are displayed in reverse chronological order. Users may vote on a story by "Digging" it. Digging a story a story saves it to a user's history (obviously a given user may Digg a particular story only once). There is also the possibility to "bury" a story, if one considers it to be spam or inappropriate material.

When a story collects enough votes, it is promoted to the *Popular* section, which is also the front page of the site. The vast majority of people who visit Digg daily or subscribe to its RSS feeds, mostly read the front page stories; thus the story exposure to the online public increases steeply, once it is transferred to the Popular section. The exact promotion mechanism is not disclosed to the public and is modified periodically in order to prevent malicious efforts of artificially promoting a story. The service moderators state that consensus by many independent users is required in order for a story to become popular.

Stories are categorized by media type (i.e. news, videos, images, and podcasts) and topic. Additionally, there is a predefined two-level topic hierarchy available for use, which is specified in Table 3. Apart from these story browsing capabilities, the application also features user-based story browsing, i.e. one can browse through the stories dugg by a particular user. Finally, it enables users to form social networks, by adding other users to their list of "friends". Such "friendship" relations are one-way (i.e. it takes both users to add each other to their friends list in order to have a mutual relation).

Apart from the basic SBS functionality mentioned above, the application offers a set of features for personalized reaction to content, more specifically it enables users to comment on stories, approve/disapprove of comments of others and blog on stories (i.e. write and submit a post to their own blog through Digg). Also, it is worth noting that a story recommendation engine has been recently launched (in July 2008) which recommends news items to users based on their past activity.

The bulk of the click stream generated by the masses of Digg users is made publicly accessible via a RESTful API. The analyses presented in the subsequent sections have been based on data downloaded via this API. The downloaded data contain information about the stories (title, description, container, topic, number of Diggs, number of comments, etc.), the users (username, subscription date, and friends) and the Diggs collected by stories (story, username, and timestamp). A first set of stories was collected by constantly monitoring the stories submitted to the site during the week between 24 and 30 April 2008. A set of 109,360 stories, S_0, were collected during this phase. This set of stories was submitted by a set of 34,593 users, U_0, who were used as seeds to collect data about a total of 354,150 users by requesting for the friends and the friends' friends of each user u belonging to U_0. Finally, the full Digging history for a random sample of these users was collected (both the Diggs and the stories that were dugg). In that way, a total of 98,034,660 Diggs given to 2,084,498 stories were collected. We will refer to

Table 3. Topic hierarchy of Digg

Container	Topic
Technology	Apple, Design, Gadgets, Hardware, Industry News, Linux/Unix, Microsoft, Mods, Programming, Security, Software
World & Business	Apple, Design, Gadgets, Hardware, Industry News, Linux/Unix, Microsoft, Mods, Programming, Security, Software
Science	Environment, General Sciences, Space
Gaming	Industry News, PC Games, Playable Web Games, Nintendo, PlayStation, Xbox
Lifestyle	Arts & Culture, Autos, Educational, Food & Drink, Health, Travel & Places
Entertainment	Celebrity, Movies, Music, Television, Comics & Animation
Sports	Baseball, Basketball, Extreme, Football (US/Canada), Golf, Hockey, Motorsport, Olympics, Soccer, Tennis, Other Sports
Offbeat	Comedy, Odd Stuff, People, Pets & Animals

the sets U_0 and S_0 of users and stories that were gathered in the first data collection phase as the *core* dataset, while the rest of the dataset will be referred to as *extended* dataset. It occasionally happened that stories or users were removed from the system (probably due to spamming behavior) in which case they were also removed from the local dataset.

Statistical Analysis of Digg Usage

The first step of our analysis involved the study of the heavy-tail nature of several variables of interest arising through the mass usage of Digg. The following distributions were examined:

- Diggs collected by stories.
- Comments collected by stories.
- Diggs given by users.
- Friends in the Digg social networks of users.

Figure 3 provides logarithmic plots of the aforementioned distributions. The figure renders clear the heavy-tail nature of the depicted distributions, by overlaying on top of the observed distributions their power-law fits according to the fitting method presented by Clauset et al. (2007). The proposed method employs an approximation to the Maximum Likelihood Estimator (MLE) for the scaling parameter of the power law:

$$\hat{a} \cong 1 + n \left[\sum_{i=1}^{n} \ln \frac{x_i}{x_{min} - \frac{1}{2}} \right]^{-1}$$

(6)

This estimator assumes that the value x_{min} above which the power law holds is known. In order to estimate this value, the authors recommend the use of the Kolmogorov-Smirnov (KS) statistic as a measure of goodness-of-fit of the model with parameters (a, x_{min}) with the observed data. The KS statistic is defined as the maximum distance between the CDF of the data $S(x)$ and the fitted model $P(x)$:

Figure 3. Four heavy-tail Digg Cumulative Distribution Functions (CDF) and their power-law approximations: (a) Diggs per story, (b) comments per story, (c) Diggs per user, and (d) Digg friends per user.

$$D = \max_{x \geq x_{\min}} | S(x) - P(x) |$$

$$(7)$$

Apparently, the plain power-law model is not sufficient for accurately fitting all of the observed distributions. For instance, the shape of the distribution of Diggs per user in Figure 3(c) indicates that a truncated log-normal distribution would be a better fit for the observed variable. Further, by inspection of the number of friends per user, a few conspicuous outliers can be identified that deviate significantly from the fitted power-law.

Temporal Analysis of Content Consumption

The temporal study of story popularity curves and user activity of Digg was carried out by means of the temporal representation and aggregation framework presented in the previous section. Based on that, a first noteworthy observation about the popularity of submitted stories in Digg is that they typically evolve in two ways: (a) they reach a plateau of popularity while in the 'Upcoming' section of the site and remain there until they are completely removed in case they do not receive any Diggs for a long time, (b) they attain the 'Popular' status after some time and they are moved to the 'Popular' section, where they undergo a second phase of popularity growth at a much higher intensity. Figure 4 depicts the cumulative number of Diggs, $N(t)$, collected by a sample popular and a sample non-popular story during their lifetime. For convenience, we denote the set of unpopular stories as R_U and the set of popular stories as $R_P{}^{f}$.

After establishing by inspection the difference of temporal evolution between popular and non-popular stories, we then proceed with comparing the distributions of their Digg arrival times. To this end, the time series, $n(t)$, of 5,468 non-popular and 852 popular stories, which were normalized by means of the transformation of Equation 5, were aggregated[8]. This resulted in the distributions

of Figure 5. Together with the distributions we present the areas of confidence for their values; more specifically, around each instance $n(t)$, we draw the interval $[n(t)-\sigma_n/3, n(t)+\sigma_n/3]$. In 6(a), the time series of the number of Diggs $n(t)$ is normalized with respect to the total number of Diggs throughout the whole lifetime of each story. In that way, it is possible to directly compare the local temporal structures of popular stories to the ones of the non-popular stories. In Figure 5(b), we present the absolute number of Diggs per hour in order to provide a complete picture of the comparison between the popular and the non-popular stories.

Figure 5 clearly illustrates the fact that while the non-popular stories gather the majority of their Diggs during the very first moments of their lifetime (first two bins in the histogram), the popular ones are characterized by two growth stages: (a) a first growth stage which is similar to the full lifetime of the non-popular stories, i.e. it is characterized by a monotonically decreasing trend, (b) a second growth stage, which takes place once a story is moved to the 'Popular' section of the site and is characterized by a steep increase in the number of votes that a story receives.

The intensity of popularity growth for the stories that become members of R_p can be attributed to the high exposure that these stories get for a few minutes after they are moved to the 'Popular' section (which happens to be the front page of Digg). Also, one should note that big search engines regularly index and rank favorably the most popular stories of Digg (and stories coming from other SBS and social media applications) and thus they act as a secondary source of exposure for these stories, which contributes to sustain their popularity growth for some time.

After analyzing the temporal evolution of story popularity, we apply a similar analysis on the user Digging behavior. For such a study, we investigate the structure of the time series that are formed from counting the number of Diggs given by users to stories that fall within the interval $[t-\Delta t,$

Figure 4. Two possible popularity evolution patterns. Note the two different phases in the popularity evolution for stories that are selected for the 'Popular' section of the site

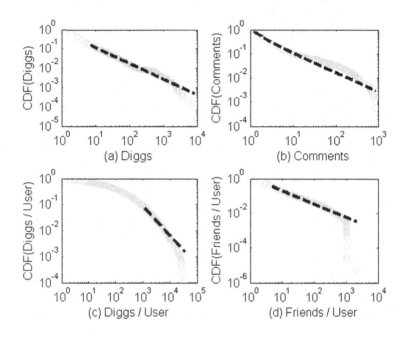

Figure 5. Digg arrival time distributions of popular vs. non-popular stories

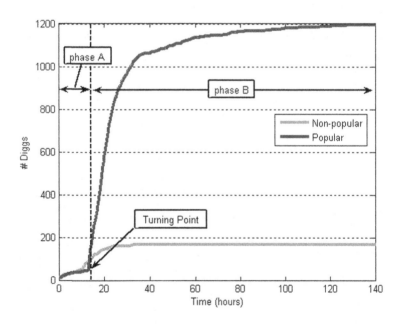

t+Δt]. Figure 6 presents the result of aggregating the user activity over 539 users drawn randomly from the set of users belonging to D_0^9. Inspection of the outer diagram reveals that Digg users are intensively active during the very first period after subscription to the service (note the extremely high number of Diggs occurring in the first 5-10% of the users' lifetime). This is not particularly surprising since users are more enthusiastic and eager to explore the service once they discover it. As time goes by, their enthusiasm wears off resulting in more stable usage patterns.

A further noteworthy observation can be made by comparing the aggregate user activity time of Figure 6(a) series with the three sample activity time series of Figure 6(b) which come from three individual users. It appears that the individual activity time series do not present any distinct pattern. On the other hand, the aggregate activity is quite stable (though the high variance indicated by the magnitude of the shaded area in 6(a) implies the instability of the individual time series). Thus, it appears that a set of independent behavior patterns of individuals leads to a stable mass behavior when aggregated.

Semantic Aspects of Digg Story Popularity

In this section, we are going to employ the previously discussed feature selection and text classification techniques in order to investigate the potential of popularity prediction based on text features. For that reason, we consider large samples of stories out of the dataset collected from Digg. The majority of Digg stories are written in English, with few stories being in German, Spanish, Chinese and Arabic. We filtered out such non-English text items by means of checking against characters or symbols that are particular to those languages (e.g. characters with umlaut, non-ASCII characters, etc.).

First, a random sample of $N = 50,000$ English Digg stories was drawn from the extended dataset and was processed to extract the text features. For each story, the information on whether it became popular or not was available, so, after extracting

Figure 6. Aggregate user Digging behavior. In subfigure 6(a), the embedded graph contains a zoomed view of the [0.1, 1.0] interval

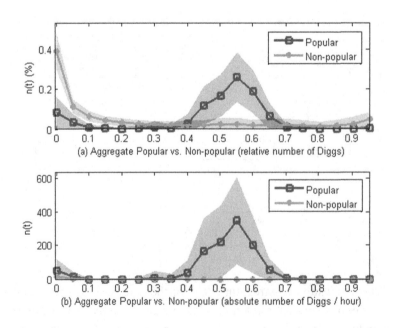

all terms from the Digg stories, it was possible to create the two-way contingency matrix of Table 4 for each term *t*. According to this, *A* is the number of popular stories containing term *t*, *B* the number of non-popular stories containing *t*, and *C* and *D* are the number of popular and non-popular stories respectively that don't contain term *t*.

Then, the χ^2 statistic is calculated based on the following equation:

$$\chi^2(t) = \frac{N \cdot (A \cdot D - C \cdot B)^2}{(A+C) \cdot (B+D) \cdot (A+B) \cdot (C+D)}$$

(8)

The χ^2 statistic naturally takes a value of zero if term *t* and the class of Popular stories are independent. The measure is only problematic when any of the contingency table cells is lightly populated, which is the case for low-frequency terms. For that reason, we filter low-frequency terms prior to the calculation of Equation 8. In addition, stop

words and numeric strings were also filtered out of the feature selection process. In order to keep the experiments simple, no stemming or other term normalization was carried out. Table 5 lists the top 30 terms of this story set along with their χ^2 scores. Although not very informative to the human inspector, these keywords can be considered as the most appropriate (from a text feature perspective) for use in making the distinction between Popular and Non-popular stories.

In order to get a more fine-grained view of such keywords per topic, we also calculate the χ^2 scores on independent corpora that contain stories only from particular topics. Table 6 provides such a topic-specific χ^2-based ranking of terms.

After ranking the terms of each corpus based on their class separation ability, it is possible to select the top *K* of them and use them in an automatic text classification scheme. Table 7 presents the results achieved by such a classification scheme, i.e. the success of predicting the popularity of Digg stories, where three classifiers are compared, namely a Naïve Bayes classifier, an SVM and a C4.5 decision tree. The dataset used consists of 50,000 randomly selected stories and the performance metrics were calculated by use of 10-fold cross validation (i.e. repeated splitting of the dataset to 10 parts and usage of nine of them for training and one of them for testing).

Table 4. Two-way contingency table of term t

	Popular	Non-popular
Term exists	A	B
Term doesn't exist	C	D

Table 5. Top 30 text features based on χ^2 statistic

#	Term	χ^2 (10⁶)	#	Term	χ^2 (10⁶)	#	Term	χ^2 (10⁶)
1	see	61.5	11	seen	7.7	21	news	4.2
2	drive	60.4	12	nintendo	7.6	22	making	4.1
3	japanese	28.5	13	program	5.6	23	breaking	4.0
4	video	17.2	14	way	5.4	24	amazing	3.5
5	google	12.9	15	gets	5.2	25	say	3.4
6	long	11.7	16	computer	4.9	26	coolest	3.4
7	cool	11.0	17	need	4.8	27	release	3.3
8	term	9.9	18	want	4.7	28	right	.9
9	look	8.8	9	play	4.7	29	xbox	2.8
10	high	7.9	20	job	4.3	30	looks	.5

Table 6. Top 10 features ranked by χ^2 statistic for four Digg topics. The respective topic corpora consist of 50,000 documents each

#	Technology Term	χ^2	World & Business Term	χ^2	Entertainment Term	χ^2	Sports Term	χ^2
1	Apple	1215.88	Bush	2532.04	RIAA	1457.53	Amazing	1264.88
2	Windows	1080.11	president	1456.52	Movie	1346.79	Nfl	1181.59
3	Linux	995.02	Iraq	1182.86	movies	1015.56	game	1158.17
4	Google	945.72	house	1016.15	Industry	940.50	baseball	1146.77
5	Firefox	919.13	years	974.60	Time	727.12	time	1040.09
6	Just	784.83	administration	964.33	Just	672.92	history	975.46
7	Digg	773.09	congress	872.78	Show	671.09	year	972.57
8	Mac	756.55	officials	841.12	Says	647.37	just	894.85
9	OS	715.56	war	27.25	ilm	635.63	Top	892.82
10	check	643.97	federal	18.37	Lost	628.37	player	877.17

Table 7. Popularity prediction results, namely Precision (P), Recall (R) and F-measure (F). Classifier abbreviations used: NB → Naïve Bayes, SVM → Support Vector Machines and C4.5 → Quinlan's decision trees. Tests were carried out with the use of 500 features on a 50,000 story randomly selected corpus and by use of 10-fold cross validation to obtain the recorded measures

Classifier	Accuracy (%)	Popular P	R	F	Non-popular P	R	F
NB (CHI)	67.21	0.160	0.426	0.233	0.903	0.705	0.791
NB (DF)	88.32	1.000	0.001	0.003	0.883	1.000	0.938
SVM (CHI)	88.10	0.130	0.003	0.006	0.883	0.997	0.937
C4.5 (CHI)	88.18	0.222	0.004	0.008	0.883	0.998	0.937

Although in terms of accuracy, the combination of Naïve Bayes with DF-selected features appears to perform best, a closer examination of the Precision and Recall measures obtained separately for the classes Popular and Non-popular provides a different insight. Specifically, it appears that all classifiers have trouble achieving descent classification performance when the input stories are Popular. That means that classifiers can predict accurately that a story will remain Non-popular (when indeed that is the case), but they usually fail to identify Popular stories. The combination of Naïve Bayes with CHI-selected features is bet-ter in that respect. The aforementioned problem is related to the well recognized *class imbalance* problem in machine learning (Japkowicz, 2000). Indeed, in the 50,000 stories of the evaluation dataset the ratio of Popular to Non-popular stories is 0.132, i.e. there is almost only one Popular story for every ten Non-popular ones.

Similar results are also obtained for the case that the feature selection and classification process is applied separately per topic. The results of Table 8 provide the respective evidence.

Social Impact on Digg Story Popularity

The last part of our case study involved the estimation of the distributions for the social influence measures of Definitions 4 and 5, namely the SS of Digg users, as well as the story SIG values. These estimations were based on a subset of users and stories randomly selected[10] from the core dataset. From Equations 4 and 5, it is clear that these computations require data that fall outside the core data set (e.g. the Personomies of the users' friends); it was for this reason that the extended dataset was collected.

The estimation of the SS distribution was based on a random sample of 672 users, of whom the SC and SS values were computed. Inspection of the scatter plot of the SC versus the SS of these users, cf. Figure 7(a), reveals that social susceptibility closely follows social correlation. That means that in most cases, when a story has been dugg by both a user and one or more of his/her friends, it is likely that the one or more of the user's friends dugg the story before the user. Few users deviate from this behavior and can thus be considered as the *opinion leaders* of the system (the more a point in Figure 7(a) deviates from the unitary straight line the more the user represented by this point can be considered an opinion leader).

Furthermore, a look into the user SS distributions as presented in Figure 7(b) indicates that the majority of circumstantial Digg users (these users that have dugg a story less than 200 times) present low social susceptibility. In contrast, Digg users with more intense activity tend to be influenced by their social network at a higher frequency. This may indicate that the more users are active within the system the more they rely on their online friends as a source of potentially interesting content.

Finally, insights into the mechanism of story promotion employed by Digg are provided through study of the story SIG patterns. Figure 8 clearly depicts the difference in the SIG distributions between the popular and the non-popular stories. These distributions were estimated by sampling 830 popular and 5076 non-popular stories and computing their respective SIG values. The histograms indicate that the event of a story with $I_r >$ *0.35* becoming popular is highly unlikely while in contrast it is very common for non-popular stories to take SIG values in the interval *[0.2, 0.7]*. This could support the hypothesis that high SIG for a story implies low probability of becoming popu-

Table 8. Popularity prediction results when features are selected per topic. Classification was done by means of the Naïve Bayes classifier with the use of 500 features selected based on CHI. For each topic, 50,000 stories were used as dataset and 10-fold cross-validation was used to obtain the performance results

Topic	Accuracy (%)	Popular			Non-popular		
		P	R	F	P	R	F
Entertainment	71.39	0.108	0.418	0.172	0.943	0.737	0.827
Gaming	70.26	0.152	0.389	0.218	0.910	0.740	0.816
Lifestyle	72.53	0.121	0.432	0.189	0.943	0.749	0.835
Offbeat	69.03	0.124	0.409	0.191	0.925	0.718	0.809
Science	64.71	0.141	0.444	0.214	0.909	0.672	0.560
Sport	65.79	0.079	0.538	0.138	0.964	0.664	0.787
Technology	67.53	0.159	0.415	0.230	0.902	0.710	0.794
World & B.	65.84	0.098	0.457	0.161	0.941	0.674	0.786

Figure 7. (a) Scatter plot of social correlation vs. social susceptibility, (b) Social susceptibility distributions for frequent vs. circumstantial users

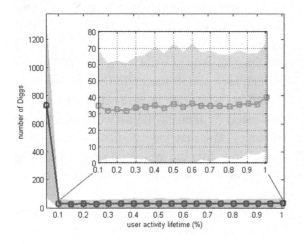
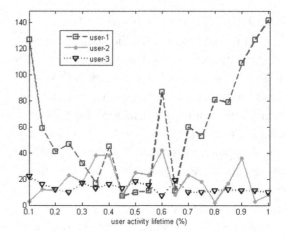

lar; however, instead of the above conclusion, we would rather speculate that Digg employs filters based on social measures similar to I_r to prevent groups of 'friends' from gaining control over which stories appear in the 'Popular' section[11].

FUTURE TRENDS

The startling success of social web applications may be just the preamble in the new era of information and communication technologies we are

currently entering. Although it is extremely risky to attempt even rough predictions concerning the future of Social Web, we would like to take this chance and provide a sketch of the future trends in systems involving the creation, discovery, rating and organization of digital content by masses of users.

In the short term, we anticipate the proliferation of existing social media applications such as Digg, reddit and newsvine, as well as the take-off of mobile social web applications, such as Twitter, used for micro-blogging through mobile devices

Figure 8. Distribution of story social influence gain (SIG) for popular and non-popular stories

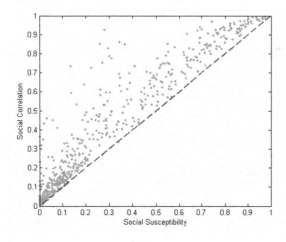
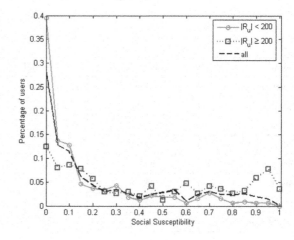

(Java et al., 2007). Further, existing and new applications will incorporate personalization and context-awareness features, thus meshing with the daily reality of people. Thus, data will be recorded that will capture all aspects of people's lives, such that new insights into human behavior will be possible through "reality mining" (Eagle & Pentland, 2006), raising new concerns about privacy. By closely monitoring the actions of the individual, machine learning will be employed to predict future consumption patterns, e.g. in order to enable effective personalized advertising schemes (Piwowarski & Zaragoza, 2007) or to spawn social interactions between strangers based on profile matching (Eagle & Pentland, 2005).

There is already evidence that the analysis of data coming from social bookmarking usage can be beneficial for search engine tasks, such as new website discovery and authoritative online resource identification (Heymann et al., 2008). In the long run, advanced information extraction and semantic analysis techniques, e.g. automatic quality evaluation of user contributed content (Hu et al., 2007), are expected to be deployed in real-world applications (e.g. Wikipedia) and provide the basis for even more advanced collaborative applications, such as innovation management platforms (Perlich et al., 2007). The requirements of such applications will in turn instigate research into underlying technology disciplines, i.e. database systems for the support of online community services and collaborative platforms (Ramakrishnan, 2007), as well as frameworks for scalable knowledge discovery from streaming data (Faloutsos et al., 2007).

CONCLUSION

The widespread adoption of SBS has transformed online content consumption due to the powerful features that such systems offer to their users. The possibility for users to submit links to content of their interest, tag, rate and comment on online resources submitted by other users as well as to form relations with each other has stimulated intensive user activity in SBS, such that massive amounts of web activity data capturing the content consumption patterns of users are produced in a streaming fashion. This novel content consumption paradigm has spawned a series of interesting research questions related to the generation and evolution of such patterns. These questions pertain to the distributional attributes of online resource popularity, the temporal patterns of content consumption by users, the semantic as well as the social factors affecting the behavior of the masses with regard to their preferences for online resources.

This chapter presented an overview of existing research efforts that are germane to these questions and provided additional insights into the phenomena taking place in the context of an SBS by carrying out an analysis of a large dataset collected from Digg. The power-law nature of web resource popularity was established in accordance with previous studies of similar online systems (Cha et al; 2007, Hotho et al., 2006a; Halpin et al., 2007). Furthermore, a set of characteristic temporal patterns of content consumption were revealed which confirmed previous findings about social media content popularity evolution (Lerman; 2007). In addition, a preliminary investigation into the semantic elements of content popularity lent support to the hypothesis that popularity is affected by the semantic content and the linguistic style. What is more, it was empirically shown that users of SBS are socially susceptible, i.e. they tend to express interest for online resources that are also considered interesting by their online "friends".

Finally, the chapter provided an outlook on the exciting new prospects for online content publishing and mining on the massive amounts of data produced in the context of SBS and related applications.

ACKNOWLEDGMENT

This work was supported by the WeKnowIt project, partially funded by the European Commission, under contract number FP7-215453.

REFERENCES

Aberer, K., Cudré-Mauroux, P., Ouksel, A. M., Catarci, T., Hacid, M. S., Illarramendi, A., et al. (2004). *Emergent Semantics Principles and Issues.* (LNCS Vol. 2973, pp. 25-38). Berlin: Springer.

Agichtein, E., Castillo, C., Donato, D., Gionis, A., & Mishne, G. (2008). Finding high-quality content in social media. In *Proceedings of the international Conference on Web Search and Web Data Mining,* Palo Alto, CA, February 11 - 12, 2008 (WSDM '08, pp. 183-194). New York: ACM.

Anagnostopoulos, A., Kumar, R., & Mahdian, M. (2008). Influence and Correlation in Social Networks. In *Proceedings of the 14th ACM SIG-KDD international Conference on Knowledge Discovery and Data Mining,* Las Vegas, Nevada, USA, August 24 - 27, 2008 (KDD '08, pp. 7 – 15). New York: ACM.

Barabási, A.-L., & Albert, R. (1999). Emergence of Scaling in Random Networks. [Washington, DC: AAAS.]. *Science, 286*(5439), 509–512. doi:10.1126/science.286.5439.509

Bi, Z., Faloutsos, C., & Korn, F. (2001). The "DGX" distribution for mining massive, skewed data. In *Proceedings of the Seventh ACM SIG-KDD international Conference on Knowledge Discovery and Data Mining,* San Francisco, California, August 26 - 29 (KDD '01, pp. 17-26). New York: ACM.

Cha, M., Kwak, H., Rodriguez, P., Ahn, Y., & Moon, S. (2007). I Tube, You Tube, Everybody Tubes: Analyzing the World's Largest User Generated Content Video System. In *Proceedings of the 7th ACM SIGCOMM conference on Internet measurement,* San Diego, CA.

Clauset, A., Shalizi, C. R., & Newman, M. E. J. (2007). *Power-law distributions in empirical data.* Tech. Rep. submitted to arXiv on June 7, 2007 with identifier: arXiv:0706.1062v1.

Cormode, G., & Muthukrishnan, S. (2005). Summarizing and mining skewed data streams. In *Proceedings of the 2005 SIAM International Conference on Data Mining,* (pp.44-55). SIAM.

Cristianini, N., & Shawe-Taylor, J. (2000). *An Introduction to Support Vector Machines and other kernel-based learning methods.* New York: Cambridge University Press.

Dave, K., Lawrence, S., & Pennock, D. M. (2003). Mining the peanut gallery: opinion extraction and semantic classification of product reviews. In *Proceedings of the 12th international Conference on World Wide Web,* Budapest, Hungary, May 20 – 24, (WWW '03, pp. 519-528). New York: ACM.

Duda, R. O., Hart, P. E., & Stork, D. G. (2001). *Pattern Classification.* Chichester, UK: John Wiley & Sons, Inc.

Eagle, N., & Pentland, A. (2005). Social Serendipity: Mobilizing Social Software. *IEEE Pervasive Computing / IEEE Computer Society [and] IEEE Communications Society, 4*(2), 28–34. doi:10.1109/MPRV.2005.37

Eagle, N., & Pentland, A. (2006). Reality Mining: Sensing Complex Social Systems. *Personal and Ubiquitous Computing, 10*(4), 255–268. doi:10.1007/s00779-005-0046-3

Faloutsos, C., Kolda, T. G., & Sun, J. (2007). Mining large graphs and streams using matrix and tensor tools. In *Proceedings of the 2007 ACM SIGMOD international Conference on Management of Data*, Beijing, China, June 11 - 14, (SIGMOD '07, pp. 1174-1174). New York: ACM.

Golder, S., & Huberman, B. A. (2006). The Structure of Collaborative Tagging Systems. *Journal of Information Science, 32*(2), 198–208. doi:10.1177/0165551506062337

Gómez, V., Kaltenbrunner, A., & López, V. (2008). Statistical analysis of the social network and discussion threads in slashdot. In *Proceeding of the 17th international Conference on World Wide Web,* Beijing, China, April 21 - 25, (WWW '08, pp. 645-654). New York: ACM.

Halpin, H., Robu, V., & Shepherd, H. (2007). The complex dynamics of collaborative tagging. In *Proceedings of the 16th international Conference on World Wide Web*, Banff, Alberta, Canada, May 08 - 12, 2007, (WWW '07, pp. 211-220). New York: ACM.

Heymann, P., Koutrika, G., & Garcia-Molina, H. (2008). Can social bookmarking improve web search? In *Proceedings of the international Conference on Web Search and Web Data Mining,* Palo Alto, CA, February 11-12, 2008, (WSDM '08, pp. 195-206). New York: ACM.

Hotho, A., Jäschke, R., Schmitz, C., & Stumme, G. (2006). Information Retrieval in Folksonomies: Search and Ranking. In *The Semantic Web: Research and Applications*, (pp. 411-426). Berlin: Springer.

Hotho, A., Jäschke, R., Schmitz, C., & Stumme, G. (2006). *Trend Detection in Folksonomies.* (LNCS 4306, pp. 56-70). Berlin: Springer.

Hu, M., Lim, E., Sun, A., Lauw, H. W., & Vuong, B. (2007). Measuring Article Quality in Wikipedia: Models and Evaluation. In *Proceedings of the Sixteenth ACM Conference on Conference on information and Knowledge Management*, Lisbon, Portugal, November 06 - 10, (CIKM '07, pp. 243-252). New York: ACM.

Japkowicz, N. (2000). The class imbalance problem: Significance and strategies. In *Proceedings of the 2000 International Conference on Artificial Intelligence* (ICAI 2000).

Java, A., Song, X., Finin, T., & Tseng, B. (2007). Why we twitter: Understanding the microblogging effect in user intentions and communities. In *Proceedings of WebKDD / SNAKDD 2007: KDD Workshop on Web Mining and Social Network Analysis, in conjunction with the 13th ACM SIGKDD International Conference on Knowledge Discovery and Data Mining* (KDD 2007, pp. 56-66).

Kaltenbrunner, A., Gómez, V., & López, V. (2007). *Description and Prediction of Slashdot Activity.* Paper presented at the LA-WEB 2007 5th Latin American Web Congress, Santiago, Chile.

Kaltenbrunner, A., Gómez, V., Moghnieh, A., Meza, R., Blat, J., & López, V. (2007). *Homogeneous temporal activity patterns in a large online communication space.* Paper presented at the 10th Int. Conf. on Business Information Systems, Workshop on Social Aspects of the Web (SAW 2007), Poznan, Poland.

Lerman, K. (2007). Social Information Processing in News Aggregation. *IEEE Internet Computing, 11*(6), 16–28. doi:10.1109/MIC.2007.136

Leskovec, J., Adamic, L., & Huberman, B. A. (2007). The Dynamics of Viral Marketing. *ACM Transactions on the Web* (ACM TWEB), *1*(1).

Mika, P. (2005). Ontologies are us: A unified model of social networks and semantics. In *The Semantic Web – ISWC 2005*, (pp. 522-536). Berlin: Springer.

Mitzenmacher, M. (2004). A Brief History of Generative Models for Power Law and Lognormal Distributions. [Wellesley, MA: A K Peters, Ltd.]. *Internet Mathematics*, *1*(2), 226–251.

Newman, M. E. J. (2005). Power laws, Pareto distributions and Zipf's law. *Contemporary Physics*, *46*, 323–351. doi:10.1080/00107510500052444

Pang, B., Lee, L., & Vaithyanathan, S. (2002). Thumbs up? Sentiment classification using machine learning techniques. In *Proceedings of the Acl-02 Conference on Empirical Methods in Natural Language Processing - Volume 10*, (pp. 79-86). Morristown, NJ: ACL.

Papadopoulos, S., Vakali, A., & Kompatsiaris, I. (July, 2008). *Digg it Up! Analyzing Popularity Evolution in a Web 2.0 Setting.* Paper presented at MSoDa08 (Mining Social Data), a satellite Workshop of the 18th European Conference on Artificial Intelligence, Patras, Greece.

Perlich, C., Helander, M., Lawrence, R., Liu, Y., Rosset, S., & Reddy, C. (2007). Looking for great ideas: Analyzing the innovation jam. In *Proceedings of WebKDD / SNAKDD 2007: KDD Workshop on Web Mining and Social Network Analysis, in conjunction with the 13th ACM SIGKDD International Conference on Knowledge Discovery and Data Mining* (KDD 2007), (pp. 66-74).

Piwowarski, B., & Zaragoza, H. (2007). Predictive User Click Models based on Click-through History. In *Proceedings of the Sixteenth ACM Conference on Conference on information and Knowledge Management,* Lisbon, Portugal, November 06 - 10, 2007, CIKM '07, (pp. 175-182). New York: ACM.

Quinlan, J. R. C4.5 (1993). *Programs for Machine Learning*. San Francisco: Morgan Kaufmann Publishers.

Ramakrishnan, R. (2007). Community Systems: The World Online. In *Proceedings of CIDR 2007, Third Biennial Conference on Innovative Data Systems Research*, (pp. 341), Asilomar, CA.

Richardson, M., & Domingos, P. (2002). Mining knowledge-sharing sites for viral marketing. In *Proceedings of the 14th ACM SIGKDD International Conference on Knowledge Discovery and Data Mining*. Las Vegas, NV. New York: ACM Press.

Salton, G., Wong, A., & Yang, C. S. (1975). A vector space model for automatic indexing. *Communications of the ACM*, *18*(11), 613–620. doi:10.1145/361219.361220

Seshadri, M., Machiraju, S., Sridharan, A., Bolot, J., Faloutsos, C., & Leskovec, J. (2008). Mobile Call Graphs: Beyond Power-Law and Lognormal Distributions. In *Proceedings of the Eighth ACM SIGKDD International Conference on Knowledge Discovery and Data Mining*, (pp. 61-70), Edmonton, Canada. New York: ACM Press.

Song, X., Chi, Y., Hino, K., & Tseng, B. L. (2007). Information flow modeling based on diffusion rate for prediction and ranking. In *Proceedings of the 16th international Conference on World Wide Web* (Banff, Alberta, Canada, May 08 - 12, 2007). WWW '07, pp. 191-200, ACM, New York, NY, USA.

Turney, P. D. (2001). Thumbs up or thumbs down?: Semantic orientation applied to unsupervised classification of reviews. In *Proceedings of the 40th Annual Meeting on Association For Computational Linguistics,* Philadelphia, PA, July 07 - 12, (pp. 417-424). Morristown, NJ: ACL.

Wu, F., & Huberman, B. A. (2007). Novelty and collective attention. *Proceedings of the National Academy of Sciences of the United States of America*, *104*(45), 17599–17601. doi:10.1073/pnas.0704916104

Yang, Y., & Pedersen, J. O. (1997). A Comparative Study on Feature Selection in Text Categorization. In D. H. Fisher, (Ed.), *Proceedings of the Fourteenth international Conference on Machine Learning* (July 08 - 12, pp. 412-420). San Francisco: Morgan Kaufmann Publishers Inc.

Zhang, J., Ackerman, M. S., & Adamic, L. (2007). Expertise networks in online communities: structure and algorithms. In *Proceedings of the 16th international Conference on World Wide Web,* Banff, Alberta, Canada, May 08 - 12, WWW '07, (pp. 221-230). New York: ACM.

Zhang, Z., & Varadarajan, B. (2006). Utility scoring of product reviews. In *Proceedings of the 15th ACM international Conference on information and Knowledge Management,* Arlington, VA, November 06 - 11, (CIKM '06, pp. 51-57). New York: ACM.

ENDNOTES

[1] An estimate of the allocation of internet users' time to different online activities is provided by the Online Publishers Association through the Internet Activity Index (IAI) in: http://www.online-publishers.org.

[2] http://www.compete.com

[3] http://www.quantcast.com

[4] http://www.youtube.com

[5] http://ucc.daum.net

[6] Although the semantics of a digital resource can be also conveyed by other kinds of features (e.g. audio, visual), we restrict our study to the semantics conveyed by textual features of the content.

[7] Whether a story jumps to the 'Popular' section or not does not solely depend on the number of Diggs it receives (although it is certainly taken into account). The Digg administrators make this decision on the basis of a set of proprietary criteria and heuristics, which they keep secret since sharing such knowledge would render the system prone to malicious attacks (e.g. to artificially boost the popularity of a story).

[8] Only stories with $|H_r| > 20$ were studied to prevent the 'noisy' time series from distorting the resulting aggregate time series of the non-popular stories.

[9] *Users with $|R_u| < 20$ were not considered in the sample selection in order to prevent users with sparse (and therefore noisy) activity to affect the aggregate activity time series.*

[10] The filtering rules of $|R_u| > 20$ and $|H_r| > 20$ (same as above) were applied here too.

[11] The post in http://blog.Digg.com/?p=106 provides further evidence in favor of this speculation.

Chapter 12
Using Data Mining Techniques to Probe the Role of Hydrophobic Residues in Protein Folding and Unfolding Simulations

Cândida G. Silva
University of Coimbra, Portugal

Pedro Gabriel Ferreira
Center for Genomic Regulation, Spain

Paulo J. Azevedo
University of Minho, Portugal

Rui M. M. Brito
University of Coimbra, Portugal

ABSTRACT

The protein folding problem, i.e. the identification of the rules that determine the acquisition of the native, functional, three-dimensional structure of a protein from its linear sequence of amino-acids, still is a major challenge in structural molecular biology. Moreover, the identification of a series of neurodegenerative diseases as protein unfolding/misfolding disorders highlights the importance of a detailed characterisation of the molecular events driving the unfolding and misfolding processes in proteins. One way of exploring these processes is through the use of molecular dynamics simulations. The analysis and comparison of the enormous amount of data generated by multiple protein folding or unfolding simulations is not a trivial task, presenting many interesting challenges to the data mining community. Considering the central role of the hydrophobic effect in protein folding, we show here the application of two data mining methods – hierarchical clustering and association rules – for the analysis and comparison of the solvent accessible surface area (SASA) variation profiles of each one of the 127 amino-acid residues in the amyloidogenic protein Transthyretin, across multiple molecular dynamics protein unfolding simulations.

DOI: 10.4018/978-1-60566-816-1.ch012

INTRODUCTION

Molecular dynamics (MD) is one of the most realistic simulation techniques available to study protein folding *in silico*. In MD simulations, the structural fluctuations of a single protein can be tracked over time by numerically solving Newton's equations of motion (Adcock & McCammon, 2006). When using molecular dynamics simulations to study protein folding and unfolding processes, multiple simulations need to be considered to probe the large conformational space and multidimensional potential energy surface available to the polypeptide chain, and obtain significant statistical mechanical averages of the system properties (Brito, 2004; Kazmirski, 1999; Scheraga, 2007). Even though the computational power available keeps increasing, it is still a major challenge to simulate protein folding or unfolding processes in its real time scale (hundreds of µs to seconds or more). However, it has been suggested that performing multiple short simulations (usually 5 to 10) provides better sampling of the conformational space than having a single long simulation (Caves, 1998). Thus, performing multiple simulations on the 10 to 100 ns time scale is becoming routine, which generates huge amounts of data to be analysed and compared. Furthermore, a large set of structural and physical properties (such as root mean square deviation, radius of gyration, secondary structure content, native contacts, and solvent accessible surface area) is usually calculated from the MD trajectories to characterize the conformational space explored.

Most of the structural and physical properties calculated from the MD trajectories are easy to extract. However, the next challenge for data analysis in multiple MD simulations is to identify, among the properties, those that are essential in describing the protein unfolding or folding processes. Additionally, it is important to define the relative importance of each property along the folding/unfolding pathway. It is expected that some of the properties best describe initial stages of the processes under study, while others may be more sensitive to later stages. Looking at a wide range of properties and experimental conditions further increases the amount of data generated by such simulation models. Analyzing and interpreting these data requires automated methods such as data mining. These issues have been addressed before by Kazmirski *et al* (1999) and Brito *et al* (2004). While Kazmirski *et al* (1999) presented several methods based on structure and property data to compare different MD trajectories, Brito *et al* (2004) discussed the usefulness of data mining techniques, which include machine learning, artificial intelligence, and visualization, to address the data analysis problem arising from multiple computational simulations, including protein folding and unfolding simulations. Figure 1 depicts a general overview of this process, from the initial system under study to the interpretation of the results using data mining tools. The researcher begins by performing multiple MD simulations, starting from the same experimental structure (same atom coordinates) but different initial atom velocities. For each simulation, a set of varying atom coordinates and velocities over time (a trajectory) is obtained. At the end of each simulation, a collection of molecular properties may be calculated to characterize the structural variation of the protein during the process. Finally, the molecular property variation profiles may be subjected to analysis using data mining tools.

The solvent accessible surface area (SASA) is one of the molecular properties that might be calculated for each MD trajectory. SASA reports on an important parameter from the protein conformational stability point of view: solvent exposure and protein compactness. Its value may be calculated for the entire protein, but also for subsets of amino-acid residues, accounting for example for the polar or non-polar contributions. Furthermore, the study of the SASA variation of each individual amino-acid residue provides a greater level of detail on the individual contributions for the folding or unfolding processes.

Figure 1. Overview of a "data mining pipeline" applied to the analysis of data arising from multiple molecular dynamics simulations

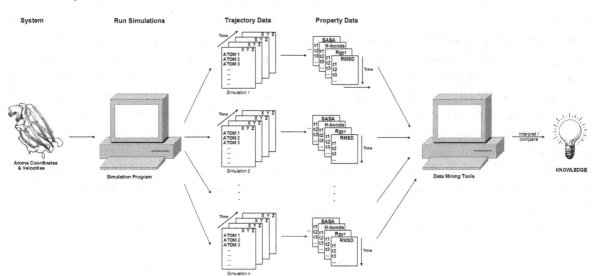

Thus, the study of SASA variation profiles of different amino-acid residues along multiple MD unfolding trajectories may shed light on potential coordinated behaviour of residues far apart in the protein primary structure, or even far apart in the three-dimensional structure.

In recent years, we have made a significant effort in developing a series of comparative-based approaches to analyze SASA variation profiles of individual amino-acid residues in protein unfolding simulations (Azevedo, 2005; Ferreira, 2006, 2007). In this chapter, we show the application of two different methods – clustering and association rules – to study the solvent accessible surface area profiles of individual amino-acid residues across multiple MD unfolding simulations of the amyloidogenic protein transthyretin in search of groups of amino-acid residues playing a coordinated role in protein unfolding. The identification of clusters of residues that change solvent accessible surface area (SASA) concurrently during one unfolding simulation or across several unfolding simulations might prove important in shedding new light in the highly complex problem of protein folding, unfolding and misfolding (Brito, 2004).

In the following sections, we first introduce a general overview on molecular dynamics unfolding simulations of the protein transthyretin (TTR). Then, we describe the main ideas associated with the application of two data mining techniques to the study of solvent accessible surface area variation of individual amino-acid residues upon protein unfolding. Next, we present and analyse the results obtained by the application of these methods, and show their usefulness in the interpretation of this type of data. In closing, we discuss the need and advantages of using data mining tools to analyse data arising from protein folding and unfolding computer simulations.

MOLECULAR DYNAMICS UNFOLDING SIMULATIONS OF TRANSTHYRETIN

In many fatal neurodegenerative diseases, including Alzheimer's, Parkinson's and spongiform encephalopathies, proteins aggregate into fibrillar structures to form insoluble plaques known as amyloid. More than 40 human diseases have been

Figure 2. Schematic secondary structure representations of the WT-TTR monomer along a typical 10 ns molecular dynamics protein unfolding simulation. The structure at the left represents the experimental crystal structure (PDB entry 1tta). The eight β-strands are labelled A (residues 12 to 18), B (residues 28 to 35), C (residues 41 to 49), D (residues 54 to 55), E (residues 67 to 73), F (residues 91 to 97), G (residues 104 to 112) and H (residues 115 to 123). The simulated time along the MD trajectory is indicated underneath each structure

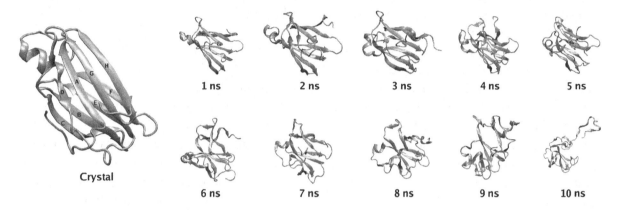

associated with the formation of amyloid deposits of different proteins. Human transthyretin (TTR) is a homotetrameric protein involved in amyloid pathologies such as familial amyloid polyneuropathy (FAP), familial amyloid cardiomyopathy (FAC) and senile systemic amyloidosis (SSA). Each TTR monomer consists of 127 amino-acids arranged in a well-characterized β-sandwich topology comprising β-strands DAGH and CBEF (Figure 2). Several single point mutations enhance the amyloidogenicity of TTR and lead to disease. Of all known mutations, Leu55→Pro (a proline replacing a leucine in position 55) is one of the most amyloidogenic, and Val30→Met (a methionine replacing a valine in position 30) is one of the most prevalent (Brito, 2003).

In recent years, we have been dedicating particular attention to the characterization of the molecular species present in the aggregation pathway of transthyretin, using both experimental (Quintas, 2001) and computational (Correia, 2006; Rodrigues & Brito, 2004; Rodrigues, 2009) methodologies. To explore the unfolding routes of monomeric species of TTR, high temperature molecular dynamics simulations were performed

in our laboratory. MD high temperature simulations are able to capture the essence of the unfolding process without changing the unfolding behaviour of the protein (Day, 2002), and allowing for shorter simulation times (tens of ns). As an example, 10 representative structures along one unfolding trajectory are shown in Figure 2, where it is clear the loss of native secondary structure and the loss of the β-sandwich topology of TTR, as the simulation progresses.

MD Simulations Details

We performed five independent molecular dynamics unfolding simulations of wild-type transthyretin (WT-TTR). For all simulations, the initial atom coordinates were taken from chain B of the WT-TTR structure (PDB entry 1TTA; Hamilton (1993)), and hydrogen atoms were added. The final system also included solvent water molecules and Na^+Cl^- ions. The initial atom velocities were assigned by a random number generator using the constraint of the Maxwell-Boltzmann distribution, and were different for each simulation. The NAMD (Phillips, 2005) molecular dynamics code was used in this work, with well-validated empirical potentials implemented in the CHARMM27 forcefield (MacKerell, 1998). Simulations were performed at 500 K in the NVE (constant number of particles, constant volume and constant energy) ensemble, using periodic boundary conditions. The length of the simulations for this study was 10 ns using a time step of 2 fs. Coordinates for the whole system were saved every 1 ps. Short-range non-bonded interactions were calculated with a 12 Å cut-off with the pair list distances evaluated every 10 steps. Long-range electrostatic interactions were treated using the particle mesh Ewald summation algorithm and were computed at every step. The system details and other relevant simulation parameters can be found elsewhere (Rodrigues & Brito, 2004; Rodrigues, 2009).

MD Simulation Analysis

The microscopic data obtained from MD simulations, such as the atomic positions and velocities, can be used to calculate macroscopic properties following changes in the structure of the protein being simulated (Adcock & McCammon, 2006). Some of the time-dependent properties commonly monitored are the radius of gyration, the root mean square deviation, the number of hydrogen bonds, and the native contacts. Here, the solvent accessible surface area (SASA) of each individual amino-acid residue of the protein TTR along the MD unfolding simulations was calculated in order to study potentially correlated behaviour among different amino-acid residues.

The solvent accessible surface area (SASA) of a protein is defined as the locus of the centre of a probe sphere (representing a solvent molecule) as it rolls over the surface of the protein (Lee & Richards, 1971). The relative SASA of a residue reflects the percentage of the surface area of the residue that is accessible to the solvent. It is defined as the ratio between the SASA of the residue (X) in the three-dimensional structure of the protein and its SASA in a tripeptide (Ala-X-Ala) in ex-

tended conformation. SASA was computed with the program NACCESS (Hubbard, 1993) using a spherical probe of 1.4 Å radius, mimicking a water molecule.

METHODS

Clustering

Cluster analysis is an exploratory technique which might be applied to group a collection of objects into subsets or clusters, such that objects within each cluster are more closely related to one another than objects assigned to different clusters. Cluster analysis has proven to be a valuable instrument in life sciences, namely in genomics (Boutros, 2005; Zhao, 2005) and proteomics (Meunier, 2007), allowing to interpret changes in the expression of entire groups of genes and to discover functional relationships among them. For the particular problem of protein folding or unfolding, it is particularly interesting to understand how amino-acid residues relate to each other during the process. Indeed, to discover groups of residues that change solvent exposure in a coordinated fashion across several unfolding simulations might be crucial to define the folding nuclei of a protein (Brito, 2004; Hammarström & Carlsson, 2000).

Clustering algorithms belong to the class of unsupervised methods, *i.e.* they do not require prior classification of the training data. They are mainly used for pattern discovery, providing the identification of novel and unexpected patterns in the data set. From this class of algorithms, agglomerative hierarchical clustering is one of the most commonly used. The agglomerative hierarchical clustering algorithm works by successively grouping the most similar pairs of objects. The algorithm starts by comparing each pair of objects, then selects the two objects with the most similar characteristics, groups these together into a node, and repeats the procedure with the remaining objects. This process continues until every object has been placed in a tree, also called dendrogram. After the selection of the algorithm, another critical issue in cluster analysis is the choice of the "best" metric for assessing the degree of similarity between the individual objects being clustered. The cosine function, Pearson's correlation, Jaccard's coefficient or Euclidean distance, are some of the commonly used metrics. The Euclidean distance and correlation measures have a clear biological meaning, with Euclidean distances being applied when the goal is to look for identical patterns, while correlation measures are used in the cases where trends of the patterns are the subject of the analysis (Eisen, 1998; Heyer, 1999). Cosine and correlation based measures are well suited for clustering of both low and high dimensional datasets (Zhao, 2005) and are data scale independent, which is not the case of the Euclidean distance.

In the interest of grouping residues showing similar SASA profiles along a MD unfolding simulation, a hierarchical tree – dendrogram – was built reflecting how the residues of the protein cluster together, using as similarity measure the Pearson´s correlation coefficient. The hierarchical clustering procedure identifies sets of correlated residues with similar solvent exposure profiles in each of several MD unfolding pathways, but yields the cluster information in a tree-like structure. This makes the identification of the "correct" number of clusters in the hierarchical clustering solution very difficult. We devised a method to help the researcher identify the clusters with well differentiated characteristics (Ferreira, 2007). Additional information on the amino-acid residues is used to annotate all the nodes of the dendrogram, and the clusters are determined taking into consideration not only the SASA pattern similarity, but also minimizing intra-cluster variation and maximizing inter-cluster variation based on the data enriching the dendrogram. The information used describes the amino-acid residues chemical characteristics and behaviour along the MD unfolding trajectories, and consists of the following properties:

(P1) the distance of the residues in the protein linear sequence; (P2) the spatial distance between the residues along the MD unfolding trajectory, which quantifies the overall spatial variation of the cluster, and measures the deviation of each residue in relation to a central point of the cluster; and (P3) the hydrophobic character of the residue (Radzicka & Wolfenden, 1988). The method can be summarized in four major steps:

1. A dendrogram is constructed based on the SASA variation profiles of the 127 residues, through agglomerative hierarchical clustering and using as similarity measure the Pearson's correlation coefficient.
2. Each node of the dendrogram is annotated with data on properties P1, P2 and P3 related to the chemical characteristics and behaviour of the amino-acid residues along the simulation, by performing a bottom-up traversal of the dendrogram (the information of a parent node is calculated based on the values of the child nodes, reflecting the variability of the properties of the residues constituting the cluster).
3. In a top-down manner, perform a traversal of the annotated dendrogram: split a cluster in two when significant inter-cluster variation is detected (above user defined threshold). Recursively apply the procedure to the obtained clusters, unless the number of residues in the clusters reaches a user defined minimum threshold.
4. Retrieve the clusters and the information on their properties.

Association Rules

Association rule mining finds interesting associations and/or correlations among large sets of data items (Agrawal and Srikant, 1994). Association rules show attribute/value conditions that occur frequently together in a given data set. They hold a simple and clear semantics and are of the form:

$$C \leftarrow A_1 \& A_2 \& \ldots \& A_n$$

An association rule is a pair of disjoint itemsets (set of items): the antecedents ($A_1, A_2, \ldots, A_n$), and the consequent (C). In general, the consequent may be a set of items but here we only consider rules with single item consequents. In the specific problem of SASA data analysis an item is represented by the pair residue/SASA. Each association rule is associated with two values expressing its degree of uncertainty. The first value is called the *support* for the rule, and represents the frequency of co-occurrence of all items appearing in the rule. The second value is the *confidence* of the rule that represents its accuracy. *Confidence* is calculated as the ratio between the *support* of the rule and the *support* of the antecedent.

Finding relations between amino-acid residues belonging to the same and/or different chemical classes is of great interest in the understanding of the protein folding problem. In the present work, the amino-acids were divided in five different classes (hydrophobic, hydrophilic, polar with positive charge, polar with negative charge and aromatic), and association rules were extracted among the five classes to study relationships linked to the main forces driving the folding process: (i) association rules among hydrophobic residues, (ii) association rules among hydrophilic and hydrophobic residues, (iii) association rules among aromatic residues, and (iv) association rules among polar charged residues. Rules were extracted using CAREN (Azevedo, 2003). CAREN is a Java based implementation of an association rule engine that uses a new variant of the ECLAT algorithm (Zaki, 2000). Several features for rule derivation and selection are available in CAREN, namely antecedent and consequent filtering by item or attribute specification, minimum and maximum number of items in a rule, and different metrics. The χ^2 test is one of such metrics. It was applied during itemset mining as it significantly reduces the number of relevant itemsets.

Although, several types of relationships between amino-acid residues could have been studied, in this work we focused on the hydrophobic residues. The hydrophobic effect is considered to be one of the major driving forces in protein folding (Dill, 1990; Kyte, 2003; Lins & Brasseur, 1995; Pace, 1996). It arises from entropically unfavourable arrangements where non-polar side chains contact water, thus favouring polypeptide arrangements in which the side chains of hydrophobic amino-acids are packed in the interior of the protein. In fact, about 80% of the hydrophobic residues' side chains are buried inside a protein when it folds (Pace, 1996). Thus, hydrophobic residues usually exhibit small values of solvent exposure (below 25%) in the protein's folded state. We set out to find groups of residues, in particular hydrophobic ones, which change solvent exposure in a coordinated fashion during one unfolding simulation or across several unfolding simulations, which might be important in defining folding nuclei for a protein (Brito, 2004; Hammarström & Carlsson, 2000). For each data set, association rules were extracted such that only hydrophobic residues with SASA values $\leq 25\%$ were involved. Because interactions between hydrophobic groups are weak, it was imposed that association rules should involve a minimum of four residues. Association rules were extracted with minimum support of 30% and minimum confidence of 90%.

RESULTS

Here, we report and compare the results obtained by the application of two data mining techniques – hierarchical clustering and association rules – to the analysis of solvent accessible surface area (SASA) variation profiles of individual amino-acid residues of the protein transthyretin across five molecular dynamics unfolding simulations.

Data Sets

Five independent MD unfolding simulations of WT-TTR were studied. The monomer of WT-TTR has 127 amino-acid residues, and each simulation is represented by a trajectory constituted by 10,000 time frames (one frame per picosecond simulated). Thus, for each simulation a data set was generated comprising 127 SASA time series, one per residue, with 10,000 time points each. Overall, we analysed five data sets reflecting the SASA variation of the 127 amino-acid residues

of WT-TTR along the five MD unfolding simulations. Each data set, named Run 1 to Run 5, is stored in a different file structured in a tabular fashion, with columns identifying residues, and rows representing time frames. Figure 3 shows the SASA behaviour of nine amino-acid residues across different MD unfolding simulations of WT-TTR. We can point out that, although different SASA profiles are observed, some residues have the same SASA profiles in the same simulation (Panels A and C), or in different simulations (Panels A and B).

Figure 3. Variation of the solvent accessible surface area (SASA) of different residues along multiple MD unfolding simulations of WT-TTR. Representative SASA profiles of nine residues are shown. The data plotted is originated from different data sets. The profiles for residues Leu12 and Glu42 are calculated from simulation 1, while Ala36 and Val71 depict data from simulation 2. Residues Phe33 and Trp41 were plotted with data from simulation 3, whereas the data from simulation 4 was used to plot the SASA profile of residues Asp39 and Ile107. Finally, data from simulation 5 was used to describe the behaviour of Lys70

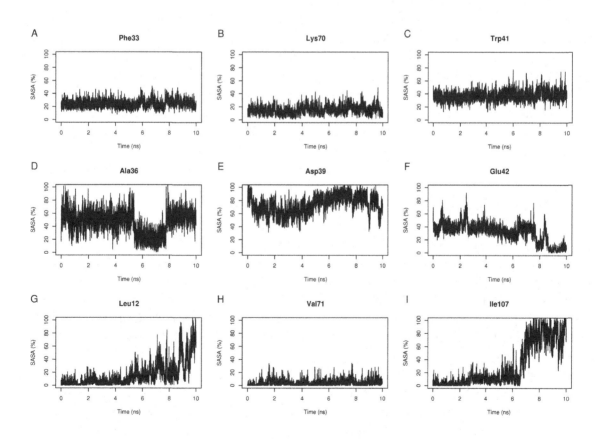

Clustering

A hierarchical clustering procedure was applied to each one of the five data sets to search for residues exhibiting similar SASA variation profiles. Prior to computation of the clustering solutions, each data set was normalised using the classic zero-mean and unit-standard deviation technique. Following the clustering procedure, we searched for prevalent correlations among the clusters determined for each data set.

Dendrogram Construction

Clustering solutions using the agglomerative paradigm were computed with the program *vcluster*, distributed with the clustering toolkit CLUTO (Karypis, 2003). For each data set, the similarity between the solvent accessible surface area (SASA) variation profiles of the 127 residues of WT-TTR was assessed using the Pearson correlation coefficient. Different parameters were chosen to produce the best clustering solution. The option *crfun* was selected to improve intra-cluster quality, and the internal criterion function *i2* was chosen to maximize the similarity between each residue and the centroid of the cluster it is assigned to. CLUTO requires the number of desired clusters to be defined, and this parameter was empirically set to 10.

Dendrogram Annotation

Following the construction of the dendrograms, each non-leaf node was annotated by performing a bottom-up traversal of the tree, i.e. from the leaves (residues) to the root. The annotation consists of a triple with information on the following properties: (P1) the distance of the residues in the protein linear sequence, (P2) the spatial distance of the residues along the MD unfolding trajectory, and (P3) the hydrophobic character of the residues. For each non-leaf node (NLN), the calculation of properties P1 and P2 depends

on its composition. Three scenarios are possible. First, if NLN is formed between two leaf nodes (i.e. two residues) then P1 is calculated as the difference of the positions of the two residues in the protein linear sequence, and P2 as the average value of the Euclidean distances between the coordinates of the C_α atoms of the two residues along the simulation. Second, if NLN is the root of a leaf node (residue) and another subtree, the properties are assigned with the average of two values: (i) the Euclidean distance between the property value in the residue and the centroid of the subtree, and (ii) the property value in the subtree. Third, when NLN is composed by two subtrees, properties P1 and P2 are calculated as the average of the property values annotating the roots of the two subtrees. Property P3 is always calculated as the average value of the residues present in the leave nodes of the subtree of which NLN is the root.

Cluster Assessment

For each data set, the annotated dendrograms were top-down traversed and the clusters determined based on two criteria: (i) a cluster must be composed by at least four amino-acid residues, and (ii) two clusters should differ by a threshold of 0.8. The dissimilarity of two clusters is calculated based on the Euclidean distance between the triples annotating the root of the subtrees that defined them.

The number of clusters obtained for the five data sets is different, ranging between 16 and 24, with the number of amino-acid residues per cluster spanning from 4 to 10.

Searching for Cluster Conservation across Multiple Data Sets

Notwithstanding the importance of the clusters found, correlating the SASA variation profiles of the individual amino-acid residues in each of the five data sets, if one was able to find groups

Table 1. Identification of WT-TTR residues present in the most prevalent correlations among all computed clusters. The five data sets are identified as Run 1 to 5, corresponding to the five MD unfolding simulations. Each gray row defines the set of residues under consideration. Properties P1, P2 and P3 correspond to the average 1D distance (number of residues), the average 3D distance (Å) and the average hydrophobicity (kcal/mol), respectively, for the cluster considered

	Run 1	Run 2		Run 3		Run 4	Run 5
Phe33, Lys70							
(P1) Average 1D distance	41.88	28.06		42.12		35.50	20.25
(P2) Average 3D distance	12.70	10.80		24.85		7.42	10.95
(P3) Average hydrophobicity	-0.76	-0.06		-1.75		-1.76	-1.11
Ala36, Asp39, Glu42							
(P1) Average 1D distance	14.09	2.50		12.12		4.88	17.19
(P2) Average 3D distance	17.00	16.17		17.12		29.81	14.92
(P3) Average hydrophobicity	-5.36	-2.40		-0.57		-7.60	-3.03
Leu12, Val14, Val71, Ile107, Ala109, Leu111							
(P1) Average 1D distance	42.06	7.62	38.50	13.25	49.00	11.24	45.69
(P2) Average 3D distance	10.73	4.43	4.83	7.49	11.19	5.63	9.41
(P3) Average hydrophobicity	2.86	1.00	4.26	4.39	0.16	0.16	2.88

of residues co-occurring in the same clusters across multiple data sets, one could speculate on the cooperative role of the correlated residues in the unfolding process of the protein WT-TTR. In order to find groups of residues conserved in the same clusters across multiple data sets, an itemset mining algorithm was applied (Agrawal & Srikant, 1994). This type of algorithms allows the discovery of elements that co-occur a number of times equal or greater than a threshold value – minimum support. In the context of this work, minimum support corresponds to the minimum number of data sets for which a group of residues is expected to co-occur.

After comparing the clusters of the five data sets, we discovered two groups of residues with prevalent correlations in all data sets: (i) Phe33 and Lys70, and (ii) Ala36, Asp39 and Glu42. Additionally, we found ten pairs of residues clustered together in four of the five data sets, with most of the pairs involving at least one of the following hydrophobic residues: Leu12 and Val14 (β-strand A), Val71 (β-strand E), and Ile107, Ala109 and

Leu111 (β-strand G). Table 1 presents the properties P1, P2 and P3 of the clusters containing the groups of residues identified above, for each data set (Run 1 to Run 5).

For the clusters containing residues Phe33 and Lys70, the data show that the average linear distance between residues (P1) in these clusters is high which indicates that stronger correlations appear first between residues far apart in the protein linear sequence; however the residues seem to appear in close spatial proximity (low values for property P2). Moreover, the residues composing these clusters are mainly hydrophobic, with most of them positioned in β-strands B, C and E. As for the properties characterizing the clusters containing residues Ala36, Asp39 and Glu42, for Runs 1, 3 and 5 higher correlation values are observed between residues far apart in the protein linear sequence, whereas for Runs 2 and 4 precisely the opposite happens. The values of average spatial distance (P2) are more or less of the same order of magnitude in all data sets, except for Run 4, where residues are close in the sequence but are spatially more distant (~ 30 Å). These clusters comprise mainly polar residues, in particular negatively charged.

Considering the clusters containing residues Leu12, Val14, Val71, Ile107, Ala109 and Leu111, co-occurrences can be found in four data sets for some residues, and in three data sets for other residues. For this reason, for Runs 2 and 3 two clusters are described. For all data sets, the clusters are constituted by hydrophobic residues (positive values of P3) that tend to be close in spatial proximity. On the other hand, to what relates to the values of property P1, two distinct patterns are observed. The residues in each of the clusters are: (i) far apart in the protein sequence (Run 1; Run 2, cluster 16; Run 3, cluster 16; Run 5), or (ii) close in the protein sequence (Run 2, cluster 1; Run 3, cluster 14; Run 4).

From these observations, it is clear that the annotation of the dendrograms, obtained by a classical hierarchical clustering procedure, with additional information on protein sequence (P1), composition (P3), and dynamics (P2) helped in the discrimination and characterization of well differentiated clusters.

How do the SASA Values of Clustered Groups of Residues Vary Throughout the Unfolding Simulations?

To establish if a particular group of residues change their solvent accessible surface area (SASA) in a synchronised fashion during the unfolding process of a protein is an important piece of information, but the analysis of the magnitude and direction of these changes is also crucial to the understanding of the unfolding process. In particular, knowing which amino-acid residues remain unexposed to the solvent or which amino-acid residues rapidly move from positions of low exposure to positions of high exposure may reveal important clues on the role those residues play in the stabilization of the protein. Figure 3 shows the SASA variation profiles of the residues co-occurring in the same

clusters in several data sets (Table 1). Two main observations can be made: (i) Phe33 and Lys70 exhibit the same SASA variation profile in all data sets; and (ii) although Ala36, Asp39 and Glu42 are clustered together in all data sets, three different SASA variation profiles are observed.

Residues Phe33 (β-strand B) and Lys70 (β-strand E) exhibit the same average solvent exposure across all MD unfolding simulations: constant solvent exposure around a mean low value (Figure 3, Panels A and B). In Runs 1, 3 and 4, residue Trp41, located in β-strand C, shows a SASA variation pattern similar to residues Phe33 and Lys70. However, the relative solvent accessible surface area of this residue is higher than the former two residues (Figure 3, Panel C).

On the other hand, Ala36 (β-strand B), Asp39 (turn BC) and Glu42 (β-strand C) are identified in the same clusters across the various data sets, but two distinct behaviours of solvent exposure are found. In Runs 1 and 5, throughout most of the trajectory, these residues favour values of solvent exposure higher than in the native structure of the protein, but become buried in the last 2 ns of the simulation, assuming values of solvent exposure lower than in the native structure (Figure 3, Panel F). In Runs 2, 3 and 4, Ala36, Asp39 and Glu42 become buried (Figure 3, Panel D) or less exposed (Figure 3, Panel E) at different time points and for different time intervals. In Figure 3, Panel D, the SASA profile of Ala36 is displayed. Its SASA value in the native structure is 27.2%, but it rapidly moves to positions of greater exposure. Until the 5th nanosecond, the SASA value of Ala36 varies around 52%. Interestingly, between the 5th and 8th nanosecond of the simulation, the residue becomes buried. It then becomes exposed again in the last 2 ns of the simulation. The profile described can be observed for this group of residues in Run 2 and Run 3. In Run 4, the SASA profiles are slightly different as can be observed in Panel E of Figure 3 for Asp39. During the first half of the simulation, the residues exhibit SASA values varying around a mean value lower than their initial SASA value. On the second half of the simulation, the accessible surface increases and begins to vary around a SASA value close to the one in the native structure of TTR.

Panels G to I of Figure 3 depict the variation of the solvent accessible surface area of residues Leu12, Val71 and Ile107, respectively. The SASA profiles shown are representative of the different profiles observed for these residues, across the five data sets. In simulation 1 (Panel G), the residues are buried during most of the simulation, but in the last nanoseconds become progressively exposed. In Runs 2, 3 and 5 (Panel H), the residues are buried in the interior of the protein throughout the simulation, displaying a very small accessible surface to the solvent, even late in the simulations when the protein is already denatured. Finally, in Run 4, the residues show low solvent accessibility until the ~ 6th ns of the simulation and then get highly exposed to the solvent (Panel I).

Association Rules

Association rules were extracted from five data sets (Run 1 to Run 5) describing the solvent accessible surface area (SASA) variation profiles of each one of the 127 amino-acid residues that constitute the monomer of WT-TTR throughout five independent MD unfolding simulations. All data sets were discretised to evaluate three levels of solvent exposure: low ([0, 25]), medium (]25, 75[) and high ([75, 100[).

Association Rules Extraction

Association rules were extracted using CAREN (Azevedo, 2003), an association rule engine with several rule derivation and selection features. As we were interested in sets of association rules characterising the relations between hydrophobic amino-acid residues with SASA $\leq 25\%$ involving at least 4 residues, we used the features for antecedent and consequent filtering, and for minimum number of items (residues) in a rule. The χ^2 test during itemsets mining was also applied, significantly reducing the number of relevant itemsets. The standard confidence metric was used to evaluate the association rules, and it was set to 90%. The minimum support was set to 30%. In Table 2, the association rules derived from the five data sets (Run 1 to Run 5) are described in terms of number of rules generated, total number of residues involved in the rules, and support and confidence intervals.

Across the five data sets, there is a large variation in the number of association rules generated, but the number of amino-acid residues identified is similar. Additionally, the support and confidence values vary within comparable intervals. As expected, support values for association rules involving more residues tend to be lower, and association rules with high support involve fewer residues.

Table 2. Characterisation of the association rules involving hydrophobic residues, extracted from the SASA variation profiles in five independent MD unfolding simulations of WT-TTR

	Run 1	Run 2	Run 3	Run 4	Run 5
No. rules	10831	407	3876	32086	758
No. residues	28	28	27	29	24
Support (%)	]30, 84[	]30, 74[	]30, 89[	]30, 85[	]30, 88[
Confidence (%)	[90, 100]	[90, 100[	[90, 100]	[90, 100]	[90, 100]

Insights on the Stability of the Hydrophobic Core of Transthyretin

We define the hydrophobic core of the protein as the group of hydrophobic residues which in the protein native structure have solvent accessible surface area values lower or equal to 25%. According to this definition, the hydrophobic core of WT-TTR is composed of 29 amino-acid residues.

In the five sets of association rules derived from the SASA variation profiles of the hydrophobic residues, a total of 33 residues are identified, of which 19 residues are present in all sets of association rules. Figure 4 shows the distribution of these residues in the native structure of WT-TTR, and it is clear that all the residues are closely packed in the interior of the protein monomer. We have previously proposed that this group of amino-acid residues may constitute the hydrophobic clusters essential to the protein folding and unfolding processes (Azevedo, 2005). In fact, we found that all the 19 amino-acid residues conserved in the five sets of association rules belong to the hydrophobic core of WT-TTR. Moreover, most of these residues participate in the formation of β-strands (84.2% in β-strands, 5.3% in α-helix, 10.5% in turns and loops), which are well defined topologies that contribute to the structural stability of proteins.

Comparison of the Sets of Association Rules

The number of association rules extracted from each data set varies considerably (Table 2). We compared the sets of association rules derived from the five data sets on the SASA variation profiles of the individual amino-acid residues of WT-TTR monomer. We found that an association rule co-occurs in a maximum of three out of the five sets of rules. Then, we investigated in more detail, the set of association rules resulting from this comparison as these rules may describe significant events in the unfolding process of WT-TTR.

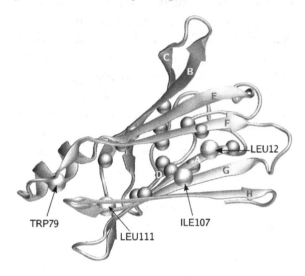

Figure 4. Schematic representation of the secondary structure of the monomer of WT-TTR. The spheres indicate the positions of the Cα atoms of 19 out of a total of 52 hydrophobic residues, co-occurring in three of the association rules sets. The four hydrophobic residues identified occur as consequents of the association rules obtained from the WT-TTR unfolding simulations.

There are 98 rules co-occurring exactly in three sets of association rules. These rules involve exactly four residues, and the average support value is 46.4%. There are 21 hydrophobic residues involved in the rules identified, all of which belong to the hydrophobic core of the protein. Moreover, these residues are mainly located in β-strands A, B, E, F and G. In Table 3, we show a selection of seven rules in the conditions described. For example, association rule AR1, states that, in Runs 1, 3 and 4, the set of residues Leu12, Ala25, Ile73 and Phe95 exhibit SASA values ≤ 25% during approximately 31%, 47% and 51% of the simulated time, respectively. Moreover, when residues Ala25, Ile73 and Phe95 exhibit SASA values ≤ 25%, then at least in ~93% of the cases Leu12 also exhibits SASA values ≤ 25%. The other association rules in Table 3 can be read in a similar manner.

Table 3. Selected association rules mined from the SASA data derived from WT-TTR MD unfolding simulations. These rules were selected from the subset of rules common to the largest number of MD simulations. All the amino-acid residues listed in each rule are hydrophobic and have SASA value between 0% and 25%. The Support value (%) for each rule in a particular data set and the lowest Confidence value (%) obtained for the association rule in the data sets are reported. Labelled with × are rules not identified in a particular data set.

				Association Rule	Support					Confidence
					Run 1	Run 2	Run 3	Run 4	Run 5	
AR1	Leu12	←		Ala25 & Ile73 & Phe95	30.709	×	47.082	51.456	×	92.966
AR2	Leu12	←		Phe33 & Ile107 & Ala109	48.819	×	37.995	42.632	×	90.127
AR3	Leu12	←		Pro11 & Val14 & Val28	51.419	×	×	56.455	37.591	98.236
AR4	Leu12	←		Val16 & Val32 & Leu58	48.569	×	×	52.281	64.721	97.828
AR5	Trp79	←		Val32 & Ala91 & Ala108	32.271	×	70.754	53.093	×	90.663
AR6	Ile107	←		Ala25 & Ile73 & Leu111	34.521	×	50.531	53.093	×	93.892
AR7	Leu111	←		Leu12 & Phe64 & Ala109	44.569	×	×	71.766	30.305	94.040

Although in Table 3 only 7 out of a total 98 rules co-occurring in three of the sets of association rules are shown, it generally describes the structure of the rules obtained. We found out that only a small subset of the hydrophobic residues appears in the consequent member of the rules: Leu12 (57 rules), Trp79 (17 rules), Ile107 (23 rules) and Leu111 (1 rule). The distribution of these residues in the native structure of WT-TTR is shown in Figure 4. Furthermore, we also observed that (i) all 98 rules can be derived for data sets Run 1 and Run 4, (ii) none of the 98 rules can be derived for data set Run 2, and (iii) if one rule is derived for data set Run 3, then it was not derived for data set Run 5, and vice-versa. Driven by these observations, we analysed the residues involved in these association rules, and their SASA behaviour.

First, for the amino-acid residues involved in the 98 rules co-occurring in three of the sets of association rules two major SASA variation profiles are observed: (i) the amino-acid residues maintain the same values of solvent exposure throughout the entire simulations; or (ii) at some point of the simulation the amino-acid residues move rapidly from positions of low exposure (≤ 25%) to positions of high exposure (~ 100%).

This is the most frequent SASA variation profile observed. Furthermore, these rules are describing mainly events in the beginning of the simulation when the conformations are more closely related to the native structure of WT-TTR. Thus, for most rules what we observe is the point in time in the unfolding process that an event occurs which drives the rupture of some structures, mainly in β-strands A, B, F and G, causing the residues to move to positions of high exposure to the solvent. The data also shows that a group of residues associated with Trp79 maintains positions of low exposure to the solvent till late in Run 3 and Run 4 (~ 6th ns), but in Run 1 they move to positions of high exposure much earlier, around the 3rd ns.

Second, particular subsets of rules occur disjointly in different data sets. This seems to indicate a degree of similarity/dissimilarity between different simulations. In a sense, it is shown that specific subsets of hydrophobic residues undergo different unfolding routes: particular groups of hydrophobic residues relate in a similar manner in some simulations, but not in others. Based on the 98 association rules found to occur in three data sets, we identified the group of residues responsible for the differences observed: Pro11,

Ala25, Phe33, Leu58 and Ala91. On one hand, association rules derived for Runs 1, 3 and 4, describe associations between residues that show a high increase of SASA values around the 4th ns of simulation, but in these data sets Ala25, Phe33 and Ala91 start with SASA values close to 0% but move almost immediately to positions of solvent exposure around 30-40%. On the other hand, in SASA variation profiles described by data sets 1, 4 and 5, the residue Pro11 moves rapidly to positions of high exposure, and Leu58 fluctuates between positions of low and medium exposure. Thus, it is clear that some residues exhibit conservative behaviour across all data sets, while others follow alternative routes.

DISCUSSION

The packing of amino-acid residues in proteins is very important in determining protein stability (Samanta, 2002). The solvent accessible surface area (SASA) variation profile of an amino-acid residue during unfolding simulations provides a way to assess the changes in residue packing upon protein unfolding. Hence, careful analysis of SASA variation profiles and even more importantly the identification of residues that vary their SASA profiles in a synchronised manner, may allow a better understanding of the unfolding process in proteins, and in particular in amyloidogenic proteins.

Here, we demonstrated the application of two distinct data mining methods to identify clusters and association of residues showing similar global solvent exposure profiles across multiple MD unfolding simulations. The two methods were applied to five data sets originated from five independent MD unfolding simulations of the protein WT-TTR. The results reported demonstrate that the methods are particularly helpful when used to compare and contrast multiple data sets allowing the identification of interesting correlations among different sets of amino-acid residues.

The results show that residues in β-strands A, B, E and G of the WT-TTR monomer display strongly correlated solvent exposure behaviour, which is consistent with previous experimental work by Liu (2000), where it is suggested that β-strands A, B, E and G of WT-TTR undergo a cooperative unfolding process, and that most of the residues coupling β-strands B with E, and A with G, play a critical role in the stabilization of TTR. The distribution of these residues in the secondary structure elements of WT-TTR leads us to believe that these residues may play a central role in the folding and unfolding processes of the protein. Moreover, Hammarström & Carlsson (2000) stated that detecting residual structures in unfolded proteins can yield important clues for the identification of initiation sites of protein folding. It has been shown that a substantial number of studied proteins possess residual structure in hydrophobic regions clustered together in the protein core which may work as seeds in the folding process. Thus, the residues identified here using both hierarchical clustering and association rules may in high probability be regarded as hydrophobic seeds in the folding/unfolding process of TTR.

Another interesting result regarding the role of residues Ala36, Asp39, and Glu42 on the stabilization of the N-terminus of β-strand C was obtained by the use of the hierarchical clustering procedure. This issue has been discussed before by other authors (Liu, 2000; Yang, 2006). It has been reported that the unfolding of WT-TTR starts with the disruption of β-strand D, followed by the unfolding of β-strands F and H. Prior to the complete unfolding of the protein, a residual structure comprising the N-terminus of β-strand C and β-strands B and E can be identified (Rodrigues, 2009; Yang, 2006). Particular attention has been given to the stability of the N-terminus of β-strand C. Liu (2000) using an experimental approach, found that the residues in the C-terminus of β-strand C are weakly protected from the solvent, while residues in the N-terminus, Trp41 and Glu42, are highly protected. These experimental results do not provide evidence of further correlated behaviour between these two residues. However, the same authors proposed that the stability at the N-terminus of β-strand C might be enhanced by the relatively short turn connecting β-strands B and C (turn BC). Our data show that, although with different solvent exposure profiles across the five MD trajectories, residues Ala36 (β-strand B), Asp39 (turn BC) and Glu42 (β-strand C) are found to be in the same clusters, showing that these residues tend to have the same collective behaviour, and indicating that in fact the residues at the end of β-strand B, turn BC, and beginning of β-strand C could belong to the same *folding unit*.

CONCLUSION

One of the challenges for data analysis in multiple protein unfolding simulations is to identify, among several physical and structural properties those that are essential in describing the unfolding and folding processes. Looking at a wide range of properties and experimental conditions further increases the potential amount of data generated by such simulation models. Analyzing and interpreting these data requires automated methods such as data mining.

Here, we showed the application of two data mining methods for the analysis and comparison of the solvent accessible surface area (SASA) variation of each one of the amino-acid residues in the amyloidogenic protein Transthyretin, across multiple molecular dynamics protein unfolding simulations. Some of the identified residues have been previously recognized by experimental and computational approaches as important in the unfolding process of TTR and may shed some new and helpful insights in the understanding of TTR amyloidosis. The ability to find and characterize clusters of amino-acid residues with correlated solvent exposure behaviour upon protein unfolding in amyloidogenic and non-amyloidogenic proteins may help identify critical residues and critical

interactions in the pathways to form the molecular intermediates responsible for protein aggregation and amyloid formation. The identification of such residues and interactions is vital for the detailed understanding of the molecular mechanisms of amyloid diseases and for the development of rational approaches towards anti-amyloid drugs. Moreover, the use of a physics-based simulation approach and the identification of correlated behaviour in SASA variation patterns upon protein unfolding across several protein structural classes, may help in the future the development of new and improved knowledge-based potentials for protein unfolding, protein folding and protein structure prediction studies.

ACKNOWLEDGMENT

The authors acknowledge the support of the "Fundação para a Ciência e Tecnologia", Portugal, and the program FEDER, through grant PTDC/BIA-PRO/72838/2006 (to PJA and RMMB) and the Fellowships SFRH/BD/16888/2004 (to CGS) and SFRH/BPD/42003/2007 (to PGF). We thank the Center for Computational Physics, Physics Department, University of Coimbra and Computer Science and Technology Center, Informatics Department, University of Minho, Braga, Portugal, for the computer resources provided for the MD simulations.

REFERENCES

Adcock, S. A., & McCammon, J. A. (2006). Molecular dynamics: Survey of methods for simulating the activity of proteins. *Chemical Reviews*, *106*(5), 1589–1615. doi:10.1021/cr040426m

Agrawal, R., & Srikant, R. (1994). Fast algorithms for mining association rules. In *20th International Conference on Very Large Databases* (pp. 487-499). San Francisco: Morgan Kaufmann.

Azevedo, P. J. (2003). *CAREN - A Java based apriori implementation for classification purposes* (Tech. Rep.). Braga, Portugal: University of Minho, Department of Informatics.

Azevedo, P. J., Silva, C. G., Rodrigues, J. R., Loureiro-Ferreira, N., & Brito, R. M. M. (2005). Detection of hydrophobic clusters in molecular dynamics protein unfolding simulations using association rules. In J. L. Oliveira, V. Maojo, F. Martin-Sanchez, & A. S. Pereira (Eds.), *6th International Symposium Biological and Medical Data Analysis:* (LNCS Vol. 3745, pp. 329-337). Berlin: Springer.

Boutros, P. C., & Okey, A. B. (2005). Unsupervised pattern recognition: An introduction to the whys and wherefores of clustering microarray data. *Briefings in Bioinformatics, 6*(4), 331–343. doi:10.1093/bib/6.4.331

Brito, R. M. M., Damas, A. M., & Saraiva, M. J. (2003). Amyloid formation by transthyretin: From protein stability to protein aggregation. *Current Medicinal Chemistry - Immunology, Endocrine & Metabolic Agents, 3*(4), 349–360. doi:10.2174/1568013033483230

Brito, R. M. M., Dubitzky, W., & Rodrigues, J. R. (2004). Protein folding and unfolding simulations: A new challenge for data mining. *OMICS: A Journal of Integrative Biology, 8*(2), 153–166. doi:10.1089/153623104138831

Caves, L. S. D., Evanseck, J. D., & Karplus, M. (1998). Locally accessible conformations of proteins: Multiple molecular dynamics simulations of crambin. *Protein Science, 7*(3), 649–666.

Correia, B. E., Loureiro-Ferreira, N., Rodrigues, J. R., & Brito, R. M. M. (2006). A structural model of an amyloid protofilament of transthyretin. *Protein Science, 15*(1), 28–32. doi:10.1110/ps.051787106

Day, R., & Daggett, V. (2003). All-atom simulations of protein folding and unfolding. *Advances in Protein Chemistry, 66*, 373–803. doi:10.1016/S0065-3233(03)66009-2

Dill, K. A. (1990). Dominant forces in protein folding. *Biochemistry, 29*(31), 7133–7155. doi:10.1021/bi00483a001

Eisen, M. B., Spellman, P. T., Brown, P. O., & Botstein, D. (1998). Cluster analysis and display of genome-wide expression patterns. *Proceeding of the National Academy of Sciences of the United States of America, 95*(25), 14863-14868.

Ferreira, P. G., Azevedo, P. J., Silva, C. G., & Brito, R. M. M. (2006). Mining approximate motifs in time series. In N. Lavrac, L. Todorovski, & K. P. Jantke (Eds.), *9th International Conference on Discovery Science* (LNAI Vol. 4265, pp. 77–89). Berlin: Springer.

Ferreira, P. G., Silva, C. G., Brito, R. M. M., & Azevedo, P. J. (2007). A closer look on protein unfolding simulations through hierarchical clustering. *2007 IEEE Symposium on Computational Intelligence and Bioinformatics and Computational Biology* (pp. 461–468).

Hamilton, W., Steinrauf, L. K., Liepnieks, J., Braden, B. C., Benson, M. D., & Holmgren, G. (1993). The X-ray crystal structure refinements of normal human transthyretin and the amyloidogenic Val-30-Met variant to 1.7 Å resolution. *The Journal of Biological Chemistry, 268*(4), 2416–2424.

Hammarström, P., & Carlsson, U. (2000). Is the unfolded state the rosetta stone of the protein folding problem? *Biochemical and Biophysical Research Communications, 276*(2), 393–398. doi:10.1006/bbrc.2000.3360

Heyer, L. J., Kruglyak, S., & Yooseph, S. (1999). Exploring expression data: Identification and analysis of coexpressed genes. *Genome Research, 9*(11), 1106–1115. doi:10.1101/gr.9.11.1106

Hubbard, S. J., & Thornton, J. M. (1993). *NACCESS, Computer Program* (Tech. Rep.). London: University College, Department of Biochemistry and Molecular Biology.

Karypis, G. (2003). *CLUTO - A clustering toolkit* (Tech. Rep.). Minneapolis, USA: University of Minnesota, Department of Computer Science & Engineering.

Kazmirski, S. L., Li, A., & Daggett, V. (1999). Analysis methods for comparison of multiple molecular dynamics trajectories: Applications to protein unfolding pathways and denatured ensembles. *Journal of Molecular Biology, 290*(1), 283–304. doi:10.1006/jmbi.1999.2843

Kyte, J. (2003). The basis of the hydrophobic effect. *Biophysical Chemistry, 100*(1-3), 193–203. doi:10.1016/S0301-4622(02)00281-8

Lee, B., & Richards, F. M. (1971). The interpretation of protein structures: estimation of static accessibility. *Journal of Molecular Biology, 55*(3), 379–400. doi:10.1016/0022-2836(71)90324-X

Lins, L., & Brasseur, R. (1995). The hydrophobic effect in protein folding. *The FASEB Journal, 9*(7), 535–540.

Liu, K., Cho, H. S., Hoyt, D. W., Nguyen, T. N., Olds, P., Kelly, J. W., & Wemmer, D. E. (2000). Deuterium-proton exchange on the native wild-type transthyretin tetramer identifies the stable core of the individual subunits and indicates mobility at the subunit interface. *Journal of Molecular Biology, 303*(4), 555–565. doi:10.1006/jmbi.2000.4164

MacKerell, A. D., Bashford, D., Bellott, M., Dunbrack, R. L., Evanseck, J. D., & Field, M. J. (1998). All-atom empirical potential for molecular modeling and dynamics studies of proteins. *The Journal of Physical Chemistry B, 102*(18), 3586–3616. doi:10.1021/jp973084f

Meunier, B., Dumas, E., Piec, I., Béchet, D., Hébraud, M., & Hocquette, J. F. (2007). Assessment of hierarchical clustering methodologies for proteomic data mining. *Journal of Proteome Research, 6*(1), 358–366. doi:10.1021/pr060343h

Pace, C. N., Shirley, B. A., Mcnutt, M., & Gajiwala, K. (1996). Forces contributing to the conformational stability of proteins. *The FASEB Journal, 10*(1), 75–83.

Phillips, J. C., Braun, R., Wang, W., Gumbart, J., Tajkhorshid, E., & Villa, E. (2005). Scalable molecular dynamics with NAMD. *Journal of Computational Chemistry, 26*(16), 1781–1802. doi:10.1002/jcc.20289

Quintas, A., Vaz, D. C., Cardoso, I., Saraiva, M. J., & Brito, R. M. M. (2001). Tetramer dissociation and monomer partial unfolding precedes protofibril formation in amyloidogenic transthyretin variants. *The Journal of Biological Chemistry, 276*(29), 27207–27213. doi:10.1074/jbc.M101024200

Radzicka, A., & Wolfenden, R. (1988). Comparing the polarities of the amino-acids: Side-chain distribution coefficients between the vapor phase, cyclohexane, 1-Octanol, and neutral aqueous solution. *Biochemistry, 27*(5), 1664–1670. doi:10.1021/bi00405a042

Rodrigues, J. R., & Brito, R. M. M. (2004). How important is the role of compact denatured states on amyloid formation by transthyretin? In G. Grateau, R. A. Kyle, & M. Skinner (Eds.), *Amyloid and Amyloidosis* (pp. 323–325). Bocca Raton, FL: CRC Press.

Rodrigues, J. R., Simões, C. J. V., Silva, C. G., & Brito, R. M. M. (2009). Potentially amyloidogenic conformational intermediates populate the unfolding landscape of transthyretin: insights from molecular dynamics simulations. *(submitted)*.

Samanta, U., Bahadur, R. P., & Chakrabarti, P. (2002). Quantifying the accessible surface area of protein residues in their local environment. *Protein Engineering*, *15*(8), 659–667. doi:10.1093/protein/15.8.659

Scheraga, H. A., Khalili, M., & Liwo, A. (2007). Protein folding dynamics: Overview of molecular simulation techniques. *Annual Review of Physical Chemistry*, *58*, 57–83. doi:10.1146/annurev.physchem.58.032806.104614

Yang, M., Yordanov, B., Levy, Y., Brüschweiler, R., & Huo, S. (2006). The sequence-dependent unfolding pathway plays a critical role in the amyloidogenicity of transthyretin. *Biochemistry*, *45*(39), 11992–12002. doi:10.1021/bi0609927

Zaki, M. J. (2000). Scalable algorithms for association mining. *IEEE Transactions on Knowledge and Data Engineering*, *12*(3), 372–390. doi:10.1109/69.846291

Zhao, Y., & Karypis, G. (2005). Clustering in the life sciences. *Molecular Biotechnology*, *31*(1), 55–80. doi:10.1385/MB:31:1:055

Chapter 13
A Geostatistically Based Probabilistic Risk Assessment Approach

Claudia Cherubini
Politecnico di Bari, Italy

ABSTRACT

Most data required for cleanup risk assessment are intrinsically characterized by a high degree of variability and uncertainty. Moreover, typical features of environmental datasets are the occurrence of extreme values like a few random 'hot spots' of large concentrations within a background of data below the detection limit. In the field of environmental pollution risk assessment constitutes a support method for decisions inherent the necessity to carry out a procedure of remediation of an area. Therefore it would be adequate to provide the analysis with elements that allow to take into account the nature of the data themselves, particularly their uncertainty. In this context, this chapter focuses on the application of an uncertainty modeling approach based on geostatistics for the parameters which enter as input in the probabilistic procedure of risk assessment. Compared with a traditional approach, the applied method provides the possibility to quantify and integrate the uncertainty and variability of input parameters in the determination of risk. Moreover, it has proved to be successful in catching and describing in a synthetic way the relations and tendencies that are intrinsic in the data set, characteristics that are neglected by a traditional classical approach.

INTRODUCTION

The risk assessment is an efficient decision support method in the evaluation on the necessity to remediate a contaminated area; it serves as a tool for the definition of the concentration value to be

DOI: 10.4018/978-1-60566-816-1.ch013

reached by means of remediation interventions for human health protection. Nevertheless, in the execution of a risk assessment, the required data are characterized for the most part by a high degree of variability and in most cases, especially when a in-depth site assessment study is not carried out, also by a substantial level of uncertainty. Moreover, in many environmental applications, a few random 'hot spots' of large concentrations coexist with a background of data below the detection limit (censored observations) (Goovaerts, 1999). An alternative approach to the probabilistic analysis based on the methods of the classical statistics can be that of analyzing and quantifying the spatial uncertainty using geostatistical techniques. Geostatistics offers a series of extremely useful instruments to operate any decisional processes in that it allows to recognize the structures that normally characterize the spatial distributions of the studied properties.

This paper is aimed at providing a geostatistical method for modeling the uncertainty connected to the input parameters in a probabilistic procedure of risk assessment. It is structured in such a way: the first section will provide some legislative notions on risk assessment's role within the remediation procedure of a contaminated area, the intermediate sections will deal with how to treat uncertainties in risk assessment, whether with classical (stochastic), or geostatistical approaches. In this part the application of geostatistics is described for the delimitation of the potentially contaminated area, the determination of the Source Representative Concentration, and also of the optimal sampling designs for site characterization, an important phase of the remediation procedure. In the final part three case studies are proposed, in which the concepts explained in the theory are applied to contaminated areas.

The Risk Assessment in the Current Italian Legislation

The risk assessment procedure is considered by the current Italian legislation (D.lgs 152/06) as a support tool to establish first of all if it is necessary to remediate an area or not and, if so, the remediation targets to reach in order to annul eventual harmful effects for human health according to the predefined acceptability criteria. When an area is subjected to investigations in order to ascertain the eventual state of contamination, one decisive step concerns the delimitation of the potentially contaminated area, to be submitted to risk assessment and subsequently to eventual remediation treatments.

The current Italian legislation makes reference to two thresholds criteria of interventions: the former is the Threshold Concentration of Contamination (CSC) that is considered as an alert limit, that, once exceeded, makes it necessary to carry out a risk assessment; the latter is the Risk Threshold Concentration (CSR), that identifies the acceptable levels of residual contamination, on which to plan remediation interventions. An area is potentially contaminated if the pollutant concentrations exceed the CSC values (tabulated); it is declared contaminated if the pollutant concentrations exceed the CSR values, obtained by means of a risk assessment, to be carried out on the basis of the results of the investigations.

Uncertainty and Variability in Risk Assessment Data

The legislative decree n. 152/06 attributes a great importance to risk assessment and defines the general criteria for its elaboration; the risk is estimated in unquestionably deterministic terms and is expressed by a single numerical value. The principle at the basis of the procedure is that of considering always the "Worst Case" that assures conservative estimation values, in that it provides higher values than the average estimated ones, in favour of the environment and human health. Nevertheless, in the execution of a risk assessment the most conservative result is not always guaranteed as the data on which the analysis is based are characterized for the most part by a high degree of variability and often also by uncertainty. The character of uncertainty and variability of the risk assessment, an intrinsic property of this procedure, is explicitly recognized by the D.lgs 152/06 that reports: "the elaboration of the analytic results has to express the uncertainty in the concentration value determined for each sample..".

When the obtained risk is close to the acceptability limit, the estimation of a defined value of the risk may not be exhaustive because it doesn't take into account the uncertainty and variability that have characterized the various phases of the analysis (U.S. EPA, 2001).

Within a procedure of risk assessment there are many sources of uncertainty (U.S. EPA, 2001):

- uncertainty in the parameters (due to the error measurement and the parameters' spatial and temporal variation);
- uncertainty in the models (due to the imprecision in the structures of the models applied for contaminants propagation and in the dose- response relationships);
- uncertainty in the scenery (due to scarceness of data regarding the area and its level of pollution).

In other words the uncertainty comes from the lack of cognitive information on parameters, phenomena or models and can be reduced, at least partly, by means of the study and the acquisition of new cognitive elements. Instead, the variability characterizes each parameter within its domain of existence and is linked to the complexity and heterogeneity of the physical and chemical processes involved in the analyzed phenomena.

In those cases, the most appropriate approach is a probabilistic analysis in which the aleatoriety of the environmental variables can be described and interpreted by means of probability distributions that provide both the interval of values and the probability of exceeding a threshold value for each contaminant. The choice of the most adequate probability distribution for each of the input parameters in risk assessment is based on the evaluation of the available data and on the specificity of the analyzed parameters, as well as on the case studies reported in the specialized literature.

PROBABILISTIC RISK ASSESSMENT: CLASSICAL APPROACH

The main probabilistic approach to risk assessment is the Monte Carlo method (U.S. EPA 2001; APAT 2008). This method implies a random sampling of each variable of the assumed probability distribution, considering frequently all the variables mutually independent and is developed in successive phases. Each parameter is described throughout a Probability Density Function (PDF). At each iteration, by means of an algorithm of calculation, a random value between zero and one is generated that allows to extract a value for each variable of the correspondent probability distribution. It could be noticed that each number has the same probability to be sampled. The obtained values are inserted in the risk assessment model that generates in turn a number representing one of the possible risk values. At the next iteration the procedure is repeated originating another result for the risk; in this way a curve of the probability distribution of the risk values is obtained, each characterized by a determined probability of occurrence.

Once the risk probability function is determined, an accepted level of the risk has to be defined. The simplest criterion is that of considering acceptable the risk in the case in which the value correspondent to the 95° percentile is lower than the acceptable limit, both for the toxic hazard index and the carcinogenic risk. If otherwise the acceptable limits are comprised between the 50° and the 95° percentile, it is necessary to carry out a more in-depth study; in these cases a valid help is given by a sensitivity analysis (US EPA, 2001) that allows to individuate the parameters present in the risk assessment that mostly condition the final result that is to say the ones whose light variation impacts in a significant way on the curve of the distribution of risk. The available monetary resources will be addressed to those parameters in order to gain more knowledge and reduce the uncertainty by means of a more accurate sampling.

PROBABILISTIC RISK ASSESSMENT: GEOSTATISTICAL APPROACH

Geostatistical approaches have proved to be very useful in the case of environmental variables where the prediction uncertainty is required to support decision-making regarding remediation and the eventuality to proceed with further sampling in some areas.

In a risk assessment procedure a fundamental step is that of the characterization of the source of contamination both as far as its spatial definition and its Representative Concentration (CRS) are concerned. Many environmental investigations are aimed at making important decisions, as for example declaring an area potentially contaminated. A commonly used procedure consists in circumscribing all the locations in which the contamination exceeds a given value retained tolerable. The application of Indicator kriging permits to determine and to map the value of the probability of exceeding a given threshold value. This helps the responsible of the decisional process to delimit the vulnerable areas on the basis of the knowledge of the uncertainty associated to the examined phenomenon. The Indicator Kriging lends itself well also to the analysis of qualitative variables, allowing integration with data of quantitative nature.

Modeling the Spatial Pattern of a Continuous Attribute

Consider the problem of describing the spatial pattern of a continuous attribute z, say a pollutant concentration in groundwater. The information available consists of a set of n observations {z(u_α), α=1,2,….n, that can be explained in such a way:

- **Concentrations:** Z=values of the continuous variable (pollutant concentration in groundwater);
- **Locations:** u_α is one of n locations, with α=1,2,…,n;
- **Concentrations at locations:** $z(u_\alpha)$ is the value of Z at location uα (pollutant concentration in groundwater at location u_α).

Spatial patterns are usually described using the experimental semivariogram γ(h) which measures the average dissimilarity between data separated by a vector h. It is computed as half the average squared difference between the components of data pairs (Goovaerts, 1999):

$$\gamma(h) = \frac{1}{2N(h)} \sum_{\alpha=1}^{N(h)} \left[z(u_\alpha) - z(u_\alpha + h) \right]^2 \quad (1)$$

where N(h) is the number of data pairs within a given class of distance and direction. The semivariogram is theoretically a function that has to begin from 0 because coincident samples have the maximum similarity; anyway it shows a discontinuity at origin due to the nugget variance, that is to say the random component not spatially correlated, connected to the error measurement.

In environmental decision making processes there is often the necessity to know the locations where a variable exceeds a certain limit. The characterization of the spatial distribution of z-values above or below a given threshold value z_k requires a prior coding of each observation $z(u_\alpha)$ as an indicator datum $i(u_\alpha; z_k)$ defined as (Goovaerts, 1999):

$$I(u_\alpha; z_k) = \begin{cases} 1 & \text{if } z(u_\alpha) \geq z_k \\ 0 & \text{otherwise} \end{cases} \quad (2)$$

Indicator semivariograms can then be computed by substituting indicator data $i(u_\alpha; z_k)$ for z-data $z(u_\alpha)$ in Eq. (1) (Goovaerts, 1999):

$$\gamma_1\left(h;z_k\right) = \frac{1}{2N\left(h\right)}\sum_{\alpha=1}^{N(h)}\left[i\left(u_\alpha;z_k\right) - i\left(u_\alpha + h;z_k\right)\right]^2$$

(3)

The indicator variogram value $2\gamma_1(h; z_k)$ measures how often two z-values separated by a vector h are on opposite sides of the threshold value z_k. The greater is $\gamma_1(h; z_k)$ the less connected in space are the small or large values.

Kriging

The variogram, expressing the statistical dependency of two points as function of their distance is used by kriging, a sort of improved form of inverse distance weighting, in order to optimize prediction. Kriging consists essentially in a weighted moving average for the estimation of a not sampled point z(u) from the nearby points $z(u_\alpha)$. In the case of strictly stationary random function, with global mean *m*, the linear estimation kriging, referred to as Simple Kriging, assumes the form:

$$z^*(u) = \sum_{\alpha=1}^{n} \lambda_\alpha z\left(u_\alpha\right) + \left[1 - \sum_{\alpha=1}^{n}\lambda_\alpha\right] m$$

(4)

Where the symbol * indicates the calculated value; n is the number of measured values $z(u_\alpha)$ that take part in the estimation of the interpolated value, λ_α are the weights and m the global mean, supposed known and constant in all the examined area.

The most commonly used form of kriging is Ordinary Kriging, that takes into account the local fluctuations of the mean, limiting therefore the condition of stationariety to a neighbourhood of a point u. Differently from Simple Kriging, the mean is not supposed known and the algorithm of interpolation assumes the form:

$$z^*\left(u\right) = \sum_{\alpha=1}^{n}\lambda_\alpha z\left(u_\alpha\right)$$

(5)

The estimation implies therefore the determination of the weights in such a way as to satisfy the following two conditions:

1. the condition of unbiasedness of the estimator:

$$E[z^*(\mathbf{u}) - z(\mathbf{u})]$$

(6)

Where z*(u) and z(u) are, respectively, the estimated and the true value in the interpolated point u; the (6) lead to the following relation:

$$\sum \lambda_i = 1$$

(7)

That ensures that kriging is an exact interpolator, in the sense that in the sampled points it returns the measured value.

2. the condition of minimum variance, that implies the minimization of the estimation variance.

An important property of kriging is that the estimation variance depends only on the semivariogram model and on the configuration of the data locations in relation to the interpolated point and not on the observed values themselves.

Another property of kriging is represented by the fact that the interpolated value can be used with a degree of confidence, because an error term is calculated together with the estimation.

Anyway it needs to be pointed out that kriging is optimal and unbiased only on the condition that the model is correct. This can represent both one of the strengths of the procedure of kriging but also a weakness, because error variances can be seriously affected by the choice of the model.

In the case of randomly sparse sampling it is quite probable that estimation variances will be large and additional sampling will be necessary. Nugget or random variance, though it does not influence estimation, sets a lower limit to estimation precision at any krigged location. If the nugget variance is large, it may produce undesirable large estimation variances (Castrignanò, 2008).

Modeling of Local Uncertainty

The value of the attribute z at an unsampled location u is certainly affected by uncertainty.

The common geostatistical approach to model local uncertainty implies the calculation of a kriging estimate and the associated error variance. A more rigorous approach is to model the uncertainty about the unknown z(u) before and independently of the choice of a particular estimate for that unknown (Goovaerts, 1999). This means modeling the uncertainty about the z value at location u through a random variable Z(u) that is characterized by its distribution function (Goovaerts, 1999):

$$F(\mathbf{u}; z |(n)) = \text{Prob}\left\{ Z(\mathbf{u}) \geq z |(n) \right\} \qquad (8)$$

where the notation "|(n)" expresses the conditioning to the n data $z(u_a)$. The function F(u;z|(n)) is called conditional cumulative distribution function (ccdf). The ccdf fully models the uncertainty at location u since it gives the probability that the unknown is greater than any given threshold z (Van Meirvenne & Goovaerts, 2001). In order to determine a ccdf it is possible to make use of parametric or non - parametric approaches.

In a parametric approach, the determination of the ccdf is straightforward by means of the assignation of an analytical model that results completely defined by some parameters characteristic of the type of distribution. On the contrary, the non parametric algorithm is not based on an a-priori assumption about the form of the analytical expression of F(u;z|(n)), therefore it is more flexible. It consists of estimating the value of the ccdf for a series of K threshold values z_k, discretizing the range of variation of z (Van Meirvenne & Goovaerts, 2001):

$$F(\mathbf{u}; z_k |(n)) = \text{Prob}\left\{ Z(\mathbf{u}) \geq z_k |(n) \right\} \quad k = 1,2,...K$$

$$(9)$$

A non-parametric geostatistical estimation of ccdf values is based on the interpretation of the conditional probability (eq. 9) as the conditional expectation of an indicator random variable I (u; z_k) given the information (n) (Van Meirvenne & Goovaerts, 2001):

$$F(\mathbf{u}; z_k |(N)) = E\left\{ I(\mathbf{u}; z_k |(n) \right\} \qquad (10)$$

with I (u; z_k)=1 if Z(u)≥ z_k and zero otherwise, can be considered as the conditional probability in Eq.5. Ccdf values can thus be estimated by means of ordinary kriging of indicator transforms of data.

Indicator Coding in Presence of Soft Data

The indicator approach requires a preliminary coding of each observation $z(u_a)$ into a series of K values indicating whether the threshold z_k is exceeded a or not. If the measurement errors are assumed negligible compared to the spatial variability, observations are coded into hard (0 or 1) indicator data (Van Meirvenne & Goovaerts, 2001):

$$i(u_\alpha; z_k) = \begin{cases} 1 & \text{if } z(u_\alpha) \geq z_k \\ 0 & \text{otherwise} \end{cases} \qquad k = 1,2,...K$$

$$(11)$$

The major advantage of the indicator approach is its ability to incorporate in the algorithm of calculation different types of information: "soft" information, that is to say qualitative information, less precise, e.g., soil map or qualitative field observations such as the smell or color of contaminated soil in addition to direct measurements on the attribute of interest, that corresponds to the "hard" information. The only requirement is that each soft datum must be coded into a vector of K local prior probabilities of the type:

$$\Pr ob\left\{Z\left(u\right) \geq z_k \middle| specific\ local\ \inf ormation\ at\ u\right\} \quad k = 1,.....K$$

(12)

Goovaerts and Journel 1995 showed how these probabilities in Eq. 12 can be derived from the calibration of a soil map and expressed as the proportion, for each category of soil, of the sampled points exceeding the critical threshold in order to map the risk of overcoming the regulatory threshold in the soil.

Cokriging in Presence of Soft Data

Some properties are mutually dependent and this dependency can be used in the estimation process. When one or more variables are estimated as linear combination, exploiting both the spatial dependence and the one among the variables, the technique is called cokriging. Given a point u where the variable $z_i\left(u\right)$ has to be estimated, the ordinary cokriging estimator can be expressed:

$$Z_i^*\left(u\right) = \sum_{i=1}^{N} \sum_{\alpha_i=1}^{n_i(u)} \lambda_{\alpha_i} z_i\left(u_{\alpha_i}\right)$$

(13)

Where i indicates the index relating to the variable and α_i the one relating to the position.

When measurements are sparse or poorly correlated in space, the estimation of the primary attribute of interest is generally improved by accounting for secondary information originating from other related categorical or continuous attributes. This secondary information is said to be exhaustively sampled when it is available at all primary data locations and at all nodes of the estimation grid, e.g., a soil map or an elevation model. Secondary data can be incorporated using a multivariate extension of the kriging estima-

tor which is referred to as cokriging, where the global mean is replaced by local means derived from a calibration of the secondary information (Goovaerts, 1999):

$$Z_1^*\left(u\right) - m_1\left(u\right) = \sum_{i=1}^{N} \sum_{\alpha_i=1}^{n_i(u)} \lambda_{\alpha_i}\left(u\right)\left[Z_i\left(u_{\alpha_i}\right) - m_i\left(u_{\alpha_i}\right)\right]$$

(14)

where Z_1^* (u) is the cokriging linear regression estimator, m is the local mean, $\lambda_{\alpha 1}$(u) is the weight assigned to the primary datum $z_1(u_{\alpha 1})$ and $\lambda_{\alpha i(}$u) i>1 is the weight assigned to the secondary datum $z_i(u_{\alpha i})$. Cokriging is much more demanding than kriging in that N(N+1)/2 direct and cross semi-variograms must be inferred and jointly modeled, and a large cokriging system must be solved.

Delimitation of Potentially Contaminated Area (Indicator Kriging)

This approach consists in delineating all locations where the pollutant concentration is above the threshold value; this requires the estimation of the contaminant concentration in not sampled points and therefore the delineation of those areas enclosed inside the isoline corresponding to the threshold value. Such a procedure doesn't exclude the presence of uncertainty because, due to the existence of the estimation error, the risk can be run to declare "potentially contaminated" a "clean" area and vice versa "clean" a "potentially contaminated" area and, in the latter case, to return it to legitimate uses. Those two types of erroneous classifications can be evaluated from the probability that the value of the variable z for the concentration of the contaminant in a not sampled point u doesn't exceed a given threshold z_k, (Castrignanò & Buttafuoco, 2004). Indicating with F the conditional cumulative distribution function of probability, it follows that:

1. the risk α(u) (of a false positive or of over-estimation), that is to say the probability of declaring erroneously a location u "potentially contaminated" is given by:

$$\alpha(u) = \Pr ob\left\{ Z\left(u\right) \leq z_k \middle| z^*\left(u\right) > z_k\left(n\right) \right\} = F\left(u; z_k \middle| \left(n\right)\right)$$

(15)

For all the locations u such that the kriging estimation z*(u)>z$_k$. The symbol (n) means conditional to the n sampling survey data. In other words α(u) measures the probability that the effective value Z(u) is lower than the critical threshold z$_k$, whereas the kriging estimated value z*(u) exceeds it;

2. the risk β(u) (of a false negative or of under-estimation), that is to say the probability of declaring erroneously a location u "clean" is given by:

$$\beta(u) = \Pr ob\left\{ Z\left(u\right) > z_k \middle| z^*\left(u\right) \leq z_k\left(n\right) \right\} = 1 - F\left(u; z_k \middle| \left(n\right)\right)$$

(16)

For all the locations u for which the kriging estimation z*(u)≤z$_k$. More explicitly, β(u) measures the probability that the effective value is higher than the critical threshold, while the kriging estimation is lower. A logical deduction defines the risk β(u) where the risk α(u) is zero and conversely.

By means of the maps of probability of exceeding a threshold fixed by the legislation it is possible to govern the acceptable risk level. The major difficulty found in this approach consists in choosing an appropriate level of probability for each type of risk such to initialize any intervention on the area (Goovaerts, 1999). The decision proves to be easy in the areas where the probability is high or low, while it gets more complicated in the other areas where it assumes intermediate values variable from 0.3 to 0.7. The threshold value of probability is absolutely subjective and variable according to the specificity of the case study.

Source Representative Concentration (CRS): UCL Method

The Source Representative Concentration, together with the data coming from the characterization, constitutes the input for a site specific risk assessment. Being its value directly proportional to the calculated risk, it can be easily inferred how its estimation accuracy is fundamental for the correct execution of the whole Risk Assessment procedure.

The Upper Confidential Limit UCL 95% of the mean value provides a representative estimation of the Source Representative Concentration; statistically the UCL 95% of a mean is defined as a value that, when calculated repeatedly for randomly drawn subsets of site data, equals or exceeds the true mean 95% of the times (U.S.EPA, 2001). This value is used for calculating the Source Representative Concentration as it represents a highly conservative estimation of the true mean value, moreover it takes into account the uncertainty linked the estimation of the mean, due to limited sampling data.

Calculation of UCL for Normal Distribution: Student' s T Method

The calculation of UCL of the mean varies according to the type of data distribution. If the data distribution can be approximated as normal, the most used method for the calculation of the UCL95 is the Student's T method, according to which:

$$UCL_{95} = C_m + t \times \bar{\varepsilon}$$

(17)

Cm represents the mean concentration and t the Student' s T value, tabulated in function of the level of approximation required (in case of UCL 95% the level of approximation is 0.05).

This procedure is articulated in the following phases:

1. calculation of the mean concentration
2. calculation of the error
3. determination of Student's t value
4. calculation of UCL95 of the mean
   1) Using the data measured during a characterization campaign it is possible to represent the punctual concentration values on the nodes of a regular-mesh grid (Figure 1) and their corresponding errors. The C_m value is given by the relation (Dacquino, 2004):

$$C_m = \frac{\sum_{i=1}^{n}\sum_{j=1}^{m} C_{ij} b_{ij}}{B} = \frac{\sum_{i=1}^{n}\sum_{j=1}^{m} C_{ij}}{n \times m} \quad (18)$$

In which C_{ij} represents the concentration calculated by means of the application of kriging in correspondence of node ij (row i, column j), n and m are respectively the rows and the columns of the grid, b_{ij} is the area of the mesh ij (Figure 1) and, being the grid regular:

$$b_{ij} = \cos t = \frac{B}{n \times m} \quad (19)$$

2) From the (18) it is possible to obtain the error value by means of the relation (Dacquino, 2004):

$$\bar{\varepsilon} = \sqrt{\frac{\sum_{i=1}^{n}\sum_{j=1}^{m} \varepsilon_{ij}^2 b_{ij}^2}{B^2}} = \sqrt{\frac{\sum_{i=1}^{n}\sum_{j=1}^{m} \varepsilon_{ij}^2}{\left(n \times m\right)^2}} = \frac{\sqrt{\sum_{i=1}^{n}\sum_{j=1}^{m} \varepsilon_{ij}^2}}{n \times m} \quad (20)$$

In which ε_{ij} represents the smallest possible error, calculated through application of kriging at node ij.

Figure 1. sampling points on a regular–mesh grid

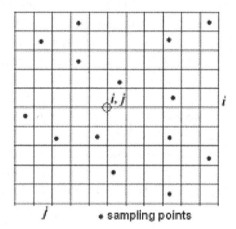

3) In the Student table (Gilbert, 1987) the t value is found, univocally determined once known the level of approximation, that is 0.05 and n×m-1, where n×m is the number of cells. In the table, for n×m-1≥ 120, tn×m-1,0.95 = N0.95, where N is the normal distribution of the data.

In this way the Source Representative Concentration can be obtained from the formulation:

$$C_R = UCL_{95} = C_m + t_{n \times m -1, 0.95} \times \bar{\varepsilon} = C_m + N_{0.95} \times \bar{\varepsilon} \quad (21)$$

Geostatistics for Characterization and Monitoring

By means of the application of geostatistical techniques it is possible to get to the definition of a model able to describe the spatial variability of parameters, in order to make operations of inference in localizations where no information is available, estimating also the associated error. The knowledge of the structure of the variability and of the variance of the estimation permits to improve soil and groundwater sampling campaigns, in terms of lower costs both for sampling and for laboratory analyses. Moreover the application of geostatistical techniques makes it possible to design a sampling scheme making reference to optimization criteria in function of the pursued aim. The geostatistical criterion can allow to insert new points where the knowledge is more approximate and to eliminate others where the information is redundant.

Uncertainty assessment is a preliminary step in decision-making processes, such as delineation of hazardous areas. In the process of characterization and remediation, multistage sampling involves an interruption of the sampling process until the data are available for estimating contaminant concentrations at unsampled locations, which will guide the selection of locations where additional data are needed (Castrignanò, 2008). This can improve the cost-effectiveness of a sampling campaign.

Optimal Sampling Design for Characterization

In the field of optimizing the efficiency of sampling, the pursued aim is that of minimizing the estimation error; a typical optimal sampling problem consists in searching for a set of samples which satisfies the criterion of optimization based on the minimization of the estimation variance (Castrignanò, 2008). The expression of the Kriging variance depends uniquely on the semivariogram of the variable, and not on its punctual values. Therefore if the semivariogram has been identified, the kriging variances can be determined independently from the knowledge of the values that the variable assumes in correspondence of different points. This is an important property on which the "fictitious-point method" (Delhomme, 1978) is based. This method consists in adding a fictitious point, with a value of the variable arbitrarily fixed, calculating the Kriging variance and comparing it with the previous one. Once added a fictitious point in a position

(u) of the domain, a "gain in precision" P can be defined as the ratio:

$$P = \frac{\left[\sigma_1^2\left(u\right) - \sigma_2^2\left(u\right)\right]}{\sigma_1^2\left(u\right)}$$

(22)

where $\sigma_1^2(u)$ represents the Kriging variance in the point (u) calculated on the basis of a number of measurements and $\sigma_2^2(u)$ the one after adding the fictitious point.

It is then possible to trace curves of isoprofit of precision to define, in correspondence of the maximum values, the preferential localization of the new measurement points.

The procedure of eliminating the redundant measurement points has been applied in Tuscany (Beretta et al., 1995) by means of an inverse procedure to the one proposed by Delhomme (1978). This method consists in removing points from the network estimating the value of the variable in the single eliminated points on the basis of the values of the variable assumed in nearby points; consequently the isoloss of information is evaluated by means of the relation:

$$I = Z_i^* - Z_i$$

(23)

where Z_i^* represents the value of the estimated variable after suppressing the value Z_i. One fixed the maximum number of measurable points, on the basis of technical-economical evaluations, this procedure is applied by means of a "trial and error" method up to the achievement of a configuration that gives the minimum loss of information.

Sampling design has to be considered therefore as a multi-stage procedure. This means that in order to optimize sampling the variogram has to be known, but the variogram itself must be obtained by sampling. It is necessary therefore to split the sampling resources between those required for establishing the variogram and those

Figure 2. geostatistics within the process of characterization and monitoring

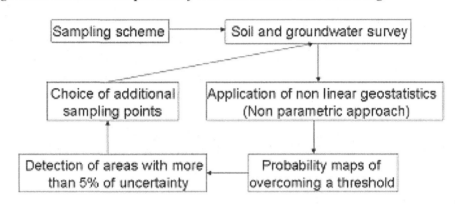

required to complete the sampling procedure (Castrignanò, 2008).

Monitoring

The evolution of the level of contamination in an area has to be monitored in time, in such a way as to guarantee that the temporal trend of pollutant concentrations corresponds to what was planned in the remediation project.

The application of geostatistics permits to define the degree and geometry of regionalization of the pollutants in a specified area and represents therefore a useful tool during the monitoring phase for planning data sampling in order to maximize the information at parity of costs.

The block diagram in Figure 2 schematizes this procedure. Once completed the monitoring of the area by means of soil and groundwater survey, the application of non parametric geostatistics permits to determine the probability maps of overcoming a specified threshold. The delineation of that portion of the area characterized by a probability higher than 0.05 that the concentration values of the study variable exceed a given threshold of intervention (both the CSC for the delimitation of the potentially contaminated areas and the CSR for the delineation of the areas to remediate) proves to be a useful tool to determine further points in which to intensify the sampling. In order to predict

polluted (or potentially polluted) zones generally the areas with a probability higher than 5% of exceeding the CSR (or CSC) values are delineated. As it is highly improbable that parts of the areas with low probability of exceeding this value are polluted, these are excluded from further sampling. In this way both the geostatistical (reduction of the estimation variance) and the field knowledge, both fundamental in the planning phase, increase progressively during the sampling, in contrast to the case of non-interactive procedures in which the data can be evaluated just "a posteriori", once all samples have been conclusively collected.

Garcia and Froidevaux (1997) used as a measure of uncertainty the absolute difference between the probability of exceeding the critical threshold z_k and the closest of the two low and high risk probability thresholds 0.2 and 0.8; they considered that the uncertainty is negligible at locations where the probability of contamination is either high (>0.8) or low (<0.2). This method doesn't take into account the uncertainty in the predictions of the site-specific threshold zk.

Van Meirvenne & Goovaerts (2001) proposed as a sampling criterion the ratio of the standard deviation to the absolute value of the mean of the local cumulative distribution of the difference (D(u)) between the pollutant concentration and the threshold:

$$u \text{ is sampled if } CV(u) = \frac{\sqrt{Var\left[D(u)\right]}}{\left|E\left[D(u)\right]\right|} \text{ is } l\arg e$$

(24)

This type of coefficient of variation CV is large if the denominator is small, that is if the simulated pollutant concentrations and threshold values are close and so the uncertainty about the exceedence of that threshold becomes large. For the same average difference, the CV will be larger if the variance of the distribution of differences is large (Van Meirvenne & Goovaerts, 2001).

STOCHASTIC SIMULATIONS

The explained geostatistical approach bases itself on the estimation of the kriging variances that are independent from the calculated values, depending uniquely on the geometric disposition of the samples and the adopted variogram model. In most studies on polluted areas, the observed variances show a proportional effect on the measured values, therefore their utilization in the calculation of confidence intervals can result somewhat fishy (Castrignanò et al., 2002). A development on geostatistics that represents an alternative technique of spatial modeling, is the stochastic simulation, particularly adapt in those applications in which more importance is attached to global statistics rather than to local accuracy. In fact the simulation attempts at reproducing the basic statistical characteristics of the data, such as the histogram and the spatial continuity, calculating a series of alternative stochastic images (equiprobable) of the random process (simulations) and thus carrying out a statistical analysis on them for the evaluation of the uncertainty.

These techniques were developed on purpose in order to give an answer to the inadequacy of the measures of spatial uncertainty according to the traditional statistic methods, unluckily are still neither sufficiently known nor applied either in scientific or in operative contexts (Castrignanò et al., 2002). Even this approach may be defined probabilistic, as it recognizes explicitly the uncertainty associated to the estimation of any environmental variable and permits to evaluate this uncertainty from the analysis of a series of stochastic simulations carried out on the area. Each of these simulations provides a map of the pollutant concentration in the study area and is consistent with the set of data and their structures of spatial continuity: each map consequently can be considered as an equally probable description of the unknown reality.

CASE STUDIES

Case Study I: Combination of Indicator Kriging and Land Use Information

This example is taken from a study of Castrignanò et al. (2004). An application of the indicator variable approach is made to a pollution case study, regarding a derelict manufacturing factory located in Apulia Region (South- East of Italy).

Arsenic and Land use Indicator Coding

The following information available over the study area has been combined:

- $z(u_\alpha)$ = Values of arsenic concentration in groundwater (expressed in μg/l) at n location u_α, α=1,2,…,n;
- $l(u_\alpha)$ = Land use information, at all locations within the area.

The z-values represent hard information in the sense that they are direct measurements of arsenic content. On the contrary, land use information provides only indirect (soft) information about the values of the variable Z. Using both hard and soft data the approach is aimed at assessing the probability that the value of z at any unsampled area u is greater than a given critical threshold z_k. Indicating with F the conditional cumulative distribution function (ccdf) of the variable Z, according with the (9) it results:

$$F (u; z_k |(n_1+n_2))=\text{Prob}\{Z(u) \geq z_k|(n_1+n_2) \} \quad (25)$$

where the notation $|(n_1+n_2)$ expresses the conditioning to n_1 hard data $\{z(u\alpha); \alpha=1,2,\ldots,n_1\}$ and n_2 soft data $\{ l(u_\alpha); \alpha=1,2,\ldots, n_2 \}$ retained in the neighbourhood of u.

In this approach the probability distribution is regarded, according with the (10), as the conditional expectation of the indicator random variable $I(u;z_k)$, given the information set (n_1+n_2):

$$F(u; z_k |(n_1+n_2)) = E\{ I(u; z_k)|(n_1+n_2) \} \quad (26)$$

$$\text{with } I(u_0;z_k) = \begin{cases} 1 & \text{if } Z(u_0) \geq z_k \\ 0 & \text{otherwise} \end{cases} \quad (27)$$

The ccdf $F(u; z_k|n_1+n_2))$ can be estimated by (co)kriging the indicator $I(u;z_k)$ using indicator transform of hard and soft data.

The indicator approach requires a preliminary coding of the hard and soft data into local hard and soft "prior" probabilities:

$$\text{Prob } \{Z(u) \geq z_k | \text{ local information at u} \} \quad (28)$$

The term "local prior" means that the probability in Eq. 28 originates from hard and soft information at location u, prior to any updating based on neighbouring data. The final target of this approach is updating this local prior probability in the posterior probability (Eq. 26). Thus, the prior information can take one of the following forms:

- local hard information data $i(u_0;z_k)$, with binary indicators defined by Eq. 27;

- local soft indicator data $y_1(u_0; l_k)$ assuming values within the interval [0,1].

The next step has been the codification in indicator variable of the different types of information available. For $z(u_a)$, being a continuous variable, the critical legislative threshold value of 10 µg/l has been used. The soft variable has been calibrated by estimating the marginal distribution of the samples with concentrations higher than 10 µg/l relatively to each type of area, as proposed by Goovaerts & Journel (1995). The marginal proportions of exceeding the critical value of 10 µg/l, relatively to each homogeneous area are reported in Tab 1.

As illustrated before, the random function approach amounts to modeling the two unknown values as realizations of two spatially dependent random variables. According to this approach, the local hard and soft indicator data $i(u_0;z_k)$ and $y_1(u_0; l_k)$ are interpreted as realizations of two correlated random functions, $I(u_0;z_k)$ and $Y_1(u_0; l_k)$ that can be processed together by cokriging, where $I(u_0;z_k)$ is the primary variable and $Y_1(u_0; l_k)$ the secondary variable.

Cokriging of Hard and Soft Data

Figure 3a shows the spatial distribution of arsenic concentration in groundwater obtained by means of Ordinary Kriging.

It is possible to observe that the concentration of arsenic is higher in the middle and in the southern zone, whereas the values decrease below the critical value at north and north-east.

The arsenic distribution seems to be concentrated in specific areas and for this reason it has been decided to investigate further introducing the soft information, represented by land use information and evaluating the probability of risk. On the basis of the available information about the activities that characterized each section of

Figure 3. a) Map of the krigged estimates of arsenic concentration in groundwater b) Homogeneous areas according to land use information (modif. from Castrignanò et al, 2004)

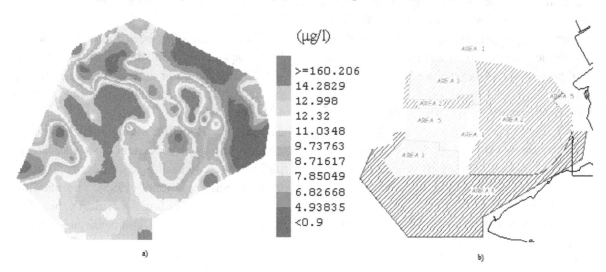

(μg/l)

>=160.206
14.2829
12.998
12.32
11.0348
9.73763
8.71617
7.85049
6.82668
4.93835
<0.9

a)

b)

the study area in the past, distant areas that were similar for activity have been pooled, arriving at the definition of 5 homogeneous areas (Figure 3b) defined in such a way:

- Area 1: deposit;
- Area 2: oil storage tank;
- Area 3: free area;
- Area 4: external area;
- Area 5: water treatment and implantations.

Applying the indicator variable (co)kriging, two types of maps have been obtained:

- Probability map of arsenic exceeding the compulsory threshold (Figure 4a);
- Marginal probability map of arsenic exceeding the compulsory threshold relative to each area (Figure 4b).

The risk of As pollution, expressed as probability of exceeding, is greater than 80% in two specific areas, the area 4 and the area 5 along the coast line. The risk α of a false positive is contoured in Figure 5a and shows that the probability of overestimation is mostly smaller than 40%. The risk β, or of a false negative, is contoured

in Figure 5b and shows that the probability of underestimation is mostly smaller than 30%, with the exclusion of a small area westbound where the probability is 60%. The impact of the risk α can be easily evaluated because it is linked to the cost of an unnecessary remediation, but it does not directly involve other considerations of non-monetary type, such as human health, that are more difficult to be estimated and are instead involved in the risk β.

CONCLUSION

In this paragraph an approach has been described where the available information, both hard and soft under the form of prior probability distribution, is coded as a set of indicator variables. The non-parametric method yielded in two specific areas (area 4 and area 5) a high probability of exceeding the critical threshold for arsenic pollution in groundwater. The presence of this pollutant is not linked with the past activities of the manufacturing factory, because from information given by the control authorities of the district, high concentra-

Figure 4. a) Probability map of arsenic exceeding the compulsory threshold b) Marginal probability map of arsenic exceeding the threshold relatively to each area (modif. from Castrignanò et al, 2004)

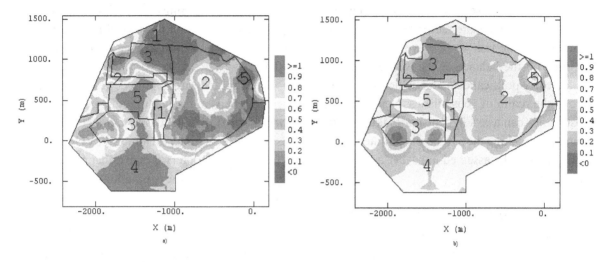

Figure 5 Contoured map of the risk α (a) and β (b) (modif. from Castrignanò et al, 2004)

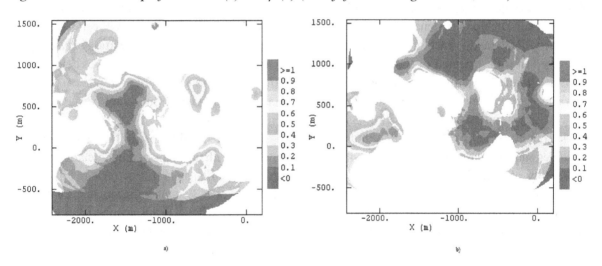

Table 1. Marginal proportions of exceeding the critical value of 10 µg/l, relatively to each homogeneous area (Castrignanò et al, 2004)

Homogeneous Areas	N. of Piezometers	Samples exceeding threshold	Exceedance Proportion
Area 1	18	7	7/18=0.38
Area 2	24	6	7/25=0.24
Area 3	20	5	5/20=0.16
Area 4	20	12	12/20=0.60
Area 5	12	9	9/12=0.75
	Σ = 94	Σ = 40	

tions were found in many samples of water drawn from other zones of the region, even not close to the study area. These probability distributions have allowed to estimate the risk α, or of a false positive, and the risk β, or of a false negative. Deciding on the balance of the two risks α and β is a clearly political decision, which falls well beyond the realm of geostatistics. Nevertheless, geostatistics can assist in decision-making management by ranking the potentially polluted areas on the basis of the assessed impact (Castrignanò et al., 2004).

Case Study II: Indicator Cokriging in Presence of Censored Data

This example is taken from a study of Castrignanò et al (2007). In the case study, the examined variables are the concentrations of Vinyl Chloride (VC), cis-1,2-Dichloroethylene (cDCE), Trichloroethylene (TCE) and Tetrachloroethylene (PCE), expressed in µg/l, detected in a wide industrial district located in Apulia. These pollutants are characterized by some values below the detection limit of the instrument. Their elaboration has been carried out by means of cokriging of the indicator variables and for each single pollutant the map of probability of exceeding the detection limit has been drawn up. From the analysis of these maps (Figure 6) it is possible to make some considerations on the spatial variability of the data:

- VC concentrates much of the values below the detection limit (0.05 µg/l) in the northern part;
- cDCE shows a low number of values below the detection limit (0.005 µg/l) concentrated in a more central area;
- TCE and PCE show values below the detection limit (0.02 and 0.05 µg/l, respectively), mostly concentrated in a central area.

The next phase of the analysis has concerned the drawing up of concentration maps applying kriging (or co-kriging) for each contaminant in those areas in which the probability of exceeding the detection limit proves to be higher than 90%.

In Figg. 7-8 are reported, respectively, the krigged maps in the mean, in the best and in the worst scenario of potential contamination obtained using confidence interval limits, for VC and cDCE. The confidence interval maps, that represent the variation range for the contamination values with an error of 5%, show a spot area to the south for both pollutants.

As far as TCE and PCE are concerned, the areas in which the values are higher than the detection limit prove to be wider than for VC and cDCE. Moreover, from the visualization of the maps, a high similarity between the spatial distributions of the contaminants TCE and PCE can be detected. The existence of a high correlation between TCE and PCE, confirmed by their values being jointly low in some zones and high in others (Figure 6) has allowed to carry out a multivariate analysis on the two variables.

The cokrigged maps of TCE and PCE look coherent with the maps of the indicator variables, showing similar spatial structures. In Figure 9 are shown the TCE concentration maps, obtained through co-kriging, in the mean, in the best and the worst scenario of potential contamination, drawn up by making use of 95% confidence interval limits. The confidence maps show large differences between the maximum and the minimum values, nevertheless, they identify a spot area of higher values down south.

In Figure 10 are shown the same concentration maps obtained for PCE, in the mean, in the best and the worst scenario of potential contamination. The last two maps show very different PCE values, but they detect two common spot areas, one more southern and the other one more northern, with an error $\leq 5\%$. In this way it has been possible to

Figure 6. maps of the probability of exceeding the detection limit for PCE, TCE, cDCE and VC (modif. from Castrignanò et al, 2007)

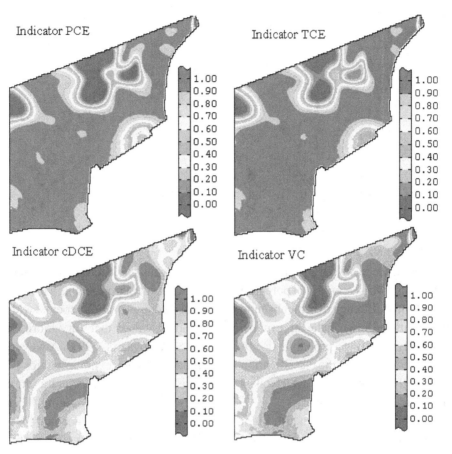

Figure 7. Maps of krigged VC concentration in the mean, in the best and in the worst scenario of potential contamination, with the spot area highlighted (modif. from Castrignanò et al, 2007)

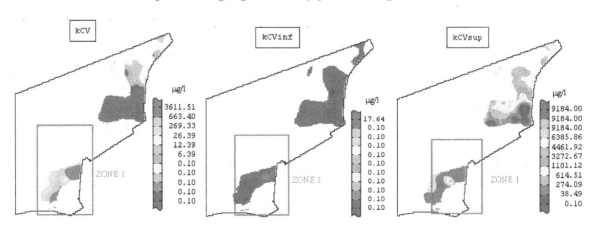

Figure 8. Maps of krigged cDCE concentration in the mean, in the best and in the worst scenario of potential contamination (spot area highlighted) (modif. from Castrignanò et al, 2007)

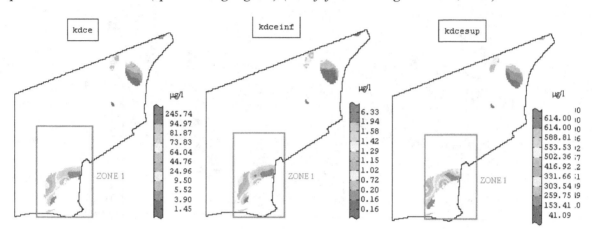

obtain three different scenarios for the areas: the mean, the best, and the worst scenario of potential contamination. The high differences in the absolute values of concentration, shown in the three maps, remark the necessity to follow a probabilistic approach (confidence interval) in the classification process of potentially polluted areas, which takes into account the prediction uncertainty.

Synthesizing the information obtained through the interpolation of the considered substances, it is possible to conclude observing that two principal spot areas can be identified; one more northern (Zone 2), the other one more southern (Zone 1), which suggest the presence of two centers of hazard (Castrignanò et al., 2007).

Conclusion

The application of indicator kriging in presence of censored data has proved to be a useful tool for the interpretation of the physical processes controlling contamination and therefore in decision-making processes, such as delineation of hazardous areas. In the study case, the application of this procedure has allowed to identify two principal spot areas which suggest the presence of two centers of hazard.

In many environmental applications, as in the two case studies presented, a few random hot spots of large concentrations coexist with a background of small values that vary more continuously in space (Goovaerts, 1999). A way to attenuate the impact of these extreme values is to use robust statistics and estimators such as the non parametric approach of indicator kriging. The application of this approach can also account for secondary data through a soft indicator coding of information, as done in the first case study.

Case Study III: Comparison of Different Approaches

In this study different geostatistical elaborations have been carried out for the determination of the dimension of the Source Representative Area and Concentration and the achieved results have been compared with the ones obtained by a classical deterministic approach. The case study regards a dismissed industrial area located in Apulia, for which an analysis has been carried out for the determination of the risk in relation to groundwater contamination by arsenic. The analysis has pertained to the determination of the potentially contaminated area and the individuation of the

Figure 9. Maps of cokrigged TCE concentration in the mean, in the best and in the worst scenario of potential contamination (spot area highlighted) (modif. from Castrignanò et al, 2007)

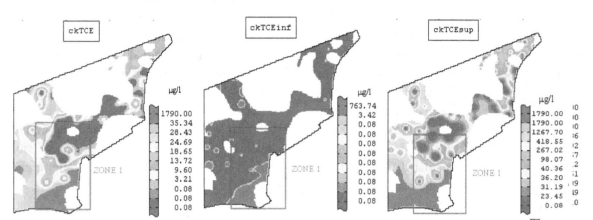

Source Representative Concentration value in correspondence of the source of pollution in groundwater. The examined approaches are:

- I approach: elaborations carried out following the classical risk assessment approach, according to the indications of ARPA Manual (2008) and the software ProUCL (U.S. EPA, 2007).
- II approach: area delimited by the isochon (CSC) of 10µg/l, obtained by means of geostatistical interpolation and determination of the Source Representative Concentration on the basis of the representative UCL value obtained from the estimated values of the variable inside this area.
- III approach: for defined values of probability of exceeding the CSC of the variable, the most vulnerable areas are delimited; the Source Representative Concentration values for each defined area are determined as representative UCL values obtained from the estimated values of the variable inside each area.

Figure 10. Maps of cokrigged PCE concentration in the mean, in the best and in the worst scenario of potential contamination (spot areas highlighted)(modif. from Castrignanò et al, 2007)

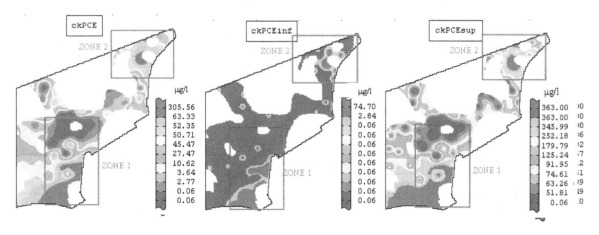

Approach 1: Classic Risk Assessment

The base map of the location of piezometers has been drawn up (Figure 11a) in order to evaluate the uniformity in their spatial distribution and therefore the possible presence of clusters and/or of not sampled areas. The statistical parameters reported in Table 2 have been determined: mean, standard deviation, coefficient of variation, skewness and kurtosis, and the histogram of the relative frequencies has been calculated (Figure 11b). From table 2, concerning the basic descriptive statistics, it can be pointed out how the distribution of the pollutant shows high positive values of skewness and kurtosis; the histogram of the relative frequencies is not symmetric because of the presence of high outliers, that means that the variable has considerable displacements from the normal distribution. The Source Representative

Concentration value has been obtained by means of Chebyshev's inequality. The tests carried out by means of software ProUCL have recognized as representative a value of the Source Representative Concentration equal to 53,0779 μg/l, that corresponds to the 97.5% of the mean. For this approach, the surficial extension of the potentially contaminated area is individuated from the area delimited by the most external sampling meshes containing a point in which at least one contaminant has been detected with a concentration higher than CSC (APAT, 2008).

Approach 2: Geostatistical Approach: UCL Method

The area in which the concentration values exceed the CSC value for arsenic in groundwater (10μg/l) has been determined by means of geostatistic

Figure 11. a) Base map of georeferenced arsenic values b) histogram of relative frequencies of arsenic

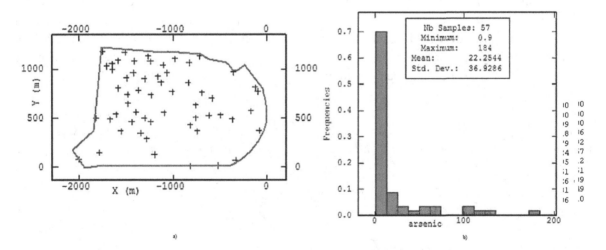

Table 2. Significant statistical parameters

Var	Mean μg/l	Min μg/l	Max μg/l	StD. μg/l	Skewness	Kurtosis	Coeff of variation (%)
As	22.25	1	184	36.93	2.54	9.22	1.66

Figure 12. a) experimental and theoretic variogram b) map of the estimated values for arsenic (in µg/l) with isoline of threshold value 10µg/l

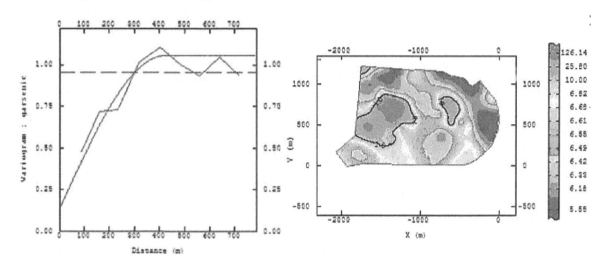

elaboration. The original variable has been preemptively normalized and standardized at mean zero and unitary variance by means of Gaussian anamorphosis. The analysis of the variogram map of arsenic didn't reveal particular anisotropies, therefore the process has been assumed as isotropic. The experimental variogram of the normalized standard variable has been calculated and a theoretic model has been adapted to it, characterized by nugget effect and a spherical structure with range = 422.09 m (Figure 12a).

The compatibility between the amount of data and the structural model has been verified by means of a cross-validation test. The map of arsenic concentration has been obtained after back transforming the values of the standard Gaussian variable interpolated by means of Ordinary Kriging and is reported in Figure 12b. In the same figure the black line evidences the area of the Source of Contamination included in the isochon 10 µg/l.

The Source Representative Concentration for this area can be obtained by means of the UCL method: considering the values of the variable estimated by means of polygonal kriging inside

the study area, tests with ProUCL software are carried out in order to determine the corresponding value of UCL. Considering the source area in Figure 12b, and carrying out tests (with ProUCL software) on the data estimated by means of polygonal kriging inside the area, the obtained Source Representative Concentration value is equal to UCL = 40.58 µg/l.

Approach 3: Geostatistical Approach: Indicator Kriging

The application of Indicator Kriging has implied the codification of the variable arsenic into a binary indicator variable, that assumes either the value 1 or 0 according as it exceeds or not the CSC of 10µg/l. After the codification the variogram of the indicator variable has been constructed and it has been modelled by means of a set of authorized theoretic functions (Figure 13a). A theoretic variogram has been determined, made up of three structures: 1) nugget effect; 2) spherical model with range=209.17m; 3) spherical model with range=567.13m. The application of Indicator Kriging has permitted to represent the

Figure 13. a) experimental and theoretic variogram of the variable b) map of the error

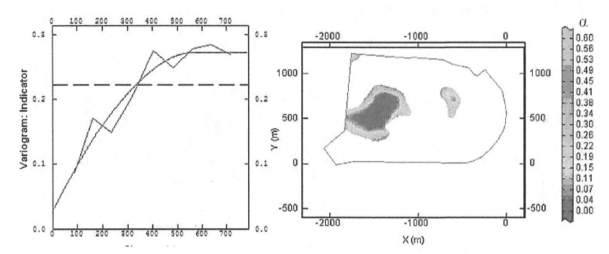

lines at equal probability of exceeding the CSC, each delimiting an area of specific geometry. Starting from the values estimated by means of polygonal kriging inside each area it has been possible to determine the probability distribution of the considered variable. It can be pointed out that the acceptation of a finite probability of exceeding implies admitting the presence of an "overestimation" (α) or an "underestimation" error (β): for the examined case, the map of the α error is reported in Figure 13b.

In Figure 14 are shown the areas enclosed by the different curves of probability of exceeding the threshold value. In correspondence of a high probability (close to 1) the area is much more restricted and circumscribed than in correspondence of a low probability (0.3). For each of these source areas it is possible to determine the Source Representative Concentration value with the UCL method.

In table 3 is reported, for each probability, the maximum width (S_w) in direction orthogonal to flow, of the areas enclosed by the corresponding isolines and the value of UCL determined by means of a test carried out with data estimated applying polygonal kriging inside those areas.

The tests show above all, for all the examined probabilities of exceeding, that the probability

density curve referred to the values is not parametric.

The graph in Figure 15a proposes the polynomial regression between UCL and probability of exceeding; it is possible to point out that, in relation to the latter the values of the former increase up to the maximum value of 59.42 µg/l in correspondence of a probability of exceeding the CSC of 90%. In Figure 15b analogous regression is proposed between the width of the Potentially Contaminated Area and the probability of exceeding.

Probabilistic Risk Assessment

Once having obtained through geostatistics the probability distributions that characterized the most significant variables, it is possible to proceed with Monte Carlo Analysis to determine the risk probability function and subsequently to define the acceptable risk level. Once fixed a specific scenario of exposure, the expression of the risk depends on the transversal dimension of the source of contamination (S_w) and on the concentration in the point of exposure (CPOE) that, in turn, depends on the value of Source Representative Concentration.

Making explicit in the analytic expression of

Figure 14. Areas enclosed by the curves of probability of exceeding the threshold value

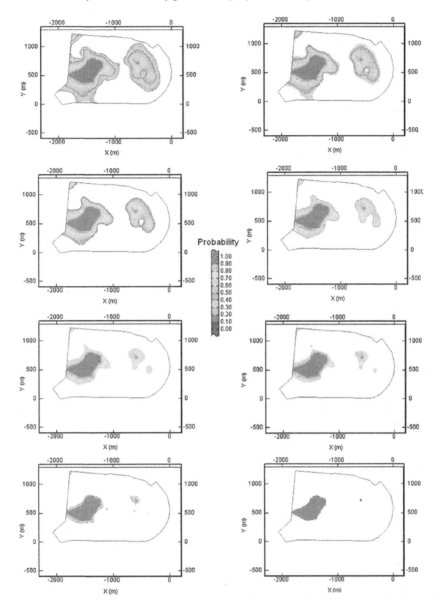

Figure 15. a) UCL as a function of probability of exceeding the threshold value of arsenic and corresponding polynomial regression law b) S_w as a function of probability of exceeding the threshold value of arsenic and corresponding linear regression law

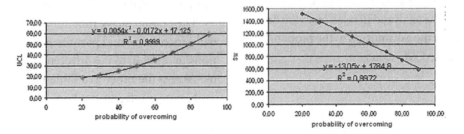

Table 3. Synthesis of the UCL values and the S_w dimension for different probability values

Probability of exceeding %	UCL (µg/l)	S_w (m)
20	18.74	1517
30	21.68	1375
40	25.29	1269
50	29.74	1138
60	35.44	1027
70	42.22	882
80	50.45	746
90	59.42	582

Figure 16. Risk in function of the probability of exceeding the CSC value 10µg/l

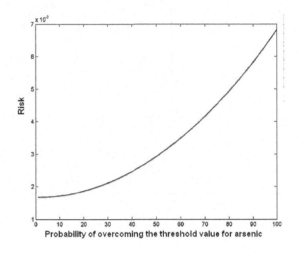

the risk the formulations obtained previously for the two parameters S_w and Source Representative Concentration, it is possible to analyze the variability of the risk throughout the variability of these parameters.

The distribution of the concentration C(x) along the longitudinal direction of flow x in contaminated groundwater can be expressed by the Domenico solution (APAT, 2008)). In the hypothesis of an aquifer of limited thickness in which the vertical dispersion can be neglected, with a source of contamination characterized by a width $S_w \geq 8\sqrt{\alpha_y x}$, assuming the value of the error function equal to 1, the Domenico equation assumes a simplified form. For the industrial area in study, fixed a defined area source of contamination in groundwater with corresponding representative concentration, assuming groundwater ingestion as only modality of exposure, by means of inserting the Domenico simplified expression in the risk formulation it is possible to obtain the "Risk Function" whose expression can be analyzed in relation to the decisions chosen for the assumption of the probability of exceeding the CSC value.

$$R = C_R \exp\left\{\left(\frac{x}{2\alpha_x}\right)\left[1 - \sqrt{1 + \frac{4\lambda_1 \alpha_x R_i}{v_e}}\right]\right\} \cdot erf\left[\frac{S_w}{4\sqrt{\alpha_y x}}\right] * EM * T \quad (29)$$

Being:

E_M = daily effective exposure;

T = pollutant toxicity;

α_x = longitudinal dispersivity [L];

α_y = transversal dispersivity [L];

v_e = groundwater effective velocity [L·T^{-1}];

λ_1 = 1st order decay coefficient for the contaminant in dissolved phase [T^{-1}];

R_i = delay coefficient in groundwater

In the case study, assuming the values of the exposure parameters recommended by APAT Manual (2008) and considering, according to the legislation, the point of compliance distant 500 m, expressing the risk in function of the probability of exceeding the Threshold Concentration of Contamination, the function reported in Figure 16 can be obtained.

The obtained risk function appears monotonically increasing and permits to carry out evaluations in relation to the different operable choices, using also the other available information.

For example, in case in which elements of

verification are needed for the eventuality of accepting the risk value corresponding to the probability of overcoming of 90%, it could be possible to ascertain that, outside the surface area enclosed by this probability (Figure 14) not relevant underestimation errors are detected, that is to say values flatly lower than 10% in most of the area reaching values of 40% just in some restricted zones.

Conclusions: Comparison of Three Approaches

This study is aimed at offering alternatives to the classical risk assessment that bases itself on the "worst case" principle, providing the possibility to quantify and integrate the uncertainty and variability of input parameters in the risk assessment procedure by means of the application of geostatistical techniques.

In this study the following elaborations have been carried out:

• determination of Source Representative Concentration by means of classical and geostatistic methods
• delimitation of potentially contaminated areas by means of Indicator Kriging in terms of map of probability of exceeding the Threshold Concentration of Contamination and evaluation of overestimation and underestimation error

Both the classical and the geostatistical approach lead to the determination of one single value of Source Representative Concentration, the former clearly higher than the latter, due to the smoothing effect of Kriging in attenuating extreme values. The geostatistical approach of Indicator Kriging on the contrary, lead to determine a range of Source Representative Concentration values and subsequently to estimate and diagram the risk in function of the probability of exceeding the threshold value.

In the field of cleanup risk assessment it is operatively impossible to know exactly the boundaries of a "potentially contaminated" area for the exceeding of the admissible concentration, as the available data contain a certain degree of uncertainty. In this context geostatistics proves to be versatile in providing elements that take into account the nature of the data themselves, particularly their uncertainty.

FINAL CONCLUSION

Geostatistics has proved to be a useful decision support tool in order to treat in an efficient way huge quantity of data and to cross various order of information. Through the application of geostatistical techniques it is possible to catch and describe in a synthetic way the relations and tendencies that are intrinsic in the data set, characteristics that are neglected by a traditionally used classical approach.

The aim of this paper is to present different case studies that focus on the utility of the application of geostatistical approaches within risk assessment. Geostatistics intervenes in this procedure first of all in the calculation of the probability distributions characterizing the most significant variables that condition the expression of the risk. It follows that an accurate characterization of these parameters is of priority before carrying out a risk assessment. Geostatistics provides a useful help in this task, in that it allows to model the uncertainty associated to the estimation and its application within the decisional process can help to formulate hypothesis regarding remediation and the eventuality to proceed with further sampling in some areas. The geostatistical criterion makes it possible not only to design a sampling scheme making reference to optimization criteria, but also to improve the cost- effectiveness of a sampling campaign, allowing to insert new points where the knowledge is more approximate and to remove others where the information is redundant.

The use of indicator Kriging permits to derive, at each unsampled location, the conditional cumulative distribution function ccdf which models the uncertainty about the unknown value (Van Meirvenne & Goovaerts, 2001). Uncertainty assessment represents a preliminary step in the decision-making process, such as delineation of hazardous areas. In fact, many environmental investigations are aimed at making important decisions, as for example declaring an area potentially contaminated. In this context, the Indicator Kriging can be applied in the study of environmental phenomena for the construction of maps of exceeding the fixed threshold also in presence of coexistence of a few random 'hot spots' of large concentrations within a background of data below the detection limit (censored observations).

This helps those responsible for the decisional process to delimit the vulnerable areas on the basis of the knowledge of the uncertainty associated to the examined phenomenon. This approach lends itself well also to the analysis of qualitative variables, allowing integration with data of quantitative nature through a soft indicator coding of observations.

An alternative technique of spatial modeling, particularly adapt in those applications in which more importance is attached to global statistics rather than to local accuracy, is the stochastic simulation. The statistics obtained from postprocessing of a huge number of simulated images permits to evaluate both the uncertainty in the estimation and the consequences that this uncertainty can imply in the decision making. Therefore the principal purpose of the next study will be that of proving the feasibility and utility of the application of stochastic simulation to evaluate the probability that a pollutant exceeds a concentration value retained critical for environmental safety and/or human health.

REFERENCES

Agenzia per la protezione dell'ambiente e per i servizi tecnici (APAT), (2008). *Criteri metodologici per l'applicazione dell'analisi assoluta di rischio ai siti contaminati, revisione2*. Rome: APAT. Retrieved from http://apat.gov.it

Beretta, G. P., Colombo, F., & Pranzini, G. (1995). Progettazione e ottimizzazione di una rete di monitoraggio delle acque sotterranee nella media valle del F. Arno (Toscana) mediante l'uso della teoria delle variabili regionalizzate. *2° Convegno nazionale sulla protezione e gestione delle acque sotterranee: metodologie, tecnologie e obiettivi*, May 17-19, Nonantola, Modena, Italy.

Castrignanò, A. Cherubini Claudia, Di Mucci, G., & Molinari, M. (2004). The application of spatial modelization of the variability for the interpretation of a case regarding arsenic pollution in groundwater. *COST 629 workshop "Integrated methods for assessing water quality,"* October 21-22, Louvain-la-Neuve, Belgium.

Castrignanò, A. Cherubini Claudia, Dima, L., Giasi, C. I., & Musci, F. (2007). The application of multivariate geostatistical techniques for the study of natural attenuation processes of chlorinated compounds. In *Heat Transfer, Thermal Engineering and Environment*. WSEAS Press.

Castrignanò, A. (2008). Introduction to Spatial Data Processing. *International Short Course on Introduction to Spatial Data Processing*, University of Zagreb Faculty of Agriculture April 21-24, 2008.

Castrignanò, A., & Buttafuoco, G. (2004). Geostatistical Stochastic Simulation of Soil Water Content in a Forested Area of South Italy. *Biosystems Engineering, 87*, 257–266. doi:10.1016/j.biosystemseng.2003.11.002

Castrignanò, A., Lopez, N., Prudenzano, M., & Steduto, P. (2002). Estimation or stochastic simulation in soil science. In P. Zdruli, P. Steduto, & S. Kapur (eds.), *Selected Papers of the 7th International Meeting on Soils with Mediterranean Type of Climate*, Bari, Italy, (pp 167-182).

Dacquino, C. (2004). Geostatistica ed analisi di rischio. *ARPA EME-SIS Internal Report.*

Delhomme, J. P. (1978). Kriging in the hydrosciences. *Advances in Water Resources, 1*(5), 475–499. doi:10.1016/0309-1708(78)90039-8

Garcia, M., & Froidevaux, R. (1997). Application of geostatistics to 3-D modelling of contaminated sites: a case-study. In A. Soares, (Ed.), *geoENV I—Geostatistics for Environmental Applications* (pp. 309–325). Dordrecht: Kluwer Academic Publishing.

Gilbert, R. O. (1987). *Statistical Methods for environmental pollution monitoring.* New York: Van Nostrand Reinhold Company.

Goovaerts, P. (1999). Geostatistics in soil science: state-of-the-art and Perspectives. *Geoderma, 89*, 1–45. doi:10.1016/S0016-7061(98)00078-0

Goovaerts, P., & Journel, A. G. (1995). Integrating soil map information in modelling the spatial variation of continuous soil properties. *European Journal of Soil Science, 46*, 397–414. doi:10.1111/j.1365-2389.1995.tb01336.x

U.S. EPA (2001). RAGS (Risk Assessment Guidance for Superfund) 2001: (Vol. III - Part A, *Process for Conducting Probabilistic Risk Assessment).* EPA 540-R-02-002 OSWER 9285.7-4

U.S. EPA (2007). *ProUCL Version 4.0 User Guide.* EPA/600/R-07/038, April 2007

Van Meirvenne, M., & Goovaerts, P. (2001). Evaluating the probability of exceeding a site-specific soil cadmium contamination threshold. *Geoderma, 102*, 75–100. doi:10.1016/S0016-7061(00)00105-1

Compilation of References

Abadi, D. J., Ahmad, Y., Balazinska, M., Çetintemel, U., Cherniack, M., Hwang, J.-H., et al. (2005). The design of the borealis stream processing engine. In *Proc. 2nd Biennal Conference on Innovative Data Systems Research (CIDR),* (pp. 277–289), Asilomar, CA.

Abadi, D. J., Carney, D., Çetintemel, U., Cherniack, M., Convey, C., & Lee, S. (2003). Aurora: a new model and architecture for data stream management. *The VLDB Journal, 12*(2), 120–139. doi:10.1007/s00778-003-0095-z

Abelló, A., Samos, J., & Saltor, F. (2006). YAM²: a multidimensional conceptual model extending UML. *Information Systems, 32*(6), 541–567. doi:10.1016/j.is.2004.12.002

Aberer, K., Cudré-Mauroux, P., Ouksel, A. M., Catarci, T., Hacid, M. S., Illarramendi, A., et al. (2004). *Emergent Semantics Principles and Issues.* (LNCS Vol. 2973, pp. 25-38). Berlin: Springer.

Abiteboul, S., McHugh, J., Rys, M., Vassalos, V., & Wiener, J. L. (1998). Incremental maintenance for materialized views over semistructured data. In A., Gupta, O., Shmueli, & J., Widom, (Eds.), *Proceedings 24th International Conference on Very Large Data Bases (VLDB),* (pp. 38–49). New York: Morgan Kaufmann.

Achtert, E., Böhm, C., David, J., Kröger, P., & Zimek, A. (2008). Robust Clustering in Arbitrarily Oriented Subspaces. In *Proc. of SIAM International Conference on Data Mining (SDM)* (pp. 763-774).

Achtert, E., Böhm, C., Kriegel, H.-P., Kröger, P., Müller-Gorman, I., & Zimek, A. (2006). Finding Hierarchies of Subspace Clusters. In *Proc. of European* Conference *on Principles and Practice of Knowledge Discovery (PKDD)* (pp. 446-453).

Achtert, E., Böhm, C., Kriegel, H.-P., Kröger, P., Müller-Gorman, I., & Zimek, A. (2007). Detection and Visualization of Subspace Cluster Hierarchies. In *Proc. of International* Conference *on Database Systems for Advanced Applications (DASFAA)* (pp. 152-163).

Achtert, E., Kriegel, H.-P., Pryakhin, A., & Schubert, M. (2006). Clustering Multi-represented Objects Using Combination Trees. In *Proc. of Pacific-Asia Conference on Knowledge Discovery and Data Mining (PAKDD)* (pp. 174-178).

Adcock, S. A., & McCammon, J. A. (2006). Molecular dynamics: Survey of methods for simulating the activity of proteins. *Chemical Reviews, 106*(5), 1589–1615. doi:10.1021/cr040426m

Adiba, M. E., & Lindsay, B. G. (1980). Database Snapshots. In *Proc. Of VLDB* (pp. 86-91).

Afrati, F. N., Chirkova, R., Gergatsoulis, M., & Pavlaki, V. (2007). View selection for eal conjunctive queries. *Acta Informatica, 44*(5), 289–321. doi:10.1007/s00236-007-0046-z

Agenzia per la protezione dell'ambiente e per i servizi tecnici (APAT), (2008). *Criteri metodologici per l'applicazione dell'analisi assoluta di rischio ai siti contaminati, revisione2.* Rome: APAT. Retrieved from http://apat.gov.it

Aggarwal, C. (2006). On biased reservoir sampling in the presence of stream evolution. In Dayal et al.

Aggarwal, C. C. (2007). On Density Based Transforms for Uncertain Data Mining. In *Proc. of* IEEE *International Conference on Data Engineering (ICDE)* (pp. 866-875).

Aggarwal, C. C., & Yu, P. S. (2000). Finding Generalized Projected Clusters in High Dimensional Space. In *Proc. of ACM SIGMOD International Conference on Management of Data (SIGMOD)* (pp. 70-81).

Aggarwal, C. C., & Yu, P. S. (2008). A Framework for Clustering Uncertain Data Streams. In *Proc. of IEEE International Conference on Data Engineering (ICDE)* (pp. 150-159).

Aggarwal, C. C., Han, J., Wang, J., & Yu, P. S. (2003). A Framework for Clustering Evolving Data Streams. In *Proc. of International Conference on Very Large Data Bases (VLDB)* (pp.81-92).

Aggarwal, C. C., Han, J., Wang, J., & Yu, P. S. (2004). A Framework for Projected Clustering of High Dimensional Data Streams. In *Proc. of International Conference on Very Large Data Bases (VLDB)* (pp.852-863).

Aggarwal, C. C., Wolf, J. L., Yu, P. S., Procopiuc, C., & Park, J. S. (1999). Fast algorithms for projected clustering. In *Proc. of ACM SIGMOD International Conference on Management of Data (SIGMOD)* (pp. 61-72).

Aggarwal, C., & Yu, P. S. (2007). A survey of synopsis construction in data streams. In C. Aggarwal, (Ed.), *Data Streams: Models and Algorithms*, (pp. 169–207). Berlin: Springer.

Aggarwal, R. K., & Wu, G. J. (2006). Stock market manipulations. *The Journal of Business*, *78*(4), 1915–1953. doi:10.1086/503652

Agichtein, E., Castillo, C., Donato, D., Gionis, A., & Mishne, G. (2008). Finding high-quality content in social media. In *Proceedings of the international Conference on Web Search and Web Data Mining,* Palo Alto, CA, February 11 - 12, 2008 (WSDM '08, pp. 183-194). New York: ACM.

Agrawal, R., & Srikant, R. (1994). Fast algorithms for mining association rules. In *20th International Conference on Very Large Databases* (pp. 487-499). San Francisco: Morgan Kaufmann.

Agrawal, R., & Srikant, R. (1995). Mining sequential patterns. In *Proceedings of the Eleventh International Conference on 1995*, (pp. 3-14).

Agrawal, R., Gehrke, J., Gunopulos, D., & Raghavan, P. (1998). Automatic Subspace Clustering of High Dimensional Data for Data Mining Applications. In *Proc. of ACM SIGMOD International Conference on Management of Data (SIGMOD)* (pp. 94-105).

Agrawal, R., Gupta, A., & Sarawagi, S. (1997). Modeling Multidimensional Databases. In *Proc. ICDE* (pp. 232-243).

Agrawal, S., Chaudhuri, S., & Narasayya, V. R. (2000). Automated selection of materialized views and indexes in SQL databases. In A. E. Abbadi, M. L. Brodie, S. Chakravarthy, U. Dayal, N. Kamel, G. Schlageter, & K.-Y. Whang, (Eds.), *Proc. 26th Intl. Conference on Very Large Data Bases (VLDB)*, (pp. 496–505), Cairo, Egypt. San Francisco: Morgan Kaufmann.

Agrawal, S., Chaudhuri, S., Kollár, L., Marathe, A. P., Narasayya, V. R., & Syamala, M. (2004). Database tuning advisor for Microsoft SQL Server 2005. In Nascimento et al., (pp. 1110–1121).

Ahmed, T., & Miquel, M. (2005). Multidimensional Structures Dedicated to Continuous Spatiotemporal Phenomena. In *Proceedings of the 22th BNCOD* (pp. 29-40). Berlin: Springer.

Akoka, J., Comyn-Wattiau, I., & Prat, N. (2001). Dimension hierarchies design from UML generalizations and aggregations. *Proceedings of the 20th International Conference on Conceptual Modeling*, (pp. 442-445).

Alhanaty, M., & Bercovier, M. (1998). Curve fitting and design by optimal control methods. In *Information Visualization*, (pp. 108-113). Washington, DC: IEEE.

Allen, F., & Gorton, G. (1992). Stock price manipulation, market microstructure and asymmetric information. *European Economic Review*, *36*, 624–630. doi:10.1016/0014-2921(92)90120-L

Alon, N., Matias, Y., & Szegedy, M. (1999). The space complexity of approximating the frequency moments. *Journal of Computer and System Sciences, 58*, 137–147. doi:10.1006/jcss.1997.1545

Anagnostopoulos, A., Kumar, R., & Mahdian, M. (2008). Influence and Correlation in Social Networks. In *Proceedings of the 14th ACM SIGKDD international Conference on Knowledge Discovery and Data Mining,* Las Vegas, Nevada, USA, August 24 - 27, 2008 (KDD '08, pp. 7 – 15). New York: ACM.

Anselin, L. (1989). *What Is Special about Spatial Data? Alternative Perspectives on Spatial Data Analysis,* (Technical Report). Santa Barbara, CA: National Center for Geographic Information and Analysis.

Antoshenkov, G., & Ziauddin, M. (1996). Query processing and optimization in oracle rdb. *The VLDB Journal, 5*(4), 229–237. doi:10.1007/s007780050026

Apaydin, T., Canahuate, G., Ferhatosmanoglu, H., & Tosun, A. S. (2006). Approximate encoding for direct access and query processing over compressed bitmaps. In *Proceedings of Conference on Very Large DataBases (VLDB),* (pp. 846–857).

Arasu, A., & Widom, J. (2004). Resource sharing in continuous sliding-window aggregates. In Nascimento et al., (pp. 336–347).

Arasu, A., Babcock, B., Babu, S., Datar, M., Ito, K., Nishizawa, I., et al. (2003a). STREAM: The Stanford Stream Data Manager. In A. Y. Halevy, Z. G. Ives, & A. Doan, (Eds.), *Proc. ACM SIGMOD Intl. Conference on Management of Data,* (p. 665), San Diego, California, USA. New York: ACM.

Arasu, A., Babu, S., & Widom, J. (2003). An abstract semantics and concrete language for continuous queries over streams and relations. In *Proc. Intl. Conf. on Data Base Programming Languages.*

Arasu, A., Babu, S., & Widom, J. (2006). The CQL continuous query language: semantic foundations and query execution. *The VLDB Journal, 15*(2), 121–142. doi:10.1007/s00778-004-0147-z

Ashburner, M., Ball, C., Blake, J., Botstein, D., Butler, H., & Cherry, J. (2000). Gene ontology: tool for the unification of biology. the gene ontology consortium. *Nature Genetics, 25*(1).

Assent, I., Krieger, R., Müller, E., & Seidl, T. (2007). DUSC: Dimensionality Unbiased Subspace Clustering. In *Proc. of IEEE International Conference on Data Mining (ICDM)* (pp. 409-414).

Austin, F. I. (2000). *Austin Freeway ITS Data Archive.* Retrieved January, 2003 from http://austindata.tamu.edu/default.asp.

Azevedo, P. J. (2003). *CAREN - A Java based apriori implementation for classification purposes* (Tech. Rep.). Braga, Portugal: University of Minho, Department of Informatics.

Azevedo, P. J., Silva, C. G., Rodrigues, J. R., Loureiro-Ferreira, N., & Brito, R. M. M. (2005). Detection of hydrophobic clusters in molecular dynamics protein unfolding simulations using association rules. In J. L. Oliveira, V. Maojo, F. Martin-Sanchez, & A. S. Pereira (Eds.), *6th International Symposium Biological and Medical Data Analysis:* (LNCS Vol. 3745, pp. 329-337). Berlin: Springer.

Babcock, B., Babu, S., Datar, M., Motwani, R., & Widom, J. (2002). Models and issues in data stream systems. In L. Popa, (Ed.), *Proc. 21st ACM Symposium on Principles of Database Systems (PODS),* (pp. 1–16), Madison, Wisconsin. New York: ACM Press.

Babu, S., Munagala, K., Widom, J., & Motwani, R. (2005). Adaptive caching for continuous queries. In *Proc. 21st Intl. Conf. on Data Engineering (ICDE),* (pp. 118–129), Tokyo, Japan. New York: IEEE.

Bach, F., & Jordan, M. (2003). Learning Spectral Clustering. In *Proc. of 16th Annual Conference on Advances in Neural Information Processing Systems (NIPS).*

Ballou, D. P., & Tayi, G. K. (1999). Enhancing Data Quality in Data Warehouse Environments. [CACM]. *Communications of the ACM, 42*(1), 73–78. doi:10.1145/291469.291471

Barabási, A.-L., & Albert, R. (1999). Emergence of Scaling in Random Networks. [Washington, DC: AAAS.]. *Science, 286*(5439), 509–512. doi:10.1126/science.286.5439.509

Baralis, E., Paraboschi, S., & Teniente, E. (1997). Materialized views selection in a multidimensional database. In Jarke et al., (pp. 156–165).

Bar-Hillel, A., Hertz, T., Shental, N., & Weinshall, D. (2003). Learning Distance Functions using Equivalence Relations. In *Proc. of International Conference on Machine Learning (ICML)* (pp. 11-18).

Barret, R., Berry, M., Chan, T. F., Dongara, J., Eljkhhout, V., Pozo, R., et al. (1994). *Templates for the solution of linear systems: Building blocks for the iterative methods,* (2nd ed.). Philadelphia: SIAM.

Bassiouni, M. A. (1985). Data Compression in Scientific and Statistical Databases. *IEEE Transactions on Software Engineering, 11*(10), 1047–1057. doi:10.1109/TSE.1985.231852

Basu, S., Bilenko, M., & Mooney, R. J. (2004). A Probabilistic Framework for Semi-supervised Clustering. In *Proc. of ACM SIGKDD International Conference on Knowledge Discovery and Data Mining (KDD)* (pp. 59-68).

Bauer, A., Hümmer, W., & Lehner, W. (2000). An alternative relational OLAP modeling approach. *Proceedings of the 2nd International Conference on Data Warehousing and Knowledge Discovery,* (pp. 189-198).

Baumgartner, C., & Graber, A. (2008). Data Mining and Knowledge Discovery in Metabolomics. In Masseglia, F., Poncelet, P. Teisseire, M. (Eds.) *Successes and New Directions in Data Mining.* (pp. 141-166). Hershey, PA: IBI Global.

Baumgartner, C., Kailing, K., Kriegel, H.-P., Kröger, P., & Plant, C. (2004). Subspace Selection for Clustering High-Dimensional Data. In *Proc. of IEEE International Conference on Data Mining (ICDM)* (pp.11-18).

Bebel, B., Eder, J., Koncilia, C., Morzy, T., & Wrembel, R. (2004). Creation and Management of Versions in Multiversion Data Warehouse. In *Proceedings of*

ACM Symposium on Applied Computing, (pp. 717-723), Cyprus.

Bebel, B., Krolinkowski, Z., & Wrembel, R. (2006). Formal approach to modelling a multiversion data warehouse. *Bulletin of the Polish Academy of Sciences, 54*(1), 51–62.

Bédard, Y., Merrett, T., & Han, J. (2001). Fundaments of Spatial Data Warehousing for Geographic Knowledge Discovery. In *Geographic Data Mining and Knowledge Discovery* (pp. 53-73). London: Taylor & Francis.

Bell, M. (2008). Introduction to Service-Oriented Modeling. In *Service-Oriented Modeling: Service Analysis, Design, and Architecture.* Hoboken, NJ: Wiley & Sons Inc.

Bellatreche, L., Karlapalem, K., & Schneider, M. (2000). On efficient storage space distribution among materialized views and indices in data warehousing environments. In *Proc. 9th Intl. Conference on Information and Knowledge Management (CIKM),* (pp. 397–404). New York: ACM.

Beretta, G. P., Colombo, F., & Pranzini, G. (1995). Progettazione e ottimizzazione di una rete di monitoraggio delle acque sotterranee nella media valle del F. Arno (Toscana) mediante l'uso della teoria delle variabili regionalizzate. *2° Convegno nazionale sulla protezione e gestione delle acque sotterranee: metodologie, tecnologie e obiettivi,* May 17-19, Nonantola, Modena, Italy.

Bernstein, P. A. (2005). The Many Roles of Meta Data in Data Integration. In *Proc. SIGMOD* (pp. 792).

Bernstein, P. A., Blaustein, B. T., & Clarke, E. M. (1980). Fast maintenance of semantic integrity assertions using redundant aggregate data. In *Proc. 6th Intl. Conference on Very Large Data Bases (VLDB),* (pp. 126–136), Montreal, Canada. Washington, DC: IEEE Computer Society.

Bessembinder, H. (1999). Trade Execution Costs on NASDAQ and the NYSE: A Post-reform comparison. *Journal of Financial and Quantitative Analysis, 34*(3), 387–407. doi:10.2307/2676265

Bettis, J. C., Duncan, W. A., & Harmon, W. K. (1998). The effectiveness of insider trading regulations. *Journal of Applied Business Research, 14*(4), 53–70.

Bi, Z., Faloutsos, C., & Korn, F. (2001). The "DGX" distribution for mining massive, skewed data. In *Proceedings of the Seventh ACM SIGKDD international Conference on Knowledge Discovery and Data Mining*, San Francisco, California, August 26 - 29 (KDD '01, pp. 17-26). New York: ACM.

Bickel, S., & Scheffer, T. (2004). Multi-View Clustering. In *Proc. of IEEE International Conference on Data Mining (ICDM)* (pp. 19-26).

Bilenko, M., Basu, S., & Mooney, R. J. (2004). Integrating Constraints and Metric Learning in Semi-supervised Clustering. In *Proc. of International Conference on Machine Learning (ICML)* (pp. 81-88).

Bimonte, S., Tchounikine, A., & Miquel, M. (2006). GeoCube, a Multidimensional Model and Navigation Operators Handling Complex Measures: Application in Spatial OLAP. In *Proceedings of the 4th ADVIS* (pp. 100-109). Berlin: Springer-Verlag.

Bimonte, S., Wehrle, P., Tchounikine, A., & Miquel, M. (2006). GeWOlap: A Web Based Spatial OLAP Proposal. In Meersman, R., Tari, Z., & Herrero, P. (Eds.), In *Proceedings of the Workshop on Semantic-Based Geographical Information Systems* (pp. 1596-1605). Berlin: Springer.

Black, F. (1985). Noise. *The Journal of Finance, 41*(3), 530–531.

Blakeley, J. A., Larson, P.-A., & Tompa, F. W. (1986). Efficiently updating materialized views. In *Proceedings ACM SIGMOD International Conference on Management of Data,* (pp. 61–71). New York: ACM.

Blaschka, M., Sapia, C., & Höfling, G. (1999) On Schema Evolution in Multidimensional Databases, In *Proceedings of the International Workshop on Data Warehouse and Knowledge Discovery,* (LNCS 1676, pp. 153-164). Berlin: Springer.

Böhm, C., & Plant, C. (2008). HISSCLU: A Hierarchical Density-based Method for Semi-supervised Clustering. In *Proc. of International Conference on Extending Database Technology (EDBT)* (pp. 440-451).

Böhm, C., Berchtold, S., Kriegel, H.-P., & Michel, U. (2000). Multidimensional Index Structures in Relational Databases. *Journal of Intelligent Information Systems, 15*(1), 51–70. doi:10.1023/A:1008729828172

Böhm, C., Faloutsos, C., & Plant, C. (2008). Outlier-robust Clustering using Independent Components. In *Proc. of ACM SIGMOD International Conference on Management of Data (SIGMOD)* (pp. 185-198).

Böhm, C., Kailing, K., Kröger, P., & Zimek, A. (2004). Computing Clusters of Correlation Connected Objects. In *Proc. of ACM SIGMOD International Conference on Management of Data (SIGMOD)* (pp. 455-466).

Bollerslev, T. (1986). Generalized autoregressive conditional heteroscedasticity. *Journal of Econometrics, 31,* 307–327. doi:10.1016/0304-4076(86)90063-1

Boutros, P. C., & Okey, A. B. (2005). Unsupervised pattern recognition: An introduction to the whys and wherefores of clustering microarray data. *Briefings in Bioinformatics, 6*(4), 331–343. doi:10.1093/bib/6.4.331

Brazma, A., Hingamp, P., Quackenbush, J., Sherlock, G., Spellman, P., & Stoeckert, C. (2001). Minimum information about a microarray experiment (miame)- toward standards for microarray data. *Nature Genetics, 29*(4), 365–371. doi:10.1038/ng1201-365

Brito, R. M. M., Damas, A. M., & Saraiva, M. J. (2003). Amyloid formation by transthyretin: From protein stability to protein aggregation. *Current Medicinal Chemistry - Immunology, Endocrine & Metabolic Agents, 3*(4), 349–360. doi:10.2174/1568013033483230

Brito, R. M. M., Dubitzky, W., & Rodrigues, J. R. (2004). Protein folding and unfolding simulations: A new challenge for data mining. *OMICS: A Journal of Integrative Biology, 8*(2), 153–166. doi:10.1089/1536231041388311

Brown, P. & GoldSchmidt, P. (1996). Alcod idss: Assisting the australian stock market surveillance team's review process. *Applied Artificial Intelligence, 10,* 625–641. doi:10.1080/088395196118452

Buccafurri, F., Furfaro, F., Sacca, D., & Sirangelo, C. (2003). A quad tree based multiresolution approach for compressing datacube. *SSDBM, 2003*, 127–140.

Buneman, O. P., & Clemons, E. K. (1979). Efficiently monitoring relational databases. *ACM Transactions on Database Systems, 4*(3), 368–382. doi:10.1145/320083.320099

Buta, P., & Barletta, R. (1991). Case-based reasoning for market surveillance. *Artificial Intelligence on Wall Stree.* (pp. 116-121). Washington, DC: IEEE.

Cai, Y. D., Pape, G., Han, J., Welge, M., & Auvil, L. (2004). MAIDS: Mining alarming incidents from data streams. *International Conference on Management of Data.*

Carney, D., Centintemel, U., Cherniack, M., Convey, C., Lee, S., Seidman, G., et al. (2002). Monitoring streams - a new class of data management applications. In *VLDB*.

Castrignanò, A. (2008). Introduction to Spatial Data Processing. *International Short Course on Introduction to Spatial Data Processing,* University of Zagreb Faculty of Agriculture April 21-24, 2008.

Castrignanò, A. Cherubini Claudia, Di Mucci, G., & Molinari, M. (2004). The application of spatial modelization of the variability for the interpretation of a case regarding arsenic pollution in groundwater. *COST 629 workshop "Integrated methods for assessing water quality,"* October 21-22, Louvain-la-Neuve, Belgium.

Castrignanò, A. Cherubini Claudia, Dima, L., Giasi, C. I., & Musci, F. (2007). The application of multivariate geostatistical techniques for the study of natural attenuation processes of chlorinated compounds. In *Heat Transfer, Thermal Enginnering and Environment.* WSEAS Press.

Castrignanò, A., & Buttafuoco, G. (2004). Geostatistical Stochastic Simulation of Soil Water Content in a Forested Area of South Italy. *Biosystems Engineering, 87,* 257–266. doi:10.1016/j.biosystemseng.2003.11.002

Castrignanò, A., Lopez, N., Prudenzano, M., & Steduto, P. (2002). Estimation or stochastic simulation in soil science. In P. Zdruli, P. Steduto, & S. Kapur (eds.), *Selected Papers of the 7th International Meeting on*

Soils with Mediterranean Type of Climate, Bari, Italy, (pp 167-182).

Caves, L. S. D., Evanseck, J. D., & Karplus, M. (1998). Locally accessible conformations of proteins: Multiple molecular dynamics simulations of crambin. *Protein Science, 7*(3), 649–666.

Ceri, S., & Widom, J. (1991). Deriving production rules for incremental view maintenance. In *Proceedings of 17th International Conference on Very Large Data Bases (VLDB).* San Francisco: Morgan Kaufmann.

Cha, M., Kwak, H., Rodriguez, P., Ahn, Y., & Moon, S. (2007). I Tube, You Tube, Everybody Tubes: Analyzing the World's Largest User Generated Content Video System. In *Proceedings of the 7th ACM SIGCOMM conference on Internet measurement*, San Diego, CA.

Chan, C., & Ioannidis, Y. (1998) Bitmap index design and evaluation. *ACM SIGMOID* (pp. 355-366).

Chandrasekaran, S., Cooper, O., Deshpande, A., Franklin, M. J., Hellerstein, J. M., Hong, W., et al. (2003). Telegraph-CQ: continuous dataflow processing for an uncertain world. In *Proc. 1st Biennal Conference on Innovative Data Systems Research (CIDR),* Asilomar, CA.

Chang, H., & Yeung, D.-Y. (2004). Locally Linear Metric Adaptation for Semi-supervised Clustering. In *Proc. of International Conference on Machine Learning (ICML)* (pp. 153-160).

Chang, J. H., Lee, & W. S. (2004). A sliding window method for finding recently frequent itemsets over online data streams. *Journal of Information Science and Engineering.*

Chang, J. H., Lee, W. S., & Zhou, A. (2003). Finding recent frequent itemsets adaptively over online data streams. *ACM SIGKDD International Conference on Knowledge Discovery and Data Mining.*

Chapelle, O., Scholkopf, B., & Zien, A. (2006). *Semi-Supervised learning.* Cambridge, MA: MIT Press.

Charest, G. (1978). Dividend information, stock returns and market efficiency-II. *Journal of Financial Economics, 6*(2/3).

Charre, J., Dumolard, P., & Le Berre, I. (1997). *Initiation aux pratiques statistiques en geographie*. Paris: Masson.

Chaudhuri, S., & Dayal, U. (1997). An overview of data warehousing and OLAP technology. *ACM SIGMOD*, *26*(1), 65–74. doi:10.1145/248603.248616

Chaudhuri, S., & Narasayya, V. R. (1997). An efficient cost-driven index selection tool for Microsoft SQL Server. In Jarke et al., (pp. 146–155).

Chaudhuri, S., & Narasayya, V. R. (2007). Self-tuning database systems: A decade of progress. In Koch, C., Gehrke, J., Garofalakis, M. N., Srivastava, D., Aberer, K., Deshpande, A., et al (Eds.), *Proceedings 33rd Intl. Conf. on Very Large Data Bases (VLDB)*, (pp. 3–14), Vienna, Austria.

Chen, C., & Liu, L. M. (1993). Joint estimation of model parameters and outlier effects in time series. *Journal of the American Statistical Association, 88*, 284–297. doi:10.2307/2290724

Chen, J., DeWitt, D. J., Tian, F., & Wang, Y. (2000). NiagaraCQ: A Scalable Continuous Query System for Internet Databases. In W. Chen, J. F. Naughton, & P. A. Bernstein, (Eds.), *Proceedings of the ACM SIGMOD International Conference on Management of Data*, pages 379–390, Dallas, Texas. New York: ACM.

Cheng, C.-H., Fu, A.-C., & Zhang, Y. (1999). Entropy-Based Subspace Clustering for Mining Numerical Data. In *Proc. of ACM SIGKDD International* Conference *on Knowledge Discovery and Data Mining (KDD)* (pp. 84-93).

Cheng, L., Firth, M., Leung, T., & Rui, O. (2006). The effects of insider trading on liquidity. *Pacific-Basin Finance Journal, 14*, 467–483. doi:10.1016/j.pacfin.2006.01.006

Chernick, M. R. (1982). A note on the robustness of Dixon Ratio Test in small samples. *The American Statistician, 36*, 140. doi:10.2307/2684033

Chi, Y., Wang, H. X., Yu, P. S., & Muntz, R. R. (2004). Moment: Maintaining closed frequent itemsets over a stream sliding window. *IEEE International Conference on Data Mining*.

Choi, I., & Kim, M. (2003). Topic distillation using hierarchy concept tree. In *ACM SIGIR conference*, (pp. 371–372).

Choi, J., Yu, U., Kim, S., & Yoo, O. (2003). Combining multiple microarray studies and modeling interstudy variation. *Bioinformatics (Oxford, England), 19*(1), i84–i90. doi:10.1093/bioinformatics/btg1010

Chrisman, N. (1974). *Attributes of geographic entities*. Technical Report, Harvard Laboratory for Computer Graphics, Cambridge, MA.

Chrisman, N. (1998). Rethinking Levels of Measurement in Cartography. *Cartography and GIS, 25*(4), 231–242. doi:10.1559/152304098782383043

Chun, Y. L., Yeh, C. C., & Jen, S. L. (2002). Efficient Representation Scheme for Multidimensional Array Operations. *IEEE Transactions on Computers, 51*(3), 327–345. doi:10.1109/12.990130

Chun, Y. L., Yeh, C. C., & Jen, S. L. (2003). Efficient Data Compression Method for Multidimensional Sparse Array Operations Based on EKMR Scheme. *IEEE Transactions on Computers, 52*(12), 1640–1648. doi:10.1109/TC.2003.1252859

Chun, Y. L., Yeh, C. C., & Jen, S. L. (2003). Efficient Data Parallel Algorithms for Multidimensional Array Operations Based on the EKMR Scheme for Distributed Memory Multicomputers. *IEEE Transactions on Parallel and Distributed Systems, 14*(7), 625–639. doi:10.1109/TPDS.2003.1214316

Clauset, A., Shalizi, C. R., & Newman, M. E. J. (2007). *Power-law distributions in empirical data*. Tech. Rep. submitted to arXiv on June 7, 2007 with identifier: arXiv:0706.1062v1.

Cleveland, W., & Devlin, S. (1979). Robust locally weighted regression and smoothing scatterplots. *Journal of the American Statistical Association, 74*, 829–836. doi:10.2307/2286407

Corby, O., Dieng-Kuntz, R., Faron-Zucker, C., & Gandon, F. (2006). Searching the semantic web: Approximate query processing based on ontologies. *IEEE Intelligent Systems, 21*(1), 20–27. doi:10.1109/MIS.2006.16

Cormode, G., & Garofalakis, M. (2007). Sketching probabilistic data streams. In L. Zhou, T. W. Ling, & B. C. Ooi, (Eds.), *Proc. ACM SIGMOD Intl. Conf. on Management of Data*, Beijing, China. New York: ACM Press.

Cormode, G., & Muthukrishnan, S. (2005). Summarizing and mining skewed data streams. In *Proceedings of the 2005 SIAM International Conference on Data Mining*, (pp.44-55). SIAM.

Correia, B. E., Loureiro-Ferreira, N., Rodrigues, J. R., & Brito, R. M. M. (2006). A structural model of an amyloid protofilament of transthyretin. *Protein Science, 15*(1), 28–32. doi:10.1110/ps.051787106

Cover, T. M., & Thomas, J. A. (1991). *Elements of information theory*. Hoboken, NJ: Wiley.

Cristianini, N., & Shawe-Taylor, J. (2000). *An Introduction to Support Vector Machines and other kernel-based learning methods*. New York: Cambridge University Press.

Cui, Y., & Widom, J. (2000). Lineage Tracing in a Data Warehousing System. In *Proc. ICDE* (pp. 683-684).

Dacquino, C. (2004). Geostatistica ed analisi di rischio. *ARPA EME-SIS Internal Report.*

Dageville, B., Das, D., Dias, K., Yagoub, K., Zaït, M., & Ziauddin, M. (2004). Automatic SQL tuning in Oracle 10g. In Nascimento et al., (pp. 1098–1109).

Damiani, M., & Spaccapietra, S. (2006). Spatial Data Warehouse Modeling. In *Processing and Managing Complex Data for Decision Support* (pp. 1-27). Hershey, PA: IGP.

Dang, X. H., Ng, W. K., & Ong, K. L. (2007). Online mining of frequent sets in data streams with error guarantee. *Knowledge and Information Systems.*

Dar, S., Franklin, M. J., & Jónsson, B. Thorn., Srivastava, D., & Tan, M. (1996). Semantic data caching and replacement. In Vijayaraman et al., (pp. 330–341).

Darmont, J., Boussaid, O., Ralaivao, J. C., & Aouiche, K. (2005). An Architecture Framework for Complex Data Warehouses. *ICEIS,* (1), 370-373.

Dasgupta, D. (1998). *Artificial immune systems and their applications*. Berlin: Springer.

Datta, A., & Thomas, H. (2002). Querying Compressed Data in Data Warehouses. [Dordrecht, The Netherlands: Springer Netherlands.]. *Journal of Information Technology Management, 3*(4), 353–386. doi:10.1023/A:1019772807859

Datta, A., VanderMeer, D. E., & Ramamritham, K. (2002). Parallel Star Join Data Indexes: Efficient Query Processing in Data Warehouses and OLAP. *IEEE Transactions on Knowledge and Data Engineering, 14*(6), 1299–1316. doi:10.1109/TKDE.2002.1047769

Dave, K., Lawrence, S., & Pennock, D. M. (2003). Mining the peanut gallery: opinion extraction and semantic classification of product reviews. In *Proceedings of the 12th international Conference on World Wide Web*, Budapest, Hungary, May 20 – 24, (WWW '03, pp. 519-528). New York: ACM.

David, L., Vetterli, M., Daubechies, I., & Ron, A. (1998). Data compression and harmonic analysis. *IEEE Transactions on Information Theory, 44.*

Day, R., & Daggett, V. (2003). All-atom simulations of protein folding and unfolding. *Advances in Protein Chemistry, 66*, 373–803. doi:10.1016/S0065-3233(03)66009-2

Dayal, U., Whang, K.-Y., Lomet, D. B., Alonso, G., Lohman, G. M., Kersten, M. L., et al. (Eds.). (2006). *Proc. 32nd Intl. Conference on Very Large Data Bases (VLDB)*. New York: ACM Press.

De Sa, V. R. (2005). Spectral Clustering with two Views. In *Proc. of International Conference on Machine Learning (ICML). Workshop on Learning with Multiple Views.*

Degrene, J., & Salge, F. (1997). *Les systèmes d'information géographique*, (2nd Ed.). Paris: Presses Universitaires de France.

Dehne, F., Eavis, T., & Andrew, R. (2001). Coarse grained parallel on-line analytical processing (OLAP) for data mining. In *Proceedings of ICCS 2001.*

Delhomme, J. P. (1978). Kriging in the hydrosciences. *Advances in Water Resources, 1*(5), 475–499. doi:10.1016/0309-1708(78)90039-8

Demaine, E. D., Ortiz, A. L., & Munro, J. I. (2002). Frequency estimation of internet packet streams with limited space. *European Symposium on Algorithms.*

Dempster, A. P. Laird, N. M. & Rubin, D. B. (1977). Maximum Likelihood from Incomplete Data via the EM Algorithm. In *Journal of the Royal Statistical Society, 39,* 1-31.

Deshpande, P. M., Ramasamy, K., Shukla, A., & Naughton, J. F. (1998). Caching multidimensional queries using chunks. In L. M. Haas, & A. Tiwary, (Eds.), *Proc. ACM SIGMOD Intl. Conference on Management of Data,* (pp. 259–270), Seattle, Washington, USA. New York: ACM Press.

Deshpande, P., & Naughton, J. F. (2000). Aggregate aware caching for multi-dimensional queries. In C. Zaniolo, P. C. Lockemann, M. H. Scholl, & T. Grust, (Eds.), *Advances in Database Technology – 7th International Conference on Extending Database Technology (EDBT)*, Konstanz (LNCS 1777, pp. 167–182). Berlin: Springer.

Dhillon, I. S. (2001). Co-clustering Documents and Words using Bipartite Spectral Graph Partitioning. In *Proc. of ACM SIGKDD International* Conference *on Knowledge Discovery and Data Mining (KDD)* (pp. 269–274).

Dhillon, I. S., Guan, Y., & Kulis, B. (2004). Kernel K-means: Spectral Clustering and Normalized Cuts. In *Proc. of ACM SIGKDD International* Conference *on Knowledge Discovery and Data Mining (KDD)* (pp. 551-556).

Dill, K. A. (1990). Dominant forces in protein folding. *Biochemistry, 29*(31), 7133–7155. doi:10.1021/bi00483a001

Dimitrova, K., El-Sayed, M., & Rundensteiner, E. A. (2003). Order-sensitive view maintenance of materialized XQuery views. In I.-Y. Song, S. W. Liddle, T. W. Ling, & P. Scheuermann, (Eds.), *Proceedings 22nd International Conference on Conceptual Modeling (ER)*, (LNCS Vol. 2813, pp. 144–157), Chicago, USA. Berlin: Springer.

Ding, C. H. Q., & He, X. (2004). K-means Clustering via Principal Component Analysis. In *Proc. of International Conference on Machine Learning (ICML)* (pp. 225-232).

Ding, C. H. Q., He, X., Zha, H., Gu, M., & Simon, H. (2001). A Min-max Cut Algorithm for Graph Partitioning and Data Clustering. In *Proc. of IEEE International Conference on Data Mining (ICDM)* (pp.107–114).

Dipperstein, M. (2008). *Huffman Code Discussion and Implementation.* Received March 4, 2009 http://michael.dipperstein.com/huffman/index.html.

Dixon, W. J. (1950). Analysis of extreme values. *Annals of Mathematical Statistics, 21,* 488–506. doi:10.1214/aoms/1177729747

Donoho, S. (2004). Early detection of insider trading in option market. In *The Tenth ACM SIGKDD international conference on Knowledge discovery and data mining,* (pp. 420-429). New York: ACM Press.

Duda, R. O., & Hart, P. E. (1973). *Pattern Classification and Scene Analysis.* Hoboken, NJ: John Wiley & Sons.

Duda, R. O., Hart, P. E., & Stork, D. G. (2001). *Pattern Classification.* Chichester, UK: John Wiley & Sons, Inc.

Eagle, N., & Pentland, A. (2005). Social Serendipity: Mobilizing Social Software. *IEEE Pervasive Computing / IEEE Computer Society [and] IEEE Communications Society, 4*(2), 28–34. doi:10.1109/MPRV.2005.37

Eagle, N., & Pentland, A. (2006). Reality Mining: Sensing Complex Social Systems. *Personal and Ubiquitous Computing, 10*(4), 255–268. doi:10.1007/s00779-005-0046-3

Eapen, B. R. (2008). Ontoderm - a domain ontology for dermatology. *Dermatology Online Journal, 14*(6), 16.

Egenhofer, M., & Frank, A. U. (1986). Connection between Local and Regional: Additional Intelligence Needed. In *Proceedings of the 18th International Congress of FIGURE*

Egenhofer, M., & Frank, A. U. (1992). Object-Oriented Modeling for GIS. *URISA Journal, 4*(2), 3–19.

Eggers, S., & Shohani, A. (1980). Efficient Access of Compressed Data. In *Proceedings of sixth int'l conference on Very large Databases*, 205-211.

Eisen, M. B., Spellman, P. T., Brown, P. O., & Botstein, D. (1998). Cluster analysis and display of genome-wide expression patterns. *Proceeding of the National Academy of Sciences of the United States of America, 95*(25), 14863-14868.

Eisen, M., Spellman, P., Brown, P. O., & Botstein, D. (1998). Cluster analysis and display of genome wide expression patterns. *Proceedings of the National Academy of Sciences of the United States of America, 95*(25), 14863–14868. doi:10.1073/pnas.95.25.14863

Elmasri, R., & Navathe, S. (2006). *Fundaments of database systems* (5th Ed.). Reading, MA: Addison Wesley.

El-Sayed, M., Rundensteiner, E. A., & Mani, M. (2006). Incremental maintenance of materialized XQuery views. In L. Liu, A. Reuter, K.-Y. Whang, & J. Zhang, (Eds.), *Proceedings 22nd International Conference on Data Engineering (ICDE)*, Atlanta, GA. Washington, DC: IEEE Computer Society.

Emmanuel, J. C., & David, L. D. (1999) Curvelets - a surprisingly effective nonadaptive representation for objects with edges. In *Curves and Surfaces*.

Erwig, M., & Schneider, M. (2000). Formalization of advanced map operations. In *Proceedings of the 9th Int. Symp. on Spatial Data Handling* (pp. 3-17).

Escribano, A., Gomez, L., Kuijpers, B., & Vaisman, A. (2007). Piet: a GIS-OLAP implementation. In *Proceedings of the ACM 10th International Workshop on Data Warehousing and OLAP* (pp. 73-80). New York: ACM Press.

Ester, M., Kriegel, H.-P., Sander, J., & Xu, X. (1996). A Density-based Algorithm for Discovering Clusters in Large Spatial Databases with Noise. In *Proc. of ACM SIGKDD International Conference on Knowledge Discovery and Data Mining (KDD)* (pp.226–231).

Everitt, B. (1980). *Cluster analysis*. New York: Halsted Press.

Faloutsos, C., Kolda, T. G., & Sun, J. (2007). Mining large graphs and streams using matrix and tensor tools. In *Proceedings of the 2007 ACM SIGMOD international Conference on Management of Data*, Beijing, China, June 11 - 14, (SIGMOD '07, pp. 1174-1174). New York: ACM.

Felixson, K., & Pelli, A. (1999). Day end returns: Stock price manipulation. *Journal of Multinational Financial Management, 9*(2), 95–127. doi:10.1016/S1042-444X(98)00052-8

Feng, Y., & Hamerly, G. (2006). PG-means: Learning the Number of Clusters in Data. In *Proc. of 19th Annual Conference on Advances in Neural Information Processing Systems (NIPS)* (pp. 393-400).

Ferreira, P. G., Azevedo, P. J., Silva, C. G., & Brito, R. M. M. (2006). Mining approximate motifs in time series. In N. Lavrac, L. Todorovski, & K. P. Jantke (Eds.), *9th International Conference on Discovery Science* (LNAI Vol. 4265, pp. 77–89). Berlin: Springer.

Ferreira, P. G., Silva, C. G., Brito, R. M. M., & Azevedo, P. J. (2007). A closer look on protein unfolding simulations through hierarchical clustering. *2007 IEEE Symposium on Computational Intelligence and Bioinformatics and Computational Biology* (pp. 461–468).

Feyer, T., & Thalheim, B. (2002). Many-Dimensional Schema Modeling. In *Proceedings of the 6th East European Conference on Advances in Databases and Information Systems,* (LNCS 2435, pp. 305 – 318). Berlin: Springer

Fidalgo, R., Times, V., Silva, J., & Souza, F. (2004). GeoDWFrame: A Framework for Guiding the Design of Geographical Dimensional Schemas. In *Proceedings of 6th International Conference on Data Warehousing and Knowledge Discovery* (pp. 26-37). Berlin: Springer.

Figueiredo, M. A. T., & Jain, A. K. (2002). Unsupervised Learning of Finite Mixture Models. [PAMI]. *IEEE Transactions on Pattern Analysis and Machine Intelligence, 24*(3), 381–396. doi:10.1109/34.990138

Fishe, R. P., & Robe, M. A. (2002). *The impact of illegal insider trading in dealer and specialist markets: evidence from a natural experiment*. Technical report, Securities and Exchange Commission.

Fishman, M., & Hagerty, K. (1992). Insider trading and the efficiency of stock prices. *The Rand Journal of Economics*, *23*(1), 106–122. doi:10.2307/2555435

Flajolet, P., & Martin, G. N. (1985). Probabilistic counting techniques for data base applications. *Journal of Computer and System Sciences*, *31*, 182–208. doi:10.1016/0022-0000(85)90041-8

Fowlkes, C., Belongie, S., Chung, F. R. K., & Malik, J. (2004). Spectral Grouping Using the Nyström Method. [PAMI]. *IEEE Transactions on Pattern Analysis and Machine Intelligence*, *26*(2), 214–225. doi:10.1109/TPAMI.2004.1262185

Francis, T. (1989). Expert system tools are Wall Street's newest creation. *Wall Street Comput. Rev.*, 26-40.

Franklin, C. (1992). An Introduction to Geographic Information Systems: Linking Maps to databases. *Database*, *15*(2), 13–21.

Franses, P. & Dijk, D. (2000). *Outlier detection in GARCH models*. Econometric institute research report EI-9926/RV.

Friedrich, J. R. (2005). Meta-data Version and Configuration Management In Multi-vendor Environments. In *Proc. SIGMOD* (pp. 799-804).

Frino, A., & Segara, R. (2008). *Trade execution, arbitrage and dealing in Australia*. Upper Saddle River, NJ: Pearson Education.

Fu, T., Chung, F., Luk, R., & Ng, C. (2007). Stock time series pattern matching: Template-based vs. rule-based approaches. *Engineering Applications of Artificial Intelligence*, *20*, 347–364. doi:10.1016/j.engappai.2006.07.003

Furtado, P. (2004). Experimental evidence on partitioning in parallel data warehouses. In *Proc. DOLAP* (pp. 23-30).

Furtado, P. (2006). Node Partitioned Data Warehouses: Experimental Evidence and Improvements. *Journal of Database Management*, *17*(2), 43–61.

Ganguly, S., Garofalakis, M., & Rastogi, R. (2003). Processing set expressions over continuous update streams. In *Proc. ACM SIGMOD Intl. Conference on Management of Data*, San Diego, CA. ACM.

Garcia, M., & Froidevaux, R. (1997). Application of geostatistics to 3-D modelling of contaminated sites: a case-study. In A. Soares, (Ed.), *geoENV I—Geostatistics for Environmental Applications* (pp. 309–325). Dordrecht: Kluwer Academic Publishing.

Gardner, S. R. (1998). Building the Data Warehouse. *Communications of the ACM*, *41*(9), 52–60. doi:10.1145/285070.285080

Garfinkel, J. A., & Nimalendran, M. (2003). Market structure and trader anonymity: An analysis of insider trading. *Journal of Financial and Quantitative Analysis*, *38*(3), 591–610. doi:10.2307/4126733

Geffner, S., Agrawal, D., Abbadi, A. E., & Smith, T. R. (1999) Relative prefix sums: An efficient approach for querying dynamic OLAP data cubes. In *Proceedings of International Conference of Data Engineering (ICDE)*, (pp. 328–335). Washington, DC: IEEE CS.

Giannella, C., Han, J. W., Pei, J., Yan, X. F., & Yu, P. S. (2003). Mining frequent patterns in data streams at multiple time granularities. *Data Mining: Next Generation Challenges and Future Directions*, AAAI/MIT.

Gilbert, A. C., Kotidis, Y., Muthukrishnan, S., & Strauss, M. J. (2003). One-pass wavelet decompositions of data streams. In *IEEE Transactions on Knowledge and Data Engineering*.

Gilbert, R. O. (1987). *Statistical Methods for environmental pollution monitoring*. New York: Van Nostrand Reinhold Company.

Golder, S., & Huberman, B. A. (2006). The Structure of Collaborative Tagging Systems. *Journal of Information Science*, *32*(2), 198–208. doi:10.1177/0165551506062337

Golfarelli, M., & Rizzi, S. (1998). A methodological framework for data warehouse design. *Proceedings of the 1st ACM International Workshop on Data Warehousing and OLAP*, (pp. 3-9).

Golfarelli, M., Lechtenborger, J., Rizzi, S., & Vossen, G. (2006). Schema Versioning in Data Warehouses: Enabling Cross Version Querying via Schema Augmentation. *Data & Knowledge Engineering, 59*(2), 435–459. doi:10.1016/j. datak.2005.09.004

Gómez, V., Kaltenbrunner, A., & López, V. (2008). Statistical analysis of the social network and discussion threads in slashdot. In *Proceeding of the 17th international Conference on World Wide Web,* Beijing, China, April 21 - 25, (WWW '08, pp. 645-654). New York: ACM.

Goovaerts, P. (1999). Geostatistics in soil science: state-of-the-art and Perspectives. *Geoderma, 89,* 1–45. doi:10.1016/S0016-7061(98)00078-0

Goovaerts, P., & Journel, A. G. (1995). Integrating soil map information in modelling the spatial variation of continuous soil properties. *European Journal of Soil Science, 46,* 397–414. doi:10.1111/j.1365-2389.1995. tb01336.x

Gopikrishnan, V.P.P. & Stanley, H.E. (2005). Quantifying fluctuations in market liquidity: Analysis of the bid-ask spread. *The American Physical Society,* 1–7.

Gourieroux, C. (1997). *ARCH models and financial applications.* Berlin: Springer-Verlag.

Gray, J., Bosworth, A., Layman, A., & Pirahesh, H. (1996). Data Cube: A Relational Aggregation Operator Generalizing Group-By, Cross-Tab, and Sub-Total. In *Proc. ICDE* (pp. 152-159).

Gray, J., Chaudhuri, S., Basworth, A., Layman, A., Reichart, D., & Venkatrao, M. (1997). Data cube: a relational aggregation operator generalizing group-by, cross-tab, and sub-totals. *Data Mining and Knowledge Discovery, 1*(1), 29–53. doi:10.1023/A:1009726021843

Gray, J., Chaudhuri, S., Bosworth, A., Layman, A., Reichart, D., & Venkatrao, M. (1997). Data cube: A relational aggregation operator generalizing group-by, cross-tab, and sub-totals. *Journal Data Mining and Knowledge Discovery, 1*(1), 29–53. doi:10.1023/A:1009726021843

Gregoire, P., & Huangi, H. (2001). *Insider trading, noise trading and the cost of Equity.*

Griffin, T., & Kumar, B. (1998). Algebraic change propagation for semijoin and outerjoin queries. *SIGMOD Record, 27*(3), 22–27. doi:10.1145/290593.290597

Grünwald, P. (2005). A Tutorial Introduction to the Minimum Description Length Principle. In P. Grünwald, I. J. Mynung, & M. Pitt, (Eds.) *Advances in Minimum Description Length: Theory and Applications.* Cambridge, MA: MIT Press.

Güting, R., & Schneider, M. (1995). Realm-based spatial data types: the ROSE algebra. *The VLDB Journal, 4*(2), 243–286. doi:10.1007/BF01237921

Guha, S., & Koudas, N. (2002). Approximating a data stream for querying and estimation: Algorithms and performance evaluation. *International Conference on Data Engineering.*

Gupta, A., & Mumick, I. S. (1995). Maintenance of materialized views: Problems, techniques and applications. *IEEE Quarterly Bulletin on Data Engineering . Special Issue on Materialized Views and Data Warehousing, 18*(2), 3–18.

Gupta, A., Jagadish, H. V., & Mumick, I. S. (1996). Data integration using self-maintainable views. In Apers, P. M. G., Bouzeghoub, M., and Gardarin, G., editors, *Proc. 5th International Conference on Extending Database Technology (EDBT)*, Avignon, France, (LNCS Vol. 1057 pp. 140–144). Berlin: Springer.

Gupta, A., Katiyar, D., & Mumick, I. S. (1992). Counting solutions to the view maintenance problem. In *Workshop on Deductive Databases,* (pp. 185–194).

Gupta, A., Mumick, I. S., & Subrahmanian, V. S. (1993). Maintaining views incrementally. In P. Buneman, & S. Jajodia, (Eds.), *Proceedings of the ACM SIGMOD International Conference on Management of Data,* (pp. 157–166). Washington, DC: ACM Press.

Gupta, H. (1997). Selection of views to materialize in a data warehouse. In F. N. Afrati, & P. G. Kolaitis, (Eds.) *Proceedings of the 6th International Conference on Database Theory (ICDT)*, Delphi, Greece (LNCS Vol. 1186, pp. 98–112). Berlin: Springer.

Gupta, H., & Mumick, I. S. (2005). Selection of views to materialize in a data warehouse. *IEEE Transactions on Knowledge and Data Engineering, 17*(1), 24–43. doi:10.1109/TKDE.2005.16

Gupta, H., & Mumick, I. S. (2006). Incremental maintenance of aggregate and outerjoin expressions. *Information Systems, 31*(6), 435–464. doi:10.1016/j.is.2004.11.011

Gupta, H., Harinarayan, V., Rajaraman, A., & Ullman, J. D. (1997). Index selection for OLAP. In A. Gray, & P.-Å. Larson, (Eds.), *Proceedings of the 13th International Conference on Data Engineering (ICDE),* (pp. 208–219), Birmingham, UK. Washington, DC: IEEE Computer Society.

Guting, R. (1998). Geo-Relational Algebra: A model and query language for geometric database systems. In *Proceedings of the EDBT* (pp. 506-527).

Haas, L., Lin, E. T., & Roth, M. T. (2002). Data integration through database federation. *IBM Systems Journal, 41*(4), 578–596.

Hagen, L., & Kahng, A. (1992). New Spectral Methods for Ratio Cut Partitioning and Clustering. *IEEE Trans. Computer Aided Design, 11*(9), 1074–1085.

Hahn, K., Sapia, C., & Blaschka, M. (2001). Automatically generating OLAP schemata from conceptual graphical models. *Proceedings of the 4th ACM International Workshop on Data Warehousing and OLAP,* (pp. 9-16).

Halatchev, M., & Gruenwald, L. (2005). Estimating missing values in related sensor data streams. *International Conference on Management of Data.*

Halevy, A. Y. (2001). Answering queries using views: A survey. *The VLDB Journal, 10*(4), 270–294. doi:10.1007/s007780100054

Halpin, H., Robu, V., & Shepherd, H. (2007). The complex dynamics of collaborative tagging. In *Proceedings of the 16th international Conference on World Wide Web,* Banff, Alberta, Canada, May 08 - 12, 2007, (WWW '07, pp. 211-220). New York: ACM.

Hamdan, H., & Govaert, G. (2005). Mixture Model Clustering of Uncertain Data. In *IEEE International Conference on Fuzzy Systems* (pp. 879–884).

Hamerly, G., & Elkan, C. (2003). Learning the K in K-means. In *Proc. of 16th Annual Conference on Advances in Neural Information Processing Systems (NIPS).*

Hamilton, W., Steinrauf, L. K., Liepnieks, J., Braden, B. C., Benson, M. D., & Holmgren, G. (1993). The X-ray crystal structure refinements of normal human transthyretin and the amyloidogenic Val-30-Met variant to 1.7 Å resolution. *The Journal of Biological Chemistry, 268*(4), 2416–2424.

Hammarström, P., & Carlsson, U. (2000). Is the unfolded state the rosetta stone of the protein folding problem? *Biochemical and Biophysical Research Communications, 276*(2), 393–398. doi:10.1006/bbrc.2000.3360

Han, J., & Kamber, M. (2001). *Data Mining: concepts and techniques.* San Francisco: Morgan Kaufmann Publishers.

Han, J., Chai, Y. D., Chen, Y., & Dong, G. (2007). Multi-dimensional analysis of data streams using stream cubes. In C. Aggarwal, (Ed.), *Data Streams - Models and Algorithms,* (pp. 103–123). Berlin: Springer.

Han, J., Stefanovic, N., & Koperski, K. (1998). Selective Materialization: An Efficient Method for Spatial Data Cube Construction. In *Proceedings of 6th PAKDD Conference* (pp. 144-158). Berlin: Springer.

Hanson, E. N. (1987). A performance analysis of view materialization strategies. *SIGMOD Record, 16*(3), 440–453. doi:10.1145/38714.38759

Harinarayan, V., Rajaraman, A., & Ullman, J. D. (1996). Implementing data cubes efficiently. In H. V. Jagadish & I. S. Mumick, (Ed.), *Proc. ACM SIGMOD International Conference on Management of Data,* Montreal, Quebec, Canada, (pp. 205–216). New York: ACM Press.

Harris, L. (2003). *Trading and Exchanges, Market microstructure for practitioners.* New York: Oxford University Press.

Harrison, J. V., & Dietrich, S. W. (1992). Maintenance of materialized views in a deductive database: An update propagation approach. In *Workshop on Deductive Databases, JICSLP,* (pp. 56–65).

Hasan, K. M. A., Kuroda, M., Azuma, N., Tsuji, T., & Higuchi, K. (2005). An extendible array based implementation of relational tables for multidimensional databases. In *Proceedings of 7th International Conference on Data Warehousing and Knowledge Discovery (DaWaK'05)* (pp. 233-242). Heidelberg: Springer-Verlag.

Hasan, K. M. A., Tsuji, T., & Higuchi, K. (2006). A Parallel Implementation Scheme of Relational Tables Based on Multidimensional Extendible Array. *International Journal of Data Warehousing and Mining, 2*(4), 66–85.

Hasan, K. M. A., Tsuji, T., & Higuchi, K. (2007). An Efficient Implementation for MOLAP Basic Data Structure and Its Evaluation, In *Proceedings of DASFAA 2007*, (LNCS 4443, pp. 288 – 299). Heidelberg: Springer-Verlag.

Hauch, R., Miller, A., & Cardwell, R. (2005). Information Intelligence: Metadata for Information Discovery, Access, and Integration. In *Proc. SIGMOD* (pp. 793-798).

Heyer, L. J., Kruglyak, S., & Yooseph, S. (1999). Exploring expression data: Identification and analysis of coexpressed genes. *Genome Research, 9*(11), 1106–1115. doi:10.1101/gr.9.11.1106

Heymann, P., Koutrika, G., & Garcia-Molina, H. (2008). Can social bookmarking improve web search? In *Proceedings of the international Conference on Web Search and Web Data Mining,* Palo Alto, CA, February 11-12, 2008, (WSDM '08, pp. 195-206). New York: ACM.

Hierachical Data Format (HDF) group. (2004). *HDF5 User's Guide*. National Center for Supercomputing Applications (NCSA), University of Illinois, Urbana-Champaign, Illinois, UrbanaChampaign, release 1.6.3. edition.

Hong, F., & Breitling, R. (2008). A comparison of metaanalysis methods for detecting differentially expressed genes in microarray experiments. *Bioinformatics (Oxford, England), 24*(3), 374–382. doi:10.1093/bioinformatics/btm620

Horner, J., Song, I., & Chen, P. (2004). An Analysis of Additivity in OLAP Systems. In *Proceedings of the 7th DOLAP* (pp. 83-91). New York: ACM Press.

Hosmer, D. W., & Stanley, L. (2000). *Applied logistic regression*. Hoboken, NJ: Wiley.

Hotho, A., Jäschke, R., Schmitz, C., & Stumme, G. (2006). Information Retrieval in Folksonomies: Search and Ranking. In *The Semantic Web: Research and Applications*, (pp. 411-426). Berlin: Springer.

Hotho, A., Jäschke, R., Schmitz, C., & Stumme, G. (2006). *Trend Detection in Folksonomies*. (LNCS 4306, pp. 56-70). Berlin: Springer.

Hu, M., Lim, E., Sun, A., Lauw, H. W., & Vuong, B. (2007). Measuring Article Quality in Wikipedia: Models and Evaluation. In *Proceedings of the Sixteenth ACM Conference on Conference on information and Knowledge Management*, Lisbon, Portugal, November 06 - 10, (CIKM '07, pp. 243-252). New York: ACM.

Hu, P., Greenwood, C., & Beyene, J. (2006). Statistical methods for meta-analysis of microarray data: A comparative study. *Information Systems Frontiers, 8*(1), 9–20. doi:10.1007/s10796-005-6099-z

Hubbard, S. J., & Thornton, J. M. (1993). *NACCESS, Computer Program* (Tech. Rep.). London: University College, Department of Biochemistry and Molecular Biology.

Hümmer, W., Lehner, W., Bauer, A., & Schlesinger, L. (2002). A decathlon in multidimensional modeling: open issues and some solutions. *Proceedings of the 4th International Conference on Data Warehousing and Knowledge Discovery*, (pp. 275-285).

Hüsemann, B., Lechtenbörger, J., & Vossen, G. (2000). Conceptual data warehouse design. *Proceedings of the 2nd International Workshop on Design and Management of Data Warehouses*, (p. 6).

Hurtado, C., & Gutierrez, C. (2007). Handling structural heterogeneity in OLAP In R. Wrembel & Ch. Koncilia (Eds.). *Data warehouses and OLAP: concepts, architectures and solutions*, (pp. 27-57). Hershey, PA: Idea Group Publishing.

Inmon, W. H. (2005). *Building The Data Warehouse* (4th Ed). Indianapolis, IN: Wiley Computer Publishing Inc.

Irizarry, R. et al (2003). Summaries of affymetrix genechip probe level data. *Nucleic Acids Reseach, 31.*

Jagadish, H. V., Mumick, I. S., & Silberschatz, A. (1995). View maintenance issues for the chronicle data model (extended abstract). In M. Yannakakis (Ed.), *Proc. 14th ACM Symposium on Principles of Database Systems (PODS)*, San Jose, CA, (pp. 113–124). New York: ACM Press.

Jagadish, H., Lakshmanan, L., & Srivastava, D. (1999). What can hierarchies do for data warehouses. *Proceedings of the 25th International Conference on Very Large Data Bases*, (pp. 530-541).

Jain, A. K., & Dubes, R. C. (1988). *Algorithms for Clustering Data*. Upper Saddle River, NJ: Prentice-Hall.

Jain, P. K. (2005). Financial market design and the equity premium: Electronic versus floor trading. *The Journal of Finance, 60*(6), 2955–2985. doi:10.1111/j.1540-6261.2005.00822.x

Japkowicz, N. (2000). The class imbalance problem: Significance and strategies. In *Proceedings of the 2000 International Conference on Artificial Intelligence (ICAI 2000)*.

Jarke, M., Carey, M. J., Dittrich, K. R., Lochovsky, F. H., Loucopoulos, P., & Jeusfeld, M. A. (Eds.). (1997). *Proc. 23rd International Conference on Very Large Data Bases (VLDB)*, Athens, Greece. San Francisco: Morgan Kaufmann.

Java, A., Song, X., Finin, T., & Tseng, B. (2007). Why we twitter: Understanding the microblogging effect in user intentions and communities. In *Proceedings of WebKDD / SNAKDD 2007: KDD Workshop on Web Mining and Social Network Analysis, in conjunction with the 13th ACM SIGKDD International Conference on Knowledge Discovery and Data Mining* (KDD 2007, pp. 56-66).

Jensen, C. S., & Snodgrass, R. T. (1999). Temporal Data Management. *IEEE Transactions on Knowledge and Data Engineering, 11*(1), 36–44. doi:10.1109/69.755613

Jensen, C., Kligys, A., Pedersen, T., & Timko, I. (2004). Multidimensional data modeling for location-based services. *The VLDB Journal, 13*(1), 1–21. doi:10.1007/s00778-003-0091-3

Jiang, H., Deng, Y., Chen, H.-S., Tao, L., Sha, Q., & Chen, J. (2004). Joint analysis of two microarray gene-expression data sets to select lung adenocarcinoma marker genes. *BMC Bioinformatics, 5*, 81. doi:10.1186/1471-2105-5-81

Jiang, N., & Gruenwald, L. (2006). CFI-Stream: Mining Closed Frequent Itemsets in Data Streams. *ACM SIGKDD international conference on knowledge discovery and data mining.*

Jiang, N., & Gruenwald, L. (2007). Estimating missing data in data streams, *the International Conference on Database Systems for Advanced Applications.*

Jin, D., Tsuji, T., Tsuchida, T., & Higuchi, K. (2008). An Incremental Maintenance Scheme of Data Cubes. In *Proceedings of* DASFAA 2008: (pp. 172-187). Heidelberg: Springer-Verlag.

John, K., & Narayanan, R. (1997). Market manipulation and the role of insider trading regulations. *The Journal of Business, 70*(2), 217–247. doi:10.1086/209716

Kailing, K., Kriegel, H.-P., & Kröger, P. (2004). Density-connected Subspace Clustering for High Dimensional Data. In *Proc. of SIAM International Conference on Data Mining (SDM)* (pp. 246-257).

Kalnis, P., Ng, W. S., Ooi, B. C., Papadias, D., & Tan, K.-L. (2002). An adaptive peer-to-peer network for distributed caching of OLAP results. In M. J. Franklin, B. Moon, & A. Ailamaki, (Eds.), *Proc. ACM SIGMOD International Conference on Management of Data*, Madison, Wisconsin. New York: ACM.

Kaltenbrunner, A., Gómez, V., & López, V. (2007). *Description and Prediction of Slashdot Activity*. Paper presented at the LA-WEB 2007 5th Latin American Web Congress, Santiago, Chile.

Kaltenbrunner, A., Gómez, V., Moghnieh, A., Meza, R., Blat, J., & López, V. (2007). *Homogeneous temporal activity patterns in a large online communication space*. Paper presented at the 10th Int. Conf. on Business Information Systems, Workshop on Social Aspects of the Web (SAW 2007), Poznan, Poland.

Kannan, R., Vempala, S., & Vetta, A. (2000). On clusterings - good, bad and spectral. *IEEE Symposium on Foundations of Computer Science*, (pp. 367—377). Los Alamitos, CA: IEEE Computer Society.

Karen, C., & Gupta, A. (2006). Indexing in Datewarehouses: Bitmaps and Beyond. In Wrembel & Koncilia (Eds.) *Data Warehouses and OLAP*. Hershey, PA: IGI Global.

Kargupta, H., Bhargava, R., Liu, K., Powers, M., Blair, P., Bushra, S., et al. (2004). VEDAS: A mobile and distributed data stream mining system for real-time vehicle monitoring. *SIAM International Conference on Data Mining*.

Karypis, G. (2003). *CLUTO - A clustering toolkit* (Tech. Rep.). Minneapolis, USA: University of Minnesota, Department of Computer Science & Engineering.

Kaser, O., & Daniel, L. (2003). Attribute value reordering for efficient hybrid OLAP. In *Proceedings of DOLAP '03*, New Orleans, Louisiana, November 7, 2003 (NRC 46510).

Kaufman, L., & Rousseeuw, P. J. (1990). *Finding Groups in Data: An Introduction to Cluster Analysis*. Wiley series in probability and mathematical statistics. Chichester, UK: John Wiley and Sons.

Kazmirski, S. L., Li, A., & Daggett, V. (1999). Analysis methods for comparison of multiple molecular dynamics trajectories: Applications to protein unfolding pathways and denatured ensembles. *Journal of Molecular Biology*, *290*(1), 283–304. doi:10.1006/jmbi.1999.2843

Keim, D., & Heczko, M. (2001). Wavelets and their applications in databases. In A. Reuter, & D. Lomet, (Eds.), *Proceedings of the 17th International Conference on Data Engineering (ICDE),* Heidelberg. Washington, DC: IEEE Computer Society.

Khelif, K., Dieng-Kuntz, R., & Barbry, B. (2007). An ontologybasedapproach to support text mining and information retrieval in the biological domain. *J. UCS*, *13*(12), 1881–1907.

Kim, K., Ki, D., Jeong, H., Jeung, H., Chung, H. C., & Rha, S. Y. (2007). Novel and simple transformation algorithm for combining microarray data sets. *BMC Bioinformatics*, 8. doi:10.1186/1471-2105-8-8

Kim, M. H., & Lee, K. Y. (2006) Efficient incremental maintenance of data cubes. In *Proceedings of the 32nd international conference on Very large data bases*, (pp. 823 – 833). San Francisco: Morgan Kaufman.

Kimball, R. (2002). *The Data Warehouse Toolkit: The Complete Guide to Dimensional Modeling*, (2nd Ed.). New York: John & Wiley & Sons.

Kitano, H. (2003). A Graphical Notation for Biochemical Networks. *BIOSILICO*, *1*(5), 169–176. doi:10.1016/S1478-5382(03)02380-1

Klein, D., Kamvar, D., & Manning, C. (2002). From Instance-Level Constraints to Space-Level Constraints: Making Most of Prior Knowledge in Data Clustering. In *Proc. of International Conference on Machine Learning (ICML)* (pp. 307-314).

Koh, J. L., & Shin, S. N. (2006). An approximate approach for mining recently frequent itemsets from data streams. *The 8th International Conference on Data Warehousing and Knowledge Discovery.*

Kotidis, Y. (2002). Aggregate view management in data warehouses. In J. Abello, P. M. Pardalos, & M. G. C. Resende, (Eds.), *Handbook of Massive Data Sets*, (pp. 711–741). Norwell, MA: Kluwer Academic Publishers.

Kotidis, Y., & Roussopoulos, N. (1999). DynaMat: a dynamic view management system for data warehouses. In A. Delis, C. Faloutsos, & S. Ghandeharizadeh, (Eds.), *Proceedings of the ACM SIGMOD International Conference on Management of Data*, (pp. 371–382), Philadelphia. New York: ACM Press.

Kotidis, Y., & Roussopoulos, N. (2001). A case for dynamic view management. *ACM Transactions on Database Systems*, *26*(4), 388–423. doi:10.1145/503099.503100

Kriegel, H.-P., & Pfeifle, M. (2005). Density-based Clustering of Uncertain Data. In *Proc. of ACM SIGKDD International Conference on Knowledge Discovery and Data Mining (KDD)* (pp. 672–677).

Kruchten, P. (1995). Architectural Blueprints — The "4+1" View Model of Software Architecture. *IEEE Software*, *12*(6), 42–50. doi:10.1109/52.469759

Kulis, B., Basu, S., Dhillon, I. S., & Mooney, R. J. (2005). Semi-supervised Graph Clustering: a Kernel Approach. In *Proc. of International Conference on Machine Learning (ICML)* (pp. 457-464).

Kyte, J. (2003). The basis of the hydrophobic effect. *Biophysical Chemistry*, *100*(1-3), 193–203. doi:10.1016/S0301-4622(02)00281-8

Labio, W., Quass, D., & Adelberg, B. (1997). Physical database design for data warehouses. In Λ. Gray, & P.-Å. Larson, (Eds.), *Proceedings of the 13th International Conference on Data Engineering (ICDE)*, (pp. 277–288), Birmingham, UK. New York: IEEE Computer Society.

Lachev, T. (2005). *Applied Microsoft Analysis Services 2005*. Prologica Press.

Lakshmanan, L. V. S., Pei, J., & Han, J. (2002). Quotient cube: How to summarize the semantics of a data cube. In *VLDB* (2002), (pp. 778–789).

Larson, P.-Å., & Zhou, J. (2007). Efficient maintenance of materialized outer-join views. In *Proc. 23rd Intl. Conference on Data Engineering (ICDE)*, (pp. 56–65), Istanbul, Turkey. Washington, DC: IEEE.

Lechtenbörger, J., & Vossen, G. (2003). Multidimensional normal forms for data warehouse design. *Information Systems*, *28*(5), 415–434. doi:10.1016/S0306-4379(02)00024-8

Lee, B., & Richards, F. M. (1971). The interpretation of protein structures: estimation of static accessibility. *Journal of Molecular Biology*, *55*(3), 379–400. doi:10.1016/0022-2836(71)90324-X

Lee, H., Hsu, A., Sajdak, J., Qin, J., & Pavlidis, P. (2004). Coexpression analysis of human genes across many microarray data sets. *Genome Research*, *14*, 1085–1094. doi:10.1101/gr.1910904

Lee, V. C., & Yang, X. J. (2005). Development and test of an artificial-immune-abnormal trading-detection system

for financial market. *Advances in Intelligent Computing*, (pp.410-419). Berlin: Springer.

Lehman, T. J., & Carey, M. J. (1986). A Study of Index Structures for Main Memory Database Management Systems. In *Proc. VLDB*, (pp. 294-303).

Lehner, W. (1998). Modeling large scale OLAP scenarios. In *Proceedings of the 6th EDBT* (pp. 153–167).

Lehner, W., Albrecht, J., & Wedekind, H. (1998). Normal forms for multidimensional databases. *Proceedings of the 10th International Conference on Scientific and Statistical Database Management*, (pp. 63-72).

Leland, H. E. (1992). Insider Trading: Should it be prohibited? *The Journal of Political Economy*, *100*(4), 859–887. doi:10.1086/261843

Lemire, D. (2002). Wavelet-based relative prefix sum methods for range sum queries in data cubes. In *Proceedings of CASCON*.

Lenz, H., & Shoshani, A. (1997). Summarizability in OLAP and statistical databases. *Proceedings of the 9th International Conference on Scientific and Statistical Database Management*, (pp.132-143).

Lerman, K. (2007). Social Information Processing in News Aggregation. *IEEE Internet Computing*, *11*(6), 16–28. doi:10.1109/MIC.2007.136

Lerner, A., & Shasha, D. (2003). The virtues and challenges of ad hoc + streams querying in finance. *IEEE Data Eng Bull*, 49–56.

Leskovec, J., Adamic, L., & Huberman, B. A. (2007). The Dynamics of Viral Marketing. *ACM Transactions on the Web* (ACM TWEB), *1*(1).

Li, C., & Wang, S. (2006). Efficient incremental maintenance for distributive and non-distributive aggregate functions. *Journal of Computer Science and Technology*, *21*(1), 52–65. doi:10.1007/s11390-006-0052-6

Li, H. F., & Cheng, H. (2008). Improve frequent closed itemsets mining over data stream with bitmap. *Ninth ACIS International conference on software engineering, artificial intelligence, networking, and parallel/distributed computing*.

Li, H. F., Ho, C. C., Kuo, F. F., & Lee, S. Y. (2006) A new algorithm for maintaining closed frequent itemsets in data streams by incremental updates. *Six IEEE International Conference on Data Mining Workshop.*

Li, H. F., Lee, S. Y., & Shan, M. K. (2004). An efficient algorithm for mining frequent itemsets over the entire history of data streams. *The International Workshop on Knowledge Discovery in Data Streams.*

Li, J., & Srivastava, J. (2002). Efficient Aggregation Algorithms for Compressed Data warehouses. *IEEE Transactions on Knowledge and Data Engineering, 14*(3), 515–529. doi:10.1109/TKDE.2002.1000340

Li, J., Maier, D., Tufte, K., Papadimos, V., & Tucker, P. A. (2005). Semantics and evaluation techniques for window aggregates in data streams. In F. Özcan, (Ed.), *Proceedings of the ACM SIGMOD International Conference on Management of Data*, Baltimore, Maryland, USA. New York: ACM.

Li, J., Rotem, D., & Wong, H. K. (1987). A New Compression Method with Fast Searching on Large Databases. In *Proceedings of* 13th *international conference on Very large data bases*, (pp. 311-318). San Francisco: Morgan Kaufman.

Li, Y., Han, J., & Yang, J. (2004). Clustering moving objects. In *Proc. of ACM SIGKDD International Conference on Knowledge Discovery and Data Mining (KDD)* (pp.617–622).

Liefke, H., & Davidson, S. B. (2000). View maintenance for hierarchical semistructured data. In Y. Kambayashi, M. K. Mohania, & A. M. Tjoa, (Eds.), *Proceedings Second International Conference on Data Warehousing and Knowledge Discovery (DaWaK)*, (LNCS Vol.1874, pp. 114–125), London. Berlin: Springer.

Lin, C. H., Chiu, D. Y., Wu, Y. H., & Chen, A. L. P. (2005). Mining frequent itemsets from data streams with a time-sensitive sliding window. *SIAM International Conference on Data Mining.*

Lins, L., & Brasseur, R. (1995). The hydrophobic effect in protein folding. *The FASEB Journal, 9*(7), 535–540.

List, B., Bruckner, R., Machaczek, K., & Schiefer, J. (2002). Comparison of data warehouse development methodologies: case study of the process warehouse. *Proceedings of the 13th International Conference on Database and Expert Systems Applications*, (pp. 203-215).

Liu, K., Cho, H. S., Hoyt, D. W., Nguyen, T. N., Olds, P., Kelly, J. W., & Wemmer, D. E. (2000). Deuterium-proton exchange on the native wild-type transthyretin tetramer identifies the stable core of the individual subunits and indicates mobility at the subunit interface. *Journal of Molecular Biology, 303*(4), 555–565. doi:10.1006/jmbi.2000.4164

Liu, L., Pu, C., & Tang, W. (1999). Continual queries for internet scale event-driven information delivery. *IEEE Transactions on Knowledge and Data Engineering, 11*(4), 610–628. doi:10.1109/69.790816

Long, B., Zhang, Z., Wu, X., & Yu, P. S. (2006). Spectral clustering for Multi-type Relational Data. In *Proc. of International Conference on Machine Learning (ICML)* (pp.585-592).

Longley, P., Goodchild, M., Maguire, D., & Rhind, D. (2001). *Geographic Information Systems and Science.* New York: John Wiley & Sons.

Lopez, I., & Snodgrass, R. (2005). Spatiotemporal aggregate computation: A survey. *IEEE Transactions on Knowledge and Data Engineering, 17*(2), 271–286. doi:10.1109/TKDE.2005.34

Lucas, H. (1993). Market expert surveillance systems. *Communications of the ACM, 36*, 27–34. doi:10.1145/163298.163301

Luján-Mora, S., Trujillo, J., & Song, I. (2006). A UML profile for multidimensional modeling in data warehouses. *Data & Knowledge Engineering, 59*(3), 725–769. doi:10.1016/j.datak.2005.11.004

Luo, C., Zhao, Y., Cao, L., Ou, Y., & Liu, L. (2008). Outlier mining on multiple time series data in stock market. In *Proc. of the Tenth Pacific Rim International Conference on Artificial Intelligence (PRICAI 08), 2008.*

Luo, G., & Yu, P. S. (2008). Content-based filtering for efficient online materialized view maintenance. In *Proc.*

17th ACM Conference on Information and Knowledge Management (CIKM), (pp. 163–172), New York. New York: ACM.

Luo, G., Naughton, J. F., Ellmann, C. J., & Waltzk, M. W. (2006). Transaction Reordering and Grouping for Continuous Data Loading". In *Proc. BIRTE,* (pp. 34–49).

MacKerell, A. D., Bashford, D., Bellott, M., Dunbrack, R. L., Evanseck, J. D., & Field, M. J. (1998). All-atom empirical potential for molecular modeling and dynamics studies of proteins. *The Journal of Physical Chemistry B, 102*(18), 3586–3616. doi:10.1021/jp973084f

Madden, S., Shah, M. A., Hellerstein, J. M., & Raman, V. (2002). Continuously adaptive continuous queries over streams. In M. J. Franklin, B. Moon, & A. Ailamaki, (Eds.), *Proc. ACM SIGMOD International Conference on Management of Data,* (pp. 49–60), Madison, Wisconsin. New York: ACM.

Malinowski, E., & Zimányi, E. (2004). Representing spatiality in a conceptual multidimensional model. In *Proceedings of the 12th ACM GIS* (pp. 12-22). New York: ACM Press.

Malinowski, E., & Zimányi, E. (2005). Spatial Hierarchies and Topological Relationships in SpatialMultiDimER model. In *Proceedings of the 22th British National Conference on Databases* (pp. 17-22). Berlin: Springer.

Malinowski, E., & Zimányi, E. (2008). *Advanced data warehouse design: from conventional to spatial and temporal applications.* Berlin: Springer.

Manku, G. S., & Motwani, R. (2002). Approximate frequency counts over data streams. *International Conference on Very Large Databases.*

Marco, D. (2004). *Building and Managing the Meta Data Repository: A Full Lifecycle Guide.* New York: John Wiley & Sons Inc.

Marian, A., Abiteboul, S., Cobena, G., & Mignet, L. (2001). Change-Centric Management of Versions in an XML Warehouse. In *Proceedings of the 27th International Conference on Very Large Databases,* (pp. 581-590).

Medina, E., & Trujillo, J. (2002). A Standard for Representing Multidimensional Properties: The Common Warehouse Metamodel (CWM). In *Proc. ADBIS* (pp. 232-247).

Meila, M. (2008). The Uniqueness of a Good Optimum for K-means. In *Proc. of International Conference on Machine Learning (ICML)* (pp. 625-632).

Meulbroek, L. K. (1992). An emrirical analysis of illegal insider trading. *The Journal of Finance, 47,* 1661–1699. doi:10.2307/2328992

Meunier, B., Dumas, E., Piec, I., Béchet, D., Hébraud, M., & Hocquette, J. F. (2007). Assessment of hierarchical clustering methodologies for proteomic data mining. *Journal of Proteome Research, 6*(1), 358–366. doi:10.1021/pr060343h

Microsoft Corporation. (2005). *SQL Server 2005: books online.* http://technet.microsoft.com/en-us/sqlserver/bb895969.aspx.

Mika, P. (2005). Ontologies are us: A unified model of social networks and semantics. In *The Semantic Web – ISWC 2005,* (pp. 522-536). Berlin: Springer.

Minenna, M. (2003). Insider trading, abnormal return and preferential information: Supervising through a probabilistic model. *Journal of Banking & Finance, 27,* 59–86. doi:10.1016/S0378-4266(01)00209-6

Mistry, H., Roy, P., Sudarshan, S., & Ramamritham, K. (2001). Materialized view selection and maintenance using multi-query optimization. In T. Sellis, & S. Mehrotra, (Eds.), *Proceedings of the ACM SIGMOD International Conference on Management of Data,* (pp. 307–318), Santa Barbara, CA. New York: ACM Press.

Mitrpanont, J. L., & Fugkeaw, S. (2006). Design and Development of a Multiversion OLAP Application. In *Proceedings of ACM Symposium on Applied Computing,* (pp. 493-497), France.

Mitzenmacher, M. (2004). A Brief History of Generative Models for Power Law and Lognormal Distributions. [Wellesley, MA: A K Peters, Ltd.]. *Internet Mathematics, 1*(2), 226–251.

Moreau, Y., & Aerts, S., Moorl, B., Strooper, B., & Dabrowski, M. (2003). Comparison and meta-analysis of microarray data: from the bench to the computer desk. *Trends in Genetics, 19*, 570–577. doi:10.1016/j.tig.2003.08.006

Morzy, T., & Wrembel, R. (2003). Modeling a Multiversion Data Warehouse: A Formal Approach. In *Proceedings of the International Conference on Enterprise Information Systems,* France.

Morzy, T., & Wrembel, R. (2004). On querying versions of multiversion data warehouse. In *Proceedings of 7th ACM international Workshop on Data Warehouse and OLAP,* (pp. 92 - 101), USA.

Motwani, R., Widom, J., Arasu, A., Babcock, B., Babu, S., Datar, M., et al. (2003). Query processing, approximation, and resource management in a data stream management system. In *Proc. 1st Biennal Conference on Innovative Data Systems Research (CIDR),* Asilomar, CA.

Mozafari, B., Thakkar, H., & Zaniolo, C. (2008). Verifying and mining frequent patterns from large windows over data streams. *IEEE International Conference on Data Engineering.*

Muller, P., & Insua, D. R. (1995). Issues in bayesian analysis of neural network models. *Neural Computation, 10*, 571–592.

Mumick, I. S., Quass, D., & Mumick, B. S. (1997). Maintenance of data cubes and summary tables in a warehouse. In *ACM SIGMOD,* (pp. 100–111).

Nagesh, H., Goil, S., & Choudhary, A. (2000). A Scalable Parallel Subspace Clustering Algorithm for Massive Data Sets. In *Proc. of IEEE International Conference on Parallel Processing* (pp.477-).

Nascimento, M. A., Özsu, M. T., & Renée, J. Miller, D. K., Blakeley, J. A., & Schiefer, K. B., editors (2004). *Proc. 30th Intl. Conference on Very Large Data Bases (VLDB),* Toronto, Canada. San Francisco: Morgan Kaufmann.

Nasir, J. A., & Shahzad, M. K. (2007). Architecture for Virtualization in Data Warehouse. In Sobh. T (Ed.) *Innovations and Advanced Techniques in Computer and Information Sciences and Engineering* (pp. 243-248). Berlin: Springer.

Nasir, J. A., Shahzad, M. K., & Pasha, M. A. (2006). Transparent querying multiple version of data warehouse. *Information Technology Journal, 5*(2), 250–259. doi:10.3923/itj.2006.250.259

Nasraoui, O., Uribe, C. C., Coronel, C. R., & Gonzales, F. (2003). TECNO-STREAMS: Tracking Evolving Clusters in Noisy Data Streams with a Scalable Immune System Learning Model. In *Proc. of IEEE International Conference on Data Mining (ICDM)* (pp. 235-242).

Neville, J., Simsek, O., Jensen, D., Komoroske, J., Palmer, K., & Goldberg, H. (2005) Using relational knowledge discovery to prevent securities fraud. *the eleventh ACM SIGKDD international conference on Knowledge discovery in data mining,* (pp. 449-458). New York: ACM Press

Newman, M. E. J. (2005). Power laws, Pareto distributions and Zipf's law. *Contemporary Physics, 46*, 323–351. doi:10.1080/00107510500052444

Ng, A., Jordan, M., & Weiss, Y. (2002). On Spectral Clustering: Analysis and an Algorithm. [Cambridge, MA: MIT Press.]. *Advances in Neural Information Processing Systems, 14*, 849–856.

Ng, R. T., & Han, J. (1994). Efficient and Effective Clustering Methods for Spatial Data Mining. In *Proc. of International Conference on Very Large Data Bases (VLDB)* (pp. 144-155).

Ng, W., & Chinya, V. R. (1997). Block-oriented compression techniques for large statistical databases. *IEEE Transactions on Knowledge and Data Engineering, 9*(2), 314–328. doi:10.1109/69.591455

Ngai, W., Kao, B., Chui, C., Cheng, R., Chau, M., & Yip, K. Y. (2006). Efficient Clustering of Uncertain Data. In *Proc. of IEEE International Conference on Data Mining (ICDM)* (pp. 436-445).

Nicolas, J.-M. (1982). Logic for improving integrity checking in relational data bases. *Acta Informatica, 18*, 227–253. doi:10.1007/BF00263192

Niemi, T., Nummenmaa, J., & Thanisch, P. (2001). Logical multidimensional database design for ragged and unbalanced aggregation hierarchies. *Proceedings of the 3rd International Workshop on Design and Management of Data Warehouses*, (pp. 7).

O'Callaghan, L., Meyerson, A., Motwani, M., Mishra, N., & Guha, S. (2002). Streaming-Data Algorithms for High-Quality Clustering. In *IEEE International Conference on Data Engineering (ICDE)* (pp.685-).

O'Hara, M. (1997). *Market microstructure eheory*. London: Blackwell Publishing.

O'Neil, E. J., O'Neil, P. E., & Weikum, G. (1993). The LRU-K page replacement algorithm for database disk buffering. In P. Buneman, & S. Jajodia, (Ed.), *Proceedings of the ACM SIGMOD International Conference on Management of Data*, (pp. 297–306), Washington, DC. New York: ACM Press.

O'Neil, P. & Quass, (1997). Improved query performance with variant indexes. In *SIGMOID*, (pp. 38-49).

Otoo, E. J., & Merrett, T. H. (1983). A storage scheme for extendible arrays. *Computing, 31*, 1–9. doi:10.1007/BF02247933

Owen, K. (2002). *Compressing MOLAP arrays by attribute-value reordering: An experimental analysis*. UNBSJ ASCS Technical Report TR-02-001.

Ozsu, T., & Valduriez, P. (1991). *Principles of Distributed Database Systems*, (2nd Ed.). Upper Saddle River, NJ: Prentice-Hall Publishers.

Pace, C. N., Shirley, B. A., Mcnutt, M., & Gajiwala, K. (1996). Forces contributing to the conformational stability of proteins. *The FASEB Journal, 10*(1), 75–83.

Palpanas, T., Sidle, R., Cochrane, R., & Pirahesh, H. (2002). Incremental maintenance for nondistributive aggregate functions. In *VLDB* (2002), (pp. 802–813).

Palshikar, G. K., & Apte, M. M. (2008). Collusion set detection using graph clustering. *Data Mining and Knowledge Discovery, 16*(2), 135–164. doi:10.1007/s10618-007-0076-8

Pang, B., Lee, L., & Vaithyanathan, S. (2002). Thumbs up? Sentiment classification using machine learning techniques. In *Proceedings of the Acl-02 Conference on Empirical Methods in Natural Language Processing - Volume 10*, (pp. 79-86). Morristown, NJ: ACL.

Papadopoulos, S., Vakali, A., & Kompatsiaris, I. (July, 2008). *Digg it Up! Analyzing Popularity Evolution in a Web 2.0 Setting*. Paper presented at MSoDa08 (Mining Social Data), a satellite Workshop of the 18th European Conference on Artificial Intelligence, Patras, Greece.

Patroumpas, K., & Sellis, T. K. (2006). Window specification over data streams. In *Current Trends in Database Technology - EDBT 2006 Workshops*, (pp. 445–464).

Paulraj, P. (2001). *Data Warehousing Fundamentals: A Comprehensive Guide for IT Professionals*. New York: John and Wiley Sons.

Pedersen, M. B., Skov, L., Menne, T., Johansen, J., & Olsen, J. (2007). Gene expression time course in the human skin during elicitation of allergic contact dermatitis. *The Journal of Investigative Dermatology, 127*(11), 2585–2595. doi:10.1038/sj.jid.5700902

Pedersen, T. B., & Jensen, C. S. (1999). Multidimensional Data Modeling for Complex Data. In *Proc. ICDE* (pp. 336-345).

Pedersen, T. B., & Tryfona, N. (2001). Pre-aggregation in Spatial DataWarehouses. In *Proceedings of the 7th International Symposium on Spatial and Temporal Databases* (pp. 460-478).

Pedersen, T. B., Jensen, C., & Dyreson, C. (2001). A foundation for capturing and querying complex multidimensional data. *Journal of Information Systems, 26*(5), 383–423. doi:10.1016/S0306-4379(01)00023-0

Pelleg, D., & Moore, A. (2000) X-means: Extending K-means with Efficient Estimation of the Number of Clusters. In *Proc. of International Conference on Machine Learning (ICML)* (pp. 727–734).

Pennec, E. L., & Mallat, S. (2000). *Image representation and compression with bandelets*. Technical report, École Polytechnique.

Perlich, C., Helander, M., Lawrence, R., Liu, Y., Rosset, S., & Reddy, C. (2007). Looking for great ideas: Analyzing the innovation jam. In *Proceedings of WebKDD / SNAKDD 2007: KDD Workshop on Web Mining and Social Network Analysis, in conjunction with the 13th ACM SIGKDD International Conference on Knowledge Discovery and Data Mining* (KDD 2007), (pp. 66-74).

Phillips, J. C., Braun, R., Wang, W., Gumbart, J., Tajkhorshid, E., & Villa, E. (2005). Scalable molecular dynamics with NAMD. *Journal of Computational Chemistry, 26*(16), 1781–1802. doi:10.1002/jcc.20289

Piwowarski, B., & Zaragoza, H. (2007). Predictive User Click Models based on Click-through History. In *Proceedings of the Sixteenth ACM Conference on Conference on information and Knowledge Management,* Lisbon, Portugal, November 06 - 10, 2007, CIKM '07, (pp. 175-182). New York: ACM.

Poosola, V., Ganti, V., & Ioannidis, Y. E. (1999). Approximate query answering using histograms. *Bulletin of the IEEE Computer Society Technical Committe on Data Engineering,* (pp. 1–10).

Pourabbas, E., & Rafanelli, M. (2003). Hierarchies. In M. Rafanelli. (Ed.) *Multidimensional databases: problems and solutions,* (pp. 91-115). Hershey, PA: Idea Group Publishing.

Procopiuc, C. M., Jonesý, M., Pankaj, K., Agarwal, M., & Muraliý, M. (2002). A Monte Carlo Algorithm for Fast Projective Clustering. In *Proc. of ACM SIGMOD International Conference on Management of Data (SIGMOD)* (pp. 418–427).

Qi, H., & Wang, J. (2004). A model for mining outliers from complex data sets. *The 2004 ACM symposium on Applied computing,* (pp. 595-599). New York: ACM Press.

Quass, D., & Widom, J. (1997). On-line warehouse view maintenance. In J. Peckham, (Ed.), *Proceedings of the ACM SIGMOD International Conference on Management of Data,* (pp. 393–404), Tucson, Arizona. New York: ACM Press.

Quass, D., Gupta, A., Mumick, I. S., & Widom, J. (1996). Making views self-maintainable for data warehousing. In

Proc. 4th Intl. Conference on Parallel and Distributed Information Systems (PDIS), (pp. 158–169), Miami Beach, FL. Washington, DC: IEEE Computer Society.

Quinlan, J. R. (1993). *C4.5: Programs for machine learning.* San Francisco: Morgan Kaufmann.

Quinlan, J. R. C4.5 (1993). *Programs for Machine Learning.* San Francisco: Morgan Kaufmann Publishers.

Quintas, A., Vaz, D. C., Cardoso, I., Saraiva, M. J., & Brito, R. M. M. (2001). Tetramer dissociation and monomer partial unfolding precedes protofibril formation in amyloidogenic transthyretin variants. *The Journal of Biological Chemistry, 276*(29), 27207–27213. doi:10.1074/jbc.M101024200

Radzicka, A., & Wolfenden, R. (1988). Comparing the polarities of the amino-acids: Side-chain distribution coefficients between the vapor phase, cyclohexane, 1-Octanol, and neutral aqueous solution. *Biochemistry, 27*(5), 1664–1670. doi:10.1021/bi00405a042

Rafanelli, M. (2003). Basic notions. In M. Rafanelli. (Ed.) *Multidimensional databases: problems and solutions,* (pp. 1-45). Hershey, PA: Idea Group Publishing.

Rafanelli, M., & Ricci, F. (1983). Proposal of a logical model for statistical databases. In *Proceedings of the 2nd International Workshop on Statistical and Scientific Database Management,* (pp. 264-272).

Ramakrishnan, R. (2007). Community Systems: The World Online. In *Proceedings of CIDR 2007, Third Biennial Conference on Innovative Data Systems Research,* (pp. 341), Asilomar, CA.

Raman, V., Deshpande, A., & Hellerstein, J. M. (2003). Using state modules for adaptive query processing. In *Proceedings of the 19th International Conference on Data Engineering (ICDE),* pages 353–366, Bangalore, India. Washington, DC: IEEE Computer Society.

Rao, F., Zhang, L., Yu, X., & Li, Y. & Chen, Y. (2003). Spatial hierarchy and OLAP-favored search in spatial data warehouse. In *Proceedings of the 6th ACM International Workshop on Data Warehousing and OLAP* (pp. 48-55). New York: ACM Press.

Rao, P., & Moon, B. (2006). Sketchtree: Approximate tree pattern counts over streaming labeled trees. In L. Liu, A. Reuter, K.-Y. Whang, & J. Zhang, (Eds.), *Proceedings 22nd International Conference on Data Engineering (ICDE),* Atlanta, GA. Washington, DC: IEEE Computer Society.

Ratsaby, J., & Venkatesh, S. S. (1995). Learning from a mixture of labeled and unlabeled examples with parametric side information. In *proceedings of the Eighth Annual Conference on Computational Learning Theory,* (pp. 412-417).

Ravat, F., Teste, O., & Zurfluh, G. (2006). A Multiversion based Multi-dimensional Model. In *Proceedings of Data Warehousing and Knowledge Discovery,* (LNCS 4081, pp. 65-74). Berlin: Springer.

Rhodes, D., Barrette, T., Rubin, M., Ghosh, D., & Chinnaiyan, A. (2002). Interstudy validation of gene expression profiles reveals pathway dysregulation in prostate cancer. *Cancer Research, 62,* 4427–4433.

Richardson, M., & Domingos, P. (2002). Mining knowledge-sharing sites for viral marketing. In *Proceedings of the 14th ACM SIGKDD International Conference on Knowledge Discovery and Data Mining.* Las Vegas, NV. New York: ACM Press.

Rigaux, P., & Scholl, M. (1995). Multi-Scale Partitions: Application to Spatial and Statistical Databases. In *Proceedings of the 4th International Symposium on Advances in Spatial Databases,* (pp. 170-183). Berlin: Springer-Verlag

Rigaux, P., Scholl, M., & Voisard, A. (2002). *Spatial databases with applications to Gis.* New York: Academic Press.

Rivest, S., Bédard, Y., Proulx, M., Nadeaum, M., Hubert, F., & Pastor, J. (2005). SOLAP: Merging Business Intelligence with Geospatial Technology for Interactive Spatio-Temporal Exploration and Analysis of Data. *Journal of International Society for Photogrammetry and Remote Sensing, 60*(1), 17–33. doi:10.1016/j.isprsjprs.2005.10.002

Rizzi, S. (2003). Open problems in data warehousing: 8 years later. *Proceedings of the 5th International Workshop on Design and Management of Data Warehouses.*

Rizzi, S. (2007). Conceptual Modeling Solutions for the Data Warehouse. In J. Wang, (Ed.), *Data Warehousing and Mining: Concepts, Methodologies, Tools, and Applications* (pp. 1-26). Hershey, PA: IGI Global Publishers.

Rizzi, S. (2007). Conceptual modeling solutions for the data warehouse. In R. Wrembel & Ch. Koncilia (Eds.). *Data warehouses and OLAP: concepts, architectures and solutions,* (pp. 1-26.) Hershey, PA: Idea Group Publishing.

Rodrigues, J. R., & Brito, R. M. M. (2004). How important is the role of compact denatured states on amyloid formation by transthyretin? In G. Grateau, R. A. Kyle, & M. Skinner (Eds.), *Amyloid and Amyloidosis* (pp. 323–325). Bocca Raton, FL: CRC Press.

Rodrigues, J. R., Simões, C. J. V., Silva, C. G., & Brito, R. M. M. (2009). Potentially amyloidogenic conformational intermediates populate the unfolding landscape of transthyretin: insights from molecular dynamics simulations. *(submitted).*

Rosenberg, A. L. (1974). Allocating storage for extendible arrays. *Journal of the ACM, 21,* 652–670. doi:10.1145/321850.321861

Rosenberg, A. L., & Stockmeyer, L. J. (1977). Hashing schemes for extendible arrays. *Journal of the ACM, 24,* 199–221. doi:10.1145/322003.322006

Ross, K. A. (2004). Selection conditions in main memory. *ACM Transactions on Database Systems, 29,* 132–161. doi:10.1145/974750.974755

Ross, K. A., Srivastava, D., & Sudarshan, S. (1996). Materialized view maintenance and integrity constraint checking: Trading space for time. In H. V. Jagadish, & I. S. Mumick, (Eds.), *Proc. ACM SIGMOD Intl. Conference on Management of Data,* (pp. 447–458), Montreal, Quebec, Canada. New York: ACM Press.

Rotem, D., & Zhao, J. L. (1996) Extendible arrays for statistical databases and OLAP applications. In *Proceedings of Scientific and Statistical Database Management,* (pp. 108-117). Washington, DC: IEEE Computer Society.

Rotem, D., Otoo, E. J., & Seshadri, S. (2007). *Chunking of Large Multidimensional Arrays.* Lawrence Berkeley National Laboratory, University of California, University of California, 2007, LBNL-63230.

Roy, P., Seshadri, S., Sudarshan, S., & Bhobe, S. (2000). Efficient and extensible algorithms for multi query optimization. In W. Chen, J. F. Naughton, & P. A. Bernstein, (Eds.), *Proceedings of the ACM SIGMOD International Conference on Management of Data,* (pp. 249–260), Dallas, Texas. New York: ACM.

Rundensteiner, E. A., Koeller, A., & Zhang, X. (2000). Maintaining Data Warehouses over Changing Information Sources. *Communications of the ACM, 43*(6), 57–62. doi:10.1145/336460.336475

Sa, S., Valdez, P., Wu, J., Jung, K., Zhong, F., & Hall, L. (2007). The effects of il-20 subfamily cytokines on reconstituted human epidermis suggest potential roles in cutaneous innate defense and pathogenic adaptive immunity in psoriasis. *Journal of Immunology (Baltimore, MD.: 1950), 178*(4), 2229–2240.

Salton, G., Wong, A., & Yang, C. S. (1975). A vector space model for automatic indexing. *Communications of the ACM, 18*(11), 613–620. doi:10.1145/361219.361220

Samanta, U., Bahadur, R. P., & Chakrabarti, P. (2002). Quantifying the accessible surface area of protein residues in their local environment. *Protein Engineering, 15*(8), 659–667. doi:10.1093/protein/15.8.659

Samos, J., Saltor, F., Sistac, J., & Bardes, A. (1998). Database Architecture for Data Warehousing: An Evolutionary Approach, In *Proceedings of 9th International Conference on Database and Expert Systems Applications,* (LNCS 1460, pp. 746-75612). Berlin: Springer.

Sampaio, M. C., Sousa, A. G., & Baptista, C. (2006) Towards a logical multidimensional model for spatial data warehousing and olap. In *Proceedings of the 9th ACM international workshop on Data warehousing and OLAP* (pp. 83-90). New York: ACM Press.

Sapia, C., Blaschka, M., Höfling, G., & Dinter, B. (1998). Extending the E/R model for multidimensional paradigms. *Proceedings of the 17th International Conference on Conceptual Modeling,* (pp. 105-116).

Sarawagi, S. (1997). Indexing OLAP Data. *IEEE Data Eng. Bull., 20*(1), 36–43.

Sarawagi, S., & Stonebraker, M. (1994). Efficient organization of large multidimensional arrays. In *Proceedings of International Conference on Data Engineering (ICDE),* (pp. 328-336). Washington, DC: IEEE CS.

Sawires, A., Tatemura, J., Po, O., Agrawal, D., Abbadi, A. E., & Candan, K. S. (2006). Maintaining XPath views in loosely coupled systems. In *Dayal* et al. (2006), (pp. 583–594).

Scheraga, H. A., Khalili, M., & Liwo, A. (2007). Protein folding dynamics: Overview of molecular simulation techniques. *Annual Review of Physical Chemistry, 58,* 57–83. doi:10.1146/annurev.physchem.58.032806.104614

Scheuermann, P., Shim, J., & Vingralek, R. (1996). WATCHMAN: A data warehouse intelligent cache manager. In Vijayaraman et al. (pp. 51–62).

Schinasi, G. K., Drees, B., & Lee, W. (1999). Managing global finance and risk. *Finance & Development, 36*(4), 38–41.

Seamons, K. E., & Marianne, W. (1994) Physical schemas for large multidimensional arrays in scientific computing applications. In *Proceedings of Scientific and Statistical Database Management,* (pp. 218–227). Washington, DC: IEEE Computer Society.

Sellis, T. K. (1988). Multiple-query optimization. *ACM Transactions on Database Systems, 13*(1), 23–52. doi:10.1145/42201.42203

Serlin, O. (1993). The history of DebitCredit and the TPC. In J. Gray, (Ed.), *The Benchmark Handbook.* San Francisco: Morgan Kaufmann.

Seshadri, M., Machiraju, S., Sridharan, A., Bolot, J., Faloutsos, C., & Leskovec, J. (2008). Mobile Call Graphs: Beyond Power-Law and Lognormal Distributions. In *Proceedings of the Eighth ACM SIGKDD International*

Conference on Knowledge Discovery and Data Mining, (pp. 61-70), Edmonton, Canada. New York: ACM Press.

Shekar, S., Lu, C., Tan, X., Chang, S., & Vatsrai, R. (2001). Map Cube: A Visualization Tool for Spatial Data Warehouses. In *Geographic Data Mining and Knowledge Discovery* (pp. 74-90). London: Taylor & Francis

Shi, J., & Malik, J. (2000). Normalized Cuts and Image Segmentation. *IEEE Transactions on Pattern Analysis and Machine Intelligence, 22*(8), 888–905. doi:10.1109/34.868688

Shimada, T., Fang, T., Tsuji, T., & Higuchi, K. (2006). Containerization Algorithms for Multidimensional Arrays. *Asia Simulation conference*, (pp. 228-232). Heidelberg: Springer-Verlag.

Shin, S. J., & Lee, W. S. (2007). An online interactive method for finding assoication rules data streams. *ACM 16th Conference on Information and Knowledge Management.*

Shmueli, O., & Itai, A. (1984). Maintenance of views. In *Proceedings ACM SIGMOD International Conference on Management of Data*, (pp. 240–255). New York: ACM.

Shoshani, A. (1997). OLAP and statistical databases: Similarities and differences. In *Proceedings of ACM-PODS Conference,* (pp. 185–196).

Shukla, A., Deshpande, P., & Naughton, J. (1998). Materialized view selection for multidimensional datasets. In A. Gupta, O. Shmueli, & J. Widom, (Eds.), *Proceedings 24th International Conference on Very Large Data Bases (VLDB),* New York. San Francisco: Morgan Kaufmann.

Silberschatz, A., Galvin, P., & Gagne, G. (2002). *Operating System Concepts*, (6th Ed.). New York: John Wiley.

Silva, J., Times, V., Salgado, A., Souza, C., Fidalgo, R., & Oliveira, A. (2008). A set of aggregation functions for spatial measures. In *Proceedings of the ACM 14th International Workshop on Data Warehousing and OLAP* (pp. 25-32). New York: ACM Press.

Sismanis, Y., & Deligiannakis, A. Roussopoulus, & Kotidis, Y. (2002). Dwarf: Shrinking the petacube. In *ACM SIGMOD 2002*, (pp. 464–475).

Slonim, N., & Tishby, N. (2000). Document clustering using Word Clusters via the Information Bottleneck Method. In *Proc. of International ACM/SIGIR Conference on Research and Development in Information Retrieval* (pp. 208-215).

Smith, B., Ashburner, M., Rosse, C., Bard, J., Bug, W., & Ceusters, W. (2007). The obo foundry: Coordinated evolution of ontologies to support biomedical data integration. *Nature Biotechnology, 25*(11), 1251–1255. doi:10.1038/nbt1346

Smith, C. R. (1995). Tracking the elusive insider. *Wall Street and Technology, 12*, 48–50.

Smith, J. (1981). *The probability distribution of market returns: a logistic hypothesis*. PhD dissertation, University of Utah.

Song, I., Rowen, W., Medsker, C., & Ewen, E. (2001). An analysis of many-to-many relationships between facts and dimension tables in dimensional modeling. *Proceedings of the 3rd International Workshop on Design and Management of Data Warehouses*, (pp. 6).

Song, L., Smola, A. J., Gretton, A., & Borgwardt, K. M. (2007). A Dependence Maximization View of Clustering. In *Proc. of International Conference on Machine Learning (ICML)* (pp.815-822).

Song, X., Chi, Y., Hino, K., & Tseng, B. L. (2007). Information flow modeling based on diffusion rate for prediction and ranking. In *Proceedings of the 16th international Conference on World Wide Web* (Banff, Alberta, Canada, May 08 - 12, 2007). WWW '07, pp. 191-200, ACM, New York, NY, USA.

Srivastava, D., Dar, S., Jagadish, H. V., & Levy, A. Y. (1996). Answering queries with aggregation using views. In Vijayaraman et al. (pp. 318–329).

Srivastava, U., & Widom, J. (2004). Flexible time management in data stream systems. In A. Deutsch, (Ed.), *Proc. 23rd ACM Symposium on Principles of Database*

Systems (PODS), (pp. 263–274), Paris, France. New York: ACM.

Stabno, M. Wrembel R. (2007). RLH: bitmap compression technique based on run-length and huffman encoding. In *DOLAP 2007*, (pp. 41-48). New York: ACM.

Staudt, M., & Jarke, M. (1996). Incremental maintenance of externally materialized views. In Vijayaraman et al. (pp. 75–86).

Stefanovic, N., Han, J., & Koperski, K. (2000). Object-Based Selective Materialization for Efficient Implementation of Spatial Data Cubes. *IEEE TKDE*, *12*(6), 938–958.

Stockinger, K., & Wu, K. (2007). Bitmap indices for data warehouses. In R. Wrembel & C. Koncilia, (Ed.), *DataWarehouses and OLAP: Concepts, Architectures and Solutions*. Hershey, PA: Idea Group Inc.

Stoeckert, C., Causton, H., & Ball, C. (2002). Microarray databases: standards and ontologies. *Nature Genetics*, *32*, 469–473. doi:10.1038/ng1028

Stoer, M., & Wagner, F. (1997). A Simple Min-cut Algorithm. *Journal of the ACM*, *44*(4), 585–591. doi:10.1145/263867.263872

Stonebraker, M., Çetintemel, U., & Zdonik, S. B. (2005). The 8 requirements of real-time stream processing. *SIGMOD Record*, *34*(4), 42–47. doi:10.1145/1107499.1107504

Szockyj, E., & Geis, G. (2002). Insider trading pattern and analysis. *Journal of Criminal Justice*, *30*, 273–286. doi:10.1016/S0047-2352(02)00129-0

Tao, Y., & Papadias, D. (2005). Historical spatio-temporal aggregation. *ACM Transactions on Information Systems*, *23*(1), 61–102. doi:10.1145/1055709.1055713

Terry, D. B., Goldberg, D., Nichols, D. A., & Oki, B. M. (1992). Continuous queries over append-only databases. In M. Stonebraker, (Ed.), *Proc. ACM SIGMOD International Conference on Management of Data*, (pp. 321–330), San Diego, CA. New York: ACM Press.

Theodoratos, D., & Sellis, T. K. (1999). Designing data warehouses. *Data & Knowledge Engineering*, *31*(3), 279–301. doi:10.1016/S0169-023X(99)00029-4

Theodoratos, D., Ligoudistianos, S., & Sellis, T. K. (2001). View selection for designing the global data warehouse. *Data & Knowledge Engineering*, *39*(3), 219–240. doi:10.1016/S0169-023X(01)00041-6

Thomsen, C., Pedersen, T. B., & Lehner, W. (2008). RiTE: Providing On-Demand Data for Right-Time Data Warehousing. In *Proc. ICDE* (pp. 456-465).

Timmis, J., Bentley, P., & Hart, E. (2003). Artificial immune systems. In *Proceedings of Second International Conference, ICARIS 2003*, Edinburgh, UK.

Tishby, N., & Slonim, N. (2000). Data Clustering by Markovian Relaxation and the Information Bottleneck Method. *Proc. of 13th Annual Conference on Advances in Neural Information Processing Systems (NIPS)*, (pp. 640-646).

Tishby, N., Pereira, F. C., & Bialek, W. (2000). The Information Bottleneck Method. In *CoRRphysics/0004057*.

Torlone, R. (2003). Conceptual multidimensional models. In M. Rafanelli, (Ed.) *Multidimensional databases: problems and solutions*, (pp. 91-115). Hershey, PA: Idea Group Publishing.

Toroslu, I. H., & Kocabas, F. (1997). Effective maintenance of recursive views: Improvements to the dred algorithm. In *Proceedings International Conference on Logic Programming (ICLP)*, (pp. 213–225).

Trivedi, N., Gilliland, K. L., Zhao, W., Liu, W., & Thiboutot, D. M. (2006). Gene array expression profiling in acne lesions reveals marked upregulation of genes involved in inflammation and matrix remodeling. *The Journal of Investigative Dermatology*, *126*, 1071–1079. doi:10.1038/sj.jid.5700213

Trujillo, J., Palomar, M., & Gómez, J. (2000). An Object Oriented Approach to Multidimensional Databases & OLAP Operations. *International Journal of Computer and Information Science*, *2*(3), 75–85.

Trujillo, J., Palomar, M., Gomez, J., & Song, I. (2001). Designing data warehouses with OO conceptual models. *IEEE Computer*, *34*(12), 66–75.

Tryfona, N., Busborg, F., & Borch, J. (1999). StarER: a conceptual model for data warehouse design. *Proceedings of the 2ⁿᵈ ACM International Workshop on Data Warehousing and OLAP*, (pp. 3-8).

Tryfona, N., Busborg, F., & Christiansen, J. G. B. (1999). StarER: A Conceptual Model for Data Warehouse Design, In *Proceedings of the 2ⁿᵈ ACM International Workshop on Data Warehousing and OLAP*, (pp. 3-8).

Tsois, A., Karayannidis, N., & Sellis, T. (2001) MAC: conceptual data modeling for OLAP. *Proceedings of the 3ʳᵈ International Workshop on Design and Management of Data Warehouses*, (p. 5).

Tsuda, K., & Kudo, T. (2006). Clustering Graphs by Weighted Substructure Mining. In *Proc. of International Conference on Machine Learning (ICML)*, (pp. 953-960).

Tsuji, T., Jin, D., & Higuchi, K. (2008). Data Compression for Incremental Data Cube

Turney, P. D. (2001). Thumbs up or thumbs down?: Semantic orientation applied to unsupervised classification of reviews. In *Proceedings of the 40th Annual Meeting on Association For Computational Linguistics*, Philadelphia, PA, July 07 - 12, (pp. 417-424). Morristown, NJ: ACL.

U.S. EPA (2001). RAGS (Risk Assessment Guidance for Superfund) 2001: (Vol. III - Part A, *Process for Conducting Probabilistic Risk Assessment)*. EPA 540-R-02-002 OSWER 9285.7-4

U.S. EPA (2007). *ProUCL Version 4.0 User Guide*. EPA/600/R-07/038, April 2007

Ullman, J. D. (1989). *Principles of Database and Knowledge-Base Systems*, (Vol. 2). New York: W.H. Freeman & Company.

Urpí, T., & Olivé, A. (1992). A method for change computation in deductive databases. In L.-Y. Yuan, (Ed.), *Proceedings 18th International Conference on Very Large Data Bases (VLDB)*, (pp. 225–237). San Francisco: Morgan Kaufmann.

Utgoff, P. E. (1989). Incremental induction of decision Trees. *Machine Learning, 4*, 161–186. doi:10.1023/A:1022699900025

Utgoff, P. E. (2004). Decision tree induction based on efficient tree restructuring. *Journal of Machine Learning*, 5-44. Berlin: Springer.

Van Meirvenne, M., & Goovaerts, P. (2001). Evaluating the probability of exceeding a site-specific soil cadmium contamination threshold. *Geoderma, 102*, 75–100. doi:10.1016/S0016-7061(00)00105-1

Vanichayobon, S., & Gruenwald, L. (1999). *Indexing techniques for data warehouses' queries*. Technical report, University of Oklahoma, School of Computer Science.

Vassiliadis (1998). Modeling Multidimensional Databases, Cubes and Cube Operations. In *Proceedings of 10th International Conference on Scientific and Statistical Database Management* (pp. 53-62). Alamitos, CA: IEEE Computer Society.

Vijayaraman, T. M., Buchmann, A. P., Mohan, C., & Sarda, N. L. (Eds.). (1996). *Proceedings of 22th International Conference on Very Large Data Bases (VLDB)*, Mumbai (Bombay), India. San Francisco: Morgan Kaufmann.

Vlachos, M., Wu, K. L., Chen, S. K., & Yu, P. S. (2008). Correlating burst events on streaming stock market data. [Amsterdam: Kluwer Academic Publishers.]. *Data Mining and Knowledge Discovery, 16*(1), 109–133. doi:10.1007/s10618-007-0066-x

VLDB. (2002). *Proc. 28th Intl. Conference on Very Large Data Bases (VLDB)*, Hong Kong, China. San Francisco: Morgan Kaufmann.

Voisard, A., & David, B. (2002). A Database Perspective on Geospatial Data Modeling. *IEEE TKDE, 14*(2), 226–243.

Wagner, D., & Wagner, F. (1993). Between Min-cut and Graph Bisection. In *Proc. of International Symposium on Mathematical Foundations of Computer Science (MFCS)*, (pp. 744–750).

Wagstaff, K., Cardie, C., Rogers, S., & Schroedel, S. (2001). Constrained K-means Clustering with Background Knowledge. In *Proc. of International Conference on Machine Learning (ICML)*, (pp.577-584).

Wang, S., Rundensteiner, E. A., Ganguly, S., & Bhatnagar, S. (2006). State-slice: New paradigm of multi-query optimization of window-based stream queries. In Dayal et al., (pp. 619–630).

Weber, R., Schek, H.-J., & Blott, S. (1998). A Quantative Analysis and Performance Study for Similarity-search Methods in High-dimensional Spaces. In *Proc. of International Conference on Very Large Data Bases (VLDB)*, (pp. 194-205).

Weibel, R., & Dutton, G. (2001). Generalizing Spatial Data and Dealing with Multiple Representations. *Geographic Information Systems and Science*. New York: John Wiley & Sons (pp. 125-155)

Whetzel, P. L., Parkinson, H., Causton, H. C., Fan, L., Fostel, J., & Fragoso, G. (2006). The MGED Ontology: a resource for semantics-based description of microarray experiments. *Bioinformatics (Oxford, England)*, *22*(7), 866–873. doi:10.1093/bioinformatics/btl005

White, J. B., & Sadayappan, P. (1997). On improving the performance of sparse matrix-vector multiplication. *Proc. Int'l Conf. High Performance Computing*, (pp. 711-725).

Wong, M. C. S., Cheung, Y. L., & Wu, L. (2000). Insider trading in the Hong Kong stock market. *Financial Engineering and the Japanese Markets*, *7*(3), 275–288.

Wrembel, R., & Bebel, B. (2005). Metadata Management in a Multiversion Data Warehouse, In Proceedings of *International Conference on Ontologies, Databases and Applications of Semantics*, (LNCS 3761, pp. 1347- 1364). Berlin: Springer.

Wrembel, R., & Morzy, T. (2005a). Multiversion Data Warehouses: Challenges and Solutions. In *Proceedings of the 3rd International Conference on Computational Cybernetics*, (pp. 139-144).

Wu, F., & Huberman, B. A. (2007). Novelty and collective attention. *Proceedings of the National Academy of Sciences of the United States of America*, *104*(45), 17599–17601. doi:10.1073/pnas.0704916104

Wu, K., Otoo, E. J., & Shoshani, A. (2004). On the performance of bitmap indices for high cardinality attributes. In *Proc. of Int. Conference on Very Large Data Bases (VLDB)*, (pp. 24–35). San Francisco: Morgan Kaufman.

Wu, M. C., & Buchmann, A. (1998). Encoded bitmap indexing for data warehouses. In *Proc. of Int. Conference on Data Engineering* (ICDE), (pp. 220–230). Washington, DC: IEEE CS.

Xing, E., Ng, A., Jordan, M., & Russell, S. (2003). Distance Metric Learning, with Application to Clustering with Side-information. In *Proc. of 15th Annual Conference on Advances in Neural Information Processing Systems (NIPS)*, (pp. 505-512).

Yang, J., Karlapalem, K., & Li, Q. (1997). Algorithms for materialized view design in data warehousing environment. In Jarke et al., (pp. 136–145).

Yang, L., & Sanver, M. (2004). Mining short association rules with one database scan; *International Conference on Information and Knowledge Engineering*.

Yang, M., Yordanov, B., Levy, Y., Brüschweiler, R., & Huo, S. (2006). The sequence-dependent unfolding pathway plays a critical role in the amyloidogenicity of transthyretin. *Biochemistry*, *45*(39), 11992–12002. doi:10.1021/bi0609927

Yang, Y., & Pedersen, J. O. (1997). A Comparative Study on Feature Selection in Text Categorization. In D. H. Fisher, (Ed.), *Proceedings of the Fourteenth international Conference on Machine Learning* (July 08 - 12, pp. 412-420). San Francisco: Morgan Kaufmann Publishers Inc.

Yano, S., T., B.,Walsh, R., & Blumenberg, M. (2008). Transcriptional responses of human epidermal keratinocytes to cytokine interleukin-1. *Journal of Cellular Physiology*, *214*(1), 1–13. doi:10.1002/jcp.21300

Yi, K., Yu, H., Yang, J., Xia, G., & Chen, Y. (2003). Efficient maintenance of materialized top-k views. In *Proceedings of the 19th International Conference on Data Engineering (ICDE)*, (pp. 189–200), Bangalore, India. Washington, DC: IEEE Computer Society.

Yin, R. K. (2003). *Case Study Research: Design and Methods,* (3rd Ed.). San Francisco, CA: SAGE Publications.

Yip, K. Y., Cheung, D. W., & Ng, M. K. (2005). On Discovery of Extremely Low-Dimensional Clusters using Semi-Supervised Projected Clustering. In *IEEE International Conference on Data Engineering (ICDE),* (pp. 329-340).

Yu, J. X., Chong, Z. H., Lu, H. J., & Zhou, A. Y. (2004). False positive or false negative: Mining frequent itemsets from high speed transactional data streams. *International Conference on Very Large Databases.*

Zachman, J. A. (1987). A Framework for Information Systems Architecture. *IBM Systems Journal, 26*(3), G321–G5298.

Zaiane, O. R., Man, X., & Han, J. (1998). Discovering Web Access Patterns and Trends by Applying OLAP and Data Mining Technology on Web Logs. In *IEEE Forum on Research and Technology Advances in Digital Libraries (ADL),* (pp. 19-29).

Zaki, M. J. (2000). Scalable algorithms for association mining. *IEEE Transactions on Knowledge and Data Engineering, 12*(3), 372–390. doi:10.1109/69.846291

Zelnik-Manor, L., & Perona, P. (2004). Self-Tuning Spectral Clustering. In *Proc. of 17th Annual Conference on Advances in Neural Information Processing Systems (NIPS),* (pp. 1601-1608).

Zeng, E., Chengyong, Y., Tao, L., & Narasimhan, G. (2007). On the Effectiveness of Constraints Sets in Clustering Genes. In *IEEE International Conference on Bioinformatics and Bioengineering (BIBE),* (pp. 79-86).

Zhang, D., & Tsotras, V. (2005). Optimizing spatial Min/Max aggregations. *The VLDB Journal, 14*(3), 170–181. doi:10.1007/s00778-004-0142-4

Zhang, J., Ackerman, M. S., & Adamic, L. (2007). Expertise networks in online communities: structure and algorithms. In *Proceedings of the 16th international Conference on World Wide Web,* Banff, Alberta, Canada, May 08 - 12, WWW '07, (pp. 221-230). New York: ACM.

Zhang, R., Koudas, N., Ooi, B. C., & Srivastava, D. (2005). Multiple aggregations over data streams. In F. Özcan, (Ed.), *Proceedings of the ACM SIGMOD International Conference on Management of Data,* pages 299–310, Baltimore, Maryland, USA. New York: ACM.

Zhang, Z., & Varadarajan, B. (2006). Utility scoring of product reviews. In *Proceedings of the 15th ACM international Conference on information and Knowledge Management,* Arlington, VA, November 06 - 11, (CIKM '06, pp. 51-57). New York: ACM.

Zhang. J. & Wang, J. (2003). An overview about principal curves. *Chinese journal of computers, 2,* 129-146.

Zhao, Y., & Karypis, G. (2005). Clustering in the life sciences. *Molecular Biotechnology, 31*(1), 55–80. doi:10.1385/MB:31:1:055

Zhao, Y., Deshpande, P. M., & Naughton, J. F. (1997). An array-based algorithm for simultaneous multidimensional aggregates. In J. Peckham, (Ed.), *Proceedings of the ACM SIGMOD International Conference on Management of Data,* Tucson, AR (pp. 159–170). New York: ACM Press.

Zhou, J., Larson, P.-Å., & Elmongui, H. G. (2007). Lazy maintenance of materialized views. In C. Koch, J. Gehrke, M. N. Garofalakis, D. Srivastava, K. Aberer, A. Deshpande, et al (Ed.), *Proceedings 33rd Intl. Conf. on Very Large Data Bases (VLDB),* (pp. 231–242), Vienna, Austria.

Zhu, Y. Y., & Shasha, D. (2002). StatStream: Statistical monitoring of thousands of data streams in real time. *International Conference on Very Large Databases.*

Zhuge, Y., & Garcia-Molina, H. (1998). Graph structured views and their incremental maintenance. In *Proceedings of the 14th International Conference on Data Engineering (ICDE),* pages 116–125, Orlando, Florida. Washington, DC: IEEE Computer Society.

About the Contributors

Pedro Furtado works as assistant professor of Computer Sciences at the University of Coimbra, where he teaches both undergraduate and postgraduate curricula, mostly in data management related areas. He is also an active researcher in the Systems and Software Engineering Group of the CISUC research laboratory. His research interests include data warehousing and mining, parallel and distributed database systems, with a focus on performance and scalability and data management in distributed data intensive systems. He received a PhD in computer science from the University of Coimbra - Portugal in 2000. He has a large number of research papers published in international journals, book chapters and international conferences, mostly in the subjects of parallel and distributed data warehousing. In his professional activities he also has had experiences with consultancy and in leading national research projects, as well as participating in European projects in the areas of parallel data management, quality of service in distributed systems and wireless sensor networks. He also has a large experience with reviewing, having served in editorial boards of book, journals, as well as in program committees of international conferences.

* * *

Paulo J. Azevedo received is MSc and PhD degrees in Computing from Imperial College at the University of London in 1991 and 1995. He is an Auxiliar Professor at Department of Informatics of the University of Minho. His research interests include bioinformatics, data mining, machine learning, data warehousing and logic programming.

Sandro Bimonte is researcher at CEMAGREF, at TSCF. He obtained his PhD at INSA-Lyon, France (2004-2007). From 2007-2008, he carried out research at IMAG, France. He is Managing Editor de Journal of Decision Systems, Editorial Board member of International Journal of Decision Support System Technology, and International Journal of Data Mining, Modelling and Management and member of the Commission on GeoVisualization of the International Cartographic Association. His research activities concern Spatial Data Warehouses and Spatial OLAP, Visual Languages, Geographic Information Systems, Spatio-temporal Databases and GeoVisualization.

Christian Böhm is since 2003 associate professor of computer science at the Ludwig Maximilians University of Munich (LMU). He received his diploma in informatics in 1994 from TechnischeUniversität München (TUM), his PhD. in 1998 and his habilitation in 2001 from LMU. From 2001 to 2003 he was associate professor at the University for Health Informatics and Technology (UMIT) in Hall in

Tyrol. His research interests include indexing structures for similarity search, in particular addressing the problems of high dimensional vector and metric spaces, and database mining (with focus on subspace and correlation clustering). He has more than 70 peer reviewed publications, among them several at ACM SIGMOD, ICDE, KDD, and ICDM. In 1997, he gained the SIGMOD best paper award for a distributed indexing method, and in 2008 the SIAM Data Mining Best Paper Honorable Mention Award for a correlation clustering technique.

Rui M. M. Brito is a Professor in the Chemistry Department of the University of Coimbra and Principal Investigator at the Centre for Neurosciences and Cell Biology of the same University. In his group experimental and computational approaches are used to study protein structure, folding and aggregation, in particular to understand the molecular mechanisms of amyloid diseases.

Claudia Cherubini graduated cum laude in 2003, PhD since 2007, currently Post Doc Scholarship at Polytechnic of Bari. Visiting Researcher in 2006 at Lawrence Berkeley National Laboratory (LBNL) and in 2005 at Geowissenschaftliches Zentrum der Universität Göttingen. Specific roles in important International Research Projects among which: Yucca Mountain Project of LBNL; European Research Project "KORA" of Universität Göttingen. European Project PRIMAC "Protection of coastal aquifers from seawater intrusion". Member of national Research projects financed by MIUR. Member of different International Scientific Committees of International Congresses, inserted in some International Program Committees, invited to be Rewiever and Speaker in the International Congresses. In 2008 didactic activity within the course "PhD International course on Advanced numerical modeling of flow and transport in soils and aquifers (ANMFT)", at University of Siena. Winner of international Prize "Best Student Paper" for the scientific paper "A hydrodynamic model of a contaminated fractured aquifer" presented at the Int. Conf. 5th IASME / WSEAS 2007. Only Italian Winner of an international selection of 35 experts in 2003. Winner of a Post doctorate Research Scholarship at University of Sannio; holder of a Post doctorate Research Scholarship at CNR. Attendance of several international training Courses. More than 40 papers published on Scientific Journals, International Books and Conference Proceedings and n. 2 final reports of European Research Projects. Some papers subject of international Selection. Certified knowledge of 5 foreign languages: English, German, Spanish, French, Portuguese and Japanese.

Martine Collard is Assistant Professor of Computer Science at the University of Nice-Sophia Antipolis (UNSA), France where she received Master degrees in Mathematics and Computer Science and a PhD in Computer Science. She was head of the Execo team on Data Mining and Information system modelling at the I3S laboratory, UNSA. She is currently a visitor in the Edelweiss team at INRIA Sophia Antipolis Méditerranée. Her main research interests are knowledge discovery from data e.g. extraction of rules, data management, knowledge quality, links with knowledge management, ontologies and applications in modelling, marketing and biology. She is author and coauthor of more than 60 papers in journals, books or conferences and served as a referee in program committees of international and national conferences or workshops.

Olivier Corby has a PhD in Computer Science from the University of Nice-Sophia Antipolis, France. He is the responsible of the Edelweiss team at INRIA Sophia Antipolis-Méditerranée. He performs research on Knowledge Engineering and Semantic Web. He works on mapping RDF/S, SPARQL and

Conceptual Graphs (CG) and he is the designer of the Corese system and published more than 90 articles in journals, books or conferences, organized about 10 conferences or workshops. He was member of more than 20 program committees of conferences or workshops.

Pedro Gabriel Ferreira has a degree in Systems and Informatics Engineer and a PhD in Artificial Intelligence from University of Minho in 2002 and 2007. He is now a Bioinformatics Pos-Doctoral Researcher at Center for Genomic Regulation, Barcelona, Spain. His research interests include Data Mining and Machine Learning and its applications to Computational Biology and Bioinformatics.

Sandra Geisler is a PhD student and works as a research and teaching assistant at the chair Informatik 5, led by Prof. Dr. Mathias Jarke, at RWTH Aachen University since June 2008. She received her diploma degree in April 2008 at RWTH Aachen University writing her thesis in corporation with Philips Research Europe in Aachen. She works on projects in the DFG funded Research Cluster of Excellence UMIC (Ultra High-Speed Mobile Information and Communication). Furthermore, she is entrusted with research in a project regarding road traffic management using data stream management techniques. Her research interests comprise data stream management, ontologies, data integration, schema matching and mapping, model management, data warehousing and health information systems. Her teaching activities comprise undergraduate and graduate courses on dataspaces and databases.

Jérôme Gensel is a Full Professor in Computer Science at the University Pierre Mendès France of Grenoble, France, since 2007. He received his PhD in 1995 from the University Joseph Fourier of Grenoble for his work on Constraint Programming and Knowledge Representation in the Sherpa project at the French National Institute of Computer Sciences and Automatics (INRIA). He joined the Laboratory of Informatics in Grenoble (LIG, formerly called LSR-IMAG Laboratory) in 2001. His research interests include Representation and Inference of Spatio-Temporal Information, Ontologies and Knowledge Representation, Geographic Semantic Web, and Ubiquitous Geographical Information Systems.

K. M. Azharul Hasan received his B.Sc. (Engg.) from Khulna University, Bangladesh in 1999 and M. E. from Asian Institute of Technology (AIT), Thailand in 2002 both in Computer Science. He received his Ph.D. in Information Science from the Graduate School of Engineering, University of Fukui, Japan in 2006. He is now assistant Professor at the Department of Computer Science and Engineering Khulna University of Engineering and Technology (KUET), Bangladesh. His research lies in the area of databases, and his main research interests include Data warehousing, MOLAP, Extendible and flexible database, Parallel and distributed databases, Parallel algorithms, Information retrieval, Multidimensional databases, and Software engineering.

Xuegang Huang is a computer scientist with over 6 years of experience in mobile services, database design, software architecture, and information management. As an employee of Danske Bank since 2007, he has participated in the design and implementation of data warehouse, business intelligence, data quality and metadata management platforms. He holds a Ph.D. (2006) in Computer Science and Engineering from Aalborg University and a B.S. (2000) and M.S. (2003) in Computational Mathematics from Dalian University of Technology. Prior to joining Danske Bank, he was an assistant professor at the Department of Computer Science, Aalborg University. His research interests include database system, software engineering, business intelligence, location-based service and mathematical modeling.

Nan Jiang is an Assistant Professor of Computer Science at the Cedarville University. She received her Ph.D. degree in Computer Science from the University of Oklahoma. Her research interests focus on the inter-disciplinary research between Data Mining, Software Engineering and Computer Systems; Data Warehousing and Online Analytic Processing; Database Management; Information Retrieval; Data Visualization; Information Systems and Information Security. She has published over 10 papers in peer-reviewed journals and conference proceedings. She has also been a reviewer for the leading academic journals and many international conferences in her research area. She is a member of the IEEE, ACM, and ACM SIGKDD.

Leila Kefi-Khelif has a PhD in Computer Science from the University Joseph Fourier of Grenoble, France. She is research engineer in the Edelweiss team at INRIA Sophia Antipolis Méditerranée. Her main research interests are information retrieval, knowledge extraction and management. She currently works on proposing methodological and software solutions to help biologists in the validation and the interpretation of their experiments. Her approach, based on semantic web technologies, is relying on formalized ontologies, semantic annotations of scientific articles and knowledge extraction from texts.

David Kensche received a diploma degree in computer science from RWTH Aachen University in 2004 and since then is a PhD student and a research and teaching assistant at Prof.\ Jarke's chair for information systems at RWTH Aachen University. In this position he is conducting research on representational aspects and methods for generic model management and on the DFG cluster of excellence "Ultra High Speed Information and Communication" (UMIC). David Kensche's research on model management includes generic methods for schema matching, mapping composition, view-based query rewriting, model transformation and applications in the areas of peer data management systems and generic data access layers. His teaching activities include undergraduate and graduate courses on algorithms and datastructures, databases and dataspaces.

Yiannis Kompatsiaris, received the Diploma degree in electrical engineering and the Ph.D. degree in 3-D model based image sequence coding from Aristotle University of Thessaloniki (AUTH), Thessaloniki, Greece in 1996 and 2001, respectively. He is a Senior Researcher with the Informatics and Telematics Institute, and currently he is leading the Multimedia Knowledge Laboratory. His research interests include semantic multimedia analysis, social media analysis, multimedia and the Semantic Web, multimedia ontologies, knowledge-based analysis, context aware inference for semantic multimedia analysis, personalization and retrieval. He is the co-author of 10 book chapters, 30 papers in refereed journals and more than 90 papers in international conferences. He has served as a regular reviewer for a number of international journals and conferences. He is a member of IEEE, ACM and IEE.

Xiang Li is currently a PhD student at Informatik 5 (Information systems) of RWTH Aachen University in Germany, where he also obtained obtained a master's degree in 2006. He got his bachelor's degree of computer science in 2004 from Tsinghua University, Beijing. His research lies mainly in metadata management, interoperability of heterogeneous databases, and management of autonomous data sources. Recent research of Xiang Li focuses on automatic schema merging using declarative first order mappings. He is also interested in novel data management scenarios, such as dataspaces, data streams, and DB&IR. His teaching activities include graduate level courses on database system implementation, data integration and data exchange, and seminars on cutting-edge data management techniques.

Li Liu is a Senior Research Assistant currently in the Data Sciences and Knowledge Discovery Laboratory under the Centre for Quantum Computation and Intelligent Systems, University of Technology, Sydney. She had obtained her Master of Information Technology degree at the University of New England in 1999. After that, she had been employed as tenure Associate Lecturer from 1999 to 2002. Then she had been employed as a research assistant in University of Technology, Sydney. Her current research interest is Data Mining. She has been involved in several Australian ARC Discovery grants in last six years as a research assistant. She is a co-author of more than a ten refereed papers with other researchers in Data Mining area.

Chao Luo is a PhD student in Faculty of Engineering & IT, University of Technology, Sydney (UTS), Australia. He is also a member of Data Sciences & Knowledge Discovery Research Lab, UTS Research Centre for Quantum Computation and Intelligent Systems. His research interests include data mining on stock market surveillance and exception mining on time series. He has published a dozen of papers in journals and conferences.

Dan Luo currently works as a research associate in information technology at the University of Technology Sydney, Australia. She was a PhD student in Software Engineering at the University of Technology Sydney. Her main research interest is data mining and knowledge discovery, in particular, methodologies and frameworks for actionable knowledge discovery in the real world. She has published a dozen of papers joint with colleagues in data mining area.

Elzbieta Malinowski is a professor at the department of Computer and Information Science at the Universidad de Costa Rica and a professional consultant in Costa Rica in the area of the data warehousing. She received her master degrees from Saint Petersburg Electrotechnical University, Russia (1982), University of Florida, USA (1996), and Université Libre de Bruxelles (2003), and her Ph.D. degree from Université Libre de Bruxelles, Belgium (2006). Her research interests include data warehouses, OLAP systems, geographic information systems, spatial and temporal databases.

Fotis Menemenis received the Diploma degree in Electrical and Computer Engineering in the Aristotle University of Thessaloniki (AUTH), Greece in 2007. His thesis involved the establishment of a system responsible for the personalized delivery of news content and concerned the creation and management of user profiles on mobile devices by means of probabilistic, machine learning-based techniques combined with natural language processing (NLP) methods. From February 2007 until September 2008, he worked as a researcher in the Multimedia Knowledge laboratory. He is currently an MSc student in the Department of Computing of Imperial College London. His current research interests involve optimal decision making under uncertainty and stochastic programming methods.

Yuming Ou is a PhD student in Faculty of Engineering & IT, University of Technology, Sydney (UTS), Australia. He is also a member of Data Sciences & Knowledge Discovery Research Lab, UTS Research Centre for Quantum Computation and Intelligent Systems. His research interests include sequential activity patterns mining and its applications in smart market surveillance. He has published more than 15 papers in journals and conferences. He has served as a program committee member for one international conference and a reviewer for two international conferences.

Symeon Papadopoulos received the Diploma degree in Electrical and Computer Engineering in the Aristotle University of Thessaloniki (AUTH), Greece in 2004. In 2006, he received the Professional Doctorate in Engineering (P.D.Eng.) from the Technical University of Eindhoven, the Netherlands. His P.D.Eng. thesis concerned the improvement of Digital Subtraction Angiography by means of real-time motion compensation. Since September 2006, he has been working as a researcher in the Multimedia Knowledge laboratory. His current research interests pertain to community detection in large networks and mining of social web data. He is currently a Ph.D. candidate in the Informatics department of AUTH under the supervision of prof. Athena Vakali and works towards the completion of an MBA degree in the Blekinge Institute of Technology, Sweden.

Claudia Plant was born in 1975 and received her diploma in informatics in 2004 from Ludwig Maximilians University of Munich (LMU). From 2004 to 2007 she has been a PhD student in biomedical informatics at the University for Health Informatics and Technology (UMIT) in Hall close to Innsbruck in Tyrol/Austria. Currently, she is working as a postdoctoral researcher at Klinikum Rechts der Isar der Technischen Universität München (TUM). Her major area of research is data mining with a strong focus on clustering. She has made several contributions to subspace clustering, semi-supervised clustering and parameter-free clustering which have been published at the top conferences of the field. Her research interests also include supervised data mining as well as scalability of data mining algorithms. In addition, she has contributed to application-related data mining, at UMIT focusing at applications from life sciences and medicine and currently focusing on data mining in neurosciences.

Christoph Quix is an assistant professor in the Information Systems Group (Informatik 5) at RWTH Aachen University in Germany, where he also received his PhD degree in computer science in 2003. His research focuses on metadata management, data integration, semantic web technologies, and data management in health care systems. He has about 40 publications in scientific journals and international conferences. The main research area of Christoph Quix is model management for which he develops methods for schema matching, schema evolution, mapping definition and composition based on a generic metamodel. His teaching activities include undergraduate and graduate courses on database systems, data structures, model management, and entrepreneurship. He gained practical experience in data warehouse systems through several projects and consulting activities in industry.

Khurram Shahzad, is a PhD candidate at Department of Computer & Systems Science (DSV), Royal Institute of Technology (KTH), Stockholm, Sweden. He is on study leave from COMSATS Institute of Information Technology (CIIT), Lahore, where he is working as Assistant Professor at the Department of Computer Science. Before joining CIIT he was lecturer at Punjab University College of Information Technology (PUCIT), University of the Punjab, Lahore. Khurram received a Masters of Science in Engineering and Management of Information Systems degree from KTH and a M.Sc. in Computer Science from PUCIT. He has over a dozen publications, presented on national and international forums.

Cândida G. Silva has a degree in Mathematics and Computer Sciences from the University of Minho in 2003. Currently, she is a PhD student in the Chemistry Department and the Center for Neurosciences and Cell Biology at the University of Coimbra, Portugal. Her work focus on the aspects of data management and mining applied to data originated from unfolding molecular dynamics simulations of proteins.

Van Trang Tran received his MCs degree in Applied Mathematics and his PhD degree in Bioinformatics from University of Lille, France. He followed a postdoctoral research in bioinformatics and biostatistics at University of Liège, Belgium and at University of Nice-Sophia-Antipolis, France. His research interests include combinatorial optimization algorithms and stochastic optimization based on weighted graphs, weighted trees and stochastic automata with applications in machine learning, data mining and knowledge discovery, bioinformatics and computational biology.

Athena Vakali, received a bachelor degree in Mathematics from the Aristotle University, Thessaloniki, an M.Sc. degree in Computer Science from Purdue University, USA and a PhD degree in managing data storage from the Department of Informatics at the Aristotle University. Since 1997 she is a faculty member at the Department of Informatics at the Aristotle University (currently associate professor), where she is leading the research group of Web Data Management. Her current research interests include web usage mining, content delivery networks on the Web, Web and social Web data clustering and Web data caching/outsourcing. She has co-edited 3 books, co-authored 7 book chapters, 38 papers in refereed journals and more than 60 papers in international conferences. She is in the editorial board of "Computers & Electrical Engineering" Journal and the International Journal of Grid and High Performance Computing. She has participated in more than 20 R&D projects.

Marlène Villanova-Oliver is an Assistant Professor in Computer Science at the University Pierre Mendès France of Grenoble, France, since 2003. She received his PhD in 2002 from the National Polytechnical Institute of Grenoble for her work on Adaptability to Users and Web-based Information Systems, at the Laboratory of Informatics in Grenoble (LIG, formerly called LSR-IMAG Laboratory). Her research fields include Adaptability and Adaptativity to Users, Multimedia Information Systems, Representation and Inference of Spatio-Temporal Information, and Ubiquitous Geographical Information Systems.

Yanchang Zhao is a Postdoctoral Research Fellow in Faculty of Engineering & IT, University of Technology, Sydney (UTS), Australia. He is an Australian Postdoctoral Fellow (Industry) and a chief investigator of two UTS Early Career Researcher Grant (ECRG) projects. His research interests are sequential patterns, clustering, association rules, outlier detection and post-mining. He has more than 30 publications on the above topics, including one edited book, four book chapters and six journal articles. He served as a chair of two international workshops, a program committee member for 15 international conferences, and a reviewer for 9 international journals and over a dozen of international conferences.

Index